July 2002
Edinburgh

A History of
Scottish Architecture

D0878909

Monique Brancourt Lehner

St Vincent Street UP Church, Glasgow (Alexander Thomson, 1857–9) and, right, Heron House (Derek Stephenson & Partners, 1967–71)

A History of Scottish Architecture

From the Renaissance to the Present Day

Miles Glendinning
Ranald MacInnes
Aonghus MacKechnie

RCAHMS

Edinburgh University Press

© Miles Glendinning, Ranald MacInnes and
Aonghus MacKechnie, 1996

Edinburgh University Press
22 George Square, Edinburgh

Reprinted 1997, 2002

Typeset in Ehrhardt by
Mitchell Graphics, Glasgow

A CIP record for this book is available from the British Library

ISBN 0 7486 0741 2 (hardback)
ISBN 0 7486 0849 4 (paperback)

Printed and bound in Great Britain
by Short Run Press Ltd, Exeter.

The publishers would like to thank
Historic Scotland for subsidy towards the
publication of this volume.

We gratefully acknowledge indirect subsidy through
the generous permission granted by RCAHMS to use
their photographs to illustrate this book.

The Publisher acknowledges subsidy from

THE SCOTTISH ARTS COUNCIL

towards the publication of this volume.

Contents

The Authors

Miles Glendinning Horsey (editor and co-author)

Threatened Buildings and Topographical Surveys Manager, RCAHMS. Honorary Fellow at the Department of Social Policy, University of Edinburgh. Co-author, with Stefan Muthesius, of *Tower Block* (published 1994 and awarded the Alice Davis Hitchcock Medallion for 1995).

Ranald MacInnes (co-author)

Principal Inspector of Historic Buildings, Historic Scotland. Honorary Research Fellow, Department of History and Economic History, University of Aberdeen.

Aonghus MacKechnie (co-author)

Principal Inspector of Historic Buildings, Historic Scotland. Editor of *David Hamilton, Architect* (published 1994). Co-author, with Margaret Stewart and John Dunbar, of *Minerva's Flame: The Great Houses of James Smith of Whitehill* (published 1995).

Acknowledgements

General Acknowledgements

We would first like to thank our partners and families, and our colleagues in Historic Scotland and in RCAHMS (especially the NMRS and Photographic Department), for their support and tolerance during the preparation of this book. We would also like to thank the following individuals and institutions; the names of those who have read through and commented on the text are asterisked. For acknowledgements in connection with List of Architects, see that section.

Rebecca Bailey, Geoffrey Barrow, Michael Bath*, Jenny and Ben Benjamin, Claudia Bölling, David Breeze, A. Buchanan Campbell, Ian Campbell*, Ronald Cant, Tristram Clarke, Rob Close, Lindsay Davidson, John Dunbar*, Richard Emerson*, Suzanne Ewing*, Richard Fawcett, John Gifford*, Neil Gillespie*, Andrew Gilmour*, Ian Gow*, Simon Green, Alison Horsey*, Deborah Howard*, John Hume*, Fiona Jamieson*, Tim Jilani, Warnett Kennedy*, Juliet Kinchin, Gus Lamb, Ronnie Lee*, Helen Leng, John Lowrey*, Derek Lyddon, Michael Lynch*, James Macaulay*, Norman MacDougall, Chris McGregor, Allan Macinnes*, Ian MacIvor*, Charles McKean*, Jim Mackie, Roger Mason*, Aidan Matthew*, Lady Lorna Matthew, Stuart Matthew, Debbie Mays*, Isi Metzstein*, Kathleen Munro, Stefan Muthesius*, Patrick Nuttgens, Miles Oglethorpe, Richard Oram*, David Page*, Willie Payne, Duncan Peet, Murray Pittock*, Charles Prosser, Sebastian Pryke*, John and Margaret Richards*, Alistair Rowan*, Roan Rutherford, Fiona Sinclair*, Thomas Spaven, Veronica Steele, Geoffrey Stell*, Margaret Stewart*, Paul Stirton, Sandy Stoddart, Strathclyde Regional Archive, Alan Tait*, Jane Thomas, Frank and Mary Tindall, David M. Walker*, Mark Watson, Diane Watters*, David Whitham*.

Picture Acknowledgements

Keith Adam: 4.1, 4.10
Architects' Journal: 9.20
ASSIST: 9.19
Ayr Public Library: 5.13
Bank of Scotland: 6.21
Basil al-Bayati: 9.28
B. T. Batsford Ltd: 4.18, 4.22, 5.14, 5.21
Ian Begg: 8.30, 9.23
Bodleian Library, Oxford: 3.35
A. Buchanan Campbell: 8.41
Sir J. Clerk of Penicuik: 3.14
R. Clerk: 3.29
Clydemore Exmouth: 6.25
G. Cobb: 5.25
Dennis Coutts: 8.38
Cumbernauld Development Corporation: 9.6, C.12, C.13
G. M. A. Davies: 5.36
Duke of Argyll: 3.41 (above)
Duke of Hamilton: 3.8 (right), 5.31 (left)
Earl of Rosebery: 4.11 (top), 7.27
Earl of Strathmore: 3.4
Edinburgh City Archive: 8.18
Edinburgh City Libraries: 2.37
Edinburgh College of Art: 3.14
Richard Ewing: 8.21, 9.17
Richard Fawcett: 1.4
Forth Road Bridge Joint Board: 9.1
Dr Andrew Frazer: 4.15
Mrs E. Galbraith: C.7
M. C. Gibb: 5.40
Gillespie, Kidd & Coia: 9.7, 9.18, 9.24
Glasgow District Council: 9.2
Glasgow School of Art: 7.43
Glasgow University Archives (Whitelaw Collection): 3.30
Hamilton District Library: 5.32
Historic Scotland: 1.5, 1.6, 1.11, 1.13, 1.15,

1.17–2.2, 2.6, 2.27, 2.28, 3.2, 6.39, 6.51

Hunterian Art Gallery, Mackintosh Collection: 7.42, 7.43

Hurd Rolland: 8.29

Hector Innes: 6.27

A. Johnson-Marshall: 9.10

T. Warnett Kennedy: 8.14

Kincardine on Forth Historical Society: 7.33

R. McFadzean: 6.41

C. McGregor: 1.9

Charles McKean: 2.7

E. & F. McLachlan: 9.35

Matheson Gleave: 8.12, 8.34

Aidan Matthew: 5.27, 8.32, 8.35, 8.46

Stuart R. Matthew: 8.28

Mitchell Library (Glasgow City Libraries): 5.7 (left)

Morris & Steedman: 9.4

R. J. Naismith: 5.22

National Galleries of Scotland: 2.8, 2.16, 5.24

National Library of Scotland (Trustees): 4.16

National Museum of Scotland/Benson & Forsyth/Carl Laubin: 9.30

National Trust for Scotland: 4.14

NOSHEB: 8.24 (left)

Page & Park: 9.27, 9.33

Perth & Kinross District: 3.13, 5.38

RCAHMS: 1.3, 1.7, 1.10, 1.16, 2.3, 2.4, 2.9, 2.11, 2.12, 2.14, 2.15, 2.18, 2.19, 2.21–2.24, 2.26, 2.32–2.34, 3.6, 3.7, 3.9 (right), 3.11, 3.15, 3.18, 3.19, 3.24, 3.33, 3.34, 3.36–3.38, 3.40, 3.41 (below), 3.43–3.48, 3.50, 3.52, 3.56, 4.3, 4.4, 4.6–4.9, 4.11 (bottom), 4.12, 4.17, 4.25, 4.26, 4.27, 5.1, 5.2, 5.5, 5.9–5.12, 5.16, 5.18–5.20, 5.23, 5.26, 5.28, 5.29, 5.33, 5.35, 5.37, 5.39, 5.41–5.44, 5.46, 5.48–6.15, 6.18–6.20, 6.22, 6.26, 6.29, 6.31–6.33, 6.36–6.38, 6.40, 6.42–6.50,

6.52, 6.54–7.6, 7.8–7.10, 7.12, 7.14–7.21, 7.23, 7.24, 7.26, 7.28–7.31, 7.34, 7.36, 7.38, 7.39, 7.41, 7.43, 7.45, 7.46, 7.48–7.59, 7.62–7.65, 8.7, 8.8, 8.17, 8.19, 8.22, 8.23, 8.25–8.27, 8.40, 8.44, 8.45, 8.49, 8.50, 9.5, 9.22, 9.25, 9.26, 9.31, 9.32, 9.34, C.1–C.6, C.8–C.11, C.14, L.1, frontispiece, cover

RCHME: 3.27, 4.2

Reiach & Hall: 9.29

RIAS: 3.8 (left), 5.3, 5.6, 5.31 (above), 6.24, 6.28, 6.35, 7.22, 8.9, 8.37, 9.9, 9.14, 9.15, 9.16

RMJM Scotland: 8.42, 8.43, 8.47, 8.48, 9.12

Joe Rock, photographer: 4.23, 5.8

Royal Botanic Garden: 9.11

Peter Savage: 7.25

St Andrews University: 9.8 (a)

Science Museum, London: 5.47

Scottish Colorfoto Lab: 5.45

Scottish Homes: 6.23

Scottish Housing Advisory Committee: 8.33, 8.39

Scottish National Portrait Gallery (National Galleries of Scotland): 3.1, 3.31, 7.40

Scottish Record Office: 3.17 (above), 3.22

Dmitri Shvidkovski: 4.28

Sir John Soane Museum: 4.13, 4.19, 4.20, 4.21

Staatliche Museen Preussischer Kulturbesitz, Berlin: 5.30

Stirling District Council, Architects' Department: 6.34

Strathclyde Regional Archive: 7.11, 9.3, L.2

Strathclyde University, Department of Architecture: 4.24, 5.4, 6.8

David M. Walker: 1.9, 3.51, 5.7 (above), 5.34

Mrs M. K. Warriner: 6.30

Whitfield Partnership: 9.13

Introduction

In a complex historical and geographical account such as this, it is necessary to begin with a few definitions and explanations. Historically, our book follows a simple, period-by-period plan; the sole exception is the beginning, where we start with an architectural movement – the Renaissance in Scotland. In each period, we aim both to trace trends and movements, and to provide a 'cross-sectional' record: to follow both the 'advanced' and the 'typical'. Partly because most general architectural histories have focused on the years before 1800, and partly because, quantitatively, the great majority of Scottish architecture in existence today dates from after 1800, our history is slanted, lengthwise, towards the nineteenth and twentieth centuries. Even so, because of the vast numbers of buildings of significance in those two centuries, these have had to be dealt with rather more succinctly than earlier monuments. Geographically, the long-settled borders of Scotland, compared to those of many other European countries, make our definition of 'Scottish' a simple one: all architecture in Scotland, or built elsewhere by architects based in Scotland. Cultural and social definitions of 'Scotland' and of 'architecture' have been a much more complex and less settled matter. Here, among other themes, we trace designers' and patrons' radically changing definitions of the 'nation' and the 'national' over several centuries. We witness a gradual expansion of the social scope of 'Scottish architecture', from the feudal possession of Stewart kings and a handful of clerics and nobles in the fifteenth century, to the twentieth century's involvement of many different groups and social classes as designers, patrons or both. For the benefit of readers who may not be familiar with Scottish history, we include at relevant points (especially at chapter beginnings) summaries of the contemporary social, economic and political background.

While we take full account of the effects on architectural patronage and practice of the wider social and economic transformations of the nation – especially the broad transitions from feudalism to the modernity of capitalism and 'national' statism – we do not provide a general history of all building. Our more conservative aim is to set out a history of 'Architecture' in the 'traditional' or canonical Western sense: a history of styles, of the works of key artists, and of their theories and ideas. Potentially, there is a conflict between analyses of form and of context. But, of course, architectural ideas, ever since Vitruvius, have emphasised the need to integrate visual beauty (*venustas*) with practical usefulness and good construction (*utilitas* and *firmitas*); in these pages, the consequent debates in Scotland are traced alongside the evolution of styles themselves. Where relevant to these architectural trends, other closely related areas of design are also addressed. For example, in following the response of architecture to changing ideas of the family 'home', we touch on interior decoration and furniture history. In discussing attempts to form 'national' definitions of architecture rooted in geographical, geological and demographic 'facts', we occasionally deal with landscape architecture and regional planning. And in discussing the increasingly intense concerns with the urban legacy of the past, we mention the movements of city planning and conservation. However, since we are concerned here above all with architecture, these other areas can only be dealt with in passing.

As the book is a general survey, a synthesis based largely on existing secondary material, our notes contain only references to quotations and to substantial help received from others; for other secondary sources, readers should consult the bibliographies. Although, over the last decades, great strides have been made in many areas through the scholarship of the chief historians in the field, such as John Dunbar or David Walker, the majority of Scottish architectural history still remains under-researched. Thus this volume can only be seen as provisional in its scope. Its aim is not to establish an authoritative account for all time, but to encourage further investigations by demonstrating the tremendous richness and international quality of its subject: our most fervent hope is that our text will soon be rendered out of date by the vigorous researches of others.

Chapter 1

Late Fifteenth Century to 1560

Stewart Triumphalism and the Early Renaissance

'. . . ful jurisdictioune and fre impire within his realme . . .'
1469 parliamentary act [1]

'Amid the Meid, repleit with sweit odouris,
A Palice stude with mony Royall Towris,
Quhair kyrnellis quent, feil turretis men micht find,
And goldin Thanis waifand with the wind.
Pinnakillis, Fyellis, Turnpekkis mony one,
Gilt birnest torris, quhilk like to Phebus schone,
Skarsment, Reprise, Corbell and Battellingis,
Fulzery, bordouris of mony precious stone,
Subtile muldrie wrocht mony day agone
On Buttereis, Ialme, pillaris and plesand springis.'
Gavin Douglas, *c.*1501 [2]

Introduction: Scotland and the Renaissance

We begin our 500-year story not with a date, but with a movement. We launch straight into one of the most momentous transformations in the great adventure of Scottish architecture – the coming of the Renaissance. In contrast to later parts of the book, which give equal emphasis to all the main architectural trends within each period, this short opening chapter is more selective, and singles out the forces of change. We are concerned here with the innovative and influential designs commissioned by a relatively small group of patrons, including some nobles and churchmen, but dominated by the increasingly ambitious and culturally assertive monarchs of the Stewart dynasty. It was the liberal, even reckless building programmes of the kings, especially James IV and V, that put Scotland at the cutting edge of the northern European architectural equivalent, and response, to the Italian Renaissance.

However far-reaching its eventual international impact, the variegated cultural movement of the Renaissance, on either side of the Alps, hardly represented a total break either from the immediate past, or – more important for this book – from the contemporary concerns of Europe's nascent nation-states. Certainly, the Renaissance's periodisation of history into Antiquity, Middle Ages and the present, and its embrace of the classical ideal of *humanitas*, had the effect of creating a seemingly universal, timeless canon of classical correctness. This canon was exemplified, in architecture, by the system of the Orders. But, at the same time, much of its initial driving force stemmed from the particular circumstances of Florence and the other Italian states – from the desire for patriotic assertion against external enemies, and above all against non-Italians. Chancellor Carlo Marsuppini of Florence declared in the mid-fifteenth century that 'the ancients used . . . to bestow high honours on those who delivered their fatherland from slavery into liberty'. [3] Translated north of the Alps, those ideas of patriotic *humanitas*, and of the conscious adoption of the historical past to the needs of the present, were turned on their head. Non-Italian

1

nations adapted concepts such as 'imperial Rome' to their own political and historical circumstances – including the chivalric legacy which Italians had branded the 'Dark Ages'. The story of Scottish Renaissance architecture before the Reformation – like that of its counterparts in northern Europe – is one of creative tension between the universal and the particular, between the classical and the medieval, between the cosmopolitan and the national.

What was the general condition of the Scottish nation at the dawn of the Renaissance, in the fifteenth and early sixteenth centuries? Since the previous century's successful struggle against English domination, there had been a relatively consistent return to peace at home and the emergence of a coherent political community. As part of this, at first the status of the Stewart monarchs had been very much that of *primus inter pares* among the powerful nobles. But from the mid-fifteenth century, and especially after James II's destruction of the powerful Douglas family in 1451–5, the kings began to enjoy a new and overarching stature. During this period, there were extensive international trading links, especially with the Low Countries and the Baltic. However, the overall economic position was one of deep stagnation: the grandiose building projects of the Stewart monarchy were gestures of cultural assertion in the face of economic adversity. During these years, political and military links were especially close with France, but there was also remarkable two-way cultural traffic between Scotland and Italy, above all by clerics. The early and mid-sixteenth century saw economic and military reverses, including two serious defeats by the English (at Flodden in 1513, and Pinkie in 1547), following which the ruling classes became polarised between pro-French and pro-English factions. By the end of the period, dynastic and religious pressures were gradually pushing Scotland and England closer together.

It was in the fifteenth-century context of renewed national self-confidence that the first influences of Renaissance culture emerged. In talking of expressions or definitions of the nation in this period, we are talking not of modern nationalist mass-movements but of the largely dynastic and religious concerns of a small ruling élite within a highly hierarchical society – which would only begin to expand significantly (although not to break down) in the sixteenth century. Within this élite, the intellectual class was the clergy. It was the investigations and writings of a succession of historian-priests that formulated the national epos, or origin myth, which shaped Scotland's early Renaissance culture. The most powerful constraint shaping this ideology was the relationship with England, where the military efforts of the previous century were now replaced, for the moment, by a war of origin myths. Eventually, by the mid- and late sixteenth century, the growth of a Stewart imperial unionism, focused on the English succession, would lead to attempts to reconcile the opposed national myths.

The Scottish epos was unusual in Europe in sidestepping straightforward dependency on either the Middle Ages or Rome – in the same way that, as we will see, the architecture of this period also avoided both strict 'classicism' and 'Gothic'. John of Fordun (*c.*1320–*c.*1384), Walter Bower (*c.*1385–1449) and Hector Boece (*c.*1465–1536) contested English claims of overlordship by tracing a line of rulers back to Fergus MacFerquhard in 330 BC, descended from a Greek prince, Gathelus, and Scota, daughter of an Egyptian pharaoh. During these millennia, the historians asserted, Scotland had never been conquered, and a range of invaders, including the Romans, had been repelled. But the focus of the epos was on more recent events. For Fordun and his successors, the unchallenged golden age of Scottish 'fredome' [4] had been the years of the MacMalcolm dynasty (1058–1286), an era followed by the 'dark ages' of wars with England. The invaders were portrayed as a Gothic barbarian horde, pillaging the nation's cultural treasures: Boece claimed that the English King Edward had ordered the burning of 'all the chronikles of Scotland' so that 'the memorie of Scottis suld peris'. [5] However, there were counter-tendencies: the myth of King Arthur potentially pointed to 'British' dynastic unity, and there were rival 'round tables' in both countries. Against this complex background, a definition of national community and kingship gradually evolved, moving, under humanist influence, away from its origins in chivalric-religious duty towards a classical concept of citizenship: the 'commonweal and liberty of the realm'. [6] The influence of Renaissance humanism became dominant in the work of Boece (a friend of Erasmus), who was chosen by Bishop William Elphinstone in 1505 to head his new university, King's College, Aberdeen.

It was in this context that the new cultural elaboration of Scottish identity began to affect architecture, and contribute to the beginnings of Renaissance tendencies. This movement had two phases: first, a renewed and selective use of Romanesque forms in ecclesiastical architecture (from the early fifteenth century); and second, a full-blown Renaissance movement of palace-building by the Stewart kings (from the late fifteenth century). In both cases, our account draws extensively on recent innovative research by Campbell. This chapter does not attempt a general account of late fourteenth-, fifteenth- and early sixteenth-century architecture; for that, readers should consult Fawcett's standard work. [7] However, one basic material characteristic of Scottish architecture throughout those centuries should be mentioned here, for its potential relevance to the onset of the Renaissance. This was the fact that, within high-class, permanent buildings, favourable geological conditions and building economics, and shortage of timber, encouraged construction almost exclusively in stone; in religious buildings, ashlar was the rule, while in secular buildings harled rubble was used in most cases, with highlights of ashlar. What is by no means clear is precisely how (or even whether) this material constraint, or opportunity, directly influenced the rather heavy, monumental forms of Scottish élite buildings – an architecture of mass, which in some ways resembled that of the Mediterranean rather more than that of northern Europe. Certainly, there was no lack of building freestone in some other north European countries with very different architectural traditions of Gothic slenderness and framed construction, such as France or England. [8]

The Renewal of Romanesque in Church Architecture

It was within the Church that the first cultural elaborations of the new patriotic historical canon emerged. The Great Schism of 1378–1417 (in which Scotland and England supported opposite 'sides') encouraged the separation of the Scottish and English Churches, already underway since the twelfth century. After 1417 there was constant traffic between Rome and Scotland, its 'special daughter' since 1192; 47 Scots and 197 attendants were granted safe conducts for land journeys to Rome in 1453 alone, and there were visits to Scotland by eminent Italian clerics such as Aeneas Sylvius Piccolomini (in 1435–6; later, Pope Pius II). The culmination of this process of religious autonomy, including researches into an array of Scottish saints, was the publication of a Scots liturgy, the *Breviarum Aberdoniense*, by Bishop Elphinstone in 1509–10, with the support of King James IV. In this religious context, the first architectural steps towards the Scottish Renaissance were taken when the late fourteenth-century revival of architectural building activity began to assume the form of a low, massive, rather static architecture prominently featuring the selective use of round arches and round columns. These features strongly resembled elements of the Romanesque architecture of the MacMalcolm 'golden age'. It is not clear whether the new tendency was actually a conscious 'revival' of old forms. Certainly, it spread above all in the centres of patriotic historical research and liturgical developments: Aberdeen, Dunkeld, St Andrews and Dunfermline. In formal terms, this new architecture was most closely paralleled in Europe by the round-columned churches of the Duchy of Brabant (from the 1340s), with which Scotland had well-established trading links; it was sharply divergent from the contemporary English trend of slender, gridlike 'Perpendicular' Gothic.

There is no space here to explore in detail this phenomenon of massive, round-arched building, which preceded the 'Renaissance proper'; we can only touch on three key examples. In the third quarter of the fourteenth century, when Fordun was writing his chronicle as a chantry priest at Aberdeen, the first and, arguably, most monumental setpiece of the style was begun: the nave of St Machar's Cathedral, with its stocky round columns and its crushingly massive west facade, whose round-arched doorway and line of seven slender round-arched, cusped windows are flanked by heavy machicolated towers [1.1]. The first securely dated example was at Dunkeld, a centre of the cult of St Columba; here the nave, with circular columns and round-arched triforium, was begun in 1406 by Bishop Robert de Cardeny, who later built a nearby palace described (in 1515) by Alexander Myln as being in a 'Scottish', or, perhaps, 'Highland' style. [9] And, at the other end of the fifteenth century – demonstrating the way this style became ingrained over time – the chapel (1500–9) of Elphinstone's new King's College [1.2] featured a prominent round-arched window (containing rounded, somewhat Netherlandish tracery) and a

corner tower with imperial crown steeple; we will return later to the significance of the latter motif.

Within late fifteenth-century church architecture as a whole, the selective inclusion of features of generally 'Romanesque' appearance (of course with 'modern' rather than 'authentic' mouldings) in otherwise Gothic buildings became an established pattern. Prominent examples included the round arch and twin doorway in the west facade of St Mary's, Haddington (probably from the 1460s), and the round columns of the nave of Stirling's Holy Rude Church (1450s–70s). The latter church, however also included a detail, dating possibly from James IV's marriage to Margaret Tudor in 1503, which hinted at another sort of 'patriotic' ideology: an archway, leading to the (later demolished) St Mary's Aisle, decorated with carved thistle and rose. By the end of the sixteenth century, as we will see in Chapter 2,

1.1 St Machar's Cathedral, Aberdeen, west facade, view from R. W. Billings's *Baronial and Ecclesiastical Antiquities of Scotland*, 1845–52.

Renaissance symbolism would become increasingly bound up with the 'assimilative nationalism' of triumphal Stewart unionism.

New religious foundations built in the sixteenth century perpetuated the framework of renewed Romanesque or highly simplified Gothic: for example, at Biggar Collegiate Church (built 1545 by Malcolm, Lord Fleming, with support from Kelso Abbey: the last pre-Reformation collegiate foundation in the country). At Midcalder, the choir (started before 1542) has a half-hexagonal apse and windows with round-arched loop patterns. 'Correct' classical architecture, by then appearing in secular buildings, was only hinted at indirectly, if at all. In some cases, a church with a conventional medieval plan featured innovative or cosmopolitan detail: for example, William Sinclair's Roslin Chapel (built probably over a number of decades after 1446) included a range of unusual features perhaps of indirect or unconscious 'classical' inspiration, such as heavily lintelled aisle bays and a 'coffered' ceiling. In other cases, centralised cruciform plans were adopted, but without any suggestion of classical style, as at James IV's own foundation at Ladykirk (*c.*1500; Nicholas Jackson, mason) or the collegiate chapel at Tullibardine (founded 1446 with a fairly rare dedication to Our Saviour, and expanded to its present form just before 1500). A pattern found in many classical rural churches of the seventeenth and eighteenth centuries – a rectangular box with square headed windows and symmetrical front gable – was presaged at Innerpeffray (a collegiate chapel dating, in more or less its present form, probably from 1506–7) [1.3]. A more dramatic centralised plan of the late fifteenth century, the hexagonal Chapel Royal of St Triduana, Restalrig, is discussed later. Among funerary monuments,

1.2 West facade of King's College Chapel, Aberdeen (1500–9), Billings view.

1.3 Innerpeffray Collegiate Church (*c.*1506–7)

a rare example of explicitly classical design seems to have been the tomb of Bishop Elphinstone in King's College Chapel, Aberdeen, constructed by Bishop Gavin Dunbar around the 1520s, and probably derived from Antonio Pollulaiolo's tomb of Sixtus IV, erected 1493 in St Peter's.

'The Palace of Honour': James IV, James V and the Architecture of Imperial Power [10]

Just as Brunelleschi's patriotic revival of Tuscan Romanesque forms in early fifteenth century Florence paved the way for a full-blown Renaissance, so these Scottish forms, evocative (perhaps unconsciously) of MacMalcolm Romanesque, would be followed by a more comprehensive and explicit Renaissance architecture – here bedded in the secular rather than religious field, in the imperial ideology of the increasingly assertive and prominent Stewart kings. The main driving force of this ideology was a growing conception of Stewart royal authority, based on two elements: the role ascribed to them, within the kingly origin-myth tradition, of upholders of national 'fredome' and the 'commonweal'; and the reality of their growing power *vis-à-vis* the nobles and the Church. This made possible James IV's forfeiture of the mighty Lordship of the Isles in 1493 – a step which was followed by a burst of castle-building in that area, both by the crown (at Tarbert Castle, enlarged *c.*1494, or Rothesay, 1512–14) and by its supporters, such as David Hamilton, Bishop of Argyll (at Saddell, *c.*1508).

As a result, Stewart monarchs were able to broaden their attention from purely internal political preoccupations to the fostering of a cosmopolitan court culture and the cultivation of a growing international profile through arms spending, high-profile diplomacy, increasingly prestigious dynastic marriages, and general imperial display – a process based on a 'once-only' exploitation of taxation and forfeiture revenue. In this, a growing awareness of classical antiquity was fed by the close links with Italy. In contrast to the later sixteenth century, there was not yet much interest in a reticent, Stoic conception of antiquity; what appealed above all was a vision of Roman imperial power and authority. In 1469 a parliamentary act declared that James III possessed 'ful jurisdictioune and fre impire within his realme . . .' [11] The king was portrayed in Renaissance form on a groat coin of the 1480s.

At the same time as this new emphasis on classical antiquity, there was also, paradoxically, a growing fascination with medieval and Arthurian chivalry. The nostalgic nature of this preoccupation can be seen in the enduring prominence of images of the Crusades and of Jerusalem, at a time when actual crusading had been replaced by peaceful pilgrimages: the heart of James I had been taken to the Holy Sepulchre in 1437, and large numbers of Scots travelled the Venice–Jaffa sea route in the late fifteenth century. Across Europe in the fifteenth and early sixteenth centuries, tournaments were transformed from quasi-battles into courtly displays: the second half of James I's reign, for example, saw a 'cult of honour'. [12]

This cosmopolitan and neo-chivalric royal image-making reached its first major climax in the career of James IV, whose bold interactions with the contemporary 'great powers' of Europe were played out in the field of culture and diplomacy – including the building of showpiece palaces. To understand his architectural policies (and those of his son) we need to outline, more generally, the multi-faceted character of his kingship. There was James the 'humane prince', patron of musicians and poets, and founder of the country's first printing press, set up in 1507 to produce mass books 'efter our awin Scottis use'. [13] There was James the courtly prince, who revelled in hunting and martial display (including spectacular tournaments of 1507–8 at Holyrood) and died a chivalric death at the head of his army in 1513. And there was James the hard-headed statesman, cautiously working to raise the international profile of Scotland, through a mixture of diplomacy and calculated pomp, on resources far slenderer than those of rich countries such as Spain, Portugal or England. During his reign, continuing tension with England was offset by the beginnings of a new trend towards closer relations, seen in James's dynastic marriage and the beginnings of an implicitly unionist Stewart 'pan-British' symbolism: we noted above the thistle and rose carvings in Holy Rude Church, which may have dated from his reign. The Arthurian legend of British kingship was a particular preoccupation. James's 1508 Edinburgh tournament included a 'counterfuting of the round tabill of King Arthour', and his son was named Arthur the following year; a poem of 1508 by Walter Kennedy refers, possibly for the first time, to the hill overlooking the tournament site as 'Arthuris-Sete'. [14] The king's most cherished project was the building-up of Scotland as a naval power, culminating in 1511 in the construction of the largest ship of the era, the 1,000-ton *Michael*. James, who designated himself admiral-in-chief in 1506, bolstered his naval drive with rhetorical appeals in 1509 for the mounting of a new crusade, soliciting papal and Venetian help. His cosmopolitanism was not indiscriminate, but was above all directed towards Italy. He spoke Italian, had an Italian alchemist, craftsmen and musicians, received gifts from three successive popes, and two of his sons – Alexander and Robert – studied at Padua under Erasmus in 1507–8.

James's humanistic Italophilia and his fascination with the imagery of chivalry both found expression in a campaign of palace-building. For one of the central pillars of the Stewart kings' cult of grandeur was an ambitious programme of architectural works, designed to provide a more monumental physical setting for court life. The latter was now anchored firmly in the central belt, with Edinburgh increasingly regarded as the capital.

Within the Stewarts' particular interpretation of 'imperial' Renaissance architecture, there was

no question of any importation of the 'correct' or 'strict' classicism of the Orders, as happened, for instance, in Poland, where Florentine architects were hired in 1502 to rebuild Krakow's Wawel Castle: it was in fact only in the 1670s that tiered and giant Orders were used in a royal project for the first time, by Sir William Bruce at Holyrood. Rather, there was a deliberate fusing of tradition with new ideas – in the same way that another, far wealthier monarch obsessed with maritime power, Portugal's king Manuel I (1495–1521), devised a lavishly decorated, turreted style evocative of Portuguese seaborne imperialism (which replaced the stricter Italian Renaissance style of his predecessor, John I). The architecture of James III, IV and V evoked a similarly wide range of sources and associations – although it would be misleading to describe these using words such as 'eclectic' or 'romantic', whose connotations are based on post-eighteenth-century concepts such as scholarly stylistic precision or individualistic, emotion-based appreciation of architecture.

The most easily and directly symbolic works were often the least substantial: the erection of temporary pavilions or decorations, or permanent ornamental features of heraldic or imperial character. We already encountered an architectural expression of one of the key symbols of regal power on the new Aberdeen college chapel (*c.*1500). Boece described this as 'a stone arch in the shape of an imperial crown'. [15] Other crown spires included those of St Giles, Edinburgh (*c.*1486) and of several large burgh kirks. Even here, there was not a rejection, but a transformation of medieval forms. Some English churches of the fifteenth century, for instance, had sported spires composed of flying buttresses. Although these were of a verticalised, Gothic character, the Scottish designers could have adapted that image to their own Renaissance purposes. Similarly, the pomp of royal ceremonial processions involved the transformation of the medieval city gate into an antique and neo-chivalric triumphal arch. When, in 1503, the princess Margaret arrived in Edinburgh for her marriage to James IV, 'at the entering of the said town was made a gate of wood painted, with two tourelles and a window in the midst. In the which tourelles was at the windows revested angels

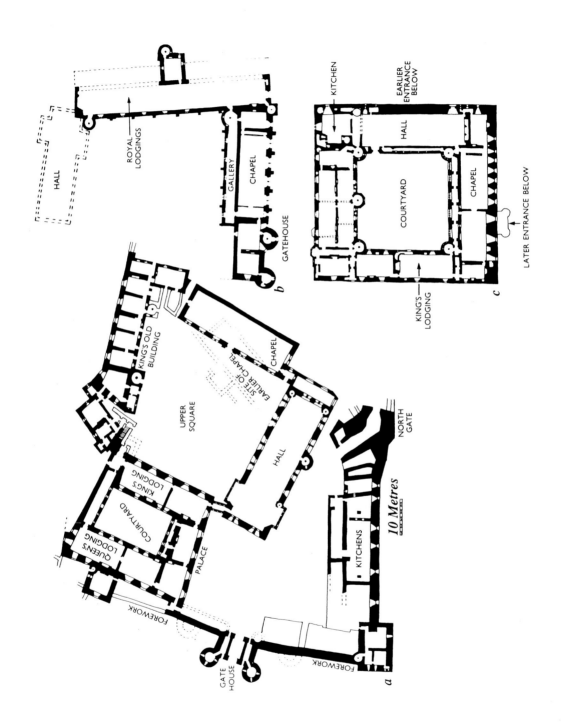

1.4 Plans of royal residences, from R. Fawcett, *Scottish Architecture from the Accession of the Stewarts to the Reformation*, p. 302 (1994): (left) Stirling Castle, the main royal complex; (above right) Falkland Palace; (below right) Linlithgow Palace.

singing joyously for the coming of so noble a lady, and at the said middle window was likewise an angel, presenting the keys to the King and Queen.' [16] A second arch was classically decorated with the cardinal virtues triumphing over their enemies. By the time of the arrival of James V's second queen in 1538, the imagery was more explicit: 'sche was receivit at the New Abbay yet; upon the eist syde theirof thair wes maid to hir ane trieumphant arch by Sir David Lindsay of the Mount, knicht, alias Lyon Kyng at Armis, quha caussit ane greyt cloud to cum out of the hevins down abone the yeit; out of the quhilk cloude come downe ane fair Lady most lyk ane angell, having the keyis of Scotland in hir hand, and deliverit thayme to the Queinis grace in signe . . .' [17]

We now pass to the palaces themselves, where the years 1500–10 had already seen the erection at Stirling Castle, by James IV, of a permanent gateway in the form of a triumphal arch, constructed of ashlar – a building method in itself evocative, in secular architecture at that time, of antiquity. In discussing the palace-building of the kings, it is necessary to caution that, despite the pioneering efforts of the editors of the Masters of Work accounts and other texts, documentary analytical research is far from complete; thus this account can only be a provisional one. Parts of the palaces, especially at Linlithgow, are still in a ruinous state, and little evidence of their interior decoration survives. The tinted harling which (as in the castles of the nobility) covered the palaces' rubble stone construction, and contrasted with the areas of expensive ashlar, has fallen off, and the external colouring (including profuse gilding and coloured paintwork) has vanished. External details such as fenestration are now a matter of conjecture; most window ingoes, for example, were probably checked for glass, and openings were filled with timber boarding in the lower half, leaded panes above. What can be said with reasonable confidence, as a starting point, is that most, if not all, of the six principal royal palaces – Linlithgow, Edinburgh, Holyrood, Stirling, Falkland and Dunfermline – were not new projects, but enlargements of previous complexes. In all these cases, subsequent rebuilding has made it very difficult to establish the contributions made by James I (who reigned 1406–37) and James II (1437–60) [1.4].

The architectural showpiece, in many ways, of the Stewarts' building drive was Linlithgow, first reconstructed by James I under Master of Work John de Waltoun in 1425–37, and referred to from 1429 as a 'palace' – apparently the first use of this description in Scotland. [18] Of the present quadrangular complex, the east quarter and parts of the north and south quarters seem to have been built at this time. During the reign of James III (1460–88) the south quarter was continued, ending in a square tower, and the west quarter was begun, probably with the aim of forming a quadrangular palace. Linlithgow's use of castellated architecture was anything but a novelty in fifteenth-century Europe, but here the 'Italianising' preoccupations of the 'imperial' monarch were beginning to prompt a far more specific interaction with advanced Renaissance architectural trends. The form of Linlithgow, as extended by James III and completed by James IV, conformed to the most fashionable pattern of Italian signorial palaces of the fifteenth and early sixteenth centuries: the quadrangular, corner-towered *palatium ad modum castri* (castle-style palace), with its combination of symmetrical, rather 'classical' stateliness and neo-chivalric imagery. [19]

It seems highly likely that Italian masons were working on the palaces by this time: an Italian mason named Cressent was recorded in royal service *c.*1511, and a family of masons with the Lombard-sounding name Merlzioun (Marliano?) worked in Scotland from the 1460s to the 1530s. But, as demonstrated in Campbell's research, a far more direct and elevated link was provided by James III's close confidant Anselm Adornes, a Brugeois merchant of Genoese descent who made an extensive voyage to Italy and Jerusalem with his son Jean in 1470–1, and presented an account of his journey (dedicated to the King) to James III on his return in 1471–2; in 1477, Adornes moved to Scotland and was made keeper of Linlithgow Palace. In his account (and in a later version prepared by Jean in 1510), several signorial palaces of the Linlithgow type are favourably remarked on: for instance, the Castello Visconteo at Pavia, described as a 'very beautiful and large castle, square with a great tower at each side and a park behind'. [20] In several private audiences held with Pope Paul II, Adornes had an opportunity to inspect the most prestigious of all *palatia ad modum castri*, the Palazzo Venezia in Rome (begun 1464). The cosmopolitan influence of Adornes's travels was also evident in one of the main ecclesiastical works of James III's reign: the Chapel Royal of St Triduana at Restalrig (*c.*1477–87), a two-storey hexagonal chapel, with (in its upper, principal chamber) no central supporting pillar [1.5]. This most unusual centralised plan may have been inspired by a newly built pair of hexagonal chapels seen by Adornes at Phileremos in Rhodes. St Triduana's Chapel was, presumably, very lavishly decorated, as its destruction was specifically ordered at the Reformation: only its lower floor, with rounded perimeter arches, survives today. In further evidence of Linlithgow's cosmopolitanism, and links to Rhodes, the town also contained (up to its demolition in the nineteenth century) a substantial, stone-built town residence of the Knights Hospitallers of Torphichen, built in the late fifteenth and early sixteenth centuries. This comprised a courtyard complex with two-storey hall wing and five-storey tower at one corner – like a miniaturised fragment of the nearby Palace.

As we might expect, it was the reign of James IV that saw the climax of building at Linlithgow, along with the most vigorous activity at the other palaces [1.6, 1.7]. His work combined greater regularity (and even symmetry) than before, and use of certain classical details, with neo-chivalric creations of turreted fantasy. His ideal of the classical/courtly palace was evoked most tellingly in Gavin Douglas's poem of *c.*1501, 'The Palice of Honour', dedicated to the 'triumphant' monarch. [21] Douglas's poem, groaning with allusions to classical mythology and the Bible, culminated in a description of the fantastic turreted palace of Honour personified, the 'greitest Empreour'. Arranged around a courtyard, its jewelled interior recalled St John's vision of the New Jerusalem and Ovid's description of the Palace of Apollo in the *Metamorphoses*:

> That heunlie Palice all of Cristall cleir,
> Wrocht as me thocht of poleist beriall stone.
> Basiliall nor Oliab, but weir,
> Quhilk Sancta sanctorum maid maist riche and deir,

> Nor he that wrocht the Tempill of Salamon,
> Nor he that beildit the Royall Ylion,
> Nor he that forgit Darius's sepulture,
> Culd not performe sa craftelie ane cure. [22]

In a manner hardly paralleled at this date in North-West Europe, Linlithgow now assumed the monumental regularity of an Italianate palace, as James completed the *palatium ad modum castri* mapped out by his father, in a programme of work lasting throughout his reign. In 1509, during the height of this campaign, James was able to appraise himself of the latest Italian fashions in architecture from his son Alexander, newly returned from a year's tour of Italy in the company of his and his brother's tutor, Erasmus. It was seemingly James IV who added, or heightened, the remaining three corner towers and some of the present battlements: the 'battaling' of the west quarter was built in 1504. [23] The Great Hall, or Lyon Chalmer, was made far more grandiose, with new fenestration (possibly in 1511–12) including a huge east window to light the dais, and cavetto-moulded, round-headed windows of somewhat Florentine character to the inner courtyard; there was also a large new fireplace with squared-off, entablature-like lintel. Elsewhere, an imposing sequence of apartments was formed in the south and west quarters, including a full-height range of galleries overlooking the courtyard. The king's lodging was mainly in the west quarter, and probably comprised a hall, inner and outer chamber, and closet. The queen's lodging was either on the floor above or in the north quarter. In these lodgings we see, perhaps for the first time, the creation of architecturally considered sequences of rooms with specialised private and public functions – a concept, beginning here at the level of royal status, which would later (in the late seventeenth century) extend to the 'state apartment' of large landowners' houses. A chapel (in the south quarter) was under construction in 1492, and was fronted by a St Machar-like range of round-arched lights.

James's most spectacular gesture at Linlithgow was reserved for the east (front) facade, with its central entrance archway beneath the Lyon Chalmer. This was transformed into a ceremonial

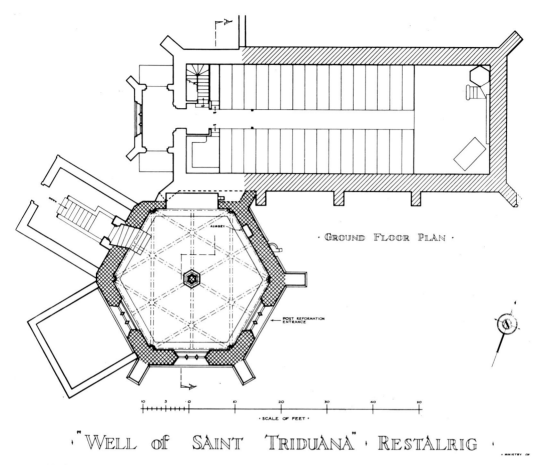

· GROUND FLOOR PLAN ·

POST REFORMATION
ENTRANCE

· SCALE OF FEET ·

· "WELL of SAINT TRIDUANA" · RESTALRIG ·

1.5 Restalrig Church and St Triduana's Chapel Royal (c.1477–87), 1957 ground floor plan.

approach of an imposing, even bombastic character, by the construction across the facade of the 'Outer Great Bulwark', an array of massive turrets – including the largest of any of the round towers built at the palaces. Today, there survive only the foundations of the three northern towers, with their outsize dumb-bell gunloops, but a southern stub wall indicates that a fourth existed (framing the main entrance, with drawbridge). The symmetrical eight-towered composition built by James at Stirling (see below) suggests that a similar arrangement may have prevailed here, but no evidence has emerged in excavation. Behind the Bulwark, the main entrance, originally formed by James I, was subsequently enriched, possibly by James IV, with a scheme of sculptural decoration, including a large coat of arms with cusped hood and flanking image tabernacles [1.8].

The latter are surmounted by finials in the shape of tiered buildings, resembling conventionalised images of the Church of the Holy Sepulchre and the Dome of the Rock (Templum Domini) found on the coinage and seals of the twelfth-century Crusader kingdom – for instance, on a seal of Amalric I (1162–74). Evocations of Jerusalem were of course ubiquitous at this time, but we should bear in mind that these were precisely the years of James's navy-building drive, and of his rhetorical calls for a new crusade. In 1508, Archbishop Blacader had set out on his behalf on a pilgrimage to Jerusalem, but died *en route*. Above the inner (courtyard) face of the entrance arch are further tabernacles (depicting as yet unidentified subjects) and a cusped hood [cf. C.3].

James IV's Linlithgow, although small by the standards of Europe's more opulent rulers, was

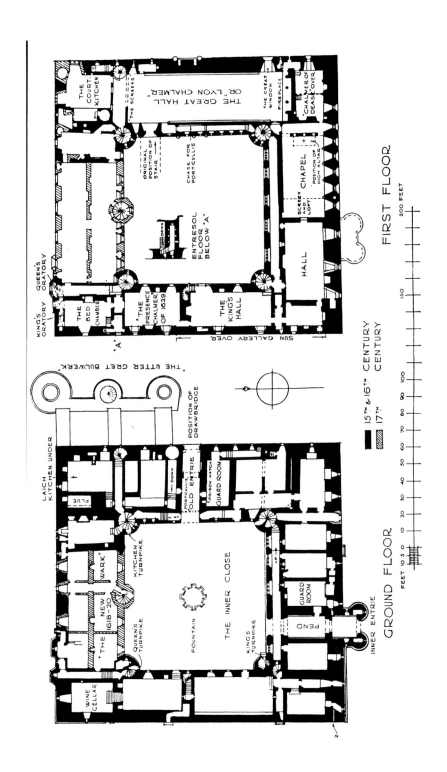

1.6 Linlithgow Palace, ground- and first-floor plans (J. S. Richardson, *Linlithgow Palace*, 1948).

1.7 Linlithgow Palace, aerial photograph from south-east. The Bulwark remains are on the right, and the James V entrance, outer entry and St Michael's Parish Church (with 1964 crown spire by Geoffrey Clarke) on the left.

unique and precocious for its date, in its combination of the sophistication of Renaissance Italy with a dash of the romance of Camelot and the *Très Riches Heures*. By comparison with its quadrangular monumentality, contemporary French work, such as the Louis XII wing at Blois (1498–1503), seemed rather irregular and 'Gothic' in character. It was only towards the mid-century that Linlithgow-like designs were built elsewhere in northern Europe: for instance, Sebastiano Serlio's Ancy-le-Franc (from 1546) or Kronborg Slot in Denmark (built from 1574 under the direction of two expatriate Scots).

We have dwelt at length on the works at Linlithgow Palace because of its monumental and iconographic intensity. But what is astonishing about the work of James IV and James V – considering the country's limited taxation base – was the high level of simultaneous building

activity at *all* the royal palaces. All of these complexes were arranged round courtyards, mostly (except at Linlithgow) of a rather loose and open character. In most cases, the main work comprised the creation of specialised public and private living-spaces, including halls and extensive lodging blocks. At Stirling Castle, a childhood home, James IV founded a new Chapel Royal (later rebuilt); constructed a palace block, the two-storey, octagonal-towered King's House [24] (completed 1496 by Walter and John Merlzioun); and built the grand Hall (completed *c.*1500), with its paired rectangular windows and hammerbeam roof, and entrance at ground-floor level. The sumptuousness of his fitting out of Stirling (partly in view of his impending marriage) was suggested by accounts of 1501 for 'scarlate' silk and 'damas', and 'welwous' (velvet) hangings for the 'Kingis inner chamir' and in

1.8 Linlithgow Palace, east quarter, outer facade, detailed drawing of main gateway as completed by James IV (J. Ferguson, *Linlithgow Palace*, 1910).

further towers on either side – one round and one square), its Roman-style ashlar finish, and its symmetrical, triumphal arch-like arrangement of openings; the composition recalls the triumphal arch entrance of the Castelnuovo in Naples (1452), remarked on in Adornes's account of his travels. The Forework's present-day, toy-castle-like appearance stems from its truncation by the British army in the eighteenth and nineteenth centuries, during their use of the palace as a barracks. Stirling Castle overlooked an extensive garden, probably begun by James in 1501. This included the 'King's Knot', subsequently expanded into a Renaissance-style parterre, con-structed of massive earth embankments. The raised octagonal centrepiece of the King's Knot was also referred to as the 'round table', and may have been the focus of Arthurian ritual, as part of the Stewarts' rivalry with the English kings as upholders of this legend. The prestige and influence of the royal gardening works is sug-gested by records of the laying-out of a hawthorn plantation at Tullibardine in the shape of James's flagship, the *Michael*, during the early sixteenth century.

James IV's works at Edinburgh Castle and Holyrood were only slightly more modest in character. At the former he built a lodging quarter (perhaps similar to that at Stirling) and another Great Hall, again of generous dimensions, and featuring cyma recta profile classical consoles, some inscribed with James's cypher in Arabic numerals, from which rises a hammerbeam roof with cyma profile [1.10, 1.11]. At Holyrood, where James's most famous chivalric tournaments were held, his architectural contribution is still unclear. He may have left the palace as a fully enclosed courtyard, including a north quarter courtyard front of uniform, somewhat classical appearance. In 1503, an extensive series of tapestries depicting scenes from the *Iliad* and from Greek mythology was set up, and in 1512, *all'antica* glass roundels with wreaths were installed in the queen's oratory: the only surviving roundels of this type are the later examples in Magdalen Chapel, Cowgate (begun 1541), bearing the arms of Mary of Guise. The extensive royal gardens at Holyrood are the subject of current detailed research. [26]

1503 for 'the Quenis chamir'; and in 1503 for 'verdeouris [tapestry with rural scenes] bocht for hyngingis of galloryis and stares'. [25] Italian embroiderers involved included the Florentines Simon and Francis Nicholai, much of whose work was done in gold thread. The frontispiece of James's remodelled Stirling was his lofty, towered Forework, built *c.*1500–10 by the masons John Yorkstoun and John Lockhart [1.9]. This com-bined the neo-chivalric and the classical-imperial in its four round angle towers (flanked by two

A less formal, monumental image was conveyed by James's country palace at Falkland, which had become a royal possession on its forfeiture by James I from Murdoch Stewart, Duke of Albany. Three quarters, probably incorporating some earlier work, were laid out on the south, east and north sides of a courtyard; the royal residence was in the east quarter, the Great Hall probably in the (now demolished) north quarter, and the buttressed chapel (completed 1512) in the south quarter. Asymmetrical variations in details such as gun holes suggest that the main gatehouse, at the south-west corner – another twin-towered composition reminiscent of Stirling and Linlithgow – may have been begun by James IV; it was completed by his son James V in 1541 (mason, John Brounhill) [1.12]. The classical roundels on the courtyard facade of the east quarter probably date from James V's time.

In a poem of 1530, before the campaign of building by James V had begun, Sir David Lindsay of the Mount wrote an address of leave-taking,

1.9 Stirling Castle, James IV's Forework Gateway (at centre and right) and James V's palace block (on left), reconstruction as at *c*.1600 by Chris MacGregor (in collaboration with Duncan Peet), based on a drawing by Professor D. M. Walker.

which conveys something of the atmosphere of leisured imperial dignity, with both antique and Arthurian overtones, to which these palaces aspired:

> Adew, Edinburgh, thow heych triumphant toun, . . .
> Adew, fair Snawdoun! [Stirling] with thy touris hie,
> Thy Chapell Royall, Park, and tabyll rounde.
> May, Iune, Iuly walde I dwell in the,
> War I one man, to heir the birdis sounde,
> Quhilk doith agane thy royall roche redounde.
> Adew, Lythquho, quhose palyce of plesance
> Mycht be one patrone [design] in Portingall or
>   France.
> Fair-weill Falkland, the fortrace of Fyfe;
> The polyte park, under the Lawmound Law.
> Sum-tyme in the I led ane lustye lyfe,
> The fallow deir, to see thame rak on rawe. [27]

In contrast to James IV's wide-ranging, but distinctly Italophile work, James V, in reflection of his dynastic policy, gradually swung the balance towards an affiliation with France, where his future father-in-law, François I, was now engaged in building palaces such as Chambord (from 1519) on a scale unattainable in Scotland – even if their spiky skylines still hinted at the Flamboyant Gothic. The unsuccessful war against the English, which abruptly curtailed James IV's reign, was followed, under the Governorship of the Duke of Albany (1515–17 and 1521–4), by a reinforced French alliance and the beginning of a burst of defensive building on coasts vulnerable to

English attacks. Albany's campaign included the construction of 'blockhouses' (fortified artillery towers) under the guidance of French or Italian engineers. First to be built was the polygonal blockhouse at Dunbar (1514–23) followed by others including rounded examples at St Andrews (from 1523) and Aberdeen (probably from 1533). Following a long tradition, royal interventions also continued to encourage nobles and other property owners in border and coastal areas to strengthen their houses against English invasions. In the same way that a 1481 act had authorised supply of ordnance to castles such as Tantallon, St Andrews, 'and sic vth castell and strenthis as may be keepit and defendit fra our Ennemyis of Ingland', an act of 1533 ordered coastal towns to build 'bulwerkis and strenthis' and another of 1535 encouraged the 'bigging of strenthis on the bordouris' – including, doubtless, the utilitarian pele-houses ubiquitous in the area. Military-type fortification, unlike normal castellated house-building, was always tightly controlled: an act of 1528 forbade the building of fortifications in the Borders without royal consent. [28] However, some features of these military programmes were picked up, for display purposes, in mainstream secular architecture, including wide-mouthed gun holes (first used at Dunbar).

By 1528, this transitional phase of instability was largely over and the 16-year-old James V had launched into a palace-building campaign almost

1.10 Edinburgh Castle, 1912 view from south, with Great Hall at left of centre, photograph dated 1912.

1.11 Edinburgh Castle, Renaissance corbel from Great Hall, with initials of James IV.

as extensive as that of his father. This was made possible by a continuation of the windfall era of royal revenue, now stemming both from forfeiture and from the growing secularisation of church estates. In 1541, the crown estates reached their greatest ever extent. Where James IV's reign had ended in armed confrontation with a military alliance including the papacy, his son's loyalty to Rome was secured at a heavy financial price to the Church: by the end of his reign the Church had become almost 'a sub-department of the royal household'. [29] By now, Edinburgh was fully established as the permanent centre of government, and James V's first major work was at Holyrood, where the present north-west tower was built, probably by John Aytoun, master mason, in the form of a Stirling Forework-like quadrangular block with *chemin-de-ronde* turrets at (probably) all four corners, and containing a sumptuous apartment on each of the two upper floors [1.13]. In 1535–6, by contrast, a west extension of apartments was added, whose tall windows and glazed oriels recalled the contemporary palaces of Tudor England. Pitscottie described the completed group as 'ane fair palice . . . and ane greit towre to him self to rest into quhene he plessit to come to the toun'. [30]

James's marriage in 1537 to François I's eldest daughter, followed (after her death) by his marriage to Marie, daughter of the Duc de Guise, was accompanied by a sharp change of architectural direction. Before his first marriage, James had travelled in France with a French mason already in his service, Mogin Martin – whose job was doubtless to look out for innovations applicable to Scotland. Later, the Duc de Guise sent two further masons from France, including Nicholas Roy. Pitscottie reported that when Marie first saw Linlithgow in 1538, 'quhilk pallace the queine highlie commendit, saying, shoe nevir saw a more princlie pallace'. [31] But in his new work at Falkland (designed principally by Roy), James turned away from the castellated, chivalrous imagery prominent at Linlithgow towards a more explicit classicism, involving use of the Orders (in the form of pilaster buttresses fronted by columns) to articulate facades. The model here was clearly contemporary French work such as François I's own house at Villers-Cotterêts (1533). Of the two ranges now surviving, the east quarter was slightly restyled by the addition of pilasters and buttresses. In front of the south quarter a new addition, containing galleries (in the manner of James IV's Linlithgow), was constructed, fronted in the same classical manner, with stone roundels flanking the first-floor windows [1.14]. From 1538, an open royal tennis court was built (other examples being at St Andrews, Stirling, Linlithgow and Holyrood). Organization of work at Holyrood and Falkland was the responsibility of John Scrymgeour of Myres, appointed to the post of Master of Work in 1537. He was, among other things, an expert on heraldry, and in the same year prepared a transcript of Gilbert of the Haye's Buke of Knychthede.

At Linlithgow and Stirling, James entrusted overall control of his alterations to a second Master of Work, Sir James Hamilton of Finnart, a nobleman who was closely related to the King, and wielded considerable power and authority until his fall from grace and execution in 1540. In Finnart's own private works, discussed later, we witness the first important example of a subsequently important figure: the aristocratic designer/patron. There, he energetically took up

1.12 Falkland Palace, Billings view of south quarter and Gatehouse (completed 1541).

and developed the new monumental architectural trends being developed at the court. [32] Within the royal programme itself Finnart, who had travelled widely in France, also acquired considerable influence, eventually being appointed in 1539 to the new post of 'maister of werk principale to our souverane lord of all his werkis within his realm now bigg and to be biggit'. [33] Finnart's scheme at Linlithgow (with master mason Thomas French, begun 1534) was relatively modest, and chiefly involved the addition of a new and more convenient, but still chivalrically imposing south entrance, set on a regularised wall-plane and approached through two squat gatehouses. Finnart's preoccupation with the imagery of fortification was expressed in the wide-mouthed gun holes that studded these new works, and the south facade of the south-west tower. Inside the palace, there were modest alterations, and in the courtyard an elaborate fountain composed of tiered imperial crowns was erected. An exuberant scheme of painted and gilt ornamentation was implemented, including decorative glass and wrought iron, and arresting external colouring. The outer window surrounds,

for example, were painted orange, and the harling was doubtless brightly tinted. Ever since the palace was gutted by Hanoverian troops during the 1745–6 war, it has remained in ruins, although partial restoration and re-roofing is now proposed [cf. 1.7].

James V's (and Finnart's) most original creation was the palace block at Stirling (built from 1538), a compact quadrangular group around a central courtyard, containing two floors of lodgings and a basement floor below, set on a raised site which exploits the Forework as a terrace wall; the palace was also linked to the Great Hall by a bridge [1.15]. James's construction of this new and lavish accommodation, only four decades after the completion of his father's own lodgings, demonstrates the speed with which expectations of domestic comfort and room specialisation were racing onwards, at the level of royalty. The new palace block's battlemented facades were articulated through a startlingly original arrangement of stepped wall-planes, with broad, pier-like projections linked by cusped arches – perhaps inspired by the entrance hood-arches on the Linlithgow east quarter – which contain statues on balusters and columns, echoed by further small statues above the cornice. This design not only anticipated one of the key decorative patterns in later houses of the nobility, in its spindly shaft-like mouldings and stringcourses, but also established one of the most memorable single images of Scottish Renaissance architecture – an image which would continue to inspire direct imitations even in the twentieth century, such as Robert Lorimer's Scottish National War Memorial (see Chapter 8). The palace was described in 1583 by Sir Robert Drummond as enjoying 'the best and maist plesand situatioun off ony of his hienes palayes be ressone it will hawe the maist plesand sycht of all the four airthis'. [34] Internally, the two lodgings had ceilings decorated with wooden roundels (some possibly carved by French craftsman Andrew Mansioun) of similar pattern to the stone or glass examples already encountered

above, and stone fireplaces of explicitly French inspiration, one decorated with thistles [1.16]. The internal courtyard may have been used as a formal pleasure ground, or as an exercise yard for beasts of the royal menagerie, which included a lion obtained from Flanders in 1539. Lesser-known palace-building work by James V included his conversion of the royal guesthouse at Dunfermline into a palace in *c.*1540, with a tall, heavily buttressed facade overlooking a deep glen.

The generally peaceful and architecturally confident reign of James V was followed, after the latter's death in 1542, by the unsettled period of the governorships of the 2nd Earl of Arran and Mary of Guise. During those years the polarisations between pro-French and pro-English parties rose to fever pitch. Fresh English invasions in the 1540s, in support of dynastic claims, prompted a fresh spate of fortification-building

1.13 Holyrood Palace, north-west tower.

1.14 Falkland Palace, courtyard facades of east (left) and south (centre) quarters as remodelled by James V after 1537, view from John Slezer's *Theatrum Scotiae*, 1693.

1.15 Stirling Castle, view of south facade of James V palace block (from 1538).

on modern polygonal European lines, both by English armies (for example at Eyemouth, 1547) and by French and Scottish builders of defence works (as at Luffness and Stirling); the English works were mostly designed by Sir Richard Lee and Thomas Petit, with help from Italian engineers, while Italians also advised on some of the defences (for example Migiorino Ubaldini, at Edinburgh, 1547–8, or Peter Strozzi, at Leith, 1548). Architecturally, court patronage continued to feed voraciously off the wealth of the Church. It was claimed that the first governor after James's death, the Earl of Arran, 'haldis ane greit houss and is at mair sumpteous expens' than even the

1.16 Stirling Castle, James V palace block, reconstruction of King's Presence Chamber in the time of James V, by Geoffrey D. Hay.

late king himself. From 1553, Arran built himself a 'palice' [35] at Kinneil: this ambitious complex was subsequently reconstructed, but two rooms retain painted decoration, in imitation of tapestries, from Arran's period. This includes New Testament scenes (with Jerusalem-like backdrop) and wreathed, antique-style portrait busts and columns [1.17].

Early Renaissance Architecture of the Landed Classes and Higher Clergy

In the wake of the achievements of Stewart architecture, the early sixteenth century saw the beginnings of the spread of Renaissance ideas to the other key area of secular patronage: the houses of landowners and churchmen. Despite the new prestige of the kings from the mid-fifteenth century, the power of the great nobles had not diminished; the legitimacy of the Stewart monarchy largely continued to rest on the principle of delegation. While the position would substantially change after the Reformation, for now the situation was that the high clergy and the nobility were able to build on a large scale, but still below that of the crown in size and sophistication. The work of Hamilton of Finnart for James V and on his own account seemed to point the way to two new types of landed 'designer' detached from the process of building – the patron-designer, and the designer working for a patron. But there is, at present, insufficient evidence to draw any general conclusions about these trends prior to 1560.

Among the nobility and lairds, the building of new castellated houses in stone (usually harled) reached an all-time peak in the period 1480–1560, as the research of Stell and (most recently) Zeune has indicated. This reflected not only rising living standards, but also a sense of security stemming from strong government and the granting of permanent tenure through feuing of kirklands (encouraged from the fifteenth century onwards) and crown lands (under an act of 1504). Even in 1521, Major observed that rural tenants with leases of 4–5 years 'do not dare to build good homes, though stone abound'. [36] The feuing

1.17 Kinneil House, view of 'Parable Room' including mid-sixteenth-century paintings of biblical subjects, and seventeenth-century timber ceiling.

system would, ultimately, underpin mass urbanisation in the eighteenth and nineteenth centuries. But, for now, the beneficiaries were landowners building on their country estates. Spanish ambassador De Ayala reported back in 1498 that 'the houses are good, all built of hewn stone and provided with excellent doors, glass windows and a great number of chimneys. All the furniture that is used in Italy, Spain and France is to be found in their dwellings'. [37] Of course, by the standards of, say, the 19th century, furnishings of castles were rather sparse and un-specialised.

This chapter does not provide a general survey of pre-1560 castle-building, for which the reader should consult Fawcett or MacGibbon and Ross. Here we are concerned, more narrowly, with the new Renaissance tendencies pioneered in the court. As with the kings, we are not dealing with a sharp architectural change. Just as the heraldic symbolism of the aristocracy of feudal power was preserved but modified in its transition to a court nobility, so the architectural form of the castellated house in Scotland as in many other countries (such as Italy) was subtly transformed by evocative, courtly imagery. The earliest surviving licence to crenellate, that of 1424 for Dundas Castle, already suggested cultural as well as security motives, referring to 'a castle with the crenellations, etc., usual in a fortalice of this sort according to the manner of the Kingdom of Scotland'. [38] Security considerations seem to have remained prominent only in the Borders and in occasional other cases, such as that of a 1537 royal licence to erect a 'tour, fortalicis' on Little

Cumbrae, plagued by pirates and bandits.

Among landowners, the forms of castellated royal setpieces such as the Stirling Forework – or even of works with a genuine military aspect, such as Albany's blockhouses – enjoyed increasing prestige. As with the royal works, the most immediate and extravagant expression of these ideas was in temporary buildings. In 1531, for instance, the Earl of Atholl built, at vast expense, a temporary quadrangular pavilion with corner turrets in the hills to welcome James V on a hunting trip with the queen mother (Margaret Tudor) and a papal envoy:

> quhilk was buildit in the midis of ane fair medow ane faire palice of greine tymmer wond witht birkis [birches] . . . quhilk was fesnitt in foure quarteris and everie quarter and nuike thairof ane greit round [tower] as it had been ane blokhouse quhilk was loftit and iestit [joisted] the space of thrie house hight; the fluir laid witht greine cherittis [grass] witht sprattis [rushes] . . . as . . . in ane gardin. Farder thair was tua greit roundis in ilk syde of the zeit [gate] and ane greit portcullis . . . and ane greit fowsie [moat] . . . and also this palice withtin was weill syllit and hung witht fyne tapistrie and arrasis of silk, and sett and lightit witht fyne glassin wondowis . . . as it had bene his awin palice royall at hame.

After three days of hunting and nights of 'bancat and triumph', the party departed and the pavilion was ceremonially burnt down: 'The hieland men sett all this fair palice in ane fyre that the king and his ambassadouris might see thame'. [39] We should remember that some of the most splendid of permanent Renaissance palaces in northern Europe, such as the quadrangular, angle-towered Chambord, were *châteaux de chasse* intended to be occupied only for short periods, sometimes only for days, at a time.

In general, the absence of direct evidence of the intentions of the patrons of castellated dwellings means that, pending more exhaustive research, we have to be cautious in tracing the transition to 'Renaissance' tendencies. This difficulty extends even to nomenclature. Recent historians, competing in their rejection of the 'military' interpretation of these buildings (a rejection which, it should be admitted, also strongly colours this account), have devised increasingly ingenious alternatives to

the traditional name 'castle' – including, even, 'château'. In the absence of any definitive semantic study of the numerous and incessantly changing names for these buildings in the fifteenth to seventeenth centuries (whether in Scots, Latin, Gaelic or English), we have kept an open mind on the problem, using 'palace' or 'house' as well as 'castle' – which itself, after all, by the late seventeenth century, was increasingly used as the label most evocative of chivalric antiquity. [40]

Nevertheless, among the houses of the higher nobility and clergy during this period, there appears to have been one clear architectural indicator of both social status and advanced Renaissance tendencies: the degree of horizontal spread, and segregation of functions, that was provided for in permanent stone buildings. The simplest and least prestigious pattern was the single tower standing on its own or with timber annexes. The most prestigious plan was the royal palace-like courtyard complex with separately articulated ranges of residential, hall and ancillary accommodation, allowing for a degree of separation of public and private, and formation of grouped 'apartments'. This rule of thumb allowed for almost limitless variations and contradictions. Among James IV's palaces, the most architecturally unified and 'advanced', Linlithgow, was also the most densely massed; and many of the most prestigious courtyard palaces also included a tower as a prominent element. But, as we will see in the following four chapters, landowners' rejection of medieval habits of semi-communal living for a more specialised and horizontal use of space would continue inexorably throughout the following four centuries, and would eventually spread to all other social classes.

Among courtyard-plan castles, the transition from medieval complexes such as Bothwell (built between the late thirteenth and early fifteenth centuries), the quasi-royal Doune (*c.*1380–1425) or Darnaway (with its hammerbeam-roofed Great Hall of *c.*1450), to designs showing Renaissance influence was gradual. The impact of James IV's work is perhaps perceptible in the twin-towered 'foirwerk . . . above the yet' [41] added by Lady Janet Seton to the courtyard-plan Seton Palace in the early/mid-sixteenth century, as well as, perhaps, the two round towers at the

corners of the King's College Aberdeen quadrangle (completed *c.*1514). James V's work at
Falkland, with its applied Orders and roundels, or
at Stirling, with its more idiosyncratic vigour, may
have inspired the facade ornament of Archbishop
Hamilton's post-1550 rebuilding of St Andrews
Castle, with its classical entrance surmounted by a
formal composition of panels, roundels, twin
shafts and friezes (like the slightly earlier Azay-le-
Rideau) [1.18]. Inside the courtyard was an
arcaded loggia – a feature which would later see
wide use in both country houses and urban street
frontages. St Andrews Castle had previously
been developed by Hamilton's predecessor,
Cardinal David Beaton, with symmetrical round
towers (before 1546). Where Falkland's somewhat
more 'correct' columnar arrangement remained
an isolated setpiece, Stirling Palace's typically
Northern Renaissance distribution of shafts,
friezes, balusters and other classical decoration
across a facade would be widely influential,
especially after 1560 [cf. 1.14, 1.15].

A far more idiosyncratic Renaissance castle
was built by Hamilton of Finnart in the 1530s
at Craignethan, Lanarkshire, in the extravagant
form of a mock-artillery fortification, of a kind
common also in France during this period (for
example Maulnes-en-Tonnerrois, 1566). Finnart's
house, set on a clifftop spur above the River
Nethan, comprises a castellated lodging block
with near-symmetrical facade and an unusual
ground-floor hall of approximately double-cube
proportions. [42] This was set in a fortified
courtyard with gun-platform, fronted by a wide
halsgraben ditch with caponier across the neck of
the spur. In contrast with contemporary military
fortifications, with their irregular, polygonal
bastions, Finnart's symmetrical complex, with its
ponderous masses of masonry, seems to hark back
to earlier patterns, such as the designs of Dürer
[1.19]. Around 1530, he had also been involved
with a similarly designed and situated house at
Cadzow for the 2nd Earl of Arran (later
Governor), with courtyards and towers. Possible
involvements by Finnart in the design of other
buildings are being researched by Charles McKean.

In practical terms, there was a significant
overlap between the courtyard or palace type of
dwelling and the smaller 'tower house', especially

1.18 St Andrews Castle, main front as rebuilt by Archbishop
Hamilton (after 1550), view of main gateway.

in cases where a hall or lodging range was added
to a tower with courtyard attached. Examples of
the latter included Balgonie, *c.*1496, by Lord High
Treasurer Sir Robert Lundie; Castle Campbell,
where a long, uniform hall range, rather like
James IV's Falkland work and with Stirling-like
octagonal-top stairtower, was added by the 2nd
Earl of Argyll, probably between 1493 and 1513;
and Edzell, where a late fifteenth-century tower
was augmented in 1553 by a lower wing with
rectangular windows and entrance arch in the
style of the Linlithgow east facade. During the
sixteenth century, the pattern of the tower with
integral lower hall wing became more and more
popular, the lower buildings showing an increasingly regular, even classical appearance: the
earlier phases of Linlithgow may have been
influential in this respect. After around 1510,
many royal licenses to build included the
expression *'mansio cum aula'* (mansion and
hall). [43] Examples built by the nobility included
pre-1556 work at Huntly, with hall/chamber and
tower, and the 4th Earl of Atholl's work at
Balvenie, where a massive blockhouse-like round

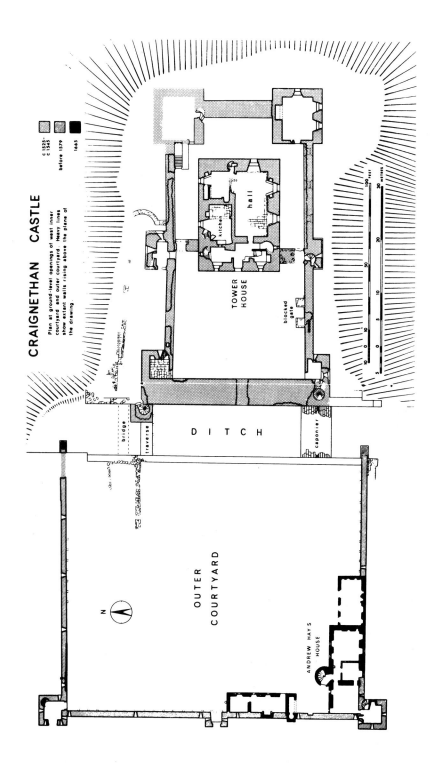

CRAIGNETHAN CASTLE

Plan at ground-level openings of west inner
courtyard and outer courtyard. Heavy lines
show extent walls rising above the plane of
the drawing.

c 1525-
c 1545

before 1579

1665

TOWER
HOUSE

hall

kitchen

blocked
gate

bridge

traverse

DITCH

caponier

N

OUTER
COURTYARD

ANDREW HAY'S
HOUSE

1.19 Craignethan Castle, Lanarkshire, 1993 plan.

tower was combined with a hall and chamber block with regular facade. This pattern also proved popular with the higher clergy: square-tower and hall groups were built at the courtyard-plan Chaplain's Court, Aberdeen (by Gavin Dunbar, bishop 1518–32, for the vicars choral), and Melgund Castle (constructed in two stages, including work by Cardinal David Beaton, after 1543). It is not clear from these examples whether there was any difference in prestige between round and square towers.

Within houses of less than palatial dimensions, patterns such as this offered one solution to the problem of how to accommodate the new demands for greater, and more specialised, space. The problem had become visible in particularly acute form in the monumental tower houses of the earlier fifteenth century, whose internal planning had become more and more elaborate. The huge block of Borthwick Castle, built after 1430 by the future Lord Borthwick with two balancing front wings (seemingly for visual rather than defensive reasons), featured within its starkly regular exterior not only a grandiose, two-storey hall but a maze of segregated spiral stairs, linking various upper parts of the structure; there were about a dozen fireplaces, their flues gathered into six large chimney stacks. From now on, the thickness of walls and the overall height and width of towers was steadily reduced. Additional complexity stemmed from the growing concern to provide fireplaces in individual rooms, with resulting networks of separate flues – a tendency which would reach its climax in the tenement blocks of the nineteenth century.

Pressure to find more space grew more intense. One solution, as just mentioned, was to separate out the hall in a spacious wing, permitting a degree of regularity (even within an overall asymmetrical facade). But there were other, more verticalised and less regular alternatives, including the pushing-out of full-height jambs (wings), containing stairs and other apartments. An alternative expedient, the adoption of plans two rooms in depth, would come later in the sixteenth century. The simplest type of full-height exten-sion was a single wing, forming an L-shaped plan, notably as at David's Tower, Edinburgh Castle (1368–77). From the mid-sixteenth century,

however, it became increasingly popular to build tower-like wings at diagonally opposite ends of a castle, creating a three-stepped arrangement, and allowing two separate sets of chambers with their own staircases. It is not clear if this was a self-contained Scottish development, or formed part of a wider north European tendency: in Danish-ruled Skåne (now part of Sweden), numbers of castles were built on quadrangular courtyard plans with two diagonally opposite corner towers, as for instance at Torup (1545). Perhaps the most extreme realisation of the first, relatively utilitarian phase of extruded castle architecture was Elcho (lower two floors built *c.*1555, upper floors built late sixteenth century), where two round and two square towers project from the main structure, plus a range of corbelled stair-towers leading to the upper floors. The result, although picturesque from today's viewpoint, can hardly be termed either classical or chivalric in its image. By contrast, the elaborate castellated compositions of the late sixteenth and seventeenth centuries – usually rebuildings of castles built before 1560 – were, as we will see in Chapter 2, a very different matter.

While this aristocratic building activity was especially vigorous around Edinburgh, the relative economic decline of the burghs up to the mid-sixteenth century meant that the capital and the other large burghs did not share in this picture of stone-built prosperity. There was as yet no class of wealthy burgesses, although (as we will see in Chapter 2), the position would change rapidly from the later sixteenth century. The grandiose layout of the wide High Street and the Canongate – stretching from Edinburgh Castle to Holyrood – and the narrow flanking burgage plots was already established; the mason Walter Merlzioun was responsible for paving the High Street in 1532. But the homogeneous, tall stone-fronted tenement houses, which we now take for granted, were a thing of the future [cf. 2.30]. In fact, following an act of 1508, most Edinburgh High Street houses, although structurally of stone, were faced with wooden galleries and front annexes, and were only two or three storeys high; their subdivision into flats through pressure of density had not yet begun. In the Canongate, density was even lower, and there were extensive gardens. The most important, all stone-built urban house of this period to have survived until recently was the Knights Hospitallers townhouse at Linlithgow, already mentioned above.

Conclusion

This golden age of royal palace-building had been partly financed by mechanisms of feuing or land transfer, which would eventually have the effect of raising the landed classes' spending power at the expense of the Church and the crown. After the Reformation of 1560, the nobles and lairds would begin to catch up with, and overtake, the patronage of the monarchy. From that point it would be increasingly their responsibility to continue the development of the Scottish Renaissance in secular architecture, with its potent mixture of classical allusions and the imagery of feudal power.

Chapter 2

1560–1660

Nobility and Urbanity

'Nobis haec invicta miserunt 106 proavi' [106 generations of
kings have left these to us, unconquered]
Inscription placed at Edinburgh Castle and
Holyrood Palace, early seventeenth century [1]

'By any meanes do not take away the battelment . . . for that is the
grace of the house, and makes it looke lyk a castle, and henc so
nobleste, as the other would make it looke lyk a peele.'
Sir Robert Kerr, 1632 [2]

'Alexander Seton, a man of high culture and urbanity, has laid
out and ornamented this villa and gardens near the city, for his
own pleasure and the pleasure of his noble descendants, and of
everyone of culture and urbanity. This is no place of warfare,
designed to repel enemies. Instead, there is a welcoming and
kindly fountain of pure water, a grove, pools, and other amenities
– everything that could afford decent pleasures of heart and
spirit.'
Inscription at Pinkie House, 1613

Introduction

While the architecture of the late fifteenth and
early sixteenth centuries was dominated by the
rhetorical creations of James IV and James V, the
patronage of the century which followed was
shaped by a rather more fluid social, religious
and political situation. Its highlights were the
Reformation of 1560, the regal union with England
in 1603, and the signing of the National Covenant
and the outbreak of the Bishops' Wars in 1638–9.
Although there were only the tentative beginnings of the complex and specialised secular
architectural patterns that would predominate in
the nineteenth and twentieth centuries, the system
of architectural patronage that had prevailed
during the feudal era was now becoming desta-
bilised by a growing imbalance of power and
wealth in favour of the landowning class.

Externally, the almost forty-year personal reign
of James VI saw an unprecedented reduction of
tension with England – in 1623 the privy council

hailed 'a dilictible tyme of peax under your
majesteis regne' – and a growth of links with
Protestant Northern Europe, especially after
James's marriage to Anne of Denmark in 1589.
The reduction of cultural intercourse with
Catholic Europe was gradual. Only after the 1627
war between England and France did the 'Auld
Alliance' begin to atrophy. At home, James VI
attempted to extend support by ennoblement of
the greater lairds on an unprecedented scale
(with 29 peerages created, for instance, between
1603 and 1625). There was an accelerating
transfer of royal and clerical lands and wealth to
the aristocrats and lairds – who were beginning
to concern themselves with agricultural and
industrial improvements, such as mining and salt
manufacture – and also to the burgher class in
towns. By the early seventeenth century, and
especially following Charles I's Act of Revocation
of 1625, which alienated many aristocrats, the
monarchy had been transformed from a guarantor
of stability to a source of political and religious

29

instability. Intellectually, as elsewhere in northern Europe, the legacy of the Renaissance was no longer seen as a kind of royal property, to be used in defence of the feudal nation against an external enemy. Instead, it was devolved to the parties contesting the great issues of the day within Scotland: whether sovereignty lay with the monarchy or a wider society; what form the growing *rapprochement* with England should take; and whether the Reformation should be reinforced or watered down.

Beginning with Queen Mary's 1566 baptismal 'triumph' for her son at Stirling, [3] the royal house (whose name Mary had changed to the French spelling 'Stuart') tried to reinforce its claims to power through imperial and origin-myth imagery, and Renaissance trappings which were now redefined in Augustan terms of reconciliation and peacemaking: the Arthurian romance prominent in James IV's evocations of 'British' kingship was now replaced by imagery of classical antiquity. Even before his accession to the English throne in 1603, James had set himself up, Apollo-like, as the leader of a 'Castalian Band' of court poets; had begun to write texts on the philosophy of divine kingship; and had started to stage classical triumphal ceremonies. He entered the English capital in 1604 through temporary triumphal arches in the manner of a Roman emperor, and subsequently endorsed an assertive classicism as an expression of his new British nation-building efforts, notably in masques and architecture designed by Inigo Jones. Reconciliation between Scotland and England also, more controversially, included the strengthening of episcopalian and ceremonial elements at the expense of Presbyterianism. There was a confidence among some of James's courtiers that union with England could be achieved on Scotland's terms – that their king 'his brand all Britayne to obey sall bring'. [4]

Opposing this Horatian or Virgilian optimism concerning Stewart power was a new Tacitean scepticism, which stemmed from a reformulation of the idea of the 'commonweal' by an emergent grouping of nobles and Presbyterian ministers. They were inspired above all by the writings of George Buchanan, whose *History of Scotland* (1582) redefined the national epos in anti-monarchical terms, claiming that Scottish history

had been characterised by an incessant checking of royal power by the nobility. What had now, of course, disappeared altogether was the old-style Catholic Scottish nationalism of the pre-Reformation years.

Faced with these new, complex polarities of views, and the revival in religious oppositions, landed patrons of architecture could choose a variety of ideological positions. Between the extremes of vociferous support for James's and Charles's British episcopalian *imperium*, and vociferous support for the counter-movement leading to the National Covenant, the compromise solution of most landowners was to assert their 'roots'. There was an explosion of interest in chivalric and heraldic matters. In some cases, this was expressed with James IV-like gusto, including conspicuous consumption on architectural status symbols. The heraldic framework allowed expressions of measured support for the monarchy's unionist nationalism, through the inclusion, in decorative schemes, of motifs such as thistles and roses, or the Stuart British royal arms.

The same framework also allowed a limited scope for the expression of religious dissent by closet Catholics, while others chose to conceal their beliefs behind a facade of Stoic modesty. With the polarisation of religious opinion, in Scotland just as elsewhere throughout Europe, the Renaissance values of liberal cosmopolitanism were most effectively safeguarded by a secular class of lawyers, tutors and state servants, and by the politicians they served, whether Catholic or Protestant. It was in the *otium* of their houses that these figures took consolation and refuge from the hectic life of urban *negotium*.

Religious Architecture in the Age of the Reformation

The rise of secular society and its patronage implications, in replacing churches by palaces as the dominant type, was a Europe-wide phenomenon. But the relative decline in patronage of large-scale religious architecture was undoubtedly sharper in Protestant countries. In 1560, Scotland's variegated religious patronage system, with its emphatic requirement for architectural elaboration, was replaced by a simple parish-based system with no architectural requirements other than a simple *Predigtkirche* – a box to preach in. The campaign by James VI, from the mid-1580s onwards, to impose an erastian and less militantly Presbyterian framework on the Kirk did not substantially alter that fact. There were now many more churches than were needed, and the main task now was to alter old churches for the new use, by sweeping away symbolic ornament and centralising their internal arrangement, with pulpit and communion table in the middle. More and more often, a three-winged or T-shaped plan was formed by adding a wing on one of the long walls, often for the use of the new church patron – the local laird. On occasion, lairds determined the architectural appearance of additions or of whole new churches, as at Falkland, in 1620. The most notable laird's aisle of this period was the Dunfermline Aisle added *c*.1610 by Alexander Seton, 1st Earl of Dunfermline, to St Bridget's Church, Dalgety Bay. This secular looking, somewhat classical block has a triangular-gabled angle tower and sumptuous raised and fielded stone panelling and cornice inside [2.1].

The type plans and stylistic trends of the post-Reformation century are analysed in Howard's recent book; [5] this chapter can only present a summary of the main developments. While in a few cases there is evidence as to the precise relationship between plans or style and the religious architecture of the period, the lack of documentary evidence mostly keeps us in ignorance. For example, might the Maxwell burial aisle at Terregles (1573), with its eastern position, its mixture of rounded and pointed arches, and its polygonal end, have been a conscious recollection of pre-1560 architecture by a Catholic family? Among the few new churches built in the immediate post-Reformation period, the most common plans were three-winged T-plans or simple rectangles, all 'centralised' in their use. Early examples include Stenton (*c*.1561) and Prestonpans (1596); the dates of the aisles in both cases are uncertain, and, in general, it is unclear precisely when the T-plan became common. The simple pitched-roof rectangular pattern, still a common type in the countryside (for example at Durness, 1619, and Nigg, 1626), received prestigious endorsement in 1594, when James VI

2.1 Dunfermline Aisle, St Bridget's Church, Dalgety Bay (*c*.1610), 1974 view.

built a new Chapel Royal in this form at Stirling for the christening of his son, already envisaged as a possible king of Britain. In contrast to most parish churches, whose doorways were normally set in or near gables, the Chapel Royal's symmetrical facade had a central entrance, its triumphal arch-like twin-columned portico flanked by paired windows in round openings – an arrangement conveying a rather secular impression reminiscent of fifteenth-century Florentine palazzi [2.2]. Inside, the walls were decorated with wall paintings, and hung with tapestries, pictures and sculptures. The christening ceremonies (overseen by Master of Work William Schaw) included chivalric displays and an exotic banquet ceremony. The centre-doored arrangement was subsequently more or less confined to private chapels built over the next century, such as Ferniehurst (probably of early seventeenth-century date, in a secular style closely resembling the new north quarter at Linlithgow, 1618–20s), George Heriot's Hospital Chapel in Edinburgh (from 1628), and the later Michael Kirk, Gordonstoun (1705) [cf. 2.36].

Elsewhere, there were attempts at more thoroughgoing centralised planning. At Portpatrick, built 1622–9 on the lands of an Irish landowner, Sir Hew Montgomerie of the Great Ardes, there was a Greek-cross plan and the curious feature (given the church's location and patronage context) of a seemingly older round tower, incorporated as a symmetrical west steeple;

2.2 Chapel Royal, Stirling Castle (W. Schaw, 1594), view of main elevation.

a similar tower was incorporated in the Munro Aisle of Kilmuir Easter Parish Church, 1616. And at St Columba's Church (1589–96), Burntisland, the new affinity between parish-based Kirk and burgesses bore fruit in a daring, square-plan project, arcaded around a central space, and originally crowned by a pyramidal roof and wooden steeple (finished 1600); the mason was probably John Roche [2.3]. The extreme centralised planning of Burntisland would not be matched again in Scotland until the twentieth century – and then, paradoxically, by designs for the Roman Catholic Church!

With the stability which, for the moment, followed the imposition of erastian and episcopalian policies by James and his son Charles I, an increasing number of fairly large new churches was commenced. These included many three-winged plans, as well as rectangular examples with symmetrical west steeples, as at Dirleton (1612: a long rectangle with round-arched windows, battlemented steeple, and the 1664 classical Archerfield Aisle) and Anstruther Easter (from 1634: with square west steeple set within the church); the original form of Greyfriars Church, Edinburgh (from 1602) is less clear, but seems to have been an aisled double-square plan with axially placed steeple. Stylistically, the already weak commitment to Gothic before the Reformation may have paved the way for the use of simplified Gothic in the early seventeenth century, while Romanesque-like forms became less prominent. Heavy Gothic windows, usually with looped or Y-shaped tracery, were common in the south: for example, at Pencaitland (1631, pointed windows

with no tracery), Duddingston Aisle (1631, looped tracery), the rebuilt Holyrood Abbey (1633, by Masters of Work James Murray and Anthony Alexander, with reticulated tracery resembling one window in Heriot's Chapel) and South Queensferry (1633, with heavy Y-tracery).

The effects of James's heightened anti-Presbyterian stance around 1620 emerged in a handful of key projects. For his visit in 1617, James ordered the Chapel Royal (by now at Holyrood) to be recast according to episcopalian liturgical requirements, with the assistance of Nicholas Stone and other English craftsmen. The scheme included portraits of the apostles, a private loft and double organ. In 1621, following the passing of the Five Articles of Perth (1618–21), James's ally, Archbishop Spottiswoode of St Andrews, primate of Scotland, built a model church at Dairsie in conformity with the Five Articles. It had a plan like the Stirling Chapel Royal, but was aligned east-west, with classical main west doorway, corbelled angle turret, and the rare feature of plate-traceried windows – perhaps to emphasise episcopacy's claims of antiquity [2.4]. Inside, it was richly furnished, including a choir screen. Spottiswoode later boasted, probably concerning the liturgical arrangement, that he 'publicly and upon his own charges built and adorned the church of Darsy after the English form' as 'one of the beautifullest little pieces of church work that is left to that now unhappy country'. [6] The Tron Kirk, Edinburgh (1636–47, built by John Mylne) also used hybrid Gothic/classical detail, but in the completely different form of a highly centralised Presbyterian church, much influenced by contemporary Dutch

(Calvinist) architecture. It had a three-wing plan with axial steeple fronted by a tall, pilastered portico-like composition [2.5].

Funerary monuments, incorporated in lairds' aisles or outside in churchyards, provided a quasi-religious building outlet for the aristocracy; a pioneer of the pattern of the detached aisle was the burial enclosure built by Sir James Melville at Collessie Parish Church (1609). From the late sixteenth century, a new type of funerary monument emerged, with recesses framed by paired pilasters or columns, sometimes with smaller aedicules above. The earliest variant of this pattern was horizontally proportioned, like medieval tomb-recesses; the earliest known surviving example is the Moray monument in St Giles's,

2.3 St Columba's Parish Church, Burntisland(1589–96).

2.4 St Mary's Parish Church, Dairsie, (1621), view from north-east.

2.5 Tron Church, Edinburgh, 1753 drawing (after William Maitland), including low spire added in 1671 by Thomas Sandilands.

Edinburgh (1569, recast 1864 by David Cousin). From the 1620s came a new, upright type, probably influenced by book frontispieces and the works of James Murray. The richest concentration of early seventeenth-century external monuments stands against the walls of Greyfriars churchyard. Some of its monuments were made by master masons William Wallace (for example the Byres of Coates monument of *c.*1629, with broken-pedimented Corinthian aedicule) and William Aytoun (for example the Foulis of Ravelston monument of 1636, with Ionic aedicule and smaller caryatid-columned aedicule above). Among the most prestigious individual examples elsewhere, some monuments to key supporters of James VI and Charles followed the English fashion for recumbent effigies: for example, that of George Home, Earl of Dunbar, at Dunbar Church (1611, by Maximilian Colt) or the Lauderdale monument, Haddington (before 1638, and possibly of English manufacture). Others featured standing figures, such as the monument to Chancellor George Hay, in the Kinnoull Aisle, Perth (1635). The most spectacular of all was the Skelmorlie Aisle, Largs, built by Sir Robert Montgomery for himself: a laird's aisle incorporating a structure in the shape of a triumphal arch, containing tomb below and family loft behind and above. The scheme was not quite completed, as no effigy was installed [2.6]. The coffered archway, decorated with obelisks and strapwork, seems to have been inspired chiefly by a monument built by James VI to Queen Mary at Westminster Abbey, London (1612). This period also saw the first freestanding secular monuments. An early example was the monument at Pitmedden (1637) to Duncan Liddel, physician to the Duke of Brunswick and benefactor of Aberdeen University: it comprised a two-stage rectangular tower with pyramid top and finial.

Secular Architecture and the Royal Building Programme

The post-Reformation shift in building patronage from religious to secular architecture would eventually, by the nineteenth century, express itself in a bewildering variety of building types, predominantly in an urban context. At first, however, the chief beneficiary was the mainly rural palace- and castle-building of the landed classes and the monarchy. Here the building activity of the latter, although still highly prestigious, was curbed by lack of money. It should be borne in mind that secular building types were still fairly unspecialised: country houses also served as local law courts and centres of administration. Like that of earlier Stewart monarchs, the landed and royal building of the post-Reformation century was driven forward by a mixture of image-making and practical requirements. On the one hand, there was a drive for greater stateliness and ornament. On the other, there was the desire for more space, and for greater segregation and specialisation in its use. Here we witness 'the beginnings of the modern world, with its distinctive conception of comfort and privacy in family life'. [7]

Within the two main existing categories of dwellings – the courtyard palace and the compact tower house – this led to a drive towards ever more coherent horizontal planning arrangements, and towards the development of new, specialised plan types. These included the self-contained blocks of lodgings, as at Linlithgow (north quarter) and Dunnottar, that allowed guests to be accommodated away from communal areas, and the development of the galleries of royal palaces into self-contained rooms (as at Culross Abbey House and Pinkie). The period also saw a percolation among aristocrats and lairds of the more theatrical architectural devices up to now largely monopolised by the kings, such as towers, gatehouses, bristling bartizans, oriels, huge armorial panels, and others such as stone scale and platt staircases. The spread of wealth was not such that, as in nineteenth-century Baronial, all construction could be in exposed freestone: the general rule was still harled rubble with ashlar dressings. But, partly inspired by the refined stonework of a new generation of royal palace works from 1615, high-quality sculptural detail became much more widespread. Because there was now a larger building stock of big stone houses, there was also a practical preference for piecemeal, lower-height addition to old structures, rather than new building.

In analysing the external architectural expression of these buildings, we should avoid

2.6 Skelmorlie Aisle, Largs.

judging the period according to the precise architectural formulae of later centuries. All buildings of this period are 'eclectic' by nineteenth-century standards. But, at the same time, particular forms could have clear cultural and ideological connotations; the main difficulty for us today, in assessing them, is simply lack of evidence. Within residential architecture as a whole, it appears that there was a growing polarisation between two extremes: a flamboyantly castellated architecture, building on the innovations of the early Scottish Renaissance with an at times brash confidence not unlike the nineteenth-century Baronial architecture which it inspired; and a new trend of more 'correct' classicism, pursuing such features as horizontal facade disposition, flat roofs, and regular fenestration detailed with elements of the Orders. From *c*.1600 to the revolution of 1638 this latter tendency was,

in the hands of some patrons, associated with an enthusiastic espousal of James's and Charles's ideology of unionism and episcopalianism. This, however, was a relatively small grouping. Most landowners, whatever their position on religious or political matters, built in patterns which drew on both castellated and classical ideas, with rather more diffuse ranges of symbols and connotations. In plan types, for example, there was much in common between some castellated buildings of a horizontal and symmetrical type, such as the late sixteenth-century Duntarvie, and more openly classical designs such as Culross Abbey House (1608) [cf. 2.19]; even an unambiguously tower-like design such as Newark (1597–9) could also contain a symmetrical facade (with central corbelled stair turret). Within Scottish architecture of this period, there was no stylistic schism or change remotely as radical as, for instance, in contemporary Portugal, where the defeat of Portuguese naval power by the Netherlands was paralleled by the collapse of the Manueline architectural style and the rise of an austere, Sienese or Palladio-influenced tendency.

In royal and landed building, an increasingly common formula was provided by the application of various types of classical detail, including columns, pilasters, pediments and balustrades, to even the most spectacular vertical castle designs, such as Castle Fraser or Amisfield [cf. 2.12]. The spread of printed French or Italian pattern books, by authors such as Serlio (available in one volume from 1566) or du Cerceau (1576–9), had for the first time given all patrons and masons throughout northern Europe – not just those who had travelled in the Mediterranean, access to an internationally conventionalised range of detailing. This included 'correct' (by antique standards) use of the Orders alongside a proliferation of more recent, northern variants of classically based decoration, designed often to fill bare walling with semi-abstract or *all'antica* patterns. Strapwork decoration, for instance, first used in the late 1530s at Fontainebleau, was commonly employed in prestigious Scottish buildings of the early seventeenth century. Pattern books could even be used as sources of entire plans. The design of Drochil Castle (*c*.1578) with its double-depth, central-corridor layout (an ultimately Italian plan type) and two diagonal angle towers, may have been influenced by plans of châteaux such as Chenonceau or Martainville, illustrated in du Cerceau's *Livre d'Architecture* (1559) [cf. 2.15].

Within the Northern Renaissance, different countries and regions could develop their own variants of ornamental vocabulary. The easiest way was through the prominent use of national or family heraldic motifs, such as the giant facade panel of Castle Fraser (1617–18) or the Huntly Castle doorway (1602). We saw in Chapter 1 how royal precedents such as the idiosyncratic shafted and panelled decoration of Stirling Castle's palace block had sparked off a fashion, among the higher clergy and nobles, for ornament comprising spindly shafts, stepped friezes and hoodmoulds, and roundels [cf. 1.15]. In the west, a regional variant of this ornament developed around 1570–1600, using cable mouldings and conglomerations of crammed mouldings (as seen, for instance, at Haggs Castle, 1585–7). In the north-east, the spectacular castles built by the Bel family of masons (see below) concentrated their pediments, turrets and other decorative features above a heavy, stepped corbel course; other details characteristic of the region included waisted baluster shafts (as on the door surrounds of Fyvie) [cf. 2.12].

Internally, the decorative tendencies of the previous century continued up to the early seventeenth century, with tapestry-hung or painted walls and painted ceilings (either flat or between timber joists). Furnishings were relatively sparse, by the standards of the country houses of later centuries. But gradually there was a change in the interior provisions and fittings concerned with comfort and domesticity: plastered walls rather than tapestries on stone walls; carpets and rugs; glazed windows; and table glass. Among the richest interiors, the spread of the new *all'antica* decoration was seen for instance in the grotesques of the frieze of Queen Mary's apartment in Holyrood (1558–9) or on the 'Prestongrange Ceiling' (1581); a more sober note was struck by the stone panelled gallery of Culross Abbey House (1608). A radical change in interior decoration (replacing flat with three-dimensional designs, and colouring with whiteness) came in the second decade of the seventeenth century, in the importation, from England, of ribbed ceiling plasterwork, arranged in geometrical patterns, sometimes with heavy suspended bosses; the first examples of such ceilings, dated 1617, were at Edinburgh Castle's palace block and Kellie Castle. Decoration of these ceilings included heraldic features, such as British royal symbols (for example at the Binns, *c*.1630).

The building programme of the monarchy combined a continuing high prestige with steadily shrinking scale, compared to the frenzy of activity under James IV and James V. The major works were those carried out by James VI at Dunfermline (in the 1590s, for his new queen), the Stirling Chapel Royal (1594), the Edinburgh Castle palace block (1615–17) and the Linlithgow north quarter (1618–1620s) [cf. 2.2, 2.7]. As with Scrymgeour and Finnart under James V, the royal Masters of Work played a linchpin role in this programme. The most important in our period were William

Schaw (Master of Work 1583–1602), James Murray of Kilbaberton (1607–34) and Sir Anthony Alexander (appointed alongside Murray from 1629; sole Master of Work 1634–8). At this time, none of the agents involved in the organisation of architectural projects precisely corresponded to the present-day architect. The two main groups were: landowners, and other representatives of patrons, who were involved in overall design and oversight of projects; and non-landed masons who combined the present-day role of contractor with some design tasks. In contrast to present-day organisational patterns such as 'design and build', the relative power of the two groups was not codified, but depended on the status and circumstances of each individual job. In royal works, an elaborately hierarchical system of control was overseen by the Masters of Work; the master masons seem to have worked in an operative role. Schaw was appointed in 1583 'grit maister of all and sindrie his hines palaceis, biggingis and reparatiounis, and grit oversear, directour and commandar'. [8] His stay in Denmark as one of the party organising James's 1589 marriage seems to have inaugurated a closeness in Scottish-Danish architectural relations. [9] His general authority in relation to the masons is shown by the fact that it was he who reorganised and codified the masonic craft in 1598–9, organising a national system of lodges for the first time. Murray, unlike Schaw, was not a laird but an artisan in origin; he was the son of a master wright in the royal works. He superintended and, in all likelihood, designed the new works at Edinburgh Castle and Linlithgow (working with William Wallace, royal master mason 1617–31), as well as other projects such as the new Parliament House, Berwick House and his own house, Kilbaberton.

Within the most prestigious non-royal projects, a similar system seems to have applied. For example, at George Heriot's Hospital (from c.1628), Wallace and his successor as royal master mason, William Aytoun, seem to have acted as contractors, and the former may have been involved in preparation of a 'modell and fram'; [10] a layout plan, which may have been that eventually adopted, was supplied by an absentee representative of Heriot's trust, Walter Balcanquhall; while stylistic features (but no

documentary evidence) suggest some involvement by Murray in the architectural design. However, in the case of country houses and other less prestigious projects, masons played a much more direct design role, as in the case of some of the Aberdeenshire castles built by the Bel family of masons. In other instances, such as the houses of Schaw's powerful friend Alexander Seton, the patron doubtless exerted a more forceful architectural role. During the early seventeenth century, under Wallace and Aytoun, the prestige of the royal master masons rose steadily; for much of the mid- and late century, the Mylne dynasty of master masons enjoyed a period of unbroken prominence.

Passing over the now largely vanished and piecemeal contributions of Mary and her Master of Work, William MacDowell – chiefly a reconstruction of the James IV palace block in Edinburgh Castle (c.1566) – the first major burst of royal palace-building during this period began after 1590 under Schaw's direction at Dunfermline, where he made additions following James VI's marriage to Anne, who had been given Dunfermline as her jointure house. These works included, it appears, a symmetrical castellated palace block with central tower. By 1616, in anticipation of James's first visit home since his accession to the English throne, alterations were put in hand at Falkland, Stirling and Edinburgh. At the latter (1615-17), the palace block was rebuilt. Its dominant outward face was made symmetrical, with ashlar front overlooking the town, flat roof, and domed turrets linked by a crenellated parapet. To the courtyard and side there were half-engaged polygonal staircase towers. Inside, it was intended that there should be superimposed king's and queen's apartments, on the Holyrood pattern. At Linlithgow, Murray had a freer hand, and a completely new plan-pattern resulted [cf. 1.6]. He replaced the former north quarter (collapsed 1607) with a completely new range of self-contained lodgings. The new five-storey block was built between 1618 and the 1620s, its tall, uniformly fenestrated facades seeming to anticipate the austerely classical urban tenements of later centuries – although it was, in fact, brightly painted and gilded when new. To the courtyard, a centrally placed, polygonal stairtower of

Edinburgh type was flanked by ranks of pedimented windows and surmounted by battlements and a near symmetrical range of chimneys [2.7]. To the outside, ranges of mullioned and transomed windows conveyed a more sober impression. Inside, there was symmetry too. There was a double-depth plan, with rooms off a cross-corridor on each floor: the ground floor is unvaulted. Both at the Edinburgh palace and at Holyrood, to emphasise that the old origin-myth foundation of royal castellated architecture had a central place in James's new unionist monarchy, an inscription was placed: 'Nobis haec invicta miserunt 106 proavi' (106 generations of kings have left these to us, unconquered). [11] As to the inspiration of this symmetrical, classical-castellated style, although the palaces themselves provided a powerful precedent, it was the contemporary royal palaces of Queen Anne's native Denmark that seemed to provide the closest parallel, their symmetrical facades punctuated with stairtowers and pedimented, mullioned/transomed windows: for instance, at Rosenborg Slot (c.1613–33).

Charles I, on his accession in 1625, immediately set about heightening the ceremonial decoration of the palaces. In 1628–9, when a royal visit was anticipated, the new north quarter of Linlithgow was richly painted and decorated, with payments recorded for 'laying over with oyle collour and. . . for gilting with gold the haill foir face of the new wark with the timber windowis and window brodis staine windowis and crownellis with ane brod for the kingis armes and houssing gilt and set of and . . . gilting and laying over with oyle collour the four orderis abone the utter yet and furnishing all sortis of gold oyle'. [12] For Charles's coronation visit of 1633, there was great expense to ensure a suitably triumphal appearance. Portraits of all the kings since Fergus I, painted by George Jamesone, were mounted at the west end of the Edinburgh tolbooth, while at the Tron, a huge double-peaked timber Parnassus 'stopit full with books' displayed representations of 'the ancient worthies of Scotland for learning'. [13] Murray designed a range of fanciful embellishments to James V's tower and palace at Holyrood, including an array

Firlithgow Palace.

2.7 Linlithgow Palace, nineteenth-century drawing showing south elevation of north quarter (J. Murray, 1618–1620s) and sections of east/west quarters.

of spires, turrets, finials and crowns. Despite the relatively limited scale of royal patronage, it still exerted considerable architectural influence, as we will see. More generally, the establishment of Edinburgh as the undisputed royal capital had, by the time the Stuarts moved to England, produced a dense clustering of satellite houses of landowners.

The Renaissance of Aristocratic Building

Gradually, and above all in the years of absentee monarchy after 1603, the aristocracy took the king's place as the effective pinnacle of Scottish society. If the century after 1455 had seen the Stewarts establish a degree of dominance, now the aristocracy and lairds caught up again with a vengeance. They began to steer the process of improvement and industrial development that would eventually lead Scotland from a feudal to a capitalist society. Sir George Bruce's pumping mechanism at his underwater Culross mine was regarded as such a wonder of the time that James VI was taken to inspect it on his 1617 visit. The building programmes of landowners expressed the way in which trade in commodities was beginning to run in parallel with trade in the symbols of power and order – although, in some cases, rash building projects led to serious financial indebtedness. And this architecture reflected the beginnings of tension between material progress and the James IV-like evocation of a glorious chivalric past. The 3rd Earl of Winton, a thrusting promoter of mining and salt panning, and builder of a harbour at Port Seton, substantially rebuilt Winton House in a classical style with some castellated features, and details loaded with personal and unionist royal symbolism [cf. 2.24, 2.25]. While the 7th laird of Glenorchy, Sir Duncan Campbell, was one of the first to begin estate improvement in the Highlands around 1600, his son Sir Colin devoted much time to ornamenting the family castle of Balloch (on the site of the present Taymouth) [cf. 5.38]. His enhancements included furniture, tapestries, and a series of over forty paintings (by George Jamesone and an unnamed German artist), depicting himself and his ancestors (all in knightly armour), the old kings of Scotland, and Charles, 'King of Great Brittane'. [14]

Among nobles and lairds, even within the court, the years after 1603 saw relatively little 'anglicisation' – with a few prominent exceptions such as George Home (Lord Berwick), or Lord Bruce of Kinloss. Even key supporters of James's unionist and episcopalian efforts, such as Sir William Alexander, the industrialist George Hay, or Robert Ker of Ancram, invested profits from their time in London back home in Scotland. It is difficult to trace any consistent relationship between patrons' political affiliations and the architectural forms of their houses. A few of the nobles espoused a classical architectural style perhaps related to James's 'British' classicism, as elaborated in London. Alongside this, the neo-chivalric 'cult of honour' continued, its traditional expressions such as jousting gradually giving way to less showy forms integrated with family-living patterns, such as heraldic or family history research. This period also saw the beginning of a wider antiquarianism, led by early/mid-seventeenth-century figures such as Sir James Balfour of Denmilne and Sir John Scott of Scotstarvit. While these chivalric and antiquarian ideas contributed, at a national level, to a distancing of the nobility from the monarchy in the lead-up to the signing of the National Covenant, they also helped distance the nobility as a whole from lesser lairds; and they served the particular interests of factions within the landed class throughout the entire period, whether *arrivistes* newly ennobled or established on church land, or older nobles trying to detach themselves from the rich newcomers.

As in the case of political affiliations, religious differences among landowners do not seem to have been directly or consistently reflected in the architecture of their dwellings: the builder of the aggressively classicising Caerlaverock courtyard extension and the builder of the ostentatiously castellated addition to Huntly (*c.*1600–10) were both Roman Catholics [cf. 2.13, 2.20]. Overall, despite the progressively more disruptive effects of Scotland's religious realignment on relations with Catholic Europe, the aim was still to combine a national-centred chivalry with cosmopolitan *humanitas*. The poet William Lithgow bragged in 1628 that 'as for as the nobility and gentry of the Kingdom, certainly, as they are generous, manly and full of courage; so they are courteous, discreet, learned scholars well read in the best histories, delicate linguists, the most part of them being brought up in France or Italy'. [15] Symbolic ornament was a slightly different case from architectural style: recent research has revealed prolific counter-Reformation symbolism in the decoration of the sixteenth-century castles of Catholic landowners in the north-east, including Gight, Craig of Auchindoir, Delgaty and Towie Barclay. [16]

The figure whose patronage and values epitomised the uncertainties of the age, and who built two of its most important projects – the remodelling of Fyvie Castle (1596–9) and of Pinkie (1613) – was Alexander Seton (1555–1622) [cf. 2.10, 2.21]. His career included appointment as Chancellor of Scotland, creation as Earl of Dunfermline, and the assignment of a leading role in the abortive 1604 union negotiation. We briefly encountered his patronage earlier, with the Dunfermline Aisle at Dalgety Bay Church [cf. 2.1]. Seton was a member of the family that built Barnes Castle, Winton, and extended Seton Palace; and he was apparently a patron and friend of Schaw and Murray [cf. 2.8, 2.18]. Thus, he was a pillar of the Stuart political and architectural establishment. Yet, in those unsettled times, he was at the same time an outsider. As a closet Roman Catholic, who had received a clerical education by Jesuits in Rome and had studied law in France, Seton was part of that world of liberal, Europe-wide cultural exchange which was now threatened by political and religious polarisations. In 1584, for instance, he and Schaw (also a Catholic) accompanied Seton's father on an embassy to Henri III to re-establish and reorganise the appointments to the 'Scotch Archers' – the French kings' royal body-guards. After his death, Seton was hailed as 'a great humanist in prose and in poecie, Greek and Latine, well versed in the mathematicks and had great skill in architecture and herauldrie'. [17] We will see in due course, in discussing his major works at Fyvie and Pinkie, the sharply contrasting expressions chosen by this humanist landowner to reflect both his power and his vulnerability.

'Gentimenis Places and Gret Palices': The Heyday of Castellated Architecture [18]

Where, in previous years, nobles' dwellings in most European countries remained generally faithful to castellated patterns, now there was a marked divergence. In France, for example, châteaux up to around 1640 adhered to the old quadrilateral plan, but increasingly discarded fortified forms. Alone among the Northern Renaissance countries, late sixteenth- and early seventeenth-century Scotland saw a bold reassertion of castellated architecture, spreading the vigorous classical-chivalric forms of the James IV/V royal palaces across the country. In neighbouring England, some lavish new castellated houses were built during this period (for example Wollaton, 1580, by R. Smythson; or Bolsover, from 1612, by J. Smythson) but their brittle squareness and symmetry differed sharply from the massive monumentality of Scottish Renaissance castles. In planning terms, these castles on the whole main-tained the long-established pattern of vaulted ground floor for service purposes, and principal floor above; the principal floor lost much of its baronial character of collective living and assumed some of the elegance of a *piano nobile*. Often, there was a new, grandiose stone staircase from ground floor to principal floor, for instance scale and platt examples at Careston (*c*.1580), Newark (1597–9) or Scalloway (1600); only exceptionally, as at Crichton (scale and platt, after 1581), or Glamis (turnpike, completed 1606), did a stair rise the full height of a building.

As is made clear in one of the most detailed documents of aristocratic attitudes in this field – Sir Robert Ker's letter of 1632 to his son, the Earl of Lothian, offering advice on the remodelling of the family castle at Ancrum – the guiding context of almost all Scottish castellated housebuilding projects by this date was the extension of old towers rather than new building. At a time of unprecedented wealth, this principle was prompted both by sentiment and by the practical aim of 'leaving always place for a better resolution'. On the one hand, there should be estate improvement and building extensions on a 'squair' or symmetrical plan; tenants' crofts and activities like football should be banished from the vicinity of the house. Yet regarding the old tower at the centre of the complex, there were different associations, of fortified chivalry, to be safeguarded – the more so as the house's proximity to the English border might pose the real security risks of invasion or 'nyghtbour feud' at some future date. Ker's advice on this point carefully distinguished between utilitarian and symbolic fortification. On the one hand, 'because the world may change agayn', windows should be kept small on the ground floor and a well should be maintained inside the house. On the other hand, he advised that 'By any meanes do not take away the battelment . . . for that is the grace of the house, and makes it looke lyk a castle, and henc so nobleste, as the other would make it looke lyk a peele'. [19]

What forms did this revitalisation of castellated architecture take? On the whole, the hierarchy of the previous period, with courtyard or palace dwellings at the top and simpler towers, was maintained, but with much greater elaboration and quantitative growth in numbers at both levels. 'Place' or 'Palace' became an increasingly common term. Bishop John Leslie claimed in 1578 that 'Gentimenis places and gret palices ma sal ye find in na place than in Fife'. [20] These newly developed 'palices' showed much overlap with classical houses in their horizontal elements, their galleries and lodging blocks and suites of apartments. The use of the Great Hall became less promiscuous and more formal or symbolic; with the development of more 'refined' eating habits, meals were eaten in the family rooms, using tables and chairs, and kitchens began their move away to remoter parts of the house.

All over the country, courtyard houses were being formed or expanded. At what was still one of the grandest, Seton Palace, the years after 1585 saw the reconstruction of the north-east quarter, in a regular, classical manner, under the super-intendence of Schaw and Alexander Seton – who provided a 'contryveance' for Robert, Lord Seton (later the Earl of Winton); however, the palace as a whole still remained an irregular agglomeration, to judge by later views, such as Clerk of Eldin's (admittedly romanticised) eighteenth-century picture [2.8]. In other palace rebuilding schemes, there were constant echoes of the great Stewart residences of the previous hundred years. The prestige of the quadrangular, towered arrange-

ment of Linlithgow was taken up by clergy (at Monimail, country palace of the bishops of St Andrews, enlarged c.1578) and aristocracy (in the quadrangular court envisaged for Edzell in the late sixteenth century, its entrance front asymmetrically balancing the square original tower with a new round angle tower). Linlithgow's courtyard and James V's gatehouse were also evoked in the 'new wark' [21] built by William Forbes, laird of Tolquhon in 1584 in the form of four quarters round a courtyard, with a gallery on two sides, entered by a stumpy twin-towered gatehouse; the house itself was stuffed with books, furniture and tapestries. A similar plan, combined with rather regular, classical fenestration, as at Balvenie, was employed at the new-built House of Boyne (1575–80), a palace with round angle towers and tower-flanked entrance, erected by Sir George Ogilvie of Dunlugas in 1575–80. Likewise Dudhope Castle, Dundee, built from 1580, had a twin-towered entrance and round towers at the angles. A more miniaturised two-tower gatehouse, set into the front of a small courtyard block built around a hall-house of c.1530–40, was erected at Rowallan in 1567. Highly horizontalised or regular-plan courtyard groups included Aberdour Castle, whose tower house acquired big extensions c.1570 (by Regent Morton) and c.1635, set above earlier terraced gardens; the extensive quadrangle of self-contained lodgings, hall and gallery added to Dunnottar Castle from c.1575 onwards; and the quadrangular, corner-towered Earl's Palace, Birsay, begun c.1574 by Robert Sinclair, Earl of Orkney, and completed by Earl Patrick – who later (1606–7) started another, more sumptuous quadrangular palace at Kirkwall, with massive oriel windows on either side of its main block [2.9].

The only one of these courtyard-based castle schemes to challenge the scale of the James IV/V works was another Seton project: the rebuilding of Fyvie Castle by Alexander Seton, begun in 1596 at the height of his first great period of power as chairman of the committee of 'Octavians' charged with regulating the royal finances [2.10]. Working with a member of the Bel family of masons and (very possibly) with Schaw, Seton spectacularly embellished an old house, dating probably from the thirteenth century, which had already been

2.8 Seton Palace, late eighteenth-century view from the north-west by John Clerk of Eldin, showing Schaw's north-east block (after 1585) on the left.

described in 1578 (by Bishop Leslie) as an 'insigne palatium'. It is likely, but not certain, that the house's Linlithgow-like quadrangular plan dates from this period, and that two of the four quarters were never completed. [22] What is indisputable is that Seton transformed the south quarter into a new show facade. In a crushingly symmetrical composition of turrets and bartizans, the new frontage comprised flanking corner towers (Preston and Meldrum), similar to the earlier Bel scheme at Midmar, and a massive centre block (the Seton tower), formed of two round towers joined by a soaring arch and capped by a gable and bartizans. This ingenious transformation of the twin-towered formula of the royal palaces or, indeed, of Seton Palace could have been intended as a baronialised evocation of the triumphal arches of Italy, but one should also recall the famous Porte Dorée of Fontainebleau (c.1528) with its triple-decker arches sandwiched between towers. Inside, a spectacular new ceremonial approach was constructed, in the form of a sweeping stone staircase contained within a 20-foot square space. But even as his triumphal seat at Fyvie was under construction, a series of political miscalculations nearly ruined Seton's career, and caused him to adopt a much more conciliatory posture in future, further concealing his Catholic sympathies.

In our second category of castellated architecture – castles dominated by a tower – the generally more restricted area available presented a much bigger obstacle to the practical aims of horizontal expansion and greater internal stateliness. One response to this was to continue the development of traditional plan types, such as the combination of hall and tower. The latter was, for instance, perpetuated at Carnasserie, Argyll, where an earlier structure was massively enlarged in 1565–72 by John Carswell, Bishop of the Isles, using masons and the latest shafted court-style classical decoration from the east [2.11]. At a slightly smaller scale, Ferniehurst Castle (rebuilt 1598) combined a two-storey main block and a four-storey tower, including a round library in its east tower; the Place of Kilbirnie (c.1627) juxtaposed a massive pre-existing tower with a somewhat classical, regularly windowed, bartizaned jamb with projecting porch.

The formula of adding more space through full-height or taller wings was further exploited. In some cases, there were developments tending towards a kind of classical regularity – a tendency

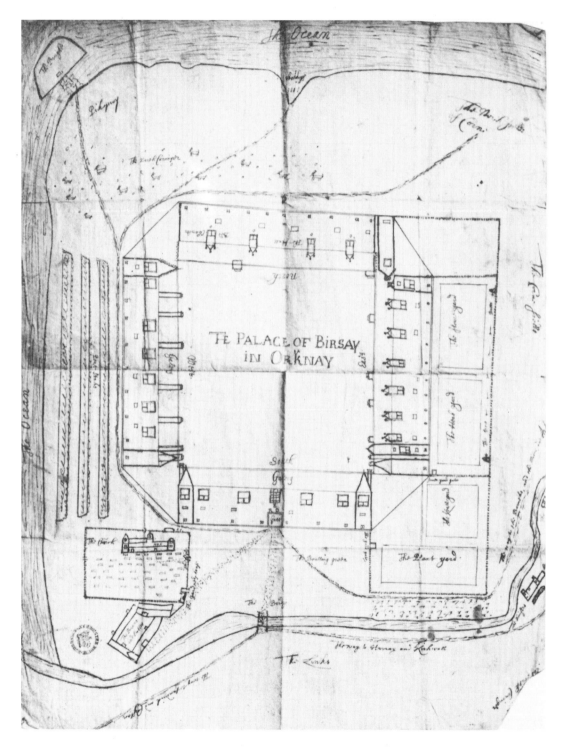

2.9 Earl's Palace, Birsay, Orkney (from *c*.1574), seventeenth-century drawing showing composite plan/elevations.

2.10 Fyvie Castle, main facade following rebuilding by Alexander Seton (from 1596), Billings view.

which anticipated one of the most important plan types of the late seventeenth century. For example, at the late sixteenth-century Duntarvie, a four-storey hall-type block of elongated plan was given, on one side, five-storey square towers at either end, creating a more or less symmetrical U-shaped plan, with a centrally placed straight flight of stairs to the first floor. A wilful asymmetry of elevation, fronting a symmetrical plan, was displayed in the Earl and Countess of Moray's Castle Stewart (1619–25), a U-shaped house with contrasting front wings (one crowstepped and turreted, the other square); here there was considerable overlap with the patterns seen at classical Winton House (dealt with later in this chapter).

Still much more popular, however, were the un-classical plan types which added one side wing to a main block, or extended it with two diagonal towers (the three-stepped or Z-shaped plan). The larger examples of the latter became increasingly grandiose after 1560; private rooms of some pre-tension, especially bedrooms, were usually housed in these towers. Sometimes large staircases were incorporated (for example at Scalloway, 1600, or the large turnpike stair at Glamis, 1606). Noltland (1560–71), built by Gilbert Balfour, an Orkney magnate described by Knox as a man with 'neither fear of God nor love of virtue', [23] featured a

2.11 Carnasserie Castle, Argyll (enlarged 1565–72).

diagonal-towered castle with attached courtyard. It contained a spacious first-floor apartment, while rivalling Finnart in warlike display with an awesome array of over seventy wide-mouthed gunports in the three lower storeys.

The most monumental realisations of the diagonal-towered pattern were in the north-east. At the early seventeenth-century Gordon Castle (now mostly demolished) an arcaded loggia ran round the outer wall of the main block at *piano nobile* level: loggias seem to have been a more common feature in country houses than the few present-day survivors suggest. At Castle Fraser, the three main stages of development were clearly distinguished: first, an old-style rectangular tower as the core; second, the addition of diagonal wings (one square, one round) by *c.*1592; and third, in 1617–18, the elaboration and heightening of this three-stepped group into a monumental composition by John Bel, mason, for Andrew Fraser. Bel heightened the round tower by four storeys, finishing it with a balustrade, and raised the remainder of the building to match. A corbel table zigzagged around the castle, topped by a forest of turrets and pedimented dormers. A roughly symmetrical approach was formed by the building of flanking wings with turrets – the 'laich biggings', 1621–36, with a regular, classical row of alternately segmental and triangular pediments – overlooked by a huge armorial panel at the top of the main building [2.12]. The most grandiloquent of all diagonal-towered north-east castles was Huntly, a house which followed the same three-stage process as Castle Fraser, culminating in a phase of work by George Gordon, 1st Marquis, *c.*1600–10. Gordon, the most openly Catholic among the greater aristocracy, created suites of apartments on two upper floors (above the Great Hall), with inner chambers in the huge round corner tower and a line of oriels, spiky dormers, and tall frieze inscribed with his name and that of his wife, Henrietta Stewart [2.13]. There was a particular emphasis on heraldic carving, including an individualistic vertical panel above the main entrance (with lavish Catholic imagery, smashed by a Covenanting army in 1640), and decorated chimneypieces inside.

Slightly smaller north-eastern castles by the Bel family, featuring only a single wing, but the same

2.12 Castle Fraser, Aberdeenshire, view from north, showing main tower (completed 1618) in background, Laich Biggings in front with conical turrets, and crowstepped pavilions of *c.*1820 in the foreground.

2.13 Huntly Castle, Aberdeenshire (completed *c.*1610), Billings drawing.

visual treatment of corbel-table and bristling castellated/classical skyline, included Crathes and Craigievar. Crathes was built 1553–96, and contained a notable 1599/1602 scheme of ceiling paintings of classical figures and warrior kings, with accompanying inscriptions including verses in praise of the 'Auld Alliance' with France.

Craigievar, a six-storey tower bought (partly completed) in 1610 by William Forbes, a wealthy Baltic trader, was finished (1626) with the help of John Bel. Originally enclosed by a small courtyard, Craigievar still followed the late medieval principle of cellular planning, with a Great Hall, eighteen other apartments and interlinking upper-floor

gallery plan

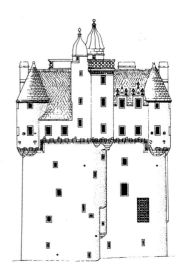

east elevation

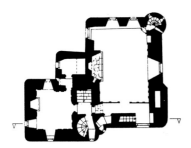

first-floor plan

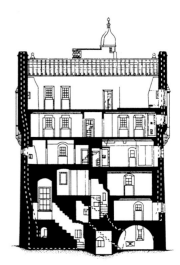

section

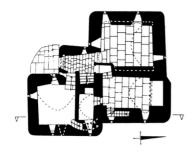

ground-floor plan

2.14 Craigievar Castle (completed 1626), plans, sections and elevations of *c*.1975 by Geoffrey D. Hay.

staircases fitted ingeniously into a confined, verticalised envelope, but its exterior was ornamented with a typically Scottish Renaissance mixture of corbel-table, pediments, turrets and balustraded viewing platform [2.14]. On the garden side of the building, and (read diagonally) on its splayed side, the castle is roughly symmetrical. Inside, Craigievar's Great Hall features a vault with heavy strapwork plaster decoration, and a fireplace with large plaster royal arms above.

Another way of trying to increase accommodation in tower-based plan types was by deepening the main tower into a plan two rooms deep, with spinal corridor, as at Drochil (from *c.*1578, for Regent Morton) [2.15] and at the reconstruction of Spedlins (*c.*1605); in the latter

instance, this double-depth plan was externally expressed by twin gables. Elsewhere in northern Europe, similar transformations were in progress within traditional formulae: for instance, mid-sixteenth-century Danish manor houses such as Egeskov featured double-depth plans and corner turrets for 'best' rooms. There were also attempts to express classical ideas of symmetry and regularity within this more compressed form, which was destined to become much more important from the late seventeenth century. At Craigston, rebuilt 1604–7 by John Urquhart, the link with Fyvie is obvious, in the use of the same mason and the same device of towers linked into a triumphal arch form, topped by a balustraded viewing platform; the U-shaped layout had elements of

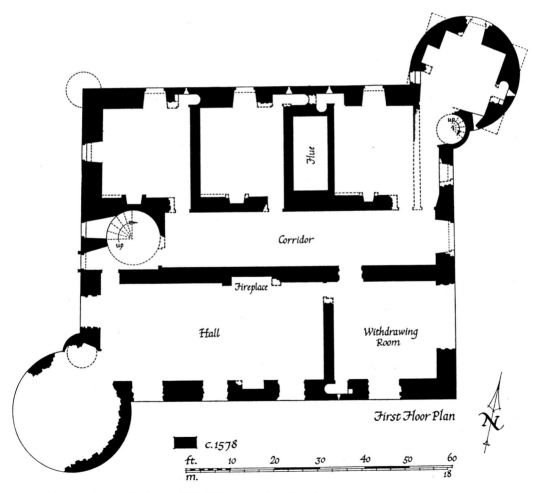

2.15 Drochil Castle, Peeblesshire (from *c.*1578), 1967 RCAHMS plan of first floor.

double-depth planning, especially at top-floor level, where there was a full-width gallery [cf. 2.10].

The most idiosyncratic of all the extended-tower castle plans of this era was the extraordinary Thirlestane, built *c.*1590 by John Maitland (who was Chancellor 1585–95 and created Baron Maitland, 1590) and partly rebuilt in the late seventeenth and mid-nineteenth centuries. Constructed on the site of a 1540s English artillery fortification, this house took the attempts to combine symmetry and horizontal apartment planning with castellated architecture to an extreme. Symmetrical on both axes, it comprised a tall, elongated block containing a processional range of rooms, with private rooms terminating at either end in a pair of complex rounded towers; the side facades were articulated by a range of shallow rounded projections rather like giant pilasters [cf. 3.6].

The lowest level of country house architecture at which castellated stone building was affordable (other than in the border area, with its austere or temporary pele-houses) was that of the lesser lairds' houses. Here, in this period, the cellular tower, even with wings, began to seem intolerably cramped and outmoded: the plan-form of the smaller diagonal-towered examples had to be more or less the same, whatever the external expression. In some cases, a semi-fortified form was combined with the beginning of a move towards a more symmetrical, classical treatment: a more regular, reposeful expression of the central block is already perceptible, for instance, at the diagonal-towered Kilmartin, built probably towards the end of the sixteenth century. During the second quarter of the seventeenth century, the Craigievar fashion of splayed plan with square balustrade-topped stairtower, at the centre, was further regularised at buildings such as Castle Gogar, 1625, Hill House, Dunfermline, 1623, and Innes House, 1640–53 (built by William Aytoun, master mason at Heriot's Hospital, and resembling the general facade disposition of Heriot's north quarter) [cf. 2.36]. At Innes House the main scale and platt stair does not stop at the first floor, but ostentatiously carries on, right up to the balustraded terrace. In Chapter 3 we will return to the elaboration of this splayed type in the mid-seventeenth century. Elsewhere, there was a gradual departure from verticalised forms in favour of more sprawling

patterns such as that of Fountainhall, a three-storey, informally villa-like grouping with some classical features (for example pedimented dormers) built, in its present form, in 1638 for an Edinburgh lawyer, Robert Pringle. Craig Castle, Angus, comprises a more complicated group, including an L-shaped two-storey and attic house (rebuilt in its present form in 1637), and an extensive courtyard complex with low, battlemented towers, an arched gateway, stables and walled garden.

Occasionally, the gradual trend away from the smaller tower turned into a sharper rupture. At Amisfield in Dumfriesshire, for example, work of *c.*1600 created one of the most dramatically compressed of small Renaissance tower houses, crowned by an outcrop of gables, rope-mouldings and columned dormer decoration: inside, one room retains a classical ceiling frieze with roundel-like motifs. But within thirty years, Amisfield's tower house had been replaced as the principal residence, by a completely new, detached three-storey classical house (1631) placed right across it and blocking it from frontal view; the new dwelling had an austere, uniformly arranged main facade and pedimented windows [2.16].

The First Classical Country Houses

By the beginning of the seventeenth century, some grander patrons were experimenting with a more radical move towards classical house design. This included attempts to evoke, albeit imprecisely, some elements of contemporary or recent Italian classicism, with a more literal use of the Orders, as against the exuberant freedom of Northern Renaissance detailing. In these cases, as in James VI's palaces, it was much easier to provide for horizontal living arrangements. These classical efforts can be divided into two main groups. The first was a series of palace-like designs built, in some cases, by patrons with a strong connection either directly with the Mediterranean, or with the somewhat Italianising tendencies of James VI's Scottish and English court architecture. The second was a tendency, pioneered particularly by James Murray, which sought to apply the classical regularity of the early seventeenth-century Scots royal palaces to more longstanding plan types.

2.16 Amisfield, Dumfriesshire, late eighteenth-century watercolour by John Clerk of Eldin, showing tower (centre) and replacement house of 1631 (at right).

The first group began with a heterogeneous group of designs or interventions in the 1580s and 1590s. The first of these was also the most idiosyncratic: a new north quarter added to Crichton Castle by the 5th Earl of Bothwell, Lord High Admiral of Scotland, during the decade following his return from Italy in 1581. Bothwell was a swashbucklingly contentious figure, who was eventually exiled in 1595 for a series of reckless attacks on the royal palaces, and died in exile in Naples. His new building at Crichton was equally provocative, being studded with diamond-faceted rustication (potentially inspired by any of a number of Italian or Italianate German buildings of the sixteenth century) and rising from an arched loggia, with round columns [2.17]. Fenestration fronting the main hall/dining room section of the facade was regular, and to the left an array of double windows fronted another urbane touch – a grand scale and platt staircase rising the full height of the building. Equally cosmopolitan, and near-symmetrical inside and out, was a design commenced in the 1590s by one of Alexander Seton's relatives, Sir John Seton of Barnes, on his return from service as master of the household of King Philip II of Spain, but left uncompleted in 1594. Perhaps inspired by the layout of symmetrical Spanish palaces, its long, rectangular main body had end wings, walled forecourt, and a long outer face with corner pavilions and uniform window bays [2.18]. Taller, but in some ways similar in plan, was the old Hamilton Palace, whose front block was seemingly a larger and more elaborate version of the Duntarvie formula, and with an associated datestone (1590) of the same period. The symmetrical facade was dominated by four large chimneys with pediments on top, and flanked by taller, projecting towers a single bay in width. More modest in height (two storeys), but extensive on plan, Scone Palace (c.1602) featured a symmetrical, uncastellated front facade with crowstepped, arched centre and side pavilions.

At James VI's move to England in 1603, a small group of houses or extensions was built by close supporters of his and his son's new ideology of regal unionism. These included two of the most indefatigable anglicisers, both appointed by James to key English government posts in the run-up to abortive negotiations for a closer political union: George Home, Lord Berwick (an English title, from 1604) and Earl of Dunbar (from 1605); and

2.17 Crichton Castle, north range
(after 1581), Billings view.

Edward, Lord Bruce of Kinloss. The forceful and
ruthless Home, appointed Treasurer in 1601 and
English Chancellor of the Exchequer in 1603, was
the mainstay of the King's episcopal and erastian
religious policies; although a lesser laird by origin,
his rapid ennoblement and rise to power catapulted
him far ahead of any of the traditional aristocracy.
In or slightly before 1607, to celebrate the regal
union, Dunbar commissioned James Murray to
design 'a sumptuous and glorious palace', Berwick
House, [24] overlooking the Tweed (shortly to be
spanned by a new stone bridge also instigated by
Home). The scanty surviving evidence concerning
Berwick House suggests that it was a flat-roofed,
regularly fenestrated, square-pavilioned building
with large mullioned and transomed windows – not
unlike the north quarter of Linlithgow – with a

top-floor gallery. It was praised by George Chawoth
at the time as 'the greatest squadron by much in
England; and of that exceeding heyght, and yet
magnificent turrets above that heyght, a goodlye
front. . . and that uniforme proportion everye waye
generally, as wold stodye a good architector to
describe'. [25] The English traveller Sir William
Brereton described, in 1636, 'a stately, sumptuous
and well-seated house, or castle. . . a most stately
platform. . . a fair long gallery joiced [with open
joisted roof], not boarded, wherein is the largest
mantle-tree [fireplace lintel] I have seen, near five
yards long of one piece; this [gallery] leaded over,
which gives the daintiest prospect'. [26]

    The following year (1608), Bruce of Kinloss,
who had been promoted by King James to Lord of
Session in 1597 and English Master of Rolls in

1603, began a similar, but more modestly sized palace, Culross Abbey House [2.19]. This comprised a two-storey block (later heightened to three storeys), with tall outer single-bay pavilions flanking a uniformly windowed, 13-bay front (the first floor windows with pediments and attenuated Tuscan pilasters) with centre doorway. The present cornice moulding suggests the house may originally have

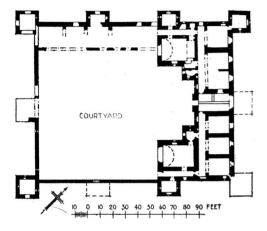

2.18 Barnes Castle, East Lothian (1590s), plan from RCAHMS *Inventory* of East Lothian.

been flat roofed, but in any case there was a strong horizontal emphasis; the block may have been intended to occupy two sides of an (uncompleted) courtyard. The plan was double-depth, with unvaulted ground floor, and *piano nobile* gallery with stone panelling on its south wall. Buildings possibly influenced by the designs of Culross and Berwick included Preston Lodge, Cupar (*c*.1623; a miniature version of the type) and pre-William Adam work at Floors Castle, whose precise dating and building sequence is still unclear.

Bucking the trend of aristocratic alienation during the reign of Charles I, one major classical design was erected by a prominent Catholic supporter of the King's religious policies: a major extension to Caerlaverock Castle built by Sir Robert Maxwell, 1st Earl of Nithsdale. The Italophile Maxwell, sent to Rome in 1624 to obtain papal dispensation for the King's marriage to Henrietta Maria, was prominent in the wave of Catholic optimism which surrounded Charles's coronation visit in 1633, and immediately afterwards he began to build striking classical additions within the courtyard at Caerlaverock. The surviving section includes symmetrical

2.19 Culross Abbey House (1608; third storey added 1670 and rebuilt in reduced form 1954–6 by Robert Hurd & Partners), mid-twentieth-century photograph prior to Hurd scheme.

facades with regularly arranged windows surmounted by large, almost Baroque segmental and
triangular pediments containing allegorical reliefs
[2.20]. Maxwell's optimism was mistaken, and the
castle was besieged and sacked by Covenanters in
1640. The building of classical show-houses by
unionist grandees was paralleled in contemporary
Ireland, where the Lord Deputy, the Earl of
Strafford, built an enormously long block at
Jigginstown, near Naas, in 1636–7 in anticipation
of a royal visit. Designed by the Dutch architect
John Allen, the double-depth house's two-storey
facade was subdivided in a semi-regular manner by
pilaster-like chimneys.

A strong contrast to these bold, even aggressive
designs was presented by the most ideologically
complex of all classical country house projects
commissioned by post-1603 establishment figures:
the enlargement of Pinkie House by Alexander
Seton in 1613, during the years of his quiet, non-
confrontational ascendancy following the death of
his rival George Home in 1611. Pinkie projects an
image neither of brashly flat-roofed rectangularity,
nor of hectoring castellation, as at Seton's own
earlier Fyvie [cf. 2.10]. Rather, the main east
quarter takes the form of a studiedly sober range,
extended out of an old tower house with a range
of classically disposed windows (originally more
regular in appearance than at present), stringcourses and seven prominent, plain chimneys
[2.21]. The facade overlooks a symmetrical walled
garden, with semi-polygonal garden house opposite. The layouts of this garden are now for the
most part lost, but it was described in 1668 by
John Lauder of Fountainhall as 'a most sweit
garden, the knot much larger than that at Hamilton
and in better order'. [27] The only external
architectural features of the house suggesting

2.20 Caerlaverock Castle, Dumfriesshire
(rebuilt after 1633), Billings view of
courtyard looking north.

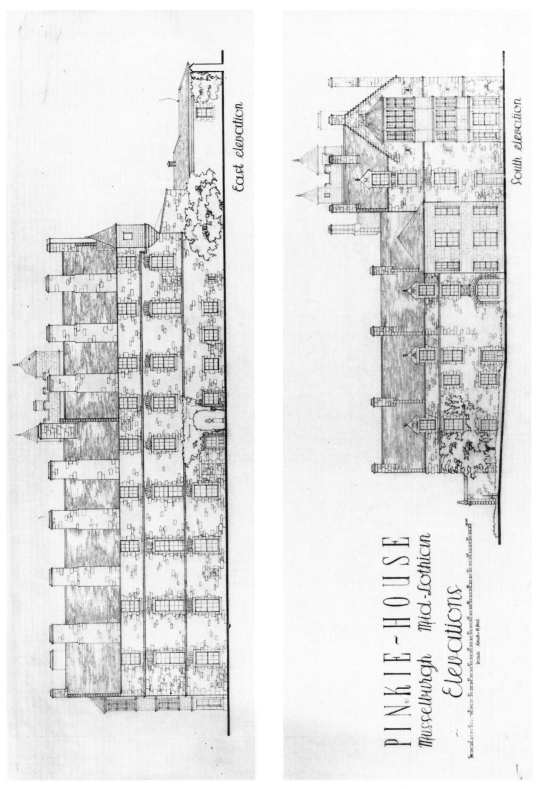

East elevation

South elevation

P I N K I E · H O U S E
Musselburgh Mid-Lothian
Elevations

2.21 Pinkie House (enlarged 1613), 1947 drawing of east and south elevations by Stanisław Tyrowicz.

opulence are a three-storey oriel window at one end, and a classical fountain with imperial crown on the entrance side – although the array of chimneys, hinting at large numbers of coal-burning fireplaces, would itself have subtly pointed to Seton's wealth. A lower, dormered wing extends to the west; a further, north-west extension, forming a U-shaped courtyard plan, may have been intended, but was not built. Inside, the ground floor of the new section was unvaulted, like Culross and Linlithgow. The second floor contained plaster-ceilinged rooms and, at the south end, the showpiece of a gallery painted in the manner of a rustic loggia, with *trompe-l'œil* 'arched' and 'glazed' ceiling, studded with moralistic illustrations of antique or mythological scenes, and accompanied by Stoic quotations from Horace and other writers [2.22]. Seton's visit to France in 1584, of course, would have allowed him to inspect personally the most prestigious gallery scheme of northern Europe, at Fontainebleau. It is not clear how much of the house's design was Seton's own, or whether he drew on the assistance of Murray.

As an extensive programme of inscriptions and mottoes makes clear, Pinkie was a comprehensively conceived expression of the Renaissance concept of the villa and garden as an intellectual and moral sanctuary from the hubbub and vices of the city. An inscription at the entrance sets a tone of conspicuous modesty: 'Alexander, Lord Seton, built this house in 1613, not as he would have wished, but as his fortunes and the size of the site permitted'. Inside, one of the gallery mottoes chided that: 'A happy home is preferable to a large home. Often toil and sorrow dwell in palaces, peace and happiness in cottages.' The principal inscription, now set in the garden wall, emphasised the house's peace-loving dedication to Renaissance ideals of *humanitas* and *urbanitas*:

> Alexander Seton, a man of high culture and urbanity, has laid out and ornamented this villa and gardens near the city, for his own pleasure and the pleasure of his noble descendants, and of everyone of culture and urbanity. This is no place of warfare, designed to repel enemies. Instead, there is a welcoming and kindly fountain of pure water, a grove, pools, and other amenities – everything that could afford decent pleasures of heart and spirit. [28]

To Seton, steeped in the world of the Italian aristocratic home, the conventions of external sobriety and internal display which governed Pinkie's design would have been just as much second nature as the castellated display of Fyvie. Seton's theme of Augustan Stoicism was also of particular relevance in the early seventeenth-century context, not only to his own predicament as a Catholic government official, but to the changing *Weltanschauung* of the nation as a whole: hesitantly following their 'king of peace' in rejecting martial confrontation with the English in favour of an uneasy negotiated accommodation. Pinkie was a location with considerable historical resonances in its own right. It stood within a few hundred yards of the site of a Roman tomb (discovered in 1565 and 'utterlie aboloschit', doubtless at the hands of Protestant iconoclasts, by 1593); [29] and it was, of course, near to the location of the battle of Pinkie, fought seventy years before. If the pomp of Linlithgow epitomised the early Scottish Renaissance confidence in the 'nation at arms', the sobriety of Pinkie seemed to symbolise a growing pragmatism, although no reduction in cosmopolitan internationalism, on the part of the nation's ruling élites.

Whether or not Murray was directly involved at Pinkie, he shortly after played a key role in a more modest architectural campaign. A more domestic-scaled version of his royal palace architecture was introduced in a series of three houses, begun shortly before the completion of the new Linlithgow north quarter: his own house, Kilbaberton (1623, now known as Baberton); Pitreavie (1630, built for his friend, and Queen Anne's chamberlain, Sir Henry Wardlaw); and Winton (1620–7, built by the mining magnate Lord Seton). Only at Kilbaberton is Murray's direct oversight certain; at Winton, there is only evidence of Wallace's involvement. In all three cases, the house forms a U-shape around a shallow court-yard, with entrance door situated in one or two of the angles. At Kilbaberton and Pitreavie, the entrance facade is symmetrically arranged, with flanking triangular, uncrowstepped gables – not unlike that of the Dalgety Aisle, but surmounted by chimneys. Decoration at Kilbaberton included buckle quoins, obelisks, and windows topped by floral-ornamented pediments. At Pitreavie, the

2.22 Pinkie House, late nineteenth-century painting of part of gallery ceiling, by T. Bonnar.

internal planning is symmetrical, and the near–symmetrical garden front is fronted by a curvilinear gable, suggestive of Dutch influence, of the type that became popular later in the century [2.23]. Clearly, these houses overlap substantially with the more symmetrical variants of castellated architecture, as at the end-winged Duntarvie, or

2.23 Pitreavie House Fife (1630), view taken *c.*1890.

the small, splay-planned post-castellated houses, such as Innes House, with their arrangement of public stair to first floor and turnpike above. This overlap was carried rather further at the third of the group, Winton (an enlargement of a pre-1540s' tower), whose flanking wings are treated in an asymmetrical but balanced manner almost reminiscent of Castle Stewart, with crowstepped gable and polygonal re-entrant stairtower on one side and a balustraded tower and corner turret on the other [2.24]. External details, such as the window surrounds and strapwork, echo Heriot's Hospital [cf. 2.36]. Inside, the first floor contains a sequence of three rooms with sumptuous plaster ceilings featuring Stuart royal symbols; the largest room has a huge heraldic stone fireplace with the unionist royal arms [2.25]. This lavishness of internal heraldic decoration was only matched at Careston Castle, begun by Sir Henry Lindsay *c.*1586 and remodelled *c.*1620–3, including a range of five great armorial chimneypieces (one with royal arms), and a large scale and platt stair in a wing.

A link between the planning of the 'Kilbaberton' series of houses and that of Pinkie is provided by the now demolished Wrychtishousis, near Edinburgh, recently researched by Charles McKean: this apparently early seventeenth-century house, encrusted with gables, towers and Murray-like details, had a deeper U-plan like a 'completed' Pinkie, with high wings and lower connecting block. It was reputedly decorated with heads of Roman emperors and of the Virtues, and with heraldic motifs, including several pseudo-medieval date inscriptions (surviving examples being dated 1399, 1450 and 1513). Another modest classical Lothian house of this period was House of the Binns, built from 1612 as the Scottish seat of Thomas Dalyell (an Edinburgh merchant who moved to London in 1603) and extended later in the seventeenth century. There was sumptuous ceiling plasterwork (*c.*1630), again dotted with unionist royal motifs, but here actually executed by

English craftsmen (under Alessandro Blanco) in anticipation of Charles I's visit in 1633.

The period covered by this chapter coincided with the maturing, across Europe, of the formal Renaissance garden, with its statues, fountains and arbours. In Scotland the ideal seems to have been a combination of walled gardens, formal aligned layouts and terracing overlooking avenues, but only fragments of schemes survive today. At Drummond Castle, only the outline form remains of the 2nd Earl of Perth's parterre of 1630, completely reconstructed in 1839 (see Chapter 5). At Murthly, the slightly later walled garden (1669) features geometrical arrays of clipped box hedges and yew trees. At Seton Palace, the sixteenth-century turreted walled garden is still traceable. Improvements to the royal King's Knot at Stirling also continued throughout the period (for example

2.24 Winton House (1620–7), nineteenth-century view of exterior.

2.25 Winton House, drawing room, Billings drawing.

in 1628). There seem to be no intact Scottish examples from this period of the formal vista, a concept which stemmed ultimately from the villas outside Rome, aligned towards the dome of St Peter's, and which (as we will see in Chapter 3) would reach its grandest scale in the France of Louis XIV. The 1629 house at Balcaskie, famous for its remodelling by Bruce, appears to have been aligned on the Bass Rock, while the flank of Prestonfield (a 1684 rebuilding of an earlier fire-damaged house) is aligned on Craigmillar Castle. The most notable surviving Renaissance geometrical garden is that added to Edzell Castle in 1604 by Sir David Lindsay, Lord Edzell. Lindsay, a cosmopolitan lawyer and tireless improver, pioneered large-scale afforestation and mining on his estate, inviting German engineers as consultants. His garden was surrounded by walls (with summer-house and bath-house), originally decorated with pilasters, pediments, Stuart unionist royal symbols and carved panels depicting the planetary deities, the Virtues and the Arts. Interest in geometrical, symbolic gardens throughout northern Europe had been encouraged by the Danish astronomer Tycho Brahe's castle,

Uraniborg (1576–80), visited by James VI in 1590. The spirit of the scientific garden was also expressed by another feature commonly found as a focal point in Scottish parterres: the sundial. The multi-faceted polyhedral variant was only made possible by John Napier's discovery of logarithms in Edinburgh in 1614: an early example, ornamented with thistles and roses, was carved by royal master mason John Mylne for the coronation visit of Charles I in 1633. The most elaborate and earliest dated sundial in the country, loaded with Renaissance ornament of the Murray pattern, was built in 1623 by Sir Walter Dundas at Dundas Castle. It comprises a fountain with three basins on each side, a heavy entablature above, and a baluster sundial above, accessible by a flying stair [2.26].

Town Houses and Civic Architecture

This was a time of almost unprecedented urban expansion. By the late seventeenth century, the four cities of the present day had established a clear population lead over their nearest challengers, with Edinburgh reaching a population of over 30,000; the other three largest towns

2.26 Sir Walter Dundas's fountain-sundial (1623) at Dundas Castle.

(Glasgow, Dundee, Aberdeen) totalled between 10,000 and 12,000 inhabitants each. In the first half of the seventeenth century, Edinburgh had strengthened its dominant position, whether in population, commerce or credit, but in the second half the other towns began to catch up. Burgh government was not democratic government, in the modern sense. Small groups of burgesses held power in the towns, while in the country small burghs of barony were dominated by local landowners. For the urban élites, the seventeenth century represented a peak of power not to be surpassed until the very different days of the late eighteenth century and nineteenth century. Architecturally, this period saw the building not only of prominent individual projects, including the mansions of the rich, but also the effective beginning of that tradition of monumental urban architecture, including public buildings and collective dwelling groups, which would reach a climax in the nineteenth and twentieth centuries.

In contrast to the increasingly distinctive forms of higher density urban dwelling groups (see below), the townhouses of the very rich were in some respects quite similar to country houses: the largest were like microcosms of the royal palaces or other courtyard houses, while others resembled U-shaped houses of the Winton/Kilbaberton type, or turreted castles. Of the houses built by aristocrats or lairds in the larger towns, the two most imposing surviving examples are located in Stirling: Mar's Wark, townhouse of the Earl of Mar, 1570–2, and

Argyll's Lodging, built for Sir William Alexander in the early 1630s. The unfinished Mar's Wark, possibly designed by the Master of Work Sir William MacDowell, was an example of a courtier building erected close to a royal palace, and closely imitating royal patterns [2.27]. It also served as a backdrop for the processional route up to the castle, for which the Earls of Mar were hereditary keepers. This public-ceremonial function informed its detailed design. The near-symmetrical facade comprised a pair of polygonal towers forming a triumphal-arch gateway, in obvious reference to the Forework, while the adjoining facade echoed the James V palace block (a style paralleled elsewhere, for instance at Carnasserie) with attenuated shafts and advanced/recessed panels. Argyll Lodging, probably designed by Sir William Alexander's son, Sir Anthony (joint royal Master of Work) and subsequently enlarged in 1674 by the Earl of Argyll, was another project undertaken in anticipation of a call by King Charles on his 1633 visit. The 1632 work comprised the extension of an L-shaped block into a Kilbaberton-like U-layout – only deeper in plan, more profusely turretted, and fronted by a screen wall and rusticated gateway like a French hôtel; detail included richly strapworked facades and a porch near-identical to the doorcase at Kilbaberton [2.28].

In and around Edinburgh, slightly more modest examples survive. A Canongate townhouse which was (originally) more or less L-shaped, with a small courtyard in the angle, is Acheson House, built 1633 by Sir Archibald Acheson of Clonekearney, Co. Armagh, and Baronet of Nova Scotia. The nearby Moray House, later extended, was built *c.*1625 for the Dowager Countess of Home. It has a gateway with pyramidal-capped piers, and gabled street facade with heavily corbelled balcony. The rapid urban growth of the capital also stimulated the building of suburban and smaller country houses nearby: Henri, Duc de Rohan noted of Edinburgh in *c.*1600 that 'more than a hundred country-seats are to be found within a radius of two leagues of the town'. [30] These houses varied, from the extremely elaborate, such as Wrychtishousis, to the modest and plain, such as the small, castellated Easter Coates (1615, for John Byres), a slightly old-fashioned two-storey L-shaped block with pedimented dormers and angle turret.

2.27 Mar's Wark, Stirling (1570–2).

2.28 Argyll Lodging, Stirling (enlarged 1632 and 1674), early twentieth-century view.

In the smaller burgh of barony, the townhouse could assert local aristocratic power in a very direct way. A prominent example was Maybole Castle, built from the late sixteenth century as the townhouse of the Earls of Cassilis, hereditary bailiffs of Carrick – a tall, L-shaped tower, with crowstepped gables, dormer detailing of the western 'Haggs' pattern, and angle turrets. The house is surmounted by a panelled prospect room at the top of the south wing, with three-sided ashlar oriel allowing the earl to survey 'his' burgh [2.29].

The houses built by prosperous merchants and tradesmen usually adopted similar forms to those of landowners. In Aberdeen's Schoolhill stood (until last century) a prominent house with bartizaned tower flanked by wings with regular fenestration, all in ashlar; it was occupied in the early seventeenth century by the painter George Jamesone, but probably built a little earlier. Nearby Provost Skene's House, probably built in 1622–41 and enlarged in the later sixteenth century by the merchant Sir George Skene of Rubislaw, has a flat-roofed main block (originally balustraded) and turreted side wings; its rather horizontal plan-form, with end wings, resembles country houses such as Duntarvie. The early seventeenth-

2.29 Maybole Castle (late sixteenth-century), Billings view.

century house of Provost James Pierson in the Greenmarket, Dundee, on the other hand, resembled older royal palaces in the massive round towers at three of its corners; the fourth corner contained a scale and platt staircase, and the ground floor was arcaded.

Alongside these setpiece dwellings, building patterns shaped specifically by the communal aspects of burgh life were now becoming prominent, especially in Edinburgh and in a burgh which was, by the third quarter of the seventeenth century, gradually emerging as the country's second largest town: Glasgow. Along the wide space of Edinburgh's High Street, merchants' houses were tightly packed alongside one another, confined by the narrowness of the burgage plots. The street was, increasingly, lined with high,

gabled facades, some crowstepped in a manner paralleled in Baltic and Netherlandish towns, and with their rooflines running back at right angles. Many of these street facades rose from arched, open loggias (referred to as 'piazzas') [2.30]. These may have been adapted from country houses such as Crichton, although the unified urban developments of Paris (for example, the Place Royale, 1605–12) or London's Covent Garden may also have been of influence. As in other densely developed European cities, the buildings behind the facades were now mostly subdivided both vertically and horizontally. For example, by the later sixteenth century, the upper floors of John Knox House in the High Street (a much rebuilt three-storey structure mainly dating from the mid-sixteenth century) formed a structurally separate

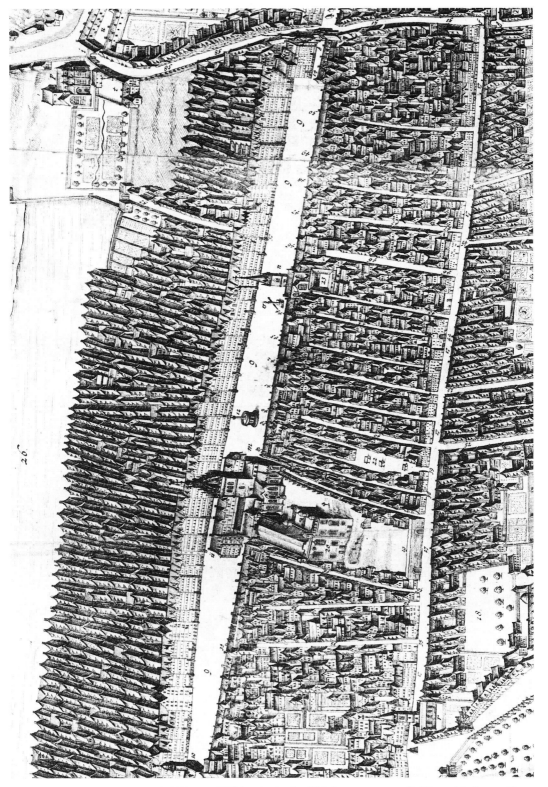

2.30 Detail of Gordon of Rothiemay's 1647 map of Edinburgh, showing High Street tenements, St Giles and Parliament House at left centre, and Netherbow Port on the right.

house reached by a newel stair. Access to upper floors might be by external forestairs. Some new buildings were even purpose-built in the form of new tenement blocks. The position at mid-century was recorded in Gordon of Rothiemay's view of Edinburgh/Canongate: tall blocks in Edinburgh High Street, much lower and more intermittent elsewhere. In Glasgow, the French traveller Jorevin de Rocheford commented in 1661 that 'the streets. . . are large and handsome, as if belonging to a new town'. [31] As rising living standards began to make masonry more affordable, timber frontages were phased out. In their place, there spread a stone monumentality increasingly shaped by the quasi-municipal development controls exercised by the Dean of Guild Courts. Following extensive fires, the town councils of Edinburgh (in 1674) and Glasgow (in 1677) made stone compulsory for all new buildings, including facades.

Most other towns were still much less densely built up: a visitor to Aberdeen in 1658 noted that 'the whole town. . . looks as if it stood in a garden or little wood'. [32] In these burghs' dwellings, a smaller scale prevailed, with a constant play between the individuality of gables, turrets and inscriptions, and the collective, harled expression of the streets. Especially rich was Culross, a centre of seventeenth-century industry, including coal-mining, salt-making, quarrying and handloom weaving. The group around the Mercat Cross (1600, with new top, 1902) has as its centrepiece a house of 1633 ('The Study') with generally uniform fenestration but corbelled out, crow-stepped stair turret [2.32].

Equally characteristic of burgh growth, and contributing to the burghs' lively, typically Northern Renaissance spired skylines, was the building of a variety of new secular public buildings, and the beginning of the idea that the 'palace' or 'noble dwellinghouse' architectural form could be used for communal or civic purposes. There was not yet by any means a precise specialisation of building forms, as in later centuries. This was clear in that most characteristic burgh building type, the tolbooth, which housed functions of local government and commercial administration and law enforcement, as well as a public clock: Kirkcudbright town council declared

2.31 Edinburgh, 45–53 High Street ('John Knox House'), late nineteenth-century photograph.

2.32 Culross, The Cross, 1980 view (showing condition following National Trust for Scotland restoration schemes, commenced from 1932).

in 1642 'the necessity of ane steple and bellhouse to keep their knok and bell quhilk is a special ornament belonging to every burgh, and which they are bound by the ancient laws of this kingdom to maintain and uphold'. [33] The most popular tolbooth plan-form, related to smaller castellated dwelling-types, was of two storeys, with forestairs, the first floor containing the main meeting room, and chambers and cells contained in the steeple. Few examples antedate this period. The squat steeple at Crail Tolbooth, for example, may date from the early sixteenth century, but the present two-storey hall block, with forestair, was probably added from 1598, and the steeple rebuilt in the eighteenth century [2.33]. Leith Tolbooth (built 1564 on Queen Mary's instructions) also featured a forestair, as did the more substantial examples at Musselburgh (1590) and Canongate (1591). Both the latter had two bell steeples, in Canongate's case with bartizans. The three most ambitious early seventeenth-century tolbooths in royal burghs were Aberdeen (where the present 'wardhouse' tower was formed in rebuilding of 1616–30, and extended to the rear in 1704–6 to designs by James Smith); Edinburgh (extended in 1609–10 with projecting staircase, in the Dunfermline/Linlithgow palace manner); and the similar,

but larger, design at Glasgow (1625–7). Glasgow Tolbooth was like a chunk of the Linlithgow north quarter, but with the stairtower at one end, topped by a crown spire (symbolising, doubtless, royal burgh status). The main, five-storey building was rebuilt in 1814, and then demolished in 1921, leaving the seven-storey steeple standing on its own [2.34]. Glasgow's Merchants' House (1659) boasted a multi-tiered, tapering steeple, set centrally on its rear facade. Other structures dedicated to civic and commercial intercourse included mercat crosses, the most architecturally precocious being that of the small burgh of Preston (1616–17), with Murray-like detailing including Tuscan pilasters and shell niches. Of the town gateways of the period, the most prominent was Edinburgh's Netherbow, reconstructed in the 1570s and 1606 in a symmetrical, turreted and steepled form, closely linked, architecturally, to the twin towers of the royal palaces [2.35].

A number of individual burgh public monuments were of an importance which set them above the more everyday civic monuments; they took their inspiration even more directly from the palaces. First and foremost was George Heriot's Hospital in the capital, financed by a legacy of Queen Anne's jeweller. As we saw above, following Heriot's death in 1624, his nephew Dr Walter Balcanquhall provided a plan ('paterne and prescript') [34] for a quadrangular block, seemingly based on a plan in Serlio's seventh book; this plan, although for a different site, may have formed the basis of the present layout, with its Linlithgow-like corner towers. The execution of this prestigious project was largely overseen by the royal master masons William Wallace (from start of building in 1628 to his death in 1631) and William Aytoun (from 1631), but what is not clear is who was responsible for the architectural design [2.36]. Much of the detail, and the rich strapwork, or larger features such as the Vignola-like hall door, could have been culled from French or Italian pattern books, but other features, such as the buckle quoins, were obtained closer at hand. The elevational treatment, resembling Linlithgow's north quarter in its window disposition and polygonal turrets, suggests an involvement by James Murray. In general, the form of Heriot's, which combines regular classical detail with

2.33 Crail Tolbooth (sixteenth–eighteenth centuries), 1936 photograph taken by Ian Lindsay.

2.34 Glasgow Tolbooth steeple (1625–7). Behind the steeple is the early twentieth-century civic improvement scheme for Glasgow Cross, comprising the quadrant building by A. G. Henderson (from 1922) and flanking City Improvement Trust warehouses (1912–16).

2.35 Netherbow Port, Edinburgh (as remodelled in the 1570s and 1606, and demolished in 1764), elevation from W. Maitland's *History of Edinburgh*, 1853.

symmetrical towers and turrets, and Gothic windows to the chapel, recalls the contemporary architecture of the Danish royal palaces; Jorevin de Rocheford remarked in 1661 that 'there is no-one but would at first sight take it for a palace'. (35) A much smaller example of the same pattern, of endowment by a rich merchant, was Cowane's Hospital, Stirling, 1639, a U-shaped building with central ogee-domed steeple, designed seemingly by the royal master mason John Mylne. Statues of benefactors, set in prominent locations on the buildings, were found at Heriot's, Cowane's and some other institutions of this sort.

The elevation of municipal patronage to an unparalleled level was seen in 1632–9 in Edinburgh Town Council's construction of a Parliament House adjacent to the High Street, to the designs of James Murray. The project was the result of both royal pressure and a fear that the legal profession, evicted from St Giles's by King Charles, might quit Edinburgh. It is important to avoid an anachronistic nineteenth- and twentieth-century conception of the Parliament House as a specialised institution invested with supreme state symbolism. This building served not only the (intermittent) sittings of parliament itself but also some government functions and law courts, and its building was a testimony as much to the rise of the legal profession as to parliamentary authority, and was modelled on aspects of royal palaces and more prestigious country houses. Externally, it recalled Winton in its splayed plan with ogee towered angle staircase, and Edinburgh Castle's palace block in its flat roof, regular fenestration, square bartizans and parapet [2.37]. Inside were 'several large halls, well covered with tapestry'. (36) The most ambitiously palace-like element of the Parliament House was the Great Hall on the first floor: its elaborate arch-braced roof was constructed, and possibly designed, by master wright John Scott in 1634–9.

In Glasgow, the greatest mid-seventeenth-century project of civic patronage was the reconstruction of Glasgow College, begun in 1630 with the aid of a subsidy from the burgh and nationwide collections and benefactions. This extensive complex was arranged around two courtyards (the second being finished by *c*.1660). Like Heriot's, it was designed in the court-sanctioned style of the royal Masters of Work; Sir Anthony Alexander had previously been a student at Glasgow and Sir William was associated with the project. The mason initially in charge was John Boyd (who also worked on Glasgow Toolboth). There was a lofty clock steeple with cupola similar to the 1633 Holyrood scheme, while an oriel window in the inner court was a spired version of the Heriot's chapel oriel; the fenestration was regular, and there were numerous turrets and pedimented dormers. The Glasgow College and Tolbooth steeples were, in the seventeenth century, the tallest in the country. Glasgow College

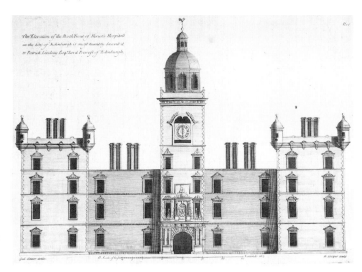

2.36 George Heriot's Hospital, Edinburgh (from 1628), north eleva tion from *Vitruvius Scoticus*.

2.37 Parliament House, Edinburgh (Murray, 1632–9), view of *c.*1740, by John Elphinstone.

(demolished for railway yards in the late nine-teenth century) was significant not only as a major public monument, but as a pointer to the urban housing patterns of the future. Its shallow-plan, uniformly windowed ranges, especially the northern three bays of the 1658 'fore worke' to the High Street, [37] in some respects anticipated the astylar row-houses and tenements which, in the next century, would replace the deep, dense plan types of the traditional burgh [2.38].

Conclusion

Our period ends in the two chaotic decades of the 1640s and 1650s, following a politico-religious revolution against Charles I's rule in 1638, which resulted in the signing of the National Covenant and the abolition of episcopacy by the Glasgow general assembly. In the series of wars that followed, mutual political, religious and military interventions between Scotland, England and Ireland grew more intense and threatening, culminating in the Cromwellian military occu-pation of 1651–60. Although some architectural projects carried on throughout this period, notably Glasgow College (as well as lesser projects such as Cramond Parish Church, 1656), the con-sequences of those two decades were extremely damaging for architecture. The revival of militant Presbyterianism in the late 1630s and 1640s fuelled a new wave of iconoclasm, now including churches of recent decades. Dairsie was stripped out as was

The COLLEDGE of GLASGOW

2.38 Glasgow Old College (from 1630), view looking eastwards, from Slezer's *Theatrum Scotiae*.

(in 1642) James VI's Holyrood chapel interior. The north-east, previously a redoubt of episcopalianism and Catholicism and less affected in 1560, was now included as well: Bishop Elphinstone's tomb was smashed by Protestant militants and St Machar's interior was stripped (in 1640).

Other than Glasgow College, the chief building projects of these turbulent decades were a series of extensive garrison citadels built from 1652 by the English occupying army. These structures, with their advanced polygonal plans and triangular bastions, included Inverness and Ayr (built from 1652 to designs of German engineers, respectively Joachim Hane and Hans Ewald Tessin), and Leith (1656–7). Only after the ending of occupation and the re-establishment of effective monarchy in 1660 would large-scale civil building resume, and this in an architectural era which saw much continuity with older patterns, but also forces of change driven by very different, increasingly comprehensive 'classical' ideals.

Chapter 3

1660–1760

The Country Seat

'. . . the chief introducer of Architecture in this country'.
                Sir John Clerk, on Sir William Bruce, 1717 [1]

'Where I make any designe I have no regard to . . . any old matter wch. are oblique & not agreeable to a modish and regullar
designe.'
                                Sir William Bruce, 1694 [2]

'Three kinds of structure then shall be my Theme
And each adapted to a Country Life,
The first may be defin'd a House of State
The Second for Convenience and Use
The third a little Villa where we may
Taste every minute's blessing sweet and gay
And in a soft retirement spend the Day.'
Sir John Clerk, 'The Country Seat', manuscript poem, 1726– 7

Introduction

This was a century of gradual, but fundamental change in the orientation of the Scottish nation: from a north-west European country preoccupied with religious and dynastic issues, to a secular-orientated society increasingly committed to world-wide British imperialism. During this time, the clashes over religious and national status which had emerged in the late sixteenth century reached their climax. Their focus was the fortunes of the Stuart dynasty and of its post-1690 political arm, Jacobitism. The first half of the period, 1660–1715, was dominated, on the whole, by the Stuart and Jacobite formula of assertive absolutist monarchy and regal union between Scotland, England and Ireland – a formula which became increasingly embattled and, in 1715, suffered a significant defeat. The second half of the period, from 1715 to 1760, saw the growing ascendancy of an opposed formula: a monarchy chosen for its conspicuous Protestantism and limited power, and a closer union between Scotland and England. Economically and socially, there was much common ground between the two phases.

In both, there was a continuation and acceleration of modernisation through agricultural and commercial 'improvement', and an emphasis on the maintenance of order through the landed élite and their allies in the emergent professional and mercantile classes. In architecture, too, this was a period which combined vigorous change with the continued upholding of images of tradition and stability. The role of the aristocratic private house as *the* emblematic building type of the post-medieval era was strengthened, but transformed through the steady infusion of more rigorous classical ideals and a growing insistence on ashlar-faced monumentality of construction.

The structure of this chapter stems from the dominance during this period of the landed classes, and of their main architectural pre-occupation – the building of their country houses. Never in Scottish architectural history, before or since, has a single building type overshadowed all others to the same extent. Most of the chapter, therefore, presents an account of the development of post-1660 Scottish classical architecture seen almost exclusively through the lens of country house design. This account is subdivided chronologically into three main periods: the years of Stuart revival and final decline, 1660–1715; the time of the establishment of Hanoverian ascendancy, immediately around 1715; and the years of Hanoverian and Whig consolidation, 1715–1760. We will see that while these oppositions and fluctuations in political affiliations had a dramatic effect on building patronage patterns, they were only imprecisely echoed in the development of architectural ideas. At the end of the chapter, a separate section deals with all other building types (including urban architecture as a whole): one characteristic of post-1560 architecture which continued throughout this period was its strongly secular orientation.

The 'Restoration' of Classical Architecture, 1660–1715

The re-establishment of royal government in 1660 was followed by a new wave of improvement. The vast majority of Scots still lived in the countryside, where the landed classes, bolstered by heritable jurisdictions, accelerated their work of agricultural enclosure and industrial ventures such as coal-mining or salt-making – a range of modernising activities, pursued almost continuously since the sixteenth century, which were now nearing a critical mass for a decisive transition to a deve-loped economy. For the moment, the old continental trading links, especially with the Low Countries, were still dominant.

Politically and socially, the years after 1660 saw a vigorous attempt to 'restore' a hierarchical system headed by a powerful monarchy, backed by a reinvigorated aristocracy. Across Europe, this was the heyday of the system of absolutist monarchy, as seen above all in the rule of Louis XIV in France. Late Stuart rule in Scotland was a kind of branch absolutism, a subsidiary arm of a multi-national monarchy based in England. This was reflected in a markedly authoritarian system of government and patronage, set up initially by a favourite courtier of Charles II, John Maitland, 2nd Earl (from 1672, Duke) of Lauderdale, the virtual viceroy of Scotland between 1667 and 1680. His patronage system was then taken over by James, Duke of Albany and York (King James VII

after 1685), who established an intermittent residence in Edinburgh between 1679 and 1682 – the first royal court in the capital since 1603. After the overthrow of James in 1689 and the instal-lation of monarchs with more limited powers, a more fluid situation ensued: landed power was maintained, and Parliament and state institutions became more prominent.

As part of the post-1660 reassertion of the hierarchical system of absolute monarchy, there were also energetic attempts to restore the cultural prestige of the landed classes, through continuing comparisons with the authority and stability of antiquity. The Stoicism of Alexander Seton had been succeeded by the ideal of the virtuoso, a gentleman steeped in classical learning. Scottish 'virtuosi' formed part of an international, French-led cultivation of manners, while equally defending the Stuart tradition of national antiq-uity. And these years also furthered the cause of urban enlightenment. During James's residence in Edinburgh in 1679–82, he aimed to foster a royalist and episcopalian/Catholic culture there, and to enlist for this the support, among others, of the rising professional classes. These partisan efforts, and the general political and cultural development of Edinburgh as a capital in the late seventeenth century, had much longer-term effects. For example, a 1688 initiative by King James, sug-gesting the building of new streets and a bridge north of the High Street, would eventually be realised in the Hanoverian 1760s in the form of the New Town[cf. 4.15, 4.17].

Architecturally, the later seventeenth century was for a long time regarded as a period of revolutionary transformation. In terms of levels of building, the importance of 1660 was clear, as marking the resumption of large-scale projects after a 20-year gap. In the field of architectural ideas, the changes were more subtle, with substantial elements of continuity. The most obvious break with the past was the full establishment in Scotland, for the first time, of a 'mainstream' European classicism, stemming ultimately from the Italian Renaissance. This fully-fledged or strict classicism comprised probably the most systematic formal vocabulary ever devised, integrating as it did layout, elevation and decoration into a single system encapsulated in the five Orders. The Orders were here seen less as decorative motifs than as symbols of a wider order and harmony, whose physical proportions were ultimately derived from ideal Platonic forms. And they were also used as a means of articulating large-scale projects and giving meaning to new building types and tasks. The international history of classicism up to the eighteenth century was a constant battle between the latter, modernising tendency and counter-appeals to the supposed purity of the antique, and to the authority of the Roman originals. The first concerted assertion of antique purity against 'debased' modern classicism in northern Europe was that in the seventeenth century, which displaced the busy individualism of the gabled Northern Renaissance, with its use of the Orders as applied decoration. In Scotland, although there were pioneering earlier efforts such as Culross Abbey House, this occurred, on the whole, after 1660.

To later generations of Scottish architects, these developments of the 'Restoration' years seemed like a new beginning: that much was accepted even by those of very different political or ideological persuasions. The first great architectural figure of the post-1660 period, Sir William Bruce, was acclaimed in 1717 by the Whig gentleman-architect Sir John Clerk of Penicuik as no less than 'the chief introducer of Architecture in this country'. [3] The competition between classical adaptation and authority had been explicitly articulated in a vigorous late seventeenth-century debate in France, between so-called Ancients, who regarded the antique as a complete and self-contained source of precedent, and the Moderns, led by Claude and Charles Perrault, who held that classical strictness and stateliness could be modified in the interests of modern convenience, introducing an element of cultural relativism and cultural nationalism. The imprecision of archaeological knowledge of classical antiquity allowed a bewildering range of evocations of it, drawing also on the work of those Italian Renaissance architects, such as Palladio and Scamozzi, who claimed to have been particularly faithful to ancient precedent.

One of the most significant aspects of the intellectual renaissance fostered by the renewed Stuart monarchy was the beginning of the emergence of Scottish architects as a distinct social group, with its own values and traditions. Despite the efforts of Schaw and Murray, it was only now that numbers of 'named architects' began to gain wide national recognition. During the period of Stuart resurgence after 1660, the structure of architectural patronage and practice was fundamentally shaped by the culture of the court. The money to pay for the most prestigious projects stemmed from government service or connections, and architectural prestige was bound up with courtier status. Conversely, key architectural works helped to bolster the political status of figures such as Lauderdale, or of the restored Stuart monarchy as a whole. After 1689, the centralisation of much government activity (including the royal works establishment) in London encouraged a new phenomenon of Scottish expatriate architects working in London – a modification of the centuries-old tradition of Scots working abroad. (In the following chapters, we include the work of such architects only if they also built in Scotland, and their non-Scottish work is only dealt with selectively.) But the replacement of royal or state direction by private initiative – a trend which would gather pace until the mid-nineteenth century – in any case diminished the importance of government patronage. Much more detailed research is needed into the complex relationships of architects, patrons and building finance during this period of fast-moving political and personal alliances.

Until the late eighteenth century, there was no decisive move towards the emergence of a demarcated architectural profession, or the establishment of architects as a 'middle-class' group. The ambiguous relationship between the gentleman-architect and the mason-architect continued. Key aristocrats and lairds still played a direct and prominent architectural role, especially, during the Restoration period, if connected with the court; this activity was facilitated by the custom of prolonged study-tours on the Continent (in France, the Netherlands and northern Italy). Correspondingly, masons who became architects aspired to landed status and values. The mid-seventeenth century had, on the whole, been dominated by the Mylne family of master masons. John Mylne, King's Master Mason until 1668, was succeeded on his death by his nephew Robert. These relationships are strikingly illustrated in the ascendancy of the two chief architects of the post-1660 years: Sir William Bruce and James Smith.

Bruce was a newly knighted politician whose architectural activities and status stemmed directly from his role as a courtier [3.1]. Widely travelled in the Low Countries, England and (probably) France, and possessor of a large and cosmopolitan architectural library, Bruce had been a close supporter of the exiled Charles II, and enjoyed some political influence in the 1660s and 1670s as a protégé of Lauderdale: in 1670–1, he was in charge of the customs and excise. Bruce established himself as a landowner in 1665 at Balcaskie and in 1675 at Kinross; he became a baronet in 1668 and in 1671 was commissioned to design the rebuilding of Holyrood Palace, being appointed to a new post of Surveyor-General and Overseer of the King's Buildings in Scotland (a 'restoration' of the old Schaw and Murray function). From that point, he became the most highly esteemed architectural consultant and arbiter of taste for the pro-court landed classes of the period, designing a number of key houses himself and advising on many others – as well as pursuing his own building projects at Balcaskie and Kinross [cf. 3.14, 3.15]. As a gentleman-architect, Bruce seldom directly superintended a project, but employed others, such as the clergyman Alexander Edward, to draw up his plans. His relationship with the masons was similar to that of, say, Murray and Wallace earlier in the century: at Holyrood, as a royal project, even the royal mason Robert Mylne worked in a clearly operative role. For some key projects, including his own house at Kinross as well as Hopetoun, Craigiehall and Mertoun, Bruce and his clients employed the mason Tobias Bachop. His dependence on his courtier status was shown by the rapid decline in his fortunes after the downfall of Lauderdale and, even more, after the dethronement of the Stuarts, when he was reduced to a relatively hand-to-mouth architectural existence, subject to constant official harassment.

James Smith was a more complex character who was less closely tied to the courtier system, and in some ways anticipated the professionalism of the future. The Forres-born son of a Catholic master mason, he studied for the priesthood at the Scots

3.1 Sir William Bruce, oil portrait by Michael Wright, *c*.1710.

College in Rome in 1671–5, where he almost became a Jesuit. Ultimately, he gave up his studies and became an apostate, returning home after extensive travel in Italy and France, marrying a daughter of Robert Mylne and (in 1678–9) taking on a contract to build the new front gateway of Holyrood Palace. With his direct experience of Italy, Smith made a swift transition to the status of architect. In 1683 he was appointed to the royal surveyorship, and three years later acquired an estate at Whitehill, near Musselburgh, building a small house there. He went on to design some of the most important houses of the age, succeeding Bruce as the most favoured establishment architect after the latter fell from favour; some of his clients, such as the 3rd Duke of Hamilton or the 1st Earl of Melville, had been ambiguous or even hostile in their relationship to the Lauderdale ascendancy. After around 1700, Smith often worked in collaboration with Alexander McGill (whom Bruce also employed to draw out plans for him, at that time). Alongside his architectural work, Smith continued to work as a mason-contractor, constructing some of his own house designs, and working often with his cousins James and Gilbert. Smith also engaged in speculative building of high-class tenement complexes in Edinburgh, as well as dabbling (ultimately, to his financial ruin) in industrial ventures such as coal-mining and canal design, and representing Forres in Parliament in 1685–6 – for which his candidacy was supported by the Earl of Mar (father of the architect).

The influence of Bruce and Smith was pervasive in this period. Between them, they firmly established in Scotland the new view of classicism and the Orders as a comprehensive system of values rather than as a vocabulary of applied detail. As we will see, their country house designs answered many of the functional and symbolic demands of the landed classes for more stately, yet also more 'convenient' houses – the latter being one of the central preoccupations of the French Moderns, as well as of the English and Dutch designers of compact houses. At the same time, they formulated a Scottish variant of the European classical ideology of the antique, with its appeals to 'purity' and 'simplicity'. In houses of the highest status, harled walls were gradually replaced by ashlar refinement, and there were experiments with monumental centralised plans and elevations. But alongside these variegated classical endeavours, the imagery of Scottish national tradition, for the moment, retained a central place.

The Rebuilding of Holyroodhouse and New Developments in Country House Planning

The 1670s were the last period in which the monarchy itself embarked on large-scale building: these were the years of the virtually total remodelling of Holyrood Palace (from 1671; by then commonly known as 'Holyroodhouse'), which we will discuss shortly in greater detail. And, at the same time, the patronage of the landed classes saw an unprecedented growth, both in its overall wealth and in its internal hierarchical complexity, with a vast range of building sizes and solutions. By the 1680s and 1690s, the top of the patronage hierarchy was represented by a series of projects of vice-regal status, including the reconstruction of Dalkeith and Hamilton Palaces and Drumlanrig Castle, while at the bottom was a new range of compact small houses or villas for minor lairds [cf. 3.7, 3.8, 3.9]. Perhaps paradoxically, the patronage of this highly hierarchical age was an

outstanding exception to the male domination which has prevailed, over the centuries, in the building and design of Scottish architecture. Powerful aristocratic women controlled some of the key palace-building projects of the era, including Hamilton and Dalkeith.

To understand the driving forces behind the new scale and opulence of the larger houses and palaces, we should begin with the internal and external context of their architecture – with the way the landed home was organised, and the way it related to the wider landscape. During the mid- and late seventeenth century, the demand steadily grew for a more ordered and dignified lifestyle, with private activities separated, socially and physically, from the public 'keeping of state', that is, the provision for reception and accommodation of visitors of 'quality' – above all, the king himself. While some put a patriotic cast on the 'revived' dignity of the post-1660 Scottish aristocracy, as an aspect of the Restoration, others branded it an 'English' fashion. Already in the late 1640s, the royalist Aberdeenshire laird Patrick Gordon of Ruthven had complained that 'once that English devil, keeping of state, got a haunt amongst our nobility, they began to keep a distance, as if there were some divinity in them'. [4] In fact, the new trends formed part of a Europe-wide revolution of polite society and manners under the absolutist monarchy system, led by the France of Louis XIV. Architecturally, the 1640s had seen a transformation of French country house and hôtel planning, in response to the twin ideals of grandeur and convenience. The old, relatively undifferentiated halls and chambers, with their sparse furniture and tapestry-hung walls, were replaced by highly specialised public rooms, such as dining rooms, withdrawing rooms and salons. These were arranged much more formally in linked apartments, decorated in a more architectonic manner, lavishly furnished, and backed up by service rooms and corridors. The most prestigious rooms increasingly conformed to precise proportional formulae: 'cube', 'double cube', and so forth.

These arrangements had to be fitted into a symmetrical and imposing plan. There was a gradual trend away from apartments arranged in straight lines, and towards more compact arrangements, which increasingly required houses to be two or three rooms deep. The most prestigious plan was a symmetrical arrangement comprising a central circulation area flanked by a private apartment on one side and a 'state' apartment (sufficiently grand for the reception of the king) on the other. This arrangement was epitomised by Le Vau's Vaux-le-Vicomte of 1652, with its apartments flanking a central salon, and its lavish internal amenities (including a private bathroom). Strictly speaking, a fully-fledged state apartment was intended only for the king's use. It was thus almost exclusively for show, and was only appropriate in houses of vice-regal status. In most houses, room use was less formal, and there was much overlap between show rooms, grand reception rooms and large private rooms. In this wider context the term 'great apartment' was often used instead; its individual rooms were also prefixed with 'great'. Vaux-le-Vicomte also showed how this new internal order could be projected far beyond the house into the landscape. Its gardener, Le Nôtre, abolished the old enclosed gardens in favour of an openness of 'unity and grandeur', [5] with vast avenues stretching to the horizon, and, closer to the house, parterres and terracing.

Scotland, in the age of Bruce and Smith, embraced these ideas of house-planning with relish. The creation of self-contained apartments, first pioneered in the royal palaces of James IV, was pushed forward: the state/great apartment concept provided an ideal symbol of the post-1660 emphasis on resurgent absolutist royalism, as well as of landed power both before and after the overthrow of the Stuarts. By 1700 a typical Scottish great apartment might begin with a stair on the model of Holyroodhouse, followed by a Great Dining Room (the largest room), drawing room, and bedchamber with dressing-room and closet; sometimes, as at Panmure (from 1666), an anteroom or lobby might be provided between dining and drawing rooms [cf. 3.10]. Existing principles of floor distribution, with the first floor long established as the principal floor, needed little alteration, although ground-floor vaulting was abandoned. The horizontal division of, or within, the new apartments was a different matter. As we will see shortly, in many cases houses which looked new and classical on the outside incorporated large

chunks of existing castellated house fabric. In such cases, the creation of symmetrical paired private and state apartments was almost impossible, and more often the task was that of squeezing large new spaces into, and around, intractably thick-walled shells. At Dalkeith, for example, the most stately room, the double-height Great Dining Room, had to be put on a different floor from the rest of the state apartment.

The decoration of large house interiors became steadily more sumptuous, attesting to their patrons' increasing ability to afford luxury goods and specialised room uses. Within many seventeenth-century great apartments, the rooms became successively grander and more ornate until the climax of the bedchamber. The existing patterns of plaster ceilings and panelled wainscoting were augmented with other even more lavish finishes, such as gilt leather hangings. This, for the time being, reinforced the dependence on foreign craftsmen (usually Dutch, English or French). There was often very little correlation in degree of lavishness between exterior and interior. At James Smith's Melville House (1697–1702), for example, a severely plain exterior concealed one of the richest interiors of the age, with features such as a huge canopied bed of state, almost certainly made by a French craftsman [cf. 3.17, 3.18]. And even in an 'un-reformed' tower, Kinnaird Castle, a 1690s inventory listed 162 chairs, 33 beds, and other miscellaneous furniture, especially in the second-floor state-rooms. Conspicuous consumption was equally displayed in the collecting and display of paintings, which in the late seventeenth and early eighteenth centuries were overwhelmingly of Dutch origin. And it fuelled more prosaic functional improvements, such as the spread of water-closets, or the change from hinged windows to the new vertically sliding, counterweighted 'sash' window – an invention, apparently, of the English Office of Works around 1669, allowing a window to be left open by any amount, which was first used in Scotland by the Duke of Lauderdale in the mid-1670s.

Outside, the gardeners of late seventeenth century Scotland energetically pursued the new ideals of 'unity and grandeur', but in a manner allowing for the country's changeable climate. Adjacent to the house, the older small walled compartments, or 'yeards', were thrown together into unified, but still walled, gardens, containing larger parterres (most thickly dotted with statues) and features such as wildernesses. Terracing and garden pavilions, often with ogival slated roofs, provided an outlook on to the wider landscape: the most spectacular garden pavilion of all was built much later at Dunmore Park, Airth in 1761, with a colossal, domed roof detailed like a giant pineapple. The landscape beyond was often ordered through vast axes formed by woodland plantations, which also served for hunting. More expensive schemes might include, for example, waterworks such as canals; to create grand vistas, it was increasingly necessary to remove inconvenient old service buildings, or even entire villages, such as the settlement of Kinneil in 1696. Ultimately, the scale of the landscaping might begin to dwarf that of the architecture, with houses sitting as tiny specks in the middle of colossal plantations [cf. 3.8, 3.14].

How were the new ideals of house-planning expressed architecturally? Later in this book, we will encounter some remarkable innovations of uncompromisingly classical design in late seventeenth-century Scotland. First, however, we have to deal with a different, and more prevalent approach during that period: the design of country houses in a way which continued to evoke openly, although now more imprecisely, images and forms of the castellated past. We saw in Chapter 2 how the early seventeenth-century revivals in the popularity of courtly ceremony coincided with a flowering of nostalgic castellated architecture, usually in the context of the rebuilding and enlargement of existing houses. In the years following 1660, the revival in royal and aristocratic confidence was celebrated in yet another phase of neo-chivalric revival, including jousting tournaments. The lawyer John Nicoll gushed in 1661 that 'it was the joy of this natioun to behold the flower of this kingdome, quhich for samony yeiris hath bene overcloudit, and now to sie thame upone brave horses, pransing in thair acustomat places in telting, ryning of races, and suchlyke'. [6] In the building or replanning of country houses, this was reflected in a revival of interest in heraldry and heritage, which manifested itself, for instance, in painting collections or decorative motifs. The

fiercely royalist Sir John Wauchope, on rebuilding his house, Niddrie Marischal, in 1662, installed a remarkable scheme of plasterwork and panelled portraits which linked his family and the Stuart restoration to the patriotic tradition of kings, proclaiming that 'nobis haec invicta miserunt 108 proavi'. [7]

Architecturally, however, this revival of royalism and heraldry was matched not by any straightforward revival of castle-building, but instead, more subtly, by a preference for the continued adaptation of existing old dynastic homes, and their modification in accordance with classical principles. Partly, this was a simple economic matter. As in earlier periods, the solidity of stone construction made it far easier and cheaper to modify rather than build anew, and in many cases, improvement schemes comprised simply internal alterations and landscaping works. Where new building was called for, its form was influenced by a shift in the material culture of the Stuart monarchy and aristocracy towards more overtly and exclusively classical forms. Of course, Roman or Augustan imagery had been present for centuries, but by the late seventeenth century, this shift was so far advanced that irregular castellated shapes were becoming seen by many as unfashionable as a model for new architecture – a view that became steadily more accentuated for nearly a century. Contact with countries where castellated architecture had been phased out a century before, such as France or England, only reinforced this feeling. The Marquess of Lothian, writing from southern England to his wife in 1693, commented of their ancestral home, Newbattle Abbey, that 'when I see houses heir it seems a skandalous thing to keep that rotten thing upp'. [8] Many aristocrats also owned properties in both Scotland and England, and the latter (as, for example, the Duke of Lauderdale's Ham House) sometimes acted as a conduit for advanced French ideas of house-planning (and garden design). Yet at the same time, there was a residual feeling that to allow a dynastic base to disappear completely was disreputable, and the old houses, now often referred to as 'castles', [9] began to acquire a kind of nostalgic prestige. The most favoured solution to this dilemma, between the 1660s and 1680s, was to 'reform' them, retaining suggestions of baronial

3.2 Palace of Holyroodhouse, c.1920 view of western facade after post-1670 rebuilding, including Bruce's new south-west tower at the right.

antiquity in their verticality and lively skyline, but subordinating these to a far greater order and symmetry.

Just as the most prestigious palace project in Europe – Louis XIV's Versailles – was a reconstruction by an absolutist king (on a vast scale) of an older château, so in Scotland the showpiece of this kind of 'reformed' design was the Stuart absolutist king's own project, steered through by Lauderdale, to rebuild the fire-damaged Holyroodhouse in 1671–9 [3.2]. It may not be entirely coincidental that this project of reassertion of Scottish royal prestige was started immediately following the failure of a scheme (in 1669–70) for incorporating union with England. For three years, the reconstructed palace – in effect, the first new royal palace built since the time of James IV and James V – was occupied on its completion by the satellite court of the Duke of Albany and York. While the King, Lauderdale, and the master masons, may have contributed to some key design decisions – John Mylne sur-veyed the existing palace in 1663, and King Charles insisted on a revision of early proposals – the main responsibility was Bruce's. The king wrote to him that 'You shall . . . designe and order the building thereof in pillar worke conforme to and with the Dorick and Ionic orders and style'. [10] The crucial design decision, which essentially dictated the form of the entire project, was to retain the James V tower, but to incorporate it in a new, symmetrical composition, building a second, identical tower at the south end [cf. 1.13]. According to John Mylne, such an extension had already been contemplated by both James V and Charles I. The two towers were linked by a classical central palace block with courtyard behind, possibly incorporating elements of the James IV palace. The overall symmetry of the group was carried further still, as the abbey on the north was duplicated by a new nave/aisles kitchen block (now long demolished) on the south side of the complex. The new central range was flat-roofed and balustraded, its central aedicule (built by Smith's team of quarriers and masons) being framed with giant paired freestanding columns – a monumental feature somewhat unusual, for northern Europe, at this date – and surmounted by a heraldic panel and lantern with imperial crown [cf. 1.2]. Overall, the centrepiece was similar in character to some of the motifs in Alexandre Francini's *Livre d'Architecture* (1631). The courtyard was much plainer, with idiosyncratic triglyph detail of Murray type.

Inside the new Holyroodhouse, a stone-built cantilevered and open-welled square staircase gave direct access to royal apartments: the king's on the south and east side of the courtyard, the queen's on the west side. These interiors were richly decorated by a range of craftsmen. The Dutch artist Jacob de Wet painted a ceiling panel and several overmantel panels; ceiling plasterwork was by two English plasterers, John Hulbert and George Dunsterfield; the Dutch carver Jan van Santvoort made the most elaborate woodwork, such as overmantels and doorcases. While the climax of the original decorative scheme was the king's bedchamber, the later picture gallery (com-missioned 1684) developed further the Restoration theme of Stuart and origin-myth royal symbolism: it was specially designed around a series of pictures of the kings since the apocryphal Fergus I. The royal works at Holyrood were completed in 1686–8, when James VII ordered conversion of the council chamber into a Roman Catholic Chapel Royal, and commissioned James Smith to convert the abbey for the use of the revived Order of the Thistle. The latter opulent scheme included twelve Corinthian-columned and canopied stalls for the knights, marble flooring, and a magnificent throne at the east end under an armorial canopy; carving was by William Morgan and Grinling Gibbons [3.3].

'Reforming' the Dynastic House

The formula evolved at Holyroodhouse, namely the retention, but regularisation, of an old dynastic home, and the installation of stately classical interiors, became the most common basis of late seventeenth-century Scottish country house design – perhaps not surprisingly, in view of the involvement there of most of the court-connected establishment of architects and masons. We can identify two main ways of achieving the desired 'reforms'. First, in a minority of cases, an arguably more conservative approach of making an asym-metrical castle seem symmetrical by realigning the main axis on to a diagonal. Second, the more

3.3 Interior of Holyrood Abbey as refitted by James Smith (1686–8), plate from *Vitruvius Scoticus*.

straightforwardly classical method of building wings or annexes to create symmetry, sometimes by the blunt expedient of simply building a new classical block in front of the old tower – as in the case of the Earl of Glasgow's extension to Kelburn Castle of *c.*1700, sitting at an angle and across the old section [cf. 2.16].

The first fashion, that of the symmetrical splay plan, stemmed from a reappraisal, rather than a rejection, of the old L-shaped castellated type plan, whose increasing regularity, earlier in the seventeenth century, we noted in Chapter 2. In 1661 the last fully-fledged castellated house of this kind, Leslie House, was built, its rectangular angle stair turret (containing a scale and platt stair) resembling Innes House; it was equipped with a moat, enclosure wall, gatehouse, corbelled bartizans and gun holes. Crichton House (*c.*1650) and Auchenbowie (1666) were smaller and more domestic, with swept-down eaves and octagonal stair turret. An almost complete internal symmetry, and a first-floor apartment of dining room, drawing room and bedroom/closet, was provided at Clounie Crichton Castle of 1666. But what was more important still was that the entrance should be set diagonally (something already seen at Braemar Castle, 1628) and combined with landscaping on the same diagonal axis.

By the late seventeenth century, all these examples would have seemed rather old-fashioned. However, a far more novel and spectacular example of this pattern was provided in the rebuilding of

Glamis Castle by the 3rd Earl of Kinghorne (from 1677, Earl of Strathmore and Kinghorne) in 1670–9 [3.4]. The Earl, an ally of Lauderdale's from the mid-1670s, was typical of the royalist aristocracy in his conflicting emotions about his castellated home. On the one hand, he insisted 'that everie man who hes such houses would reform them, for who can delight to live in his house as in a prisone'. Indeed, there was 'no man more against these old fashions of tours and castles than I am'. Yet he was 'inflam'd stronglie with a great desyre to continue the memorie of my familie' by retaining the core of the old structure, containing as it did 'my Great Hall, which is a room that I ever loved'. His solution was to re-orientate and extend the castle into a symmetrical splay plan, by adding a new west quarter to match the tower's existing eastern jamb: both wings were given gables, flanking balustrades symmetrically, and the roof was heightened. An aedicular entrance was set at the centre, and a new diagonally aligned system of courts and vistas was laid out. By this means, a stolid tower house was converted into a composition of overpowering, almost Baroque dynamism – a startling and (for Scotland) unprecedented solution. Of his design, the Earl commented laconically that 'Tho' it be an old house and consequentlie was the more difficult to reduce the place to any uniformitie yet I did covet extremely to order my building so that my frontispiece might have a resemblance on both syds'. Internally, a new great apartment was formed in the expanded shell of the castle; 'my

The frontispiece of the Castle of Glammiss, given by King Robert the first of the Stewarts, in y.e year 1376 with his daughter to John Lyen Lord Glammiss, Chancellor of Scotland. As it is now reformed by Patrick Earle of Strathmore his Linead heir: and Successour An.Dom.1686.

R. 1.

3.4 Glamis Castle, 1686 elevation of main front: copper plate engraved by R. White after Slezer drawing.

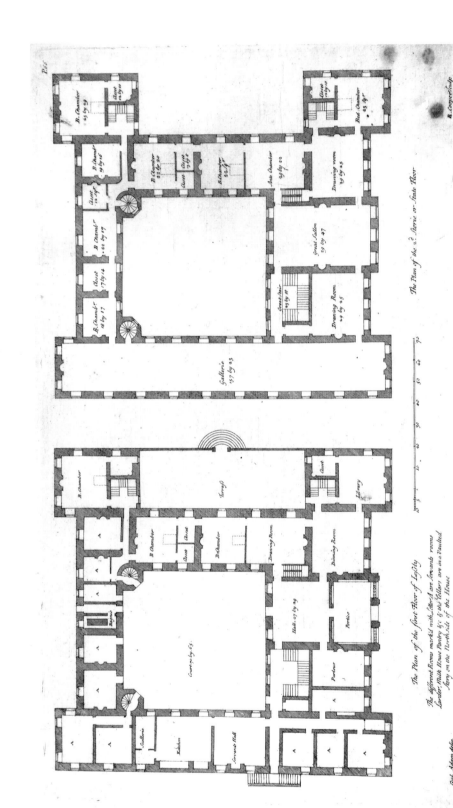

3.5 Leslie House (rebuilt 1667–72, J. Mylne), first- and state-floor plans, from *Vitruvius Scoticus*.

Great Hall' was converted into a drawing room. Kinghorne designed the whole scheme himself, having decided not to 'call in such as in this age were known and reput to be the best judges and contrivers . . . Public Architecturs'. [11]

The *tour de force* of Glamis had no immediate followers, although the eighteenth century would see more persistent attempts to develop the splay plan idea. In the third quarter of the seventeenth century, it is perhaps unsurprising that the most popular way of 'reducing' a castle to 'uniformitie' instead followed the Holyroodhouse pattern: that of an old tower extended into a larger, symmetrical complex, often in the form of a gabled 'U' with infilled centre, or angle towers flanking a lower, parapeted and balustraded centre. However, this most favoured compositional formula did not actually begin at Holyrood, but built on the existing tradition of angle towers and U-shaped plans (as at Duntarvie or Kilbaberton). These precedents were first modified into the new form in 1663–4 in the reconstruction of Methven Castle, probably by John Mylne. Methven's remodelled plan was square and double-depth, with Spedlins-like spinal plan and circular towers at all four angles. On the entrance facade, gables flank the balustraded central section, which contains a grand scale and platt stair. Constructed of harled rubble in the old fashion, the ground floor is un-vaulted and the garden facade comprises a severe grid of windows. At Leslie House, in 1667–72, the 7th Earl of Rothes, a government member (but by then out of favour) and wealthy coal-mine owner, carried out a major quadrangular rebuilding scheme to the designs of John Mylne and (after his death) his nephew Robert, with the advice of Bruce [3.5]. Here, a symmetrical gabled style, not unlike that of Murray or Glasgow College, was married to elements of symmetrical state-apartment planning and segregation of public and private activity. Heavily furnished and decorated, the principal floor included a centrally positioned 'great Sallon', and a gallery filling the entire north quarter, hung with family portraits. We will deal later with Mylne's related design for a new house at Panmure (from 1666) [cf. 3.10]. The last of this series of expanded and regularised towers of the 1660s was Bruce's own first country house, Balcaskie, which he rebuilt in 1668–74 with John

Hamilton (mason) and Andrew Waddel (wright). Here he recast an L-shaped house into a double-depth, symmetrical block with pavilions at each corner. The main facade comprised angle towers and crowstepped gables with lower central section, probably balustraded; the pavilions were quoined in the manner of earlier seventeenth-century French chateaux. Balcaskie's main vista was aligned on the Bass Rock. Inside, plasterwork in the two main rooms was by Holyrood craftsmen Dunsterfield and Hulbert.

Naturally, the personal building work of the Maitland/Lauderdale family contributed some of the most influential works in this growing movement of expanded and 'reformed' houses. Between 1664 and the early 1670s Charles Maitland, the earl's younger brother, and privy councillor, enlarged his (L-shaped) castellated dwelling, Hatton House, on two sides, forming symmetrical, turret-flanked compositions. The new south facade was dominated by a massive four-storey block with piended roof at the centre, and faced out on to a large walled parterre with angle pavilions and terracing. The east facade was symmetrical, with flanking gables. Subsequently, Maitland's son, probably influenced by Holyrood, infilled this facade with a flat-roofed, balustraded section and porch [cf. 3.2]. In 1670 the Earl of Lauderdale himself, together with (from 1672) his new and powerful wife, the Countess of Dysart, began the remodelling of their main Scottish home, Thirlestane Castle [3.6]. This was the first reliably documented work of Bruce; Robert Mylne acted as contractor. Lauderdale was at the peak of his power, having been appointed King's Commissioner to Parliament the previous year, and he may have wished to outdo his brother's Hatton efforts. The existing plan of the house was already unusual in its symmetry and linear processional character on the principal floor. Now this floor was converted into a lavish state apartment of five rooms, while the ground-floor service area was turned into a second great apartment, for the Earl and Countess. To accommodate the displaced service rooms, the house was expanded by additional pavilions, quoined and with splayed roofs, flanking the entrance end. The new entrance facade was fronted by a raised terrace and surmounted by a pediment: a hierarchical,

3.6 Thirlestane Castle (central block *c.*1590, expanded with pavilions in 1670–7 by Sir William Bruce, and Baronialised in 1840–1 by William Burn and, later, David Bryce). Early twentieth-century view of main front in its condition following Bryce's work.

classical solution, composed of towered elements of fairly traditional character. Inside, there was rich decoration, including plasterwork by Dunsterfield and Hulbert. Other, minor works designed by Bruce at Lauderdale's other properties included the extension of the L-shaped Brunstane House into a U-planned 'very convenient lodge' (1672); [12] and the building of quoined classical annexes at Lethington (Lennoxlove) in the 1670s under the supervision of John Slezer. In 1673, Lauderdale employed two Dutch joiners to install sash windows ('double chaussees') at Lethington [13] and possibly (to judge from drawings by Slezer) on the entrance front at Thirlestane. From that point the use of the old hinged windows among the Scots landed classes, as with their equivalents in the Low Countries, England and Ireland, was progressively phased out.

After the overthrow of the Stuarts, the design principles of this earlier phase in Bruce's work were perpetuated in a number of schemes for Jacobite lairds in Angus, executed and in some cases designed by Alexander Edward. At Kinnaird Castle, the 4th Earl of Southesk commissioned two unexecuted schemes for enlargement of the house, and landscaping, in 1695–8. The first of the schemes, designed by Bruce and drawn by Edward, envisaged a double-depth house with angle towers of the Balcaskie kind, while the second, probably drawn by Slezer (perhaps for

James Smith), proposed a five-bay pedimented centrepiece and grand, Dutch-style double-return staircase inside. A more modest extension by Edward at Brechin Castle, planned in 1704 and finished in 1711, formed a new, symmetrical pedimented front flanked by round towers. At Careston Castle, again possibly to Edward's designs, an L-shaped tower was expanded in 1702 into a symmetrical, U-planned block, including a new first floor apartment.

Although some of Bruce's later alteration schemes included bold classical elements, such as the loggia and segmental pediment inserted between the wings at Craighall, Fife (1697–9), his most innovative designs were in the field of completely new houses. It was, rather, in the work of James Smith that the most daring classical 'reforms' of country houses occurred. From the very beginning, exploiting slightly different establishment circles from Bruce's pro-Lauderdale clique (and despite his Catholic background), Smith was able to command the patronage of some of the country's most powerful landowners. It seems likely that it was he who designed for Anne, Duchess of Hamilton, the symmetrical recasting of the main, Regent Arran tower of Kinneil House (completed 1677), as a home for her eldest son, the Earl of Arran. In a reversal of the predominant pattern of wings and low balustraded centre, here a tall, central, flat-roofed section of five storeys, balustraded and uniformly sash-windowed, was flanked by shorter turreted 'pavillions'. [14] In a far more ambitious scheme of 1679–90, Smith recast Drumlanrig Castle for the 1st Duke of Queensberry – a key government figure during most of the 1680s, who was seeking to enlarge his house to match his new status. Mylne and Bruce may also have advised on the scheme. Although one section clearly dates from the sixteenth century, it is not clear how much else of the present complex is new and how much is older. The 1615 plans of the 'unreformed . . . Place of Drumlangrig' appear to show a looser, but already quadrangular grouping, with a tower at one corner. [15] As 'reformed', Drumlanrig assumed a massively quadrangular, symmetrical form with bartizaned corner towers in the Heriots and Fyvie tradition – a design which stands alongside Glamis as one of Scotland's great setpieces of castellar/Baroque palace-design [3.7]. The main entrance facade boldly recalls Holyrood in its combination of stepped-down outer towers and balustraded central section, with coroneted cupola. Windows are pedimented in a Murray-like fashion, while the facade's central section features, in a somewhat French manner, giant fluted Corinthian pilasters and a richly swagged porch with segmental pediment; below is a terrace and loggia with a horseshoe perron. The house was surrounded by extensive terraced gardens, including pavilions. Although Queensberry was deprived of his principal offices in 1685, he may have had a hand, two years before then, in Smith's elevation to the royal Surveyorship. In 1686 he also bought (from Lord Hatton) a townhouse in the Canongate: we will return to that later. Two other very similar, slightly later schemes are associated with Smith. The first, possibly by him, was the symmetrical south front added to an old castellated house, Keith Hall, in 1697–9 for Lord Kintore (a Jacobite friend of Smith's). The new facade had bulky ogee-roofed towers flanking a flat roof, in a composition not unlike the early seventeenth-century Redbraes Castle, Berwickshire (although the latter's main facade had, Heriot-style, three rather than two towers). The second, definitely by Smith, was an unrealised project of *c.*1695 by the 4th Earl of Traquair (a Catholic Jacobite) to make his old tower symmetrical by constructing a second, large wing; the scheme proved too ambitious and, instead, Smith tidied up Traquair's garden front with detached, ogee-roofed pavilions, and rebuilt the forecourt.

In striking contrast to these projects, in the 1680s–1700s Smith also designed two of the most uncompromisingly monumental classical projects of the age: the remodelling of Hamilton Palace, from 1684 to *c.*1700, for the 3rd Duke and Duchess of Hamilton, and that of Dalkeith Palace, 1702–5, for Anne, Duchess of Buccleuch and Monmouth. At Hamilton, in 1684, the Duke (formerly leader of the opposition to the now-deceased Lauderdale) and Duchess began a staged rebuilding programme with the construction of new offices and stables; they had already got descriptions of recent

3.7 Drumlanrig Castle (James Smith, rebuilt 1679–90), early twentieth-century photograph of entrance front.

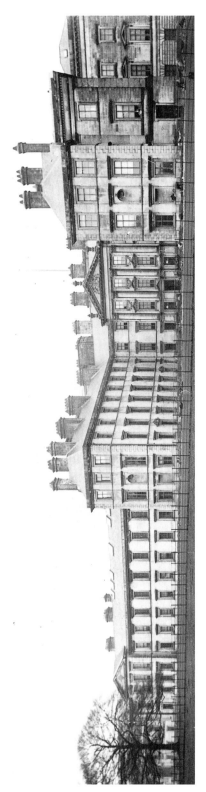

French houses from their son on his Grand Tour. From 1691 the main house, with its quadrangular, single-depth plan, was tackled [3.8]. For this the Duke consulted and travelled widely, securing advice, for instance, from Bruce and Sir Christopher Wren. Eventually, the decision was taken to retain some of the old house at the north, and to build in front of it a new, open, U-shaped courtyard, whose long, single-depth wings echoed the old layout and evoked the air of a great French

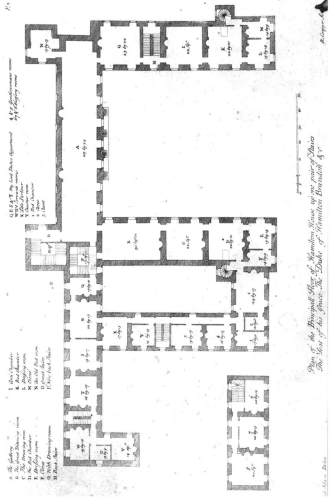

hôtel. The vertical grouping of the windows recalled the work of Pierre Le Muet, a copy of whose *Manière de Bien Bastir* was bought by Smith's cousin in Hamilton in 1698. In a telling sign of the craze for state apartments among the higher aristocracy, it was the west, state wing that was built first (finished 1693); the family lived in that while the duplicate, east wing was finished (1696). By then the Duke had died, but the Duchess ploughed relentlessly ahead with the

3.8 Hamilton Palace (remodelled 1684–*c.*1700 by Smith): (left) south front, view of *c.*1890; (middle) principal floor plan drawn by William Adam *c.*1730, and reproduced in *Vitruvius Scoticus*; (right) garden layout by Alexander Edward, 1708.

remainder of the scheme, including the linking north quarter and the interiors (completed 1701). Of the north block, Smith commented at the time that 'Her Grace is content that we should make it as fine as possible so as the same may be not gaudy or exceed the rules of proportion and true symmetry with the rest of the work'. [16]

The air of refined splendour aimed at by the Hamiltons in this, the largest country house building project of the age, was epitomised in the dominant feature of the main ashlar south frontage: a three-storey tetrastyle Corinthian portico. The sheer scale of this, as well as the setting-back of its smooth-shafted two-storey columns in curved recesses, and the positioning of its pediment in a freestanding position above the wallhead, hinted at a somewhat 'antique', 'Italian' monumentality. We should remember that although Sir Christopher Wren had just built (1682–9) a giant portico at Chelsea Royal Hospital, no columnar portico on this scale had hitherto been built in a domestic or palace context in Scotland or England; even the France of Louis XIV – the stronghold of the superimposed Order – offered no direct precedent. Not for nothing were the Hamiltons the nation's premier landed dynasty! Hamilton Palace's interiors were decorated in a more ostentatious, yet still sombre

manner, with much use of richly carved dark oak by William Morgan. On the principal floor, the north quarter was taken up with a gallery; the state and private apartments in the wings were planned identically, and each comprised a dining room, drawing room, bedchamber, dressing-room and closet. The existing garden and park was north of the palace, but in the 1690s a vast landscaping scheme was begun, arranged around a north-south grand axis with the palace at the centre; the north avenue was underway by 1692 while the south avenue, linking the low and high parks, was being contemplated from 1694. Both parks were intended for a range of activities, including hunting, deer rides and walks. In 1708, following a continental tour (1701–2) taking in Marly and Versailles, Alexander Edward surveyed the policies of Hamilton and proposed the construction of a network of vistas, incorporating this grand north-south axis on either side of the palace.

Smith's Hamilton Palace, with its use of giant columns, had introduced, for landowners of the top rank, a new standard of austere architectural grandeur. A year after Hamilton's completion, in 1702, this stone monumentality was echoed, on a slightly more restricted budget, by the Duchess of Buccleuch. She commissioned Smith to rebuild the old Dalkeith Castle into a new 'Palace of

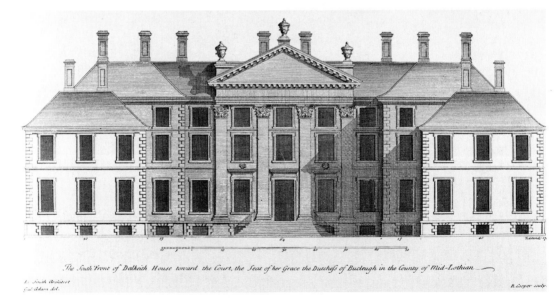

3.9 Dalkeith Palace (rebuilt 1702–5 by Smith): (above) main elevation, from *Vitruvius Scoticus*; (right) 1929 RCAHMS ground-floor plan, including state apartment and the Duchess's chambers, and showing how the old tower is embedded in the new design.

Dalkeith', [17] equipped with state apartments on a level which would reflect her close royal connection. When proposals for a completely new house proved too expensive, the Duchess was forced to settle for the expedient of scooping out a U-shaped space from three sides of the existing house's old courtyard, and distributing new apartments round this space to form a new sash-windowed facade – commanding a grand axial landscaping scheme cut through the policies [3.9]. In contrast to the serene horizontality of Hamilton, at Dalkeith there was a more dynamic massing, building up from low wings to the climax of the giant pedimented tetrastyle Corinthian portico. However, it was only this centrepiece that was of ashlar; the remainder was harled. Contrasting strongly with the soberly un-accented horizontality of Hamilton, this pyramidal and

tightly integrated composition was the closest approach of Scottish classicism to the mainstream continental Baroque. As recognised by the English visitor John Macky in 1723, Dalkeith's telescopic plan in some ways resembled the Dutch royal palace of Het Loo, as rebuilt by Jacob Roman *c*.1692. If the outside was heavily architectonic, Duchess Anne's new interior was theatrical in character. The entrance hall and staircase were profusely lined in white marble. On the ground floor was the main state enfilade, and above, in isolated glory, and approached by the main stair, the Great Dining Room (later a picture gallery). Most woodwork in the principal rooms was carved by William Morgan and Isaac Silverstyne: decoration was especially rich in the private apartment. Again in emphasis of the Duchess's semi-royal status, the house was one of the most

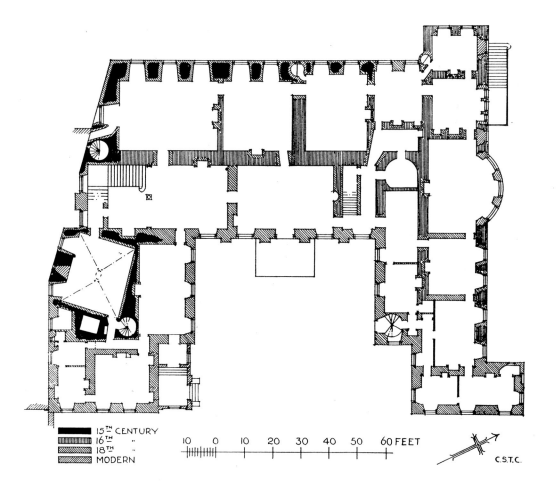

15TH CENTURY
16TH   "
18TH   "
MODERN

10   0   10   20   30   40   50   60 FEET

C.S.T.C.

richly furnished of its generation: some of the contents were brought from the Duchess's English mansion, Moor Park.

'Proper, Modish and Convenient':
The New Classical Country House (18)

Where the amalgam of new and old in the period's rebuilding schemes was motivated by a mixture of dynastic pride and expediency, fewer constraints applied in the case of new classical houses – a category of project which was less prominent at first than the Holyrood-style 'reforms', but in the long run was perhaps more significant. Here we witness the development, again led by Bruce and Smith, of a new and radical country house architecture, keeping pace once more with advanced international trends. For major new houses, the keynote was a severe monumentality which fused the grandeur of the Italian 'antique' – already encountered above, in the reconstructions of Hamilton and Dalkeith – with a renewed and heightened Scottish ashlar austerity. For the newly prominent class of lesser lairds, on the other hand, a compact, villa-like house emerged, planned for convenience as well as grandeur. On the whole, it was easier to contemplate building anew in those cases where an existing ancestral house was not involved.

This process of evolution in new house architecture was only gradual. At first, developments ran closely in parallel with that of the 'reformed' older houses such as Leslie and Balcaskie, and were dominated by symmetrical U-plans. The first major setpiece of this type, Panmure House, was built from 1666 by the 2nd Earl of Panmure, to the designs of John Mylne (who also acted as contractor); the work was superintended after Mylne's death by another Edinburgh mason, Alexander Nisbet, and probably completed in 1671 [3.10]. This was a very important house, which set out a number of planning themes later elaborated in much grander projects. To begin with, the plan of its double-depth main floor represented the closest Scottish attempt, at that early date, at a symmetrical arrangement of matching apartments on either side of a great salon, which here stretched the full depth of the house; even the elevation had a suggestion of Vaux in its overlapping outer pavilions and high roof. And the placing of a large room on the top floor, above the salon, anticipated a favourite eighteenth-century theme: here it was a billiard room, but a library was more common in later cases. Panmure was extensively landscaped on all sides, including covered walks and labyrinths nearby, and vistas radiating out through the surrounding woods. Although Panmure was an essentially non-political landowner, the

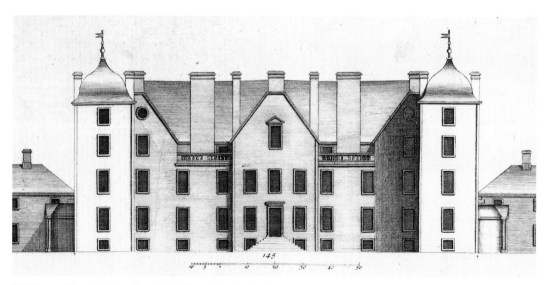

3.10 Panmure House (J. Mylne, from 1666), *Vitruvius Scoticus* drawings: (right) plans of first, principal and roof storeys; (above) elevation.

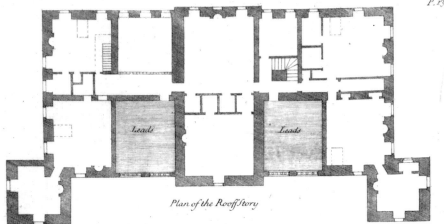

Plan of the Rooff Story

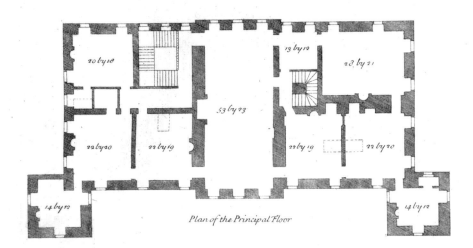

20 by 18

13 by 12

23 by 21

53 by 23

22 by 20   22 by 19

22 by 19   22 by 20

14 by 12

14 by 12

Plan of the Principal Floor

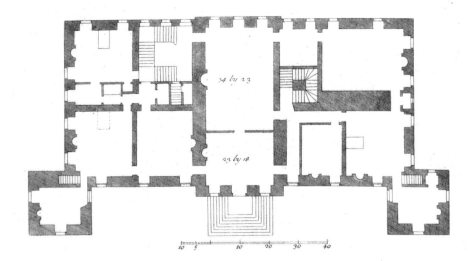

34 by 23

23 by 18

10 5   10   20   30   40

involvement of Bruce was recorded in several aspects of the project – the designing of gates (1672), and advising on offices (1693). However, it is not clear whether the layout or elevation of the house owes anything to his influence; the drawings and contracts were handled by Edward. A closer Bruce link is suggested by the fact that the house was flanked by convex quadrants – a rare feature later repeated in Bruce's Hopetoun, and pointing to an interest in the villa plans of Palladio.

A similar architectural grouping, less ambitiously classical in its internal planning, was found in two houses – New Tarbat and Royston – built by George Mackenzie, Viscount Tarbat, a prominent episcopalian and grain trader from Easter Ross who (like Smith) managed with a degree of success to transfer his allegiance from James VII to William II. Although Tarbat was a friend of Bruce, he probably designed New Tarbat himself, and built it *c.*1663–70, on a shallow, corner-pavilioned U-plan with stairtowers in the angles and first floor state apartment. Here we see the process of aristocratic architectural emulation at work: in 1670 George Dunsterfield was engaged to travel to Milton to install plaster ceilings 'conform to my Lord Hatoun's House', [19] while by 1688 joiners were busy installing sash windows. By then, however, the attention of the newly ennobled Tarbat had turned elsewhere, to the construction of an extensive house just outside the capital at Royston (now Caroline Park). Although we deal with it here because of its patronage connection, Royston was not a new house, but an enlargement of a tower house bought by Tarbat in 1684 on a scale almost amounting to a new building. We will return later to the increasing phenomenon, at that time, of the building of villa-like houses near the capital by those seeking a rural setting near Parliament and law courts. Following the death of Lauderdale, Tarbat's political fortunes were rising and, like Seton at Pinkie following Dunbar's death, he felt confident enough to indulge in an exercise of conspicuous modesty. The tower house was enveloped in a new courtyard, like Leslie on plan. An inscription by Tarbat and his wife declared that this 'tuguriolum' (cottage) was built 'for their own comfort and that of their friends'. In 1693–6 a new south facade was added, in which the French affiliations of the

Panmure tower-flanked pattern were made more explicit, with square end pavilions and high domed roofs, and banded pilasters flanking the entrance hall. Inside, a staircase with elaborate iron balustrade led up to the first-floor great apartment [3.11].

Many new houses built by lesser lairds between the 1660s and 1690s followed these patterns in a simplified manner, consolidating the earlier developments of the Murray years but not, as yet, aspiring to the sash-windowed prestige of Lauderdale's works. A notable U-planned laird's house, with separate pyramidal-roofed pavilions and taller main block, was Gallery, Angus, where a 1677 contract between Sir John Falconer and Thomas Wilkie, an Edinburgh mason, specified 'ane double house' with 'two jams . . . ane galleryie the full lenth of the said house . . . storme windowes . . . caisements' and 'ane large scale staire'. [20] The plan was double-depth, with more or less symmetrical room-disposition and a modest great apartment on the first floor. Smaller equivalents of the gable-flanked 'infilled U' plan

3.11 Caroline Park House, Edinburgh, view of 1690s state stair, with wrought-iron work perhaps by Alexander Gairdner.

3.12 Dunkeld, view from Slezer's *Theatrum Scotiae*, showing the house (Bruce, 1676–84) at the centre and the cathedral on the left.

type were built at the crowstepped Bargany (1681), Prestonfield (1681–9, a total rebuild of a damaged house with shaped gables and balustraded centre), and Cammo (1693, also with shaped gables). Lesser versions of the gabled H-shaped layout of the 1670s included Philpstoun (1676) and Bannockburn (1674, with Murray-style wallhead dormers).

The mid-1670s saw a sharp break, at the hands of Bruce, from this evolutionary approach, in two moderate-sized houses in Perthshire: Dunkeld (1676–84) and Moncrieffe (finished 1679). [3.12, 3.13] Here austere harled facades derived from the laird's house tradition – unadorned except for quoins, stringcourse, pedimented doorcase and cornice – were remarshalled in a new classical form which was influenced by the 'convenience' of contemporary small-house design fashions in north-west Europe, but which also, in its low attic windows, aspired to something of the heavy dignity of an Italian palazzo. The essence of these houses lay in their innovative plan. Both were three-storey and basement blocks with a deep, nearly square plan divided by cross walls into three units stretching from front to rear, allowing a central salon to be combined with two or three rooms on either side. This compact layout, along with the piended roof with central lantern, echoed recent English and Dutch houses (by Inigo Jones, Jacob van Campen and others); the plan also resembled contemporary French *maisons de plaisance* such as Pierre Bullet's Château d'Issy of

1681. Dunkeld House was built as a winter-retreat for Lauderdale's supporter, the Marquess of Atholl, to replace a house destroyed by English troops in 1654. It incorporated the residually 'castellated' features of angle-turrets and parapet, and overlooked a landscaped vista aligned on the tower of the cathedral. Moncrieffe, built by Thomas Moncrieffe of that Ilk, contained a full-depth first-floor central Great Dining Room flanked by five main rooms, closet, and open, Holyrood-like stair. It was described by Macky as 'a neat little Seat . . . very neatly wainscoted and furnished within'. [21]

3.13 Moncrieffe House (Bruce, finished 1679).

The most decisive visual development of this compact, yet monumental dwelling-type came in 1679–93, in Bruce's construction of a new country home for himself: Kinross House [3.14, 3.15]. Working at a leisurely pace dictated by his declining political fortunes and increasing indebtedness in the 1680s, Bruce here achieved his most carefully crafted synthesis of planning, architecture and landscape. The project began with the building of a forecourt and outbuildings (by 1686), followed by the main block's structure (1686–90) and furnishings (1690–3); its workforce included two Dutch masons, Peter Paul Boyse and Cornelius van Nerven. The plan of Kinross,

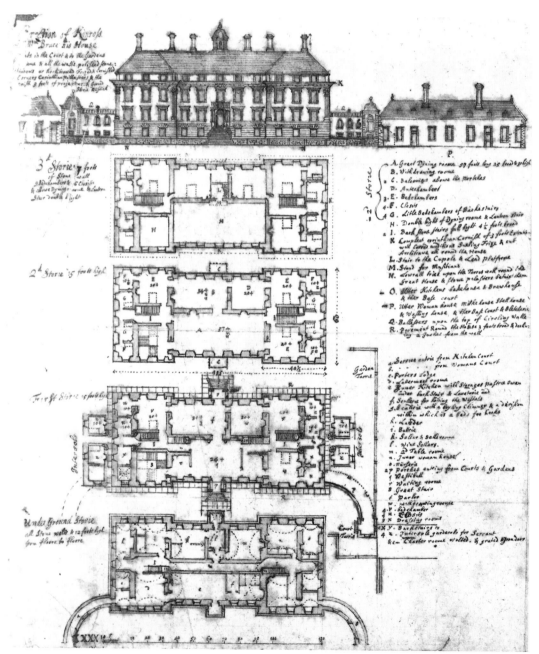

3.14 Kinross House (Bruce, 1679–93), drawings probably by Edward: (above) plans, elevation; (right) landscaping layout.

intended by Bruce to rank in status as a major country house despite its relatively limited size, was far more complex than the simple tripartite plan of Moncrieffe and Dunkeld. In some practical aspects, as so often, the empirical ingenuity of English architecture provided inspiration: the vaulted service floor was modelled on the double-depth plan, with a continuous spinal corridor, built at Coleshill (from *c.*1650). On the three floors above, the double-depth and corridor plan was confined to the sides: at the centre, a more formal and grandiose effect was achieved by channelling cross-communication through a central vestibule (on the first floor) and a great, double-height Salon

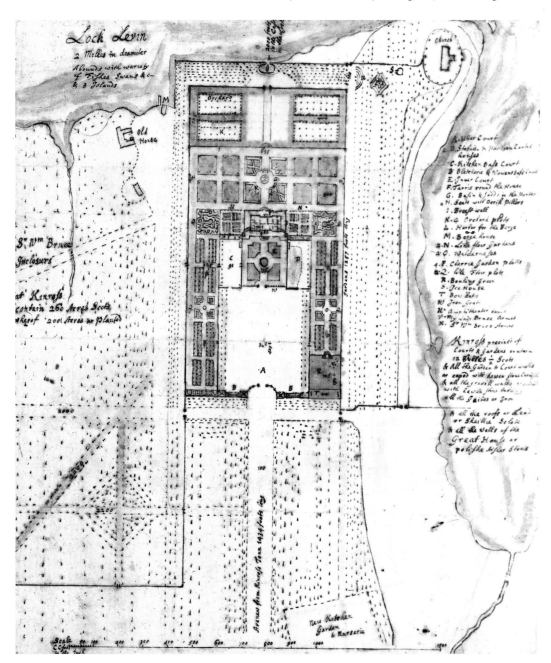

3.15 Kinross House, east front.

(on the second, state floor). The great apartment, which was never, in the event, fully fitted up, comprised drawing and dining rooms behind the Salon, with flanking bedroom suites and end mezzanines.

When it came to the exterior of Kinross, the homely classicism of the contemporary English houses was hardly a suitable model for Bruce's monumental 'seat'. Instead, he set out to intensify an image of heavy, almost palazzo-like grandeur, with relatively widely spaced windows. The house comprised a shallow H-plan block, standing on a channelled rusticated basement (a new feature), with its pavilion corners articulated by single Corinthian pilasters. The entire composition was topped by a continuous entablature and cornice, a row of low attic windows and a piended roof with central lantern. The house was incorporated in an extended layout of quadrant links and courts in the Palladio manner. Although all suggestion of the castellated tradition had been purged from the house itself, the centrepiece of Kinross's extensive landscaping scheme was an axial vista aligned on the ruined tower of Lochleven Castle, in which Queen Mary had been imprisoned. Here, we see a link emerging between the earlier tradition of dynastic piety, and the early eighteenth- and nineteenth-century conception of historic or castellar forms as something separate, and complementary, to classicism.

The decisive contribution of Kinross to Scottish domestic architecture was to tip the balance against harled rubble construction, pattern-book added decoration, and features directly evocative of the castellated past, as elements acceptable within top-rank houses. It established a new type of stone monumentality, based on full articulation through the Orders, and, where possible, on the use of ashlar. The latter, where even the largest Renaissance palaces in Rome had normally used render, seemed to point to ancient, rather than modern, Roman inspiration. Of course, ashlar building was already many centuries old within Scotland, stretching back to twelfth-century (or earlier) examples such as St Rule's Church, St Andrews. [22] But there is no indication that the new phase of classical architecture represented by Kinross was inspired by those precedents. Although for the moment confined to the most prestigious houses, and even there by no means universally used, the new framework would gradually percolate down (often in astylar form) to less elevated social groups over the following two centuries.

In the new houses that followed, Bruce refined the planning aspects of this compact yet stately deep-plan classical pattern. Craigiehall (1698–1701) was built as a suburban villa for Bruce's distant relation, the 2nd Earl of Annandale, to replace a small castellated house. Here, in a complex relationship typical of Bruce's later years of political opposition and restricted freedom, he was faced with the involvement of James Smith (now royal Surveyor) as a rival consultant. Spurred on by this rivalry, Bruce pioneered elements of the grander centralised planning that would later mature at Hopetoun. As recorded in correspondence of 1694, Bruce's original proposal for demolition of the old house and construction of a new, symmetrical, formal design – 'a convenient little house, gardings and courts' [23] –was undermined by Smith, who argued for a straightforward replacement of the old tower and retention of an orchard of which the Earl was fond. Bruce, in turn, attacked Smith's proposal as too small and 'in a meaner manner yn is befitting a gentleman under your Lop. condition and quality'. By comparison with his earlier works, Bruce's attitude to the clash of classical regularity and older patterns was now uncompromising: 'Where I make any designe I have no regard to . . . any old matter wch. are oblique & not agreeable to a modish and regullar designe . . . If your Lo. will have things proper, modish and convenient, you must not concern yourself for anything old in ye way yrof'. [24] Eventually, a compromise was reached: a deep tripartite plan on the precedent of Bruce's Dunkeld and Moncrieffe, but an external form, piend-roofed with two-bay pedimented frontispiece, which was possibly influenced by Smith. The basement was constructed of banded masonry and the building was bounded by piers at the sides. Internally, there was a near-central staircase, lit by the cupola.

In view of Bruce's increasing personal and political difficulties after 1689, it is not surprising that some of his later houses were, essentially, recapitulations of earlier themes. At Harden, for example (1703; now Mertoun), a double-depth house of Kinross-like plan was fronted by a small pediment. A more original design, House of Nairne (*c*.1709–12), was seemingly drawn up jointly with Lady Nairn and Alexander McGill, with advice from the Earl of Mar. Like some later designs of Mar and William Adam, Nairne had a tall, compact central block of three storeys and basement; there were slim, pyramidal-roofed turrets recessed on the side walls, and flanking wings.

From 1698, Bruce began a last major commission, Hopetoun House, which would rival the greatest works of Smith in classical originality and grandeur [3.16]. Hopetoun was built in two stages. First, in 1698, Lady Margaret Hope commissioned the building (by Bachop), to Bruce's designs, of a new house for her son, Sir Charles Hope (later Lord Hopetoun). This block was centrally planned around an octagonal staircase hall, its principal floor arranged in a Greek cross (externally expressed by pedimented projections) and containing, in effect, two flanking apartments. The high roof was flat and balustraded at the centre, with a lantern above the staircase. In this arrestingly novel plan, Bruce enriched his existing concepts of compact house planning with geometrical centralised ideas evocative of Italian Renaissance and antique grandeur, as more recently and monumentally realised in the Royal Pavilion of Louis XIV's Marly. As we shall see shortly, James Smith had been increasingly fascinated by Italian centralised-planning ideas, while Edward visited and drew Marly on a visit in 1701–2. A recently discovered painted ceiling in the staircase octagon also attests to the original design's Italian preoccupations.

In 1702, Bruce was brought back to recast the first Hopetoun in a new and more imposing form for the young Lord Hopetoun. Full-height angle pavilions were added – forming a U-shaped front of three storeys and basement on the by now familiar pattern – and the entire front was given overall channelled rustication, with a ground-floor arcade at the centre. Convex Tuscan colonnades (a highly unusual feature) were to join the main building to service blocks. The revised scheme now clearly aspired to the dignity of a major country house; the channelled rustication and general arrangement, with its large, complex main block, conveyed something of the air of a great French or Dutch hôtel. However, by the 1720s, before the Bruce scheme was fully complete, Lord Hopetoun would already have begun completely refacing it to a still grander design of his own, assisted by William Adam. The landscaping of Hopetoun, continuing the theme of monumental order, included a vista of extreme ambitiousness, aligned (on the east) on North Berwick Law and (on the west) on Abercorn Church.

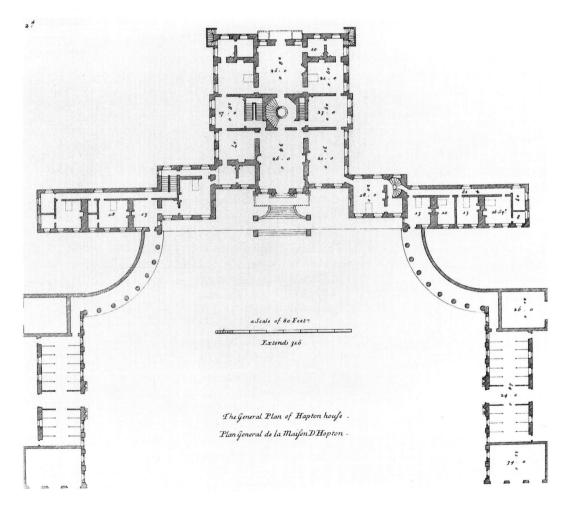

3.16 Hopetoun House, final form of Bruce design (1702), illustrations from *Vitruvius Scoticus*: (above) east entrance elevation; (below) principal floor plan.

While Kinross and Hopetoun gave Bruce the opportunity to indulge his increasingly uncompromising and experimental classical tastes, Smith had a rather more frustrating time in his new commissions. A collection of unexecuted designs by Smith, later owned by Colen Campbell, contains projects for houses and villas based on a wide range of Italian sources, doubtless inspected at first hand by Smith. The designs include a group of large palazzo-like houses, with superimposed Orders, and various centralised villas. A number of the plans pertain to medium-sized country houses, including permutations of the Leslie/Panmure arrangement of central full-depth salon and side wings [cf. 3.5, 3.10]. But Smith could only realise those ideas in heavily modified form.

For example, several sets of unexecuted proposals, including two by Smith, survive for Melville House, a piend-roofed, shallow H-plan house built by the 1st Earl of Melville in 1697–1702: Smith was contractor, and probably also the main designer of the house as completed (although Bruce was also involved, in a consultant role, and Edward helped draw up plans). One of the unexecuted Smith proposals envisaged a three-storey Corinthian portico, and another an arrangement of outer pavilions and central two-storey loggia in the manner of Palladio's Villa Trissino. The corresponding plans provided for a central toplit circular or square hall. Another drawing, not by Smith, also suggested a double loggia. The Earl, a cautious lawyer, vetoed all these plans, and the exterior was built in a more austere, harled and unpedimented style – effectively, as a plainer and narrower version of Kinross [3.17]. He reserved the opulent display of his newly ennobled wealth for the interior. Inside, there was a symmetrical H-plan. On the principal floor, the central salon (or Great Dining Room) was of nearly double-cube proportions, and filled with family portraits; it gave access to two flanking apartments. The state apartment was wainscoted in oak by east coast craftsmen, including Edinburgh wright Thomas Kyll; the finest carvings in the house were by William Morgan. Melville was furnished as profusely as any royal palace, including as the centrepiece the Great Leven and Melville State Bed. The other main apartment (Lord Melville's) was finished in pine [3.18].

Key elements of the Melville design were repeated, again probably by Smith, at Dryden House, built some time before 1715 by a close political ally of his: George Lockhart of Carnwath, a wealthy, energetically improving Jacobite laird with extensive coal interests. It, too, was arranged on an H-layout with piended two-bay wings and quoins, but deeper plan, with either arm of the 'H' being five bays in length. A more elaborate proposed design for Dryden envisaged an (unrealised) tall tetrastyle portico and raised pediment; Lockhart's major political patron in the early 1700s was, significantly, the 4th Duke of Hamilton. An even more arresting example of external plainness and internal richness, Yester House, was designed by Smith for the Marquess of Tweeddale. Its pavilions were begun in 1699 and the main block *c*.1710. As originally conceived by Smith, Yester comprised a nine-bay piend-roofed box of two storeys and basement with severely flat elevations and ogee-roofed flanking pavilions. Building on the precedent of Bruce's second Hopetoun, the walls (above a rusticated base) are channelled all over – the epitome of refined severity. The original internal layout, only partly executed, included a principal floor with salon and hall each rising two floors; later, William Adam began forming a great apartment on the first floor.

Alongside his enlargements of Hamilton and Dalkeith, setting as they did new standards of classical grandeur, Smith also made a decisive contribution to the evolution of a new type of house of even more compact character than the Dunkeld/Moncrieffe pattern, suitable for the homes of minor lairds or professionals (such as himself) who aspired to landed status, or as villas or lesser houses of more wealthy landowners. For those wanting to build new houses, the late seventeenth century's refined norm was represented by Blairhall, Fife, a two-storey, five-bay design of astylar classical uniformity, with steep roof and crowsteps. Smith's contribution was to introduce a degree of 'antique' monumentality to the exterior of this single-depth house type, through pediments and more up-to-date classical detailing, and internally to introduce more complicated plans, including specialised service-spaces, corridors, and a limited degree of public and private separation. In other words, Smith

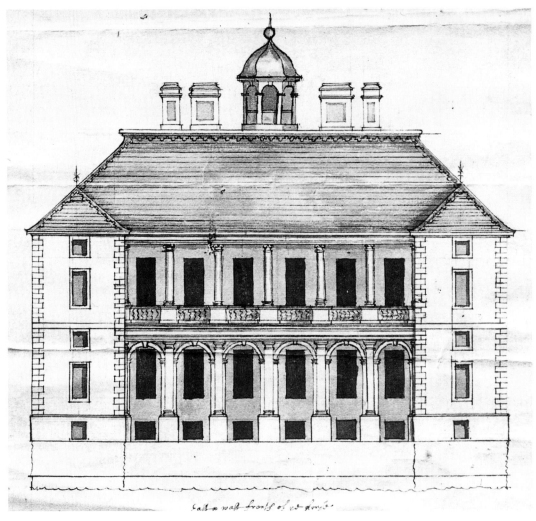

3.17 Melville House, Fife: (above) unexecuted design drawing of *c*.1697; (right) principal floor plan and elevation as largely executed (1697–1702; the house was built with cupola, and non-aedicular entrance), from *Vitruvius Britannicus*, vol. 2.

designed villa-sized houses as miniature versions of large country-seats. Not surprisingly, he first attempted this on his own estate of Whitehill (after 1686), in a dwelling for himself and his family: a two-storey house, with quoins and tall piended roof, advanced centrepiece and pediment above the wallhead. The garden doorway, approached by a double forestair, is flanked with pilasters tapered at the base in a somewhat Michelangelesque manner. Internally, the staircase was set off-centre, and the first floor accommodates a principal apartment of four rooms ingeniously arranged in spiral form, from staircase to bedroom. The house was renamed Newhailes in 1707 and subsequently

greatly expanded by Sir David and Sir James Dalrymple [3.19].

In two other houses, Strathleven (attributed) and Raith, Smith developed the same ideas in houses of deeper plan. In the seven-bay facade of the later Strathleven (1708), the central pediment contains oculi and armorial panel and a full entablature behind. Raith (1693–6, for a son of Lord Melville) was originally intended as a miniature Hamilton, with vertical window-bay units flanking statue niches, but a simpler design was actually executed. It seems likely that the 'antique' gravity of Palladio's villas (as well as the compact planning of more recent small houses in

The Elevation of Melvin houſe in the Shire of Fyfe in Scotland, the Seat of the Rt. Honble. the Earl of Leven —
to whom this Plate is moſt humbly Inſcrib'd.
Elevation de la Maiſon de Melvin dans la Comté de Fyfe en Ecoſse.

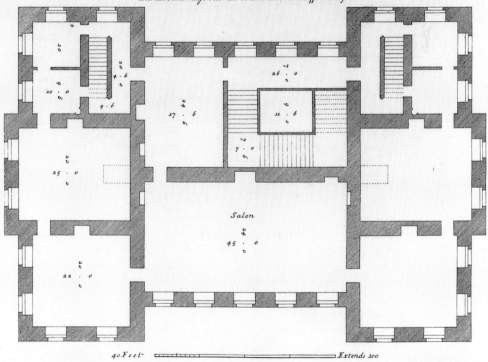

Salon

40 Feet   Extends 100

Plan of the principal Floor ..
Plan du principal Etage.

Ca: Campbell Delin   H. Hulſbergh Sc:

3.18 Melville House, state bed, seen before removal from the house.

north-west Europe) was a stimulus to Smith's development of this new type plan of the monumental small classical house – a framework which would prove highly influential over the following decades, even centuries.

'1715': Lord Mar and 'The True Ancient Simple Taste' (25)

On 6 September 1715, John Erskine, 11th Earl of Mar, commenced an armed insurrection in support of the Jacobite claimant to the throne, James Francis Stuart, who arrived in Peterhead on 22 December. The position of Mar – previously a political high-flier under Queen Anne, as Secretary of State for Scotland from 1705 – and of the Scottish political establishment as a whole had been undermined to the point of open revolt by the sweeping changes which followed the Hanoverian succession in 1714. However, the campaign which he led rapidly lost impetus and collapsed, leaving Mar to join James in exile on the Continent.

What concerns us, in this account, is not Mar's attributes as a political and military leader, but the fact that he was (and remained, during his exile) one of Scotland's most important architects. And this political/architectural overlap was not just an isolated case. Ever since Smith's interiors at Holyrood Abbey Church, along with the Chapel Royal, had been sacked by Calvinist militants in December 1688 [cf. 3.3], the steady strengthening of Presbyterian unionism, especially through the 1707 incorporating union and the Hanoverian succession, had alienated, to varying degrees, virtually the entire establishment of Restoration architecture. Bruce's disaffection was openly displayed, leading to twenty years of virtual house-arrest, and even harsher measures on occasion. He was arrested in 1696 in connection with plots to assassinate King William II, and in 1708 was secured 'upon suspition' in Edinburgh Castle at the time of an attempted Jacobite invasion. For the non-juring episcopalian minister Alexander Edward, by contrast, the events of 1689–90 widened, rather than curbed, his opportunities. Ejected from his ministry in Fife in 1695, he took up full-time architectural and garden design [cf. 3.8]. In 1701–2, he was sent on a tour of France, England and the Low Countries by a group of Jacobite noblemen, headed by Mar, with instructions to 'view, observe and take draughts of the most curious and remarkable Houses, Edifices, Gardings, orchards, parks, plantations, land improvements, coall works, mines, water works and other curiosities of nature and art'. (26) Edward's visit to France had another purpose, however – to visit James Francis Stuart at St Germain, and deliver a letter in cypher from the 4th Duke of Hamilton – reporting, no doubt, on Jacobite fortunes in Scotland. Following the Jacobite defeat in the 1715–16 war, Mar occupied his exile not only in political activity but in preparing utopian architectural schemes of vast ambitiousness. Among the Scottish architects who had chosen to move to London to seek work, there were similar experiences. Mar's protégé James Gibbs, a closet Catholic who (like Smith) had studied briefly for the priesthood at the Scots College in Rome, and had received architectural training from Carlo Fontana, was deprived of a major public commission of church-building after

1714; whereas the career of another architect who openly embraced Whig Hanoverianism, Colen Campbell, enjoyed a meteoric rise – partly at Gibbs's expense.

Clearly, in terms of architectural *patronage,* the downfall of the pre-1714 *ancien régime* had a direct, even revolutionary impact. Predictably, however, there was very little direct correlation between these dramatic events and the course of architectural *ideas*: there was no 'Jacobite architecture' as such. The Earl of Mar was as prominent a figure in the architectural developments of the years around 1715 as he was a political and military leader. But those developments were characterised not by revolution, but by a consistent thread of evolution, which linked the tendencies of the Bruce 'Restoration' years to the architecture of the years of Hanoverian ascendancy.

The central theme in this continuing evolution within Scottish classicism was the development of a new and more explicitly articulated view of antiquity, building on the formal and seemingly un-theoretical innovations of Bruce and Smith. In this age, of course, direct knowledge of ancient monuments was largely focused on a few set-pieces in and around Rome. Wildly inaccurate speculations were rife about other parts of the ancient world. *Le Grand Marot* of *c.*1670, for example, pictured a 'Greek Temple' as a vast courtyard structure, with polygonal bastions and multi-storey domed apses – a kind of cross between the Louvre and the Temple of Solomon. Just as each country made its own reconstructions of the Antique, it was open to each country's classical architecture to make its own accom

modation between ideals of ancient purity and modern social, political and economic conditions. And whereas, in France, this 'modern' context was still one of absolutist national development, Scotland was now increasingly running in parallel with England in stressing landed, private-led 'improvement' – of whatever political or dynastic complexion.

The main theme of the architectural expression of early eighteenth century Scottish landed power was a new insistence on exclusively classical design. From the beginning of the eighteenth century, it became even less acceptable than before, in the buildings of the Scottish landed classes, for old parts of houses to be publicly displayed. References to national or family heritage were separated out into complementary areas such as sculpture and landscaping. Driven forward by the ideas of a new generation of landed architects and commentators, who broke with the courtly ideals of the Bruce generation, the form of early eighteenth-century classical architecture built on the experiments of Bruce and Smith by making more overt allusions to the antique. In particular, it exploited the legacy of Palladio and Scamozzi in evocations of Roman grandeur. While these efforts led, on occasion, to architecture of a dramatic, scenographic character – especially the fantastic designs made by (and for) Mar in exile – the legacy of this period of experimentation for the mid-eighteenth century would, on the whole, be one of respect for architectonic order. The principles of four-square ashlar monumentality established by Bruce and Smith would be retained. Scotland would conform in all significant respects to the

3.19 Newhailes House (Smith, after 1686), original garden front; the central block is Smith's original Whitehill.

north-west European early eighteenth-century trend towards monumental sobriety, as opposed to central Europe's voluptuous illusionism and dynamic rupturing of linear or right-angled forms.

The first of the turn-of-the-century gentlemen-designers to attempt to formulate a theoretical position was Mar's friend, the indefatigable agricultural improver Sir Andrew Fletcher of Saltoun. Fletcher was a militant republican and opponent of the parliamentary union with England, believing that English Whiggery was a philosophy of decadent commercialism. To him, improvement must be based on the values of antiquity and inspired by the 'great and stupendous public works' achieved by the private wealth of the Romans. [27] What Fletcher himself actually designed, or advised on, is not yet clear. Like Smith, he developed an interest in compact villa planning, seemingly inspired by Italian examples. In 1699, Fletcher wrote that the 'magnificency' of such buildings, with their dignified, heavy facades and sparing window-openings, provided a framework of design for domestic architecture 'not inferior to what the Greeks had for their temples'. By contrast, he condemned the 'meanness' of the typical irregular-windowed, old-fashioned Scottish house, 'struck out all in opens like a pigeon-house', and claimed that 'that glaring, staring light with which we illuminate our houses . . . dissipates all thought'. [28] We saw above, for instance at Bruce's Kinross, attempts at a relatively sparsely windowed, palazzo-like treatment. The problem of combining domestic fenestration with a monumental facade would exercise many future architects, including Robert Adam and Alexander Thomson.

The ideas of Mar himself focused on the relationship between improvement-led modernity and the antique. By 1700, he was established as an 'adviser' [29] on architecture and landscape-gardening, of a status equal to Bruce. The source of his expertise is uncertain: perhaps a combination of Fletcher, Smith and Edward. Mar appears to have provided designs for a variety of new country houses, especially near his own home at Alloa – including the rebuilt House of Alva (after 1700), and perhaps Tullibody, Tillicoultry and Blairdrummond (with which McGill was also associated). He also designed agricultural improvement schemes: for example, in 1707 for the Earl of Kinnoull at Dupplin. At Craigiehall, Mar advised on the building of courts after 1701, and in 1708 remodelled the house's surroundings, designing a gate which may survive, repositioned, in the massive Doric portico and segmental pediment of the 1759 Craigiehall Temple pavilion. A link with Bruce was also suggested by his role in advising on the design of House of Nairne.

Mar's most tireless efforts were reserved for his own estate at Alloa, from which he had directed, since 1689, an extensive range of industrial and agricultural improvement enterprises. By around 1700, he had decided to retain and regularise the old tower house, chiefly for economy's sake, and to concentrate his new works in a vast strategy of landscaping. By 1706, Edward was at work on the house carrying out Mar's rebuilding scheme, including reroofing and installation of sash windows. The tower was regularised and made symmetrical outside, with a big doorcase, and wings were built, while inside it was remodelled with a great circular staircase and a 'Grand Sall' at first-floor level. His apologetic feelings about his ancestral home, and his improvements to it, reflect the rapidly increasing unfashionability, yet also the continuing sentimental hold, of the old towers. Writing in retrospect (in 1726), he recalled that 'I was to blame . . . for going about repairing the old House of Alloa, wch. was more fitt to be made a quarrie'. But there was 'something in the old Tower, especially if made conforme to the new designe, wch. is venerable for its antiquity and makes not a bad appearance'. And after his remodelling works, the house, while still 'not pretending to Architectur', nevertheless 'is now in such a way to be made a tolerable good and agreeable one within, tho not very beautiful and regular without, with no great charge'. [30]

The Alloa landscaping works were unprecedented not only in their scale, but in the fact that they were directly interrelated with a scheme of industrial development. In 1701, Mar started to enlarge an existing formal garden into a gigantic complex covering four square miles, and organised around three avenues radiating, Versailles-like, from the house, with subsidiary axes in other directions. He began work on one avenue in 1701, and was further emboldened by Edward's reports on his 1701–2 mission to France. Vistas were focused on a variety of distant buildings (including some of national historical resonance, such as Stirling Castle and Old Stirling Bridge) and on natural features such as the Ochil Hills. The extensive waterworks were serviced by a hydraulic pump designed and built by the Earl in 1710, powered by a giant waterwheel which also drained his coal-mines; this was scrapped in 1713 and replaced by a dam. Mar's great scheme of classico-historical landscaping and industry was much visited and admired by other members of the landed élite. For example, Sir John Clerk of Penicuik – who would succeed Mar, in the 1720s, as the 'Maecenas' of Scottish 'improvement' architecture -visited Alloa in 1708 and acclaimed the garden as a 'sweet place'. [31]

Despite Mar's exile from 1716, his architectural career, far from atrophying, took a revitalising change of direction. With the opportunity and leisure to build up an unrivalled knowledge of recent and ancient continental architecture, especially in Italy and France, his imagination was set free, and he embarked on a succession of astonishing utopian projects. In 1717 he wrote that 'I am infected with the disease of building and planting'. [32] In the time-honoured aristocratic fashion, he employed a variety of Italian and French draughtsmen or architects to produce his drawings – but the overall conceptions were of course his. Typically of advanced classicists across northern Europe at the time, Mar's projects were dominated by calls for a 'return' to 'simplicity' – a concept based on the claims of antique purity and modern debasement. In 1718 he lauded 'the remains of the old Roman greatness, which all in these ages comes far short of, St Peter's excepted', and condemned recent Baroque architecture, whether in Italy or England. He scorned 'the degeneracy of the present Romans from the old in their architecture'. They had abandoned antiquity, 'in all its noble simplicity, for gimcrack insignificant ornaments, worthy of nobody but Vanbruge'. The antidote to the 'extravagancies' of Borromini was to revive the 'true ancient simple taste', by using the 'Streight Line without any Breaking'. [33]

Mar acknowledged similar ideas to his own in other countries: for example, in late seventeenth-century French monumental classicism, where 'Lewis Le Grand has a great thought and good taste in everything'; [34] or in the recent 'perfection' of antique-inspired architecture in England at the hands of his friend, Lord Burlington. His own interpretation was different from all these, combining theatrical and compactly verticalised evocations of the antique with an aversion to Baroque fragmentation of the straight line. He became preoccupied with the more exact use of antique originals. For example, he based the column proportions of a project of *c.*1718 for a Stuart royal palace on the dimensions of the Maison Carrée in Nîmes. But there was also an increasing concern to build in the *spirit* of the grandest Roman monuments. This was evinced especially in his preoccupation with vast, domed structures – a pattern influenced by the later interpretations of Palladio and Michelangelo (at St Peter's), or by the drum-topped compositions of Le Pautre.

There is no space here to list in detail the many grandiose unbuilt projects of Mar's exile, for which readers should consult Stewart and Friedman [35] – but they fall into two general categories of scale. The first was that of large houses, including a series of designs for London palaces for James Francis Stuart between 1718 and 1728, and schemes for the rebuilding or replacement of older houses, including Drumlanrig and his own Alloa, in which he developed his ideas for the interpretation of the Scottish heritage in classical terms. The second was that of designs for more compact landed houses, whose planning was determined by values of 'convenience' more than by grandeur.

In all his schemes for large houses, the most common pattern was a square plan with central hall, often polygonal with Greek-cross arrangement of flanking arms – 'cross pearced' in Mar's own words. [36] While the obvious and closest precedent was of course Bruce's Hopetoun, Mar's travels had allowed him to examine at first hand the most renowned continental examples of houses of royal status designed on compact and 'antique' lines. He was most influenced by Hardouin-Mansart's Pavillon du Roi at Marly (begun 1679), with its centralised plan, giant pilastered elevations, and soberly rectangular outline. Writing of Marly in 1717, Mar reported to James Francis Stuart that he 'could not help . . . turning it in my head to suit and accommodate such a design for [James's] service in another place'. [37] Throughout the 1720s, he designed a series of houses for James's hoped-for return to London, explicitly based on Marly, but with elaborated vertical features including a central octagonal 'Grand Sall' surmounted by a domed library and belvedere balcony [3.20, 3.21].

As to how this grandiose architecture might be applied to Scottish conditions, Mar gave two more specific clues in the 1720s. The first came in a series of projects for the 'reforme' of old quadrangular seats, including Drumlanrig and two English houses. In each case, the centre was to be ·roofed over by a vast domed superstructure. Concerning his 1722 project for 'amending and improving' Drumlanrig, Mar commented that the house 'at present is a very inconvenient one but

capable of being made very convenient, handsome and agreeable . . . by . . . building a Sall, wt. a Dome over it for a library' [cf. 3.7]. [38] These schemes were, perhaps, slightly frivolous in character. By the early eighteenth century, the only truly serious and credible solution to the problem of adaptation of Scottish houses was total concealment or removal of the old fabric, alluding to national or family heritage indirectly, and in classical form. In 1712, Mar himself had undertaken a search in London for old Scottish historical records, in the hope of finding 'mighty discoveries of the Celticks and Druids' which might give 'some insight into the character that was used in this country, which J. Caesar speaks of as being something like the Greek'; the national origin myth, of course, had a 'Greek' element in the form of the apocryphal prince Gathelus. [39] In a 1730 proposal for replacement of his house at Alloa, Mar envisaged a rectangular-plan structure with the usual gigantic

3.20 Design for a 'Royal Palace' by Lord Mar (1720s), published in *Vitruvius Scoticus*: one of the main elevations.

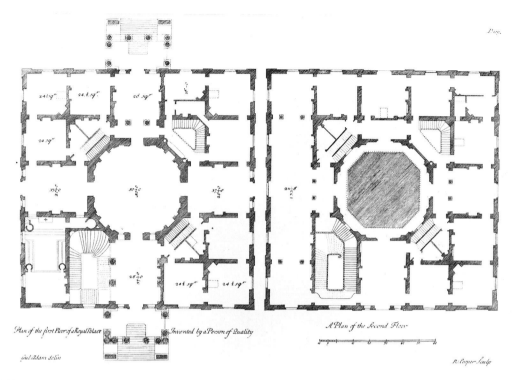

3.21 Lord Mar's 'Royal Palace', first- and second-floor plans.

central space, octagonal superstructure and belvedere, but treated in a relatively cubic and severe fashion, with columns confined to central porticoes. Each facade employed a different Order along with symbolic sculpture: Roman Doric and the just war; Ionic and the Erskine family heritage; Corinthian and fruitful peace; and Tuscan Doric and the patriotic Highlands (including two outsize statues in Highland dress). Here we see presaged the 'national' or Ossianic classicism which would become so prominent from the late eighteenth century onwards.

Bold and in some ways precocious though Mar's schemes were, we must bear in mind that they were never intended as practical building propositions, and that their direct influence on Scottish architecture was uncertain and posthumous: he sent one plan to William Adam in the 1720s, and the remainder of the collection was returned to Alloa after his death in 1732. The only one of Mar's post-1716 designs which was largely built fell not into the palace category but into the class of the smaller landed home: a new house at Dun, planned from the early 1720s, for his kinsman David

Erskine, who had become 13th laird in 1710. In 1717 Mar explained what he saw as the minimum requirements for a 'small' house of this type, which made it clear that something larger and more stately than Smith's villa type was intended: a 'neat' house with 'one little good apartment and a spare room or two for a friend who may stay a night on occasion, and other conveniences for servants, is all I would wish'. Small size must not lead to meanness. The house must be 'regular [with] one tolerable large room in it where one can breath freely indoors'. [40] At House of Dun, Mar got the opportunity to put these ideas into practice, working in collaboration with executant architects in the form of McGill and William Adam – the latter being a designer who would subsequently popularise many of the same ideas of dramatic classicism seen in Mar's work. From 1723, a series of plans by McGill and Adam were vetted by Mar in Paris. He criticised McGill's first effort as more suited to a villa near a town than a country house, and produced alternatives. His first design (1724) was a centralised plan, highly verticalised and including a five-room main apartment and Marly-like terraced landscaping [3.22]. Mar insisted that his design, though 'only a Pavilion', [41] must have stone dressings at least. His second scheme, a far more economical and modest composition, appears to be modelled in its overall dimensions (although not in plan) on Bullet's Château d'Issy. Construction began in 1730, substantially to Mar's plan, although with a triumphal-arch frontispiece added [3.23]. Internally, a remarkable plasterwork scheme was installed in 1742–3 by Joseph Enzer. This, it seems, comprises a complete Jacobite decorative cycle. The climactic groups, in the Salon, pointed openly to a future overthrow of Hanoverian rule by military force, and portrayed the Augustan peace that, in the opinion of Jacobites, would follow restoration of the Stuart monarchy[3.24].

The Contribution of James Gibbs and Colen Campbell

Some idea of the form that Mar's post-1715 architecture might have taken, if it had ever actually been built on a large scale – austerely grandiose, but with richly decorated highlights or centrepieces – can be gauged above all from   the career of his former protégé, the Aberdonian James Gibbs. Trained in Rome by Fontana (1705–8), at a time of growing reaction against Baroque dynamism, Gibbs realised in his built designs (almost all in England) a similar conception of the Antique to that of Mar. Gibbs held that the 'August Remains' of Rome should inspire 'a more grand appearance' in new buildings; this would be secured not by 'wrong-judged Profuseness' but by 'Proportion . . . whether entirely Plain, or enriched with a few ornaments properly disposed'. [42]

Many of Gibbs's country houses, built for Whig as well as Tory landowners, followed the Smith/Bruce pattern of external plainness and internal lavishness, while his public buildings, on the whole, attempted to convey an air of Roman gravity. Although Gibbs's first church, St Mary-le-Strand in London (1714–17), was a densely aedicular and essentially Baroque design, his slightly later proposal for St Martin in the Fields (1720) turned sharply towards a supposedly antique monumentality and geometry by com-

3.22 House of Dun, Angus, 'Dun A' project designed by Lord Mar in Paris in 1723.

bining a Pantheon-like circular body and portico with a parish kirk-like front steeple. As built (1722–6), St Martin's was redesigned for economy with a rectangular body [3.25]. Equally 'antique' was the plan of King's College New Building, Cambridge (1724–49), which combined an austerely astylar main facade with a thermal window and portico at centre. Another building proposed for the same complex, but unbuilt, would have had a gigantic octostyle portico. Gibbs's secular works in Scotland are relatively few and plain: for example, Balvenie House (1724), a compact house of harled rubble.

A different, and (in the event) more mainstream role in the development of early eighteenth-century English classicism on 'antique' or 'Roman' lines was played by another Scottish architect, Colen Campbell. His calls for 'antique simplicity' and attacks on the 'affected and licentious' Baroque, [43] while in themselves hardly different from Mar's rhetoric, were linked to a more literal and prescriptive reading of the villas and other works of Palladio, as well as the works of Inigo Jones. Although Campbell's success, in patronage terms, partly stemmed from his aggressive espousal of Hanoverian Whiggism, his architectural ideas were powerfully shaped by the studies of James Smith, especially in small-villa planning and Palladio-like centralised designs. In 1712, having built the Shawfield Mansion – a compact, pedimented villa of Smith type in Glasgow for the prominent Whig banker and slave-trader Daniel Campbell – Colen Campbell began practice in London [3.26]. There he popularised the idea of an 'English tradition' of classicism in his three-volume *Vitruvius Britannicus* (1715–25) and in his designs for an influential series of houses and villas. These began with Wanstead (1714–20), whose raised, porticoed central section aimed 'to introduce the Temple Beauties in a Private Building'. [44] Some later Campbell designs, such as the angle-towered Houghton Hall (1722–35, with tower domes – ironically – added by Gibbs), built for Prime Minister Robert Walpole at the peak of his powers, were based rather more closely on the seventeenth-century patterns of Scottish classicism, but recast the latter in the motifs of Inigo Jones [3.27]. Although the prescriptive impact of English Palladianism depended partly on the resonances of its evocations of Inigo Jones, it was also informed by an element of Augustan cosmopolitanism, promoted especially by Lord Burlington: the latter, it has recently been argued, was a closet Jacobite, for whom Jones's work symbolised the pre-civil war years of Stuart peace. [45]

In Scotland, the interpretation of the antique to shape post-1715 architecture most strongly would not be Campbell's and Burlington's 'Palladian' formula – despite the influence of Smith's ideas in the genesis of that formula – but the more variegated and dramatic, although never truly 'Baroque', ideas presaged in the work of Gibbs and Mar. There was a substantial continuity between many of Mar's ideas and the later course of Scottish architecture. We will see, in Chapter 4, that he even set out, as early as 1728, a basic prospectus for what would later become the Edinburgh New Town. What is still uncertain is the extent to which his work directly influenced that of William Adam, the leader of the next generation of Scottish architects. It is to the work of Adam and his contemporaries, and the very

different conditions of patronage under which they operated, that we now turn.

'Improvement' and the Country Seat, 1715–1760

Despite the defeat of the 1715–16 Jacobite insurrection and the subsequent consolidation of Whig and state Presbyterian power, the following decades at first saw continuing tension over the national/dynastic question. Only after the final, unsuccessful Jacobite invasion of 1745–6, with its aftermath of Hanoverian state repression in the Highlands, did real political stability begin to take root. Economically, the incorporating union with England, by creating a free-trade zone, at first sparked off economic difficulty, lasting to the mid-century, while benefiting a few groups, such as the Glasgow tobacco merchants. The imposition of a malt tax in 1725, for example, triggered disturbances which led to the sacking of the house of one of its main supporters – Daniel Campbell's Shawfield Mansion [cf. 3.26]. As a result, two years later, there began the first government intervention aimed at fostering long-term economic recovery, in the form of the creation of the Board of Trustees for Manufactures. Their economic initiatives – which, as we will see in the next two chapters, included the promotion of design and of design education – would, however, take a long time to gestate.

Paralleling this government initiative were the efforts of private landed improvers, whose efforts differed little from the ideas of Jacobite improvers such as Mar. While the Treaty of Union had removed many grandees to London, it boosted the lifestyle of their men of business back home, and provided legal sinecures for government supporters. 'Improvement' was now seen as part of an integrated Enlightenment ideal, in which antiquity served as a model of rationality rather than deference to authority. In the same way that the last years of Louis XIV's reign had witnessed the abandonment of antique and divine authority in favour of an ideal of historical progress, so in Scotland the origin-myth tradition of antique kingship was now increasingly pushed aside by the growing cry for modernising improvement and

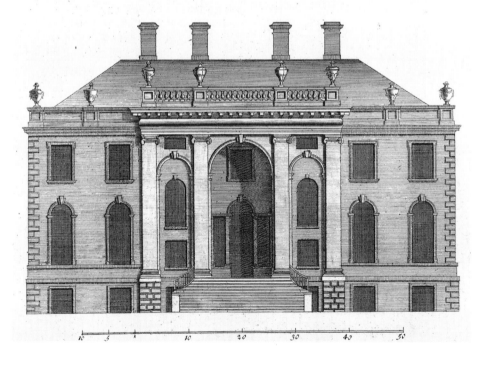

The South Front towards the Garden

These Fronts of the 2 Design being more ornamented than
the former are executing according ly

3.23 House of Dun (Mar/W. Adam, from 1730), as built and published in *Vitruvius Scoticus*: (above) main facades; (right) upper floors.

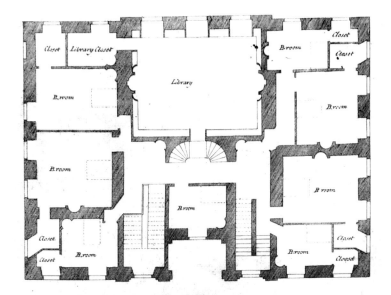

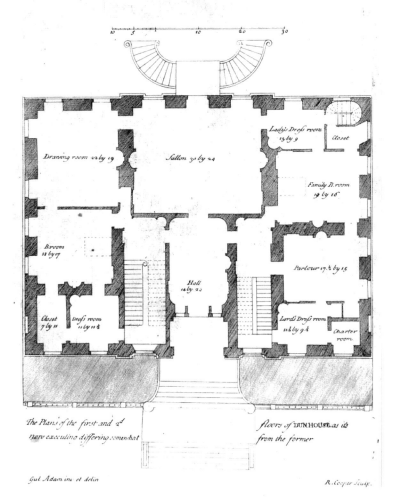

Closet   Library Closet   B.room   Closet   Closet

Library

B.room   B.room

B.room   B room

B.room

Closet   Closet

Closet   B.room   B.room   Closet

Drawing room 22 by 19   Sallon 30 by 24   Lady's Dress room 13 by 9   Closet

Family B. room 19 by 16

B.room 23 by 17   Parlour 17½ by 15

Hall 14 by 23

Closet 7 by 11   Dress room 11 by 11½   Lord's Dress room 11½ by 9½   Charter room

The Plans of the first and 2d   floors of DUNHOUSE as it
now executino differing somewhat   from the former

Gul Adam inv et delin   R. Cooper Sculp.

3.24 House of Dun, salon, east wall.

capital accumulation, and an increasingly close alliance between the Scottish landed-mercantile élite and their English counterparts. The concentration of industry in the central Lowlands was not yet complete, with major developments at locations elsewhere, such as Bonawe (the Lorn Furnace ironworks, 1753).

The changing economic and social conditions were naturally reflected in the position of architects themselves – although the powerful force of freemasonry may have provided a behind-the-scenes way of perpetuating some architectural values of the Stuart era. The improving landowner-architects, in the Mar tradition, remained figures of power and authority, as we shall see above all in the case of Sir John Clerk of Penicuik. Now these were joined by growing numbers of designers from non-landed backgrounds, whether professional (such as James Gibbs) or operative (such as John Baxter or Robert Mylne). Especially in the post-1707 years of economic difficulty, there was a marked tendency, on the part of this type of architect, to move to England in search of work. But the most forceful and innovative of the period's 'new architects', William Adam, stayed at home and set about 'improvement' with a vengeance. Exploiting every element of the Hanoverian state and economy, Adam rose to become not only the country's pre-eminent architect of these years, but also one of its

more powerful industrialists – a giant figure, straddling all aspects of early eighteenth-century architecture and building. Adam's social background spanned the landed and non-landed categories: he was the son of a Kirkcaldy mason, but the grandson of a peer, and the son-in-law of a laird. In his work, although architecture was still mixed up with 'trade' in a way that would become unacceptable in later centuries, we see the beginning of a separate social status of the architect, as opposed to the earlier status vicariously derived from landed values. In the course of an exchange with the Marquess of Tweeddale over the remodelling of Yester House in 1730, for example, Adam wrote that 'Now I think I have fully answered your Lordship's [objections], and will conclude with the reverse of yours, that this is my trade and I like it.' [46]

The ability of architects to practise their 'trade' on a semi-professional basis was enhanced by a rapid growth in the number and diversity of illustrated source books, drawn from across Europe, and providing accurate illustrations and plans of ancient, Renaissance and recent buildings. Where the earlier pattern books had been linked to the copying of motifs or of generalised precedent, now architects could begin to synthesise their concepts of classical architecture into complete systems of values, expressive of wider cultural norms or of individual, personal style. Although it

The West front of S.t Martins Church .

3.25 St Martin's in the Fields Church, London, elevation as built (1722–6), from James Gibbs's *Book of Architecture*.

is uncertain precisely which books in the Adam family library at Blair Adam were acquired by William and which by his descendants, it seems that, in his day, the library included an extensive range of French, English and Italian architectural books, along with French treatises on building technology, and monographs of individual key buildings (such as Amsterdam Town Hall or Versailles). It was on this foundation that the archaeological eclecticism of the late eighteenth

century would be built – especially by William's own son, Robert Adam.

What were the effects of these political, social and economic developments on the design of the building type which still remained dominant: the country house? After 1715, the old style of castellated house or palace reached the nadir of its reputation among most landowners: with the exception of Holyrood, the royal palaces were left to decay or (at Edinburgh and Stirling) were turned into barracks. The ideal solution seemed to be a completely new house – although some, such as Sir John Clerk of Penicuik, still held that, 'old families ought to preserve their old Towers as monuments to their Antiquity'. With the economic troubles of the early eighteenth century, the number of houses built rose only gradually: nearly twice as many were constructed in the 1790s (over sixty) as between 1700 and 1720. At first, therefore, just as previously, the only affordable solution was 'reform'. Now, however, this often took a far more radical shape. For example, the 2nd Duke of Atholl employed the architect James Winter to remodel Blair Castle in 1747–58 into an asymmetrical, but regularised sash-windowed mansion; on completion of what was referred to as the 'clipping of the Castle', the building was renamed Atholl House (only to be re-'Baronialised' by the 7th Duke, to David Bryce's designs, a hundred years later). [47] An even more thoroughgoing 'reform' of the former Taymouth Castle in 1743–50 by the architect John Douglas was praised by a visitor, who remarked that the building 'looks well in its new coat and sash windows'. [48]

Cost constraints applied more forcibly in the more restricted field of lairds' houses. In 1719, the agricultural improver Sir Archibald Grant of Monymusk considered with dismay his ancestral seat, with 'battlements and six different roofs of various heights and directions, confusedly and inconveniently combined, and all rotten, with . . . granaries, stables and houses for all cattle and of the vermine attending them, close by'. [49] Although Grant's friend, the architect Alexander Jaffray, offered to design a 'little comodius house' to replace this 'prodigious confused rooffe', [50] instead the course of regularisation was chosen. Writing in 1734 of the proposed rebuilding of Quarrell, Stirlingshire, the owner, John

The Elevation of Daniel Campbell of Shawfield Efq.ʳ his houfe in the City of Glafgow in Scotland.
to whom this Plate is moft humbly Infcrib'd.

Elevation de la Maifon du Mʳ Campbell Sieur de Shanfield a Glafgow en Ecoffe.

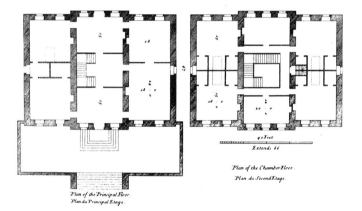

Plan of the Chamber Floor.
Plan du SecondEtage.

Plan of the Principal Floor.
Plan du Principal Etage.

3.26 Shawfield Mansion, Glasgow (C. Campbell, 1712), plan and elevation from *Vitruvius Britannicus*, vol. 1.

Drummond, declared that 'I . . . desire no more vaults nor any grates to the windows'; the house was to be transformed from 'echoes of ruines' into 'a convenient little habitation,. . . done frugally and effectively', with the dictates of fashion balanced against the economy of re-use. [51] In some cases, the heightened emphasis on 'convenience' and newness emphasised by a full-height or almost full-height ground floor, without basement: for example, at Touch House (1747), where a pedimented new block was built in front of an old tower.

In the internal planning of the country house, whether new or remodelled, the overriding principle of the great apartment began to be subtly modified: often, as at Arniston or Yester, it was the last part of the house to be completed. In the prestigious case of William Adam's rebuilding of Hopetoun House (from 1721), the paired arrangement of flanking state and private apartments, laid out in linear fashion, was expanded to an extreme. The huge size of the state rooms (intended to display a newly acquired painting collection) dictated, in effect, the building of an enormous show frontage on the outside. More frequently, however, there were determined attempts to break up linear sequences into more complex and compact patterns of more equally sized main rooms. In smaller houses such as Mavisbank, the spiral planning of Smith's more compact plans

3.27 Houghton Hall, Norfolk (C. Campbell, 1722–35), England.

was reproduced. Some began to suggest that potentially conflicting activities should be separated: for example, in William Adam's drawing of his unbuilt scheme for Newliston in 1723, the central salon separated the dining and drawing rooms – one of the first examples of the arrangement of three public rooms spanning the entire frontage of a house [cf. 3.37]. In the Newliston design, the outer rooms were smaller than the central one, but subsequently the reverse usually applied, as at Pollok House or in Adam's unbuilt Buchanan designs.

Within Scottish great apartments, the grandest rooms were now the dining and drawing rooms rather than the bedchamber: very often, the dining and drawing rooms were of equal size. In the 2nd Duke of Atholl's lavish internal remodelling of Blair in the 1750s, with plasterwork by the Clayton family (a scheme simultaneous with the external 'clipping' overseen by Winter) – we see the rise in the status of the drawing room in progress: the original dining room was converted, before its completion, to the drawing room, and vice versa. Developing the theme of the great room at the top of the house, pioneered at Panmure and developed in Mar's designs, an increasingly popular planning feature in the early eighteenth century was a library in the lodging storey: the most notable example was the library above the hall in William Adam's Arniston House, 1726–33 [cf. 3.33]. The advance of internal mod cons of a more prosaic nature continued. In 1734, for instance, Adam proposed the installation of a 'Water Closet with a marble Stooll' by the lord's bedroom at Yester; for the servants, there was a 'House of Office' in the courtyard. (52)

The decoration and furnishing of the greatest apartments now aspired to an unprecedented splendour, not even matched in turn-of-the-century works such as Dalkeith (but itself, correspondingly, less lavish than the eclectic interiors of the nineteenth century). This increasing richness in no way threatened the north-west European insistence on monumental order, established so firmly in Scotland by Bruce and Smith. With prominent exceptions such as the drawing room at Marchmont House, interior designs steered clear of Central European Rococo's assaults on architectonic clarity. In conformity to the growing emphasis on antiquity, interiors as well as exteriors were often now articulated by ranges of giant pilasters and arches, while decorative features, however overpowering, were kept strictly separate from structural elements: we witness this rigour in an accentuated form in Enzer's scheme at Dun [cf. 3.24]. Although the quantity and diversity of luxury furniture reached an unprecedented level, the way it was arranged became subject to highly formalised rules. When out of use, most pieces were arranged in rigidly controlled patterns around the edges of rooms; some furniture, like pier glasses, was designed as a fixed element of the architecture. Status was increasingly denoted by the quantity of gilding on ornaments, ranging from ceiling mouldings to picture frames, pier tables and glasses. Around the setpieces of framed paintings, walls were covered in lavish fabrics, such as crimson silk damask, while the liking for panelled interiors continued almost unabated, and was integrated with a new fashion for ingenious painted schemes of imitation marbling and graining. From the 1720s, there was also a vogue for landscape painting in country house interiors. William Adam, from this time, employed the

Edinburgh housepainter James Norie the elder and his sons on all his large houses, to paint idealised, Italian-style landscapes in the panels of interior schemes. In a link with government design and manufactures sponsorship, Norie was also appointed 'Master Painter to the Board of Ordnance in North Britain' during this period. Other Scottish craftsmen whose work flourished to distinction under the patronage of figures such as William Adam or Sir John Clerk of Penicuik included the cabinetmaker Francis Brodie. In an indication of the rise in social status of the makers of luxury goods, Brodie, although from a legal family with landed connections, chose to enter the furniture-making trade, where he produced pieces of an assertively architectonic, 'antique' character for the most stately interiors, alongside plainer furniture for household use. At the more modest scale which formed the bulk of most landed building of the period, there was often no 'great' apartment as such; the most elaborate rooms were the main private apartments. Visitors were often received in the family bedchamber, and from the 1730s wallpaper provided an economical alternative to plasterwork or panelling.

Sir John Clerk and Mavisbank

The continuities and changes in the design and patronage of the Scottish country house after 1715 were encapsulated in the activities of Sir John Clerk of Penicuik, an improving laird, musical composer and arbiter of taste; he was described in 1725 by the antiquary and humanist scholar Alexander Gordon as 'Scotland's Maecenas'. [53] His principal work of architectural design, and arguably the most important single example of early eighteenth century Scottish architecture, was Mavisbank House, built in 1723–6 in collaboration with William Adam [3.28, 3.29].

In Clerk's work, the improving and the antique preoccupations of generations of lairds were heightened to an unprecedented degree. Politically, and economically, he was a forthright defender of Whig mercantilism and unionism, and exploited with voracity the coal reserves of his own land at Loanhead; it is worth noting, from today's perspective, the exceptionally harsh working conditions, of near-slavery, which prevailed in parts of the mining industry during the eighteenth century. Clerk was also in the forefront of the new wave of agricultural improvement: he planted three million trees on his Penicuik estates in thirty years. In parallel with these aggresively modernising activities, Clerk pursued a highly elaborated neo-Roman lifestyle of Pliny-like *honestum otium*, including a modified version of the traditional landed interest in architectural design and consultancy. His record of a 1724 trip to Hadrian's Wall, for example, noted a pioneering Newcomen colliery engine alongside Roman antiquities. Already in 1683–4, Clerk's father (also Sir John) had constructed a tall, pyramidally roofed mausoleum, inspired by antique tombs, in

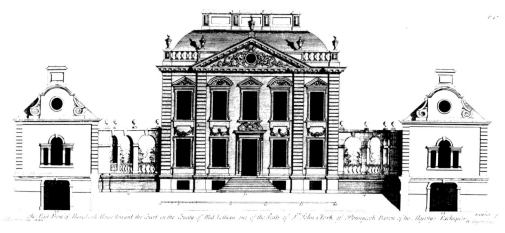

3.28 Mavisbank,(Clerk/W. Adam, 1723–6) *Vitruvius Scoticus* drawings: (above) entrance facade; (right) principal and vestibule floor plans.

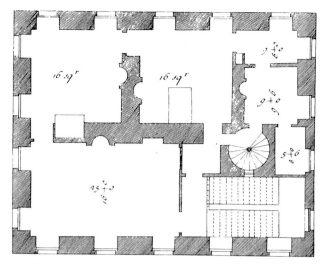

Plan of the Second Story or principal floor

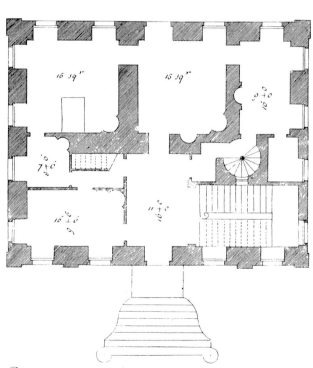

Plan of the Vestible floor of Mavisbank House

Gul. Adam inv. et delin

Penicuik churchyard. Clerk himself had had a legal education at Glasgow and Leiden, and subsequently (unusually for that date) had visited Rome, where he was instructed in architecture and drawing, and studied antiquities, classical literature and music. From that point, the primacy of antiquity and antique-orientated Renaissance designers became his preoccupation. He explained in 1727 that his readings of 'the Classicks' had taught him that 'the antient Greek and Roman structures, or the Designs of them by Palladio and others, ought to be standards fit for the imitation of our modern Architects'. [54] All northern European efforts at antique grandeur were to be judged by this yardstick of taste, severe and yet susceptible to dramatic about-turns. On Clerk's visit to Paris, for example, 'Everything I saw seem'd only to be a copy from some great original I saw there [Rome]. Houses, palaces, villas, gardens, statues, pictures, were all mean in comparison with what I had observed in Italy.' [55] Likewise in England, the interpretation of 'antique simplicity' by the 'Palladians' was looked at critically: Burlington's Chiswick House, while 'all in the ancient manner', was 'rather curious than convenient', and his York Assembly Rooms were 'disproportionable'. [56] At home in Scotland, the previous generation's efforts at a monumental classicism were not spared criticism: of Kinross, Clerk noted in 1717 that 'whatever Sir William's talents were, the ornament of this house show

nothing of them. Several gates and avenues are wrong placed, and the orders of Architecture are ill contrived and worse executed.' Twenty years later, by contrast, Kinross was praised by Clerk as 'in an Italian form . . . a very fine house' [cf. 3.14, 3.15]. [57] The precise reasons for Clerk's reversal of opinion about Kinross are unknown.

As is clear from the above, Clerk's antique conceptions differed from those of predecessors such as Saltoun and Bruce both in his demand for more first-hand antiquarianism – he was an obsessive archaeologist, and spent much time excavating Roman antiquities on his estate – and also in his ability to put his thoughts down on paper. He even went so far, in 1726–7, as to prepare a manuscript poem, 'The Country Seat', setting out his ideas on country house architecture and landscaping. Sir George Mackenzie of Rosehaugh had already, in the late seventeenth century, written a poem on a similar theme ('Caelia's Country-house Closet', first published in 1709), but Clerk's architectural description and analysis was far more explicit and systematic. The central argument of Clerk's text was that landed status and activity must be expressed through a much more specialised gradation of house sizes and amenities than hitherto – in all cases, based on 'how the antients formed their rural Seats'. There should be four distinct types of house: the 'Royal Palace', the 'House of State', the 'Usefull House', and the 'Villa'. The most assertively antique was of course

3.29 Mavisbank in its setting, 1860s' photograph.

the first, whose grandeur would be secured, Mar-like, by avoiding the 'mean practice' of super-imposed Orders in favour of devices such as 'huge Columns . . . stately Porticos,/ High tow'ring Cupola's, bold Pediments . . .' The three other types were designed for 'a Country Life'. The House of State was a smaller, aristocratic country version of the royal palace, while the Usefull House – like Mar's Dun – was planned around an economical minimum of public space. For the Villa, a retreat from urban hubbub, a more compact and exotic form than the sprawling Pinkie or Royston pattern was desirable: 'that always is the best/Which the Pavilion of a Persian King/in bulk and Beauty may resemble most' [cf. 3.20, 3.21, 3.22]. [58]

Clerk's most innovative work, Mavisbank, was built for himself, and provided a telling indication of the growing importance of his smallest category of house – the 'Little Villa' – within the spreading social scope of classical architecture. Although Clerk had long intended to recast his own old house, Penicuik, as 'a very fine uniform house', he instead decided to build a new 'summer pavilion' at Loanhead, from which he could superintend more closely his nearby coal-mine. The site had already been selected by his father, who had prepared a succession of designs in 1696–8, beginning with a tall, linear, laird's tower plan and ending with a square-plan, piend-roofed and balustraded block with symmetrical plan.

In his partnership with William Adam in the design of Mavisbank, Clerk seems to have been, on the whole, dominant: for instance, he provided Adam with a copy of Palladio and the works of Jones. The design eventually 'concocted' between Clerk and Adam [59] comprised a five-bay villa of two storeys and basement, its angles defined by channelled pilaster strips, and its three-bay centrepiece surmounted by a sculpture-laden pediment and domed roof. Adam described his initial design of 1723 as 'a very small Box, and Genteell too'. [60] He suggested adding a storey, breaking with Italian Renaissance proportions towards a more verticalised, Mar-like form, but Clerk refused: 'If I had complied, the fabrick wou'd have lookt like a Touer, and been quite spoiled, but however, the Architecture may please or displease, it is oueing chiefly to my self.' [61]

Even without the extra storey demanded by Adam, the executed design was markedly compact and vertical in its massing. Clearly, the proportions of the house were of great concern to Clerk, as a composer. In retrospect, Clerk also held that Mavisbank had been too densely sculptural in its ornamentation. As early as 1724, he decided to expand the house with pavilions. These piend-roofed, Venetian-windowed blocks were linked to the house by curved, open quadrants seen as evocative of Pliny. The house had an unusual site, tucked into a bank with, in effect, a single aspect; to the rear was an archaeological site believed by Clerk to be Roman. Internally, the house contained ground-floor services, a 'Family Apartment' above, and a great apartment (planned in spiral form) on the second floor. The supervision of construction was entrusted by Clerk to John Baxter, a competent architect and contractor who later went on to design numbers of houses himself. It was decorated in 1726–9 with rich decorative plaster-work, and painted by James Norie. His designs included, in the hall and staircase, 'landscap and imitation-whyte marble and Mahogany Colours' with a gold sun on a blue and white ground in the staircase ceiling. While the house's architecture, in its compact richness, strongly recalled the small houses of the wealthy which dotted the outskirts of Paris (as well as Dutch examples such as Marot and Roman's De Voorst, completed 1697 and seen by Edward in 1701), its overall conception was that of a microcosmic realisation of the Plinian villa of *honestum otium*. Mavisbank was an elaboration and reformulation, on a smaller scale, of the ideal that had motivated the building of Pinkie a century earlier. While the nineteenth century would come to regard Classical Edinburgh as above all a city of Greece, Mavisbank reminds us that the capital and its surroundings enjoyed a previous, equally potent phase of classical association, focused on the Italian villa and the 'suburban' surroundings of Rome. In 1739 a visitor to Mavisbank, Roger Gale, remarked that 'you would there think yourself rather in a valley near Tivoli'. [62]

In addition to his own projects, Clerk carried on the grand old tradition of the adviser to landed friends. Some schemes were for the aristocracy, such as two designs for a cascade at Drumlanrig prepared for the 2nd Duke of Queensberry in

1732. In other cases, he performed the role of cultural mentor, cajoling friends in remoter parts to accept new standards of both modernity and antiquity. For example, in the negotiations which followed the fire at Glasserton, the home of his nephew Lord Garlies, in 1734, Clerk suggested to Garlies the building of a new 'family house' to replace the 'cold, unwholesome' old tower. In reply, Garlies protested that 'when you mention Cubes and rooms of 18, 16 or even 19 feet high you write indeed like ane architect . . . it is impossible to have what you call ane apartment in a little house, without taking up a whole story and that I cannot spare'. Rather, 'A little house with good lodging pavilions is what I like best'; and, 'as to houses of office, knowledge of that kind would be useful for a Galloway man, for as yet we are absolutely ignorant of office houses'. Eventually, with much advice from Clerk and John Douglas, John Baxter designed the new Galloway House (built 1740–5), with its four-storey, pedimented centre block; the latter Baxter felt to be too high, protesting that 'I am sorry to build such a high Modrin Castell'. (63)

William Adam and His Contemporaries

As we have already noted, 1715 marked a watershed in the patronage of Scottish architecture. Even James Smith, who had agilely survived the 1689–90 changes, was gradually eased to the sidelines; he managed to secure a commission as designer of post-1715 garrisons for the Board of Ordnance (to be discussed later), but was sacked from that post in 1719, complaining in a letter that he had been 'disgracefully turn'd out of his Majesty's service in the 73d. year of his age'. (64) In response, he and McGill expanded their collaboration in country house work. McGill, sometimes with Smith, designed a series of austere, sometimes grandiose commissions which mostly reworked earlier themes. Although much more research into this period remains to be done, commissions so far identified include Blairdrummond (1715–17), a tall, harled block fronted by an elaborate series of outer, inner and flanking courts; Elphinstone (attributed, *c.*1718), a long double-depth block with narrow tetrastyle portico; Mount Stuart (1718–22), pedimented with advanced two-bay ends in Melville fashion;

Donibristle (1719–23), with Smith-like centre pediment and flanking gables, and lavish garden ironwork. Other tall, pedimented houses possibly by Smith include Kilkerran and Craigie (both *c.*1730) in Ayrshire, while House of Gray (1714–16), possibly by McGill, harked back to the corner-tower fashion. A project for Broomlands (1719), possibly by Smith, contained an octagonal hall and toplit tribune. A very ambitious scheme of this period was the new frontage built on to Woodhall House, Lanarkshire, by Daniel Campbell in the early eighteenth century. The three-storey facade contained a basement rusticated in two differently patterned layers, arched and Venetian windows on its principal floor, and a heavy pedimented attic [3.30]. This congested compilation of motifs from Roman Renaissance palaces could have been built immediately after Campbell's acquisition of the estate in 1711, in which case the architect might have been James Smith or Colen Campbell: it bears a general resemblance to some of Smith's unidentified palace-type designs. If built after the burning of the Shawfield Mansion in 1725, it could have been designed by Colen Campbell (or by Daniel Campbell himself, using motifs culled from *Vitruvius Britannicus*).

Despite these late works, the careers of Smith and McGill were now unmistakably in decline. Correspondingly, the new star of William Adam rose in spectacular fashion: after his death, he could be recalled by John Clerk of Eldin as 'the universal Architect of his country' [3.31]. (65) Readers seeking a detailed account of his career should consult Gifford's book. The foundation of Adam's success, and that of his sons, was not his social status, but his achievements as a successful industrialist and contractor who exploited the opportunities offered by the new Hanoverian regime. His rise began with a survey of the Holyroodhouse roof (steered his way by Clerk, as Baron of Exchequer), and proceeded to building of Highland fortifications (as Mason to the Board of Ordnance from 1730), and to entrepreneurial development of forfeited Jacobite estates. From 1728, Adam secured the leases of the Winton estate of the dispossessed Setons, including the two baronies of Tranent and Cockenzie, and embarked on a massive programme of coal-mining and salt production. In 1728 Clerk hailed 'the enterprising

3.30 Woodhall House, Lanarkshire, main facade.

3.31 William Adam, portrait by William Aikman.

from 1720 and rapidly built up a large and cosmopolitan architectural library. By 1730 he was able to explain patiently to the Marquess of Tweeddale about the correct design of a portico in accordance with the 'strick rules of Architecture', adding reproachfully that 'this is a Coledge on Architecture which I'm sorry your Lordship does not like better'. [67] But his advice might equally include the large-scale development of collieries, harbours and drainage engines, which kept constant pace with classical architecture in the accelerating landed drive for 'improvement'. In 1737 one of his key clients, the Duke of Hamilton, wrote to Adam: 'Of my coal: perhaps it may turn out as you seem to flatter me it will; if so cubes, temples, obelisks etc., etc. will go the better on.' [68]

The inventive variety of William Adam's architecture and house-planning, which would provide such a stimulus for the eclectic individualism of his son Robert, makes it difficult to pick out any overriding theme. Although he designed some houses on the largest scale for the nobility, most of his clients were middle-rank lairds enriched, for instance, from legal practice or time in the army. In his building or (as often) rebuilding schemes for them, he continued Smith's quest for a more rhetorically expressive, but compact and 'convenient' house. And just as Smith built for clients of various political and religious persuasions, so Adam (baptised William in 1689) built for Jacobites as well as Hanoverian Whigs: we

temper of the proprietor who had at this time under his own care near to twenty general projects – Barley Mills, Timber Mills, Coal Works, Salt Pans, Marble Works, Highways, Farms, houses of his own a–building and houses belonging to others not a few'. [66] Adam was much in demand as a discerning consultant and contractor for country house improvement. He styled himself architect

have already encountered the seemingly anti-government plasterwork installed by Enzer for Lord Dun in the 1740s under Adam's supervision, and Adam included one of Mar's palace designs in his proposed compilation of Scottish classical architecture, *Vitruvius Scoticus*, begun in 1727 but not published until *c.*1812 [cf. 3.20, 3.21, 3.24].

Externally, the more imposing appearance desired in these middle-sized houses was achieved chiefly by heavier ornament and modelling. The use of giant pilasters became more common; Adam added a pilastered tetrastyle frontispiece to Smith's austere block at Yester (1730), arguing that it would 'take off the Plainness of the ffront'. [69] A wide range of more emphatic motifs was employed, some drawn from other countries. Channelled pilaster strips and arched windows, and Le Pautre-like monumental pilastered compositions, evoked France, while arched rusticated ground floors were inspired by the work of Inigo Jones in England. Adam clearly admired Jones, using his well-known portrait on his personal seal from around 1740. But the most emphatic influences were probably those of Scottish architects. The work of Gibbs, published in his *Book of Architecture* of 1728, was of special impact on William Adam. Heavy blocked openings became a favourite motif, and an entire circular garden temple (at Eglinton, designed possibly *c.*1738) was seemingly copied from Gibbs's book. In terms of decoration and facade architecture, a design such as that for Kenmure (unexecuted) of *c.*1744, for example, features a bewildering array of quoins, urns, pediments and Venetian windows, with a two-storey and basement entrance facade combined with high, four-storey side facades. In planning terms, the compressed and centralised concepts of Mar, of which Adam was probably aware from the late 1720s, may also have exerted some influence.

William Adam's own architectural development began, conservatively, from the patterns established by others in the seventeenth century. It is possible that Adam himself designed Gladney House, Linktown (1711), the house he and his family occupied until 1727. The double-depth U-plan house was flanked by closet towers with shaped gables, its recessed centre containing a raised and flat-ended pediment supported by a single pilaster at either side; the now rather old-fashioned gable-flanked pattern recurred occasionally in later Adam projects, such as the unexecuted plan for Fasque (probably 1730s). Adam's Makerstoun (*c.*1715), with its large semicircular pediment, platform roof and quadrant-linked pavilions, superseded an initial plan by McGill. In Adam's rebuilding of Floors (1721–6, for the 1st Duke of Roxburgh), there was a more horizontal solution. The double-depth, angle-towered plan returned more openly to the formula of Culross Abbey House or Panmure, but now with pedimented towers in (what was thought to be) the manner of Inigo Jones; its even fenestration resembled Gibbs's slightly later King's College building at Cambridge. Subsequently, the pattern of a long block, either with or without end wings, was repeated in Adam's unexecuted plan of *c.*1740 for Preston Hall. Its most grandiose realisation, however, was earlier in his career: at Hopetoun (1721–48), where Adam was brought in by Bruce's patron, the Earl of Hopetoun, to remodel completely Bruce's house even before it had been completed. Hopetoun had already become dissatisfied with Bruce's complex design. Having since toured the Continent, he would have been aware that the most stately European designs for palaces, ever since Bernini's Louvre proposals of the 1660s, had insisted on a low, unbroken horizontality. From 1721, therefore, Hopetoun had the front of the Bruce composition demolished, and substituted a completely new entrance front; both old and new facades were in ashlar [3.32]. Its enormous width stemmed from its symmetrical arrangement of flanking apartments (a state apartment and a luxurious and more intimately planned private apartment). It is likely that the arrangement here was the same as at Mavisbank, with the Earl himself making key design decisions (perhaps with outside advice from someone such as Gibbs or Mar), and Adam acting in a semi-executant capacity. The main part of the new front was a shallow U-plan, with full entablature and Versailles-like balustraded attic along its entire length. The outer pavilions were defined, Kinross-style, by giant angle pilasters, while the central section was more profusely pilastered, with an (unbuilt) tetrastyle portico. Internally, variety in the sequence of state rooms

The (general) Front of Hopeton House toward the Court, The Seat of the (Right Honourable) the Earl of Hopeton in the County of LINLITHGOW

3.32 Hopetoun House, east facade of William Adam's design (from 1721) as drawn for *Vitruvius Scoticus*. It was completed by Adam's sons with alterations, especially the omission of the portico (cf. 3.16)

was obtained by staggering the alignment of these sumptuous, double-height spaces; the doors were aligned to provide a strict enfilade.

Country houses comprising such long ranges formed only a minority in William Adam's output. More common were compact designs either of medium scale, in the tradition of Dunkeld and Kinross – Clerk's 'Usefull House' – or of Whitehill-like villa size [cf. 3.12, 3.14, 3.19]. Here, if there was any attempt to include formal apartments, this was often achieved by spiral-type plans. In Adam's work, Mavisbank's only rival in elaboration, although not in architectural significance, was Somerville House (1726–34, later renamed The Drum) – a show villa intended to re-establish a family 'seat' for the 12th Lord Somerville. Flanked by service wings, its plan was a simple tripartite one, but with a canted projection for the staircase on the garden front. The facade was loaded with heavy decoration of the Gibbs type, including blockings and rustication in all possible locations. The centrepiece was a Venetian window emphasising the great drawing room on the principal floor. This floor, labelled the 'state floor' on the *Vitruvius Scoticus* plan, also contained a great bedchamber and sumptuous Clayton plasterwork.

The first of Adam's more ambitious medium-sized house designs was his unrealised project of 1723 for Newliston, designed for one of his most powerful patrons, the 2nd Earl of Stair, as a nine-bay block, with Inigo Jones-like rusticated arched staircase surmounted by a single-storey pediment. The plan was cruciform with central tribune flanked by staircases, and 'sallon' at the rear flanked by drawing and dining rooms. This was followed by a succession of commissions for houses of this general size, many far more austerely treated, such

as Haddo (1732–5), where Adam's plain, seven-bay pedimented block, with wings, was built by John Baxter. Other designs included Cumbernauld (1731), Torrance (*c.*1740), Tinwald (1738) and Buchanan (1741). The most confident of Adam's medium-sized houses was Arniston, begun in 1726 and partly completed in 1733 for the influential lawyer Robert Dundas; it was fully completed to a modified plan in 1754–8 [3.33]. Built of rubble with ashlar highlights, Arniston's main facade is again in a somewhat Gibbs-like manner, its recessed centre portico comprising a trio of round-headed openings and engaged Ionic columns, with a wide stair in front. Inside, the upstairs principal rooms were reached by a grandiose arcaded entrance hall, square on plan and moulded in plaster by Joseph Enzer; its pierced upper arcade, clustered pilasters and pointed arches strongly recall the theatrical effects of German Baroque (of which Adam perhaps learnt in his copy of Paul Decker's *Fuerstlicher Baumeister* of 1711), without, however, overrunning the integrity of structural elements. [70] At the top of the house, hidden away in a retreat above the hall, is the library, pilastered and lined with busts. This was another example of the persistent feature, in Scottish country houses, of an important room at high level, placed centrally on the front, (for instance, at Culross Abbey House or Craigston).

In the 1730s, Adam began the three most significant of his later designs – Chatelherault, Minto House and Duff House – whose conflicting affiliations to a verticalised, almost Baroque drama and a horizontal monumentality typified the rich diversity of his work. Chatelherault was a ducal hunting and banqueting lodge built (from 1731, with rich plasterwork of 1740–2 by Thomas Clayton) to provide a terminal feature for the great

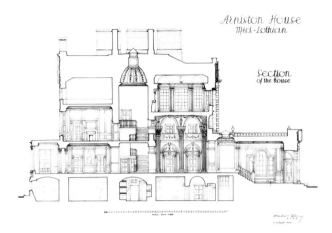

Arniston House
Mid-Lothian.

Section
of the house

3.33 Arniston House (W. Adam, from 1726), cross-section by Stanislaw Tyrowicz, 1946.

south vista of Hamilton Palace. This avenue, included in Edward's 1708 proposal, was completed as part of Adam's 'Great Plan' of 1728 [cf. 3.8]. [71] Referred to in one eighteenth-century engraving as a 'villa', [72] Chatelherault comprised an elaborate screen wall linking two pairs of tall pavilions – a composition of highly theatrical character, yet almost 'neo-classical' in its lack of central emphasis [3.34].

Minto House (*c*.1738–43) was not a new house but a remodelling and vast expansion of a sixteenth-century tower, for Gilbert Elliot, Lord Minto. The rebuilt house had a V-shaped splay plan symmetrically arranged around a central axis comprising a circular entrance hall and octagonal garden room at the centre, flanked by three main rooms on each side – a layout perhaps influenced by Gibbs's abortive plan (after 1708) for an X-shaped house with domed central hall at Dupplin, or by the more recent example of Filippo Juvarra's cross-planned Stupinigi Castle, 1729–33. The hall was domed and the end gables were curved. Minto's principal influence would be not in classical architecture but in the novel field of 'new castles' [3.35; cf. 3.4].

Where Minto's splay plan reacted away from the pyramidal dynamism of Glamis towards a prismatic severity, at the same time Adam was engaged in the most boldly plastic of all his major designs: Duff House. Duff, whose main block (but

3.34 Chatelherault (W. Adam, 1731–42).

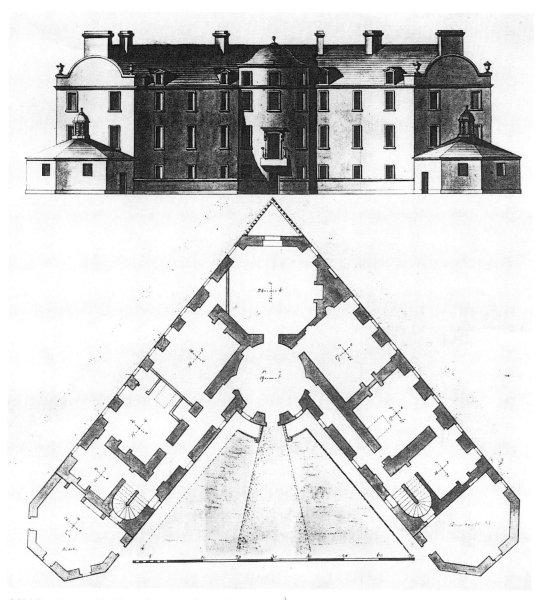

3.35 Minto House, mid-eighteenth-century plan and front elevation as expanded by William Adam (*c*.1738–43); the pavilions at the end of the wings were unexecuted proposals.

not planned wings) was built in 1735–40 for Lord Braco, was an unhappy commission that ended in litigation. In this compact yet massive block, of four main storeys, Adam was at last able to build a great house in the form of a 'touer' [3.36]. The design's Mar-like verticality was accentuated by the turret-like angle pavilions, with their super-imposed Corinthian pilasters in the Kinross manner, and their acceptably 'antique' belvedere domes (echoing the small turrets added to the

Pantheon) [cf. 3.20]. After at first insisting on the omission of the attic, Braco, rapidly losing enthusiasm, changed his mind, he told Adam, 'because the want of it would Spoill the Looks of such a Monstrous house and indeed I wish you and the house had been at the D— before it had been begun'. The show facades were built of Queensferry stone shipped up by Adam, who boasted of the Marly-like ranges of giant pilasters that 'they gave the ffront a grand appearance'. [73]

The pomp of the exterior was matched internally, with a cruciform plan and great open-plan staircase. The family and state apartments were separated not horizontally, but vertically; the first floor comprised the former, the second the latter (including a thirty-foot cube saloon); the attic contained a gallery. The interior of Duff was never finished: because of the acrimony over costs between Adam and Braco, work was stopped in 1740, and the enraged owner lowered his coach blinds whenever he drove past the unfinished shell. Duff was the climax of William Adam's pursuit of architectural grandeur, and of his fertile ability to combine interior spaces in new and arresting plan-forms. This vigorous and 'enterprising' [74] world outlook would, in due course, be recast in a cosmopolitan form by his son Robert.

Dwarfed until now beneath the colossal shadow of William Adam, the work of other country house architects during the years from 1720 to the 1760s is a conspicuously under-researched area. In some cases, the old relationship of landed patron-designer and executant architect-mason continued. Sir John Clerk's son, James, employed John Baxter the elder to carry out the eventual rebuilding of

Penicuik House itself, in the form of a long, porticoed block (1761–9), while John Baxter the younger drew out Clerk's plans for Rossdhu House in 1772–8. Baxter the elder went on to design some houses on his own account, including, as we have seen, Galloway House, as well as Hawkhead House (*c*.1738) and Mayshade House, near Loanhead (1753, for his own occupation). He also built as contractor, for the 6th Earl of Wemyss, the new Amisfield House, East Lothian (1756–9), a seven-bay, Ionic-porticoed design by the English Palladian architect Isaac Ware. Another similar scheme concerned Marchmont House, where the 2nd Earl of Marchmont had initially (1724) considered renovating Redbraes: 'To make it a house, then, the steeple, Closets upon the Roof, great Stairs and Balasters upon the Leads and other great weights must be taken quite away.' [75] After canvassing Campbell, Gibbs and perhaps Mar, and obtaining several proposals from William Adam, the 2nd Earl decided to do nothing, and it was left to his son to build a new house at Marchmont in 1750–3, with Thomas Gibson as executant architect: rather like Floors, the new house was low, harled and unaccented at the centre,

3.36 Duff House (W. Adam, 1735–40), view showing pedimented main facade on left, and side facade (including additional, subsidiary storeys) on right.

with Venetian-windowed wings. At Newhailes, Sir David Dalrymple, the man who bought the modest villa from James Smith and renamed it in 1709, began to enlarge it in the 1710s; the library was built in 1718–21, and a new great apartment (with rich Thomas Clayton plasterwork) was created in 1733–43 [cf. 3.19]. In the north-east, Alexander Jaffray, laird of Kingswells, carried out some architectural work (including the already mentioned advice to Grant of Monymusk); it is uncertain whether the severe, nine-bay three-storey front added to Culter House after 1721 was designed by him or by James Gibbs. A similar role in the south-west was played by William Craik of Arbigland, in designs including his own house of *c.*1753, and Mossknowe of 1767.

The only other figure who remotely rivalled Adam as a professional architect was John Douglas, who enjoyed a long and successful career as a designer of new or remodelled country houses. In the latter, his approach, like Adam's, was one of relentless surgery, or alternatively of concealment. A prime example of the first category was Finlaystone, where, in 1746–7, the centre of the old castellated house was cleared away to make space for a small 'new house of three stories' [76] containing the highly compressed main apartment; it was, unexpectedly, in the flanking pavilions that parts of the old house were retained, and remodelled into family accommodation. The result was a completely new-looking, symmetrical group of central house and flanking wings, linked in a straight line. At Archerfield (1744–5), Douglas adopted the alternative solution of planting a new range in front of the existing house, projecting Hopetoun-style at either end to obscure it completely from view. On the principal floor, the new front range was symmetrically arranged, with vestibule and flanking (equal-sized) drawing and dining rooms [3.37]. The facade, with its central canted bay carried up above the wallhead, was vigorously loaded with details culled from Gibbs, including arched windows and blocked surrounds; ornament was especially concentrated around the centre.

In the west and north, a number of major houses, in addition to Woodhall, are still unattributed to any designer. Pollok (from 1747), a severe, piend-roofed block, may be by Allan Dreghorn; but there is no evidence about the

architect of Auchinleck (*c.*1760), an expanded version of Smith's compact villas with giant pilasters and heavily sculptured pediment. In some cases, there was overlap with patterns already outlawed by high fashion. In the north, the rebuilding of Foulis Castle (1750–92) resulted in a house whose rear elevation was not unlike Marchmont's old Redbraes, U-shaped with a tall tower at the centre. At Arbuthnott (from 1754) an old house was restructured in a compressed version of a standard late seventeenth century formula, with flanking harled gables and a pedimented ashlar centrepiece. The design appears to have been by the owner, Viscount Arbuthnott, and the contractor was a Montrose wright, John Ferrier. By the end of the eighteenth century, the simple pedimented pattern of small, two-storey-and-basement house introduced by Smith had become the generalised pattern for lesser lairds' houses. A typical example was Straloch, Aberdeenshire (*c.*1790), with pedimented centre and quadrant wings in the form of a rear service court.

After William Adam's death in 1748 (and, in effect, for some years beforehand), the architectural fortunes of the Adam dynasty passed to his children – especially, at first, to his oldest son John, who succeeded his father as laird of Blair Adam, the family home, and took charge of his architectural and contracting practice. Although John immediately took into partnership his younger brother Robert, whose reputation would later far outstrip his own, at this stage he was not only the business manager of the partnership, but a competent designer within the formulae established by his father. The Adam children inherited not only William's great wealth and entrepreneurial verve, but also his extensive connections within the Hanoverian establishment. John promptly succeeded to William's post of Mason to the Board of Ordnance, and over the next decade the brothers undertook large military building contracts in the Highlands, providing not only profit but valuable grounding in management of large-scale building operations. After 1748 John Adam spent weeks at a time in the north on military work, and often used his spare time to design country houses nearby. Examples included the new Banff Castle (*c.*1749–50), a three-storey five-bay house of tripartite plan 'rough cast in

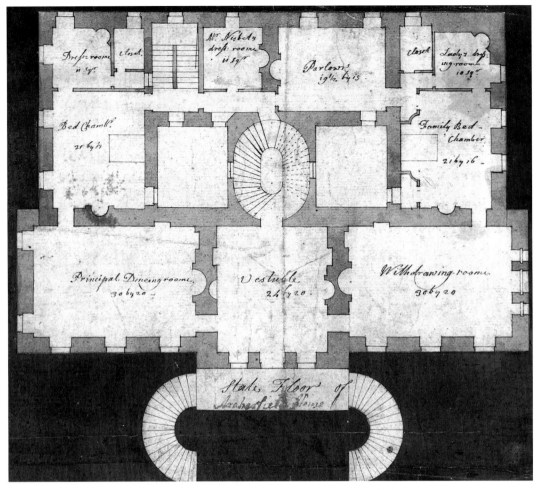

3.37 Archerfield House, plan by John Douglas of the state floor, as expanded by him (in 1744–5).

order to defend the Storms', [77] or the rebuilding of Castle Grant (from 1753) with extended rear service wings and a new, starkly austere block on the other side – perhaps the most arresting example of the mid-eighteenth century desire to conceal an irregular older building with a completely regular addition [3.38]. A number of designs by the brothers, still led by John, comprised reformed variants of the popular, Palladio-inspired layout of main block and quadrant wings. Paxton House (1757–63), with its seven-bay, tetrastyle-porticoed central block of two storeys and basement, was built by the mason James Nisbet; either he or the Adam brothers may have prepared the design. At Dumfries House (1754–9), where Robert Adam superintended the work before departing for Italy, a slightly taller and larger main block of nine bays, with astylar pedimented centrepiece, combined tripartite and cruciform floor plans, somewhat as at Duff [3.39]. The brothers may also have designed the similar, but slightly smaller Cochno House (*c*.1757). Their Moffat House of 1761–7 resembled Banff Castle in its basement-less, five-bay piended form.

The brothers' most lavish scheme in this period was the completion and modification of their father's design at Hopetoun, for the 2nd Earl (who had inherited the unfinished scheme in 1742 with the great north apartment still a shell). John Adam and Lord Hopetoun designed and supervised the interiors of the two main state rooms, the Great Dining Room and Great Drawing Room, with delicate, almost Rococo plasterwork and lavish furniture mostly made in Edinburgh or on the estate (by Thomas Welsh). Externally, the colonnaded links and redesigned pavilions were complete by 1746 and the new, more sober frontispiece (without portico) by 1751 [cf. 3.32]. At Yester, a basic architectural design by William Adam for the salon – with coved ceiling and tabernacle doors – was sumptuously executed by Robert, including coffering in the coving and classical landscapes by William Delacour (completed 1761) set in panels: here we see the transition to the more assertively 'antique' imagery of Robert Adam already underway.

3.38 Castle Grant, John Adam's new north elevation of 1753-6 .

While the Adam brothers' pre-1760 work built on and refined the work of their father, they were also indirectly involved, as contractors for the 3rd Duke of Argyll's new Inveraray Castle (from 1746), in a new and innovative phase in country house design: the building of 'new castles'. This would complicate the (up until then) growing polarisation of the relationship between classical architecture, whether 'modern' or 'antique', and the castellated heritage. Here we must briefly review the early development of landscape-gardening, in which some of the new ideas had been presaged.

The concept of the imposition of geometrical order upon the landscape had been challenged in early eighteenth-century England by a new concept of the 'natural' or 'informal' garden, to be judged by subjective intuition rather than hierarchy and precedent – an early example of Romantic ideas. This concept rapidly became popular throughout Europe, not least in Scotland: for an account of its spread, readers should refer to Tait's *The Landscape Garden in Scotland*. [78] Here, however, its influence was mingled with two other proto-Romantic ideas. One was the ambiguous status of old Scottish castellated houses – architecturally stigmatised, yet still emotionally valued. The other was a growing appreciation of the 'Sublime' in Scottish landscape, including the

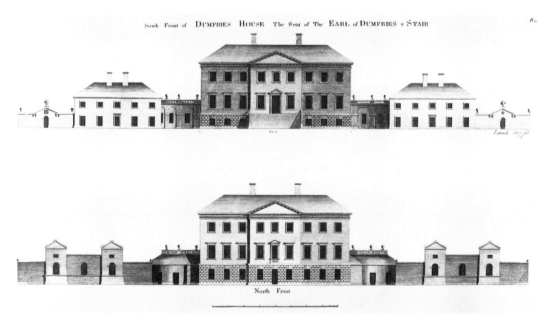

3.39 Dumfries House (J. Adam, 1754–9), main elevations, from *Vitruvius Scoticus*.

creation of artificially wild features as a foil to
classical houses; Bruce and Mar had already
aligned some of their landscape vistas on historic
remains, and others on natural landmarks. Clerk's
'Country Seat', while still insisting that a house
should be immediately surrounded by parterres,
also advocated the incorporation within landscaping of 'other harsh and frightfull objects' such
as 'High tow'ring Rocks and noisy Cataracts'. [79]
In a series of improvements at Penicuik, he
introduced wild landscaped walks, including an
artificial 'frightful cave'. [80] A similar scheme was
completed in 1757 at Dunkeld Hermitage by the
prodigious improver and former Jacobite general,
Lord George Murray. From the early eighteenth
century, a growing number of schemes had
juxtaposed sublime landscape and old remains
with formal elements, including developments of
the banqueting house building-type. In 1708, Sir
James Carmichael of Bonnington built a small
classical view-house overlooking the dramatic
Corra Linn falls on the Clyde and the ruinous
Corra Castle; it was linked by a long, straight
terrace to the gardens around Bonnington House
[3.40]. And Adam's Chatelherault, while commanding a grand, axial view to the front, backed
immediately on to the steep gorge of the river Avon
and the ruins of Cadzow Castle.

From the mid-eighteenth century, a further step
was taken, which actually began infiltrating the
nascent Romantic attitudes into the field of new
building. This new step was to build new houses in
the style of castles, while, of course, continuing to
incorporate into them up-to-date symmetrical
plans and modern conveniences. The first showpiece of this movement was the new house built at
Inveraray from 1746 by Archibald, 3rd Duke of
Argyll. Argyll, a staunch champion of Whig
unionism who (with his brother the 2nd Duke) had
dominated Scottish politics for several decades,
embarked in the 1740s on an extensive programme
of estate improvement, including the demolition of
his old castle and the building of a new seat [3.41].
In the building of the latter, he may have been
anxious to display a combination of confident
progressiveness and ancestral roots. As early as
1720, McGill had made plans for adding wings to
the old castle. Now, however, a completely new
design was drawn up, probably in 1744, by the

3.40 Corra Linn Pavilion (1708; overlooking Falls of Clyde), New Lanark.

military engineer Dugal Campbell, who designed
the crowstepped, classical Governor's House at
Edinburgh Castle in 1742, and who would later
take part in the anti-Jacobite war of 1745–6.
Campbell's plan envisaged a 'House . . . designed
in the Castle Stile', with a polygonal fort-like outer
wall and symmetrical splay-planned *corps de logis*.
He was an acquaintance of William Adam, and his
design strikingly resembled some recent work of
the latter – notably, the splay plan of Minto, and
the bastions he added (as contractor) to various
Highland castles [cf. 3.35]. Campbell's proposal
was not built, and instead the Duke engaged the
English architect Roger Morris (whom he had
previously employed on work in London). Morris
consulted William Adam in Edinburgh in 1744 and
built the new house in 1746–9. His design retained
Campbell's castellation and dry moat. It comprised
a simple square box with pointed windows and
central tower – a plan-type somewhat reminiscent
of Mar's designs – and round towers at the angles.
Inside, the house had classical interiors, later richly
remodelled by Robert Mylne from 1780.

The two designs for Inveraray – by Campbell
and Morris – between them anticipated many of
the future permutations of new castle-building.
This fashion would only catch on slowly – the
next really large example was John (and probably
James) Adam's Douglas Castle of 1757, a tall, U-
plan design of which only one side was built – but
it would eventually be taken to a new pitch of
elaboration by Robert Adam. What distinguished

this castle-building from the old, seventeenth-century affection for dynastic homes was its roots in a combination of classical order and the beginnings of a Romantic reliance on the irrational. As we will see in Chapter 4, this complex new world-outlook would become far more prominent in the late eighteenth-century era of Ossian.

Urban, Public and Religious Architecture, 1660–1760

It is a measure of the dominance of the 'Country Seat' in this period that all other building types, including urban buildings as a whole, can be dealt with together. The great explosion of urban and public building which would eventually dwarf the patronage of the landed classes in scale and diversity lay some distance ahead. But the urban architecture of the late seventeenth and early eighteenth centuries was full of promise of this spectacular future, especially in its insistence on a co-ordinated or planned approach to urban settlement: the most renowned example would be the late eighteenth-century realisation of James VII's and Mar's concepts of a planned extension to Edinburgh, but there were numerous less obvious, but equally significant pointers to later developments.

Throughout these years, the country continued to extend its tentacles of power and patronage into the town, in the form of the townhouses of the aristocracy and lairds. There was no building campaign as lavish and consistent as, for instance, that of the aristocratic town palaces which dominated the centre of Warsaw from the late seventeenth century. However, during the period of Stuart absolutist reassertion in the 1660s–80s, the Canongate enjoyed a period of great popularity as a place for courtiers' townhouses. The foremost example was Queensberry House, built from 1681 as the town lodging of Lauderdale's brother, Charles Maitland (Lord Hatton), and sold on, in 1686, to the 1st Duke of Queensberry; James Smith acted as mason in its construction. This 'great mansion with garden and orchid', [81] was originally a harled U-plan block of three/four storeys with ogee-roofed wings, and mansarded centre. Elsewhere, townhouse building was more episodic. In the late seventeenth century, some houses of merchants or professional men kept up the old gabled fashion, such as the four-storey, crowstepped Provost Norie's House, Stirling (1671), while others, such as Tobias Bachop's own house at Kirkgate, Alloa (1695), showed the influence of the new, regular classicism.

The move towards greater classical stateliness in early eighteenth-century country houses was mirrored in the towns, where mezzanines and complex plans were often needed to fit grand public rooms into small envelopes. Alexander McGill's reconstruction of the Duke of Montrose's townhouse in Glasgow (1718–19) comprised a flat-roofed, balustraded block faced entirely of horizontally channelled masonry. It contained an apartment planned in spiral form, like Mavisbank's principal floor. In the capital, William Adam's townhouse for Lord Minto (1738–43) resembled his exactly contemporary country house for the same client in its refined geometry and grandeur: a cubic, piended block with polygonal side projections, and two double-height great rooms. Also boasting two grand public rooms, on its garden front, was Lord Milton's house in the Canongate, by John Adam (1754–8). [3.42] And the same architect's Hawkhill villa (1757), with only one main floor, was an even greater marvel of compact planning. In the north, a typically severe, dignified example of the type was the harled, five-bay Balnain House, Inverness (1726).

Examples such as Hawkhill could just as easily be classified villas, or retreats, as townhouses – for, as we noted above in the case of Mavisbank, this was a time when the environs of Edinburgh were increasingly thickly dotted with the villas of the rich. Some were simple, small classical houses, such as the two-storey 'Hermits and Termits', St Leonards (just outside Edinburgh), built in 1734 for William Clifton, Solicitor of Excise. Before long, grouped settlements of villas began to form, in the manner which would become ubiquitous in the nineteenth century: an early example, developed from the early seventeenth century, was Inveresk, where surviving examples include the square-planned, pyramid-roofed Halkerston Lodge (1638–42), built for the Edinburgh merchant John Rynd; other places such as Prestonpans and Haddington also acquired quantities of villa-type houses and gardens.

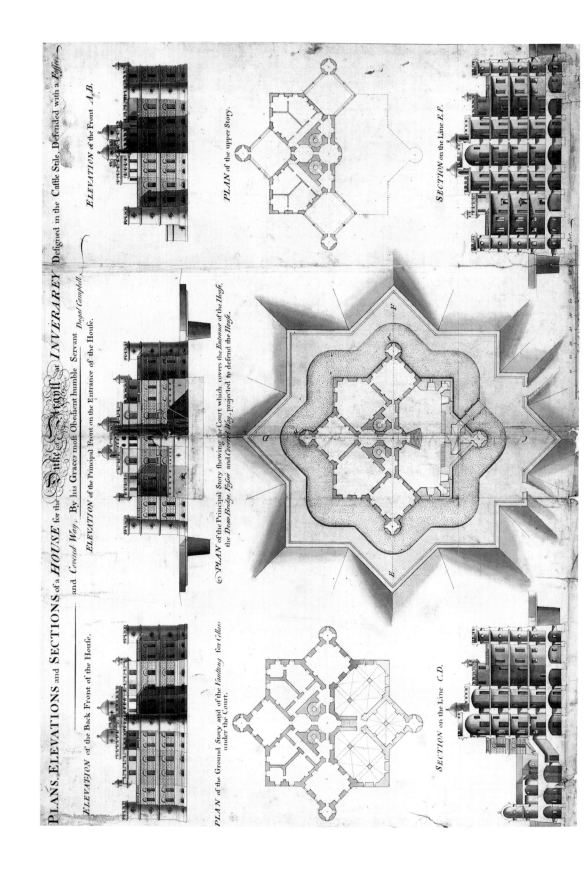

PLANS, ELEVATIONS and SECTIONS of a HOUSE for the Duke of Argyll at INVERARY. Designed in the Castle Stile, Defended with a Fossee and Covered Way. By his Graces most Obedient humble Servant Dugal Campbell.

ELEVATION of the Front A, B.

PLAN of the upper Story.

SECTION on the Line E, F.

ELEVATION of the Principal Front on the Entrance of the House.

⊙ PLAN of the Principal Story shewing the Court which covers the Entrance of the House, the Draw Bridge, Fossee and Covered Way, projected to defend the House.

ELEVATION of the Back Front of the House.

PLAN of the Ground Story and of the Vaulting for Cellars under the Court.

SECTION on the Line C, D.

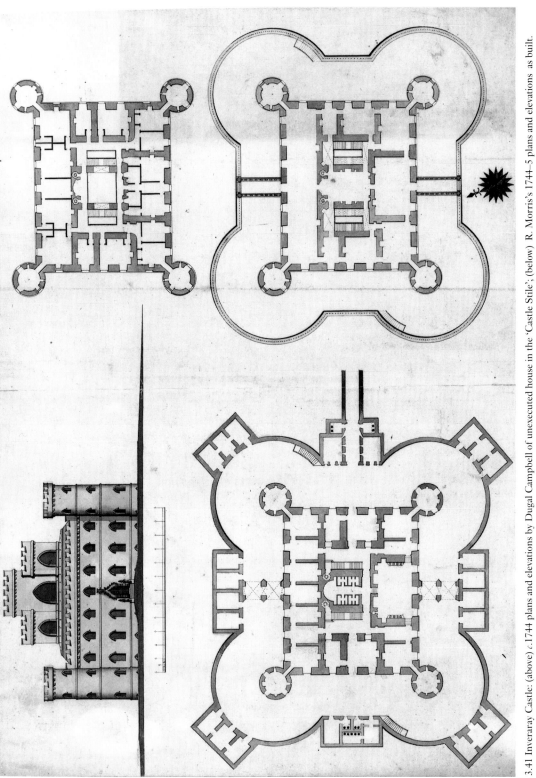

3.41 Inveraray Castle: (above) c.1744 plans and elevations by Dugal Campbell of unexecuted house in the 'Castle Stile'; (below) R. Morris's 1744-5 plans and elevations as built.

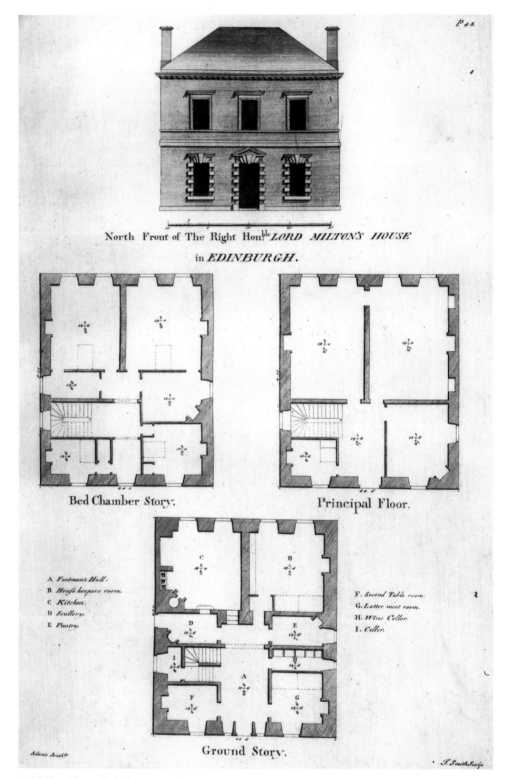

North Front of The Right Honᵇˡᵉ *LORD MILTON'S HOUSE* in *EDINBURGH.*

Bed Chamber Story.

Principal Floor.

A. *Footman's Hall.*
B. *House keepers room.*
C. *Kitchen.*
D. *Scullery.*
E. *Pantry.*

F. *Second Table room.*
G. *Latter meat room.*
H. *Wine Celler.*
I. *Celler.*

Ground Story.

Adam Arch⁺

T. Smith Sculp.

3.42 Milton House, 90 Canongate (J. Adam, 1754–8), elevation and plans, from *Vitruvius Scoticus*.

The beginnings of the villa formed part of a growing reassessment of concepts of urban settlement. The economic fortunes of the existing towns during this period were mixed. The epochal change in trade patterns from east to west, towards transatlantic trade, began to benefit Glasgow at the expense of the east coast ports. In 1723 Macky described the typical Fife coastal burgh as presenting 'a good appearance at a distance, like an old lady in Decay; but when you come into it, those large Stone white Houses, which seem like Palaces far off, prove to be Heaps of Decay when you approach them'. [82] In the capital, the late seventeenth century had been a time of prosperity. Infrastructural and social improvements such as installation of piped water supply, spread of luxury goods and creation of a service sector reinforced its cultural status as a capital city, even as its political role diminished. After the 1707 union, by contrast, there were several decades of economic stagnation.

It was above all in Edinburgh that, during the late seventeenth and early eighteenth centuries, the patterns of urban development (as opposed to suburban or villa development) which would pass into mass production in the nineteenth century were first worked out: the dense tenement block, and the individual dwelling built in rows. The eighteenth and nineteenth centuries would see the emergence of mass urban housing as an architectural type characterised by sharp national differences. In north-west Europe, the roots of these divergences lay back in the seventeenth century. During that time, the new planned urban spaces of Paris, such as the Place Royale (1605–12) or the Place Louis le Grand (from 1699) had pioneered the idea of grouping lines of dwellings behind architecturally unified facades. The plots behind were developed intensively with courtyard-plan houses, a dense pattern later extended to high tenement blocks. In Amsterdam and London, the late seventeenth century saw the development of hollow street blocks lined with narrow, deep row-houses with back gardens. In Scotland, a formula different from any other country gradually emerged: the building of strips of dwellings around the perimeter of street blocks (with large open back courts) as in the Netherlands and England, but using broad and relatively shallow house plans. Scottish urban housing layouts were distinctive,

above all, in the thoroughness of their renunciation of the narrow, deep burgage plot.

We already saw, in Chapter 2, the nascent tendency of building in rows in the plans of Glasgow College [cf. 2.38]. Now this was applied to urban housing. It was in the centre of Edinburgh (and in Leith) that there first began to emerge a classically monumental type of purpose-built collective dwelling-block, prompted by the capital's burgeoning professional/mercantile society and service/industrial economy, and the consequent demand for spatial segregation of the dwellings of the rich from those of the poor – which were increasingly identified with the old, haphazardly subdivided developments of the burgage plot [cf. 2.30]. The first, tentative steps in this process were taken from the 1670s in a series of speculative tenement blocks. The first developments were carried out in the vicinity of the Parliament House from 1671 onwards by the energetic speculative builder Thomas Robertson (who was associated with James Smith). Then followed several blocks built by none other than Robert Mylne and James Smith. The first of three tenements built by, and named after, the former was Mylne's Land, Leith (1678), a four-storey block with attic and basement, double-depth plan and scale and platt staircase. Mylne's Square, in Edinburgh's High Street (1684–8) was the first project to break out from the old medieval layout by demolishing and building across several older closes in a new unified design – here, a big open square. Also important for the future, as an urban parallel to Bruce's designs at Kinross, was the monumentality of ashlar facing (rubble at rear) and uniform fenestration. The houses, intended exclusively for the rich, attempted to compress elements of a great apartment into an even tighter setting than Smith's small villas: accommodation varied from dining room, three bedrooms, closet and kitchen to dining room, outer hall, four bedrooms, closet and three cellars.

Mylne's Square was an instant success, many of the houses being snapped up by lawyers; Mylne kept one of the houses himself. In 1690, he began his last and most monumental speculation, Mylne's Court, in the Lawnmarket, beginning with a front (south) block six storeys and attic high, and later extending this with rear blocks and a

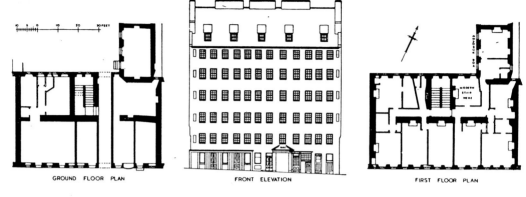

GROUND FLOOR PLAN   FRONT ELEVATION   FIRST FLOOR PLAN

3.43 Mylne's Court, Lawnmarket, Edinburgh (R. Mylne, from 1690), 1951 front elevation and floor plans of south section.

courtyard [3.43]. In the front range of Mylne's Court, key features of later Scottish middle-class tenements were charted out. This broad, shallow building, arranged along the street building line, is faced in ashlar, with plain unbroken eaves. Inside, a scale and platt staircase gives access to two houses on each floor, one on either side: the flats are two rooms in depth, from front to back, with small service rooms and corridors along the spine-walled centre. Smith's Land, a large tenement built at roughly this time by Smith, the architect on the north side of the High Street (in the present-day Paisley's Close) was similar in its open layout and double-depth internal planning, as were some early eighteenth-century tenements, such as James Court (built 1723–7 by James Brownhill, wright) or 312–28 Lawnmarket (two tenements, built 1726–52). An equivalent development of high-income flats in the Canongate was located in Chessel's Court (from 1745). Elements of the old deep-plot planning were retained in some developments with a succession of courtyards: for example, in Paterson Court (built before 1724), with its 'fore court' and a 'back court'. By the end of the eighteenth century, the Lawnmarket and much of the High Street had been transformed into a succession of broad, ashlar tenements devoid of gables, projections or even the relatively recently established arcades; at the rear, on the steeply sloping ground, some tenements were of great height, of ten storeys or more [cf. 2.30]. In these houses, as in the similar, but lower, tenement blocks built for the merchant classes of nineteenth century Glasgow, there was a rapid increase in specialised room use – reflecting rising urban manners – and lavishness of furniture and other fittings (such as carpets); dining tables and large matching sets of chairs became common. The popularity of press beds reflects the demands put on limited space by these rising expectations.

Where, in the densest areas, the renunciation of the deep-plot pattern took the form of multi-storey tenements arranged in rows or squares, for those of the wealthy who sought a greater segregation from the dilapidated central areas but could not afford to build separate villas, a compromise solution was arrived at: to build individual dwellings in rows. This was a kind of hybrid between villa and tenement, resembling the row dwellings of the Netherlands or England, but avoiding those countries' extreme verticality and compression of plan. The first such developments were planned in squares, influenced perhaps by those of Glasgow College or contemporary London [cf. 2.38]; early examples included Argyle Square (completed *c.*1742) and Brown and Adam Square (both of the 1750s). Brown Square was built by architect-speculator James Brown, who in 1766 began to develop the town's largest square: George Square (named after the architect's brother rather than the king); most of its houses were built by Michael Nasmyth [cf. 5.18].

The accelerating march of the philosophy of improvement also prompted a growing interest among landowners in the creation of planned settlements, especially with the aim of attracting craftsmen and industry, and fostering centres of commerce. Examples from the late seventeenth century included Newton Stewart (1670s) or Gifford, while the early eighteenth century saw the beginnings of a campaign of village-building in the north-east. The most ambitious effort was a project by the Duke of Argyll at Inveraray, as part of his vast campaign of agricultural and estate improvements. The building of his new castle involved the demolition of a village located inconveniently close to its site, and the enforced removal of tenants to a new planned town [3.44]. The first buildings of the relocated Inveraray were commenced by John Adam in 1751, in the form of a grand and roughly symmetrical 'facade' to the north, made up of a town house and an inn flanking the arched entrance to an estate 'mall'; the eventual, cruciform plan (at the heart of which was a church) was drawn up by Robert Mylne in 1774 and developed by rows of dwellings, including tenement blocks. It was only from the late eighteenth century that privately driven urbanist developments of this kind were built in really large numbers.

During the economic uncertainty of the earlier part of the century, a significant role in regularised or planned settlement – especially of a kind which would later be applied in denser, more urban settings – was played by public building programmes. An example of a planned settlement organised by the Board of Manufactures was the construction of a French weaving colony, named 'Picardy', to the north-east of Edinburgh. The settlement, built in 1730–1 to McGill's designs, comprised a symmetrical row of single-storey cottages with a two-storey block at its centre. In the Highlands, a more significant part was played by the military building programmes of the Hanoverian state. While military architecture prior to the eighteenth century had essentially comprised the building of bastions and fortifications, the emergence of the barracks as a specialised building type led to an element of convergence with domestic architecture. The first post-1707 steps were taken by James Smith, during his tenure of the post of 'Surveyor and Chief Director for Carrying on the Barracks in North Britain' in 1718–19. Following the government's decision in 1717 to replace the independent Highland companies with regular troops, Smith was asked to design four garrisons in the north: Ruthven (built 1719–22), Cille Chuimin (1718–21, later Fort Augustus), Glenelg (or Bernera, 1720–3) and Inversnaid (1718–20). [3.45] The contractor at Inversnaid and Cille Chuimin was Smith's cousin Gilbert Smith. All comprised square or

3.44 Inveraray, distant view of new town (from 1751) from Dun na Cuaiche.

rectangular enclosures, containing two tenement blocks of three storeys and cellar facing each other; the tenements at Cille Chuimin and Bernera were double-depth, while the other two were single-depth.

Under the patronage of General Wade, the army commander-in-chief in Scotland from 1724, William Adam subsequently assumed Smith's former role, with his appointment as 'Mason to the Board of Ordnance in North Britain' in 1730, and benefited from a share of the massive government road – and bridge-building programme of 1725–37. His proudest achievement of this strategic programme was the five-arched Aberfeldy Bridge over the Tay (1733–5), with its obelisk-crowned cutwaters [3.46]. An inscription on the bridge, composed by the English churchman and scholar Robert Freind, invited the onlooker to

> admire this military way which extends for 250 miles beyond the Roman frontiers, striding over deserts and marshes, cutting through rocks and mountains, and crossing the impatient Tay. George Wade, prefect of the forces in Scotland, completed this audacious crossing work in the year 1733, by his cleverness and the immense labours of his soldiers. See what the royal protection of George II is worth!

While recent claims by Jane Clark that General Wade was a covert Jacobite [83] leave it open to speculation that this ringing declaration may have contained a note of irony, what is incontestable is that the rhetoric and architectural monumentality associated with the Antique continued to exert a mesmeric hold on all 'improvers' (whether Hanoverians or Jacobites).

After the 1745–6 war, Adam was awarded his biggest military contract of all, intended as a final, crushing demonstration of Hanoverian power in the Highlands: the building of a small fortified town, Fort George, for the main Highland garrison [3.47]. Designed in 1747 by a military engineer, Colonel William Skinner, to accommodate two battalions and a resident artillery unit, this enormous complex was built over two decades (1748–69) under the supervision of successive members of the Adam family: first William; then John, Robert and James. Fort George was so extensive that it required the physical removal of a nearby hill (in 1766). Its outer fortifications, designed according to the norms of post-sixteenth century European military engineering, comprised a series of overlapping polygonal bastions; the pedimented gatehouse was ornamented with a heavy Hanoverian coat of arms. Inside was an axially planned layout, centred on a square (Barrack Square, 1753–64) flanked by two identical U-plan three-storey tenements. A chapel was built at one end of the main axis (1763–7), with nave and aisles plan, and Roman Doric columns. Although, by the time it was complete, the complex was militarily obsolete, its highly structured planning concept would exert an enduring influence.

While, in the field of residential architecture, Glasgow College's squares contributed to the growing fashion for building in squares and rows, the form of its lofty, rectangular steeple influenced a different area of urban architecture: that of public buildings. Here a greater architectural uniformity was now increasingly demanded. In the planning of tolbooths, the basic pattern of a

3.45 Ruthven Barracks (Smith, 1719–22), view from west.

3.46 Tay Bridge, Aberfeldy (W. Adam, 1733–5).

3.47 Fort George (W. Skinner, 1748–69).

meeting room above a vaulted ground floor, with steeple, was retained, but a new element of formality was introduced in Bruce's design for Stirling Town House (1703–4). Here, on the front facade, a campanile-type tower similar to that of Glasgow College, with yawning entrance archway, was married to a three-storey and attic, three-bay classical block not dissimilar to the ashlar classicism of later Edinburgh New Town row-houses [cf. 2.34, 2.38]. The Glasgow College model of tolbooth steeple remained highly influential as a model for civic order, even into the eighteenth century: for instance at Dumfries (built from 1705 by Bachop, who substantially amended designs by John Moffat) [3.48]. In 1727, for example, Auchtermuchty Town Council had noted 'how uneasie and troublesome' was 'the want of a good tolbooth with a clock and bell and steeple', [84] and the following year built a new tolbooth with tall rectangular steeple and spire. An alternative, more strictly classical option was presented by Linlithgow (1668–70, by John Smith): a regularly windowed front facade, grand staircase, and low, balustraded tower at the back. Bruce also introduced a stricter classicism to another type of public building, in his columnar design for the Edinburgh Exchange, built from *c*.1680 by Thomas Robertson; the mason was James Smith. The Exchange was burnt down in 1700; the replacement (built from 1753) is described in Chapter 4.

The early eighteenth century saw a gradual move towards greater horizontality in the planning of public buildings, including a convergence, in the steepled tolbooth, with the porticoed, highly modelled pattern of ecclesiastical architecture pioneered by Gibbs at St Martin's in the Fields Church [cf. 3.25] ; from the 1750s, the use of Gibbs-like steeples was also extended to country house stable courtyards (for instance at Penicuik, 1762–5). In Edinburgh, although the depressed first decades of the century left McGill, appointed City Architect in 1720, with 'no publick work of importance' by 1725, [85] the 1730s saw a series of increasingly ambitious public commissions by William Adam, all with long, austerely windowed frontages (in the Gibbs King's College manner) and elaborate pedimented centrepieces: the Orphans' Hospital (1734), George Watson's

3.48 Dumfries Town House (from 1705).

Hospital (1738), and the Royal Infirmary (1738–48; later incorporated in David Bryce's Royal Infirmary). Adam's Glasgow University Library (1732–45) conveyed a somewhat ecclesiastical air, with pedimented front and small Corinthian portico. In the field of civic architecture, his Dundee Town House (1731–34) displayed a clear debt to Gibbs, in its central steeple and pedimented frontispiece; these lent the building an ordered monumentality previously rare in the tolbooth tradition, while the ground floor was arcaded and provided with rusticated channelling [3.49]. Adam's more modestly scaled tolbooth at Sanquhar (1735–7) was of two storeys with central pediment and low octagonal steeple above; its double forestair recalled those of earlier country houses such as Drumlanrig or Whitehill. John Douglas's Campbeltown Town House (1758–60) has a set-forward steeple and rich blocked, round-arched detail typical of the architect.

Late seventeenth- and early-eighteenth century

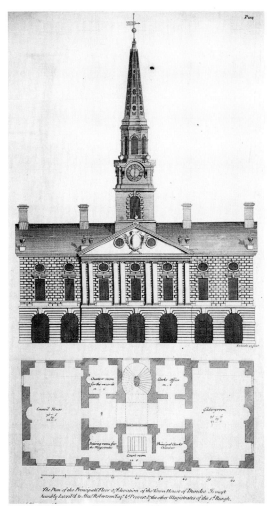

3.49 Dundee Town House (W. Adam, 1731–4), principal floor plan and front elevation, from *Vitruvius Scoticus*.

religious building, in town and country, was comprehensively overshadowed by the now well-established secular orientation of Scottish architecture. With the one outstanding exception of James VII's refitting of Holyrood Abbey in 1687, [cf. 3.3] church architecture was now firmly bedded into its reformed tradition of plainness and modest size – a tradition to which, in general, both the Presbyterian and episcopalian wings of Scottish Protestantism conformed. There would be no outbreaks of Baroque extravagance in Scottish churches, but instead an austere classicism, sometimes with Gothic elements. A centralised plan with two or three arms, in a rectangular or T-planned arrangement, was still the rule. Larger examples sported a steeple, situated either centrally on the long axis in the Edinburgh Tron Kirk manner (as at Gifford, *c.*1710, possibly by Smith and McGill) [cf. 2.5], or on an end gable, in the pre-Reformation manner seen recently at Anstruther Easter Church (1634–44). One of the most monumental examples was Polwarth Church (1703), built by the 1st Earl of Marchmont (possibly incorporating earlier remains), with massive harled steeple and round-arched doorway. The form of steeple, with concave cap, pioneered by Murray and Alexander at Holyrood in 1633 and used at Glasgow College, continued its popularity; the steeple of South Leith Parish Church was rebuilt in 1674 by Robert Mylne with wavy parapet and concave belfry.

Within such a simple, well-established framework, it is sometimes difficult to make exact correlation between any architectural innovation and the religious controversies of the period. Lauder Church, for example, was built by Bruce in 1673 on the instructions of the Duke of Lauderdale, who was at that time in charge of the drive, backed by King Charles, to enforce episcopacy. Lauderdale instructed Bruce that 'I would have it decent and large enough, with a handsom little steeple'. [86] But it is difficult to correlate the resulting design – a Greek-cross plan with simple Gothic tracery – with its liturgical-ideological context [3.50]. Did the Gothic windows signify Stuart emphasis on antiquity, and did the centralised plan reflect episcopalian liturgy? Another architecturally adventurous variant of this centralised planning was designed just after 1715: the rebuilding of Durisdeer Church (in 1716–20, attributed to Smith and McGill) for the 3rd Duke of Queensberry. The reconstruction retained the domed burial aisle which already contained one of the period's most exotic funerary monuments, the Berniniesque pedimented baldacchino of the 1st Duke of Queensberry – built from 1695 and probably designed by James Smith. The rest of the church was demolished and replaced by a new T-plan church (the Queensberry aisle becoming the latter's fourth aisle), which was adjoined by a massive laird's retiring apartment designed like a small, piend-roofed country house, and surmounted by a steeple and (originally) spire [3.51, 3.52].

3.50 Lauder, St Mary's Church (Bruce, 1673, on left) and tolbooth (on right; eighteenth–century) 1990 aerial view of the centre of this planned burgh.

3.51 Durisdeer Parish Church, Dumfriesshire, montage by Professor David M. Walker of the original design (as rebuilt 1716–20).

3.52 Queensberry monuments (Smith, 1695), Durisdeer Church.

It was perhaps in response to the drive for episcopalian forms of worship that the later seventeenth century saw experiments with more linear patterns, including deep rectangular plans with pulpit on the end opposite the entrance – a design for which Edinburgh's Greyfriars offered a precedent, with nave and flanking aisles. Also sometimes used was the Latin cross, a form increasingly popular in the Counter-Reformation Catholic Church. It may have been no coincidence that when James Smith, who had nearly become a Jesuit himself in his youth, was allowed to design Canongate Parish Church in 1688 (to take over the parish church function of Holyrood Abbey on completion of its conversion), he designed a Latin cross plan, un-steepled and with bell-shaped, sweepingly curved facade, recalling, in a highly restrained way, the two-tiered nave and aisles pattern popular in the continental Baroque [3.53]. However, Canongate Church never saw episcopal worship, as it was still incomplete at the time of the Presbyterian revolution of 1689–90; the chancel was blocked up unused.

The years after 1715 saw, in many cases, a continuation of the older-established patterns. T-shaped churches with a steeple on the long side included Smith and McGill's monumental New Church, Dumfries (1724–7), its tall Glasgow College-like steeple crowned by a splayed spire; and the same architects' more modest Newbattle Parish Church (1727–9), which closely resembled the nearby church at Carrington (1710). Experiments with centralised plans continued, most notably at William Adam's Hamilton Parish Church (1729–32), comprising a Greek cross inscribed in a circle, one arm being porticoed; and at John Douglas's octagonal Killin Church (1744). These older patterns were now increasingly transformed by the new, more assertively 'antique' monumentality introduced by Gibbs at St Martin's Church in London, with its combination of a massive, steepled portico and rectangular, side-aisled plan [cf. 3.25]. At St Andrew's Parish Church, Glasgow (1737–59) – designed by Allan Dreghorn, the influential Glasgow architect-businessman, in collaboration with the mason Mungo Nasmyth – a giant portico was matched with a steeple slenderer than Gibbs's. [3.54] Not unsurprisingly, when Gibbs himself returned to Aberdeen to design a church there himself – St Nicholas West, in 1752–5 – he followed the same rectangular plan, designing a nave-and-aisles, barrel-vaulted layout with superimposed pedimented front. At the smaller Donibristle Chapel (completed 1731), designed by McGill for the Earl and Countess of Moray, a rectangular plan, along with blocked Gibbs-type detailing, was reproduced in reduced form, with an arcaded octagonal belfry and pedimented gable with armorial panel [3.55]. McGill's (attributed) early eighteenth-century chapel at Mount Stuart, Bute, on the other hand, recalled the James VI Stirling Chapel Royal in its symmetrical front facade, high roof and paired windows; it was T-shaped with a rear wing [cf. 2.2].

After several decades of outlaw status, episcopalians began building a limited number of new chapels after the passing of the Toleration Act in 1712. In episcopacy's north-eastern heartland, Alexander Jaffray designed St Paul's chapel in Aberdeen as early as 1721, while a meeting house designed by McGill was inaugurated in Montrose in 1724. In the central Lowlands, an Edinburgh chapel opened in 1722; what is probably the oldest surviving example, St Andrew's by the Green in Glasgow (1750–2), designed by the masons William Paull and Andrew Hunter, comprises a simpler version of the Gibbsian pedimented rectangular plan, concealing the chapel's religious function behind a domestic-looking exterior.

As we noted in the case of Durisdeer, burial aisles and funerary monuments continued to provide an outlet for more elaborate, even Baroque decoration. Among the freestanding aisles, some were roofed, such as Robert Mylne's 1710 aisle in Greyfriars churchyard for the Trotters of

3.53 Canongate Parish Church, Edinburgh (Smith, 1688, photograph of *c.* 1920).

3.54 St Andrew's Parish Church, Glasgow (A. Dreghorn, 1737–59).

Mortonhall, or the two-storey, harled, domed aisle at Milton of Campsie (1715). The grandest and most cosmopolitan was, appropriately, designed and built by James Smith: the Greyfriars mausoleum of Sir George Mackenzie of Rosehaugh, persecutor of the Covenanters ('Bluidy Mackenzie'). Erected in 1691, this comprised a circular, Corinthian-columned, ogee-domed structure [3.56]. Among aisles attached to churches, a fairly elaborate example was the 1664 Archerfield Aisle at Dirleton, a massive block with deep rusticated quoined angles, pedimented doorway and round-arched, traceried window. The pattern continued of aisles incorporating retiring rooms with a vault: for example, at the pyramidal-roofed Abercorn Aisle, built in 1707–8 by Bruce (attr.) for the Hopetoun family. Funerary monuments increasingly adopted an upright aedicular form, influenced by book designs. The greatest concentration of the latter was in Greyfriars churchyard, including Robert Mylne's

3.56 Greyfriars Churchyard, Edinburgh, monument to Sir George Mackenzie of Rosehaugh (Smith, 1691).

1674 monument to his uncle John, based on the frontispiece of Francini's *Livre d'Architecture*; a comparable design was used for the Riccarton monument at St Nicholas's churchyard, Aberdeen (1696). Even more elaborate was the black and white marble monument to Archbishop James Sharp in Holy Trinity Church, St Andrews. Erected in 1679, the year of Sharp's assassination by Covenanters, it comprises a huge Corinthian-columned aedicule flanked by doused torches. By the eighteenth century, more classically 'correct' designs were the rule.

Conclusion

The classical country house architecture, which dominated the century from 1660 to 1760, answered the practical and symbolic requirements of the 'improving' landed classes (and also, at first, of the 'restored' Stuart monarchy) in its potent mixture of antique stateliness and modernity. It

3.55 Donibristle Chapel, Fife (McGill, completed 1731).

was Bruce and Smith who firmly established in Scotland the new view of classicism and the Orders as a comprehensive system of values rather than as a vocabulary of applied detail; and Mar and Adam who gave that classicism a more variegated character, highly attuned to the thrusting ideals of improvement.

While the controlled polarisation of this period – between the modern and the ancient – did not for now seriously threaten respect for classical authority and precedent, we will see in the next chapter that the later eighteenth century would bring great changes. In particular, the archaeological discovery that there was no single 'antiquity' would open the way to the nineteenth century's romantic individualism and eclecticism.

Chapter 4

1760–1800

Rationalism and Irrationalism

'I believe this is the historical Age, and this the historical Nation'.

David Hume, 1770 [1]

'. . . that greatness and simplicity of composition, which, by imposing on the imagination, strikes the mind.'

Robert and James Adam, 1776 [2]

'August, around, what PUBLIC WORKS I see!
Lo! Stately streets, lo! Squares that court the breeze!
See! Long canals, and deepened rivers join
Each part with each, and with the circling main
The whole enliven'd Isle.'

James Craig, 1768 [3]

Introduction

In this short chapter, we trace the beginnings of a double revolution, in both the context and the ideas of architecture. The growing wealth of society, especially in the towns, pointed to a new diversity of patronage. And the undermining of classical authority by history-based 'neo-classical' relativism led to a transformation in architectural concepts: there arose widely varied, even conflicting tendencies, including the rationalism of the Edinburgh New Town, and the cult of the irrational artistic genius, spearheaded by Robert Adam.

Economic Revolution and the Transformation of Classicism

In 1763, the staggering victories in the Seven Years War left Britain, for the first time, as the most powerful state in Europe. And after the secession of the United States, and the conquests in India, a new British Empire began to emerge, which Scots felt belonged to them as much as to the English. With Jacobitism now a spent force, people's efforts were redirected to exploiting these unprecedented imperial and commercial opportunities. Between 1750 and 1800 Scottish overseas commerce grew by 300 per cent – far faster even than that of England. At home, the mobilisation of civil society during the 1745–6 war had paved the way for accelerated improvement. *The Scots Magazine* of 1752 recorded that the entire nation was infected by 'zeal for the improvement and prosperity of this country . . . a truly patriotic and national spirit'. [4] The rule of law and the security of the moveable goods of the merchant were the pillars of this new 'free' society, motivated by its own drive to transform itself.

These economic and industrial advances, which accelerated after 1790, were reflected in major building campaigns, both urban and rural, whose decentralised private patronage was fuelled by the rise in credit, and by government help – for instance, from the Board of Manufactures. In the country, landowners' outlook shifted towards a more open modernity, perhaps because of the failure of the 1745–6 rising and the abolition of heritable jurisdictions. The power of the landed classes, if anything, expanded, and the building of planned settlements accelerated dramatically. The scope of country house building was widened by the demands of *arrivistes*, such as those who had enriched themselves from plunder in the East

147

Indies, for relatively small, but prestigious 'seats'. But this rural activity was increasingly matched by a growth in the momentum of improvement in the towns and among their rising merchant classes. In Edinburgh, Glasgow and elsewhere, an array of private institutions and societies was created, to further the course of urban order and to provide opportunities for display of status. Soaring wealth demanded development for added rental value and more sophisticated services, and led to the beginnings of a new diversity of building tasks. Never again would there be a single dominant type within architecture, as with churches before the Reformation and country houses since then. Instead, there was a widening variety of types, along with a new, overarching conception of the entire city as a monument.

Such developments as these greatly expanded the scope of the work available to architects. In 1750, Robert Adam declared that Scotland was a 'narrow place' [5] where little could be achieved. But by the 1780s and even more, the turn-of-the-century, the position was beginning to change. Adam was increasingly able to work at home and, in the last year of his life, designed no fewer than eight major public buildings in Scotland. James Playfair's largely Scottish practice (from 1783) was still based in London, whereas his son, beginning practice at home in Edinburgh over thirty years later, enjoyed a leading status among the city's intellectuals, and designed a series of prestigious public monuments. The only top-rank early nineteenth-century architect who moved away to England was, significantly, the country house specialist William Burn. Growing wealth also had more specific material effects within architecture: for example, by squeezing out non-ashlar construction from high-status projects.

The social status of the architect was gradually evolving into that of an economically independent urban professional, emancipated from landed patronage and values, and able to deal with a wide variety of building tasks. The Adam family was still closely involved with trade: from 1764, the four brothers ran a contracting and speculative-building company, William Adam & Co. (named after the fourth brother). But from the start Robert set his face against the profession's other major overlap of responsibility – that with the landowner-designers. He explained that 'All the gentry of the country are Architects, they know, or think they know much more than any Professional man, be he ever so eminent. It has been my constant study to try if I can root out this absurd idea of theirs and I flatter myself I am rather gaining ground on them.' [6] Adam's innovative architecture did much to establish the new formula of the architect as an individualistic artist, who distilled a personal manner from study of a wide range of stylistic sources.

In the field of architectural ideas, the late eighteenth century was a period of rapid change across Europe in attitudes to classicism. This was a time when the dethronement of antique authority, first proposed by Charles and Claude Perrault in the late seventeenth century, began to become a reality. Broadly speaking, there was a break from the concept of classicism as a unitary, cumulative tradition, within which the only differences could be those of competing claims of fidelity to ancient first principles. Faced with the growth of historical relativism, with archaeology's discoveries that there was no single antiquity, and with the proliferation of accurate architectural source books, this 'great tradition' now began to fragment. The spontaneous range of its local variants gave way to a deliberate competition of different classical and, even, non-classical 'styles'. There was a growing diversity of views about the past, and a feeling that the architecture of each period and each nation had its own internal validity.

The fragmentation of classical authority facilitated the spread of the Romantic conception of the individual artist. Although the Italian Renaissance had itself laid a high emphasis on artistic personality, the heaped-up, monumental compositions published by Giovanni Battista Piranesi from the 1740s greatly strengthened the status of intuitive genius, and of the Romantic aesthetic principles of the Sublime and Picturesque, in interpreting the new, relativistic antiquity. Alongside this individualism, there were attempts to find a fresh system of overarching order to replace classical precedent. At the same time, formally speaking, there was a general reaction within classicism away from hierarchical, extroverted Baroque compositions towards more static or repetitive conceptions of monumentality. With the gradual dissolution of the Enlightenment concept of integrated understanding and improvement, a range of rationalist and emotionalist concepts of order were on offer. Rationalists such as Laugier and Lodoli, for example, attempted to apply a clinical reason to architecture, ideas reflected in the extreme geometrical solutions of some late eighteenth-century French projects. Others began to emphasise the social, moral and historical context offered by the nation. It is this ferment of conflicting ideas – still faithful in general to the forms of classicism, but all the time questioning and decomposing its old certainties – that we, today, know as neo-classicism.

The mounting tension between the rational and irrational was especially significant in Scotland, whose intellectuals saw themselves in a vanguard role in promoting the concept of historical progress: in 1770, David Hume declared that 'this is the historical Age, and this the historical Nation'. [7] The cult of historical progress was both furthered and undermined by the complexities of the nation's own historical position. Affection for the old, national-epos patriotism still persisted alongside, and in tension with, the unprecedented new participation in modernising improvement and overseas British victory. This was, for instance, an age of growing interest in antiquities, with the Society of Antiquaries being founded in 1780 by the 11th Earl of Buchan: its first accession (a Bronze Age hoard) was described as a 'quantity of Roman Arms'. The late eighteenth-century's modernising sense of disjunction also singled out Scotland as a country which would play a central role in formulating, chiefly through literary media, the international Romantic conception of nationality. The sense of loss of pre-modern innocence, now habitually identified with the Stuart monarchy and the Jacobite cause, was also linked to an aestheticisation of that most unchanging, and therefore basic physical component of 'national identity': the natural landscape. It was above all the *Ossian* poems of James MacPherson (a client of Robert Adam), which fixed the principles which later guided the spread of romantic nationalism across modernising Europe and North America. We will return later to the Scottish attempts to devise a specific architecture for Romantic landscape – a develop-

ment of the earlier landscape concepts, of Bruce and others, that were traced in Chapter 3.

The 'Adam Revolution' and the Classical House

These new ideas of pluralistic antiquity and individualism were powerfully developed by Piranesi's friend and pupil, Robert Adam [4.1]. He reformulated the 'antique' into a tradition of Scottish Romantic classicism which would endure for the next century and a half, in the work of W. H. Playfair, Alexander Thomson and beyond. Adam's architectural ideas were intermediate between the classical eighteenth century and the eclectic nineteenth century. In his classical work, he developed – out of different sources – a recognisable personal 'style', with internal and external variants, which could be modified to different purposes. This was the first stage in the development of that eclecticism, both 'typological' (in its use of different styles for different building types) and 'synthetic' (in its merging of different sources within itself), which would come to dominate European architecture in the nineteenth century.

4.1 Robert Adam, portrait attributed to Pécheux.

Although there was still a reluctance to embrace the fully-fledged forms of Greek antiquity – James Adam described Paestum as 'an early, an inelegant and unenriched Doric, that afford no detail' [8] – Robert consistently used Ionic capitals modelled on the Erechtheion (as published by J. D. Leroy), as well as Greek Doric column shafts (for example at Alva Mausoleum, 1789, and Westerkirk Mausoleum, 1790). And beyond these classical innovations, Robert Adam began the break-up of secular architecture into competing 'styles' (a word he frequently used), not least by vigorously promoting the design of new country houses as 'castles'. Adam's patronage, too, was intermediate between the eighteenth and nineteenth centuries: where the first part of his career was dominated by the country and town houses of the Scottish and English landed classes, after the 1770s he also showed a growing concern with design of monumental public buildings in Scotland.

Robert Adam, although a standardbearer for the new stress on artistic personality, was no isolated genius. Instead, as we saw in Chapter 3, he sprang from the heart of the Edinburgh architectural establishment – rather like that equally dominant figure of mid-twentieth-century Scottish architecture, Robert Matthew. Born in 1728 in Kirkcaldy, the second of William Adam's architect sons, Robert's upbringing and early work left him steeped in the world of entrepreneurial Hanoverian improvement, with all its government and military patronage connections [cf. 3.39, 3.41, 3.47]. And the profits of William's industrial and contracting work left him, like his brothers and sisters, a rich man. By the 1750s, through these partly vicarious means, Robert, alongside his brother John, had become one of the most prominent architects in Scotland. But he was not content with this worthy status of prominence. His appetite for Baroque and antique grandeur had, doubtless, been whetted by the cosmopolitan architectural library at Blair Adam. And he hankered after more lavish projects than Scotland at that time could provide. Adam therefore decided to augment the imaginative calibre of his monumental classicism, and the status of his patronage, by direct experience of the Mediterranean; in 1754, he set off in pursuit of 'the Antique, the Noble & the Stupendous'. [9]

The years 1755–7 Robert spent in Italy, studying Roman and Renaissance architecture: in 1757 he jokingly wrote to Allan Ramsay as 'your Roman friend Bob'. [10] The climax of this work was a trip across the Adriatic to make drawings of the Roman palace at Spalato (Split), in Croatia. While in Rome, he cultivated friendships and links which would enable him to develop new strengths: Charles-Louis Clérisseau familiarised him with French standards of decorative refinement; Jean-Baptiste Lallemand trained him in landscape painting; while Piranesi, whom he boasted in 1755 had 'become immensely intimate with me', [11] provided a vision of Roman grandeur to complement his own evolving sensibilities.

To Adam, antiquity, and its potential contribution to 'taste', were still the all-important objects of his travels; but the meaning of both terms had changed. Now they no longer represented unquestioned authority, but the reverse: a stimulus to individualistic licence and 'picturesque' invention. Adam's ideas formed part of the new tendency of individual, aesthetic or formal reaction to architecture that was beginning to emerge in the eighteenth century, and which, within Scotland and England, was above all denoted by the labels 'Picturesque' and 'Sublime'. These concepts were profoundly shaped by contemporary developments in literature and landscape painting. Adam's own Picturesque was conceived in terms of sharp contrasts between 'Architectonick' order and wild romanticism. Within this context, study of the antique, and the subsequent definition of 'taste', was a matter not of archaeological accuracy and strict rules but of the subjective, even emotionalistic collaging of motifs. In 1756, Robert wrote back to his family that Rome was 'horribly antique and pleasing'. 'This is the most intoxicating Country in the world, for a pictoresque Hero, would you have agreeable smiling prospects, they are here in abundance. Would you dip into wild caverns, where glimmering light aggravate the horrid view of Rocks and Cavitys & pools of water. Here there are many of them, such indeed as my wildest imagination had never pictured to me'. [12] In the architecture of the antique, it was above all the Sublime that Robert valued. In 1755, his first letter home to his mother from Rome praised above all the Pantheon for its 'Greatness, and Simplicity of Parts', which 'stamps upon you the Solemn, the Grave and Majestick'. Like Mar, he contrasted these qualities with the 'gaity, or Frolick' of 'our modern buildings', but exempted St Peter's from that criticism. [13]

Having completed his Italian stay, Robert Adam moved to England in 1758, largely working from London for the next fifteen years; he practised jointly with his brother James between the latter's completion of his own continental travels in 1763 and his effective retiral from practice in 1773. At that time, a move to London was inevitable for a young architect of Robert's ambition, given the stark imbalance in the 1750s between continuing economic uncertainty at home, and the swaggering ostentation of the London élite in the morning of British power. Adam set about this next stage of his career with relish, writing jokingly home in 1758 as 'my dearest Mother's British boy', and warning that he was 'an architect who expects to despise Inigo Jones as he did Deacon Jamieson'. He published his Spalato work in 1764 as a folio (with perspectives by Clérisseau), in order 'to introduce me into England with uncommon splendour'. In his own work for the London ruling classes, he recognised that he would, above all, have to design for show, to 'blind the world by dazzling their eyesight with vain pomp'. [14]

Although, in 1761, Adam was appointed jointly with William Chambers to the post of Surveyor to the King, the work that was on offer in London was above all concentrated in the field of domestic architecture – just as at home. In England, as in Scotland, there was no large state programme of public monumental building. This posed a potential problem. As Robert and James made clear in their published *Works*, while houses offered ample scope for 'elegance and delicacy of . . . ornamental decorations', they lacked, in the Adams' view, the 'real greatness' of public buildings, which were 'the most splendid monuments of a great and opulent people'; externally, 'the frequent, but necessary, repetition of windows in private houses, cuts the facade into minute parts, which render it difficult, if not impossible, to preserve that greatness and simplicity of composition, which, by imposing on the imagination, strikes the mind'. [15] But the emphasis

on domestic architecture also provided an opportunity. The Adams were greatly advantaged by the fact that, following the spate of large-house construction in early eighteenth-century England, most available work was for remodelling existing houses – the approach which, as we have seen, had long been the norm in Scotland. One of the chief skills of William Adam and others had been to create both classical grandeur and modern 'convenience' inside an, at first glance, unsuitable shell.

In the practical business of house-planning, Robert and James, like their father before them, took their basic principles from French practice, asserting in 1778 that 'a proper arrangement and relief of apartments are branches of architecture in which the French have excelled all other nations: these have united magnificence with utility in the hotels of their nobility, and have rendered them objects of universal imitation'. [16] The balance between 'magnificence' and 'convenience' was now swinging towards more specialised and variegated planning. Especially in view of the continuing decline in royal power, the great or state apartment now seemed a crude and outmoded concept. In Scotland, from around 1750, encouraged perhaps by the shift in landed self-perceptions towards more overt modernity, it was virtually phased out. What was demanded was a more flexible grouping of rooms of different functions, expressed architecturally through different shapes and, even, different styles; there should be tailor-made solutions for each house. Private rooms became more extensive and well equipped: we have almost arrived at the 'private wing' of the early nineteenth century.

Throughout his whole career, the architectonic essence of Robert Adam's style was a transformation of classicism, including both severely 'antique' and Baroque elements, through application of the principles of the Picturesque and Sublime. In this, he was inspired by the great antique and post-Renaissance monuments of Italy and France, by the grander works of recent Scottish and English classicism – above all those of his own father, and those of Sir John Vanbrugh (which he and James labelled 'rough jewels of inestimable value') [17] – and by castles and castellated Renaissance palaces both in Italy and

Scotland. The resulting aesthetic principles were encapsulated in the concept of 'movement', which Robert and James defined as follows: 'Movement is meant to express, the rise and fall, the advance and recess, with other diversity of form, in the different parts of a building, so as to add greatly to the picturesque of the composition . . . the same effect in architecture, that hill and dale, foreground and distance, swelling and sinking have in landscape'. [18] Adam's expression of these principles changed sharply over the course of his career. The first fifteen years were dedicated to the creation of a personal style based on cosmopolitan international classicism. After the mid-1770s, when Robert was effectively practising on his own again, and working more often back home in Scotland, he gave freer rein to his leanings towards romantic eclecticism, launching into more overtly pictorial and sentimental styles: these included both a more theatrically monumental classicism, and a castellated style for country houses.

In Robert Adam's early work in England, then, the principles of 'movement' provided highlights of splendour in work which was mainly concerned with design of suites of rooms inside country and town houses. Adam set out to achieve 'movement' in these English domestic interiors in two ways. First, by differentiating rooms in style and shape – 'a great diversity of ceilings, freezes, and decorated pilasters'. [19] Second, by devising a small-scale yet sumptuous style of patterned decoration which set motifs drawn from Roman grotesques and French Rococo into geometric, compartmented patterns. The Adams mocked the stolid 'correctness' of mid-eighteenth-century classicism: there could be 'nothing more sterile and disgustful, than to see forever the dull repetition of Dorick, Ionick and Corinthian entablatures, in their usual proportions, reigning round every apartment'. They crowed that, through their own diversity and 'movement', 'the massive entablature, the ponderous compartment ceiling, the tabernacle frame . . . are now universally exploded'. [20] We can do no more here than deal in passing with the English commissions of Robert (and James) between 1758 and the late 1770s, summarising this work under its three main episodes or phases. In each, both Robert and James were involved, but the main design innovations stemmed from Robert; the practice's combination of large output and cosmopolitan taste was assisted by the talented draughtsmen employed, including numbers of Italians.

The brothers' English work from the late 1750s to the late 1760s was dominated by country house schemes, some for Scottish aristocrats. The main

4.2 Syon House, London (R. Adam, remodelled from 1762), the anteroom.

schemes included Harewood House (remodelled 1759–71); Osterley Park (remodelled from 1763); Luton Park (1766–74, a new house for the 3rd Earl of Bute); and Kenwood (remodelled 1767–9 for the Earl of Mansfield). The two most monumental were Kedleston Hall and Syon House [4.2]. At Kedleston, working for the 1st Lord Scarsdale from 1761, Adam transformed a scheme by James Paine into an evocation of 'the private edifice of the ancients'. [21] A massive centrepiece modelled on the Arch of Constantine was added to the south front: this facade, with its dynamic interplay between the curves of the dome and the projecting staircase, and the emphatic verticals of the colonnade, showed Adam's 'movement' at its closest to the Baroque. The brothers claimed in the *Works* that 'we really do not recollect any example of so much movement and contrast, as in the south front of Kedleston house'. Inside, in replacement of (in his opinion) 'excessively and ridiculously bad' proposals by James Stuart, Adam designed a columned Great Hall and a saloon beneath the coffered dome. At Syon House (from 1762, for the 1st Duke of Northumberland), Adam's remodelled interior set out to create a 'noble and elegant habitation' [22] in the manner of a Roman palace, with rooms sharply differentiated by shape and decoration. Even the eclectic masters of the nineteenth century could hardly have outdone the contrast between Syon's delicately elegant gallery (1763–4) and the overpoweringly opulent east anteroom. The gallery's elongated plan, hardly susceptible to an architectonic treatment, Adam decorated with two-dimensional detail 'in a style to afford great variety and amusement'. [23] The anteroom was another matter. Whereas early eighteenth-century landed palaces such as Hopetoun had been content with giant pilasters to create the desired grandeur, here in the 1760s only freestanding columns, some shipped from Rome, could suffice to lend an antique weightiness to the brash wealth of the new Britain. The Adams boasted that the Ionic columns, with their idiosyncratic necks, and crowned with gesticulating gilt statues, were treated 'in the most splendid manner of which the order is susceptible'. [24]

The second phase of Robert Adam's English work, peaking in the early and mid-1770s, concentrated on remodelling of London houses such

as 20 St James Square (1771–4), Derby House (1773–4) and Home House (1773–6); most lavish of all was the glass drawing room at Northumberland House (1770).

Thirdly, and finally, from 1768 to 1771 Robert and his brothers embarked with typical confidence on a gigantic redevelopment scheme in London, named the 'Adelphi Buildings'; we will discuss this later in the context of his wider urbanist initiatives at home. By 1773 the brothers felt able to boast, of their architecture in England, that they had 'brought about . . . a kind of revolution in the whole system of this useful and elegant art'. [25]

Of the hundred or so schemes (some unexecuted) for country houses produced by Robert Adam after 1758, thirty-six were in Scotland. But it was above all from the later 1770s and 1780s that the growing economic recovery began to lead to some exceedingly large and grand Scottish commissions, such as Gosford, Mellerstain or Culzean. Among the classical houses, there was, on the whole, a somewhat Gibbs-like combination of rectilinear, even neoclassical restraint – for instance, through flanking wings set in a straight line with the main block rather then curved forward as quadrants – with emphatic, even exotic highlights, including detail culled from Spalato or other sources. Inside, the drive for more complex planning and variegated room shapes made its influence felt. A number of the schemes were for remodelling in the traditional manner. For example, at Glasserton House – a tall house of three storeys and attic built in the 1740s by John Baxter – Robert Adam proposed to add a complex central feature with a thermal window and arched niches; the scheme was eventually built more plainly. At Lauderdale House, Dunbar, a plain, seven-bay house was augmented (1790) with a pavilion at each end, and a semicircular Ionic porch in between. Some schemes involved internal work only, such as the remodelling of Archerfield (*c.*1790) including a toplit domed rotunda.

Many of the new classical commissions were medium- or smaller-sized houses, some just very plain and fairly conventional, others highly inventive in plan. On the whole, the approach was evolutionary: Adam elaborated the plans of his father's and his brother John's smaller houses, adding a touch of 'movement' with at least one

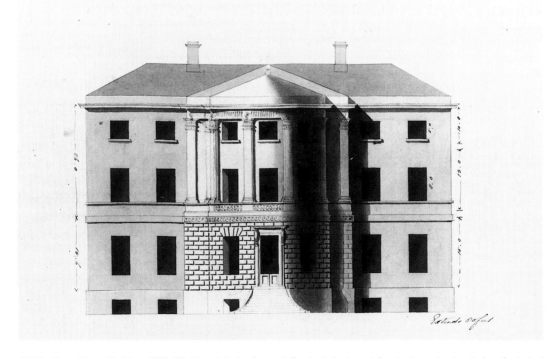

4.3 Newliston House (R. Adam, 1789–91): (above) design for south facade; (below) north facade; (opposite above) plan of principal floor; (opposite below) early 1790s sketch by Robert Adam for drawing-room; the decoration (unusually) was to be in needlework.

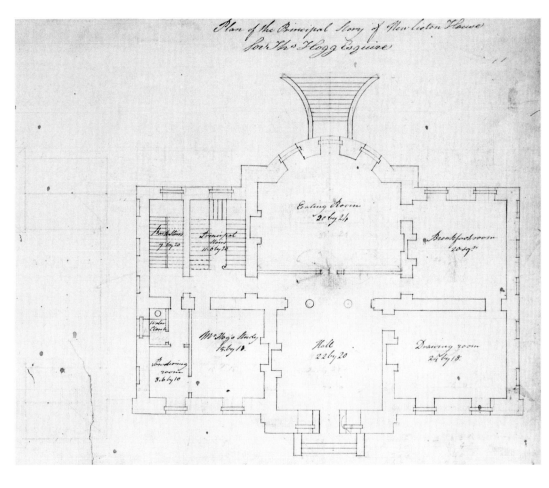

Plan of the Principal Story of New Liston House
for Thos Hogg Esquire

Eating Room
30 by 24

Breakfast room
20 by 9

Water Closet

Powdering
room
8.6 by 10

Mr Hogg's Study
15 by 18

Hall
22 by 20

Drawing room
24 by 18

room of non-rectangular (preferably oval or circular) plan. There was an increasing willingness to spice up modest elevations with pilasters or pediments. The simplest pattern was represented by examples such as Letterfourie (1773), a severe, three-storey block with spindly Corinthian porch and straight wings; Jerviston (1782), basement-less, with straight wings, pilastered entrance front, and circular room behind the hall; Barholm (1788), a two-storey block with straight wings, pediment and relieving arches, and an octagonal breakfast room flanked by dining and drawing rooms; and Balbardie (1792–3), comprising a central three-storey block with Spalato order columns and pilasters, linked to straight wings by arches with columned, apsed recesses. Some of the most severely classical houses were suburban villas – a category to which we shall return later in this chapter. Outside Edinburgh, Bellevue (1774) was a plain, piended box with Spalato order porch, and bowed projection to the garden denoting an oval drawing room on the principal floor. Outside Glasgow, Langside (1777) was pedimented with quadrant wings, pilasters and relieving arch above. A rare Scottish example of an Adam townhouse was 7 (later 8) Queen Street, Edinburgh (*c.*1770, for Lord Chief Baron Ord), a five-bay block with four/five rooms, of varying plans, on both the main floors.

In some classical houses, Adam experimented with more daring plans, and with a more dramatic profile. Where Sir John Clerk in the 1720s had rejected the 'tower' as an inappropriate form for a house, now Robert and James Adam observed that 'we learn from Pliny, that towers were no uncommon conceit even in the villas of private persons'. [26] At Sunnyside, Liberton a 1785 design proposed a tall, pyramidal core with wings, but a later revision (1786) built a flatter piended roof; the plan featured rooms of differing shapes jutting out in three spurs. At Balavil House (*c.*1790–6, for James MacPherson), there was a pyramidal-roofed rectangular tower at each corner, and plain relieving arches between. The most extreme experimental plan was that of Walkinshaw (1792), whose wedge-shaped plan had an octagonal tower at each corner, and paired, flat-roofed towers flanking the entrance; all the rooms on the main floor were curved or octagonal. At Walkinshaw, we

see Robert Adam's classicism at its closest to his 'castles' – to be discussed shortly – as well as to geometrical neo-classicism. The most notable of Robert Adam's medium-sized houses were Kirkdale (1787, for Sir Samuel Hannay), and Newliston (1789–91, for Thomas Hogg). The former, a tripartite-plan house with straight wings, was an exercise in neo-classical severity (and economy) which in some ways anticipated the plain 'Italian' houses of W. H. Playfair and others in the early nineteenth century; it had a canted bay to the garden and low-eaved roofs. At Newliston, a three storey main block featured giant paired Spalato order columns on one side, and a bowed, giant-pilastered projection on the other [4.3].

The most ambitious of Adam's classical house designs in Scotland was Gosford, commissioned in 1790 by the 7th Earl of Wemyss and built in 1792–1803. One of Adam's last and favourite works, Gosford, in its magnificent Forth-side setting, was clearly intended to evoke the majesty of Spalato, the marine palace of a Roman emperor. Its plan realised on the grandest scale the now standard symmetrical frontage of dining room, saloon and drawing room [4.4, 4.5]. These rooms were intended, as at Hopetoun, as a dramatically lit setting for a celebrated picture collection. Gosford's main (west) facade, facing out across the Forth, was treated as an uncompromising rectangular block, with central Corinthian-columned portico flanked by pilasters and with an arched Venetian window in each bay. Inside, the three main rooms, forming a vista of 136 ft, were each lit by one of these arched windows. In style and shape, Adam contrasted the three rooms in an almost theatrical fashion. The dining room was severely treated with a groin vault. The drawing room featured undulating walls and reflective glass beneath an oval dome, clasped at the corners by four marble columns. The saloon, modelled on the *vestibulum* at Spalato, was toplit by the building's central dome. Behind and in parallel to this line of rooms, bedrooms and private apartments were fitted into the overall envelope. As actually built, the design of Gosford was simplified: the three grand Venetian windows were changed to lunettes. The domed wings were demolished in the early nineteenth century by the 8th Earl, but later in the century the 10th Earl, as we will see in Chapter

4.4 Gosford House (R. Adam, 1792–1803), 1880s view of west (Forth) facade during construction of William Young's enlargement scheme.

7, commissioned William Young to rebuild them and recast the house in a more florid classicism. [cf. 7.19]

'Adam Classicism': Contemporaries and Followers

Adam's forging of a new and more individualistic classicism was based, above all, on his direct and active engagement with Roman antiquity in Rome - something that, with the downfall of Jacobitism, seemed less potentially subversive to patrons. A number of other Scottish architects followed in his footsteps to Rome – for instance, John Baxter (in 1761) and John Henderson (in 1774). In some cases, a Roman connection might still be problematic, as was shown by the unsuccessful career of James Byres of Tonley, a Roman Catholic ex-Jacobite who had served in the French army after 1745 and, during the 1760s and 1770s, made a range of wildly unrealistic proposals for grand palaces in a Mar-like style, with central courtyards – including one scheme of 1768 for Sir Lawrence Dundas. None of these was ever built, and Byres instead stayed in Rome as a *cicerone* and art dealer. The only project of any size Byres built, in his retirement back home, was very different to a Baroque palace: a pioneering Catholic seminary at Aquhorthies for Bishop George Hay (1796–9), designed in a plain, self-effacing granite domestic style.

By contrast with Byres's somewhat alienated experience, it was above all Adam's fellow 'London Scots' – during these years of voracious Scottish advances within the new Britain, and English

Wilkesite resentment at the fact – who made it their business to engage with the most advanced tendencies of continental neo-classicism. Four names, in particular, rose to prominence in this way: Robert Mylne and William Chambers (both contemporaries of Adam); and the somewhat younger Charles Cameron and James Playfair. The young Mylne, heir to the Edinburgh dynasty of master masons, triumphed in the *Concorso Clementino* of the Academy of St Luke in 1758 with a design for a great public building in a French neo-classical manner. He then launched into a career with an engineering bias, specialising in design of bridges (including Blackfriars in London, 1760–9, and Jamaica Bridge in Glasgow, 1768–72). Mylne's Scottish domestic work included plain classical houses such as the pedimented Cally House (1763–5) and the two-storey, square Pitlour House (from 1783); at a far more sumptuous level, he installed interiors at Inveraray Castle (1782–9) for the Duke and Duchess of Argyll in a lavish, Adam-like style, and laid out part of the Duke's Inveraray 'new town'.

Chambers, born of Scottish parents in Sweden, was exceptionally widely travelled (including a spell in China), and trained in Paris with Blondel. He exemplified a different kind of cosmopolitanism from Adam's, namely that of the gravity of the French classical tradition, with its greater selectivity and restraint in its embrace of the new Romantic ideas. His taste was described by Adam as 'more Architectonick than Pictoresque'. [27] Chambers, who became the most noted architectural establishment figure of the British state, as tutor to the Prince of Wales and secretary

4.5 Plan of Adam's Gosford scheme, from *New Vitruvius Britannicus*, vol. 1, 1802.

of the Royal Academy, mostly practised in England, but he built a few, influential works in Scotland. Duddingston House (1763–8), for the 8th Earl of Abercorn, was a neo-classical reformulation of the Edinburgh suburban villa [4.6]. Its highly compact tripartite plan concentrated the maximum grandeur in a full-height, coffered entrance hall. Outside, the house conveyed a basement-less, temple-like severity, with hints of the Grecian in the detailing of its fluted Corinthian order; but this was combined with a rustic note in the asymmetrical placing of the office courtyard, set back to one side. Chambers's house for Sir Lawrence Dundas in St Andrew Square (1771–4) was another matter. Situated on one of the prime axial sites in the Edinburgh New Town, its composition was more muted and evocative of English or Dutch Palladianism [4.7]. It was later transformed into a symmetrical composition with two flanking, set-forward blocks (with giant Ionic order) built in 1769 and 1781. Later in this chapter, we will return to another contribution by Chambers to the urban planning of Edinburgh: the building of row-houses in St Andrew Square to a harmonised design.

Charles Cameron, trained in London in the 1760s, was elevated to even greater heights of patronage than Adam, as one of the favoured court architects of an absolutist ruler. In 1779, following an expedition to Rome in 1768 – on which (in contrast to Adam's overtly artistic approach) he made, and later published, a detailed archaeological investigation of the Baths of Trajan and Nero's *Domus Aurea* – Cameron was engaged by the Russian Empress Catherine the Great to remodel and extend her palaces. Catherine lauded him as 'Mr Cameron, écossais de nation, Jacobite de profession, grand dessinateur, nourri d'antiquités, connu par un livre sur les bains romains'. [28] Like Adam's English work, Cameron's most lavish commissions were for the creation of novel interiors – here on an unlimited budget. He, too, relied on eclectic differentiation between apartments, combined with a personal 'style' of decoration based on Roman grotesque ornament. As he built nothing in Scotland, his work falls outside the scope of this account, and we can only briefly list his main imperial works: at Tsarskoe Selo (1779–87), remodelled apartments along with new Cold Baths and Ionic-peristyled Cameron Gallery; and at Pavlovsk, a palace for the Grand Duke Paul (1782–6) and a Greek Doric Temple of Friendship (*c.*1780).

In contrast to the far-flung riches of Cameron's work, James Playfair's practice, although based in London, mostly comprised jobs back home in Scotland. Being nearly thirty years younger than Robert Adam and over a decade younger than Cameron, his continental tours (in 1787 to Paris, and in 1792–3 to Rome) were dominated by the preoccupations of advanced neo-classicism, including visits to Paestum, and familiarity with

4.6 Duddingston House (Chambers, 1763–8), *c.*1960 view.

4.7 Dundas mansion (later Royal Bank of Scotland), St Andrew Square, Edinburgh (Chambers, 1771–4), 1962 view.

the works of Boullée and Ledoux. Playfair's short career (curtailed by his death in 1794 at the age of 39) benefited substantially from the patronage of the key politician Henry Dundas, 'the uncrowned king of Scotland', for whom, as we shall see, he built a castellated villa, Melville Castle. [29] In his classical works, Playfair showed from the beginning a tendency to compose in elemental, unornamented planes and shapes. Even conventional early houses such as the remodelled Bothwell Castle (1787–8) betrayed signs of a cubic horizontality. By 1790, in an unbuilt design for a 'Marine Pavilion' at Ardkinglas, he envisaged an overtly French-inspired rectangular block with flat centre, deep eaves, and strong vertical accents at the ends. James Playfair's masterpiece, Cairness, was built for Sir Charles Gordon, agricultural improver and heir to a Jamaica sugar fortune [4.8]. Its main block, designed from 1788 and built from 1791, was thoroughly neo-classical in its juxtaposition of side end towers (echoing the old Scots classical patterns) and underplayed horizontal centre. The building's construction in light grey Cairngall granite ensured a maximum stereometric sharpness. The court of offices, possibly designed in 1792–3, was the most elemental of all in its geometry, with semicircular plan and blind lunettes with stumpy columns. Inside, studies of 1793 by Playfair showed the development of classical eclecticism beyond the Robert Adam

stage: now Greece was the key, and there were increasingly precise references. The drawing room walls were to give the impression of looking out through the 'Frieze and Ionic Order of the Temple of Apollo Didymaeus in Ionia', including granite columns, marble bases and capitals; and the billiard room's coved ceiling would copy that in 'Nero's Baths at Baia'. [30] Although these elaborate decorations were not executed, an even more exotic, 'Egyptian' scheme was installed in the billiard room, with hieroglyph inscriptions, battered fireplace and door surrounds. Cairness provides a powerful signpost of the new directions in the classical Scottish house, influenced by the sharpness and monumental rigour of France but also exploiting archaeological/eclectic Greek and Egyptian motifs: certainly, Playfair's Cairness correspondence frequently used the adjective 'Grecian'. [31] A later and even more extreme design, the Lynedoch Mausoleum at Methven Church (1793), took the form of a squat miniature Greek temple composed of a stack of heavily rusticated strips [4.9].

If these were the most innovative figures of this period, the 'age of Adam' also saw the creation of an architectural canon which would become the consensual norm of Scottish classicism for decades, until the more general adoption of the Greek in the next century. Of the classical designs of Adam's followers, Richard Crichton's Gask

4.8 Cairness House (J. Playfair, from 1791), (left) detail of court of offices; (below) billiard room.

4.9 Lynedoch Mausoleum, Methven Parish Church
(J. Playfair, 1793).

House (1801), for instance, with its great central
arched element and single-storey portico, was
greatly indebted to Robert's own designs; John
Paterson's Coilsfield (1798), with its semi-
extruded circular section, speaks a language close
to Cameron's work at Tsarskoe Selo; while
Ardgowan House (1797–1801), by Adam's former
clerk of works, Hugh Cairncross, featured an
austerely bow-fronted, stepped composition on
its west frontage. In Preston Hall (1791), by
Robert Mitchell of Aberdeen, the conventional
front facade conceals an austerely cubic rear
elevation with low pavilions. In the north, James
McLeran's pedimented Tarbat House (1787)
carried on, in ashlar form, the earlier traditions
of refined severity. Neo-classical tendencies were
also apparent in occasional designs by English
architects, notably Thomas Harrison's Kennet
House of 1795–9, a severe block with bowed
centre projection on its garden front.

Landscape-Romanticism and the Building of New Castles

The growth of Ossianic national-Romanticism
during the late eighteenth century was at first
expressed, in the visual arts, in classical styles.
When Sir James Clerk commissioned the (Norie-
trained) artist Alexander Runciman to decorate the
ceiling of the saloon at Penicuik, he originally
requested grotesques in the 'Baths of Titus' style.
Then, changing his mind, he renamed the room
the 'Hall of Ossian', and asked Runciman to
decorate it with Ossianic themes, still in a classical
style. But ambiguity soon began to spread
outwards from that very area that was a focus of
controversy in Chapter 3 – the value put on old
castellated dynastic houses. General William
Gordon, laird of Fyvie, who was portrayed in
Highland dress, standing in triumph in front of
Ancient Rome, in Pompeo Batoni's celebrated
painting (1766), later proceeded to extend Fyvie
c.1790 by building a large new tower (the Gordon
Tower) in a style fairly accurately matching
Seton's work. In itself, that did not differ much
from the neo-chivalric castellated additions of the
seventeenth century (for example at Castle Fraser).
A far sharper break was represented by the
building of new, symmetrical castles. Here the
tradition begun at Inveraray was continued from
the 1770s – most significantly by Robert Adam.
His castles were the most obvious result of his
turn, in the mid-1770s, towards a more assertively
picturesque and romantic manner. And they were
a sign of the refocusing of Adam's attention back
towards Scotland, spurred by the country's
accelerating economic recovery, and by the
appearance of younger rivals in England, such as
James Wyatt; by 1772, Adam had already set up an
Edinburgh office.

Robert Adam's castles were new (or enlarged)
buildings which were classical in interior
decoration and even, basically, in plan, but which
were castellated outside, and were intended above
all to be seen against the background of the newly
defined 'Scottish landscape'. From the commencement of Inveraray in 1746 until 1800, thirty
castle projects were built in Scotland, of which
thirteen were by Robert Adam. Adam's castles had
their beginnings in the imaginative reaction of

Robert and his brother-in-law John Clerk of Eldin to the growth of Ossianic Romanticism, as well as to the well-established international landscape movement exemplified in the work of Claude and Poussin. That reaction linked the literary-artistic conventions of landscape to two specific architectural patterns: the castle, and the cottage-orné. Eventually, as we will see later, elements of both would be merged by Sir Walter Scott at Abbotsford.

The first response of Adam and Clerk of Eldin to the developing Scottish landscape movement was an outpouring of paintings and drawings of castles in a wild setting, mostly in a rather generalised 'Norman' style, some with round towers. Then, from around 1770, starting at Wedderburn, Adam began to design new country houses in the form of 'castles'. These took a quitej different form from his imaginative pictures – one more directly related to earlier Scottish patterns.

The most obvious and recent precedent for castellated designs was Inveraray, and John Adam's Douglas Castle [cf. 3.41]. A more indirect influence was that of the castellated palaces and houses of the Scottish Renaissance, examples of which John and Robert had directly worked on in the late 1740s, adding star-shaped bastions during fortress-conversion work in the north-east for the Board of Ordnance. Adam and Clerk had also drawn and painted (in a picturesque style) Scottish Renaissance houses [4.10; cf. 2.8]. Their views about these buildings were transitional between a more or less classical conception of them, and a view (more typical of later generations of Romantic architects) that asymmetry was a basic characteristic of the Scottish Renaissance. Clerk argued in the 1790s that, although not built for defence, such buildings still adhered to 'the principal decorations of the old castle; they were

4.10 Robert Adam, undated view of Holyrood Palace.

4.11 Barnbougle Castle, 1774 drawings by Robert Adam for unexecuted enlargement scheme: (top) perspective of north front and figures; (bottom) principal floor plan.

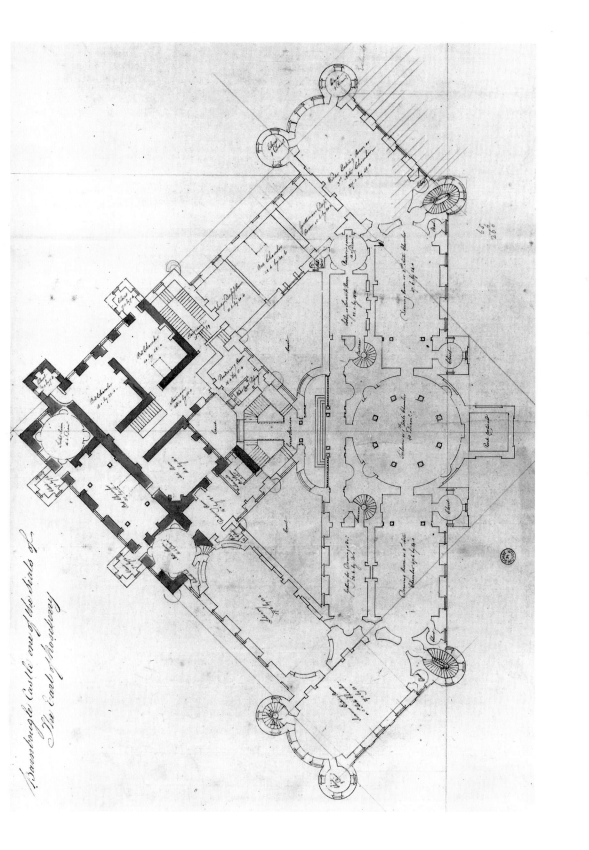

still flanked by towers and surmounted with turrets and battlements, and though their regularity and situation deprived them generally of the picturesque contour of the former yet they continued from their grandeur and effect to be pompous and interesting objects. Of this species of building we have a splendid example in the Heriot's Hospital of this city' [32] [cf. 2.36]. It was Heriot's, along with Vanbrugh's Blenheim Palace in England, that James Adam had singled out in 1762 as key exemplars for the theory of 'movement'. But in his castles just as in his classical architecture, what was important with Robert Adam was not the specific sources but the personal 'style' into which he synthesised them. Just as prominent in forming his castle style were other, more general elements in his philosophy of 'movement', stemming from the stimuli of his Grand Tour: the grandeur of the Roman *thermae*, of triumphal arches, and of Italian Romanesque, Renaissance or Baroque monuments. There was considerable overlap from the beginning between his castles and elements of his classical house architecture, including not only the general principle of symmetry and interior classicism, but also more specific external features of the classical houses: for example, the massive twin-tower gateway on the south front of Luton Park.

This change in architectural taste towards castle-building was facilitated by a spread of Romantic taste among landowners, such as Gordon of Fyvie: 'oldness' was coming back into favour. Sir John Dalrymple, for whom Adam enlarged Oxenfoord Castle in 1780–2, wrote to a friend in 1784 that 'I have repaired an old castle and by the help of Bob Adams have really made it much older than it was . . . it would suit you, who are an Antiquary, perfectly'. [33]

The castellated house designs built by Robert (and James) Adam, either from new or as extensions, fell into two phases. The first was a group of relatively plain, rectangular designs, including Mellerstain, *c*.1770–8 (a new block, with refined classical interiors, built to link existing wings), the bow-fronted, turreted Wedderburn (1771–5) and the plain, crenellated Caldwell (1771–3). From the mid-1770s, there then began a series of far freer, more Romantic designs which exploited the play of light and shade, with the

boldly geometrical shapes of towers and turrets. This second group was inaugurated by an unbuilt scheme of 1774 for the 3rd Earl of Rosebery, which envisaged the reorientation and transformation of the L-shaped tower house of Barnbougle Castle into a dramatic splay-planned block with bastion-like courtyard: in these turreted, triangular forms, there was a striking overlap with classical house design, including both his father's Minto and the neo-classical geometry of his own Walkinshaw [4.11]. A slightly later splay-plan castellated design, also unexecuted, was that for Beauly Castle (1777). Castles which were actually built in this manner included Culzean (from 1777; north elevation from 1785); Oxenfoord (1780–2), Dalquharran (from 1782, and extended 1880 to its present length), Pitfour (attr., *c*.1785), Seton (1790), Airthrey (from 1790) and Stobs (1792–3). In all these cases, severe, tower-like blocks with unadorned, almost neo-classical fenestration were arranged in symmetrical clusters and plan-forms which were designed to be suitable for axial views, but, at the same time, to be 'read' asymmetrically when seen in landscape. A largely unexecuted castellated design was that for Fullarton (1790).

The setpieces of the series of executed castellated designs are Dalquharran Castle, set in a grandiose, open landscape, with a central round tower on one main facade and twin-towered centrepiece on the other; [4.12] and the rugged, north elevation of Culzean Castle, dating from the 1785 remodelling. It was at the 'whimsical but magnificent Castle of Colane' (in the words of Clerk of Penicuik, in 1788), that Adam's patron, the 10th Earl of Cassilis, a lawyer and MP, encouraged the architect to 'indulge to the utmost his romantic genius'. [34] Adam added to Culzean, already enlarged in 1777, a new block containing a circular saloon, library and bedroom suite, and hollowed out an elliptical staircase inside the original section. This created a sequence of contrasting geometrical, classical spaces which exemplified the drama of interior 'movement', but were clad externally in the imagery of the castellated sublime, with the saloon expressed in a heavy, bastion-like round tower offset by an artfully ruinous vaulted causeway [4.13, 4.14].

Both before and after his death, Robert Adam's castellated style, with its tight massing and

4.12 Dalquharran Castle, 1971 view showing Adam central block (from 1782) and Wardrop & Reid wings (of 1880).

4.13 Culzean Castle, 1787 elevation by Robert Adam of north front, showing the new additions (including the main seaward tower).

restricted footprint, was widely imitated. The ex-Adam men John Paterson and Richard Crichton consolidated his work in a series of houses. Crichton's Rossie Castle of *c.*1800, and Paterson's Monzie (*c.*1795–1798) and Eglinton (1796–1803), were plain versions of the Adam castle style, with classical interiors, incorporating planning devices such as oval or circular rooms; Eglinton also reworked Inveraray's compactly symmetrical, corner-towered plan type [cf. 3.41]. Paterson, who had helped manage Robert and James's Scottish practice, set up on his own in 1791, and became the leading post-Adam designer of castles. His practice extended into north-east England, where

his large scheme of alterations and additions at Brancepeth (1818–19) demonstrated the vigorous potential of late Adam massing in its great curtain walls and twin entrance towers. Other lesser examples of the style include Alexander Stevens's Raehills (1782), whose terraced round tower in some ways anticipates the Culzean north tower, and Alexander Laing's Darnaway (1802), a symmetrical design with higher central block, like Mellerstain [cf. 4.13]. The house which represented perhaps the ultimate simplification of Adamesque castellated architecture is probably attributable to Paterson: Fasque (*c.*1809), a composition of stark masses, with simple crenellations and projecting front, with central canted bay (heightened *c.*1840). Here the links to classical designs such as Kirkdale were close; internally, there was a spacious circular domed staircase, the boldest in Scotland of that date. Before long, the castle style was also applied to villa-type designs near Edinburgh. The most prestigious was James Playfair's commission to build a villa-like house, Melville Castle (1786–91), for Henry Dundas. This comprised a symmetrical main block flanked by round angle towers; Playfair also remodelled Kinnaird in a castellated style (1785–93) for Sir David Carnegie. The Edinburgh villa of Charles Gordon of Cluny, Hermitage of Braid (1785), ornamented with Venetian windows, bartizans and battlements, was possibly designed by Robert Burn. We will see in Chapters 5 and 6 that Adam's innovations in castle-Romanticism would give rise to a range of offshoots of increasingly 'national' connotations, including the castellated and Romanesque work of David Hamilton, and, later in the nineteenth century, the mature Baronial of David Bryce.

The end of the eighteenth century also saw tentative efforts to formulate another response to Romantic ideas and landscape in domestic architecture: the primitive artistic cottage. This concept was also bound up with the landscape movement, in this case with the picturesque cottage-orné in the landscape and the garden retreat overlooking the landscape. The pioneering example was built by John Clerk of Eldin in the grounds of Eldin House, Lasswade, some time between 1769 and 1774: a summer-house with ingleneuk chimney and turf roof, nicknamed 'Adam's Hut' after his brother-in-law Robert. There then followed a treetrunk-supported hut at Dalquharran, built *c.*1785 by Robert Adam himself for his niece, Mrs Kennedy; and the more substantial Lasswade Cottage, Lasswade, which Clerk constructed *c.*1781 for his nephew. The latter was an extension of an existing building, and had a thatched roof, bowed drawing room, treetrunk porch and classical interior. [35] Significantly, the Lasswade cottage was rented by Walter Scott in 1798–1804 from the Clerks as his first married home – a

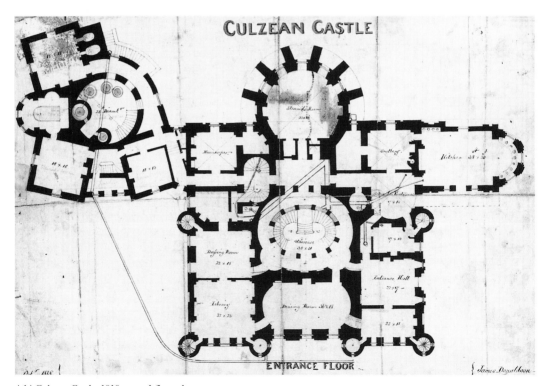

4.14 Culzean Castle, 1818 ground-floor plan.

'little place by the roadside with a view, a garden and one big living room'. [36] We shall return to Scott's role in Chapter 5, in tracing the later development of a more consciously irregular, and more overtly 'national' style of house.

The City as Monument: The Planning of Edinburgh's New Town

Throughout the previous chapter, urban architecture, although full of promise of change, remained a kind of appendix to the main story of the country house. In the next chapter, covering the early nineteenth century, the largest and most prestigious commissions are unambiguously public buildings in towns, and the city as a whole is increasingly exalted as a kind of collective monument. The present chapter thus represents a transitional period. Country houses, on the whole, still enjoyed the highest status. But a revolution was now under way in urban patronage and architecture.

In the movement for building of new communities, a national tradition was now reinvigorated by Enlightenment rationalism in architecture and in economics - for instance, in the argument of Adam Smith that the market should be harnessed through infrastructural work. Eighteenth-century Scotland, along with England, was urbanising and industrialising faster than anywhere else in Europe: the proportion of Scots living in towns rose by 50 per cent between 1750 and 1800. The contribution of architecture to the shaping of this process took the form both of urbanist interventions in existing towns – a movement spearheaded by the planning of the New Town of Edinburgh – and the accelerated creation of new communities in previously rural areas.

The age of rationalism, in established urban settings, transformed the philosophy of improvement. Internationally, the late eighteenth century saw a revitalisation of the longstanding architectural concern with 'the ideal city'. Scottish designers participated in this new phase of utopianism. In 1756, Robert Adam responded to the Lisbon earthquake by putting forward a plan for a completely replanned city laid out in a vast axial and geometrical pattern. Among projects of unified urban planning that were actually built, the grandest were still in France: the Place Louis XV in Paris, with its pediment-flanked, colonnaded ranges, was begun in 1763 by A. J. Gabriel. Alongside these ideal conceptions ran the more pragmatic and longstanding concerns of the rich. All over Europe, but especially in rapidly industrialising Scotland and England, with their privately driven campaigns of improvement, urbanisation and the growth of manufacturing were provoking demands from the landed classes and the urban wealthy for more exclusive living areas insulated from the disease and crime of the old centres. In some ways, this was simply an extension to a city-wide scale of the spatial segregation and specialisation previously seen, in microcosm, in the planning of palaces: now and for most of the nineteenth century, this spatial dynamic – ever outwards, ever more space – seemed uncontentious and accepted by all. In Edinburgh, a further stimulus to more radical change stemmed from the particular historical circumstances of the capital in the mid-eighteenth century – from the disparity between its spectacular intellectual development as a 'hotbed of genius' and its economic and physical stagnation. Although there were still many sumptuous houses in the town, increasing numbers of landowners and the rich were now giving up their houses in town for villas outside. As we saw in Chapter 3, a start had been made in the piecemeal beginnings of purpose-built tenements and row-houses since the late seventeenth century; but on the whole, the town's steep-sided site had remained a fundamental obstacle [cf. 3.43].

Now, in the 1750s, the bold decision was taken to vault right beyond those bounds, by creating a completely new, separate suburb for the rich: the Edinburgh New Town. This concept, it must be emphasised, was directly based on the protourbanist ideas of the late seventeenth and early eighteenth centuries. James VII's suggestion of 1688 had first raised the possibility that the town's dramatic geological constraints could be overcome, and even exploited, by building bridges to the north and the south. It was believed (in 1794) that Bruce had made the first designs for a northward bridge. And Mar had elaborated this idea in a proposal of 1728 to transform Edinburgh from a 'bad and incommodious situation [to] a very beneficial and convenient one', by building 'a large bridge' linking the city to a ridge to the north, on which could be built 'many fine streets' commanding 'a noble prospect of all the fine ground towards the sea, the Firth of Forth, and the Coast of Fife'. [37] It would be the job of Mar's Hanoverian enemies, following the final defeat of Jacobitism, to turn his ideas into spectacular reality.

The prime mover behind the New Town plan was the prominent local politician George Drummond, six times Lord Provost, who had largely been responsible for earlier public projects such as William Adam's Royal Infirmary. The initial proposal was drawn up by Sir Gilbert Elliott and published in 1752: the *Proposals for Carrying on Certain Public Works in the City of Edinburgh*. These proposals differed from those of Mar largely in their greater detail, and in their language, confidently couched in terms of a post-1745 triumphalism and Whig private initiative. They argued that 'now that the rage of faction has abated', the 'general industry and improvement' of Scotland must be the aim. Citing Berlin, London and Turin as examples, they claimed that the most promising catalyst would be to raise the status of the capital city, by constructing a new élite residential suburb, or New Town. With the aim of attracting the rich from their villas and from the existing town (which, from this point on, became generally referred to as the 'Old Town'), the new development would be restricted to 'people of fortune and a certain rank', with 'spacious streets and large buildings, which are thinly inhabited, and that, too, by strangers chiefly, and persons of considerable rank'. [38] It was not intended to empty the Old Town, but to attract merchants to live there: indeed, a centrepiece of the new plans was the construction of one of the most ambitious building projects ever seen there. In 1752, largely at Drummond's instigation, John Adam designed a new Merchant Exchange located in the heart of the Old Town. Built from 1753 (with detail modifications by John Fergus), and subsequently taken over by the Town Council as the City Chambers, it had a U-shaped, pedimented courtyard front of five storeys, not unlike a French or Dutch urban hôtel, while the back walls were of enormous height and sheerness.

The main impulse behind the actual implementation of the New Town plan came from the Town Council. In 1759 the draining of the valley immediately north of the Old Town began, and in 1765 the Council started the building of the three-arched North Bridge across it (designed by William Mylne, younger brother of Robert, and completed in 1772). In 1767, the royalty of the burgh of Edinburgh was extended to cover the area of the new suburb. The Town Council's competition for the layout of the New Town residential area itself, judged by Commissioner George Clerk and John Adam, was won by the young architect James Craig in 1766. Craig's original plan seems to have been in the shape of a British flag, with streets radiating diagonally and at right angles from a central square, but the eventually adopted layout (July 1767) was more severely rectilinear, with a marked east-west orientation. It had a central axis (George Street) with a square at either end; on each flank there was an open-sided street, the northern one (Queen Street) looking north to Fife, and the southern (Princes Street) looking south to the Old Town and castle. Public buildings were incorporated within the overall residential layout: churches were to terminate either end of the axis, but that at the eastern end was displaced by Chambers's Dundas mansion [cf. 4.7], and was instead built on one side of George Street (St Andrew and St George's Church, 1782–7). Other public buildings, not shown on the prizewinning plan, were added in Craig's later versions. The streets were named (or renamed) by King George after Hanoverian dignitaries, and Craig's published version of his plan (1768) was embellished with further British nationalist rhetoric drawn from a poem, 'Prospect of Britain', by his uncle, James Thomson:

> August, around, what PUBLIC WORKS I see!
> Lo! Stately streets, lo! Squares that court the
>   breeze!
> See! Long canals, and deepened rivers join
> Each part with each, and with the circling main
> The whole enliven'd Isle [4.15] [39]

The original plan of the New Town was a startling illustration of the transformation of classicism through the combined influence of urban patronage and neo-classical ideas. On paper, the axial

4.15 Edinburgh, first New Town, 1767 plan by James Craig.

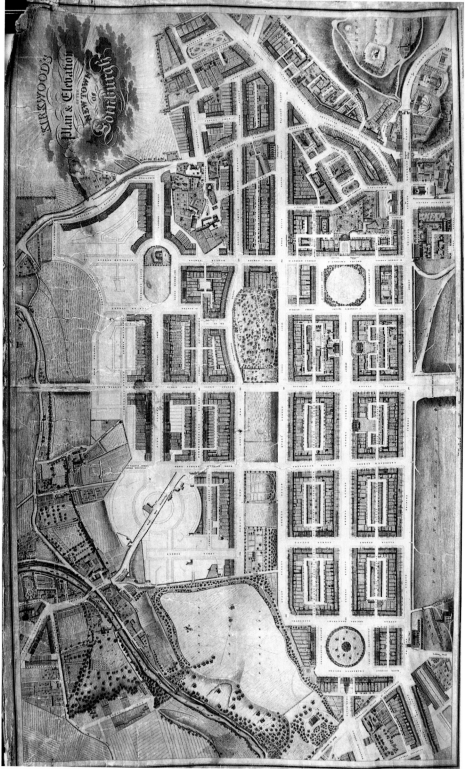

4.16 Kirkwood's 1819 plan and elevation of the first and second Edinburgh New Town developments, and the St James Square and Gayfield areas, including miniature elevations of frontages.

4.17 View from west, *c*.1780, of first New Town (left), North Bridge (centre), and Old Town (right).

layout, with its straight vistas and cross-axes, was redolent of the 'unity and grandeur' of country house landscaping schemes over the previous hundred years. But what had largely disappeared was the overwhelmingly hierarchical character of the latter – an outcome encouraged, of course, by the fact that Edinburgh was no longer the capital of a state, and thus lacked the most strongly hierarchical institutions, such as royal palaces. The public buildings of this planned city, and the dwellings which lined its streets, existed in a far more complex and open relationship. Some of the detailed planning devices of the residential New Town also seemed reminiscent of other different building types, such as the U-shaped, tenement-like barrack blocks at Fort George; austerely classical military buildings, after all, were a prominent feature of late eighteenth-century Edinburgh, with the building of the massive New Barracks on one side of the Castle (1796) [cf. 3.47]. [40]

What was just as remarkable as the formal force of this grand plan for a new 'city as monument', was the consistency with which it was carried out over the following decades, through increasingly restrictive development controls by the Town Council and the private landowners and trusts concerned. There would be six subsequent extension plans, whose execution would stretch well into the next century [4.16, 4.17]. The first streets, around St Andrew Square, were mostly built on the now established pattern of individual row-houses, with flatted tenements at the corners and in some other cases, without any attempt to impose common designs; this was little different to

James Brown's contemporary development of George Square. However, something slightly different was tried by William Chambers in a group of four houses at 23–26 St Andrew Square, built in 1770–2. All of these had three-storey, five-bay fronts faced in stucco, each unit being separated by banded pilasters. Soon the original 1767 feu guidelines were tightened, and 1782 saw the first efforts to get relatively homogeneous ashlar facades. While some large townhouses, such as Robert Adam's 7 Queen Street, were incorporated in the layout from the start, even the more everyday row-house designs became richer as George Street was extended to the west; a giant-pilastered example was 115 George Street (1790). The almost exclusive use of ashlar facade construction from now onwards was the factor which, more than anything else, would set the Edinburgh New Town apart (in general monumental consistency) from its overseas neoclassical equivalents such as St Petersburg, Berlin or Copenhagen.

A further important step towards concerted architectural design in the New Town was taken by Craig, in a scheme for an area to be developed by private speculation at the east end of Princes Street, centred on St James Square. This was the first example of the pattern which was to become dominant in later parts of the New Town, whereby an architect would produce both layout and elevations. Craig's feuing plan for St James Square was dated 1773; the north-east side of the square (1780–6) was a single unified, highly severe, design. Later, as we will see in Chapter 5, it seems that Craig was responsible for the different, even less hierarchical grid which was used in the westward extension of Glasgow. Craig's other works were relatively few, and included, in the New Town, the Physicians' Hall, George Street, 1775–9.

In 1791, an even more decisive co-ordinating initiative in street design was taken by Robert Adam, at the instigation of the Town Council, in his design for the sides of Charlotte Square in the form of grand facades with central pediment and outer pavilions, and giant Orders; similar principles had been employed by the Adam brothers in their London designs (in less monumental materials) for the Adelphi, as well as for Portland Place (from 1774) and Fitzroy Square (1790–4) [cf. 4.19]. At Charlotte Square, a mature, three-dimensional pattern was finally achieved, which would allow future phases of the New Town to be dealt with as monumental architectural and town-planning compositions [4.18]. Eventually, from the mid-nineteenth century (see Chapter 6), a decline in the relative cost of freestone would allow this unified ashlar homogeneity to be extended to rows of dwellings of all classes, across the whole country.

Despite the physical separation of the New Town from the old, and despite the radical regularity of the former's layout, the juxtaposition of the two in the view north from Princes Street established a clear relationship between them, laying the basis for an eventual revaluation of the Old Town as something inherently precious. In a series of more utopian projects by Robert Adam, in his late 'romantic' period of the 1780s and 1790s, this creative juxtaposition of old and new was carried further. The essence of Adam's proposals was that of multi-level planning around 'bridge streets', an idea influenced perhaps by Renaissance utopian schemes such as Filarete's Sforzinda or Leonardo's concept of ground-level commercial life and upper level for the use of 'gentlemen' – or by Piranesi's view of a triumphal decked 'Ponte Magnifico' in his *Prima Parte* (1743). The first practical example of multi-level planning by the Adams had been the Adelphi in London, where they speculatively built a large complex of flatted dwellings on a vaulted base, including so-called 'cottage' dwellings set in the substructures; the composition of the main river facade comprised a palazzo-like main block, with the gable ends of the terrace blocks at right angles treated as detached pavilions [4.19]. In 1771, Robert Adam had also made a design for a 'new town' at Bath, reached by a bridge (the only part of the scheme built to his

4.18 Charlotte Square, Edinburgh (R. Adam, from 1791), early twentieth-century view (following alterations of *c*.1880).

4.19 Adelphi Terrace, London, part elevation by R. & J. Adam, including upper and substructure dwellings (1768–71).

plans) with superstructure lined with shops; a similarly abortive bridge scheme, envisaging flanking housing at upper level and wharves below, was put forward for Ayr in 1785–8.

The most architecturally ambitious of these multi-level proposals, however, were made for Edinburgh. The first concerned the South Bridge, a 19-arched structure over 1,000 feet long, designed by Alexander Laing to link the Old Town with extensions to the south, continuing the line of the North Bridge. In 1785, when the Commissioners for the South Bridge were considering a preliminary proposal to line the bridge with rows of houses like those of the New Town, Adam put forward an alternative scheme for a street flanked by 'colonades [*sic*]' and a monumental substructure spanning Cowgate, with differentially treated private housing and shops. His own 'one connected Design', in which 'every separate House makes only a part of the whole', he contrasted with the Commissioners' proposals:

> The Trustees intention of taking some house in the New Town as a Model, to repeat it through the whole length of the street, would have too much sameness and produce a very unpleasing tiresome effect, especially as there is no House yet built in the New Town that an Architect would chuse as a Model for a Shop to imitate, far less to repeat it through a whole Street. [41]

Craig also put forward a more modest plan in 1786 for an octagon and crescent at the extremities of the bridge. Following an acrimonious dispute between Adam and Lord Provost Sir James Hunter

Blair, the buildings flanking the South Bridge were eventually built by Robert Kay (1786–8) in a much plainer version of Adam's unified design, including pediments at intervals. Further examples of Adam's agglomerative planning proposals included one for Leith Street in 1785, with shops, terrace and dwellings above (built in simplified form from 1786); and a daring sketch design of 1791 for a multi-level 'Bridge of Communication between the New Town and Buildings on the Calton Hill, forming an Entrance to the Old Town by the Calton Street and Leith Wynd' [4.20]. This bridge, for reasons we will return to, was envisaged in both classical and castellated versions; but it was not built. The closest approximation, among surviving buildings, to the scale and general architectural character envisaged by Adam in his multi-level schemes, is the five-storey tenement block of Gayfield Place (from 1790, by the little-known architect James Begg) – a vast rectangular, symmetrical mass with tiny pediments at the top and flanking bow windows. This formed part of the Gayfield estate (feued from 1785), one of a number of autonomous classical developments which sprang up around the edges of both the New and Old Towns.

In social terms, the hopes of the New Town promoters for a suburb of landowners' houses were not realised: although a few aristocrats did build their town houses there, merchants and professionals were by far the dominant groups. In the late nineteenth century, most of the first New Town would be converted to commercial and public use; but even in its initial, residential form,

4.20 Robert Adam, 'Bridge of Communication between the New Town and Buildings on the Calton Hill', proposal (unbuilt) of 1791; the university dome envisaged by Adam is visible on the right. Both classical and castellated versions of the scheme were prepared.

the New Town and its houses became one of the key arenas for the cultural expression of the middle classes' growing power. Inside their dwellings, a neo-classical restraint now governed decorative taste: interiors were understated, with white painted ceilings and woodwork, plain walls, cast plaster friezes and ornaments. The interests of landscaping were served by the creation of a network of pleasure grounds, especially after 1800; the first enclosure of a garden, in St Andrew Square, took place in 1770. Robert Chambers noted in 1825 that these gardens 'brought up to the very door of artificial existence, refreshing and unfailing supplies of the primitive commodities of nature'. [42]

The landed classes who had on the whole avoided the New Town, instead continued their preference for villas just outside the city, as in the case of Lord Moray at Deanhaugh; the kind of plain classicism generally used in these villas was illustrated by Robert Adam's Sunnyside. As early as 1785 the architect David Henderson made an (unrealised) proposal for 'an assemblage of Gentlemen's Villas, bounded upon the outer line by a plantation of forest trees and each Villa situated in such a manner as not to overlook another'. [43] Here the antique/Renaissance vision of Edinburgh in terms of the surroundings of Rome, as at Mavisbank, was brought right up to the edge of the town. For instance, the panoramic vista of the town commanded by David Henderson's three-storey villa for James Rocheid, Inverleith House (1774), appears to be 'aligned' on the steeple of St Giles's, in the manner of Roman

villas and St Peter's. And in 1788, Alexander Nasmyth, the renowned landscape gardener and bridge-designer, and (later) key figure in the fostering of Scottish landscape painting, designed for Lord Gardenstone a prominent eyecatcher by the Water of Leith, St Bernard's Well, which was based on the circular, columned Temple of Vesta at Tivoli.

Public Buildings in Edinburgh and Glasgow

The late eighteenth-century public buildings erected as part of the early New Town development were of relatively moderate size, but, in some cases, innovative design. At St Andrew and St George's Church, George Street, designed by Major Andrew Frazer (1782–7, with tall steeple probably also designed by Frazer, and built by Alexander Stevens in 1787), the Gibbs tradition was reinterpreted with an oval plan and tetrastyle Corinthian portico; Stevens himself probably designed the steeple of St Cuthbert's Church (1789–90). Another novel church, of neo-classical, Greek-cross plan, was built outside Edinburgh at Lasswade in 1791; it was possibly designed by Robert Adam's brother-in-law, John Clerk of Eldin. Among secular New Town buildings, a similarly adventurous neo-classical severity was shown in John Henderson's Assembly Rooms (1782–7), an austere stone rectangle, planted on a rusticated base; the pedimented portico was added later, in 1817–18, by William Burn.

A decisive expansion in scale and aspirations was brought to this field of building by Robert

Adam. Although most of his career had been devoted to the transformation of domestic architecture with his eclectic innovations, he still harboured a deep-seated 'desire to raise a great building of a semi-public nature in the monumental manner'. [44] Where the old dominant building types, such as palaces, had combined elements of the public and private, now there began to emerge the kinds of unambiguously public institutional buildings which would represent the most prestigious monumental classicism in the nineteenth century. From the mid-1770s, the economic revival of Scotland enabled Adam to become involved with a series of grand public projects in Edinburgh and Glasgow.

In Edinburgh, Robert Adam built two great public institutions – Register House and Edinburgh University – which were inspired by the model of the palace facade, and which rejected the now old-fashioned idea of the U-shaped courtyard, as seen in the Merchant Exchange of only twenty years earlier. Register House was built in an axial position commanding the northern end of North Bridge. Adam was awarded the job in his capacity as Architect of the King's Works with responsibility for Scotland; this was the first major public building commenced in either Scotland or England for several decades [4.21]. His plan (1771) envisaged a domed rotunda within a quadrangle – a concept which owed much to his own earlier proposal for Syon House and thus, ultimately, to Mar's schemes. The main facade was sober and even neo-classical; it had a plain upper storey over rusticated arches, with a relatively small

central portico flanked by turreted outer pavilions; inside was a wide, coffered dome. The first section was built in 1774–90; the whole building was completed in 1822–34 by Robert Reid.

In contrast to this restrained display, Adam's University College design conveyed a resounding, even triumphal character, reflecting Adam's move, even within the classical framework, to a more assertively romantic manner. This was not a government commission, but almost a personal crusade for Adam; he wrote in 1789 of 'this great and important Work, which I had so much at heart', and explained to the university trustees that 'I have been infinitely more activated by the motive of leaving behind me a monument of my talents, such as they are, than by any hope of gain whatever'. [45] His plan envisaged a courtyard block, the main east facade with projecting wings and a central portico featuring six giant columns formed of Craigleith monoliths. The portico's yawning central arch had pedestrian side-arches and a Gibbs-like semi-circular window above [4.22]. This was a kind of ashlar-faced grandeur that, in the Scotland of Sir William Bruce or even William Adam, could only have been commanded by kings or top nobles. The passing on of grand monumental patronage to collective secular institutions was celebrated, together with hints of the tradition of Scots royal antiquity, in a bold inscription above the central entrance: its most prominently emphasised lines associated the original foundation of the university in 1583 by decree of 'Jacobi VI Scotorum Regis' with the design of the present building by 'Architecto

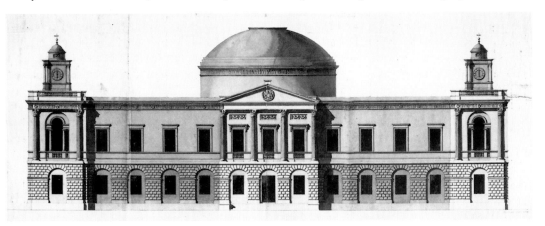

4.21 General Register House, south elevation by Robert Adam, 1776.

Roberto Adam'. Building began in 1789 but halted in 1793, for several decades, for lack of money. As Sir Nathaniel Wraxall noted in 1813, 'The front as it now stands presents a very majestic appearance, but it is more like a palace for a sovereign than a college'. [46] Adam's own romantic conception of this building was underlined in his 1791 Calton Hill 'Bridge of Communication' drawing, in which the University rears up as a vast domed structure, almost in the later manner of Alexander Thomson [cf. 4.20, C.]. The influence of the Adam style in the public buildings of others was seen in the Merchant Company Hall, Hunter Square (1788–90), with three big round-arched and over-arched windows; its architect, John Baxter the younger, was equally capable, in small burghs, of designing in a more traditional style, as shown by his stumpy, steepled Peterhead Town House of 1788.

Although the new Romantic neo-castle style was originally specifically associated with country houses, it also found gradually increasing use in urban public buildings. The first of these was located, appropriately, on the Calton Hill, a patch of wilderness right next to the town. From 1776, James Craig built the Old Observatory House, a simplified Gothic structure and the first of a cluster of pavilions and monuments on the hill: Robert Adam had suggested to Craig that the building should look like a fortification. The following year (1777), Adam himself built there a severely 'antique' circular monument to David Hume, evocative of the rugged tombs outside Rome. And in 1791, he commenced on the sides of the hill what was probably his most innovative single design: the Bridewell prison (1791–5) [4.23]. The Bridewell philosophy of incarceration, which emphasised reform over punishment, might have suggested a severely neo-classical expression. Indeed, the panopticon plan Adam designed (at the suggestion of Jeremy Bentham) for the Bridewell, with its comprehensive provisions of surveillance, was assertively rationalist. But the chosen architectural style was, in the event, a castellated manner similar to his castles, and inspired chiefly by Scottish Renaissance works: one unexecuted scheme for the jail showed the main block flanked by twin towered pavilions in the manner of Holyrood (which the Bridewell overlooked), while some aspects of the plan, such as its embedded

round tower, were also related to Adam's castle designs. None of the surviving designs for the Bridewell relate exactly to the finished building, which stood on the site now occupied by Tait's St Andrew's House. The aim of the Bridewell's romantic form was perhaps to exalt the untamed quality of Calton Hill as a foil to the rational world of the New Town. The Bridewell was also doubtless related to the castellated variant of Adam's 1791 Calton 'bridge-street' proposal.

As the 1752 document had predicted, the Edinburgh spirit soon infected other towns, big and small. In Glasgow, Aberdeen and other large centres, the large-scale town-planning extensions mainly occurred after 1800, and will be dealt with in Chapter 5. However, Glasgow also saw a flurry of proposals for great monumental buildings by Robert Adam in the last year of his life (1791–2), working with James Adam and initially assisted by John Paterson. This series of projects would be of the greatest significance for the future, in whetting the appetite of Glaswegians for a more monumental and dignified planning of their booming town.

4.22 Edinburgh University main front (R. Adam, from 1789; including 1886–7 dome by R. Rowand Anderson), view of *c*.1930.

4.23 Alexander Nasmyth, *Edinburgh, from Calton Hill*, 1825, detail showing the Bridewell (R. Adam, 1791–5) at left foreground, and the Old and New Towns in the background.

4.24 Glasgow Assembly Rooms, late nineteenth-century photograph, showing central Adam section (1796–8) and wings. The building was demolished *c*.1890, and the Adam portion was partially re-erected by Glasgow Green as the McLennan Arch.

The end of the eighteenth century was witnessing a shift in Glasgow's commercial base from tobacco to cotton, and piecemeal efforts at 'New Town' extensions had begun. St Enoch Square was laid out from 1768 (by the Town Council), George Square from 1782, and St Andrew's Square from 1786 (around the church, by William Hamilton). It was in Glasgow, with its growing capitalist vigour, that the commercial slant of Robert and James Adam's proposals struck a particular chord: most of them included ground-floor shops, rationalising a previously sporadic activity which, as today, helped finance residential and public schemes. In one scheme, for the Tron Kirk, they offered the alternative of keeping or demolishing the Tron steeple and erecting shops through which the church would be reached. Robert's earlier motif of coupled columns framing a central aedicule set on a heavily rusticated podium was used again, here in combination with a domed turret, at the Trades' Hall (1791–4); the Assembly Rooms (built 1796–8 to the Adams' designs) also had paired, advanced Ionic columns and a rusticated basement forming a triumphal arch motif, and wings with shops (not built until the early nineteenth century) [4.24]. Perhaps the most important of the Adams' rush of Glasgow public buildings was the Infirmary (1792–4; a project secured by the Adams after the death of the originally appointed designer, William Blackburn). Here, like Register House, the main elevation, with its typical late Adam relationship of wings and core, seems in some ways heavy and conservative, but also recalls the earlier, more vigorous hybrids such as the south front of Kedleston or the anteroom at Syon; as with the grand terrace fronts, the elevation bears little relation to the internal layout, which featured, on its fourth storey, a central aisled rotunda with wards on each side. In a castellated vein, Robert and James's Glasgow proposals also included an unusual scheme of 1791 for Barony Church, with a Fyvie-like triumphal arch with gable, caphouse and optional crowsteps (built in a different form and demolished 1889).

After Robert Adam's death in 1792, James Adam carried through to completion, sometimes reluctantly, Glasgow works such as the Infirmary, where the brothers had put in proposals at no profit because Robert 'was keen to have the job for fear of its being spoilt'. [47] A scheme of pedimented, four-storey tenement blocks built speculatively by the university on High Street, flanking College Street (built 1793) was probably designed by James Adam. Some of the brothers' schemes were unrealised or scaled down – but they had planted the seeds of monumental grandeur in Glasgow public architecture. Involved in some of the Adams' projects, in all likelihood, as an assistant, was the young David Hamilton, soon to become a dominant figure in the eclectic classical development of central Glasgow in the early nineteenth century.

Town Planning in the Country

The trend of settlement-creation by landowners, whose beginnings we noted in Chapter 3 in cases such as Inveraray, accelerated under the new economic conditions into a massive social and demographic upheaval [cf. 3.44]. Across the Lowlands, the late eighteenth century saw a wave of replacement of many 'fermtouns' by farms, and resettlement into villages and small towns, linked to new communications. The process was already under way by the early eighteenth century in the Lothians; by the late century, the movement of settlement-planning (or the extension of existing small burghs) was spreading like wildfire. Spurred on now by the example of the Edinburgh New Town, axial grid plans with squares and, sometimes, symmetrically placed public buildings sprang up across the whole country. The momentum thus built up would endure throughout the nineteenth century. For example, in the far north, as late as 1908, a proposal to break the building line of King Harald Street in Lerwick provoked pleas that the 'general symmetry, regularity and general appearance' of 'the principal and the model street of our New Town' should be upheld. [48] And at the other end of the country, in the far south, the grid layout of Newcastleton (or Copshawholm), founded in 1793 by the 3rd Duke of Buccleuch as a model weaving community with one main street and three squares, was still being infilled with rows of new houses (mostly single-storey) up to the First World War [4.26].

The most dramatic explosion of planned settlement-building and expansion was in the north-east. In a Moray equivalent to Inveraray, John Baxter, who had carried out a castellated remodelling of Gordon Castle in 1769–82 for the 4th Duke of Gordon, then proceeded to lay out the nearby new town of Fochabers from 1776 on a grid plan. Its central square contains a representative group of severely classical public buildings. The focus is Bellie Church (1795–7), a plain, piend-roofed box, still essentially in the Gibbs tradition, with a severe tetrastyle portico and steeple. It is flanked by a pair of two-storey blocks (with blind semicircular arcades) of *c*.1800: the townhouse and a house for the baron-bailie. The remainder of the centre of Fochabers was mainly built up in the nineteenth century. Elsewhere in the north-east, the density of settlement foundation was such that two grid-plan new towns, New Keith (founded by the Earl of Seafield *c*.1750) and Fife Keith (founded by the Earl of Fife, 1817), stand right next to each other. New settlement-building also resulted from landowners' forced movements of tenants for 'amenity' reasons, as Ker had advised at Ancrum over a century before and as Argyll put spectacularly into practice at Inveraray. Bowmore village, Islay – axially focused on a circular church – was founded in 1768 by Daniel Campbell of Shawfield and Islay to allow removal of the village of Kilarrow from next to Islay House; 110 new houses were completed by 1793 [4.26].

Some planned settlements were more specifically dedicated to industry, and here, the growing concentration of industrial effort in the 'Central Belt' became more obvious. In many cases, these projects were landowner-driven. Charlestown, in Fife, founded in the 1770s by the 5th Earl of Elgin to house workers at his nearby limeworks, was laid

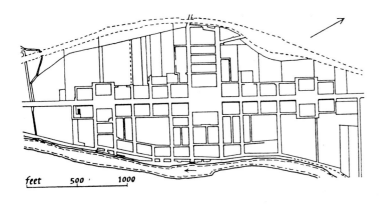

feet 500 1000

4.25 Twentieth-century plan of Newcastleton (or Copshawholm), Roxburghshire (from 1793).

4.26 High Street, Bowmore, Islay (founded 1768), 1976 picture.

4.27 New Lanark (from 1785), 1975
aerial photograph.

out as a long rectangle with 'improved' cottages. Other projects were devised by non-landed entrepreneurs. The boldest new rural industrial settlement of all, and the most symbolic of the nascent industrial might of the Clyde Valley, followed this pattern: New Lanark, an integrated group of six-storey cotton mills and workers' tenements, built from 1785 by David Dale (in partnership with Richard Arkwright) in the romantic setting of the Falls of Clyde, a precipitous gorge of Covenanting fame [4.27]. The housing at New Lanark was a simple development of the row patterns already established in late seventeenth century Edinburgh. The mills were in a similar,

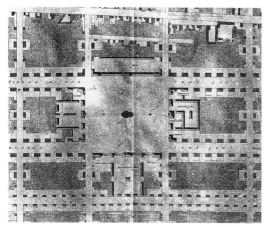

4.28 W. Hastie, plan for the central part of Tsarskoe Selo new town, 1809 (laid out near the royal palace of the same name).

plain classical manner – a style repeated in other large contemporary industrial schemes, such as the four-storey range which survives at Calderhaugh Mill, Lochwinnoch (1789).

Beyond Scotland, the New Town formula of planned settlement spread its influence far and wide. For example, William Hastie, who travelled to Russia at Charles Cameron's invitation in 1784, and assumed charge of the imperial city-planning service between 1808 and 1832, planned countless new towns across the Russian empire on the grid-like patterns established by Craig's Edinburgh scheme [4.28].

Conclusion

In this chapter, we traced how the unitary values of classicism began to break down under the pressure of conflicting ideals, including rationalist planning and irrational individualism. These were the years dominated by the multi-faceted innova-tions of Robert Adam, and by the impact of the first Edinburgh New Town. During this time, the growing wealth and urban-based diver-sity of society also started to undermine the previous hierarchical patronage relationships. Now the stage was set for a vast expansion of the building programmes of social and economic modernity, and for the flourishing of a vast range of eclectic 'styles' in which they could be expressed.

Chapter 5

1800–1840

Romantic Classicism and the Emergence of 'National' Architecture

'Imagine a city girded to the north and east by the Firth of
Forth, that backs on to a mountain at least eight hundred feet
high, whose crest is frequently hidden by clouds, and on whose
slopes, extending south and westwards, the city is built.'
                    Gustave d'Eichthal, on Edinburgh, 1828

'. . . an old-fashioned Scotch residence, full of rusty iron coats
and jingling jackets.'
    Sir Walter Scott, on his proposed house at Abbotsford, 1816 [1]

Introduction

Driven by wealth, patronage changes and the
increasing complexity of architectural ideas, the
early nineteenth-century development of Edinburgh
fused the rationalist and the Romantic in
spectacular fashion. The schematic grid of Craig's
plan was replaced by an overall concept of a
classical, especially Grecian Sublime – a city
'image' into which was integrated a more and
more complex range of building types and
planning innovations [5.1]. Edinburgh's spirit
would be rivalled by the very different urbanist
developments of Glasgow, which addressed new
building tasks and challenges even more fearlessly.
The west-east bipolar architectural culture of
modern Scotland, with all its creative tensions and
contrasts, was beginning to emerge. But at the
same time as all this diverse city-building activity,
rural architecture was also in ferment. The
clinically rational planning abilities of William
Burn reshaped the country house along more
informal, and more hierarchically efficient, lines;
while Sir Walter Scott developed a new, more
complex and in some ways anti-urban Romanticism,
which would eventually displace the individual
genius by the national community as the focus of
Romantic attention.

The Architecture of Imperial Scotland

The Napoleonic Wars provided a new, more
intense focus for British nation-building ideology:
Scotland now saw its destiny as eternally wedded to
that of England not just in trade and commerce but
even in survival. In 1803, for instance, Dr Thomas
Chalmers, the future evangelical church leader and
Tory, rallied support for volunteer battalions
against the 'cannibal banditti' of Napoleonic
France. [2] After 1815, the world-revolutionary
epoch threatened by 1789 seemed finally to have
run its course, and the way seemed clear for
stability and growth. Now, the British Empire
encompassed 20 per cent of the world's
population. Scotland, wholeheartedly welcomed
in the joint crusade of Protestant imperialism,
participated equally voraciously in its counter-
part at home: industrial expansion, concentrated
especially around Glasgow. The onward march of
'improvement' into the new industrialising urban
centres was epitomised in the work of James
Cleland, a Glasgow wright and builder who became
an indefatigable pioneer of urban improvement in
the city, both through his own entrepreneurial and
rationalistic schemes (especially during his time as
the Town Council's Superintendent of Public
Works, 1814–34) and through his internationally

5.1 Mid-nineteenth-century capriccio of the 'Monuments of Edinburgh' by David Rhind; the Royal Institution, the Free Church College and the Tolbooth Church are pictured in their actual relationship [cf. 5.10, 5.23].

renowned statistical publications, including the unprecedented innovation of a classified census of Glasgow in 1819.

But this rampant push for growth had its darker side. Industry's ability to attract workers to the new urban centres led to growing social tensions. From the end of the eighteenth century, there was an increasingly sharp differentiation between an urban bourgeoisie and, flanking it socially, the landed classes and the new category of the 'poor'. Attempts to remedy the resulting social disintegration included both political reform – culminating in the Reform Act of 1832 – and religious evangelical zeal. In the country, the scope of improvement expanded further, with the 'opening-up' of the Highlands through large-scale road and bridge building; in the first three decades of the nineteenth century, Thomas Telford built over a thousand bridges, including daring structures such as the iron-arched, towered Craigellachie Bridge (1814–15) [5.2]. The process of rural improvement was linked to large-scale emigration to the colonies – a further engine of colonial-based industrial expansion.

The architectural response to these revolutionary accelerations of improvement was a complex one, which elaborated on the themes of the Scottish Enlightenment, while at the same time devising new Romantic formulas. The concern for rationalist building construction, so strong in French architecture, enjoyed a less elevated status in Scotland: that was evident, for example, in the essentially practical researches and publications of Peter Nicholson into the systematising of building technology – a wide range of compendia, practical guides and scientific pamphlets which laid down, almost single-handedly, much of the basic principles of nineteenth-century building. Rather, the key intellectual elements of Enlightenment thinking in Scottish architecture were concerned with spatial patterns, and their relation to the continuing human activity of improvement. The results of this refined architectural rationalism were far more complex than the old formulas of planted grids of new towns or improved country-estates and seats. An emblematic built realisation of early nineteenth-century Enlightenment architectural ideals was William Playfair's Royal

5.2 Craigellachie Bridge (Telford, 1814–15), 1963 view.

Institution, a massive Greek Doric colonnaded monument built 1822–6 and extended in 1832–5 [cf. 5.1, 5.10]. Occupying a focal position in several of the axial, classical vistas of Romantic Edinburgh, the Institution – a building as grandiose as a major country house – functioned chiefly as the headquarters of the Board of Manufactures, the agency which was dedicated to the fostering of 'quality' Scottish goods for export by encouraging competitive self-improvement. By the 1820s, under its secretary James Skene, the Board had become a powerhouse of innovation, and had extended the principle of rationalist improvement to art, through the agency of its design school (founded 1760); its teachings fed reforms in such fields as interior decoration and municipal architectural design, but also contributed to the Board's task of strengthening the Scottish economy. In this chapter, we will encounter a wide variety of attempts at a rationalist spatial structuring of social activity and of improvement.

This period saw a major shift in patronage, from the landed and the rural towards the bourgeois, urban and institutional – just as the landed classes had displaced the Church and the monarchy after the late sixteenth century. Some lairds were still extensively involved in urban development through the setting of feuing restrictions as they surrendered their villas and developed the lands. And, with the unrivalled prosperity enjoyed by the landed interest around 1800, the building of country houses by aristocrats and lairds, or newly rich proprietors, was expanded. Some, notably Hamilton Palace, upheld the tradition of classical splendour, while those designed by William Burn used a variety of styles to clothe plans as rationalist as any new town layout [cf. 5.31, 5.32, 5.34]. While, socially, the landed classes became more assimilated to a unitary 'British' nobility, the relationship between this trend and the architecture of their houses was complex: the latter tended towards a more and more assertively 'national' expression. Yet all this landed building activity was progressively outpaced by the even more rapid development of urban and middle-class wealth. The post-Industrial Revolution urban building types controlled by the middle classes became larger and grander in scale than the houses of the landed classes. A whole range of public buildings was promoted by new institutional bodies, such as boards and parliamentary commissioners, or municipal authorities. Activities previously housed in utility structures were now accommodated in special monumental buildings. There was a proliferation of libraries, academies, museums, professional institutions, prisons, court-houses and other such types [cf. 5.1]. Compared to the strong central state role in some continental countries, this public patronage was at this stage relatively decentralised in Scotland, with a prominent role played by voluntary mechanisms like subscription associations. Other new urban building types directly served the interests of urban capitalism, such as banks, insurance offices, or shops; more indirect was the role of the new, specialised residential areas, ranging from speculatively built workers' and middle-class tenements to detached villas for the urban rich.

The emergence of a consolidated Scottish bourgeois 'identity' had obvious implications for architects. Both Edinburgh and Glasgow (and, to a lesser extent, Aberdeen) had now developed clusters of architects of a status ranging from the national to the local. Regional architects, too, were beginning to emerge, in other towns: designers such as Walter Newall in Dumfries, William Stirling in Dunblane, or William Robertson in Elgin handled a wide range of buildings in their areas, including country houses, churches and public buildings. While the establishment of national and regional institutions still lay in the future (in the 1840s), professional demarcation lines were hardening. By the 1820s Thomas Telford, who had previously acted as architect of a variety of buildings, had become established as head (in both Scotland and England) of the new and separate profession of civil engineering.

The post-1815 years of British triumph, paradoxically, were combined with a new and confident assertion of *Scottish* nationality, replacing the uncertainties of 'North Britain' by a new, proudly 'national' Imperial Scotland. The development of modernised capitalist and colonialist states in the nineteenth century was, as a rule, associated with the development of increasingly coherent ideological conceptions of the 'national'. Post-1815 Scotland, because of its unique position as a culturally autonomous nation within the world's most powerful state, was able to project on a global scale a new and highly specific set of images of itself. These were founded on the existing prestige of Ossian and further accentuated by the achievements of Sir Walter Scott – the world's first historical novelist, and one of the leaders of the international trend to heighten Romanticism and modify the early Scottish Enlightenment's ideas of simple, linear intellectual and material Progress. Architecture played a key part in Scott's efforts – as we can see, for example, in his organisation of the visit of King George IV to Edinburgh in 1822, when the city was itself laid out as a theatrical arena of living history; and in his building, or rather rebuilding, of his own Borders house, Abbotsford, in the image of 'an old-fashioned Scotch residence' – a project we will discuss in detail at the end of this chapter [cf. 5.46, 5.47, 5.48]. [3] Conversely, the wartime and early post-war years were also a time of unusual English influence in several areas of Scottish architecture. For example, the prolific work of William Burn was indebted in key respects to that of his master, Robert Smirke; and Gothic's lack of 'national' connotations in Scotland allowed the widespread adoption of the English 'Perpendicular' style in many new churches. As we will see in Chapter 6, the mid-century years saw a continuing English impact on some church architecture; however, by the time of Burn's move to England in 1844, the earlier links in secular architecture had almost disappeared.

The Hellenic Vision

The chief architectural expression of both the revolutionary, modernising urban society and the new, Romantic Scottish nation was at first one and the same thing: a Romantic neo-classicism. The novelty and the 'national' character of this architecture was symbolised by one element above all, namely a stately Greek style. The identification of monumental classical architecture with national identity had begun in seventeenth- and eighteenth-century France, where Claude Perrault's Louvre colonnade was hailed in 1740 as 'le portrait du caractère de la Nation'. [4] In the trabeated construction and severe, rectilinear character of neo-Grecian architecture, countries ranging from the United States to Norway and Russia saw not only a new purity but also a symbol of their national dignity. In Scotland, while there is no indication that the centrality of 'Greek ancestry' in the old national origin myth was any longer seen as significant, the images of Greek antiquity nevertheless now made an enormous impression, displacing Rome as the main inspiration for a national classical grandeur. In the building of classical Edinburgh during this period, as in the case of Washington or Helsinki, an austere Greek unity seemed the defining element.

The period of Grecian ascendancy coincided with the neo-classical insistence on treating the city, including its residential areas, as a single architectural monument. The new wealth, and the call to build public monuments, encouraged not only individual setpieces but also a new, architecturally unified expression of town planning. More prosaically, it was at just this time that ashlar classicism began to become generalised for most classes of buildings. This was due above all to the prolific availability of good building stone, helped by improvements in aspects ranging from machine tools (from the 1820s) to transportation. Increasingly the older type of rubble, wood and thatched buildings could be excluded from towns. Even within stone building, there was a trend to increasingly precise and homogenised techniques: for example, David Hamilton of Glasgow was able to specify sandstone from a single quarry for many of his principal buildings, wherever they were located.

But neo-Greek architecture never became all-embracing in its scope. It itself had stemmed from a drive for a new variety and precision within classicism, rejecting the Adamesque evocation of different classical 'moods' as no longer specific enough; and now other stylistic recipes or combinations of recipes flourished alongside it, to express the 'personalities' of all the new building types. By the 1830s, Grecian public institutions were built alongside Roman banks, Baroque churches and Gothic monumental spires; the Grecian upsurge in mid-century Glasgow would have an even more radically eclectic context [cf. 5.1].

These developments in stylistic practice were linked to a great diversification in the means of disseminating architectural information. Just as, at the end of the eighteenth century, the neo-classical architects had rejected pattern-book publications such as Chambers's *Treatise*, with their aristocratic universalism and deference to authority, in favour of artistic individualism and accurate, first-hand investigations of antique remains, so now, in the early nineteenth century, the importance of the latter faded in the face of a proliferation of published sources. These included new, eclectic pattern books – such as the encyclopaedic publications (from 1799) of J.-N.-L. Durand, professor of architecture at Napoleon's École Polytechnique – as well as books on contemporary architects of international standing. A culmination in the stress on Greek archaeology seemed to have been reached in the 1822 proposal to erect a National Monument to the Napoleonic war dead on Edinburgh's Calton Hill in the form of an exact 'facsimile of the Parthenon'. [5] To ensure accuracy, the eminent English architect-archaeologist C. R. Cockerell was engaged to draw up the designs, which were then (partly) completed under the supervision of W. H. Playfair. But this proved to be the end, rather than the beginning of a movement. Within Playfair's own consummately refined *œuvre*, which included an increasingly eclectic range of styles alongside the Grecian, Mediterranean travel played virtually no role, while study of books such as the *Sammlung architektonischer Entwürfe* of K. F. Schinkel, illustrating projects in a city (Berlin) of previously little international architectural prestige, were crucial. On his only visit to Italy, to seek medical treatment in 1842, Playfair found 'little to admire and a great deal to shudder at' in Florence. [6] The classical fastidiousness of designers such as Playfair masked a stylistic individualism which was more and more radically undermining antique propriety and precedent. And by the end of the period covered in this chapter, the force of archaeological investigation was decisively shifted, by George Meikle Kemp, to an explicit pursuit of 'national' styles at home.

The main driving force of the early nineteenth-century movement for Grecian classicism in Scotland was a reaction against the elaborate Roman geometry of Robert Adam towards lower and more severe forms, and a desire for a studied simplicity of elevations, with sharply fluted Doric and Ionic porticoes. The only standing building in Scotland up until then which provided any precedent for these aspirations was Chambers's fifty-year old Duddingston House. The 'establishment' position at the turn of the century, against which the Grecians reacted, was represented by the work of Robert Reid, who built a variety of monuments and streets in Edinburgh and Perth in a post-Adam classical style during the 1800s and 1810s, and then went on to hold the post of Master of Works and Architect to the King in Scotland between 1824 and 1839. His Adamesque public buildings (such as St George's Church, Edinburgh, 1811–14) employed the compositional devices of 'movement' in a heavier form, while his layout (with William Sibbald) of the northern extension of the New Town in 1801–4 was followed by elevations for several streets, including Heriot Row (1802–8), in a simplified Charlotte Square manner.

The architect who, more than any other, took up and carried forward (until his own premature death in 1813) the revolutionary neo-classical tendencies previously sketched out by James Playfair was William Stark. He was, significantly, based in Glasgow for almost all of his career – the first of many mentions of that city as a home of monumental classical architects. Stark's mature work, contained within the single decade 1803–13, laid down a wide range of leads for others to follow, including classicisms that varied from a severely Grecian Doric to a complex Baroque, and programmes which encompassed lunatic asylums

and a cottage-orné for Sir Walter Scott. He was born in Dunfermline, and perhaps the Adamesque work and Italian travels of his brother-in-law, John Craig, may have been an early influence. In our first record of his working career, in 1798, we find him at St Petersburg – one of the great centres of European neo-classicism. Invigorated by the architectonic power of Imperial Russia (and, doubtless, by the splendour of Cameron's works at Pavlovsk and Tsarskoe Selo), Stark returned home and began practice in 1803. He won the competition for the Hunterian Museum at Glasgow University, defeating a number of others, including David Hamilton [5.3]. In this, the first of a group of Scottish neo-classical projects which sought to express scientific or medical rationalism through centralised plans, Stark designed a domed, Roman Doric-porticoed three-storey building (erected 1804–5), to house the collections of the pioneering surgeon and anatomist William Hunter, spatially representing the unity of the human organism in its juxtaposition of antiquities, natural history, anatomy, library, pictures and coins.

In 1808, Stark turned from this rather delicate design towards the severity of the neo-Greek. An unbuilt proposal for a library and schools at Greenock blended fluted Greek Doric columns (including a hexastyle portico) with the Roman grandeur of a tall Pantheon dome and triumphal-arch outer pavilions. Such a combination of Greek porticoes and domed buildings had been not

5.3 Hunterian Museum, Glasgow, record drawing by W. H. Playfair, *c*.1817.

5.4 Justiciary Court House (Stark, 1809–14), photograph taken *c.*1890, before the rebuilding of 1910–13 by J. H. Craigie.

uncommon in recent Russian architecture: for instance, at Nikolai Lvov's Cathedral of St Joseph at Mogilev (built 1781–98 by a Scottish executant architect, Adam Menelaws). An 1808 proposal by Stark (also unbuilt) for the completion of Thomas Harrison's Broomhall for Lord Elgin envisaged a long, low, flat-roofed group, with unpedimented Greek Doric colonnades. A French neo-classical horizontality became even more pronounced in Stark's Glasgow Court House (built 1809–14; rebuilt 1910–13) [5.4]. Here he employed a giant Greek Doric order for the first time in Scotland, in a composition of brooding horizontality, with heavy hexastyle portico, channelled masonry and linking stringcourse, and anta-pilastered pavilions. At the Court House, any Adamesque ideas of 'movement' were banished by an inert massiveness; Stark's design defeated the competition entries of various architects, ranging from a Greek Doric entry by David Hamilton to a domed and cupola-crowned design by Reid.

Yet at the same time as these pioneering Greek efforts, other experimental designs by Stark were giving a new life to architectonic 'movement'. An almost Baroque dynamism, recapitulating Gibbs themes, was displayed in his compressed, obelisk-pinnacled St George's Tron Church, Glasgow (1807–8) [5.5]. Stark's most confident demonstration of St Petersburg-like grandeur came from 1812 when two of the capital's élite professional groups, the writers and the advocates, engaged him to design monumental library interiors (the Signet, and the Advocates') behind the stolid facades of

5.5 St George's Tron Church, Glasgow (Stark, 1807–8).

Reid's refaced (from 1803) Parliament Square. The highlight of his scheme was the Advocates' (now Upper) Library, a nave-and-aisles hall of Corinthian columns and clustered pilasters with central transepts and dome [5.6]. It was only fitting that, in Edinburgh's classical architectural celebration of Enlightenment, the most monumental interiors should have been those of libraries.

In another sharp contrast, the same years saw the building of two severely astylar classical projects by Stark, in which rationalistic social control through the plan was the paramount aim: the lunatic asylums at Glasgow (designed 1804–6, built 1807–20) and Dundee (1812–20). In asylum planning – always split between prison and hospital considerations – the years following Adam's pioneering Bridewell saw a range of attempts to reconcile surveillance and classification with freedom of movement. At Glasgow, Stark designed an uncompromisingly centralised Greek-cross plan with central stair and eight separate exercise yards around, with the aim that 'each class may be formed into a society inaccessible to all others' [5.7]. [7] Its severe, round-arched forms influenced many subsequent institutional buildings in the west, such as Charles Wilson's domed, round-arched John Neilson Institution, Paisley (1849–52). Stark's Dundee asylum was very different in form. Its domestic-scaled H-shaped block featured single-storey wings facing out over

planted gardens – a premonition of the lower-density 'colony' asylums of the 1890s, and an equivalent, in the microcosmic form of an institution, of the landscaped town planning layouts that Stark was beginning to advocate by 1813. He claimed that his Dundee plan allowed 'great gentleness and great liberty and comfort combined with the fullest security'. [8]

Just before his death, Stark moved to Edinburgh, where his most immediate legacy would emerge, in the refined and yet highly individualistic work of his pupil, William Playfair. Stark was also associated in his last years with the national-Romantic architectural projects of Sir Walter Scott, who (as we will see later) commissioned cottage sketches from him for the rebuilding of Abbotsford. Scott acclaimed Stark as 'a young man of exquisite taste', and after his death lamented that 'more genius has died than is left behind among the collected universality of Scottish architects'. [9] But the element of spatial rationalism in Stark's work exerted an equally pervasive, but more subtle, effect across all of early nineteenth-century Scottish architecture. Aspects of his asylum planning were echoed, for instance, in both the asylums and the country houses of William Burn – an architect whose plans showed a rationalist genius in the combination of relentless but unseen systems of classification and segregation with great 'liberty' and 'informality' for

5.6 Signet Library, Edinburgh Law Courts (Stark, from 1812), *c*.1920 view.

the upper-class owners. It was the combination of intuitive eclecticism and social rationalism in Stark's work which identifies him as Scotland's first architect of 'modern society', with all its tension between the individual and the collective.

The Building of 'Modern Athens'

In Edinburgh, Scotland's Romantic classical city planning of the first quarter of the nineteenth century achieved its most dramatic realisations. During the first decades of the century, a period when its population rose sharply from 66,000 (1801) to 136,000 (1831), the capital was transformed into an integrated Romantic city, formed of a rich overlaying of vistas and groupings of buildings of all periods and styles, in a landscape setting of unparalleled grandeur. The excitement of this transition was captured in two paintings of 1825 by Alexander Nasmyth: *Edinburgh from Calton Hill* (including the Bridewell and the Old and New Towns), and *Edinburgh from Princes Street, with the Royal Institution under Construction* (including a top-hatted W. H. Playfair directing operations) [5.8; cf. 4.23, 5.1].

It was now accepted by all that Edinburgh was becoming, or had already become, a classical city of outstanding beauty. But what *kind* of classicism did it represent? We saw in Chapter 4 that, as recently as 1788, Nasmyth's own design for St Bernard's Well had visualised the capital not as an Athens, but in Roman terms, as a Tivoli. By the 1820s, with the National Monument and other large Grecian monumental works underway, Edinburgh was dubbed 'The Athens of the North' by the poet Hugh William Williams; in 1829, T. H. Shepherd's *Modern Athens* reinforced the concept. The architectural reality was more complex. Archaeological Hellenism was insufficiently vigorous for nineteenth-century tastes. Its Sublime and Picturesque elements had to be clearly accentuated, in a way which would stand up to the spectacular natural setting of the capital. This was done in a calculated and sophisticated manner by Edinburgh's early nineteenth-century architects, acknowledging typological eclecticism by integrating classical and non-classical buildings, temples and spires, into monumental compositions and vistas – as did, later, the Ringstrasse in Vienna

[cf. 5.1]. These setpieces in their mixed styles were set against a backdrop of 'ordinary' astylar rowhouses and tenements, many of which were not so much Grecian as simply reworkings of established eighteenth-century patterns.

To achieve this collective city development required an overpowering continuity of aim, spanning many decades, and a consensus between private patrons and public authorities. To take just one example: the seemingly homogeneous, astylar Greek curve of Bellevue Crescent formed part of the first northern extension of the New Town, located on lands jointly developed by the Town Council and the Heriot Trust, and planned in 1801 by Robert Reid (then City Superintendent of Works) and William Sibbald, surveyor to the Trust. Bellevue Crescent, situated on the Council's section of the area, was designed by Reid's successor Thomas Bonnar (in 1818) and revised by his successor (from 1819) Thomas Brown to include at its centre a church, St Mary's, with Corinthian portico and tall domed steeple [5.9]. The church was built in 1824 by the Town Council, while the houses were feued out to speculative builders, working to Bonnar's elevations. The south half of the crescent was finished by 1832, but the north half was not finally completed until 1884, under the direction of John Lessels (to plans modified in 1869 by City Architect David Cousin).

At the same time as these developments of everyday New Town residential architecture, the development of the various strands of classicism of Modern Athens was also powerfully drawn forward by the more innovative works of its principal architects. Following the death of Stark in 1813, the spread of a fully-fledged Grecian style among the Edinburgh profession followed rapidly. Archibald Elliot's 1815 design for Waterloo Place confronted the axis of Princes Street with a flanking pair of Ionic porticoes, while his County Hall of 1816–19 was built with an Erechtheion Ionic (rather than the originally planned Parthenon Doric) order at the request of Sheriff Sir William Rae. William Burn, a former assistant of Robert Smirke in London, imported Smirke's office organisation and Grecian manner in a series of buildings based on the Doric portico and side pavilions formula of Covent Garden Theatre, a pioneering English Grecian design whose

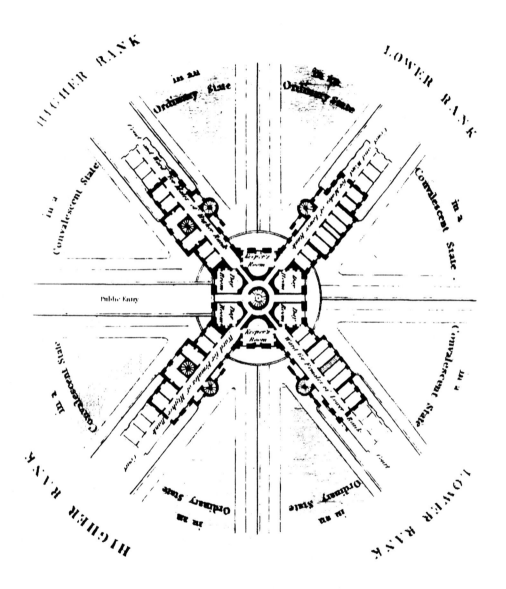

MALE PATIENTS

of the

HIGHER RANK   LOWER RANK

in an Ordinary State   in an Ordinary State

in a Convalescent State   in a Convalescent State

Public Entry

in a Convalescent State   in a Convalescent State

HIGHER RANK   LOWER RANK

in an Ordinary State   in an Ordinary State

of the

FEMALE PATIENTS

5.7 Glasgow Lunatic Asylum: (left) plan by William Stark, 1807; (above) lithograph by D. M. Walker after photograph taken *c*.1900.

construction he had himself supervised (1808–9). These included Greenock Custom House (1816–19), Edinburgh Academy (1822–4; a single-storey version) and the low, massive John Watson's Hospital (1825; built for the education of orphans of professional people). A striking Grecian alternative to the dynamism of Stark's St George's, within the Gibbs steeple/entrance formula, was Burn's design for North Leith Parish Church (from 1813, with tetrastyle Ionic portico). Related designs by other architects included David Hamilton's Falkirk Town Steeple (1813–14) and his Greek Doric Port Glasgow Town Buildings (1815–16).

After around 1820, while Burn was establishing his pre-eminent status in the rationalist planning of country houses, his and Elliot's urban Greek efforts were being swiftly overtaken by the work of

two designers, William Henry Playfair and Thomas Hamilton, who developed Stark's conception of an eclectic classicism infused with the refinement of Hellenism. By comparison with the Roman exuberance of Robert Adam's classicism and castles, their work was both more varied, in its stylistic eclecticism, and more restrained, in its outward consistency. That was a formula precisely tailored to the post-1800 collective endeavours that were needed to actually realise Adam's vision of Edinburgh, the Sublime city.

W. H. Playfair was the son of James Playfair, the architect of Cairness. Following his father's early death, the young Playfair was brought up by an uncle, the mathematician and geologist Professor John Playfair. Through him, William gained entry into the most exclusive Edinburgh Whig circles,

5.8 Alexander Nasmyth, *Edinburgh from Princes Street with the Royal Institution under Construction*, 1825 (including top-hatted W. H. Playfair directing operations).

at a time which coincided with a sharp rise in the political fortunes of the Whigs. Within this theocracy of intellect, the young Playfair enjoyed the patronage and protection of powerful friends such as the Lord Advocate, Lord Rutherford, and was able to develop, cocooned from financial and patronage pressures, a 'certain refinement and polish and a keen discernment between the chaste and the uncouth'. [10] With the exception of a single shop in George Street, Playfair designed no commercial buildings. He could concentrate on lofty projects for the city's ruling classes, lavishing minute attention and 'patient study' on architectural details, including the full-sized designs of interior fittings and furniture. In Playfair's view, 'nothing good in Architecture can be effected

5.9 Bellevue Crescent and St Mary's Church, Edinburgh (designed from 1818, completed 1884).

without a monstrous expenditure of patience and Indian Rubber'. [11] Playfair was no doctrinaire Grecian, and exploited with ease the new world of typological eclecticism, designing informal Italian or Baronial country houses with the same refinement as Grecian public buildings. His career began with a spell in Stark's office, where he imbibed the Graeco-Roman monumentality and rationalism of his master's work. In 1841, in a comment incidentally indicative of the growing west-east divergence in architectural world-outlooks, Playfair revealed that his own favourite among Stark's works was the Hunterian: 'I would rather be the author of that sweet little piece of good proportion than of all the other ostentatious Glasgow buildings put together and most of those of London' [cf.5.3]. [12] After Stark's death, Playfair appears to have spent time in the offices of Benjamin Wyatt and Smirke in London, and, in 1816, toured France with his uncle – seemingly the first Scottish architect to examine first-hand the architectural achievements of Napoleonic rule.

By then, Playfair's independent career was already under way, as, in 1815, he had won a competition to complete Adam's unfinished Edinburgh University College, halted by lack of money since 1793 [cf. 4.22]. Playfair's scheme, executed in 1819–27, proposed the exact completion of Adam's east facade design, and retained most of the other main external elements, such as quadrant colonnades in the courtyard. His own main contributions to the complex were concerned with the provision of monumental interior spaces, including a museum and the Upper Library. In the latter, an initial design divided into architectonic units in the manner of Stark's libraries was replaced (as built in 1826–7) by a more neo-classical, Schinkel-like scheme comprising a uniform range of Corinthian pilasters, with Ionic-columned screen at either end. The detail, however, was still Roman, not Greek. Playfair himself contributed to Stark's library complex at the law courts in 1819–20, with a new staircase, upper vestibule and Corinthian screen – the staircase being replaced by Burn in 1833, with a completely new imperial stair. In 1818, Playfair's university success led to a second commission in which a rationalist fascination for centralised planning was prominent: the City Observatory, a domed Greek cross built on Calton Hill for the Astronomical Institution, founded 1812 under the presidency of his own uncle. The design, possibly based on an earlier proposal by Stark, had a central dome and four arms, each with a hexastyle Roman Doric portico.

Playfair's transition to an explicitly Greek neo-classicism took place at a location away from Edinburgh, in 1818–20, at Dollar Academy – a trial-run for the capital's development of monu-mental Hellenism in a Sublime landscaped setting. Overlooked by the Ochil Hills, the Academy's main facade comprised a pedimented hexastyle Doric portico with flanking tetrastyle pavilions. Inside, the principal room was an Ionic colonnaded library. The year 1822 saw the commencement of two important neo-Grecian commissions, both already touched on above. The first was that for the Royal Institution; Playfair was asked back in 1832–5 to enlarge the building to provide complex new exhibition spaces for manufactures, and contrived, on a tight budget, greatly to augment its triumphal character with additional colonnades and porticoes [5.10]. The same year also saw the beginning of the uncompleted building of the National Monument, by Playfair, working to Cockerell's archaeologically accurate drawings – a case of Greece coming to Playfair rather than vice versa. Although only part of the stylobate and several columns were built in 1826–9, before the money ran out and the scheme was abandoned, the National Monument project established several important precedents. First, it reinforced the importance of rationalistic codes in design, adding a concern with harmonic proportions to the exist-ing spatial rationalism. Second, it helped raise the standard of Scottish building masonry from the excellent, as in James Playfair's Cairness, to the superlative [cf. 4.8]. Third, it established W. H. Playfair as an even more perfectionist and expensive architect than before. And fourth, it gave a further push to the cult of monuments to 'national heroes' and the 'heroic dead'.

The latter had been a central feature of the new concepts of the unified nation first unleashed by the French Revolution and the Napoleonic Wars. At the end of this chapter we will return to Sir Walter Scott's later definition of the 'national' in terms of non-classical styles. At this stage, how-ever, the expression of national sentiment was still channelled chiefly through classicism: Scott's own monument in Glasgow, after all, was a massive Doric column by David Rhind (1837). When the proposal for a National Monument was first made in 1817, one newspaper letter writer had suggested the Parthenon as a model in the following terms: 'What, then, can be more worthy of a nation, a building which was the boast of the country . . . from which we derive all our philosophy, all our morals, all our taste, all our love of liberty, all our eloquence, all our poetry; in short, all that is good.' [13] Another correspondent, however, countered in 1822 that a Grecian monument would be 'a perpetual and painful solecism'. [14] Many other key monuments of the period were classical, including the first monument to Wallace, a tall statue erected in 1814 at Dryburgh by the Earl of Buchan to the designs of John Smith, on a square podium. The same formula was applied in public monuments to national or even local notables; two classical monuments by Burn, with statues by Francis Chantrey, were the Dundas monument, Edinburgh (1821, a Trajanic column), and the gargantuan pedestal and statue of the 1st Duke of Sutherland, notorious for his pivotal role in the 'Clearances', erected on a hilltop at Golspie (1836–8). Chantrey was also the sculptor of the classical statues of George IV (1831) and William Pitt (1833) in Edinburgh's George Street. Playfair contributed to this movement with two further Grecian memorials on the increasingly cluttered Calton Hill. The first, commissioned by Playfair himself following his uncle's death, was the Playfair Monument (1826), a tetrastyle Greek Doric colonnade on a high podium, situated at the corner of the Observatory precinct wall. The second was the Dugald Stewart Monument (1831), a tall version of the Choragic Monument of Lysicrates.

From the late 1820s, Playfair continued on occasion to build in a monumental neo-Greek mode, as at the Edinburgh Surgeons Hall (1829–32), whose portico is ingeniously carried forward to the building line, perching on a front screen wall with entrance courtyard behind and beneath [5.11]. But an eclectic vigour became more promi-nent once again in his classical work. Arguably his most powerful contribution to Edinburgh's

5.10 Late nineteenth-century view of Hanover Street, Royal Institution (W. H. Playfair, 1822–35), Free Church College (W. H. Playfair, 1846–50) and Tolbooth Church (Graham, 1839–44) (cf. 5.1, 5.23).

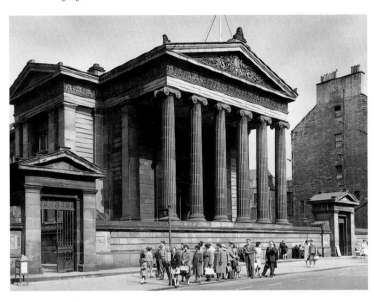

5.11 Surgeons Hall, Edinburgh (W.
H. Playfair, 1829–32), 1961 view.

Romantic urbanism was made by a classical design, which broke sharply from the horizontality of strict Grecian classicism, and returned to a Stark-like architectonic grandeur: St Stephen's Church, 1827–8. Here, presented with a similar falling site to that of the Hunterian, Playfair used the latter's pattern of pavilion-flanked side elevations to clothe the body of the church – only, now, splayed out around the centralised form of an octagon. But the main front, unlike the Hunterian, had to serve as a major vista-stopper, terminating a long falling street axis. So, instead of a 'sweet little' portico, [15] Playfair fronted St Stephen's with an enormous tower, heavily finialled like Stark's St George's Tron Church, but blocklike and sepulchral in character, in contrast to the latter's dynamic vigour, and constructed of Craigleith ashlar [5.12]. The tower comprises pilastered upper stages above a yawning arched entrance (flanked by colossal scrolls) which leads, dramatically, straight on to the gallery of the octagonal *Predigtkirche* inside; the interior decoration is sparsely Grecian. This romanticising of the neo-Greek through essentially Roman Baroque devices was widely prevalent at the time – we need only cite Hittorff's St Vincent de Paul Church, Paris (1824), with its Berniniesque lanterns.

Throughout all of Playfair's work, whether public buildings in Edinburgh or picturesque country houses, there was a common thread of obsessively scholarly attention to detail. There could not have been more of a contrast between his individual, perfectionist labours and the highly systematised logic of Burn's large practice – run with a business acumen learnt from Smirke in London. The conflicts between the isolated artist-figure and the practical designers of quantity were to be a running theme of architectural modernity, as seen later, for example, in the clashes between Mackintosh and Keppie or Burnet. In 1841, Playfair disparaged William Burn – an adversary in his Tory politics as much as in his architecture – as 'purse proud and ostentatious and overbearing – his utter want of genius . . . equalled by his copious supply of impudence'. [16] Slightly more surprisingly, Playfair described as 'full of intrigue and vulgar taste' Thomas Hamilton, the architect who was his chief rival in Edinburgh monumental architecture.

Certainly, compared to Playfair's sheltered academicism, Hamilton's classical monumental manner was characterised, throughout, by a slightly greater willingness to contemplate elements of pictorial theatricality; but the difference was not a wide one. In contrast to Playfair, Hamilton was of humbler origins – the son of a mason, who served as an apprentice with his uncle. In the meritocracy of early nineteenth-century Edinburgh, his talents were quickly recognised. His first breakthrough, however, came not in the capital but in the west,

5.12 St Stephen's Church, Edinburgh (W. H. Playfair, 1827–8), 1961 view.

where in 1818, he won, the competition to design another important example of the classical national memorial genre: the earliest of the Burns monuments, put up in 1820–3 at the poet's birthplace, Alloway (near Ayr), only a quarter-century after his death [5.13]. Hamilton's essay in Grecian was based on the Choragic Monument of Lysicrates but with open colonnade and Corinthian order derived from the temple of Castor and Pollux. He also subsequently (in 1830) added his contribution to the increasingly monument-laden Calton Hill, a circular Burns Monument heavier and richer than Alloway.

It was on the flanks of Calton Hill that Hamilton designed what was, perhaps, the single most significant single monument of Edinburgh classical Romanticism, and one of the setpieces of archaeological Hellenism in Europe: the Royal High School (1825–9) [5.14]. This project, sponsored by the Town Council, was originally envisaged as a rectilinear, pilastered composition on a podium at St James's Square, based on the model of the Theseion, which was one of Hamilton's favourite Greek monuments. For the building's eventual, abruptly rocky site, Hamilton evolved (from 1825) a more Romantic and dynamic vision, presenting the relatively small group of buildings as an overpowering array of tiered and interpenetrating temple and colonnade-like structures, which built up, in a somewhat Baroque manner, to the climax of a boldly trabeated, heavy Doric portico.

Alongside this Greek mode, Hamilton maintained a more emphatic Baroque style. This was most spectacularly demonstrated not in Edinburgh but back in Ayr, where his Municipal Buildings (1828–32) recast the traditional steepled tolbooth pattern in a composition of overwhelming power [5.15]. Its steeple, set on a massive, battered base with archway, is ringed by diagonally set, superimposed columns; the building was extended in 1878–81 by Campbell Douglas & Sellars. We will touch on Hamilton's nearby Gothic Wallace Tower (1830–3) in Ayr later. In Edinburgh, at the Dean Orphanage (1833–6), opposite Burn's John Watson's Hospital, Hamilton expressed these Baroque tendencies in a manner more closely attuned to landscape setting. In its sylvan location, separated from the western New Town on a hill

5.13 Burns Monument, Alloway (T. Hamilton, 1820–3).

above the Water of Leith, the orphanage's twin towers are often glimpsed over trees; they contain staircases (tapered internally in an ingenious device of false perspective), and chimney flues carried up into corner turrets like Playfair's at St Stephen's. In contrast to this accentuated landscape silhouette, Hamilton's last great public building, the Royal College of Physicians (1844–6), faced the task of fitting into the long, terraced facades of Queen Street. By then there was, as we will see shortly, growing discontent with the austere rectilinearity of the first New Town. In this instance, Hamilton ruptured the line of large-windowed houses with a square, tomb-like structure with blind attic, Tower of the Winds facade elements, and portico with Hellenistic aedicule above, flanked by lifesize statues by Alexander Handyside Ritchie [5.16]. Inside, the original main hall, with caryatid-supported ceiling and marbled Corinthian peristyle, conveyed a rich and heavy impression.

5.14 Royal High School, Edinburgh (T. Hamilton, 1825–9), view of *c.*1935.

5.16 Royal College of Physicians (T. Hamilton, 1844–6).

5.15 Ayr Municipal Buildings (T. Hamilton, 1828–32).

Edinburgh's New Town: The Golden Years

During the first quarter of the nineteenth century, the surroundings of the existing New Town were turned into a huge building site, as extension developments mushroomed [5.17]. The New Town's population rose from around 15,000 in 1815 to 40,000 in 1830, and its social composition became even more widely based, with lawyers and small lairds investing the profits of agricultural improvement. What is so startling to us today is that the visual unity of the expanded New Town was the result not of public regulation but of private mechanisms. The houses were built by speculators, helped by easily available finance from the capital's many private banks, and working in conformity to plans and elevations specified by the private owners of the land in their feuing conditions.

The development of the later New Town in the first three decades of the century showed there was a subtle change in both architecture and layout, compared to the most ambitious elements of the first New Town, such as Charlotte Square. Much research still remains to be done on this epic period, but it is possible to suggest some summary definitions. Architecturally, there was a gradual move from Adamesque Roman patterns to a more specifically Greek style – usually still simplified into a plain street-architecture – followed, in the 1820s, by the devising of more rhetorically monumental, or individualised, designs. In layout, the rectilinear, functionally undifferentiated type of grid seen in Craig's design, with public buildings integrated with rows of rather un-monumental dwellings, was rejected in favour of more sharply defined, self-contained residential zones, in which monumental blocks of houses were combined with irregular layouts and copious greenery. By the time Edinburgh's building boom expired in the early 1830s, these developments, between them, had laid comprehensive architectural foundations for the even more vigorous residential expansion of mid-century Glasgow.

The architectural expression of the New Town extension boom was founded on the everyday street architecture of rows of houses and tenements built on Reid and Sibbald's extension plan of 1801–4. The more prestigious streets, such as Reid's Heriot Row (1802–8) or Great King Street and Drummond Place (both 1804), still followed late Robert Adam formulae of compositional unity, such as the rusticated ground floor, central portico and advanced flanking bays pattern of Charlotte Square. In the plainer streets of tenements (mostly designed either by Thomas Bonnar or Thomas Brown), often the only ornament of the severely astylar blocks was the ground-floor rustication. The stepped tenements of Dundas Street (designed by Bonnar, started from 1807) and its continuation Pitt Street (started 1820) seemed hardly different from the plain house architecture of the mid- and late eighteenth-century, although they were now of ashlar construction, tooled rather than smooth in finish [cf. 5.23].

The Grecianising of New Town street architecture began with the scheme for Waterloo Place (1815–22, by Archibald Elliot, and engineer Robert Stevenson). This continued the line of Princes Street in a monumental manner, with twin porticoes facing west and a triumphal arch bridge over Calton Road (1816–19), realising at last Robert Adam's vision of a monumental entry to the town via Calton Hill. In parallel with this project, other extension schemes were beginning to combine generally Adamesque compositions with Greek stylistic elements. These included Robert Brown's designs for the Easter Coates lands, including the majestic axis of Melville Street (planned in 1814), with diamond-shaped intersection at the centre; this austere boulevard would later be converted into a romantic spired vista, by the construction of Sir G. G. Scott's Episcopal Cathedral (see Chapter 6) [cf. 6.52]. Artisan streets, such as Brown's William Street or St Stephen Street (both from 1824), remained as plain as before; outwith the New Town, some classical tenements, such as those by Burn in Bread Street/Lothian Road, 1820–5, were even built of rubble.

The culmination of this Greek phase of street architecture, with its continuing links to the principles of classical stateliness, was located at the north-east side of the New Town: the terraces of

Playfair's Calton scheme, above all Royal Terrace (begun 1821, redesigned 1824), facing north across London Road with a 360-metre-long facade. Royal Terrace's three-storey frontage took the palace type formula to a haughty extreme, with an array of separate colonnades ranked hierarchically: three tall Corinthian ones at the centre, two Ionic on either side [5.18]. However, in another of Playfair's street designs for the Calton scheme – Brunswick Street (designed *c*.1824) – there emerged a new and different interpretation of Adam's demand for a unified monumental treatment of groups of dwellings, combining the neo-classical demand for repetition with an increasing individuality of single units. Brunswick Street included a line of balustraded porches linked by balconies – a rectilinear, zigzagging form more typical of mid-century heaviness than of neo-Greek restraint. More conventional, but influential later in Glasgow, was a tenement block by Burn, 2–28 Henderson Row (1824–6), with channelled ground floor, individual Ionic porches to main-door flats, and balustrade. The most idiosyncratic and grandiloquent of these new monumental Greek solutions was St Bernard's Crescent, one of a group of streets designed by James Milne in 1824, on the Raeburn estate developed on the sylvan north-west edge of the New Town [5.19]. With a panache that would have been unthinkable even in the 1760s, this fairly ordinary, curved row of dwellings was fronted with a hectoring array of two-storey Doric columns crammed between giant antae – all in ashlar above sunk-storey level. The windows of dwellings peep out in between, and on either side are repetitive, colonnaded two-storey wings. J. Grant's *Old and New Edinburgh* of 1882 recorded that the crescent was 'adorned with the grandest Grecian Doric pillars that are to be found in any edifice not a public one'. [17] These individualistic interpretations of classical monumentality, in the context of middle-class urban dwellings, seem to presage some of the themes of mid-century Glasgow, especially the work of Alexander Thomson.

Although most of the streets in Reid and Sibbald's 1801–4 extension layout followed a rectangular layout, by the time the later parts of that layout were being feued out, the more concerted attempt to differentiate 'residential'

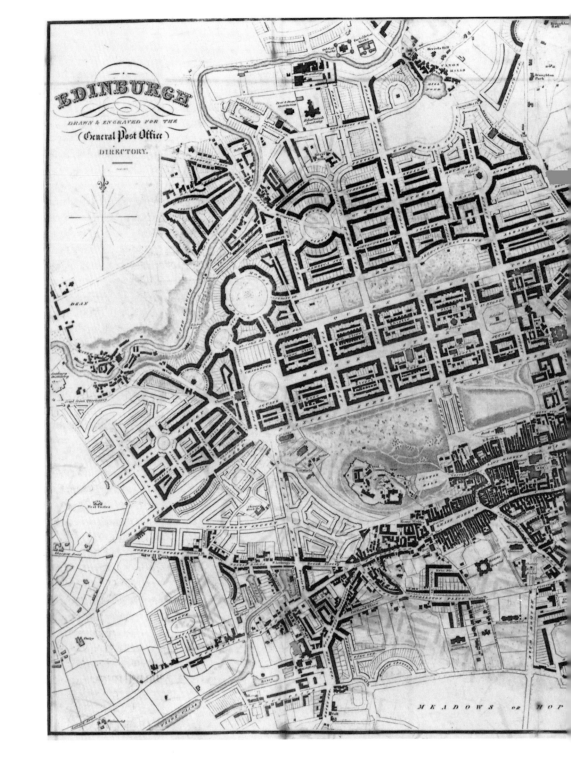

EDINBURGH

DRAWN & ENGRAVED FOR THE

(General Post Office)

DIRECTORY.

MEADOWS or HOP

5.17 General Post Office Directory map of Edinburgh (1828–9) showing the Old Town below and the New Town above, including Playfair's largely unrealised Calton scheme at top right.

zones from this outward–looking urban pattern had begun in earnest, in several proposals and developments of the 1810s and 1820s. In proposals of 1813 for an extension of the New Town on part of Calton Hill, Stark led the way. He elaborated Adam's attacks on the first New Town as monotonous, by denouncing symmetrical axes and advocating a combination of convenience and landscaped effect: there was 'in a bending alignment of street, much beauty, and perhaps the most striking effects'. He praised 'variety and unexpected change of form, both in the streets and buildings'; trees and buildings 'assimilate well together'. Playfair backed this up in a report of 1819, blasting the 'tame monotony' and 'complete uniformity of plan' seen in 'many parts of the New Town of Edinburgh'. He proposed a vast 'new Town between Edinburgh and Leith' [18] to provide for all classes except the poorest, with a radial layout, square and terraces around Calton Hill. The Calton scheme as built was curtailed, but the grand climax of Royal Terrace, mentioned above, was completed. As in the case of Stark's evolving ideas on asylum planning, these schemes tried to combine a socially comprehensive spatial structure with elements of informality and natural landscaping [cf. 5.17].

In parts of the second (northern) New Town, curved or landscaped elements were also introduced: we touched above on the curved, but monumental St Bernard's Crescent, on the Raeburn estate (developed from 1813). At the north-west end of the area, Playfair designed Royal Circus and associated streets in 1819–20 for the Heriot Trust, and built them, with his usual refinement, in 1821–3; Royal Circus comprised two great crescents facing each other, with a meandering road through a pleasure ground in the centre; it formed part of the main cross-axis in Reid and Sibbald's layout along with the straight Great King Street and the U-shaped Drummond Place. The formal planning devices in this phase of the New Town, such as crescents and circuses, were influenced indirectly by examples in France or England, such as the circular Place des Victoires, Paris (1685) or the more recent crescents of Bath. However, the Grecian ashlar gravity of the buildings erected on them, resulted in an urbanist formula of more consistent monumentality.

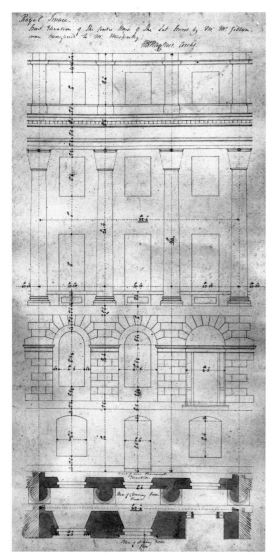

5.18 W. H. Playfair, front elevation (*c.*1824) of central house in Royal Terrace.

The trend towards a more architecturally unified, yet landscape-sensitive residential pattern in the New Town reached its climax in the development of the Earl of Moray's Drumsheugh estate [5.20]. The Earl's 1822 Articles and Conditions of Roup and Sale were unprecedentedly detailed in the architectural obligations they laid on developers of vacant stances in the area. They required conformity to ashlar elevations prepared by his architect, James Gillespie Graham, including giant columns and pediments. The Earl's wooded gardens were to be preserved as a pleasure ground for the new proprietors. The centrepiece of this development, Moray Place (1822–36) is a duodecagonal space of almost claustrophobic grandeur, ringed by stepped ranks of giant orders, in the Charlotte Square arrangement of pedimented centrepieces and two-bay pavilions. The same pattern was reproduced in straight frontage form at Albyn Place; other facades within the scheme were quieter in appearance. Almost immediately, there were proposals to extend development from the Moray estate to the Dean estate across the Water of Leith. In 1824, Lord Provost John Learmonth proposed a high-level bridge across the gorge, and, the following year, bought the Dean estate himself. In 1831–2, assisted by the Cramond Road Trustees, he commissioned Thomas Telford to design the 100 feet. high Dean Bridge, with its four segmental arches on slim, panelled piers [5.21].

The collective grandeur of Edinburgh's Grecian residential areas was matched in the splendour of the dwellings they contained. In streets such as Moray Place, the gigantic stone-built row-houses

5.19 St Bernard's Crescent, Edinburgh (J. Milne, from 1824).

5.20 Aerial photograph of the north-western Edinburgh New Town showing Moray Place (at centre), Ainslie Place (at bottom right), and Royal Circus (at top left).

and flats were designed for winter occupation by rich middle-class owners who, in all likelihood, had summer villas and seaside cottages. These houses were fit to accommodate parties of hundreds and, like the country houses of the landed class, were decorated according to well-established, consensual formulae of taste. In contrast to the levelling-up of ornament in grand Glasgow houses later in the century, these Edinburgh dwellings to some extent still maintained the old state-apartment hierarchy of decorum, culminating in the lavishly gilded drawing rooms. In the internal arrangement of these rooms, there was an increasing departure from the formality of the eighteenth century, with its furniture pulled back against the walls; Greek taste was associated with a freer disposition of couches and other furniture. But alongside this overall impulse of social conformity, these houses were also the setting of a forceful late offshoot of the Edinburgh Enlightenment. They increasingly played host to experimental schemes painted by D. R. Hay, the capital's leading housepainter, who rejected 'mere taste' for a rationalistic philosophy of 'scientific' decoration in accordance with 'the

laws of harmonious colouring'. [19] Rejecting wallpapers as too susceptible to dampness in Scotland's equable maritime climate, Hay made painted stencilwork, graining and marbling the staples of the country's elevated decorative schemes for the rest of the nineteenth century.

Alongside these further extensions to the New Town, there was the beginning of concerted architectural intervention in the Old Town, following the City Improvement Act of 1827. The project had originally been conceived by Thomas Hamilton in an article of 1817 in the *Scots Magazine* and in an 1824 report, in collaboration with William Burn [5.22]. Their concept was similar to that of 1752: to prevent the Old Town atrophying, by opening up new access routes in this case to the south and south-west (the present George IV Bridge and Johnston Terrace) and to the north, to the New Town, over the 'Earthen Mound' thrown up by building operations north of Princes Street. All were to be pulled together into architecturally monumental compositions, and new blocks were to employ the 'Flemish style'. [20] The new bridges to the south and south-west were begun with energy in 1829, under the supervision

5.21 Dean Bridge, Edinburgh (Telford, 1831–2), early twentieth-century view.

of Hamilton, who was appointed architect to the Edinburgh Improvements Commission; his successor was George Smith (a former Burn assistant). Hamilton's original proposal for an axial termination to the Mound, converting the Lawnmarket into a square with the 'Flemish' towered John Knox Memorial Church (planned 1829, not built), was later supplanted by the present curved approach. Some indication of the 'Flemish' style visualised by Hamilton for Old Town replacement buildings emerged in 1840–1, when a large five-storey block of tenements and shops, Melbourne Place, was built to Smith's designs on the west side of George IV Bridge; its main facade comprised an array of finialled gables, and featured a three-storey corbelled oriel.

These proposals by Hamilton acted as a curtain raiser to the climax of the monumental remodelling of the Mound in the 1840s and 1850s by his

rival, Playfair. Already, in 1839, the spired Tolbooth St John Church had been commenced by James Gillespie Graham at the head of the vista up the Mound. But there then intervened in 1843 the Disruption of the Established Church of Scotland, and the founding of the rival, anti-erastian Free Church of Scotland. The Free Church, which, as we will see in Chapter 6, expanded very rapidly, wanted to emphasise its centrality in the nation's life. It chose a second site at the top of the Mound, in front of the Tolbooth Church, to build its own first theological college. Following a large competition, Playfair secured the commission – perhaps unsurprisingly, as his closest friend, Lord Rutherford, the Lord Advocate, was a prominent Free Church member. He designed the main north facade as a Gothic outcrop (1846–50), whose towers, accentuated by tall pinnacles, were audaciously designed to frame and

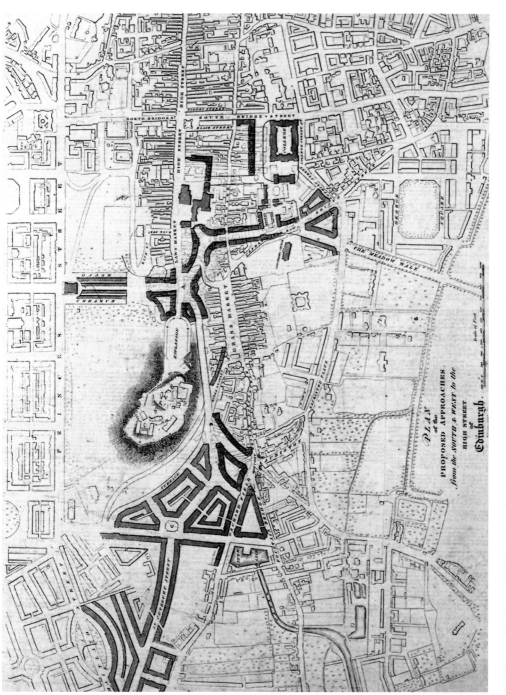

5.22 Thomas Hamilton and William Burn, plan for new approaches to Edinburgh Old Town from the west and south; *Caledonian Mercury*, 6 December 1824.

5.23 Dundas Street (formerly Pitt Street), Edinburgh, axial view from north: at the top are visible the towers of the Free Church College (W. H. Playfair, 1846–50), framing the steeple of the Tolbooth Church (Graham, 1839–44) (cf 5 1 5 10)

'capture' the steeple of the rival Tolbooth Church, when seen looming above the Doric portico of Playfair's Royal Institution at the bottom of the Mound [cf. 5.1, 5.10, 5.45]. The same classic-Gothic vista was translated into an even more rhetorical and poignant form when seen at long distance, from the bottom of Pitt Street [5.23]. There the composite silhouette, framed by ascending ranks of classical tenements, stood sentinel over the processional route that the seceding ministers had taken on the day of the Disruption, on their march down from St Andrew's Church to Tanfield Hall.

To complete the grouping on the Mound – over whose design he had succeeded, through skill and good connections, in maintaining a virtual monopoly – Playfair was asked in 1849 by the Board of Manufactures to prepare designs for a new, twin-purpose building to house the National Gallery and the Royal Scottish Academy [5.24]. This was the most singleminded of Playfair's efforts in adaptation of Hellenism to public buildings; it is worth noting that on his visit to Italy in 1842, he had described the Pitti Palace as 'about the ugliest building I ever saw . . . better fitted for the reception of some horrid ogre' than for a gallery. [21] In Playfair's final design, the two functions of the building were expressed by a double Ionic portico arrangement, subjugated overall by a severe Grecian monumentality

(which was offset slightly by rather un-Greek balustrades). An alternative design by Thomas Hamilton (1846) had proposed two separate buildings. At the laying of the foundation stone in 1850, Prince Albert hailed Playfair's design as 'a Temple erected to the Fine Arts', [22] and in 1853 Playfair wrote to Rutherford, making clear his self-conscious evocation of Hellenic purity: 'I feel sure that the architecture of this building will be too simple and pure to captivate the multitude, but I am certain I follow the right path in what I am doing and so am content'. Internally, there was a scheme of rationalistic painted decoration by Hay, including imitation graining and carefully chosen wall colours, such as deep purple, which he maintained was the 'most effective in giving clearness to works of art'. [23] In response to criticisms that no building should be erected on this sensitive location, Playfair visualised its positioning in exalted terms, as 'being like the hub of a wheel, the centre-point of the great cyclorama of North Edinburgh, which embraces the Firth of Forth and, on a clear day, the mountains of the Highlands'. [24] Playfair died in 1857, a year before the eventual opening of his Gallery. In its obituary, the *Scotsman* wrote of his 'intense fastidiousness . . . subservient to powerful genius'. [25]

The development of the Mound complex in the late 1840s and 1850s was the swansong of Edinburgh's Romantic or 'national' classicism.

5.24 W. H. Playfair, preliminary sketch design for the proposed National Gallery (1850–8).

Already, by then, the breakneck phase of development of the Modern Athens was over - brought to an end by the bankruptcy of the Town Council in 1833, its resources overstretched by the extension of Leith Docks. For nearly twenty years, housing development in Edinburgh virtually stopped and population growth slowed dramatically, and the torch of its city-planning passed to Glasgow. Before we look westwards to that even more audacious story, we must deal with the resounding echoes of the capital's developments in what was now increasingly becoming a true 'Granite City' – Aberdeen – as well as the smaller-scale improvement schemes in the city of Perth.

'New Town' Planning in Aberdeen and Perth

In Aberdeen, whose prosperity was driven by the booming agricultural economy of the north-east, the years from 1800 saw a series of bold schemes more or less following the earlier Edinburgh models of axes and bridge-streets. The first example of the latter pattern, Marischal Street,

was built down to the harbour in the 1760s, but the Aberdeenshire County Road Trustees surveyor, Charles Abercrombie, with local ratepayer support, successfully pressed for a far larger scheme for an inland road gateway: a new, axial street running south-west from the old centre for a mile, on a series of arches, with a bridge at the Denburn designed by Thomas Fletcher with modifications by Thomas Telford [5.25]. Following the passing of special legislation in 1800, the new street (later named Union Street) was laid out in 1800–5 at a total cost of £114,000. In contrast to the Adam projects, all old buildings in the way of the Union Street viaduct were demolished. Monumental classicism could have been invented for Aberdeen and for granite – the local material previously considered too hard for decorative work. The city's first fully dressed ashlar granite building (James Burn's Aberdeen Banking Company office) was built in 1801–2 at the east end of Union Street, in the Castlegate. Slightly later, by the 1830s, the cutting of granite was revolutionised by the introduction of steam-powered technology. The north-eastern granite industry expanded and even began an export drive [cf. C.5, C.6].

5.25 Castle Street and Union Street, Aberdeen, 1880s' view. Prominent buildings include (from left to centre) Union Buildings (Simpson, 1822–3), the Town House (Peddie & Kinnear, 1866–74), and the North of Scotland Bank (Simpson, 1839–42).

From the 1810s to the 1830s, this grand axis, along with new subsidiary streets, was provided with new public buildings and flanking residential areas, including the beginning of curved layouts in the Edinburgh manner. As in Edinburgh, two rival architects were responsible for the evolution of Aberdeen's granite classicism; but in contrast to the capital, the dominant architectural theme in Aberdeen's civic developments was neo-Greek from the start. Working in the city from 1804–5, and soon appointed Town's Architect, John Smith set a standard of homogeneous classical excellence in his so-called 'Facade': the colonnaded, arched St Nicholas graveyard screen of 1829. As City Architect, Smith designed a succession of Grecian public and ecclesiastical monuments like the North Church (1830), a synthesis of several sources including a Tower of the Winds steeple; and the reposeful, Doric-porticoed, single-storey Town's Schools (1840). The North Church formed part of a more general ordering of King Street as a second landward axis. Smith designed severe blocks on the east side of the street (1825–30).

The most distinguished and refined contribution to the shaping of classical Aberdeen, as well as to the building of country houses in the north-east, was made by Archibald Simpson. Returning from travels in Italy in 1813, Simpson began a series of largely Grecian public buildings, beginning with the Ionic-porticoed Medico-Chirurgical Society's Hall, King Street (1818: opposite his Gothic St Andrew's Episcopal Church, 1816–17), and the similarly porticoed Assembly Rooms (Music Hall), Union Street (1820–2). Simpson's Athenaeum (or Union Buildings), 1822–3, was a simplified version of the Robert Adam multi-level idea, on a steep, narrow site at the east end of Union Street; its great *in antis* Ionic porticoed entrance front rhetorically addressed the square around the Mercat Cross in Castle Street (newly restored by John Smith, 1820). Other Simpson commissions further enhanced the new monumental ensemble at the King Street/Union Street/Castle Street junction: the Northern Insurance Company's office at 1–4 King Street (1839–40), and the adjacent North of Scotland Bank (1839–42), whose quadrant-porticoed corner, crowned by James Giles's terracotta statue of Ceres, symbolised the triumph of agricultural improvement in the north-east. Elsewhere in the city, Simpson's Royal Infirmary (1832–40) on Woolmanhill, an H-plan block with dome and three pedimented temple fronts, provided both a romantic object in the landscape, looming over the Denburn Valley, and an essay in subtly understated Grecian; and the colossal anta-order facade of the New Market (1840–2), accompanied by the laying-out of the new Market Street, accorded an unprecedented monumentality to the act of shopping [5.26].

As in Edinburgh, the construction of public buildings in Aberdeen was matched by residential development, structured by the highly linear character of the Union Street axis (and its continuation, from 1820, into Albyn Place). The most severely monumental of these new schemes was the sheer curve of Simpson's Bon-Accord Crescent (1823), built with adjoining streets (Bon-Accord Square and West Craibstone Street) [5.27]. Aberdeen's building boom came to an end, later than Edinburgh's, with a local commercial slump in 1848. Simpson also built prominent classical monuments in other north-eastern and northern burghs: in Elgin, St Giles's Church (1827–8, with Lysicrates tower above a portico) and Anderson's Institution (1830–3). A similar Greek solidity was expressed, further west, in William Robertson's Dr Bell's School, Inverness (1839–41), with its heavy Doric portico. We will return later to Simpson's work in picturesque and neo-medieval styles.

Among the many smaller-scale new town developments on the Edinburgh model in other burghs, the most significant was that in Perth, where Provost Thomas Hay Marshall instigated a programme of improvements from 1795. Already, from the 1780s, some plain classical schemes, such as Charlotte Street, had been built. Now a range of new streets were designed, the most elaborate being in a post-Adam style. The resemblance to Edinburgh was heightened by the fact that Robert Reid, a friend of Marshall, designed some of the prime examples, including Marshall Place (1801) and Rose Terrace (1805); the corner block of Rose Terrace, Marshall's townhouse, had giant pilasters. The centrepiece of Rose Terrace was the Academy (1803–7) by Reid, with rusticated ground floor and Roman Doric colonnade above, flanked by pavilions and

5.26 Aberdeen New Market (Simpson, 1840–2), 1965 view.

5.27 Bon-Accord Crescent, Aberdeen
(Simpson, 1823), photograph taken by
Robert Matthew, c.1930.

surmounted by balustrade and clock. The year 1824 saw David Morison's building of the porticoed Marshall monument and museum, and 1836 the building of William M. Mackenzie's City and County Infirmary. In the years around 1830, there began the development of villa suburbs (for example in Barossa Place).

In Dundee, there were no developments of similar magnitude. Following proposals of 1824 by William Burn for central area improvement, one major axis was built: Reform Street, feued from 1834 to the designs of Burn's former clerk, George Angus. In 1832, Angus had already designed, the building which would terminate the new vista, the Dundee Public Seminaries, a Greek Doric group with central portico and massive anta-pilastered pavilions. The most noteworthy classical public building of this period in the town was George Smith's Exchange Coffee House (1828), a meeting place for merchants including assembly rooms, library and reading room.

David Hamilton and the Rise of Glasgow

In the first quarter of the nineteenth century, Glasgow was growing faster than any other city in Europe. Its economy and society were proudly orientated to sea and empire. The year 1825 saw the first claim that Glasgow was the British empire's 'second city', [26] while in 1840 Archibald Alison declared that 'The progress of opulence for the last half century has been unprecedented in European annals'. [27] Although, in 1825, textile workers' productivity was already two or three hundred times higher than that of eighteenth-century hand workers, this was still a time of rapid economic transition. By the 1830s a new pattern of heavy industry, focused on iron, coal and railways, was emerging. Soon urban growth would enter a more highly structured phase, with increasing municipal intervention; as early as 1818 the Town Council had become involved in provision of street gas-lighting. However, in contrast to the later phase of City Improvement Act remodelling, there was not yet a policy of systematic land assembly or area redevelopment.

This period of civic triumph was also a period of rising social and medical crisis, with a sharp increase in the mortality rate. During the first post-war decade, mushrooming Glasgow was racked by violent disturbances and radical dissent, culminating in the 1819–20 insurrection by hand-loom weavers. Secular solutions were focused on political reform, bolstering the existing power of local élites, and attempting to control the 'mob'. Alongside these ran attempts, strongly supported within Glasgow Town Council, to combat social disintegration by reasserting a 'godly common-wealth' uniting all classes. [28] Thomas Chalmers's pioneering ministry in St John's Parish, Glasgow (from 1819) propagated ideas of self-help among the poor. Already, the evangelical-capitalistic culture of mid-century Glasgow was emerging. Even prior to the 1833 municipal reforms, many Glasgow councillors were evangelicals.

Among Glasgow's capitalist élite, a marked cultural divergence from the capital developed, in areas including architecture and interior design. One commentator observed that this élite, concerned with 'public estimation . . . made fashion their model in everything, in their houses and furniture, their dress, their taste'. [29] To escape from the disease and squalor of the old centre, the ruling classes moved out of the city, first south to Tradeston (planned from 1791), then Hutcheson-town (from 1794). In Laurieston, feued out by James Laurie from 1802, Peter Nicholson designed Carlton Place, the city's first two unified classical residential row facades in the Charlotte Square manner (built in 1802–4 and 1813–18, including Laurie's own sumptuous house) [5.28]. Then, more decisively, there was a move out to new western suburbs, with the feuing out of the Blythswood estate. In 1792 or 1793, the Town Council had consulted James Craig on design of the street layout, but the result was different to his Edinburgh work. The grid was open-ended, although the uniform pattern of east-west service lanes gave a subtle linear emphasis to the layout. Blythswood was built up from 1816; the only formal, closed space was Blythswood Square (laid out from 1823 to 1829, possibly to the designs of William Burn or George Smith, and executed by John Brash).

By the 1820s Glasgow had begun, far more than Edinburgh, to assume the differentiated layout of a true capitalist city. As part of this, the original eighteenth-century extension area became

5.28 Carlton Place, Glasgow (Nicholson, 1802–18).

transformed into a centre of commerce and public monuments. The latter followed, on the whole, a more eclectic classicism than those of Edinburgh or Aberdeen, although there were large Grecian projects. In all the various classical permutations, the work of Stark offered powerful models; we noted above the early Grecian project of his Justiciary Court House of 1809.

The most influential and versatile Glasgow architect of those years was someone who had competed with Stark for the Hunterian and Court House commissions, and who would doubtless have been his main rival had Stark lived longer: David Hamilton. Hamilton, who was no relation of his Edinburgh namesake Thomas, was almost certainly employed by the Adam brothers on their range of Glasgow projects. A marked Adamesque influence, for instance, is evident in one of the designs he submitted for the Justiciary Court House competition (1809), and in the design of Hutcheson's Hospital (1802). Although Hamilton would only briefly design in an explicitly Greek mode, preferring on the whole a richer Graeco-Roman style, the sharp profiles of neo-Greek would remain prominent in his work.

Hamilton's main importance at this stage of our account lies in his central role in the post-Adam city improvement of Glasgow between the 1790s (when he first appears in the city records as architect of the Humane Society house 'for the reviving of apparently drowned persons') and the end of his career in the 1840s, by which time he was working in combination with his son James. In this respect, he often collaborated with the irrepressible James Cleland. Cleland himself was, also, directly responsible for a number of public buildings and monuments, including the Post Office in Nelson Street (1810), and the Magdalen Asylum (1812) and the High School in Upper Montrose Street (1820). He organised the reconstruction of Glasgow Green as a civic park in 1815–26, where he had already commissioned Hamilton to design a Nelson monument there in the form of an obelisk (1806, the first memorial to the British naval hero anywhere in Scotland or England).

Hamilton's early public buildings combined a taste for architectural complexity with a concern for skyline impact doubtless inherited from the Adams, and, ultimately, from the Gibbs church steeple tradition. A series of public buildings with tall spires in the tolbooth/townhouse manner included Glasgow's Hutcheson's Hospital (1802–5), with its Renaissance/Mannerist facades and its axial location; Falkirk Town Steeple (1813–14, with early attached use of Greek columns); and Port Glasgow Town Buildings (1815–16). From the late 1820s, however, we witness a far more florid architectural treatment, combined with carefully planned urban intensification. Here, a key influence was undoubtedly Hamilton's work on the enlargement of Hamilton Palace (financed, like the growth of Glasgow, by huge industrial profits), which brought him into direct contact with the most lavish and up-to-date French and Italian classicism; we will deal with that project shortly. At the Royal Exchange (1827–9), Hamilton and his son ingeniously refaced the Cunninghame Mansion of 1778–80 with a rich Greek Corinthian portico and squat cylindrical tower [5.29]. The Exchange's newsroom hall provided a public meeting place for business transactions, celebrating architecturally a collective activity of improvement which had previously taken place sporadically in coffee houses around the city; the hall's columned form doubtless echoed that of St Andrew's Church. At the same time, the Exchange played, a wider civic role, as it was designed to close the vista down Ingram Street and create a new civic space. This idea formed part of a profitable scheme of improvement devised by the Royal Bank of Scotland, who sold the Cunninghame Mansion in 1827 for rebuilding, built new premises for themselves behind it (also 1827, to the Ionic Greek designs of Archibald Elliot II, with a big portico flanked by archways), and feued off the rest of the ground for construction of the square (built 1830–9 to the designs of Hamilton and James Smith); the latter was an early example of purpose-built three-storey business chambers, rather than the prevailing pattern of houses over shops. At a more humdrum level, the 1830s saw a range of innovative Hamilton projects, including the Cleland Testimonial, Buchanan Street (1834–6), built to celebrate Cleland's retiral from his Superintendent post – a corner block of tenements and shops, with inset rounded corner like Hamilton's later British Linen Bank, which presaged a characteristic Glasgow pattern. Hamilton's last commercial and public projects, around 1840, anticipated trends of the mid-century and will be dealt with in Chapter 6.

To offset the creation of grand urban vistas, David Hamilton also emphasised the architectural design of green space in the city. The Necropolis, dramatically situated on a hill behind the cathedral, saw major Hamilton works including the gateway (1833, with massive piers derived from

Stark's Asylum), the lodge (1839–40), and the 'Bridge of Sighs' (1833–4) over which the remains of Glasgow's ruling classes were conveyed to their last, often architect-designed resting places. He also played a central architectural role in the ceremonial event which set the seal on Glasgow's new status: the 1837 visit by Sir Robert Peel to be installed as Rector of the University. A banquet for over 2,000 guests, arranged predictably by Cleland (whose definitive volume *Statistical Facts of Glasgow* was published that year), was held in a temporary pavilion in Buchanan Street. The pavilion, laden with rich British nationalist symbolic decoration, was designed by Hamilton, as the city's premier architect.

The results of the push to monumentalise the Scottish city, west and east, were assessed by an influential outside observer in 1826. In that year, one of the great European masters of early nineteenth-century classicism, Karl Friedrich Schinkel, visited Scotland [5.30]. In Glasgow he noted the 'purity' and 'splendour' of the new architecture, and in both cities he hailed the rapid

5.29 Royal Exchange, Glasgow (D. Hamilton, rebuilt 1827), unexecuted 1911 scheme for extension (visible at rear) by A. N. Paterson.

5.30 K. F. Schinkel, pen and pencil drawing of Edinburgh from Calton Hill, 1826.

march of neo-classical modernity: 'There is a wondrous contrast . . . between the stone huts covered with straw in the old parts, and the splendid streets full of palaces, twenty-foot wide pavements of the finest stone, iron railings and gaslight lamp-posts.' What seemed to Schinkel most immediately striking, in contrast to the plaster facades of everyday Prussian streets, or what he described as the 'mean' urban domestic architecture of England, was the homogeneity of 'magnificent stone' on all sides. Schinkel's romantic sensibility also responded to the juxtaposition of Edinburgh's old and new towns, to the 'picturesque' skyline effect of the Bridewell and the drama of the bridge-streets pushed through, and above, the Old Town. [30] Just as the Edinburgh burghers of 1752 had cited Berlin and other European cities as inspiration for their crusade to recreate their own capital, so Schinkel returned to Berlin from the 'Northern Athens' reinvigorated in his own quest for a monumental and 'national' classicism.

Country House and Villa Architecture: Classicism and Its Rivals

The role and function of the classical country house had historically been legitimated by a slowly evolving social and economic structure. By 1800, after the late eighteenth century's sweeping changes in agriculture had been assimilated, the landed classes emerged richer than ever, and the building of country houses expanded in quantity and quality. However, the architectural form of the kind of houses built underwent radical change, in response to demands for greater informality. The

textbook classical country house set in an informal landscape was gradually slipping from fashion, as the landed classes began to favour more romantic, irregular compositions for their rural seats. Between 1800 and 1820, the grand classical country house had its final say, in a significant burst of building.

By far the greatest of all these projects was the enlargement of Hamilton Palace in 1822-6, by Alexander, 10th Duke of Hamilton, claimant to the Scottish throne and admirer of Napoleonic authoritarianism and continental neo-classicism; in 1843 Hamilton, whom some nicknamed 'Il Magnifico', [31] married his son and heir into the French imperial family. He had begun to build up a colossal art and manuscript collection even before he succeeded to the dukedom in 1819, and (during a period as ambassador to Russia) had commissioned abortive designs for the re-modelling of the palace from Giacomo Quarenghi, then imperial Russian architect. Now his palace was to undergo a hypertrophic expansion, fuelled by the colossal revenues of his industrial developments, especially collieries in Stirlingshire and Lanarkshire: in the mid-1840s, for instance, he saw an annual profit of £10,000 from four new Motherwell mines alone. Even today, the thought of the mountain of working-class toil on which the Duke's Napoleonic vision was built is a sobering one.

In 1819, 'Il Magnifico' commissioned new designs for the remodelling from Francesco Saponieri (who proposed a porticoed design for the new north-facing main front, in the character of Luigi Vanvitelli's Royal Palace at Caserta, from 1752), before finally entrusting the project to David Hamilton, with internal work by London decorator Robert Hume [5.31; cf. 3.8]. Hamilton

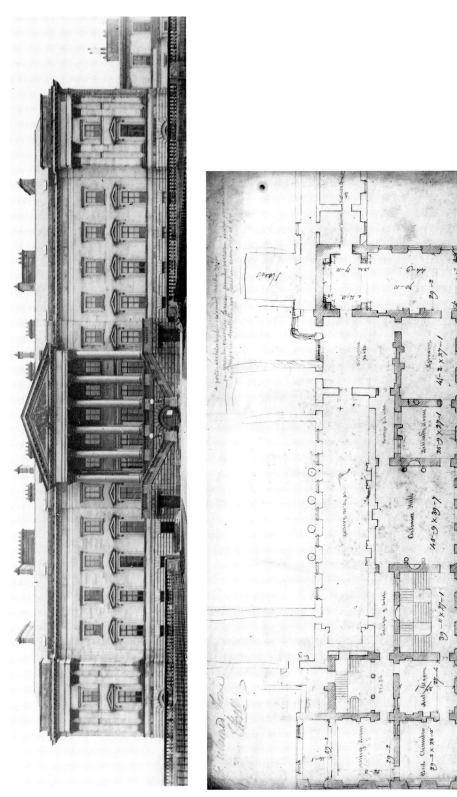

5.31 Hamilton Palace: (above) c.1890 view of the new facade designed by David Hamilton, from 1822; (left) plan by David Hamilton of principal floor of new block.

enlarged Saponieri's proposal in 1822 by adding pilastered pavilions in the manner of Stark's Court House design: he advised the Duke that 'the architectural parts of the Fronts should be executed in a bold and prominent manner, every feature being made to tell out, and affected with the fewest joints'. [32] Overall, the main facade was clearly affiliated to the long European palace tradition of rectangular, horizontal massing. The columns of the exuberantly freestanding hexastyle portico were 25-feet-high monoliths transported to the site, like those of Edinburgh University, in specially constructed vehicles, pulled by a team of thirty horses. Inside, the theme of over-powering grandeur was continued; the entrance hall, repeating the rich Corinthian order of the exterior, led to an array of state rooms crammed with art treasures; in 1828, Napoleon's former architects, Percier and Fontaine, made abortive plans for interiors in the latest French manner [5.32]. In 1844 David Wilkie panegyrised the Duke as 'the first of our peers, the first of our cognoscenti, and in his palace possessing the first gallery of art our country can boast of'. [33] Seven years later, Dr Gustav Waagen, Director of the Prussian Royal Picture Gallery at Berlin, noted on a visit that

> 'as the Duke combined in equal measure a love of art with a love of splendour . . . the whole ameublement was on a scale of costliness, with a more numerous display of tables and cabinets of the richest Florentine mosaic, than I had seen in any other palace. As a full crimson predominated in the carpets, a deep brown in the woods of the furniture, and a black Irish marble, as deep in colour as *nero antico* . . . the general effect was that of the most massive and truly princely splendour; at the same time somewhat gloomy, I might almost say Spanish, in character.' [34]

Hamilton's involvement in the lavish commission provided a conduit for the spread of a continental richness into his own later work, and nineteenth-century Scottish architecture in general. Subsequently, the Duke built a riding school at Hamilton (1838) of a strikingly neo-classical austerity. It comprised a low, rectangular block with arched openings and lunettes. The project may have been inspired by Giacomo Quarenghi's very different design at St Petersburg; its architect was probably David Hamilton.

While the richness of Hamilton Palace's classicism soon began to percolate through to lavish urban commissions by David Hamilton and others, it had relatively little influence within country house architecture, where no other patron could remotely match the Hamilton purse. Other houses still remaining faithful to classicism were relatively austere and restrained in style. But new tendencies were stirring in this area, especially in the area of practical planning, where there was a growing demand for privacy and segregation of different classes of occupants. This requirement was most satisfactorily answered by arranging public rooms in an *en-suite* sequence, preferably with the private rooms in a separate wing – a tendency already presaged in Parisian hôtels of the early eighteenth century. One way of combining this with symmetry was the splay plan: in 1809–14, Archibald Elliot reconstructed William Adam's Minto, making the house one room deeper along its entrance (concave) front and creating extensive private and public accommodation. Externally, the high roofs and gables of Adam's design were replaced by a cubic, parapeted profile, with a multi-level curved portico replacing Adam's ogee-roofed tower at the junction of the wings. Another Adam-like splay plan was used on a smaller scale at Lennel House (*c.*1820, probably by John Paterson). A further influence was the work, in the 1810s, of Robert Smirke, who devised an exceptionally dry, austere Grecian country house architecture of cubic forms. The key examples of this trend were Smirke's Kinmount (1812) in Dumfriesshire, and Whittingehame (1817–18) in East Lothian [5.33]. The former, in its original form, was an uncompromisingly blocky composition whose austere garden front confronted its setting of a tree-covered hill. In the area of practical planning, Smirke's most notable contribution, for the future, was at Newton Don (1815–18), where he devised a plan type with entrance on a side, or short facade, leading to a long axis with (on one side) a sym-metrical garden front of three public rooms (in the case of Newton Don, flanked by bow windows).

These rationalist principles of practical and rectilinear planning were raised to a peak of refine-ment in the country house work of William Burn. From the 1820s, exploiting the High Tory connections he had built up during his time with

5.32 Hamilton Palace, view of gallery (originally built by James Smith), *c.*1880.

Smirke, Burn specialised in country house design, building three or four examples each year. By 1830 he had the biggest architectural practice in Scotland, spanning the whole country without regard for east-west distinctions. An increasingly prominent force within his firm was his assistant (from *c.*1826) and partner (from 1841 to 1850), David Bryce [cf. L.1]. The latter's own, clearly demarcated architectural contributions did not, however, begin until after 1840.

Central to Burn's achievement was his mastery of the changing requirements of country house planning, setting a framework which those who followed, from Bryce to Lorimer, could reproduce and develop with little effort [5.34]. At a purely visual level, this framework displayed, as in the New Town houses, a trend from formality of layout to comfortable informality – a continuation of the trend which had begun in the mid-eighteenth century with the rejection of the state apartment. But alongside this, there was the need to provide the physical setting for the increasingly specialised social structures of the country house – just as

5.33 Kinmount House (R. Smirke, 1812), nineteenth-century engraving.

the planning of the romantic Edinburgh New Town, as a whole, also catered for more and more sophisticated patterns of segregation. As with all inhabitant-influenced dwelling forms from the nineteenth century onwards, the dominant social factor in the design of Burn's country houses was privacy – here in the context of a highly ordered spatial hierarchy in which the lifestyle of the élite inhabitants was supported by a vast pyramid of

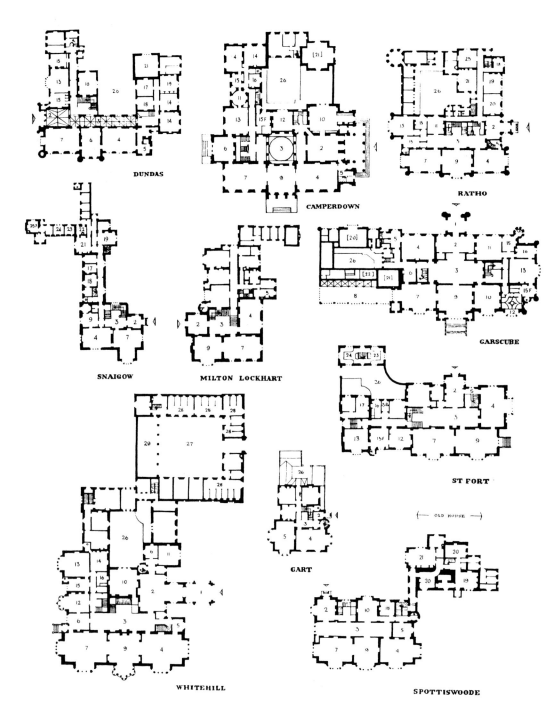

5.34 William Burn, plans of ten country houses to show comparative planning, redrawn by David Walker *c*.1974 from original working drawings. South is at the bottom except for Dundas and Whitehill. Room key: 1 carriage-porch; 2 entrance hall; 3 saloon or hall; 4 dining room; 5 dinner service; 6 anteroom; 7 drawing room; 8 conservatory; 9 library; 10 billiard room; 11 private sitting, writing, business rooms; 12 boudoir; 13 family bedroom; 14 bedroom; 15 dressing room; 16 bathroom; 17 ladies' maid; 18 butler; 19 housekeeper; 20 servants' hall; 21 kitchen; 22 scullery; 23 game larder; 24 dairy; 25 laundry; 26 servants' court; 27 stable court; 28 stables; 29 coach houses.

controlled labour. In David Walker's words,

> Rooms . . . were often linked completely en suite so that the mistress of the house never had to use the hall or the corridor unless going out. The corridor in the private suite was in fact mainly for the use of personal servants, the central saloon and main staircase more for guests than for family. The service wing, or wings, were no less carefully thought out. Male and female servants were solidly walled off from each other with their own stairs, and as far as possible the lines of communication they followed in the course of their duties were kept separate. (35)

This was the last phase of landowner-led innovation, in that movement from the communal to the segregated dwelling which had first emerged (in Scotland) in the Stewarts' palaces. Henceforth the main thrust of this movement would be its extension to smaller dwellings and other social classes.

While Smirke's Newton Don pointed to the linear planning of a country house along an axis stretching from entrance to private areas, with a symmetrical facade of public rooms to one side, it was Burn, with his roots in the Edinburgh culture of spatial rationalism, who developed the full implications of this plan for domestic privacy. At Burn's Camperdown (designed in 1821 and built 1824–6 for the 2nd Viscount Duncan), it was refined further, by placing a separate family wing at right angles at the far end of the long axis. Such an L-shaped house fitted rather awkwardly into the constraints of a formal classical plan, and was more suitable, as we will see, to a non-classical style. Camperdown had a hexastyle Ionic portico and symmetrical pilastered side facade, echoing William Wilkins's Grange Park, in England. Internally, there was an iron-framed, two-storey central saloon and toplit imperial stair. Other architects who remained faithful to an austere classicism for some of their country houses included Simpson in the north-east, who designed the Doric porticoed Crimonmogate (*c.*1825) and the Corinthian Stracathro (1827) in a chastely monumental manner, and William Robertson's Aberlour House of 1838 (with later *porte-cochère* of 1857) [5.35]. But by the late 1820s, the classical country house was in full retreat, owing not only to changing practical concepts of domestic convenience, but also to the growing impact of typological eclecticism, which increasingly associated monumental classicism with public buildings, and country houses with more informal styles. At Burn's Garscube (1826–7), for instance, the fashion-conscious client rejected a classical proposal in favour of a more irregular 'Tudor' mode: we shall examine shortly the prolific non-classical houses in which his planning ideas were fully developed.

In the search for more informal alternatives to monumental classicism in the country house, the first and most obvious choice was to maintain an element of deference to antiquity and the Mediterranean, by adopting the style of the Italian villa,

5.35 Stracathro House (Simpson, 1827).

with its low-pitched roof, its combination of general regularity with asymmetrical features such as low towers, its generally massive walls with sometimes small, round-headed windows, and its general air of harmony with the landscape. This solution – an international paradigm of the picturesque villa – had been especially popular elsewhere in northern Europe in the early nineteenth century, for instance in Germany. But as well as picturesqueness it encompassed an element of rectilinear rationalist geometry, and, for that reason, had been endorsed in the publications of J. N. L. Durand. The leading Scottish figure involved in its promotion was Playfair, in a series of designs of the late 1820s, including Belmont (1828–30), a large villa for Lord MacKenzie just outside Edinburgh, and Drumbanagher, in Ireland (designed 1829) [5.36]. His hybrid proposal of 1828 to build Brownlow, Ireland, 'in the style of a Roman villa', [36] with a symmetrical, porticoed front facade and low-eaved round-arched service wings, was rejected by the client for an 'Elizabethan' style (built 1833–5). In the more remote setting of Dunphail, Morayshire (1828–33), Playfair's tendency of low massiveness, with sweeping eaves, was carried to an extreme – described locally as 'a splendid modern mansion in the Venetian style' [37] – while at St Ronan's Well, *c.*1828, he built a cottage and tree-trunk portico in the Eldin/Adam manner [5.37]. His remodelling of Relugas House, near Forres, in 1830, with *porte-cochère*, was commented on (in memoirs written in the 1840s) by Elizabeth Grant of Rothiemurchus, who remarked that 'it had been a common small Scotch house, but an Italian front had been thrown before the old building and an Italian tower had been raised over the offices'. [38] This pattern was taken up by others, such as Archibald Simpson, who, in his last years, experimented with the design of severe, low-eaved, smaller houses across the north-east; examples included Linton House, Midmar (1835), Thainstone (1840, with tall, arched porte-cochère) and Glenferness (1844–5). John Smith followed Simpson's example at the symmetrical, harled Craigellie House (1840–1). A more asymmetrical classical design, in refined ashlar, was Keithick House, Coupar Angus (1818–23), designed by David A. Whyte of Templeton Meigle. The main

difficulty with this style was one of appropriateness: its connotations of simple rusticity robbed it of some of the ceremonial gravity needed for a major country seat. Those connotations could be seen at work, for example at Simpson's Grecian Crimonmogate (1825), whose west lodge was asymmetrical with highly simplified Doric portico and low-eaved roof. The Italian villa style was sometimes applied to smaller houses, in such rural settings, through the medium of pattern-book design. For example, St John's Cottage, Maybole, a symmetrical but low-eaved house of *c.*1810 with canted front bay, is based on a design for a 'small House in the Style of a Modern Cottage' illustrated in an English pattern book of 1803, Richard Elsam's *Essay on Rural Architecture*.

For those who wanted a more assertively picturesque and 'national' romantic image, castellated, medieval or Northern Renaissance styles seemed more appropriate: the early nineteenth century saw elsewhere in Europe (for instance in Germany, England and France) the beginnings of the 'nationalisation' of the Italian Picturesque by addition of features from the Northern Renaissance. After the eighteenth-century consensus, among landowners, on classicism and rationalist improvement, in the Romantic nineteenth century the pendulum now began to swing away from classical regularity and back towards associations of landownership with lineage. Soon Sir Walter Scott would be able to say, of John Douglas's eighteenth-century remodelling of Dalhousie Castle, that 'the old castle was mangled, I believe, by a fellow called Douglas, who destroyed, as far as in him lay, its military and baronial character and roofd it after the fashion of a Poor's house'. [39] During this period, as accurate archaeological publications on old Scottish buildings were not yet available, whereas volumes concerned with English architecture (such as John Britton's *Architectural Antiquities*, from 1805) were already appearing, attempts at 'national' romanticism at first followed generalised patterns or sometimes specifically English styles such as Elizabethan or Tudor. Later, the demand for more authentic renderings of the 'national' would lead logically to the researches of Kemp (on ecclesiastical buildings) and Billings, and to the eventual emergence of the 'Scotch Baronial' style.

5.36 Belmont, Edinburgh (W. H. Playfair, 1828–30), view of *c*.1896.

5.37 Dunphail House, Morayshire (W. H. Playfair, 1828–33), *c*.1910 view.

In quantitative terms, the years after 1800 saw a veritable boom in castle-building. Where, as we have seen, the period 1746–1800 had seen thirty castles built in Scotland, between 1800 and 1810 a further thirty were now begun. There was a wide range of castellated designs, developing the post-Adam trends seen, for instance, at Fasque or Rossie [cf. 4.12, 4.13]. The most emblematic of the neo-dynastic castles was A. and J. Elliot's central block of Taymouth, a more elaborate version of Inveraray built in 1806–9 for Lord Breadalbane with rich Gothic plasterwork inside by Francis Bernasconi [5.38; cf. 3.41]. The Inveraray resemblance was perhaps to be expected here, as its owners belonged to a cadet branch of Can Campbell. An anonymous traveller in 1819 praised Taymouth as 'a spacious, massy and lofty structure, uniting the idea of the power . . . and grandeur associated with an ancient castle and that of the conveniency, comfort and brilliancy of modern refinement'. [40] Taymouth was extended in 1818–25 by William Atkinson, and again by J. Gillespie Graham in 1834, with sumptuous decoration by Trotters of Edinburgh and the English designer A. W. Pugin.

Further, similar houses by the Elliots were Stobo (1805–11), Loudoun (1806), and Newbyth (1817, a lower-height version of the Inveraray plan). Castellated equivalents in the west were Robert Lugar's Tullichewan (1808) and massive walled additions to Balloch Castle (1809). Examples in Tayside and the north-east included Robert Smirke's Kinfauns Castle (1820–2, a squared-off castellated echo of Kinmount), Simpson's Castle Forbes (1814, completed by

5.38 Taymouth Castle (A. J. Elliot and W.
Atkinson, from 1806), 1903 picture.

John Smith), Smith's Cluny (1836), and the much
later Drummuir Castle, Keith (1848–50), by
Thomas Mackenzie. The most prolific architect of
castellated houses at the beginning of the
nineteenth century was J. Gillespie Graham: his
castles, often with a large round tower, and
sometimes including Gothic fenestration, include
Culdees (1809), Cambusnethan Priory (1816),
Duns (1818), and Dunninald (1823). Houses of a
more Gothic or ecclesiastical style (often late
English Gothic) and asymmetrical plan made their
appearance at Richard Crichton's Abercairny
Abbey (begun 1805 and completed by R. and R.
Dickson); William Atkinson's lavishly decorated
Scone (1803–12) and his smaller Rossie Priory
(1807–15) and plainer Tulliallan (1817–20); J.
Gillespie Graham's Crawford Priory (1811–13, a
completion of an 1809 David Hamilton design);
and R. and R. Dickson's Millearne House (1823–34).

A more idiosyncratic offshoot of this castellated tendency was a neo-Romanesque element.
Crichton's Rossie of *c*.1800 had included flanking
arcades, and Hamilton/Graham's Crawford
included a Romanesque-style main entrance arch
– although whether the latter was intended in
imitation of fifteenth-century ecclesiastical neo-
Romanesque (with its round-arched highlights
within generally Gothic buildings) is unclear. It
was Hamilton who, alongside more conventional
castellated designs such as Castle Toward (1820–1),

designed the most dramatic Romanesque mansion: Lennox Castle (1837–41), a broodingly
symmetrical block, rising from a castle-like
battered plinth with asymmetrical-looking skyline,
in the Adam manner. Hamilton's brief there,
from J . L. Kincaid Lennox, was to express the
latter's family's pretensions to an ancient lineage
through use of a 'Norman' style [5.39]. [41]
A smaller, similarly Romanesque project was R.
and R. Dickson's 1840 addition to Dunimarle.
Comparable work in other countries included
Thomas Hopper's Gosford Castle in Ireland
(*c*.1820) and Penrhyn Castle, Wales (*c*.1825–44).

In this period between the Adam castles and
the mid-nineteenth-century Baronial, the most
noteworthy stylistic trend in romantic country
house architecture was that of 'Tudor' or
'Jacobean'. Here, as with neo-Greek houses, some
English architects were initially most prominent:
for instance, William Wilkins (at Dalmeny,
1814–17 and Dunmore Park, 1820) or E. Blore (at
Corehouse, 1824–7). But here, too, it was William
Burn who became the key figure in relating the
style to innovations of practical planning, in
building it on a large scale, and in beginning the
transition to Baronial. His first large commission,
Saltoun (1817) had a Taymouth-like cubic
composition with plan perhaps derived from
Kinmount, but with square rather than round
corner towers. Architecturally, Burn's houses in

non-classical styles expertly balanced landowners' practical demands for a segregated informality with the potentially conflicting desire for a degree of stateliness in public rooms and main facades. A Burn country house was like a microcosm of the balance between segregation and stateliness, irregularity and symmetry, achieved in the planning of the later Edinburgh New Town [cf. 5.34]. Whereas the practical convenience of a monumental house like Camperdown had to be subordinated, in some respects, to external symmetry, picturesque house styles allowed a more economical concentration of grandeur in towers and specific highlights. But overall, the same rectilinear, almost Durand-like grid-based planning principles were retained. Burn's first non-classical efforts, after Saltoun, mostly followed a broadly symmetrical Tudor style similar to Wilkins's Dalmeny: Carstairs (1822–4), Blairquhan (1820–4) and Garscube (1826–7). There were also so-called 'cottage houses' [(42)] in a more rustic Tudor style, beginning with Snaigow (1824–7) and Freeland (1825–6). A trend towards conscious exploitation of the perceived informality of Scottish Renaissance architecture became evident at Burn houses such as Riccarton (enlarged 1823–7), and Lauriston Castle (enlarged 1827), where an old tower house was incorporated in the composition, and as a result the first floor was used as the principal living level, in the Renaissance manner – a practice that would be increasingly adopted by architects through to Lorimer.

It was from 1829, with Burn's designs of that year for Tyninghame (a large extension) and Milton Lockhart (a new house), and his 1831 designs for Auchmacoy, that we see the real beginnings of 'Scotch Baronial' architecture, with its specific references to Scottish Renaissance castellated architecture through features such as bartizans and crowsteps [5.40]. By then, as we will see later, Sir Walter Scott, with whom Burn was friendly, had made a decisive contribution to Baronial in the building of his own house at Abbotsford. In 1837, at Invergowrie, Burn was using the elements of Baronial architecture with full scenographic confidence; from 1844 he paid R. W. Billings (who had worked on Britton's *Antiquities*) £1,000 to produce his multi-volume *Baronial and Ecclesiastical Architecture of Scotland*, a series whose detailed drawings would provide a decisive inspiration to the Baronial movement. Alongside these developments, Burn also used a 'Jacobean' style derived from a slightly later period of the Northern Renaissance. Carstairs of 1822–4 had Jacobean gables, and the style reached a pitch of sophistication at Dupplin (1828–32), St Fort (1829) and Falkland (1839–44), At first many of these details were of English inspiration, but by the time of Castle Menzies (1836–40), he was also employing Scottish Jacobean detailing. The culmination of Burn's Jacobean houses was Poltalloch (1849–53), built by the Malcolm family

5.39 Lennox Castle (D. Hamilton, 1837–41), 1994 view.

5.40 Tyninghame House (Burn extended 1829), 1888 view.

(enriched from the 1790s by the profits of their Jamaican slave and cotton trading) as part of a wide-ranging programme of estate improvement and village-building. Its south (garden) facade was symmetrical, with bay windows, and the entrance facade had an elaborate tower. From 1838, drawn doubtless by the ever closer cross-border connections within the aristocracy, Burn's attention increasingly turned to England, with his commission to complete the enormous project of Harlaxton Manor in a sumptuous Baroque style (perhaps the work of Bryce). He energetically attempted to export Baronial to England with his designs for Fonthill (1847–9), but it was only in mid-century hotels, and in the later work of his pupil Richard Norman Shaw, that the style took hold there.

Other architects also made important contributions to the evolution of a more 'national' style of informal country house in the early nineteenth century. More scholarly in detail than Burn's work was a series of houses by William Henry Playfair, who increasingly resented the former's success in the field, complaining in 1841 that he 'carries all before him . . . creating blots upon the landscape'. [43] While, in 1833, Playfair eventually

built Brownlow not as a 'Roman villa' but in the Elizabethan style of a 'comfortable . . . old manor house', [44] in the mid-1830s he embarked on a series of remarkably accomplished Baronial houses or enlargements. Key examples were Craigcrook Castle (1835) and Barmore (or Stonefield, 1836–40), with its crowstepped gables and tall twin-corbelled turrets flanking the main entrance, and symmetrical garden facade arrangement of equal-sized drawing and dining rooms flanking a smaller room, in the manner common since the time of William Adam.

Gillespie Graham enlarged Brodick Castle in 1844 in a similar style. Among some Glasgow architects, there were the beginnings of attempts at a specifically 'western' Baronial. David Hamilton, for example, designed Dunlop House (1831–4) in a strikingly compressed, verticalised manner, with elaborate strapwork detailing based on seventeenth-century western sources such as the Glasgow College [5.41]. In the north-east, John Smith played a Burn-like role in propagating competently planned houses in a Jacobean/ Baronial hybrid style, at Easter Skene (1832), Balmoral (1834–9) and Forglen (1840–5); his son William Smith would carry out the influential rebuilding of Balmoral for Queen Victoria in 1853–5. In the north, W. Leslie and the Duke of Sutherland, in consultation with the English designer Sir Charles Barry, enlarged Dunrobin Castle from 1845 in a freer turreted manner.

Paradoxically, these new, more picturesque patterns of country house were linked to a revival of the popularity of *formal* gardens and parterres of the pre-eighteenth century type, whether enclosed and walled or open and axial: Sir Walter Scott was one of their most vociferous advocates. One key site where this connection was made especially explicit was at Murthly, where Gillespie Graham's extravagant project for a Jacobean-style palace (begun 1831, left unfinished 1838) was set as an axial background to the seventeenth-century walled garden. Scott visited the site in 1830 and recorded that the new house was 'planned after the fashion of James VIth's reign, a kind of bastard Grecian – very fanciable and pretty though'; subsequent family correspondence of 1839 included discussion about preservation of the ornamental trees. [45] It was at another Perthshire site, Drummond Castle, that perhaps the most elaborate example of the revival of the Renaissance garden took place, in George P. Kennedy's 1839 remodelling and embellishment of the 1630 parterres. His Italianate design, overlooked by terraces and a grand staircase, and studded with sculpture and topiaries, focuses on a three-dimensional saltire-cross pattern.

At this point, we must take a sideways glance at one area of institutional building – the design of large educational buildings – in which the same picturesque architectural styles as in country houses were used on a rather larger scale, and usually in a monumentally symmetrical arrangement. At the root of this, of course, was the image of George Heriot's Hospital (paradoxically believed by many at that time to have been designed by Inigo Jones), although the precise stylistic expression was more often a kind of English Elizabethan or Jacobean [cf. 2.36]. Most of the key examples belong at the end of our period, among them David Rhind's bristling Daniel Stewart's Hospital, with its two bartizaned towers (1848–53), William Burn's Madras College, St Andrews (1832–4) Archibald Simpson's Marischal College, Aberdeen (1837–42), and – largest of all – Playfair's Donaldson's Hospital (1841–51), a palatial quadrangular complex ranged round a courtyard with an array of towers and turrets [5.42, 5.43]. Playfair applied himself to the detailing of this project with his usual intensity, explaining to the trustees in 1839 that 'I avoid carefully all mixture of Roman mouldings with the Gothic. A picturesque effect can as well be expressed in pure language as in a grotesque and unhealthy jumble'. [46] Emphasising the overlap with country house architecture, Playfair created a similar turreted effect – although closer to the architectural style of Heriot's than to Elizabethan – in his rebuilding of Floors Castle in 1837–45, transforming it into a vast, symmetrical complex with tiers of quadrangular blocks and a forest of bartizans. The climax of this axial spikiness in school design, Bryce's Fettes College, was not built until the 1860s and will be dealt with in Chapter 6 [cf. 6.31, C.2].

As classicism in country house design for the landed classes lost impetus, there arrived in force on the architectural building scene a classical building type, the villa, that in some ways imitated the landed aspirations of the country house, yet also established its own distinct legitimacy. As we have seen in the previous three chapters, the smaller villa, as the centrepiece of an estate or as a retreat, had existed since the Renaissance, and had been powerfully reinvigorated in the eighteenth century, when its social focus gradually widened from lesser landowners to include the professional classes. The early nineteenth century still

5.41 Dunlop House (D. Hamilton, 1831–4), late nineteenth-century view.

5.42 Daniel Stewart's Hospital, Edinburgh (Rhind, 1848–53), seen *c.*1900.

5.43 Donaldson's Hospital, Edinburgh (W. H. Playfair, 1841–51): elevation by Playfair, *c.*1840.

witnessed the building of small classical dwellings in the modest laird's house tradition. For example, Burn's Craigielands (from 1817) comprised what was, in effect, a three-floor villa disguised as a single-storey villa, with Doric portico and Kinmount-like plan centred on a low, square tower. Park House, Drumoak, by Simpson (1822) was like a miniaturised version of Burn's Greenock

Custom House, with single-storey centre section and two-storey pavilions.

But the major boom area in villa-building was in a belt around the cities, at first especially Edinburgh. By 1800, Midlothian was dotted with the country retreats of the Edinburgh middle classes, who were seeking an informal summer foil to the social rigours of town life in the winter; and the same applied around Glasgow. By the early nineteenth century, as we noted above in discussing the 'Italian villa' style, in houses of this smaller size, the issue of formality versus informality seemed much less pressing than in big country seats, and a light classicism, often astylar, soon became popular. David Hamilton, for instance, designed a series of simply detailed villas on small 'estates' on the outskirts of Glasgow or on the Clyde. His Kilmardinny House (attr., *c.*1815) still shows a late Adam character; but after 1800 there was also a host of regularised classical villas such as Aikenhead (1806, extended 1823) and Camphill (*c.*1810), with central portico and panelled or pilastered end bays. Around Aberdeen, examples included a single-storey villa in Westburn Park by Simpson (1836–7), with gently sloping roof, overhanging eaves, and tetrastyle portico. In the Dunblane area, local architect William Stirling designed a mixture of smaller houses of this kind, alongside Tudor manses. Also well underway by the early nineteenth century was the large-scale development of marine summer-residence settlements. These were clustered especially on the Clyde, although in the east it had been recorded as early as 1795 that some cottages in Inveresk were being let as seabathing accommodation.

By 1820 a new trend towards the establishment of the villa as a principal residence of middle-class owners, and of the design of purpose-built suburbs of small villas on the outskirts of cities, was taking hold. Here it overlapped with the urban trend towards self-contained residential areas, noted earlier, in the 1820s' phases of the Edinburgh New Town. In the capital, for example, Arthur Lodge (*c.*1827–30) – probably by Thomas Hamilton, for the jeweller William Cunningham – was a compact, exceptionally refined single-storey suburban villa with roofline broken by a projecting temple-like attic feature. Situated close by was a small development laid out by Gillespie Graham, Blacket Place (from 1825), comprising miniature single-storey (and basement) villas, some with Greek Doric porches. Similar work in villa design was done in Dundee by the Town's Architect, David Neave (including Logie House, *c.*1813). A slightly later single-storey Graeco-Egyptian villa, The Vine, was built in Dundee in 1836 by an unknown architect, as a house and art gallery for

George Duncan, MP. A similarly restrained informality was seen inside houses such as these, as demonstrated in Alexander Carse's 1807 view of the drawing room at Midfield Cottage, Lasswade. Later, with improved transport by land and sea, especially through the railways, suburban villas were laid out on increasingly large and regularised patterns of streets, alongside high-class tenements. By this stage (unlike in the late nineteenth century) the era of purpose-built working-class tenements, of generally classical ashlar-faced appearance, had not yet arrived. Working-class people still tended to live in older areas abandoned by the middle class.

During the years 1820–40, the domination of the symmetrical villa began to be challenged, partly through the influence of the parallel developments in country house architecture, but chiefly through the rationalising of the limited space available to the villa client or speculator. A more informal, picturesque, asymmetrical style of villa architecture was well suited to housing the growing commercial classes and their attendant solicitors, teachers, doctors, and of course architects. This reassessment of the form of the villa is best illustrated in the suburban and marine developments around Glasgow and along the Clyde, where a traveller in 1826–7 noted that the shores were 'enlivened with the seats and villas of the more opulent merchants'. [47] Here, at first, the Italian villa was dominant but, after 1850, the 'national' Picturesque began to replace it, as we shall see in Chapter 6 [cf. 5.47]. In the prolific villa work of David Hamilton, the emergence of these non-classical trends can be seen in microcosm. An early, informal design of a villa-sized house in castellated form was his Castle House, Dunoon (1822), with portico, designed for the former Lord Provost of Glasgow, James Ewing. The marine resort of Largs shows a range of slightly later D. and J. Hamilton villas in informal styles: a low, asymmetrical Tudor pattern at Priory Lodge (Elderslie Hotel) 1829–30 and two other attributed examples in Largs – Warriston and Northfield – of *c.*1830; and a low-eaved, bay-windowed, asymmetrical splayed plan with diagonally-set porch at St Fillans Villa (1843, in nearby Skelmorlie); a severely classical design of the same period in Largs was Brooksby (attr., *c.*1840).

Ecclesiastical Architecture and the Rise of Neo-Gothic

The increasingly 'deep and fervid spirit' of early nineteenth-century religion stimulated a marked rise in church attendances. [48] Ecclesiastical buildings reflected this only indirectly, in a new stress on historical and archaeological accuracy. In contrast to England, France and Germany, where the identification of Gothic as 'national' gave a more precise, medievalising focus to this trend, the lesser emotional resonance of Gothic in Scotland allowed not only a thriving classical church architecture but also the use on equal terms of a wide range of medieval styles, including English Perpendicular or Flemish, and, alongside Gothic, a growing tendency of neo-Romanesque (generally referred to at the time as 'Norman'). All the medieval styles were treated still in a rather regular, symmetrical manner – on plan, not unlike the classical Lasswade or Cromarty East. It is difficult to make any hard-and-fast links between particular styles and denominations. On the one hand, classical styles were denounced by some as 'Popish' or 'pagan'. On the other hand, there was an almost opposite tension within Presbyterianism, with a growing use of neo-Gothic by the Established Church, and an attempt by the dissenting Churches to mark themselves off from this through classicism.

In Edinburgh classical churches, while the post-Gibbs steepled tradition continued in designs such as Robert Nisbet's Inveresk Church (1803–10), and was developed in Grecian form at Burn's North Leith Church of 1813, the controversies of 1816 about the style of the National Monument led to the labelling of Greek temple motifs as 'pagan'. [49] Relatively few columnar Greek churches were built after that in the capital: an example was Archibald Elliot's 1820–1 Broughton Church, with its Doric temple front. More typical were styles such as the Graeco-Baroque of Playfair's St Stephen's, or the domed Roman of Reid's St George's, Charlotte Square [cf. 5.12]. In Glasgow, there was less ideological controversy, and the grafting of porticoes on to the existing meeting-house pattern could be carried on and developed. A foretaste of the mid-century classical affiliations of the United Presbyterian Church was seen in Gillespie Graham's West George Street Independent Church of 1818, for a dissenting congregation, with portico on rusticated podium; some critics, however, described it as a 'Popish Chapel'. [50] Similarly, John Baird I's Greyfriars United Secession Church (1821) was fronted by a Roman Doric portico. Classical designs for the Established Church in Glasgow ranged from the Baroque power of Stark's St George's Tron Church (1807–8) to the quieter designs of David Hamilton for St Enoch's Parish Church (1827), with portico and retained older spire, and St Paul's Parish Church (1835) with unpedimented Ionic portico and domed tower [cf. 5.5].

Within Gothic churches, the end of the eighteenth century had seen the idiosyncratic example of the Adams' St George's Episcopal Chapel in Edinburgh (1792, with octagonal lantern on ogival arches), as well as two pioneering examples which employed characteristically Scottish medieval or seventeenth-century-style detailing: James Playfair's small, chapel-like Farnell Church of *c.*1789 (with Y-tracery) and Richard Crichton's towered Craig Parish Church of 1799 (with reticulated tracery). However, the emphasis on a 'national' neo-medievalism in church architecture would only develop fully at the end of the nineteenth century. Most of the large numbers of Gothic churches built after 1800 were treated in a thin, often spiky manner, with, if anything, English Perpendicular stylistic features: for example, Glenorchy Church (1810–11), built by the Earl of Breadalbane (client of the Elliots at Taymouth) as a kind of eyecatcher on rising ground; or John Paterson's octagonal St Paul's Church, Perth (reconstruction *c.*1800–7) and Fetteresso Church, Stonehaven (1810–12). With examples such as Gillespie Graham's Collace (1813), or David Hamilton's Old Erskine (1813–14), Larbert (1817), and St John, Bell Street, Glasgow (1817–19), we witness attempts at a more 'correct' English Perpendicular. Gillespie Graham soon established neo-Gothic church design, alongside castellated houses, as the core of his very large practice – the only rival of Burn's in scale. In working out how to adapt Gothic architecture to Presbyterian worship – the same dilemma that the post-1560 designers had faced – the solution of architects was increasingly to retain 'aisles', but to use the latter for galleries facing into the 'nave'.

Apart from a characteristically vigorous experiment by Stark in the low, massively harled design of Saline Parish Church (1809–10), it was in the cities that the first attempts at a more monumental neo-Gothic expression were taken, for it was within planned urban settings that the churches could make their mark, as populations grew and the socially disruptive effects of industrialisation increased. Celebrating the passing of the Catholic Relief Act, James Gillespie Graham designed St Andrew's Roman Catholic Chapel in Glasgow (1814–17) with an imposing 'Oxbridge college chapel' front; it was originally planned that a large neo-Gothic seminary for the teaching of priests would be built next door [5.44]. With the increase in English migrant workers, the Episcopal Church also enjoyed rapid growth. In the capital, the Episcopalians chose English Perpendicular models, at St Paul's York Place (Archibald Elliot, 1816–18), the towered St John's Chapel (William Burn, 1816–18 – doubtless inspired by the Gothic work of Smirke, for example at Lowther Castle). The English commentator Thomas Rickman criticised St John's for its 'constant repetition of small parts'; [51] but at his own St David's (Ramshorn) of 1824–6, in Glasgow, the geometrical tracery seemed hardly less thin. More significant was the Ramshorn Kirk's T-plan and symmetrical front with tall tower.

5.44 St Andrew's RC Cathedral, Glasgow (Graham, 1814–17), 1965 view.

In a series of designs, a somewhat Schinkel-like pattern of symmetrical neo-Gothic churches with tall towers closing axial street vistas was established: we recall here the similar principles of Playfair's Baroque tower at St Stephen's Edinburgh [cf. 5.12]. Axial-towered churches of this kind were built by a large range of architects in the 1820s and 1830s, including designers more renowned for their classical work. Examples included David Hamilton (Bothwell, 1825–33, and High Church of Campsie, Lennoxtown, 1827–8); John Smith (Udny, 1821); William Stirling II (for example Lecropt, 1824–6, with D. Hamilton); George Angus (Tulliallan, 1832–3); and David Bryce (Coylton, 1836, and Monkton, 1837). It is also worth noting that a steepled axial pattern became established as one of the main styles of early nineteenth-century Episcopal and Presbyterian churches in North-East America.

A smaller group of parish churches were designed on the same planning principles, but in a neo-Romanesque style. These included Gillespie Graham's Errol (1831–3) and Thomas Hamilton's spired Alyth (1837–9): Hamilton claimed in 1833 that 'the Norman style of architecture is in my opinion very suitable for a parish church; it requires little expenditure on ornament, while it presents features sufficiently characteristic of its intended purpose'. [52] R. and R. Dickson added a tall, round-arched steeple and spire to Edinburgh's Tron Kirk in 1828. Slightly later neo-Romanesque examples included William Burn's Morton Church (1839–41) and John Henderson's Stirling North Church (1841). It is not clear whether there was any awareness of the 'national' overtones of round arches in the fifteenth century: Hamilton's South Leith Parish Church (1847–8) combined round-arched openings with some Scots Gothic detailing.

Pre-eminent among the country's early nineteenth-century neo-medieval churches was one example where setting and archaeology were resoundingly brought together: Gillespie Graham's Tolbooth Church in Edinburgh's Castlehill (1839–44), already mentioned above for its townscape role [5.45]. Built to house both the Tolbooth congregation and act as a meeting hall for the General Assembly of the (pre-Disruption) Kirk, the building consists of the same basic

5.45 Courtyard of Free Church College (Playfair, 1846–50) and (to rear) Tolbooth Church steeple (Graham, 1839–44), 1930s' view.

elements as the earlier churches – hall and symmetrically planned tower – but the scale is now monumental and the detailing dense and assured. The 240-feet-high steeple, in contrast to the square lumpiness of, for example, Airth, presents an ornament-loaded cluster of soaring gablets, its mass lightened in a presentiment of the Glaswegian neo-Gothic of the 1860s and 1870s. The principal source for this design was, of course, Thomas Hamilton's 1829 John Knox Church proposal, for the same site, with a similarly rich, Flemish-inspired spire; but in much of the fertile detailing of the building (especially on the spire), Graham was helped by his young English assistant, A. W. N. Pugin – whose polemics were shortly to spark off the 'Gothic Revival' movement in his own country. In its confident massing and its vigorous silhouette – later enhanced so triumphantly by Playfair's college project for the seceding Free Church on the Mound below – the Tolbooth Church was one of the crowning architectural achievements of 'Romantic Edinburgh'. Another major steeple by Graham and Pugin had been added in 1832–4 to the boxy Old Church, Montrose (built 1791 by David Logan); its buttressed form hinted at an open crown-like form. More explicitly anticipating the later nineteenth-century revival of the crown steeple was the example added in 1818 by Robert Pollok to East Kilbride Parish Church (rebuilt 1774).

Throughout Europe, the interest in medieval architecture had now matured to such a degree that controversies arose over the condition of some of its monuments: the epoch of 'restoration' began in earnest. William Burn subjected Dunfermline Abbey Kirk to radical rebuilding (essentially as a new building) in 1821, and in 1829–33 refaced St Giles's Edinburgh, sweeping away the famous 'Luckenbooths' (medieval shops) attached to its walls. Only the tower remained largely untouched by his surgery. In 1835 Gillespie Graham produced plans for the reroofing of the Holyrood Abbey Church for use as a General Assembly Hall. These proposals proved too expensive (leading in turn to his Tolbooth Church project), as did a plan by Graham the following year to reorder Glasgow Cathedral internally (making unauthorised use of drawings by Meikle Kemp); both schemes fell through. In 1848 the

North British Railway's dismantling of Trinity College Church, Edinburgh, for the building of the city's main railway station, caused major controversy. The dismantling was supervised by Bryce and the choir was rebuilt on its present site (between High Street and Jeffrey Street) from 1872. On the whole, the national/moral passion provoked by church restoration in some countries (such as Germany or England) was less prominent in Scotland. Conservationist energy would mainly be aroused, in the later nineteenth and twentieth centuries, by secular tasks, including collective urban regeneration. In the final section of this chapter, we deal with the broad context of that secular orientation: the Romantic search for 'national' architecture, led by Sir Walter Scott.

Scott, Abbotsford and 'National' Architecture

As part of his wider influence in defining the specific images and qualities of the new world-projection of Imperial Scotland, it was Scott who played a decisive role in setting down, for the first time, precise 'national' qualities in architecture, in contrast to the more general evocativeness of, say, Robert Adam's Castle Style [cf. 4.13]. It was Scott's work that made it certain there would be no religio-nationalistic 'Gothic Revival' in mid-century Scottish architecture – although there would be some parallels to the latter in the classical work of Alexander Thomson. On the whole, it would be secular architecture that would be the focus of the quest for the 'national'.

Building on the impact of Ossian, Scott's writings played a key role in the international development of Romanticism, by fuelling the growing identification of Romantic genius with nations, as well as, or instead of, individuals. In the Scottish context, this growing pride in the nation's past was closely bound up with pride in the improving, imperialist present: Scott was a close friend of Skene of the Board of Manufactures, and argued in 1826, 'Let us remain as nature made us, Englishmen, Irishmen and Scotchmen, with something like the impress of our several countries upon each. We would not become better subjects, or more valuable members of the common empire, if we all resembled each other like so many smooth shillings.' [53] The influence Scott exerted on the development of 'national Romanticism' in architecture was not, however, purely indirect and literary. He also made a more direct and crucial impact, through the building of his own famous villa or retreat in the Borders: Abbotsford [5.46, 5.47, 5.48].

Abbotsford was Scotland's most influential contribution to the movement of Romantic 'troubadour' houses that swept Europe in the late eighteenth and early nineteenth centuries. Its building (or, rather, rebuilding, as a nondescript farmhouse formed the core of the complex) took place in two stages in 1817–23; this was preceded by a prolonged process of planning and of abortive schemes by Scott himself – a process during which Scott's own approach matured steadily from a frothy dilettantism to a greater antiquarian, and moral, seriousness. Doubtless the image Scott first had in mind for his country villa was the thatched rusticity of Clerk of Eldin's Lasswade Cottage, which he himself had rented from 1798 to 1804. [54] Scott's first architect-collaborator on the Abbotsford project was Stark, who began work in 1811 on what was envisaged as a design of 'a picturesque and original cast . . . sufficiently rural though not boorish'. Stark's death precluded the

realisation of this 'whimsical, gay, odd cabin that we had chalked out' (Scott). [55] Sir Walter then sought the assistance of William Atkinson in designing a now more ambitious non-classical design: 'an old English hall such as a squire of yore dwelt in'. [56] By 1816, the 'English' features had been expunged in favour of a still somewhat lighthearted, but specifically 'Scottish' image: the ideal of 'an old-fashioned Scotch residence, full of rusty iron coats and jingling jackets' . . . in 'the old fashioned Scotch style which delighted in notch'd gable ends and all manner of bartizans'. [57] The first building phase, in 1817–19, adopted a broadly Jacobean manner with Scottish Renaissance detailing. As in his work at Scone, Atkinson was also put to work designing the interiors, including carpets, curtains, and new furniture using medieval detail on a basically classical framework. It might seem odd that an English architect should have been involved here at all, but Scott was of course the dominant influence on proceedings. In the second phase, built 1821–3 (again with Atkinson), Scott's ideas had developed further. Externally, the completed building was now quite complex, with some explicitly Baronial features – including a Fyvie-type arch flanked by crowstepped towers on the river facade. The gardens of Abbotsford also formed part of the

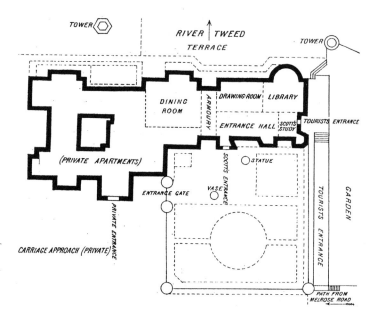

5.46 Abbotsford House, ground plan from R. Richardson, *The Land of Scott* (excursion handbook for British Association for the Advancement of Science meeting in Edinburgh, 1892). This plan was taken from Thomas Ross's personal copy.

5.47 Abbotsford (W. Atkinson with W. Scott, 1817–23), external view in 1840s.

5.48 Abbotsford, Entrance Hall, *c*.1885 photograph by Alexander Inglis.

movement to revive the 'walled garden'.

Internally, in 1824, after the house's structural completion, Scott implemented a scheme of decoration which would give the interiors – a library, study, hall and drawing room – a more evocative and serious 'old' and 'national' atmos-phere. He did this through two devices. The first was the profuse incorporation of actual old architectural fragments and pieces of furniture – effectively the beginning of 'antique' collecting in Scotland. And the second was the treatment of new surfaces so as to resemble old. In a slightly unexpected link with Edinburgh rationalism, both were organised for him by D. R. Hay, who later recalled that 'at that time, there were no shops in Edinburgh such as these where old carvings can now be easily obtained – for I believe Sir Walter's adoption of these articles as a decoration gave the first impulse to the rage for them which has since existed'. [58] In room decoration, Scott (according to Lockhart's *Life*) 'abominated the commonplace daubing of walls, panels, doors and window-boards with coats of white, blue or grey', and 'desired to have about him . . . rich, though not gaudy, hangings, or substantial old-fashioned wainscot work, with no ornament but that of carving; and where the wood was to be painted at all, it was done in strict imitation of oak or cedar'. [59] In Hay's words, 'Sir Walter desired that it should all be done in imitation of oak, not like woodwork newly fitted up, but to resemble the old oak carvings as much as possible . . . to appear somewhat weather-beaten and faded, as if it had stood untouched for years'. [60] Here we witness the beginning of the nineteenth-century concern for 'artistic' oldness in interiors. This movement would reach its climax not in the mid-century Baronial (which endorsed a Burn-like practical modernity indoors) but in the late nineteenth-century reaction *against* Baronial at the hands of Rowand Anderson and others.

The influence of Abbotsford was enormous – and not only within architecture. Where Scott's works had promoted Scotland as an international tourist attraction, Abbotsford now itself became part of that tourist circuit, alongside Melrose; in 1844, Fox Talbot photographed the house for a book, *Sun Pictures in Scotland* – only the second photographic book ever published – devoted to subjects associated with Scott and his novels. By the mid 1850s, the house received over 4,000 visitors a year, and by the mid 1870s over 2,000 Americans alone were visiting annually. Its architectural influence extended equally far eastwards, and was put to widely varying purposes. As early as the 1820s the Russian Tsar Nicholas commissioned Adam Menelaws to build Abbotsford-inspired pavilions with Gothic and 'cottage' features at Peterhof (alongside other contrasting structures such as a Turkish elephant house and Egyptian gate) and Tsarskoe Selo. Conversely, the Scott-influenced turreted mansions 'in the style of old Scots castles', built by some Polish nobles in the 1820s and 1830s, were intended to evoke 'feelings of sorrow for the forsaken power of Poland'. [61]

At home, the fame of Scott was the direct cause of, and inspiration for, the most spectacular shrine of the early nineteenth-century movement of national romanticism: the Sir Walter Scott Monument in Edinburgh [5.49]. This 200-feet-high neo-Gothic steeple, comprising a tapering, multi-pinnacled spire on an arched, diagonally buttressed and flying-buttressed base (with a statue by John Steell beneath) was built in 1840–6 at a cost of £16,000 to the designs of George Meikle Kemp. Kemp, an ex-assistant to Burn, won a two-stage competition in 1838 (which had specified the Gothic style) with a design which he claimed to be a secular adaptation of 'the purity of taste and style of Melrose Abbey'. In the 1820s and 1830s, Kemp had acquired an unrivalled first-hand knowledge of Scottish Gothic architecture through extensive sketching tours, and had made drawings for an abortive project to publish a book on Scottish ecclesiastical antiquities; the Scott Monument design was based on these studies. [62] The completed monument was hailed by a Town Council brochure as a 'Gothic temple . . . gorgeously decorated . . . perhaps the finest monumental edifice in the kingdom'; Kemp predicted that the views from it would 'create an excitement something like one of Scott's romances'. [63] Kemp's other most significant completed work, before his premature death in 1844, was the Millburn Church at Renton (designed 1840, completed 1845), an axial-plan building with a spiky spire like the Scott Monument. Immediately following Kemp's death, his crusade of antiquarian recording was taken up by Burn, who commissioned Billings (as we saw above) to resume the task of recording and publication.

Along with the Tolbooth Church, the Scott Monument was the heir to Hamilton's and Burn's 1824 call for a 'Flemish' architecture in the Old Town. In particular, it recalled the spiky openwork Antwerp spire proposed for Hamilton's John Knox Church – only this was now clothed in archaeological Scottish detail. Seen in vistas along Princes Street or glimpsed through Old Town closes, the Monument was perhaps the supreme built realisation in Europe of the Gothic-fantasy ideal which had featured so prominently, for

5.49 Sir Walter Scott Monument (1840–6), Edinburgh, drawing of *c*.1840 by George Meikle Kemp.

instance, in the paintings of Schinkel. Where Playfair, as recently as 1835, had proposed a Scott Monument in the form of a classical obelisk, now the cult of monuments to national heroes was firmly wrenched away from classicism. Thomas Hamilton, too, built a neo-Gothic national monument, in Ayr: the square, multi-stage Wallace Tower (1830–3), with niche for James Thom's statue of Wallace in a primitivist style. But soon Gothic, too, would be rejected as insufficiently 'national'.

Conclusion

All the architectural expressions of Scottish nationality during the post-1815 period – classical, neo-medieval and Baronial – seemed equally at ease within the overarching framework of the 'imperial partnership'. By 1848, as we will see in Chapter 6, it did not even seem surprising that Queen Victoria should herself acquire, and reconstruct, a Baronial mansion in the Highlands, at Balmoral [cf. 6.25]. It was the very power of British imperialism that facilitated the worldwide projection of the images of Scottish culture, including the fame of Classical Edinburgh and of 'Scott Country'. As we will see in the next two chapters, the architectural concern with 'national' values would fluctuate in character and intensity over the remainder of the nineteenth century. During the mid-century, the expression of the 'national' in secular architecture would be dominated by confidence and aggressive individualism, whereas later, an element of moral-collective utopianism would become predominant.

Chapter 6

1840–1880

Mid-Century Eclecticism and the Ascendancy of Glasgow

'. . . the present mania of fashions and styles . . .'
Building Chronicle, 9 Nov. 1854 [1]

'. . . an endeavour to realise the idea of eternity'.
Alexander Thomson, on 'the soul of Egyptian
Art', 2nd Haldane Lecture, 1874

Introduction

During the mid-nineteenth century, as the global power of the British 'imperial partnership' experienced its most triumphant expansion, Scottish society responded with an optimistic mixture of commitment to the promotion of capitalism, and confidence that its concomitant social evils could be conquered. At the end of the century, a perception of external and internal threats would encourage the development of a more unified and disciplined conception of the nation. But for now, with world-wide Scottish industrial and commercial power flourishing beneath the imperial umbrella, anxieties about national identity were at an all-time low. Responding to this climate, the nation's architects maintained, on the whole, their affiliation to monumental classicism, but subtly transformed it through a modernising, *laissez-faire* spirit. This was expressed not only, in most designers' work, through a rich eclecticism, but also, in the outstanding case of Alexander Thomson, through an unparalleled combination of religious-based emotionalism and structural logic. At the same time as these classical developments, the specifically 'national' architectural images adumbrated by Scott were expanded into the ebullient Scotch Baronial style. In many ways, however, the main achievement of the period lay not in the setpieces of high architecture, illustrious though they were, but in the sheer *amount* of everyday 'architecture'

constructed in the now established building types such as commercial or social buildings, or middle-class housing. By the end of the period, even working-class housing aspired to an unprecedented, ashlar-faced grandeur.

The Triumph of Laissez-Faire

The undermining of the political power of the old society of landed and established religious interests was now followed by a further acceleration of capitalist-led social and economic transformation. This was the era of urbanised mass development, above all in and around Glasgow – now one of the great cities of Europe – and of the building-up of a new diverse industrial base, including coal and iron production. The vast wealth created by imperial and capitalist expansion percolated down throughout much of society, including skilled workers. In some ways, this was a time of rampant individualism: in housing, for instance, the small speculator was the main engine driving the large-scale construction around the cities. The earlier building types of capitalism were refined and elaborated. Banks and insurance companies built ever more grandiose headquarters and branches in the cities, along with offices for lawyers, shipping firms and land agents; the construction of bank chambers from the 1840s (as with David Rhind's work for the Commercial Bank) constituted one of the biggest ever building campaigns in Scottish cities. Technologically advanced warehouses, dock and harbour buildings, daring road and railway bridges were constructed across the country.

This age was also a laboratory of alternatives to the iron law of the market economy – alternatives which were seen, for the moment, in embryo only. The early nineteenth-century evangelical efforts bore fruit in an explosion of religious zeal, and a diversification of the Presbyterian parish system. The deferential system of landed patronage, already eroded by dissenting city dwellers, was further undermined by the Disruption of 1843, over the issue of state control of patronage. Of 1,203 ministers, 451 walked out and created the Free Church of Scotland, unleashing one of the largest single building campaigns of the century, including exhilarating monuments like the Free Church Colleges of Edinburgh and Glasgow [cf. 5.45, 6.4]. The Free Church was a child of the nineteenth-century version of improvement – dominated by the new middle classes and the rich, and by artisans and farmers. From 1847 the merger of the various Secession churches created another wealthy, modernising denomination, the United Presbyterians; we shall return later to their special influence among the ruling classes of Glasgow. Yet, despite all their activity, the churches' ability to intervene directly in the social and public-health crises of the period was actually in decline. Following the great famines of 1846–7, even Thomas Chalmers accepted the demise of the communitarian and charity-based ideal of the 'godly commonwealth', and urged state involvement. Now the way was open to the hegemony of the two competing materialistic visions of capitalism and state-socialism – a theme which forms the backdrop to the architectural patronage of Chapters 7, 8 and 9. Indirectly, however, evangelical attitudes continued to exert influence on secular affairs, for instance through the reformist thinking of key members of Glasgow Town Council – or, as we will see, through the architectural utopianism of Alexander Thomson.

At first, state intervention in social provision mostly took the form of local boards and committees, usually of a hybrid public/private character. Only gradually did municipal or local authorities become more prominent. In education,

for instance, by the 1860s, middle-class dissatisfaction with the fragmented, private-based system led to state intervention, in the 1872 Education Act, and the imposition of formal curricula and a unified system; but the main power was still wielded by local boards. In the countryside, there was at first little erosion of the old order. The role of landowners remained a prominent one, but now under the public title of Commissioners of Supply. In this capacity, they oversaw, and mostly paid for, the building of courthouses, jails, roads and bridges. By the turn of the century, however, the local authority system would be extended to the country areas as well.

Increasingly it was the city which was seen as the key battleground for the issues of disease, vagrancy and crime: the cholera epidemic of 1848–9 administered an especially severe shock to the middle classes of Glasgow. Compared to the more pessimistic outlook which began to spread later in the century, the city was still seen as a fundamentally civilising force, which could deal with its own problems. The expansion of street lighting, for instance, allowed a completely new, more open view of the city at night. Although the increasing external projection of Scotland in terms of the anti-urban, Highland imagery of Ossian and Scott appeared to separate the urban and the 'national', the two were subtly complementary. Glasgow Town Council's choice of Scott's Loch Katrine as the source of its municipal water supply tapped the romantic purity of the Highlands. As in the case of water, municipal social initiatives at this stage concentrated on provision and control of basic physical infrastructure. In a succession of laws, from the 1862 General Police Act (inspired by the vision of Provost Lindsay of Leith) to the 1892 Burgh Police Act, police (regulatory) commissioners and town councils were welded into unified 'local authorities', whose services benefited the middle and, increasingly, the working classes. In what was beginning to emerge as a major social and health problem, working-class housing, there were attempts at police regulation of standards, though Dean of Guild Courts. The most dramatic public intervention in the built environment – the clearance and replanning work of the city improvement schemes – was at this stage initiated and controlled by separate trusts, but it pointed directly to the future interventions of municipal socialism.

How did mid-nineteenth-century buildings express the bewildering changes and challenges of the period? In the area of construction, traditional methods remained dominant, but became comparatively much cheaper. However, industrial expansion also produced revolutionary new building materials: cast and wrought iron, and, later, steel. The use of iron in 'high' architecture potentially undermined, still further, classicism's once-settled relationship of structure and decoration, based on the Orders and the trabeated principle. It also seemed to clash with the newly achieved triumph of low-cost, high-quality load-bearing stone construction. Structure and architecture now seemed potentially unrelated; it was possible to criticise eclectic decoration as 'mask architecture'. [2] Debates started: how much should iron be expressed externally? Or, more fundamentally: should architecture aim at decorated construction, or constructed decoration? In Chapter 5, we touched on one solution, in the country houses of Burn: to use iron everywhere, increasing the flexibility of planning, but to do so in a concealed or subordinated manner. Later in this chapter, we will see that some different and more explicit aesthetic expressions of structural iron were attempted in Glasgow city centre commercial developments. But after about 1860, the concealed approach became accepted as the norm, for at least the next fifty years: there was a ubiquitous structural use of iron, and later steel, behind the scenes. Exposed structural ironwork was only used in utilitarian structures such as exhibition halls, conservatories (notably Boucher & Cousland's Kibble Palace, first erected in 1863–6 at Coulport House and moved to Glasgow Botanic Gardens in 1873) or railway-station sheds (such as James Carswell's Queen Street, Glasgow, 1878–80).

In 'high' architecture, the dominant capitalist modernity of the age was expressed not through new materials but through a new, dense, cosmopolitan eclecticism, fed by an unprecedentedly prolific availability of sources. At home, although there were still close links with other professions and trades through the medium of freemasonry, the professional status of the architect was becoming ever more precisely defined, partly

through new networks of societies and professional institutions. Only now did architects acquire a generally accepted status equal, for example, to lawyers. After two attempts to found national architectural associations in 1840 (the Edinburgh-based Institute of the Architects of Scotland, which collapsed in 1841) and 1850 (the Architectural Institute of Scotland, which lasted until 1873), a relatively settled pattern emerged of consolidated western and eastern groupings (led, from 1858, by the Glasgow Architectural Association, later the Glasgow Institute of Architects, and the Edinburgh Architectural Association); regional associations were founded in Dundee in 1884, Aberdeen and Inverness in the 1890s, and Stirling in 1933. It was only a few Edinburgh practices, such as that of Bryce, which established a nationwide scope (including the west), and then only in specialised categories such as country houses; urban work was generally dealt with on a western, eastern or regional basis.

Stylistically, far wider links were now possible: the march of eclecticism had left behind classical archaeological investigations of the Adam and Cockerell kind, and substituted a combination of journals and books (as a miscellaneous and international stylistic source) and archaeological research into specifically 'national' subjects on the lines set out by Scott and Kemp. As Alexander Thomson told the Glasgow Architectural Society in 1859, the architect today was 'built about with books, containing examples of every known style. If an architect wants an idea, he does not require to fly away into the region of the imagination to fetch it – it is ready on hand on the adjoining shelf'. [3] The need for aspiring architects to be wealthy enough to afford extensive personal travel had gone. And there were also personal contacts, which proliferated especially during Glasgow's heyday of British imperial commitment and transatlantic sea traffic. Thomson's own business and family links were no more than typical, taking in as they did India (through a brother-in-law in the army), Africa (through a missionary brother) and the United States (through an architect brother-in-law). Historians today may conceivably underestimate the density of connections of ideas and styles in those years, coming as they did before the regularisation of international architectural intercourse through mass journals; much further research on the subject is necessary.

The mid-nineteenth century in no way challenged the dominance of monumental classicism within Scotland, but fundamentally changed its nature, by further complicating and undermining the precedent-led framework of the Orders, with its hierarchy of decorum both between and within buildings. The growing demand for more sumptuous decoration and richer profiles reinforced the grip of typological eclecticism – that is, the use of different styles as the main way of distinguishing between building types. Although some architects, such as Thomson, chose to evoke an antique stateliness in selected contexts, any building type could now potentially be heavily loaded with ornament. Heavier ornamentation was also bound up with a further dramatic intensi-fication of synthetic eclecticism: the mingling of different sources within single buildings. Increasingly, across northern Europe, the established sources of international classicism – the Graeco-Roman, the round-arched 'Italian' (or Romanesque) and the Baroque – were merged with elements of the 'national' or 'Northern' Renaissances from the fifteenth to the eighteenth century. And they were used in novel com-binations, in heavier, pyramidal groupings. The Second Empire style promoted by Napoleon III in France in the 1850s gave special prestige to this combination of classical ornament with more verticalised, abrupt styles suggesting medieval overtones; the pace for mainstream European eclecticism was set by the bombastically plastic silhouettes of L.-T.-J. Visconti and H.-M. Lefuel's New Louvre (1852–7), or the splendour of J.-L.-C. Garnier's Paris Opera (1861–74).

Although the *Building Chronicle* in 1854 wrote disparagingly of 'the present mania of fashions and styles', [4] and later generations rejected it even more vehemently, this double eclecticism was, in its own time, a highly sophisticated instrument. In no other age were such exact and extensive attempts made to reflect the social significance of buildings in their outward appearance. The new eclecticism, for example, allowed new building types, such as railway stations, to be made com-prehensible, and, indeed, to be given a variety of meanings: for example, the North British Railway

Station in the somewhat industrial coastal burgh of Burntisland (by Thomas Grainger and John Miller, 1847) was made to look like a severe Grecian public building, while John Miller's design for the same company at Melrose, railhead for Abbotsford on the Borders line (1847–9), imitated a miniature Jacobean country house. Eclecticism also made possible a precise visual expression of the fine social and economic differentiations between buildings and areas within the mid-nineteenth-century city – while all the time remaining within the overall framework of monumental classicism. In the building of Glasgow's prominent Woodlands Hill development from 1855 with terraced houses of the wealthy, and public buildings, the same architect, Charles Wilson, used different styles for various simultaneously built parts of the develop-ment [6.1]. In its residential buildings, a precise, rusticated, palazzo-like style was used for the inward-looking Park Circus, but a more flam-boyant, high-roofed French Renaissance for the outward-facing Park Terrace, overlooking West End Park. At the Free Church College (from 1856), a slightly later Glasgow equivalent of Playfair's college on the Mound, a round-arched, somewhat secular style was used, but combined with tall campaniles: we will return to this major monument in more detail later [cf. 6.4]. The only non-classical element was introduced by J. T. Rochead, building for a congregation in the Established Church anxious to emphasise liturgical ceremony: he contributed the spikily gableted Gothic Park Church (also from 1856). Wilson's biographer and former assistant, the architect David Thomson, contrasted Park Circus's 'clear, delicate and effective' classicism with Park Terrace's 'picturesque groupings and broken and sweeping lines' and 'profuse employment of oriels': the latter's profile, he declared, 'accords well with the swelling forms of the hill and luxuriant out-lines of the wooded park'. [5]

What these eclectic buildings in past styles stood for, then, was a comprehensive and cosmopolitan modernity, attuned to the demands of the present. However, the spread of eclecticism in the mid-nineteenth century also encouraged another, very different way of addressing those demands: the beginning of morally imbued clashes *between*

6.1 Aerial photograph of Woodlands Hill, Glasgow (built from 1855): towers of Free Church College and Park Church at upper left; at centre, Park Circus, with Park Terrace/Quadrant around, facing outwards.

styles, or of demands for completely new, non-historic styles. This tendency usually went hand in hand with new social, religious or rationalistic conceptions of the role of architecture, both in the present and in the past. Here it was emotion, not stylistic versatility, that counted. The early and mid-nineteenth century in Germany, for example, saw vehement debates between advocates of classical, round-arched and neo-Gothic styles; in England, the 'High Victorian' architects made Gothic an emblem of national identity and a vehicle for new architectural 'freedom'; and, later in the century, American architects developed the principles of free eclecticism with tremendous force. And in the twentieth century, the principles of free design and moral commitment would form a prominent component in the Modern Movement. In mid-nineteenth-century Scotland, still a stronghold of monumental classicism, it was through classical buildings that the impulse towards an emotionally-charged eclecticism was expressed, in the architecture of Alexander Thomson in Glasgow. And it is to Glasgow – the undisputed focus of Scotland's urban and architectural achievements in the mid-nineteenth century – that we now turn.

The Building of Monumental Glasgow

The continuation of Glasgow's explosive development in the mid-century was fuelled by a uniquely potent mix of religio-capitalist fervour. The logic of improvement was driven onwards, on the one hand, by entrepreneurial verve, and, on the other, by evangelical zeal among its governing élite. As an example of the city's innovative leadership, we can cite John Blackie, publisher, Provost and prime mover behind the 1866 City Improvement Act, leading member of the Free Church – and key patron of Alexander Thomson. Thomson's own church, the United Presbyterians, upheld equally strongly this dual ideology of entrepreneurial philanthropy. Within the Glasgow architectural profession, there were constant exchanges between offices and, even, dynastic-style intermarriage. This was an artistic-intellectual élite whose own commercial activities, including property speculation, linked it integrally with the capitalist ethos of the city. While we will examine in due course

the massive building programmes of Glasgow's expansion – commercial and public buildings and slum reconstruction in the centre, and suburban spread outside – we first need to set out the architectural framework.

The conduit from which the most important of the eclectic influences of mid-nineteenth-century Glasgow emerged was the late work of David Hamilton, who was known among younger architects in the west as the 'father of the profession' [6.2]. [6] Such diverse architects as J. T. Rochead, Charles Wilson or John Baird II began their careers in his office. His own work, especially following his experiences at Hamilton Palace, had by 1840 become progressively richer, repudiating neo-classical plainness. In 1857, one reviewer recalled the 'advancement' from early buildings like Hutcheson's Hospital to later works such as the Royal Exchange or the Western Club: 'The quaint forms, the stringy ornament and miserable detail of the Hospital are so widely separated from the masterly and elegant treatment of the last two mentioned edifices that one, unaware of the fact, would never for a moment suppose them the offspring of the same mind.' [7] In the field of commercial and public buildings, the later works of Hamilton and his son James, as we have seen, put down many markers to a more 'Italian' astylar treatment of new city centre types, while retaining from the Grecian a refined rectilinearity and hardness of detail. For example, 151–157 Queen Street (*c.*1834) had a grid of pilasters and over-lapping horizontal elements. Following a continental tour by James, the years around 1840 saw the building of several influential city projects. These included the Western Bank, Miller Street (1840), an idiosyncratically cubic design featuring huge doorpieces flanked by shallow two-storey bays; the three-storey, astylar British Linen Bank, Queen Street (1840–1), its recessed curved corner resembling Simpson's slightly earlier North of Scotland Bank, Aberdeen, but treated in a far heavier manner with a balconied doorway similar to the earlier Jacobean example at Dunlop House (1831–4); and the Glasgow and Ship Bank, Ingram Street (1842), with double-height Roman Doric portico crowned by six allegorical John Mossman statues. At the Western Club House (1840–1), the Hamiltons combined the palazzo form – which

6.2 Western Club House, Glasgow (D. Hamilton, 1840–1); to its right, the Stock Exchange, by John Burnet senior, 1875.

would be of ever growing importance for big urban buildings – with a bold rectangularity. Beneath the massively consoled attic and cornice are two-storey bay windows with square columns and a channelled ground floor.

Around and after the death of Hamilton in 1843, his legacy was taken forward by a variety of designers, including two major practitioners of monumental classicism. The first was John Stephen, who heightened Hamilton's tendencies of cubic massiveness in a notable series of buildings in a personal Graeco-Egyptian manner. These included St Jude's Church, Glasgow (1840), with huge battered pylon entrance; the Blythswood Testimonial School, Renfrew (1840), with multi-tiered columnar steeple; and Gartsherrie Academy, Coatbridge (1845), with low massing and round-arched windows [6.3]. A far more central and prolific figure in the mid-nineteenth century was Hamilton's former pupil, Charles Wilson. He worked in Hamilton's office in 1827–37, and would have witnessed works such as Hamilton Palace. His own career was launched in 1841 when he won a commission to design the City Lunatic Asylum at Gartnavel, built 1841–3 in a Tudor style; this commission took him on a study tour of mental institutions in France. For urban monumental public and residential buildings, Wilson developed David Hamilton's Italian Renaissance tendencies into a more intensely refined, round-arched

6.3 St Jude's Episcopal Church, Glasgow (Stephen, 1840), late nineteenth-century picture.

6.4 Free Church College, Glasgow (Wilson, 1856–61).

manner, influenced especially by the Cinquecento-style work of German classicists (with its links with neo-Romanesque). In public buildings, 1846 saw the emergence of Wilson's mature round-arched style at the Glasgow Academy, Elmbank Street. This was followed by a string of commissions in this manner, including the John Neilson Institution, Paisley (1849–52), with low dome and arched windows recalling Stark's Asylum building, and the Venetian Seicento Royal Faculty of Procurators (1854), with its paired columns and arched windows on a rusticated ground floor. The climax of the series was the Queen's Rooms (1857–8), a large pedimented structure of early Italian Renaissance character, with huge, round-arched openings, built as a temple of the arts and sciences for David Bell of Blackhall, a rich Glasgow merchant. The Queen's Rooms incorporated one of the most lavish sculptural schemes of nineteenth-century Glasgow, executed by John Mossman. The chief feature of this was a frieze symbolising Glasgow's loyalty to the union, to freemasonry and to political liberalism. The side facade features a series of relief panels depicting 'great men' in various fields; the representative of architecture was David Hamilton.

We briefly mentioned above, for its eclectic significance, Wilson's greatest work, the Free Church College on Woodlands Hill (1856–61) [6.4]. Like Playfair's Mound grouping in Edinburgh, Woodlands Hill was the scenic centrepiece of the new, mid-century Glasgow, and the college was its crowning element. Its design also set out to broadcast the power and authority of the Free Church through a tall towered silhouette, but in an open, Glasgow fashion, seen not in a structured vista but as an asymmetrical cluster visible from all directions. The college comprised a church flanked by twin engaged towers, and an asymmetrical college wing attached, with campanile above the entrance – an arrangement resembling the garden and entrance facades of a contemporary country house. All three towers are of a massive, yet exceptionally attenuated form, with slit-like patterning, giving this classical complex an eclectically romantic, even slightly medieval character. We will deal later with Wilson's large output of houses and churches.

Alexander Thomson and 'The Idea of Eternity' [8]

Forming part of this milieu – as a close friend, for example, of Charles Wilson – yet also standing apart from it, in the unique emotional intensity of his architecture, was Glasgow's greatest mid-nineteenth-century architect: Alexander Thomson [6.5]. There is no space in this book for any more than a brief survey of Thomson's work: for a detailed account, the books by McFadzean, Gomme and Walker, and Stamp and McKinstry should be consulted. Trained by Robert Foote (to 1836) and John Baird I – the latter, as we will see, a formidable exponent of iron architecture in the city centre – Thomson began his independent career in 1847, when he joined John Baird II (a former pupil of David Hamilton) in partnership. His work from that point spanned the commercial, spiritual and social needs of booming Glasgow: speculative offices and chambers, churches, tenements, suburban and marine villas. We will deal with each of these as we encounter them, thematically. But first, an architectural and ideological overview is necessary.

Thomson's architectural achievement was to revitalise the Adam tradition of the Sublime by

6.5 Alexander Thomson.

harnessing it to the capitalistic and religious driving forces of mid-century Glasgow. He naturalised this tradition in the West, and imbued it with both a new emotional and subjective intensity, and a new structural logic; his wife's grandfather was Peter Nicholson. This would allow his work to remain one of the most pervasive influences in Glasgow architecture until the mid-twentieth century. The mid- and late-nineteenth century saw a variety of attempts in Europe and America to break radically from tradition-dictated orthodoxy and devise individualistic architectures of 'freedom', linked to utopian conceptions of the past societies associated with their styles. Of these, Thomson's was unique both in its architectural form, an intensely eclectic monumental classicism, and its associated ideology – a Presbyterian intellectualism reliant on individual conscience alongside biblical authority. Thomson was in no way averse to the practical, day-to-day pursuit of capitalist modernity in mid-nineteenth-century Glasgow: his letters to his brother George show a constant preoccupation with property speculation, renting, subletting – all bound in with his practice. [9] But this was fused with the fundamental driving force of religion. His great-grandfather had been a Covenanter, and he was an elder of one of his own churches (Caledonia Road). He insisted that 'Religion has been the soul of art from the beginning'; the architect could be 'in however humble a sense, a co-creator'. [10]

Thomson explained his own ideas in the series of four Haldane Lectures he delivered in 1874, and in several other lesser publications. The cornerstone of his beliefs was the concept that progressive divine revelation, in the Old Testament sense, also applied to architecture. At the root of his architecture lay a utopian conception of antique society in terms of a kind of proto-Presbyterian purity – a picture which would have seemed unrecognisable to the gentlemanly eighteenth-century classicists, or even to Adam or Stark. For Thomson, doubtless also influenced by Masonic philosophy, the beginning of architecture lay in the society of Ancient Egypt, whose massive and repetitive architecture, with its 'expression of quietly waiting till all the bustle is over', represented part of an 'endeavour to realise the idea of eternity'; [11] the hypothetical

architecture of the Old Testament, including Solomon's Temple, was also associated with those values. Egypt's trabeated architecture of repose had been refined by the Greeks, and infused with a 'high, contemplative. . . harmony'. The buildings of the Acropolis had reached such a level of perfection that they could act as 'mediators between heaven and earth'. [12] After this climax the picture had become more complex. On the one hand, aspects of Pauline or Early Christian architecture were held to anticipate the Presbyterian *Predigtkirche*. More generally, however, the 'fleshly' and 'wordly' concerns of Rome, with its 'restless' arcuated construction, [13] had led to the barbarous Fall of the Middle Ages. Modern revivalist styles only perpetuated the moral turpitude of those societies. 'Modern Italian' reflected Rome's decadence in its 'loose composition, its gross mouldings, and. . . blown-out forms'. [14] And the modern Gothic reflected the primitive violence of its original. Here – in a curious echo of the Scottish origin-myth tradition of historiography we traced in Chapter 1 – Thomson turned on its head the 'national' argumentation of English or German Goths such as Pugin and Reichensperger, by arguing that neo-Gothic in Scotland was a barbarian interloper: 'This violent struggle of forces, this incessant struggle between stick and knock-down, may account in some measure for the favour the style has found with a cock-fighting, bull-baiting, pugilistic people like the Anglo-Saxons.' [15] The rationalistic claims of Puginian Picturesque he dismissed as 'very humble business': the vast symmetry of Solomon's Temple had not been 'controlled by any utilitarian consideration'. [16]

Despite this rhetorical opposition in his ideological vision of the 'ancients', the governing *architectural* principles of Thomson's philosophy – the 'subjective', and the Sublime – paralleled those of English High Victorianism and of the slightly later 'free' American styles of Richardson and Sullivan. In Thomson's case, the ultimate source was the qualities we first saw dramatically introduced to the Scottish monumental architecture by Adam almost a century earlier, even if his evocations of piled-up temples and colonnades were also clearly influenced by the apocalyptic paintings of John Martin and the repetitive pilastrades of Schinkel [cf. 6.40]. In 'form and conception' – the 'two most essential elements in Architecture' – Thomson vehemently argued against the conception of art as an 'objective' representation of nature. The 'subjective' was everything: 'the orderly or harmonious expression of what we feel in our hearts or conceive in our minds'. The supreme expression of the subjective architecture of divine revelation was that of grandeur – in other words, the Sublime. [17] The role of grandeur was to provide a medium of direct, individual communication with God. The desired emotional effect Thomson compared to the feelings of a mountain climber gazing out over a snow-capped, moonlit expanse in the Highlands: 'An indescribable, strange consciousness, which every instant becomes more intense, that he is standing there alone, the only living thing before God . . . His terror melts into ecstatic joy; and, exulting in the love of God, he finds new strength and passes on his way'. It was the task of a monumental Presbyterian architecture based on 'the principle of repetition' and on 'the mysterious power of the horizontal . . . in carrying the mind away into space' to evoke 'the diffusive love . . . the peace which passeth all understanding . . . the eternity which baffles and confounds all faculty of computation', and to convey 'an emanation from some mystery of endless dawn'. [18]

Thomson took special care to distinguish his individualistic, emotionalist relationship to Egypt and Greece from the previous generation's archaeology-based use of antiquity: even neo-Greek architecture 'could not see through the material into the laws upon which that architecture rested'. [19] In the early 1870s, as president of the Glasgow Institute of Architects, he called on the profession 'to abandon with all convenient expedition the whole mass of accumulated human tradition under which we have been, as it were, smothered'. [20] But this was simply rhetoric: in contrast to the early twentieth century, there was no suggestion that this combination of utopianism and emotionalism could best be expressed architecturally by jettisoning the past altogether. Instead, it was through a highly eclectic monumental classicism that Thomson attempted to realise his 'laws'. His style combined a predominance of massive, trabeated horizontality

with vertical elements of almost Baroque dynamism, including towers and other piled-up features. Just as in the work of Richardson and Sullivan, the geometrical simplicity and unity of Thomson's designs was accentuated by emphasis of the wall-mass and down-playing of windows (which were integrated into pilastrade-like bands or sunk-in surface patterns) and by the application of regular, incised surface relief. Although he attacked Puginian rationalism, Thomson's own trabeated logic and ruthless proportional discipline had strong rationalist overtones of its own. These ideas were systematically developed throughout his career. The Italian round arches of his early villas were abandoned from the early 1850s, and 1856 saw his first large church commission, Caledonia Road [cf. 6.39]. From the 1860s, there was much commercial and urban residential work. He further sharpened his antipathy to neo-Gothic in two unsuccessful interventions in competitions in the British capital, for the Albert Memorial (1862) and the South Kensington Museum (1865). The latter, punctuated by a tower at one end, took to an extreme the principle of interpenetrating temple fronts and long, Schinkel-like colonnades. In the following pages, which deal with the mid-century urban development of Glasgow in a geographically radial manner, beginning with the centre, we will repeatedly encounter Thomson's works as highlights of architectural and utopian intensity.

The Radial City: Urban Architecture and Planning in Glasgow

In the centre, cases such as Hamilton's refacing of an older mansion for the new Royal Exchange demonstrated, as early as the 1820s, how a richer and heavier classicism could be used to reflect the growing trends of land-use intensification, and of codification of urban space in terms of the private and public realm. By the 1850s, not only the older streets but even parts of Blythswood were seeing increasing numbers of redevelopment schemes with purpose-built 'chambers' and offices. In the commercial field, the sumptuous palazzo model first really took hold in the design by the Edinburgh architect, David Rhind, for the Glasgow main branch of the Commercial Bank of Scotland (1853–7), a four-storey Renaissance block bound together with rusticated vertical bands, and surmounted by a higher colonnaded section. The persistence of this pattern was seen, for example, in Campbell Douglas & Sellars's 1874 expansion of J. T. Rochead's Bank of Scotland, St Vincent Place (1867–70). Among public buildings, the continued popularity of the Grecian temple-like form was seen in W. Clarke and G. Bell's City and County Buildings (1841–71), echoing Playfair's Surgeons Hall in its portico perched on a high wall, while the new Renaissance and Italian tendencies were repre-sented in designs such as Wilson's Royal Faculty of Procurators (1854) [cf. 5.11].

The 1850s also saw a new but relatively short-lived trend among Glasgow architects, in the form of an attempt to exploit openly the new possibilities of slim cast- and wrought-iron construction, in commercial city-centre ware-houses. The basis of this was a round-arched, somewhat Venetian Renaissance style, first consistently applied to commercial architecture in 1854 at the sumptuously ornamented 37–51 Miller Street, by Alexander Kirkland (designer of the Ionic-pyloned South Portland Street suspension bridge, 1851–3). This was translated into iron at John Baird I's Gardner's warehouse (1855–6), designed with the ironfounder and patentee R. McConnel [6.6]. Here, within a round-arched

palazzo theme, the exposed iron frame offered almost uninterrupted glazing. At John Honey-man's Ca d'Oro of 1872, the Venetian prototype was imitated in a three-storey iron arcade on masonry arches. By that time, however, there was a reaction away from exposed iron towards hybrid forms: Honeyman's design was essentially one of substitution. More common was partial conceal-ment of iron, driven partly by practical consid-erations. The main department store of Wylie & Lochhead, a huge concern offering a cradle-to-grave retail service, was rebuilt by James Sellars in 1883–5 in fireproof form following an earlier fire which destroyed a cast-iron structure: its iron frontage and tall shopping hall was clad in terracotta. There was no attempt to apply an externally expressed cast-iron aesthetic to industrial buildings. William Spence's Randolph Elder's Engine Works (1856–8), for instance, was a massive, battered, rubble block.

The commercial work of Alexander Thomson conformed to these ambiguous trends, although following trabeated rather than arched patterns. Where an 1851–2 design for a Howard Street warehouse proposed a slender structure of iron and glass (in its 'Greekness', not unlike William Spence's Paisley's building, Jamaica Street, 1855–6), the Buck's Head building in Argyle Street (1862–3) offered a more hybrid arrangement of cast-iron set-forward columns with stone trabeated

6.6 Gardner's Warehouse, Jamaica Street, Glasgow (John Baird I,1855–6), 1965 view.

6.7 Grosvenor Building (Thomson, 1859–61, with later heightening of 1907), Glasgow, 1965 view.

architecture. Other Thomson designs, then and later, all but concealed the iron structure within a lithic monumentality, emphasising the trabeated principle and the theme of horizontal repetition, but substituting highly eclectic designs for the conventional storey-height hierarchy of the Orders. Key examples included the Grosvenor Building of 1859–61, a speculation by Thomson and his brother George, with giant pilasters and projecting aedicules, and attic storey of consoles [6.7]; and Grecian Buildings (1865), a corner block with end pavilions and deeply recessed top floor behind stumpy columns, the detail being largely Egyptian. The most powerful of these commercial blocks was Egyptian Halls (1871–3), a four-storey, palazzo-like block designed, horizontally, in accordance with 'the principle of repetition'. [21] [6.8] Its ground floor contained plate-glass

shopfronts, its first and second floor pilastered windows, its third (attic) floor recessed glazing behind a squat Egyptian colonnade; at the top was a deep, coved cornice concealing an attic rooflight. The concern to preserve the wall-mass was also seen in Thomson's conversion of 122 Wellington Street as his office in 1872; the attic floor was toplit to allow a masonry facing. Thomson's commercial style of gridded stone facades was influential even beyond Clydeside, as seen for instance in J. M. Robertson's India Buildings, Dundee (1874).

The development of the city centre was not just a simple matter of intensification of the uses of the regular streets built in the eighteenth and early nineteenth centuries. There was also the question of what to do with the old core, around Glasgow Cross, which the march of capitalist development had denuded of prestigious city-centre uses and

6.8　Egyptian Halls, Glasgow (Thomson, 1871–3), *c.*1890 view.

had turned into the multi-occupied slum homes of unskilled workers. Increasingly, people began to agree that there was no way in which speculators alone could solve this problem, and so, on the initiative of the Town Council, the old centre became the prototype of a daring new type of improvement: area clearance and redevelopment, or a kind of planned New Town *within* the old town. Building on the Enlightenment concepts of municipal intervention pioneered in the capital, especially the Old Town road schemes of Thomas Hamilton, the Council broadened the scope of public intervention substantially beyond police controls over building layouts, into the matter of housing conditions. In 1845, the Town Council supported abortive moves by a number of prominent citizens for a joint stock company intended to improve working-class dwellings. From that time, there were intense debates in the city, for instance, among architects (in debates of *c.*1850–90), as to what patterns of reformed working-class housing should be aimed at. Already, in controlling the design of new small tenements, the Glasgow Police Acts and the initiatives of City Architect John Carrick – the first of the great Glasgow architect-organisers – had entrenched the rather low-density (by continental standards)

pattern of tenement development around hollow squares. Some architects proposed a range of modifications to this, for central redevelopments, including the denser building of rear blocks as in Germany (James Cousland), the building of higher blocks (Honeyman), or the glazing over of streets (Alexander Thomson). Others, such as James Salmon or J. J. Stevenson (in 1860), compared all tenements with 'an ingenious shipmaster packing freight into the hold of a vessel', [22] and instead demanded that slum-dwellers should be moved out to lower-density housing, modelled on middle-class villa suburbs.

Action finally came in 1866, when the Glasgow City Improvement Act authorised the Town Council to set up a Trust to acquire and redevelop an 88-acre area centred on Glasgow Cross. In contrast to the romantic, scenographic ideas which influenced Edinburgh's redevelopment ideas, Glasgow's were uncompromisingly rationalistic. They were openly influenced by the work of Haussmann in replanning the French capital in 1853–69 by driving through new boulevards. The scheme's chief author, Provost John Blackie, headed an 1866 delegation to visit Haussmann's 'great works'; Glasgow was to become a 'second Paris'. [23] Glasgow's 1866 scheme also emphasised new street construction, with thirty-nine new routes planned by Carrick. The old secondary street pattern was erased, and new, ventilated thorough-fares were laid out, and developed with plain warehouse buildings (to serve the new railway stations). From 1880, some new tenements were built, but in contrast to the twentieth century, there was no concept of general rehousing of the large numbers of those displaced by clearance (who totalled one-eighth of Glasgow's population).

Alongside the huge efforts of the City Improvement Trust in the city centre, Glasgow's mainstream processes of city extension through new middle-class and, in some cases, working-class developments had reached a new pitch of dynamism. The main impetus of, and finance for, development stemmed from merchants and professionals moving westwards from the insan-itary, cholera-ridden centre. As in Edinburgh, there was a new demand for variety. In 1855 the *Building Chronicle* criticised the 'aristocratic dullness' of the straight streets of the Blythswood estate. (24) But none the less, the collective principles of stone-faced uniformity and shared ownership of pleasure grounds were maintained. In Glasgow and the surrounding burghs, the speculative developers of the new areas were mainly controlled through the public agency of police regulation or Town Council feuing, rather than through private feuing burdens, as in the capital. The 1830s saw the first breaks from grid patterns, with looser developments of terraces further west. These included George Smith's Woodside Crescent, Terrace and Place (from 1831 to the early 1840s); the complex, David Hamilton-like linear classicism of Alexander Taylor's Royal Terrace (1839–49), its line of rounded bays and boxy porches looking back to Playfair and forward to Thomson; and John Baird's Claremont Terrace of 1847, with individual porticoes brought together in a unified colonnade. These develop-ments built on the innovations of later Edinburgh terrace designs of the mid-1820s, such as Burn's Henderson Row or Playfair's Brunswick Street, which had shown how the individual house or tenement units could be accentuated without sacrificing overall unity of design. From now on, strict grid plans were usually confined to dense developments and, especially, to new working-

class areas. In the housing of the middle class, two major initiatives set the pace towards more open and dynamic patterns: Woodlands Hill and Great Western Road.

Woodlands Hill, which would eventually house the top families in Glasgow's merchant and political class, formed part of a Town Council-promoted plan for high-status development of a wedge of land sandwiched between two outlying burghs, and immediately north of Smith's Woodside terraces [cf. 6.1]. We discussed above the plans by Charles Wilson for Park Circus and Terrace; these formed part of an overall plan which Wilson (with surveyor Thomas Kyle) prepared in 1854 for the area, including a dramatically contoured new park (West End, later Kelvingrove, Park) below the houses. Great Western Road was a more ambitious undertaking. Formed as a result of an Act of 1836 for a road from St George's Cross to Anniesland Toll, its aim, like the North Bridge in Edinburgh, was to facilitate the development of a new, select suburb detached from the existing city, on the Kelvinside estate. This boulevard, boldly sweeping out to open horizons, was itself to be lined with terraced development in an increasingly variegated assortment of classical styles. The first develo-pment, from 1845, was Wilson's Windsor Terrace, its florid heaviness (with balconies) evoking Roman Renaissance palaces [6.9]. In the following decade, the variety of solutions was evident in two strikingly contrasting developments by one architect, J. T. Rochead: Buckingham Terrace (1852–8), reminiscent of Hamilton's Western Club in its use of bay windows (here canted) within a palazzo form, and Grosvenor Terrace (1855), whose relentlessly repetitive arched fenestration recalled the Venetian Renaissance precedent of the Procuratie Nuove, as well as contemporary Glasgow commercial buildings such as Gardner's, or Kirkland's Miller Street block [6.10]. Pre-eminent in the 1860s was Alexander Thomson's complex design, Great Western Terrace (from 1869), which comprised two palazzo-like three-storey blocks interpenetrated by a long, two-storey range. While the heavy cornice made clear its mid-century affiliation, the austere facades, Ionic porches and lack of central emphasis seemed to evoke the earlier age of Grecian neo-classicism – something which, in contrast to Edinburgh New

6.9 Windsor (later Kirklee) Terrace, Glasgow (Wilson, 1845–64).

6.10 Grosvenor Terrace, Great Western Road, Glasgow (Rochead, 1855).

Town houses of, say, 1820, had become a matter of conscious choice, among all the other 'classicisms' now available.

Great Western Road's original chief task was to provide access to new flanking suburbs such as Kelvinside and Dowanhill – although railway construction soon supplemented its transport role. Here, picturesque layouts prevailed, with villas interspersed with terraces and tenements in various eclectic classical styles. Dowanhill, laid out

by James Thomson in 1858, had as its centrepiece the great convex Roman Doric sweep of Crown Circus (1858) and the heavier classicism of Crown Terrace (1873–80). At its north-west extremity, Westbourne Terrace (1871), another late Thomson design, echoed Rochead's Buckingham Terrace in its plinth-like ground floor and canted bay windows. Hillhead, built largely from the 1850s as a small separate burgh, had a grid plan, mainly comprising terraces and tenements, with Glasgow

University's new Gothic buldings (planned from 1863 by Sir G. G. Scott) on Gilmorehill at one end. The most architecturally noteworthy of Hillhead's house developments was Thomson's Eton Terrace, Oakfield Avenue (1865), a somewhat congested design with outer pedimented pavilions, porches in between, and insistent incised Grecian decoration.

Elsewhere in the city, monumental classical terrace architecture for the middle class was carried on in a more sporadic manner; we can only touch on a few highlights here. Largest in scale was a group planned by Kirkland from 1849 at Stobcross, including the undulating elevation of St Vincent Crescent, a third of a mile long. At the other, diminutive extreme, Thomson's 1–10 Moray Place (from 1859) used rigid horizontal repetition and deeply incised modelling to provide an answer to the visual 'problem' of intrusive fenestration, posed so provocatively by Adam [6.11]. Moray Place's array of identical pilastered bays, flanked by pedimented pavilions, was designed to be seen at a sharp angle, minimising the impact of the windows. Thomson's Walmer Crescent (1857–62), built in isolation adjoining Paisley Road West, was the equal in grandeur of Edinburgh's similarly curved St Bernard's Crescent, built thirty-five years previously; however, its facade was articulated not by giant Orders but by massive rectangular bay windows, offset by the insistent horizontals of channelled rustication and mullioned fenestration [6.12].

Although Walmer Crescent was of palatial scale and at first 'occupied exclusively by rich merchants', [25] it was in fact a tenement block. Here we come to the question of the architectural treatment of the tenement – a type which, by the third quarter of the nineteenth century, was increasingly erected not only in middle-class suburbs, but in new, purpose-built areas for workers in key industries: for instance, Maryhill (a police burgh from 1856) or Govan (police burgh from 1864). Architecturally, there were many links with middle-class terraces of individual dwellings, but the overall aesthetic seemed to have remained closer to neo-classical uniformity and severity. By comparison with the ornately variegated five- and six-storey plaster facades of tenements in Central Europe, with their emphatically individual palazzo treatment of each unit and their heavy attics, the

6.11 1-10 Moray Place, Glasgow (Thomson, from 1859).

four-storey tenements of Glasgow and the other cities seemed austere and homogeneous, sharply shaved off at the roofline (except in Aberdeen), and low and horizontal in their terraced massing. What seemed outstanding, in international terms, was the ubiquity of fine masonry facing. The spread, and increasing refinement, of stone construction in Scottish architecture, which had gathered pace over the centuries from Stirling Forework, Kinross House and the National Monument, reached its climax in the seemingly endless, uniform ranges of working-class tenement blocks in Govanhill or Maryhill. Their precision of construction was in many ways superior to that of Renaissance palaces: where even the Palazzo Farnese had been of render with stone dressings, even the humblest Glasgow shopfronts were often now of ashlar. Inside, too, everyday buildings employed masonry techniques which in past centuries would have been regarded as impossibly daring and expensive for all but the richest patrons: for example, there was widespread use of geometrical (cantilevered open-well) staircases inside tenement blocks. This stylistic and constructional uniformity and systematisation, externally and internally, was just as much an expression of industrialised 'mass' society as of Scottish stone-building 'tradition' [cf. 7.57, C.7, C.8].

In tenements, the mid- and late nineteenth-century demand for more variegated and rich architectural treatment, and the problem of how to give unequal compositional weight to storeys of equal height, was partly answered through heavier

6.12 Walmer Crescent, Glasgow (Thomson, 1857–62), 1965 view.

ornament, including rusticated or channelled ground floors to give weight, consoled architraves and sill courses on the first floor to simulate a *piano nobile*. In the absence of stuck-on plaster decoration, the aim of greater horizontal variety in facades was largely achieved through two compositional devices: the bay window and uneven grouping of windows. Canted bay windows, although recorded as far back as Pinkie House in 1613, were first used on the terraces of the wealthy in the 1850s (Buckingham or Park Terrace), and then were extended, in the form of oriel bays, to tenements such as Walworth Terrace, Kent Road (1858–60). The use of grouped windows stretched back as far as Edinburgh tenements of the sixteenth or seventeenth century, or Crichton Castle in the 1580s, but recent examples such as Hamilton's Western Club were more immediately relevant: William Clarke's Granby Terrace, Hillhead (1856), for instance, included triple windows. By the 1890s, both bay and grouped windows became ubiquitous in new working-class tenements. More individual solutions of tenement design, involving ingenious use of banded and incised ornament to differentiate between storeys, were contributed by Thomson: the most notable was the long range of Queen's Park Terrace in Eglinton Street (1857–60) [6.13].

While there was overlap between middle class and working class in the architecture of terraces and tenements, the greatest area of growth in middle-class housing was not in these massive designs, but in developments of individual villas. Doubtless, the very spread of ashlar tenements to the working class had the effect of stigmatising the latter among the bourgeoisie. One of the earliest exclusively villa layouts in the Glasgow area, David Rhind's West Pollokshields (1849) was feued out in 1851, and became a police burgh in 1875. Against the background of otherwise generally plain classical villas, the area also includes a sequence of houses by Thomson, ranging from the Playfair-like round-arched and towered Italian manner of The Knowe, Albert Drive (from 1852) to the austere, cubic Graeco-Egyptian of Ellisland, Nithsdale Road (1871), with recessed lotus-headed columns at the entrance. Across the areas surrounding Glasgow, Thomson and other contemporary architects pioneered a great variety of

6.13 Queen's Park Terrace, Eglinton Street, Glasgow (Thomson, 1857–60).

approaches to villa design. The refined, eclectic mainstream of the mid-century was represented by the work of Wilson, whose large villas, building on the work of David Hamilton, paralleled contemporary continental practice in their combination of some picturesque elements with a still generally classical framework. Plans ranged from axial layouts with symmetrical front facades – in David Thomson's words, 'his early dreams of classic symmetry and spacious dispositions' – to the typical asymmetrical Burn-like country house plan of flank entrance leading to symmetrical garden front. A more compact alternative featured a central stairwell. A wide variety of styles was used by Wilson to clad these plans. Representative of the 'rich and picturesque' Baronial and castellated style was Wester Moffat House, Airdrie (1859–62), a large villa with central staircase: 'a pile of a high castellated character' resembling an 'old baronial fortalice'; we will return later to Wilson's Baronial work. To evoke a more urbane richness, an informal 'Italian' classicism might typically be used by Wilson in association with the flank-entrance plan – for instance at the Curator's

House, Botanic Gardens (1840), and at Woodside House, Paisley (1850–1) – praised by David Thomson for its 'careful and judicious adjustment of the parts, grouping and contrasting agreeably with each other, moderately rich, without redundancy, as becoming the residence of a gentleman of means and culture'. [26]

More unconventional villa solutions, as we might expect, emanated from Alexander Thomson's practice. Maria Villa, Langside (1856–7), the first of Thomson's villas composed in an uncompromisingly rectilinear manner, comprised a pair of cleverly juxtaposed 'handed' dwellings on an interlocked plan, to allow more imposing asymmetrical facades: we will return shortly to the interior decoration of this and the villa Holmwood (1857–8). Thomson's earlier villa work, before his repudiation of the round arch, was especially to be found in the burgeoning marine suburbs. Along the Clyde, for instance, at Cove and Kilcreggan (first offered for sale by the Duke of Argyll in 1849), Thomson built an earlier and more austere version of The Knowe, at Craig Ailey (1850), sited spectacularly above a rugged cliff, like Adam's Culzean [6.14]; his Seymour Lodge (1850) was in a more conventional gabled cottage-orné style. Elsewhere on the Clyde, the more forceful eclecticism of the 1870s, partly influenced by Thomson's example, was exemplified in the houses designed by his close friend, the young William Leiper, at the beginning of his extensive work in Helensburgh. Two large villas for wealthy clients, Cairndhu (1871) and Dalmore (1873), were designed by Leiper respectively in a sumptuous François Ier and a rather austere Baronial style [cf. 7.29]. At the same time, on two plots bought by Leiper himself, he built both his own house, Terpersie (1871), an austere, gabled design with a hint of polychromatic banding, and, next door, Bonnyton (*c.*1872), a gabled Grecian design in a Thomson-like manner.

In the interior decoration of their villas, the thrusting Glasgow mercantile class moved away from the conventional classical richness visible at James Laurie's 52 Carlton Place (1802–4) towards a new eclectic variety. As in Edinburgh there was a break from the leadership values of the old landed establishment. But whereas in the capital the driving force was the genteel scholarship and rationalism of the Board of Manufactures, in Glasgow the dominant ethos was the social mobility and cosmopolitan brashness of a commercial and industrial élite which used the home for business-related socialising: the dining room's importance was not diminished, but reinforced. In this context, the old classical hierarchy of rooms, differentiated by degree of decorum and ornament, was unceremoniously jettisoned and replaced by a rampant typological eclecticism. In the houses of the very rich, all main rooms were now decorated at 'drawing room level', and differentiated by stylistic sources drawn not only from Europe but from throughout Glasgow's trading empire, including the Middle and Far East. In this context, the growing expertise of Glasgow tradesmen with machine-assembly techniques was

6.14 Craig Ailey, Cove (Thomson, 1850).

6.15 22 Park Circus, Glasgow (Boucher, 1872–4) view of staircase.

avidly exploited. One of the most sumptuous examples was the house of iron manufacturer and exporter Walter MacFarlane, at 22 Park Circus, built in 1872–4 by James Boucher [6.15; cf. 6.1]. Externally, of course, Boucher's design conformed to Wilson's grave classical prescription. Internally, the house presented a triumphal procession of rooms of overwhelming opulence and craftsmanship, including an arcaded, domed ground-floor corridor, and an upper hall surmounted by a cast-iron dome. Mid-nineteenth-century mainstream villa interiors, like exteriors, steadily moved away from neo-classical sparseness towards more intense architectural frameworks and, in most cases, more crowded, heavily padded contents.

Alexander Thomson's villa interiors took up and developed these trends, in his own individual manner. He adopted the rationalist principles and techniques pioneered by Hay in the east, and made

them the basis for a forcefully architectonic and polychromatic style of stencilling, in which rooms were unified by classical trabeated elements, fusing Greek and Egyptian elements. In the machine-made modernity of Thomson's steam-engine-turned details, the contrast could not have been sharper with the deliberate 'oldness' cultivated by Scott at Abbotsford: Thomson's Haldane Lectures advocated use of the machine to obtain precision. The one eighteenth-century convention retained, or perhaps revived, was the precise placing of furniture (here often designed by Thomson). No 'Victorian clutter' of clients' moveable contents was allowed for in the designs of Thomson villas. A scheme of this kind, for example, was designed for Maria Villa (1856–7), where Thomson justified the post-and-lintel format not in rationalistic but in visual terms: 'to unite together the several parts of the room, thereby giving an effect of increased

HOLMWOOD,—CATHCART, RENFREWSHIRE.

R. Anderson Engraver

6.16 Holmwood, Cathcart (Thomson, 1857–8): (left) exterior; (right) interior details; both from *Villa and Cottage Architecture*, 1868.

PLATE LXXI.

HOLMWOOD.

SECTIONS AND DETAILS.

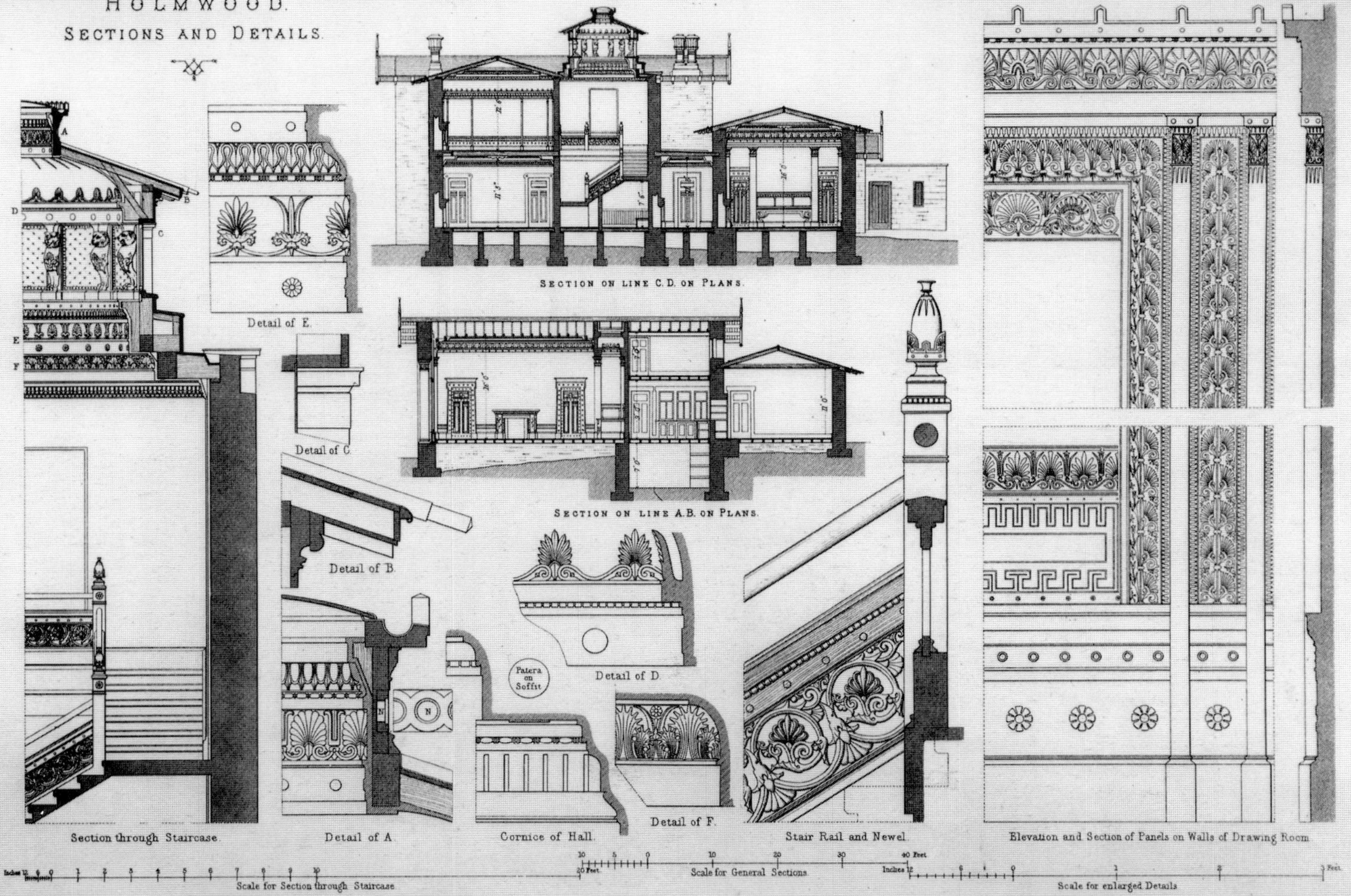

Section through Staircase.

Detail of E.

Detail of C.

Detail of B.

Detail of A.

Detail of D.

Cornice of Hall.

Detail of F.

Pateræ on Soffit.

Section on Line C. D. on Plans.

Section on Line A. B. on Plans.

Stair Rail and Newel.

Elevation and Section of Panels on Walls of Drawing Room.

Scale for Section through Staircase.

Scale for General Sections.

Scale for enlarged Details.

A. & G. Thomson, Architects.

BLACKIE & SON GLASGOW EDINBURGH & LONDON.

J. Sulpis Eng. over.

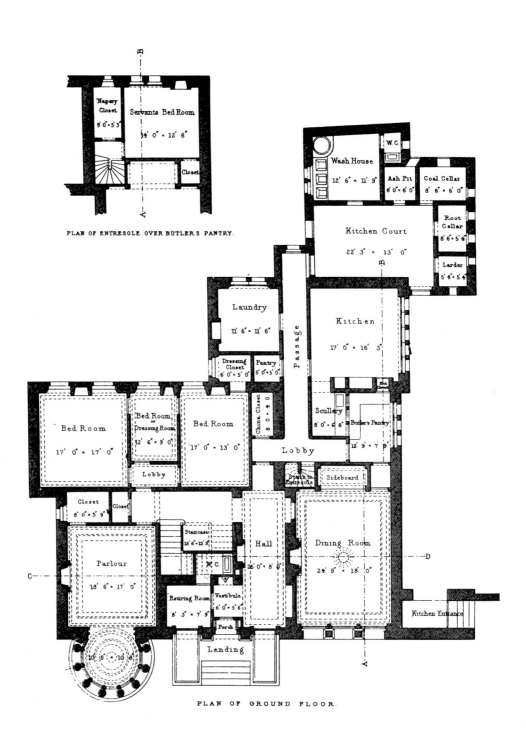

PLAN OF ENTRESOLE OVER BUTLERS PANTRY.

Plan of Entresole (upper left):
- 'Napery Closet 9' 0" × 5' 3"
- Servants Bed Room 14' 0" × 12' 6"
- Closet

Plan of Ground Floor:
- Wash House 12' 6" × 11' 9"
- W.C.
- Ash Pit 6' 0" × 6' 0"
- Coal Cellar 8' 6" × 6' 0"
- Root Cellar 8' 6" × 5' 4"
- Kitchen Court 22' 3" × 13' 0"
- Larder 5' 4" × 5' 4"
- Laundry 11' 6" × 11' 6"
- Kitchen 17' 0" × 16' 3"
- Passage
- Dressing Closet 6' 0" × 5' 0"
- Pantry 5' 0" × 5' 0"
- China Closet 8' 0" × 4' 0"
- Scullery 8' 0" × 6' 6"
- Butler's Pantry 12' 9" × 7' 9"
- Bed Room 17' 0" × 17' 0"
- Bed Room or Dressing Room 12' 6" × 9' 0"
- Bed Room 17' 0" × 13' 0"
- Lobby
- Lobby
- Closet 8' 0" × 5' 9"
- Closet
- Stair to Entresole
- Sideboard
- Staircase 18' 6" × 13' 3"
- W.C.
- Parlour 18' 6" × 17' 0"
- Hall 26' 0" × 8' 0"
- Dining Room 24' 9" × 18' 0"
- Kitchen Entrance
- Retiring Room 8' 3" × 7' 3"
- Vestibule 6' 0" × 5' 6"
- Porch
- Landing
- 10' 6" × 10' 6"

PLAN OF GROUND FLOOR.

6.17 Holmwood, ground-floor plan, from *Villa and Cottage Architecture*.

extent. The apparent height of the ceiling is also enhanced by giving force to the lower mass of the walls, and so making them serve as does a foreground to a picture.' [27] Thomson's showpiece interior was Holmwood (1857–8), designed for the mill-owner James Couper [6.16, 6.17]. Here the dining room frieze reproduced Flaxman's illustrations of the *Iliad*, but the drawing room was given a slight edge by the employment of a professional artist, Hugh Cameron, whose panels were inspired by Tennyson's 'Idylls of the King'. The stencilled, polychromatic decoration was probably executed by C. T. Bowie, Glasgow's leading interior decorator and a former pupil of D. R. Hay. After Holmwood, Thomson's collaboration with the artist Daniel Cottier, and the interiors of other architects, such as Leiper's 1870s Helensburgh villas, would see a gradual reduction in polychromatic forcefulness in favour of a new stress on 'artistic' sensitivity.

Similar processes of inner redevelopment and suburban building to Glasgow's, but on a smaller scale, were under way in Dundee. Following the appointment of a new and energetic Burgh Surveyor, William Mackison, in 1868, an Improvement Act was passed in 1871. Over the following twenty years, Mackison forced through the redevelopment of almost the entire pre-nineteenth-century centre, constructing new, Haussmannesque classical thoroughfares such as Commercial Street – a programme which laid the ground for even more ambitious civic reconstruction plans at the turn of the century. In Aberdeen, following the huge exertion of developing Union Street, improvement became more piecemeal. The late nineteenth-century setpiece was the Rosemount and Denburn viaduct scheme, later built up with cliff-like tenements such as 1–27 Rosemount Viaduct (1897, by Brown & Watt). The only mid-century rivals in splendour to the houses of the Clydeside élite were the 'jute palaces' of the Dundee mill-owners, greatly enriched following the boom in jute manufacture from the 1850s: these were, as a rule, designed by Tayside architects. Andrew Heiton's Castleroy (1867), for the Gilroys of Tay Works, was in a brittle Tudor manner, with Gothic stair-hall; James Grimond, co-founder of Bowbridge Works, employed T. S. Robertson from 1861 to extend Carbet Castle in

an anarchic turreted François Ier style, with sumptuous interiors including dining room and saloon ceilings by the French artist Charles Fréchou (1871).

The Capital at Mid-Century

The 1850s saw the beginning of a recovery in building in Edinburgh after the slump of the 1830s and 1840s. In terms of architectural innovation, the mid-century was a fairly quiet period. The work of David Hamilton and his followers in Glasgow was paralleled in the consistent development of a more sumptuous classicism for commercial and public buildings, and more picturesque styles for villas. But these were modified by a striking and at times idiosyncratic development of the Board of Manufactures' rationalistic ideology.

From the mid-1830s and early 1840s, while Thomas Hamilton and Playfair had continued to exploit the potential of explicitly Grecian architecture, William Burn, David Bryce (Burn's partner 1841–50) and David Rhind had begun to move towards an astylar, Italian palazzo-like classicism for some commercial buildings and club-houses, and a Graeco-Baroque grandeur for others – in both cases, combined with a somewhat Greek sharpness of detail. In contrast to Glasgow, there was no bold reassertion of the Grecian in the 1850s, and none of the exotic element with which the latter was mixed at the hands of Thomson; rhetorical flourishes were instead provided by a Roman or openly Baroque grandiosity. At first, the 'Italian' trend was defined by Burn's sober palazzo of the New Club (1834), whose relatively restrained style was imitated in a succession of buildings with features such as projecting door-pieces and aediculed or pedimented first-floor windows. The theme was developed by Bryce in a consistent series of palazzo-type buildings of this type in central Edinburgh over a period of more than thirty years: the Refuge Assurance Building (1840); the Edinburgh Life Assurance Company offices in George Street (1843); the Western Bank and the Exchange Bank of Scotland in St Andrew Square (both 1846, and with Burn); and, as late as 1874, the Union Bank Edinburgh office in George Street. Bryce's Edinburgh Sheriff Courthouse

6.18 Commercial Bank head office, George Street, Edinburgh (Rhind, from 1843), late nineteenth-century view.

(1863–8; subsequently replaced by the present National Library), combined a restrained, palazzo central section with the more forceful element of single-bay flanking wings with attached columns.

Soon, however, the demand for richness and pomp by banks and financial institutions became stronger. The most representative Edinburgh figure in the transition to a heavier commercial style was David Rhind. He was catapulted to prominence in 1843 when the Commercial Bank asked him to design their head office in George Street [6.18]. The confident proportions of his heavy, porticoed block, with its opulent interior plasterwork and painted decoration by D. R. Hay, reflected Rhind's personal experience of Italian architecture:. In April 1847, the *Scotsman* acclaimed 'the rich and massive architecture of the front', and the interior decoration 'in a style which is not less than gorgeous'. Rhind then proceeded to design Commercial Bank branches across the country: we noted above the Roman palazzo style of his Glasgow main branch (1853–7), with its rusticated piers and Corinthian-columned banking hall. The move away

from neo-classical austerity by the mid-century was exemplified in Rhind's design for the Life Association of Scotland (1855–8), an over-poweringly ornate Venetian Renaissance confection standing right next door to Burn's New Club [6.19]. Rhind's many sheriff courthouses also included classical designs: for example, the Italian Renaissance example at Wick (1862–8). More idiosyncratic was the massive Roman cube of his Christie Miller Mausoleum, Craigentinny (1848–56), richly decorated with sculpture by Alfred Gatley.

It was, however, in the work of Bryce that the full force of classical eclecticism in Edinburgh in due course became clear. Alongside his continuing fidelity, where required, to Burn's restrained palazzo-type manner, Bryce experimented with a wide variety of classicisms. In a monumentally lavish commission for the 10th Duke of Hamilton, Hamilton Palace Mausoleum, he produced a design (1848) of neo-classical, geometrical grandeur. [6.20] Its tall, circular tower stood on a block-like base, housing an octagonal chapel and crypt with Egyptian basalt sarcophagus bought in

6.19 Life Association of Scotland, Princes Street, Edinburgh (Rhind, 1855–8), 1966 view.

Rome for £600 by 'Il Magnifico' to serve as his own tomb. At the same time, Bryce was evolving a more assertively 'Baroque' style. In a revival of Adamesque 'movement' or Stark's architectonic power, Bryce re-emphasised the elements of column and entablature rather than the smooth, reposeful masses of Burn's earlier Grecian. This, alongside Bryce's Baronial and François Ier country house style (to be discussed shortly), became one of the hallmarks of his ascendancy in Edinburgh. By his death in 1876, Bryce was widely regarded as the east's premier architect, and many later influential figures were his pupils; his brief partnership with R. Rowand Anderson around 1873 symbolised the transmission of that status to the younger designer.

It was in the mid- and late 1830s, even before the beginning of Bryce's partnership with Burn, that this Graeco-Roman Baroque tendency began to emerge: for example, in his St Mark's Unitarian Church (1834–5) or in the spectacular Southern German Baroque interiors of Burn's Harlaxton in England (from 1838). The year 1841 witnessed the beginning of the style's extension to commercial buildings, in his Edinburgh and Leith Bank, in George Street (extended 1847), whose giant Corinthian order, with pilastrade threaded through, was influenced by David Hamilton's work in Glasgow, such as the Royal Exchange or 151–7 Queen Street. The Edinburgh and Leith Bank contributed to a roughly symmetrical composition on the north side of George Street, where it matched a heavy Corinthian colonnade added to numbers 15–19 by Bryce (1840) and MacGibbon & Ross (1879). Even bolder was Bryce's British Linen Bank (1846–51), on the east side of St Andrew Square. In a composition of Baalbek-like grandeur, six tall Corinthian columns, set forward on a massive ground-floor podium, support separate entablatures and statues by A. Handyside Ritchie; inside, the aisled and columned telling hall continued the monumental theme. Alongside St George's Free Church (1867–9), to be discussed later, the climax of Bryce's neo-Baroque, and the closest Edinburgh equivalent to Second Empire flamboyance, was his rebuilding of Robert Reid and Richard Crichton's Bank of Scotland head office (designed 1801, built 1802–6) at the top of the Mound [6.21]. Already in 1852, Thomas Hamilton

6.20 Hamilton Palace Mausoleum (Bryce, 1848).

had made abortive proposals for a rebuilding with a rusticated basement and a towered skyline; Hamilton's own Baroque tendencies had already emerged clearly at Ayr Assembly Rooms and the Dean Orphanage. In 1864–70, Bryce finally refaced and embellished Reid and Crichton's tall, plain structure. His main north front, set on a colossal basement, breaks out into a Corinthian-columned, pedimented centrepiece, crowned by statues and flanked by set-back towers; at the top is a complex, Cortona-like dome. A similarly sumptuous design by Bryce's nephew David (Junior) was the City of Glasgow Bank, Hanover Street (designed 1865–6, finished 1901 by T. P. Marwick).

The middle decades of the nineteenth century in Edinburgh, as in Glasgow, saw the beginning of a concerted institutional classicism. A range of large projects was erected by government

6.21 David Bryce perspective of Bank of Scotland rebuilding scheme (1864–70), Edinburgh.

architects, including Robert Matheson's Palm House (1855), New Register House (1856–62) and Post Office (1861–6), and the Germanic round-arched Renaissance of Captain Francis Fowke's Royal Scottish Museum (1860–1). More complex was the work of the City Architect, the Playfair-trained David Cousin. This provided one of the main architectural outlets for mid-nineteenth-century Edinburgh rationalism. The latter, like the work of Viollet-le-Duc in France, was an attempt, by people who had rejected neo-classicism, to return to classical 'harmony'. Led by D. R. Hay and by the teachings of Alexander Christie of the Board of Manufactures School of Design (responsible, among other projects, for the sumptuous decoration of J. Gillespie Graham's St Anthony's Chapel, Murthly, 1846–8), its ideas were given wider currency from 1850 by the founding of the Aesthetic Society. Cousin, trained in Playfair's office and a Free Church member, played a prominent role in the society. Through his work, the theories of 'harmonic proportion' that preoccupied the Edinburgh rationalists could be tried out at public expense. [28] His Corn Exchange, Grassmarket (1849), a palazzo-like building with asymmetrical tower, had a grid-like facade laid out on harmonic angles, with striking low-relief ornament. The Reid School of Music (1858), a heavier and plainer classical block, was designed for another Aesthetic Society member, the musician Professor Donaldson. It was decorated internally by Hay and had a coffered concert hall laid out in accordance with precise acoustic calculations. Other Cousin works possibly designed in conformity to harmonic proportions included the Scots Renaissance India Buildings, Victoria Street (1864) and the classical facade scheme conceived for the north side of the new Chambers Street in 1864 (but only partly executed).

A more idiosyncratic follower of these ideas was James Gowans, who entered the building trade in 1833 and trained as an architect in Bryce's office. A contractor for architectural setpieces such as Rhind's George Street Commercial Bank, Gowans's varied commercial and industrial career included the construction (from 1846) of large sections of the Highland Railway and (from 1871) of the Edinburgh tramway system, as well as the building-up (from 1850) of the biggest quarry-master's business in Scotland, in which capacity he pioneered the introduction of rock drilling by machines. Understandably, Gowans became a vocal upholder of the capital's status as a homo-geneous stone-built city, and participated in the police regulation of building activity, becoming Lord Dean of Guild in 1885; at the same time, he vigorously promoted the construction of sanitary working-class dwellings. Taking up the Aesthetic Society conception that 'in architecture, a geometric basis is at the root of what we admire' [29] Gowans applied it to masonry construction, believing, like Viollet-le-Duc, that he had discovered the key to medieval masonry design. As a rich man, he was able actually to build realisations of his ideas. His own Edinburgh house, 'Rockville' (1858), was built on a stone grid of two-foot squares of cyclopean rubble – supposedly designed to allow mass production of stone components – with angles based on the diagonal, and related to circles. The house's fantastically busy composition was crowned by a five-stage

tower and Bryce-like château roof [6.22]. Similar in style was the villa 'Lammerburn' (1860), while his 1866 Castle Terrace tenement development, also designed on a geometrical basis, adopted a Cousin-like free Renaissance, with palace-like twin towers. His family tomb, in Grange Cemetery (1858) was a large triangular monolith with heavy canopy. Gowans collaborated on some schemes with the architect Frederick T. Pilkington: for example, the Edinburgh Winter Garden and West End Theatre, Castle Terrace (1875), where he designed the outside and Pilkington the interior. Other Pilkington secular works in a round-arched classical style included the Venetian design of the Dundee Eastern Club (1867–70); and his own house at 38 Dick Place, Edinburgh (1865–70), with complex staircase and neo-Rococo ballroom. We

6.22 Rockville, Edinburgh (Gowans, 1858), 1964 view.

will deal later with the designs for which Pilkington is more widely known, his 1860s' churches.

From the 1850s, the middle-class residential spread of Edinburgh resumed, following similar patterns to that of Glasgow, with a combination of boulevard and crescent developments of terraces, and areas of villas. Some developments began where they had left off at the 1833 crash. For mid-nineteenth-century taste, even the more variegated New Town designs of the 1820s now seemed impossibly austere. While the English critic John Ruskin's 1853 comparison of New Town houses to 'prisons' prompted some indignation, Lord Cockburn's criticism of the New Town's 'poverty in all its details' was hardly less acerbic. [30] To many in the capital, as in Glasgow and other European cities, the individual suburban villa now seemed the best pattern, but for those who still valued monumental city life, a less severe version of the terrace seemed preferable. The western edges of the New Town were infilled with bay-windowed terraces, including the grandiosely Graeco-Italian section of Drumsheugh Gardens designed by Peddie & Kinnear (1874–8; the rest of the street was by John Lessels), and the crescents of the Heriot Trust's estate of Wester Coates (with elevations by the Trust's surveyor John Chesser, *c.*1871–9). The Dean Estate, beyond the Dean Bridge, was developed in boulevard form around Queensferry Road, flanked by bay-windowed terraces, with elevations by John Chesser, such as Buckingham Terrace (from 1860) and Learmonth Terrace (from 1873).

To the south of the Meadows and Links, a range of new areas was developed from the 1860s, including the villa area of the Grange, and the tenemental areas of Marchmont and Warrender. Here the urge for greater architectural plasticity was expressed not only, as in Glasgow, through the ubiquitous use of canted bay windows, but also – doubtless evoking the romantic image of the capital – through an explicit use of Baronial features. The latter ranged from small details such as stop-chamfered or roll-moulded window-arrises to elaborate crowstepped gables. In the development of the Warrender estate, architects such as Thomas Marwick and Edward Calvert followed with gusto the Baronial guidelines set down in an 1869 feuing plan by Bryce. Streets such as Warrender Park

Crescent or Road (both from 1876) combined a generally classical homogeneity and repetition with a proliferation of Baronial decoration [6.23]. This was, essentially, a reworking of the New Town formula at roughly the same scale and roughly the same relative distance from the Old Town, but in Baronial stylistic dress. In the north, notable Baronial groups of the 1870s and 1880s by Alexander Ross are located around Ness Walk, Inverness. Elsewhere in the east, a generally neo-classical plainness prevailed. In Aberdeen tenements, generally of two or three storeys and attic, bay windows never became very popular, but they were used widely on villas. Thomsonian incised forms were translated into granite in housing by the Aberdeen architects Pirie and Clyne, including a row of villas in Hamilton Place (1880s) and an ornate dwelling, with some Gothic detailing, at 50 Queens Road (1886) [cf. C.6].

Edinburgh and Leith working-class housing, on the whole, echoed the west in reinforcing the perimeter-type street plan with shallow plans and open back courts, and abandoning evenness of window spacing. However, bay windows were avoided, preserving a neo-classical facade flatness and austerity through to the early twentieth century; exceptions included two striking blocks by Pilkington in Fountainbridge/Grove Street with aggressively Gothic arched facades, built 1864–5 (one as a working men's home). The period from the 1850s to the 1880s, as in Glasgow, saw numerous attempts to devise lower-density patterns, often in association with some sort of philanthropic organ-isation: two-storey flats with forestairs were built by Gowans in 1854 at Rosebank Cottages (with elevations by Alexander MacGregor) and by the masonic-based Edinburgh Co-Operative Building Company from 1861 at Glenogle Road, while the tireless Gowans went on to build a two-storey demonstration block of four dwellings at the 1886 Edinburgh International Exhibition.

In 1860, a report on the housing problem by an Edinburgh committee of artisans defended the tenement pattern, claiming that 'the Edinburgh architecture – also substantially that of Paris – is based upon a far higher principle in social philos-ophy than we are accustomed to believe. The proverb that "an Englishman's home is his castle" contains a very selfish, if not impracticable idea.' In

6.23 Warrender Park Road, Edinburgh
(from 1876).

contrast to the clean-sweep modernity of Glasgow, this committee also, for the first time, advocated the 'benevolent and profitable' reconditioning of Old Town tenements 'with the idea of preserving the ancient and national character of the domiciles'. [31] The association between old burgh houses and the 'national' will recur in later chapters of our account. In fact, Edinburgh in this period saw a vigorous central redevelopment drive, based on a City Improvement Act (passed 1867), as in Glasgow or Dundee. But in this case, the Romantic and scenographic principles already established by Thomas Hamilton and Burn remained prominent, and led to the devising of an inner-urban street architecture based on Scotch Baronial [cf. 5.22]. Billings had drawn attention to the 'peculiarities and merits' of old burghs' 'street architecture . . . private dwellings ornamented by that light, graceful, angular turret which was adapted from the French château architecture'. A prototype Baronial improvement scheme had already been promoted privately in the city, by the 1853 Edinburgh Railway Station Access Act [6.24], which authorised the building of

a curving street from the High Street down to the new station. The 1853 Act specified that the new buildings must 'preserve as far as possible the architectural style and antique Character' of the area. [32] The resulting scheme, Cockburn Street (laid out 1856 and built 1859–64 by speculators to the designs of Peddie & Kinnear), had provided a new, dramatic architectural gateway to the Old Town, bristling with turrets and crowstepped gables. Following this example, the 1867 City Improvement Act proposed the formation or widening of several streets on either side of the High Street, with 'elevations . . . of plain but marked character, in harmony with those fine specimens of national architecture in many of the neglected and overcrowded areas'. [33] The resulting elevation designs, such as those for the widened St Mary's Street (from 1869) and Blackfriars Street (from 1870) were mostly by the Trust's architects, David Cousin and John Lessels, but other architects such as Robert Morham and David Clunas designed individual blocks within that framework; the overall architectural character was Baronial of a plainer kind than Cockburn Street.

6.24 Peddie & Kinnear's 1850s' presentation drawing of Cockburn Street, Edinburgh (built 1859–64); with Old Town and City Chambers behind.

David Bryce and the Heyday of Scotch Baronial

By the middle decades of the century, the confidence and power of Scottish-British imperial culture, and the effective completion of improvement at home, had both subtly altered the significance of the 'national', squeezing out the doubts felt by Scott and the Romantics about the relation between Scottish nationality and the forces of modernity: now both could be expressed together. In architecture, the style which played that role was Scotch Baronial. Although, as we saw above, used in some urban housing contexts, its climax was rural: the country houses built by the ruling classes of imperial Scotland, especially to the designs of Bryce, who combined Scottish and French elements in an eclectic synthesis of different branches of 'national' northern European Renaissance sources.

In contrast to the regionally varied expressions of classicism across Scotland, the 'national' Baronial style was relatively homogeneous across the whole country. Indeed, the Scotch Baronial country house was as much a product of cosmopolitan modernity as of 'national' characteristics, as was acknowledged slightly later by G. S . Aitken: 'Feudalistic in character, and necessarily . . . crude in conception, it has by the talent of able modern exponents been brought up to date through the happy transfusion into it of the style of the French châteaux, with which it is nearly akin'; it had been 'refined in detail and translated into forms more appropriate to our modern ideas of domestic architecture'. [34] There was no equivalent, in this 'modern' Baronial, to Thomson's idealisation of the Greeks and Egyptians as the basis for an emotionalist architecture. The Baronial patrons and designers looked on the old and new societies as diametrically opposed. As Billings put it, 'The spots chosen as the most suitable for fortifications in the old days of family warfare, though generally selected by men who never looked at scenery, and cared for nothing but eating, drinking and fighting, have often supplied exquisite pieces of scenery, adapted entirely to our modern taste'. [35] Nor did nineteenth-century Baronial mansions follow Scott's admiration for old texture; there was an emphasis on precise, hard stone finish, and plate-glass windows. Only later in the century, as we will see in Chapter 7, would a new movement, Traditionalism, begin to look on Scottish Renaissance castles with the same liking for 'old texture' as Scott, and the same utopian idealism as Thomson.

Mid-nineteenth-century Scotch Baronial, above all, formed part of an international north European movement of revision of the Picturesque, especially in the houses of the rich. Universal 'Italian' styles were rejected in favour of more accurate 'national' styles: for instance, in France, by a 'néo-Renaissance' based on the Loire châteaux. For such a movement, new, national types of source-publications were necessary – a need met in Scotland by the publication in 1845–52 (subsidised by Burn) of Billings's series, *The Baronial and Ecclesiastical Antiquities of Scotland*. Although based on accurate drawings, the finished illustrations presented dramatically shaded (and sometimes imaginatively embellished) perspectives of castles and churches. As with Adam, the subjects, even if symmetrical on plan, were presented in an irregular and asymmetrical manne. [cf. 1.12, 2.10, 2.13, 2.17, 2.20, 2.25, 2.29].

Who were the patrons of this style of picturesque, 'national' modernity? As we saw in Chapters 4 and 5, landowners' attempts to ally with, and exploit, the new Ossianic images of Scotland had become steadily more closely linked with architectural images of castellated lineage. Mid-nineteenth-century Baronial works would be commissioned both by the established aristocracy, such as the Duke of Atholl (patron of Bryce's 1869–76 alterations to Blair Castle) and by the newly rich, such as chemical manufacturer Charles Tennant (owner of Bryce's The Glen, 1855–60) or opium trader Alexander Matheson (patron of Alexander Ross's Ardross, 1880–1). For businessmen wishing to build out of income rather than capital, the characteristic Baronial project of a series of additions to an existing house was especially suitable. In all these respects, we see echoes of the castellated originals of the sixteenth and seventeenth centuries, and (although the nineteenth century did not know it) of their patrons.

Desire to imitate the monarchy was just as much a factor in this period as it had been in the earlier centuries. Queen Victoria acquired a Highland estate, Balmoral, in 1848; she praised John Smith's original house as a 'pretty little castle in the old Scottish style'. [36] In 1853–5, a new castle was built, to the designs of William Smith and Prince Albert [6.25]. The new Balmoral comprised two blocks – main and service – each with central courtyard, and linked by a massive 80-foot tower with tourelles. In 1864, the north-east-born architect Robert Kerr contrasted the 'medievalism' of its style with its planning, which displayed an 'obvious desire to provide that regular disposition of thoroughfare lines which is so important a means of convenience, and. . . that simple rectangularity of partitionment which belongs to good plain modern rooms'. [37] Inside the new Balmoral, the ballroom was flamboyantly decorated with stags' heads, but the other rooms were of plain, rather classical style. By 1855, Balmoral's Burn-like combination of rationalistic planning and loosely picturesque elevations, intended to recall the old John Smith house (and reminiscent in style of Burn's Auchmacoy, 1831, and in plan of Forglen, 1839), had been left far behind by the development of a richer, more plastic Baronialism.

The new, more full-blooded Scotch Baronial was not chiefly the responsibility of Billings, although he built one or two major projects in a harshly hard-edged style. These included a warehouse at 115–137 Ingram Street, Glasgow

(1854–6) and the reconstruction of Dalzell House, Motherwell (from 1859) and of Castle Wemyss (from 1860) in a serrated, almost Pilkington-like manner. Rather, the pivotal figure in this confident mid-nineteenth-century expression of the 'national' was David Bryce, heir to Burn's vast Scottish country-house practice [cf. L.1]. Bryce, during his period as chief clerk and (1841–50) partner to Burn, had been thoroughly grounded in the planning and practical building of country houses. Some of his early designs continued Burn's low and rather episodic Baronial manner: for instance, Tollcross (1848) or Ormiston Hall (1851). But by the early 1840s Bryce – in parallel to his urban Graeco-Roman style – was already moving to a more dynamic and heavily decorated Baronialism. The key transitional design was his large addition to Seacliffe House (1841), where Bryce transformed an original plan by Burn into a more sculptural mass, and added turrets and bay windows. The next decisive stage was reached at Balfour Castle, Shapinsay, Orkney (1846–51) [6.26]. Here, Colonel David Balfour, heir to a fortune made in India, commissioned Bryce to enlarge, indeed submerge, what had been a 'neat little villa' [38] beneath a massive battlemented and crowstepped block of public rooms; the design included, for the first time, one of the most characteristic of Bryce's trademarks – a canted bay window corbelled out to a straight gable above. Bryce's main series of large country houses

6.25 Balmoral Castle (as rebuilt 1853–5 by W. Smith and Prince Albert), early twentieth-century view.

6.26 Balfour Castle, Shapinsay, Orkney (Bryce, 1846–51), late nine-teenth-century view.

6.27 Hartrigge House (Bryce, rebuilt 1854).

exemplified, perhaps more than any other buildings of their age, the capacity of eclectic modernity to adapt familiar old motifs to new uses and combinations, and combine them with completely new features such as plate glass and gaslighting. By this time, Billings's volumes were in course of publication.

Within Bryce's varied country house *œuvre*, three basic plan types are discernible. First, there was a mainstream of large Baronial projects, developing the Burn tradition, designed in a fairly irregular manner with some symmetrical elements. Second, there was a new trend of large houses with far more pronounced symmetrical elements, and features drawn from the early French Renaissance;

and thirdly, there were small, compact houses. These varied plans, with their extensive service facilities and segregation of functions, and their plans often based on accretions to an existing core, represent the culmination of planning tendencies which began in the Scottish Renaissance - although that period's most prestigious plan type, the courtyard palace, was no longer so popular in the nineteenth-century era of privacy. In the development of the first, mainstream Baronial category, the focus is normally a massive tower, or high, castle-like range. This might be an old Scottish Renaissance tower which Bryce was adding to, or a part of a new composition, on the model established by Gillespie Graham's tower at Brodick

(1844), Playfair's at Stonefield (1836), or later Burn examples such as Buchanan (1852–4). The tower section normally forms part of an asymmetrical entrance front, while the garden-front may be symmetrical; if new, the tower normally is based on one of the sixteenth- or seventeenth-century castellated setpieces, such as the round tower of Huntly or Castle Fraser, the arched towers of Fyvie, or the high oriel gable of Maybole [cf. 2.10, 2.12, 2.13, 2.29]. For example, at both Hartrigge (rebuilt 1854) and The Glen (1855–60), the dominant feature is a Maybole-pattern tower; The Glen has a symmetrical garden facade [6.27].

In the late 1850s and 1860s, Bryce's mainstream, irregularly planned Scotch Baronial pattern reached its climax in a series of very large commissions. The first and, perhaps, most spectacular was Craigends (1857–9), built for Alexander Cunninghame. [6.28] With swaggering panache, Bryce deftly balanced an overall richness with due emphasis on the most important elements of the building. The entrance facade was dominated by a Fyvie-type tower at one end, containing the entrance. By comparison with the Seton Tower itself, this was of a far more compressed, Baroque character, built of freestone rather than harled rubble, and groaning with

additional features such as a balcony, a square balustraded tower behind it, cast-iron ornamentation, and mullioned windows [cf. 2.10]. Providing a balance at the other end of the entrance facade was a Maybole-type tower, here reduced to a clearly subsidiary role; the garden front was symmetrical, between two gables. At Castlemilk (from 1864), for Sir Robert Jardine of Hong Kong, a Fraser-style round tower was the focus, here used with *porte-cochère* and juxtaposed with a sheer, flat-fronted main block – in a stark, almost brutal suggestion of multi-period accretion. At Ballikinrain (also from 1864) for Sir Archibald Orr Ewing, another Huntly/Fraser corbelled-out round tower, of gargantuan proportions, provides the fulcrum of asymmetrical garden and entrance facades; the garden front presents a bustling array of gables and bay windows, while the stable block has a Fettes-like clock-tower. More severe designs among larger Bryce works include Glenapp (1870), and the 're-Baronialised' Blair Castle (1869–76) with its restrained sprinkling of turrets and heightened walls, and new entrance hall lined with the weaponry of the Duke of Atholl's 'private army'. Another extension to a famous old house was made at Fyvie itself by Bryce's nephew, John Bryce: in 1890 he designed

6.28 Craigends House (1857–9), perspective by David Bryce.

the new Leith Tower, with Huntly-type oriels.

Alongside this mainstream of development, the period from the mid-1850s also saw the emergence of a new Franco-Scotch Baronialism of high-roofed, spired castles, which exploited the closeness of the two countries' architectures in the early Renaissance years: Billings had claimed that Scottish Renaissance castles had been influenced by 'the airy turrets and fantastic tracery of France'.[39] As in 'néo-Renaissance' nineteenth-century châteaux in France, these projects were usually symmetrical in plan and elevation, resulting in a return to the Adam principle of symmetrical plans and asymmetrical silhouettes. The symmetrical tendencies of the Scottish Renaissance originals were obviously a stimulus: already, in 1840–1, Bryce and Burn had embellished the spiky, towered skyline of Thirlestane with further turrets and flanking wings, and a frontal ogee-roofed central tower, creating a much more boldly pyramidal composition [cf. 3.6]. At Kinnaird Castle, commissioned 1854 by the 7th Earl of Southesk, Bryce recast the castellated James Playfair house of 1785–93 in a Blois-like manner,

with Scottish details; the central building was refaced and given high roofs, and while the resited entrance was still at one end, the south front, facing a symmetrical garden, had now clearly become the main facade [6.29]. Bryce's enlargement of Cortachy Castle in 1870 for the 5th Earl of Airlie was focused on a new, symmetrical entrance facade, whose high roofs gave it an almost over-powering mass; the old house was tucked away to one side [6.30]. The climax of this tendency, and the most triumphant Scottish contribution to Second Empire monumental eclecticism as a whole, was not, however, a country house, but a large private school in the capital, Fettes College (1864–70) [6.31; cf. C.9]. This symmetrical, high-roofed composition of bartizans, towers and spires rises from a Blois/Huntly-like ground-floor loggia, with a cavernous Fyvie-pattern entrance tower providing a colossally plastic centrepiece. Bryce's own perspective presented the building asymmetrically, while the college's main, axial avenue to the south added yet another grand, spired vista to Romantic Edinburgh. Bryce's smaller houses were of somewhat different

6.29 Kinnaird Castle (rebuilt from 1854 by Bryce), late nineteenth-century view.

6.30 Cortachy Castle (rebuilt 1870 by Bryce), photograph of *c*.1878.

character, with compact plans closely based on Burn precedents (as at Ardnaseig, 1833). Examples such as Stronvar (1850) or Shambellie (1856) were built of rubble, with cheaper small-paned sash windows and relatively few turrets and excrescences; Keiss (1859–62) was harled to conform to an earlier core [6.32]. We will see in Chapter 7 that this plainer approach, here simply due to economy, would begin to acquire a new, 'artistic' prestige from the 1880s, when elaborate Baronialism began to slide from architectural fashion.

Bryce's Baronial country houses exerted a wide influence, especially through the work of his pupils, such as Charles Kinnear, James M. Wardrop, Andrew Heiton and J. T . Rochead – a body of architecture which, like Bryce's own domestic *œuvre*, spanned the whole country, without regard for geographical distinctions. While this national scope was unusual for the mid-nineteenth century, the era of landed supremacy in the seventeenth and eighteenth centuries had, after all, preceded the urban explosion and the entrenchment of the east-west cultural polarity. Baronial houses by these former pupils included Rochead's Levenford House, Dumbarton (1853) and the hard-edged, simplified Vogrie House, by Heiton (1875). Wardrop contributed the château-like enlargement of Callendar Park (1869–77) and plainer work at Nunraw (1868) and Kinnordy (1879, with Pinkie-like seventeenth-century features); Peddie & Kinnear abortively proposed a colossal, Franco-Scotch scheme at St Martin's Abbey, Perthshire,

with courtyard-palace or hôtel plan. Other large-scale Baronial castles included, in the north, Alexander Ross's Ardross (1880–1) and Ross & Macbeth's Skibo Castle (1900, for Andrew Carnegie, incorporating an 1880 house by Clarke & Bell). Among western architects, the David Hamilton practice of using specifically western seventeenth-century detail was perpetuated in the Baronial houses of Charles Wilson (who had been Hamilton's chief draughtsman at the time of Dunlop's construction), whether located in the west or the east. Examples included Shandon House (1849), St Helen's, Dundee (1850), or the larger Benmore House, Kilmun (1862, with 1874 enlargement by David Thomson). Baronial houses by other western designers included John Burnet Senior's Auchendennan (1864–6) and a foray into the style by Alexander Thomson at Craigrownie Castle, Cove (*c*.1854). Although mainstream Baronial avoided the Scott-like 'artistic' concern for 'oldness', there were idiosyncratic exceptions, which anticipated some of the characteristics of turn-of-the-century Traditionalism. These included Patrick Allan Fraser's enlargement of Hospitalfield, Arbroath (from 1850), and his building of the Arbroath Western Cemetery Mortuary Chapel (1875–80, with spiky exterior and suffocatingly massive interior), both including naturalistic detail by local craftsmen, such as stone-carver James Peters and wood carver John Hutchison; and Spencer Boyd's rebuilding of Penkill Castle from 1857 to the designs of A. G. Thomson (no relation of 'Greek' Thomson), with

6.31 Fettes College, Edinburgh (Bryce, 1864–70), axial view from south; in foreground, Comely Bank private tenements of 1938-46, designed by Stewart Kaye for Dean Property Investment Company.

6.32 Stronvar House, Balquhidder (Bryce, 1850), late nineteenth-century view by J. B. White.

6.33 Mortuary Chapel, Western Cemetery, Arbroath (P. A. Fraser, 1875–80).

noted Pre-Raphaelite murals by William Bell Scott [6.33].

The mid-nineteenth century's requirement for more accurate 'national' historical styles posed a problem for designers of the interiors of Scotch Baronial houses. The Adam formula of castellated exterior and classical interior would no longer do, but there were no accurate records of original Scottish Renaissance interiors in their complete state. Of course, even if there had been records, the originals, with their tapestries, stools and chests,

would have seemed far too sparse and dark for mid-nineteenth century-taste. In response, a new consistent Baronial eclectic interior was synthesised. The basic architectural shell was treated in a massive, even primitive manner, including plastered or rubble walls, unpainted stone fireplaces and pitch pine timberwork, crowned by seventeenth-century style compartmented plaster ceilings. Ornamental richness on the walls was provided not only by heraldic decoration, as in the Scottish Renaissance 'originals', but also by a further range of conventionalised symbols of landed power and national affiliation, including displays of tartan, weaponry and stuffed animals' heads. The reception of Queen Victoria at Taymouth in 1842 had provided a starting point for Baronial troubadour spectacles. These colourfully 'national' features were combined with fittings and services of uninhibited modernity, such as sprung upholstery, gaslighting and water-closets.

By the mid-nineteenth century, the Scotch Baronial style was spreading from its country house redoubt to public buildings and other urban contexts, again largely at the hands of pupils of Bryce, such as James C. Walker or Charles Kinnear: we saw above its use by Peddie & Kinnear from 1854 in the remodelling of a chunk of 'Old Edinburgh' (the building of Cockburn Street) [cf. 6.24]. From the 1850s, it began to be associated with projects for 'national monuments', where its confident massiveness seemed to reflect the bullishness of the culture of 'imperial partnership', and replaced the earlier classicism and Gothicism. Bryce's pupil, J. T. Rochead, was responsible for the earliest and grandest of these projects – the National Wallace Monument at Stirling, 1859–69 [6.34]. This colossal, sculptural tower was 220 feet high, set on a prominent hill, and constructed of rock-faced rubble, with extruded stair turret and heavily indented chamfering; it was topped by the imperial emblem of a crown spire, and contained a series of vaulted chambers above one another. The completion of this giant monument to Scottish imperial, unionist nationalism was greeted with telegrams of support from Garibaldi and Kossuth. The National Wallace Monument would, in turn, have been outdone by a series of unrealised projects of the late 1850s and 1860s, which marked the beginning of the campaign to convert Edinburgh Castle from a military barracks into a national monument. The first was a proposal by Colonel Richard Moody of the Royal Engineers to recast the New Barracks, Munition House and Ordnance Stores in a château-like style, to designs by Francis T. Dollman; Moody was a friend of D. R. Hay, and it seems possible that he drew up this craggy, romantic scheme in accordance with the Aesthetic Society concepts of harmonic proportion [6.35; cf. 1.10]. Then, in 1864, came proposals by Bryce to build a 165-feet-high keep on the site as a 'Scottish National Memorial to the Prince Consort'. The actual remodelling of the castle from the 1880s by Hippolyte Blanc was more modest in scale, and only in the 1920s was a symbolic 'national monument', of a quite different purpose and character, completed there by R. S. Lorimer [cf. 8.1, 8.2, 8.3, C.3].

Slightly later, Scotch Baronial began to spread into the field of mainstream urban public buildings, beginning with the series of courthouses built following the Sheriff Courthouses Act of 1860 – a programme overseen largely by land-owning Commissioners of Supply who may have seen Baronial as a natural style to signify estab-lishment authority. Peddie & Kinnear's Greenock Sheriff Courthouse, 1864–7, was a miniature Fettes-like composition with symmetrical central tower; Brown & Wardrop's Stirling (1874–6) was a symmetrical, scaled-down version of an 1864 design; while David Rhind contributed emphatic rubble designs at Dumfries (1863–6) and Selkirk (1868–70; with Castle Fraser round tower). From Baronial sheriff courthouses to Baronial municipal

6.34 National Wallace Monument, near Stirling, exhibition drawing of 1859 by J. T. Rochead.

buildings, with their established requirement for tall steeples as authority symbols, was a short and obvious step. An early pointer was Charles Wilson's Rutherglen (1861–2, with curiously shaved-off tower), followed by J. C. Walker at Dunfermline (1875) and Hawick (1883), and F. J. C. Carruthers at Lockerbie (from 1887). The proudest monument of this series, including sheriff courts as well as municipal offices, was the enlargement of Aberdeen Town House by Peddie & Kinnear in 1866–74, naturally in granite [6.36]. Its bartizaned main tower, for several decades by far

6.35 Unexecuted proposals of 1859 by Francis Dollman for a Baronial rebuilding of Edinburgh Castle.

the most prominent landmark in the city, echoed, in hugely amplified form, the old Aberdeen mansions illustrated by Billings.

The use of Scotch Baronial in other institutions and commercial buildings was less common; in the educational field, Kinnear's Morgan Hospital, Dundee (1866) resembled Fettes, and the mountainous pile of J. Macleod's Christian Institute, Bothwell Street, Glasgow (1878, extended 1895–8 by Clarke & Bell and R. A. Bryden) combined Baronial massing with some neo-Romanesque detail. Baronial was applied to the design of symmetrical, pavilion-plan hospitals by Bryce at Edinburgh Royal Infirmary (begun 1872 and finished by John Bryce 1876–9) and by John Burnet Senior at Glasgow's Western Infirmary (1871–7, with turreted centrepiece based on the gables of Glamis Castle) [6.37]. In the commercial field, an early example of Bryce's Franco-Scotch manner was the Royal Exchange, Dundee (1855), while David MacGibbon built branches for the National Bank of Scotland at Alloa, Falkirk and Forfar in 1861–3; Kinnear followed his lead, while Rochead's City of Glasgow

bank offices in Trongate (1855) were loaded with gables and other busy detailing: the *Building Chronicle* praised its 'grace, ease and picturesque fashion of outline, which gives so much interest and beauty to this peculiar cast of architecture'. [40]

Church Architecture and the Classical Vision

The church-building of the mid-century was dominated by the activity of the three Presbyterian groupings – the Established Church, the Free Church and the United Presbyterians – although the revival of Catholicism and Episcopalianism would eventually diminish that dominance.

For all three main Presbyterian denominations, the main concern, with the rapid expansion of industrial cities, was quantity. This applied most dramatically, of course, to the Free Church. The first year after the Disruption saw a frenzy of building activity. The first Free Church in Edinburgh opened three days after the Disruption, in Lothian Road; it was constructed of brick with

6.36 County and Municipal Buildings, Aberdeen (1866–74, by Peddie & Kinnear), and (on left) the 1975 Town House Extension designed by City Architect Tom Watson.

6.37 Western Infirmary, Glasgow (J. Burnet, 1871–7), 1988 view.

paper and canvas interior lining. More substantial efforts of 1843 included Archibald Simpson's 'Triple Kirks', a Marburg-spired complex built in a matter of weeks to house three congregations displaced from Aberdeen's St Nicholas's Kirk; construction was of rubble with brick dressings and spire. By the time of the first Free Church Assembly of 1844, 470 churches had already been completed. However, it remained as unclear as ever what, if any, should be the relationship of architectural form and style to Presbyterian building. There was constant debate about internal arrangements, fluctuating between the extremes of the auditorium tailor-made for preacher-centred worship, and the linear plan associated with devotional liturgy. The mainstream architectural position of this period was represented by David Thomson's observation of Charles Wilson that 'a strong sense of the fitness of things withheld him at all times from accepting the long drawn aisles to Presbyterian churches'. [41] About external architecture, there was less discussion, but just as little consensus. Perhaps because the specially privileged 'national' Gothic prominent in countries such as Germany, England or France enjoyed less status in Scotland, the most emotional, 'free' tendencies within church archi-tecture came from within monumental classicism, and the advocacy or opposition of particular styles was a relatively local and fluctuating matter.

The new classical developments of these years stemmed chiefly from the Baroque leanings of Stark and Playfair, and above all from the latter's St Stephen's Church. In Edinburgh, where, as we saw in Chapter 5, critics had attacked use of explicit Greek forms as 'pagan', other classicisms were not affected. Bryce soon developed his more densely ornamented Baroque manner first seen at St Mark's Unitarian Church (1834–5). At St George's Free Church, Shandwick Place (1867–9) – a sumptuously Corinthian-columned building doubtless intended as another urban landmark of the Free Church's authority – the complex Southern German Rococo tower remained unbuilt, and a plainer campanile by R. Rowand Anderson was later substituted [6.38]. More typical of the third quarter of the nineteenth century was the genteel Italian classicism of Peddie & Kinnear's Palmerston Place Church (1873–5), its towered and arcaded facade fronting a capacious auditorium plan. An asymmetrical, towered Lombardic variant of Italianate classicism was attempted at Sutherland & Walker's Rosehall United Presbyterian Church (UP), Dalkeith Road

(1877), with its arcaded and pedimented facades and transept-galleried, radial-seated interior. In the north-east, 'Italian' classicism appeared in a different form: at Archibald Simpson's Woodside West New Church, near Aberdeen (1846–9), a monumental clock steeple, octagonal on a cubic base, was combined with the low-eaved austerity of his informal country house style.

In the west, there was a far more forceful development of ecclesiastical classicism, led by Alexander Thomson, and including a prominent Grecian element – used now in a context not of neo-classical restraint, but of eclectic richness. We have to remember that Thomson's own church, the United Presbyterian, was the most favourably disposed towards classical auditorium solutions, although it also commissioned major neo-Gothic works, such as James Brown's profusely finialled Perpendicular design for Renfield Street Church (1848, popularly known as 'The United Presbyterian Cathedral'). [42] There were several main sources for Thomson's ecclesiastical architecture. These included the Baroque steepled tradition of Gibbs, Stark and Playfair; the Italianate villa architecture of Playfair and others, with its asymmetrical towers and wings (as seen for example at Thomson's own Craig Ailey, 1850) [cf. 6.14]; the temple-based architecture of Grecian neo-classicism; and the influence of Ancient Egypt and the Middle and Near East. These were filtered through a more general context of piled-up, interpenetrating monumentalism, as seen in the projects and works of Adam and Thomas Hamilton, and the apocalyptic paintings of Martin.

The first of Thomson's three major churches was Caledonia Road UP (1856–7) [6.39]. Here the scenographic portico and podium arrangement of the Surgeons Hall and the County Buildings was reinterpreted as an asymmetrical and introspective composition, with a sombre, block-like steeple at one side; it was just at that time that Thomson's friend Wilson was building Free Church College [cf. 6.4]. *The Building Chronicle* noted that the church's style was not 'trammelled by a rigid adherence to ancient examples'. [43] As always, the townscape role is carefully considered, not only through the axis-stopping tower but also through the integration with new adjoining

6.38 St George's West Free Church (Bryce 1867–9), late nineteenth-century view (including 1880–2 tower by R. Rowand Anderson).

tenement blocks by Thomson. Inside, he introduced polychrome decoration for the first time in United Presbyterian churches – an innovation that was adopted only cautiously by the other Presbyterian denominations.

In 1856, Thomson ended his partnership with John Baird II and formed a partnership with his brother George, an astute Christian businessman who was later to give up architecture to become a missionary in Africa. One of their first commissions was the building of the second major Thomson church, St Vincent Street UP (1857–9). Here we encounter in a striking form the interaction between religious and capitalist endeavours in mid-century Glasgow – or, more precisely in this case, between A. & G. Thomson, church architects, and A. & G. Thomson, property speculators. At this time, George Thomson

6.39 Caledonia Road UP Church, Glasgow (Thomson, 1856–7), 1965 view.

worshipped at Gordon Street Church in the centre of the city. Like many congregations in the centre, Gordon Street suddenly found that the rise in commercial land values had left them with a considerable asset. They decided to realise this by moving to a new site further out in Blythswood. The Thomson brothers, in their capacity as developers, bought the old site and erected the Grosvenor Building on it (1859–61), while in their capacity as architects, they were appointed to design the congregation's new St Vincent Street Church, along with a slightly later tenement next door to it, in order to maximise rental value [cf. 6.7]. St Vincent Street's sharply sloping site, most frequently seen from below, offered the opportunity to design a building which exceeded in monumentality even Playfair's St Stephen's, and Thomson eagerly grasped it [6.40, 6.41]. The composition comprises two elements: a main church block of crushing Baroque power, conceived as a mound-like structure of interpenetrating temple, lower 'aisles', and pylons, on an exaggeratedly tall podium; and a lofty steeple, set almost separately to one side in campanile form, its bare lower section topped by a fantastic conglomeration of Egyptian and oriental detail,

including an attenuated dome. In general, it seems likely that the high podium form of this awesome structure was intended to recall the Temple of Solomon, held at that time by many writers to have been supported on a vast platform. Throughout, Thomson's emphasis on mass is reinforced by suppression of windows into sunken embrasures or banded patterns.

Inside St Vincent Street, the auditorium extended down into the podium, while, laterally, a broad *Predigtkirche* plan was secured through the extra width of the aisles. Although this feature, in practical terms, was borrowed from neo-Gothic architecture, it seems that Thomson's own reasoning was grounded in a utopian evocation of the world of early Christianity, as well as in what was thought to have been the plan of the Temple of Solomon. Fleming's later, but apparently accurate account recalled that he was

'imbued with the thought that the classic style which was in use for all sacred structures when Paul preached was that best fitted for a presbyterian place of worship. A presbyterian Church is essentially a place for hearing in, so the first duty of the architect is to produce an auditorium. This implies that the chamber in which the audience meets should be

6.40 St Vincent Street UP Church, Glasgow (Thomson, 1857–9): (above) view of substructure, including Derek Stephenson's Heron House (1967–71) on the right ; (right) detail of top of steeple.

approximately square; but classic temples were twice as long as they were broad. The solution preferred in the present case was to increase the breadth by the addition of aisles'. [44]

The furniture and fittings, designed personally by Thomson, echoed the external emphasis on mass, with heavy single-piece pews, exploiting the machine-assembly techniques of shipbuilding, and a pulpit so architectonic that it is almost a building

in its own right, with a theatrical concealed entrance allowing the minister to appear, suddenly, in the middle of the auditorium. The scheme was completed by stencilled decoration in primary 'archaeological' Grecian colours.

In 1858, a competition entry by Thomson for St Mary's Free Church in Albany Street, Edinburgh (on a steeply sloping corner site), combined the asymmetry of Caledonia Road with a St Vincent Street-like tower and a caryatid porch. Thomson

which formed a base for the symmetrical upper work. Here the break from academic classicism seems almost complete. The detailing seems to have come out of some biblical illustration or Egypto-Babylonian fantasy of squat colonnades and insistent horizontality. The central pylon recalls the block-like form of John Stephen's St Jude's Church, while the crowning dome is an enlargement of the upper stage of the St Vincent Street tower, to proportions perhaps suggested by Stark's Asylum dome [cf. 5.7, 6.3].

Inside Queen's Park Church, Thomson's experiments in polychromatic decoration were taken a stage further, in his collaboration with the artist Daniel Cottier, who was working at that time (as we will see) with William Leiper on the design of a neo-Gothic church for a sister UP church at Dowanhill; Thomson and Leiper were also close at that time. Cottier, trained in stained-glass design in Glasgow, was a remarkable designer whose early interior schemes developed the rationalistic ideas of D. R. Hay and the Board of Manufactures in new directions. At Queen's Park, for example, primary colours were abandoned for a more complex framework of tertiary blues and reds – an aspect of the later nineteenth-century avant-garde rejection of bright eclecticism for more muted 'artistic' design. Cottier moved to London in 1869, and subsequently on to the United States; by 1873 his decorative-art and art-dealing business was disseminating 'artistic' taste across the anglophone world, with showrooms in New York, London and Sydney. The links between Scottish mid-nineteenth century interior design and the English-American Queen Anne and Aesthetic movements of the third quarter of the century have yet to be investigated: Thomson's friend J. J. Stevenson played a prominent role in the 'Queen Anne' style after he moved to England in 1873. Nor has the possibility of more general architectural interactions between Glasgow and North America, in an age of burgeoning steamship travel, been fully researched. Might there have been a direct connection, for example, between the monumental Sublime of Thomson and H. H. Richardson's ideal of a 'quiet and massive' architecture? [45]

was unsuccessful, and a dramatically verticalised Gothic design by J. T. Rochead, with three-stage tower, was built instead (1859–60). In Thomson's final large church, Queen's Park UP (1867–9), the site was flat and uninspiring [6.42]. He was forced, as at Caledonia Road, to place the pseudo-portico on a high podium to give the design monumental presence. The entrance was sited to one side of a pilastered screen articulating the awkward boundary and defining the lower adjacent halls,

Thomson's eclecticism powerfully invigorated the classical cause in Glasgow, but the next

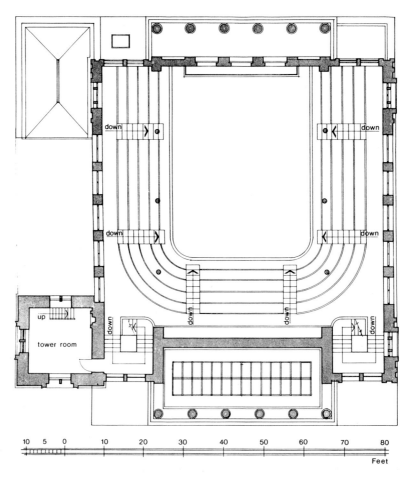

6.41 St Vincent Street UP Church, plan at gallery level.

generation of architects was not prepared to maintain the same high temperature of emotionalism. In the west, the most popular classical form for a church after the 1850s was simply a Grecian temple. A succession of refined designs, many commissioned by the UP Church, included John Burnet Senior's Elgin Place Congregational Church (1855–6, Greek Ionic) and T. L. Watson's Wellington UP Church (1882–4, Madeleine-style Corinthian) [6.43]. The grandest was H. & D. Barclay's sumptuous and massive St George's in the Fields, with its Paris Opera-style high roof (1885–6), Ionic portico and figurative pediment sculpture by Birnie Rhind; a late offshoot of Thomson's St Vincent Street false portico and aisled formula was Alexander Skirving's Langside Hill Free Church (1894–6) [6.44]. More diverse eclectic frameworks were devised by the Barclays

at Ewing Place Church (1858), with powerful Doric portico and deeply incised side facades; and by J. T. Rochead at John Street UP Church (1859–60), a huge block with rusticated basement supporting directly glazed giant colonnades, recalling the Baroque work of Rochead's master Bryce in the capital. The Free Church commissioned a classical design of a different character from Boucher and Cousland at St George's Church (completed 1865): a compact Italian Renaissance structure, equivalent in richness to their Macfarlane house at Park Circus, and with galleried Latin-cross plan. Peddie & Kinnear made a foray into the west with Sydney Place UP Church (1857), with a wide sculptured pediment and recessed portico beneath. By the 1870s, there was a tendency towards a rather more sparing, delicate aesthetic. This was exemplified in James

Sellars's somewhat Schinkelian Finnieston Free Church of 1879–80, which combined a tetrastyle Greek Ionic portico, and slender octagonal lantern, with a sober, pilastered main body [6.45]; and in the chaste Italian Renaissance of John Honeyman's Cathedral Square UP Church (1878–80, with arched facade and cupola-capped tower at one end) and Westbourne Free Church (1880–1, with two-storey superimposed portico). The classical church designs of the Barclays, Sellars and others ran in parallel with the same designers' contributions to a powerful, post-Thomson renaissance in Glasgow secular classicism; we will return to the latter at the end of this chapter.

Religious and Secular Medievalism

If Thomson's churches formed part of a comprehensive, eclectically varied classicism, embracing all building types, neo-Gothic architecture in mid-century Scotland was of more restricted scope. Here, as Gothic lacked the 'national' status of its counterparts in some other countries, we do not expect to encounter the comprehensive rationalism of a Viollet-le-Duc, nor the moral-visual intensity and scope of the English 'Gothic Revival'. Instead, the connotations of Scottish neo-Gothic remained, as in the early nineteenth century, largely visual and ecclesiastical: the clothing of preaching-church plans in 'correct' detail and dramatic, spiky skylines. A liturgically driven trend towards more devotional, medievalising plans began to emerge during this period, but its influence remained, for the moment, rather superficial.

During the 1850s, Presbyterian neo-Gothic design began to develop towards heavier forms, while remaining faithful to symmetry and preaching-church layouts. This trend can be gauged by comparing the spectacularly spiny designs of J. T. Rochead's St John's Free Church, Glasgow (1845, with Kemp-like spire) or James Brown's Renfield Street UP Church (1848), with the prolific everyday work in the next decade of the brothers John, James Murdoch and William Hardie Hay, Borderers who had settled in northern England. The Hays' many Free Churches are usually symmetrical, with a central steeple at the front, and a single-span overall roof. Examples include South Free Church, Stirling (1851–5); Well Park Free Church, Greenock (1853); Chalmers Church, Stirling (1853); St John Free Church, Gourock (1857, with later spire); East Free Church, Brechin (1856); and Buccleuch and Greyfriars Free Church, Edinburgh (1856–7), with heavy, diagonally buttressed steeple and squat belfry.

By the 1860s, some Free Church congregations had become rich and confident enough to look for a radically new pattern of neo-Gothic preaching church. That call was answered by Frederick T. Pilkington, who built (in partnership with John F. Bell) an eclectic series of churches, beginning with two influential competition wins in 1861: Trinity Free Church, Irvine, and Barclay Church, Edinburgh. Trinity mingled French and Italian Gothic in a vigorously polychromatic grouping, in which Pilkington's penchant for powerful, at times even brutal masonry detailing was given free rein. Barclay Church was an altogether more ambitious affair. The centre of evangelical life in the capital, under the ministry of Revd James Wilson, and (at the time) the tallest building in Scotland, Barclay's 250-feet-high steeple trumpeted the power of the Free Church across south Edinburgh [6.46]. A model preaching church, with heart-shaped, galleried auditorium and arched roof braces supported on four stout piers, its centralised plan was expressed externally in a massively compressed form, loosely based on Normandy Gothic prototypes and ornamented with a (curtailed) programme of naturalistic carving. In the fearless vigour of Pilkington's formal eclecticism, an obvious comparison is with Thomson - although Pilkington's work hardly operated at the same level of emotionalist power. Interestingly, A. L. Drummond's description of Barclay Church in his standard history of Protestant architecture singled out for comment Pilkington's 'Monumental Egyptian sense of Eternity and ponderous Grandeur, a sense of the "Numinous" '. [46] Other, less elaborate Pilkington Free churches of similar type included Penicuik (1862) and Kelso (1864–6).

The 1860s and 1870s saw the first comprehensive attempts to evoke the spirit of Scottish medieval architecture. Bryce's Carnwath (1865–9) was indebted to the nearby ruined collegiate chapel, while his West Coates Church of Scotland

6.42 Queen's Park UP Church, Glasgow (Thomson, 1867–9), views of *c*.1900: (above) exterior; (right) interior.

(1868–70), the first Established Church built in Edinburgh since the Disruption, adopted a heavy Scots Gothic, perhaps to suggest a conservative gravity, and at St Mungo's Church near Lockerbie (1875–7) his rugged freestone church had stumpy buttresses and a massive, defensive-type tower. Wardrop & Reid's prominently located St Mary's, Stow (1873–6) had a polygonal apse and heavy rubble masonry. The years 1877–8 saw the addition of a crown spire to St John's Gourock, by Bruce & Sturrock.

By this time, in the west, a range of younger architects was formulating a variety of new solutions to the task of combining preaching-church plans with a neo-Gothic architecture more evocative of medieval forms. The key figures were John Honeyman (trained by Burn), J. J. Stevenson

6.43 Wellington UP Church, Glasgow (T. L. Watson, 1882–4).

6.44 St George's in the Fields Church (H. & D. Barclay, 1885–6).

(trained by Bryce and Scott, and working at that time with Campbell Douglas), and Leiper (by Boucher & Cousland and J. L. Pearson), as well as the slightly older John Burnet Senior and J. T. Rochead. Honeyman's St Mark's, Greenock (1861), and Lansdowne UP Church, Glasgow (1862–3, with thin spire and John Mossman scuplture), both had wide naves and narrow, passage-like aisles, while his broach-spired Park Church, Helensburgh (1862), was triple-aisled, with central pulpit. Stevenson's campanile-towered Kelvinside Parish Church (1862) featured Italian Gothic aisles with cast-iron columns. Burnet's Woodlands UP Church (1874–5) was dominated by a tall, French Gothic spire and (inside) grandiose cast-iron-columned arcades; both this and Rochead's Park Church (1856–7) had gableted windows on the side facades, a feature inspired by Elgin Cathedral and St Giles.

An important transitional point between that group of churches, with their slender spires and still rather spiky detail, and new emphases of the 1870s was represented by Dowanhill UP Church (1865–6), a commission which launched the independent career of William Leiper at the age of 26 [6.47]. Here a massive preaching space was fronted

by an axially placed, richly modelled French Gothic steeple. Inside, the galleries face a tabernacled pulpit set high in the far wall, reached by a concealed entrance. This feature, of course, is shared with Thomson's slightly earlier St Vincent Street Church, also for the United Presbyterians. Although, in general, there seemed little affinity between Leiper's soaring design and the Semitic majesty of Thomson's architecture of mass, there was in fact another very direct link: a decorative scheme by Daniel Cottier, whose designs, at Dowanhill as at the contemporary Queen's Park, signalled the beginnings of the rejection of mid-nineteenth-century eclecticism as garish and brash. The key word was 'artistic', implying a new, rather more muted sensitivity. At Dowanhill, for example, Cottier provided a scheme of stencil work not in primary but in tertiary colours, defined in black and gold, stained glass (with foliage and Old Testament figurative subjects), and ceiling decoration of spangled stars and planets.

A series of notable Glasgow churches built in the 1870s laid the groundwork for the later evolution, by architects such as J. J. Burnet and R. Rowand Anderson, of a neo-Gothic Presbyterian Church architecture which would be both 'artistic' and monumental. Leiper's Camphill UP Church of 1875–8 was also stencilled (to designs by the

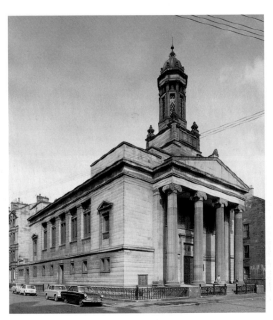

6.45 Finnieston Free Church (Sellars, 1879–80).

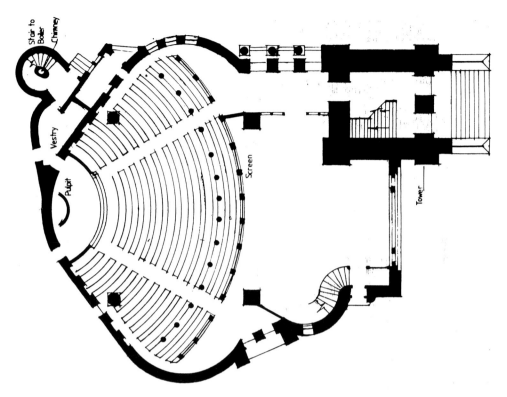

6.46 Barclay Church, Edinburgh: (Pilkington, from 1861) (left) detail of west facade; (right) ground-floor plan.

end [6.49]. The climax of Sellars's ecclesiastical Gothic designs was Belhaven UP Church (1876–7, almost contemporary with the Grecian of his Finnieston Church), a Normandy Gothic composition possibly influenced by an earlier Richard Norman Shaw design. The main front comprises three tall lancets clasped by heavy buttressed turrets; the interior, originally stencilled, contains arcaded aisles, a gallery at one end, and an apse containing an organ at the other. The Campbell Douglas partnership also participated in the growing interest in Scottish Gothic forms at St Enoch's Free Church, Old Dumbarton Road (from 1871), with tall crown spire.

The new popularity of instrumental music was first reflected in Presbyterian architecture in the 1860s, when the lifting of its prohibition was followed by a burst of organ-building. While the

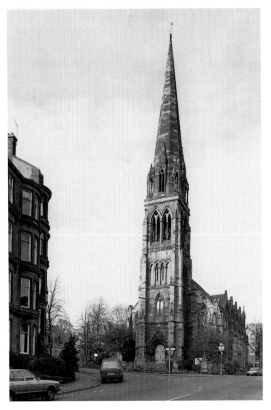

6.47 Dowanhill UP Church, Glasgow (Leiper, 1865–6).

architect), and planned around a wide nave with tall arcades and galleries behind [6.48]. Its soaring Normandy Gothic steeple, based on St Pierre, Caen (which Leiper visited specially to study for this commission), was completed in 1883. A series of churches by the Campbell Douglas partnership showed a similar combination of architectonic weight and 'artistic' aspirations. Townhead and Blochairn Parish Church of 1865–6, by J. J. Stevenson, featured a tall sculptural spire and Cottier interior (the latter's first Glasgow job, here still in primary reds and blues). Queen's Park High Church, 1872–3, by Campbell Douglas & Sellars, had a similar steeple, and may also have been designed by Stevenson before his move to England; from 1872, Sellars became a partner and the main designer in the practice. At Belmont Hillhead Parish Church (1875–6), Sellars won a competition in his own right, and designed a tall, Sainte Chapelle-like apsed structure, bristling with gablets and framed at the front with angle turrets; inside was a single vast space with gallery at one

6.48 Camphill UP Church, Glasgow (Leiper, 1875–8).

6.49 Belmont Hillhead Parish Church, Glasgow (Sellars, 1875–6).

organ at Dowanhill sat more modestly on the entrance gallery, in some other churches it had been moved to the other end, facing worshippers as a theatrical centrepiece. By then, a wider movement towards liturgical intensity and a 'renascence of worship' [47] in Presbyterianism was under way. The Church Service Society of the Established Church, for example, was founded in 1865 to study old liturgies – a movement we shall deal with in greater detail in Chapter 7. Early examples of these tendencies included the showpiece neo-Gothic parish church built to the designs of James Salmon senior at Anderston (1864–5) by Rev. Marshall Lang, one of the pioneers of the liturgical movement; this combined an auditorium plan with chancel (containing the first integrally designed organ in the country) and raised choir area with communion table. An earlier impulse towards ceremonial liturgy, stemming from within Presbyterianism, had been

the founding of the Catholic Apostolic Church by Edward Irving, former assistant of Thomas Chalmers at St John's parish; its first Glasgow church, built from 1852 in McAslin Street, had also been designed by Salmon (to a sketch by A. W. Pugin) with a sumptuously stencilled, gallery-less interior. One of the first Established Churches to dispense with galleries in favour of arcades and clerestories was Rochead's Park Church (1856–7).

While these developments were under way in Glasgow, a vigorous school of neo-Gothic church design had become established in the north-east, emphasising soaring steeples and, naturally, granite monumentality. In Aberdeen, the Established Church's construction of Rubislaw Parish Church (1874–81, by J Russell Mackenzie, with tall, spiky tower) spurred the powerful Aberdeen Free Church establishment to commission one of Pirie & Clyne's most memorable designs: Queens Cross Church, opened in 1881 and renowned as the first charge of the charismatic preacher George Adam Smith [6.50]. The Wilson-like vertical linear patterns of its tower, and hard-edged geometrical ornament, had been presaged in 1878–80 at Pirie's South Church, Fraserburgh. The 1890s saw the awarding of some very large commissions for the Free and (after the union of 1900) United Free Churches to the Aberdeen practice of Brown & Watt, one of whose partners (George Watt) had been a Sellars pupil. These included the neo-Gothic Holburn (1894) and Beechgrove (1896–1900), with tall steeple and nave and transept plan), as well as the classical Melville (1901–3, with campanile and horseshoe auditorium).

Alongside the Presbyterian use of Gothic, as one style alongside others, this period also witnessed a minority tendency, confined largely to the Episcopalian and Roman Catholic Churches, which imitated the very different trends within the contemporary English 'Gothic Revival' – often by employing English architects. This movement first manifested itself in the Episcopal Church, which saw boom years from the 1840s, owing to the combined impact of an influx of English migrant workers and an anglicising tendency among elements of the wealthier classes. The year before G. G. Scott took the English Gothic Revival to the Continent at Hamburg's Nikolaikirche (1844), the architect John Hayward was invited to Scotland by

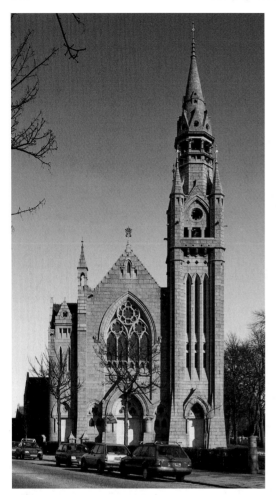

6.50 Queens Cross Church, Aberdeen (Pirie & Clyne, 1881).

6.51 St John's Episcopal Church, Jedburgh (J. Hayward, 1843–4).

the Lothian family to build a model 'Tractarian' church intended to 'express the notion of the beauty of holiness': St John's Chapel, Jedburgh (1843–4) [6.51]. [48] This was a nineteenth-century equivalent of Dairsie, but conceived in very different social and political circumstances. Its memorial stone was laid by Lady Lothian, co-foundress of the influential English pressure-group for more ritualistic Anglican liturgy and architecture, the Cambridge Camden Society; in 1844, English luminaries of the Oxford Movement attended its consecration ceremony. St John's incorporated the full range of conventions of Gothic Revivalism, including east-west alignment and liturgical-architectural differentiation of elements such as nave, chancel, vestry, porch and bellcote; even the most idiosyncratically English

features were duly included, such as a 'lych gate' (a wooden gate with its own gabled roof, with provision for storage of coffins). The interior was lavishly decorated, much of it designed by the eminent Gothic Revival architect W. Butterfield – who also built the adjacent school (1844), along with two other later showpiece Episcopal projects: the Cathedral of the Isles, Millport, and St Ninian's Cathedral, Perth (both 1849–51). Other large Episcopal commissions by English architects included G. F. Bodley's sumptuously ornamented city mission church at St Salvador's, Dundee (1865–75), and a series of churches or cathedrals by Sir G G Scott, beginning with St Paul's, Dundee (from 1852), St Mary's Glasgow (from 1871), and culminating in Scott's victory in the 1872 competition for St Mary's Cathedral in Edinburgh. The latter, paid for by the Walker trustees, was begun in 1874 as a centralised design in heavy rubble masonry with single spire, but two western spires were added (and completed 1917), creating the fantastic, Schinkel-like vista we enjoy today along neo-classical Melville Street [6.52]. In keeping with Tractarian emphasis on 'local' features, these designs by Scott or Butterfield attempted to incorporate Scottish medieval details, in the same way that Scott's Nikolaikirche had clothed its powerful spire in 'German' forms.

Scottish exponents of mid-century Episcopal architecture followed some of these principles. William Hay designed St John's Longside in 1854 with a Pluscarden-style saddleback tower. John

6.52 Melville Street, Edinburgh (planned 1814), and St Mary's Episcopal Cathedral (G. G. Scott, 1874–1917).

Henderson, previously responsible for symmetrically towered Perpendicular designs such as Holy Trinity, Dean Bridge, Edinburgh (1837–8), was by the mid/late 1840s designing asymmetrical or 'liturgically correct' churches such as St Mary's Dunblane (1844) or St Mary's Port Glasgow (1856). In 1843–51, he built a theological college for the burgeoning church at Trinity College, Glenalmond, in a quadrangled, Oxbridge style. Soon, however, these ideas began to be absorbed into more mainstream Scottish architecture. When Henderson died in 1862, his Episcopal practice was largely inherited by the young Edinburgh designer R. Rowand Anderson. After completing as executant architect (in 1862–5) a design of G. G. Scott's at St James's, Leith, Anderson first designed, in his own right, a series of Episcopalian churches (including St Michael and All Saints, Brougham Place, Edinburgh, 1865–78, and St Andrew's Church, St Andrews, 1867–9), before launching into a new and independent line of 'worshipful' architecture at the neo-Romanesque Catholic Apostolic Church, Edinburgh (1873–94); we will return to those developments at the end of Chapter 7 [cf. 7.52]. In the north, a setpiece of Episcopalian neo-Gothic was Alexander Ross's twin-towered St Andrew's Cathedral, Inverness (1866–9).

The Roman Catholic Church was also enjoying a renaissance on the strength of an influx of migrant workers from Ireland. Its churches remained faithful to the Counter-Reformation demand for a linear, but open internal space. It awarded almost all its largest commissions to English designers, including George Goldie (St Mary's, Lanark, 1856) and J. Hansom (St Mary's Lochee, 1865). In Buckie, however, the Bishop of the Northern District, the Rt Rev. James Kyle (working with A. & W. Reid of Elgin) was responsible for the grand, twin-towered design of St Peter's (1850–7), while Andrew Heiton built St Mary's Monastery, Perth (1868), in a harsh rubble Gothic, similar in some ways to his Baronial designs at Vogrie.

At this point, for convenience, we deal with two subsidiary movements within medievalising architecture in those years: neo-Romanesque churches, and neo-medieval secular architecture. The boom in popularity of Gothic during the mid-century to

some extent left Romanesque behind, but the tributary represented by earlier examples, such as Thomas Hamilton's Alyth Parish Church or Gillespie Graham's Errol, continued. In 1846, for example, Graham was commissioned by Sir William Drummond Steuart to build St Anthony's Chapel, Murthly, in a 'Saxon or Byzantine [*sic*]' style; [49] the building was later given sumptuous gilded and marbled decoration by Alexander Christie and his pupils at the Board of Manufactures design school. Some Presbyterian examples echoed the Gothic trend of dramatic, spired symmetry, as at Charles Wilson's McBride Free Church, Rothesay (1845), with its axial, steepled facade, while others adopted a heavier treatment, as at David Robertson's North Morningside Church, Edinburgh (1879–81), with its pyramidal-capped corner tower. Neo-Romanesque churches were also built for the Episcopalians – for example, David Cousin's St Thomas, Rutland Place, Edinburgh (1842–3), or John Henderson's St Baldred's, North Berwick (1861–2) – as well as for the highly ritualistic Catholic Apostolics, in the Edinburgh church by Anderson. It was designs such as Campbell Douglas & Sellars's Dysart Free Church (now St Serf's), 1872–4, combining round arches with a squat, St Monans-like profile, which seemed to point forward to the low, massive form in which neo-Romanesque would be revived at the turn of the century.

The secular use of medieval styles was limited by the same code of 'appropriateness' that, in Edinburgh, frowned on Grecian churches. David Thomson, for instance, claimed that the 'boldness and originality' of the round-arched Renaissance style used by Wilson at Free Church College was, compared to medievalism, 'more true to our modern requirements and more expressive of our aspirations in philosophy and art'. [50] Despite examples such as Wilson's own Southern Necropolis Gateway (1849) or G. E. Street's extensions to Dunecht House (1870s), the same also seemed to apply to neo-Romanesque. However, the period from the mid-1860s to the late 1870s saw a minor fashion for use of neo-Gothic on public buildings. This was seemingly sparked off by the work of G. G. Scott at the Albert Institute, Dundee (1864–7) and the new Glasgow University building

6.53 Glasgow University (Sir G. Scott, from 1864).

(1864–70, with spire 1887 by J. O. Scott) [6.53]. At Glasgow, Scott's engagement, by an English caucus on the university's Removal Committee, proved controversial, as did the Gothic style. Alexander Thomson, for example, railed against 'this invasion from the south'. [51] Scott's design followed the Tractarian formula of seeking legitimacy through Scottish details – albeit within a framework of somewhat Flemish character. He explained that 'I adopted a style which I may call my own invention, having already initiated it in the Albert Institute Dundee. It is simply a thirteenth or fourteenth century secular style with the addition of certain Scottish features peculiar to that country.' [52] Secular Gothic designs which followed included Leiper's Dumbarton Academy (1865–6); Heiton's Perth Municipal Buildings (1877); J. Burnet Senior's Glasgow Stock Exchange (1875, extended 1894); and Matthews & Lawrie's Inverness Town House (1876–82) [cf. 6.2]. Not only were these buildings relatively few in number, but their often slender, 'archaeological' character contrasted strikingly with the eclectic gusto of mainstream secular architecture, as represented by contemporary examples such as Fettes College or Aberdeen Town House.

International and National 'Renaissance' Complexities around 1880

We close this chapter by returning to the classical mainstream, and reviewing its condition around and after 1880. Despite the almost neo-classical severity of buildings such as Sellars's Finnieston Church, Scottish classicism by 1880 seemed overall to be reaching a high point of rich ornament [cf. 6.45]. The ever more complex stylistic combinations began to undermine even the new hierarchy of building types represented by typological eclecticism. This climactic phase of ornamented classicism had two main stylistic variants. One was, paradoxically, both cosmopolitan and 'national' – the 'Northern', or 'free' Renaissance. The other was more specific to the west of Scotland: a heavy 'Baroque' eclecticism drawing heavily on Thomson's work.

The Northern Renaissance style was a culmination of the element of synthetic eclecticism within the international Second Empire trend, whose bulky buildings were heavily encrusted with picturesque decoration in 'national' styles of the fifteenth to seventeenth centuries. In contrast to the specifically 'Franco-Scotch' appearance of, say, Fettes, the new style offered rather less precisely definable mixtures – although François Ier remained a key ingredient. It gained its first major footholds in Scotland in the east among architects such as Rowand Anderson or Peddie & Kinnear, who were becoming increasingly dismissive of New Town homogeneity. Change was gradual: commissions such as Peddie & Kinnear's University Club (1866), or Anderson's Conservative Club (1881–4), both in Princes Street, remained faithful to the Brycean palazzo framework, albeit with elements of asymmetry, while a more eclectic design such as Peddie & Kinnear's Craiglockhart Hydropathic Institution (1877–80) seemed to hark back to the low-eaved, colonnaded Italian villa architecture of Playfair – with touches, perhaps, of Alexander Thomson. A similar restraint was evident in Anderson's competition-winning design for the Edinburgh University extension buildings in 1874, which combined a scholarly but asymmetrical Venetian Cinquecento style with comparative Continental research into planning [6.54]. Speaking

6.54 University of Edinburgh Medical Buildings (Anderson, from 1874).

in 1884, Anderson advocated Renaissance as 'a meeting ground where these gifts of the ancients to the modern artists . . . will mingle and lead to the production of a phase of art that will respond to and be more expressive of the thought and life of the modern world than anything we have yet seen'. [53] And his Edinburgh University scheme seemed to look backwards to the New Town as much as forward, in its two- and three-storey scale and austere expanses of wall: it inspired St Aloysius College, Glasgow (1883), designed by his ex-assistant Archibald MacPherson. But in 1882–4, in the most important Glasgow commercial development of the decade – the massive Caledonian Railway headquarters block at Central Station (completed as a hotel), there was a sharper break from the academic canon [6.55]. Anderson's design was finely balanced between busily gabled facade eclecticism and a massive vertical punctuation, in the sheer, tall corner tower, crowned by gables. Journalists lauded the block for its 'artistic. . . Renaissance character, which is at the same time broad and dignified'. [54]

George Washington Browne (senior assistant to Anderson from 1879, partner 1881–5, thereafter in practice himself) brought to Edinburgh a Glaswegian swagger and love of bristling complexity, covering a full range of building types. Sometimes he designed in a specifically François Ier classicism, assisted by the expertise of his new, Beaux-Arts-trained assistant, S. Henbest Capper, as at the Edinburgh Public Library of 1887, which comprised an ornate upper structure perched on a massive, rock-faced base of sunk storeys [6.56]. But he also imported to commercial architecture the typical verticalised profile and busy application of gables, pilasters of Northern Renaissance eclecticism: for example at Redferns, Princes Street (1891), and Buchanan Street Cranston's Tearooms (1896). As we will see in Chapter 7, his later partnership (from the mid-1890s) with J. M. Dick Peddie would bring his work back to a calmer, more reposeful pattern by the turn of the century.

Perhaps the most important offspring of Anderson's Free Renaissance phase was A. G. Sydney Mitchell – one of the most versatile architects of the late nineteenth century. Mitchell, who spent five years as an Anderson pupil before setting himself up in practice in 1883 at the age of 26 (and taking on as assistant the Bryce/Anderson-trained George Wilson – his partner from 1887), was immediately launched into the world of advanced architecture and major commissions through the family connections of his father, Sir Arthur Mitchell FSAS. We will see in Chapter 7 that Mitchell's work – which included some of the biggest secular and religious commissions of the 1880s and 1890s – was a kind of microcosm of the advanced tendencies of those decades, in its easy fusion of eclecticism, grandiose scale, a new sensibility for oldness, and close study of building types. But what concerns us specifically here is his eclectic Northern Renaissance work. Like Browne, Mitchell used it as a 'house style' for a series of banks and commercial buildings, including large numbers of Commercial Bank branches built from 1883.

Browne and Mitchell also involved themselves in the design of Edinburgh private dwellings, where they brought a more picturesque freedom to the design of the classical villa or urban dwelling, or, more rarely, the country house. In the west, the 'artistic' free Renaissance villa was already well entrenched, in sumptuous examples such as

6.55 Glasgow Central Station Hotel (Anderson, 1882–4).

Leiper's François Ier 'Cairndhu', Helensburgh, 1871. Such interiors, with furniture by firms such as Wylie & Lochhead, increasingly overlapped with the fitting-up of luxury ocean liners. In some higher-rent Edinburgh tenement blocks, the residually neo-classical austerity still seen in working-class tenements was all but banished by rollicking facades of bay windows and mansarded roofs: for instance, in the long ranges built in the 1880s and 1890s along Home Street and Bruntsfield Place, Edinburgh, by architects such as Browne, H. J. Blanc, Dunn & Findlay, and T P Marwick; or isolated later prestige-blocks in smaller towns, such as W. Hunter McNab's Argyll Mansions, Oban, 1906. In larger townhouses, a restrained departure from New Town severity was signalled in Mitchell's first house, 3 Rothesay Terrace (1883), for the *Scotsman* proprietor James Ritchie Findlay – a magnate whose philanthropy

we shall encounter again. Its rich interior included elaborate marble chimneypieces made by Farmer & Bridley. A freer and later Glasgow equivalent was Lowther Terrace, with townhouses by Miller (1900) and Mitchell (1904–6).

Inside the eclectic-classical urban or suburban houses of the wealthy, cost was no longer a limit on design. Internally, the trend towards complexity reached a climax of heavy drapery, upholstery and bustling detail around 1890, with 'Renaissance' and 'eighteenth-century' detail used with a profusion and technical mastery unknown in those centuries. The influence of Aesthetic Movement taste for Japanese and Chinese styles ran alongside a rising awareness of Scotland's own heritage of decorative arts, spurred by the sale of the contents of Hamilton Palace from 1882 [cf. 5.32]. The relative lack of cost constraint allowed the differentiation of rooms by style to reach a peak of

6.56 Edinburgh Central Public Library (1887), exhibition drawing by George Washington Browne, exhibited at the Royal Scottish Academy in 1888.

sophistication and richness. And this in turn brought to fruition the centuries-long campaign by the Board of Manufactures to convert Scotland from a net importer to an exporter of design. This success was exemplified in the achievement of William Scott Morton, who in 1870 (with his brother) founded a firm in Edinburgh to produce 'Art Furniture' – systematising and commercialising the ideas of Walter Scott. Rapidly, Scott Morton diversified into house-decoration, and devised a succession of 'artistic' innovations such as, in 1881, the introduction of 'Tynecastle Tapestry' wall covering (an embossed canvas using patterns sketched personally by Morton on a trip to Italy). By 1882 he was exporting to New York, where he specialised in fitting out the palaces of industrialists with complete decorative schemes. The setpiece of Morton's 'artistic' typological eclecticism in Scotland was his firm's decoration of spirits magnate Arthur Sanderson's Edinburgh house at 25 Learmonth Terrace (1891–3) [6.57].

The external architecture of this house, by James Simpson of Leith, was essentially a sumptuous extension of the New Town tradition, with peristyled bow windows. Inside, however, in an echo of Morton's New York work, the rooms were elaborately differentiated by style: a stair-hall with replica Parthenon frieze in Tynecastle canvas, a hall with Cottier stained glass, a 'British' dining room, and Adamesque drawing room, and a Louis XIII bedroom – the decoration almost all being executed by Scottish craftsmen. By comparison with this 'artistic' density, the early nineteenth-century interiors were now seen as plain and drab: Morton wrote to Andrew Heiton in 1882 that 'Every Northern has such a cold, grey look after leaving Italy. We ought to make a desperate effort to keep up the sunshine inside if we should not have it so bright externally'. [55] Alongside Morton's international efforts, the cause of 'artistic' and 'aesthetic' interiors within the Edinburgh middle class was propagated especially

6.57 25 Learmonth Terrace, Edinburgh(1891–3), *c.*1900 view of main staircase.

by Thomas Bonnar II, whose firm, Bonnar & Carfrae, had inherited the mantle of the capital's leading decorative business after Hay's death in 1866. However, these trends also contained a germ of a reaction against mass-produced elaboration: in 1894 Scott Morton called for 'simplicity and readableness' and 'power' in colour design. [56] We will return to that reaction, in our account of the beginnings of the Traditionalist movement, in Chapter 7.

By the late 1890s, Northern or Free Renaissance had fallen from avant-garde fashion, damned by what was now seen as an indiscriminate eclecticism, in both the typological and synthetic senses. The idea that 'national' characteristics could be evoked through sheer quantity of eclectic details now seemed especially implausible. In 1897, Rowand Anderson signalled the completion of a full circle in taste, in the building which completed his Edinburgh University extension scheme: the McEwan Hall, whose sumptuous, but emphatically arcuated interior returned to a more 'Italian' and architectonic interpretation of the

6.58 McEwan Hall, University of Edinburgh (Anderson, 1897), *c.*1900 view.

Renaissance [6.58]. From now on, Northern Renaissance was increasingly confined to the everyday production of bulky, well-planned commercial buildings, laden with intricate pilasters, gablets and other detail. The relative cost of masonry preparation was at an all-time low, and huge commercial buildings could be entirely faced in ashlar. Two of the most renowned examples face each other on Edinburgh's Princes Street: W. Hamilton Beattie's Jenners store (1893–5), and the even more overbearing North British Hotel (1896–1902), a vast mound of tiny detail containing 700 rooms and 13,000 tons of stone masonry, capped by a squat, 190-feet tower. Beattie's efforts at these and other sites converted parts of Princes Street into a parade of jostling hotels. Similar in planning, in some ways, were the massive   Infantry and Cavalry Barracks built at Redford, Edinburgh, in 1909–15 to the designs of the English architect Harry B. Measures, Director of Barrack Construction. In central Glasgow's grid-iron layout, there was often only a single facade available to the designer, so the rampant Northern Renaissance outcrops, usually now in red rather than grey sandstone, were more verticalised and congested: key examples included Leiper's Sun Insurance block of 1889–94 (whose eclecticism was still sufficiently modish to win a silver medal at the 1900 Paris Exposition), and James Thomson's gigantic facade for the Liverpool, London and Globe (1898), encrusted with flat-relief intricacy.

If the Northern Renaissance, as a movement of cosmopolitan modernity, was found across the whole country, the west also saw an alternative kind of classical eclecticism in the 1870s and 1880s, which fused generalised 'Renaissance' elements with the specific legacy of Thomson (who died in 1875), expurgated of its more exotic stylistic features and of its reliance on religious-utopian idealism. This was a different matter from survivals of the earlier nineteenth-century Italian Renaissance style, such as the prolific work of City Architect John Carrick (for example at Maitland Street Northern Police Office, *c.*1890). A redoubt of post-Thomson classicism was the work of Hugh & David Barclay, who applied Thomson's architecture of mass, with inset or banded windows, to institutional and social use in a series of forty schools in Glasgow and nearby burghs.

The most common pattern in their work was a palazzo with central hall and columns or window-bands. Publicly built examples include Abbotsford (1879), Govanhill (1886), Jean Street, Port Glasgow (1883–4), and Clune Park, Port Glasgow (1887), while the private Glasgow Academy (1878) was a more sumptuously colonnaded variant on the theme. A more individualistic solution, reminiscent in its curved plan and cubic mass of Thomson's Walmer Crescent, was the pedimented Rutland Crescent School of 1883. For a much larger public commission, namely the Greenock Municipal Buildings (1881–9), the Barclays chose a more conventional classicism, but the enormously tall, domed steeple echoed some

6.59 Greenock Municipal Buildings (H. & D. Barclay, 1881–9), *c.*1900 photograph.

6.60 St Andrew's Halls, Glasgow (Sellars, 1873–7), late nineteenth-century photograph.

of the features of St Vincent Street Church [6.59]. The work of Sellars (mostly under the aegis of the Campbell Douglas practice) was more complex and variegated. His most grandiose commission, St Andrew's Halls (1873–7), is dominated by its heavy west facade, divided into three sections, with a monumental array of giant Ionic columns surmounted by outer pavilions containing caryatids; these and other sculptures are by John Mossman [6.60]. Inside, the main hall was like an enormous Thomson church interior, galleried on three sides, elaborately stencilled, and with heavy, flat ceiling. Also evoking an image of Grecian severity, Kelvinside Academy of 1877 returned to the interpenetrating temple theme of Thomas Hamilton's High School; Sellars's only public school design was Milton School (1877–8, for Glasgow School Board), a monumental reworking of Moray Place's twin-pavilion formula [6.61]. But in Sellars's contemporary City of Glasgow Bank and New Club (both 1878), there emerged a

6.61 Milton School, Glasgow (Sellars, 1877–8), 1972 view.

heavier and more congested Renaissance classicism [6.62]. The giant Corinthian colonnaded central section of the bank facade seems to anticipate the Baroque vigour of some turn-of-the-century work of J. J. Burnet, such as

6.62 New Club, West George Street,
Glasgow (Sellars, 1878).

Waterloo Chambers. Contemporary journalists
praised the 'extreme delicacy and crispness' of
these designs, and their 'dignified proportion and
massing, and refined detail'. [57] Other architects
in the west made varying uses of the eclectic
classical legacy of the mid-nineteenth century.
John Honeyman's porticoed Paisley Museum
(1866 and 1881) and his Coats Observatory (1883,
with complex ramped plan) followed some late
Thomson works in returning to a neo-classical
dignity, whereas (as we will see in Chapter 7)
William Young's Glasgow Municipal Buildings
(1883–8) was more heavily ornamented [cf. 7.2].
By comparison with the Barclay palazzi, James
Thomson's Garnethill Public School (1878)
remained more faithful to a looser Italian type of
composition, with central tower. The most startling Thomson 're-use' of all came later, in 1907,
when Clarke, Bell & Craigie incorporated an actual
Thomson block (the Grosvenor Building) within
a heaped-up, heightened composition, topped by
colonnades and domes [cf. 6.7].

Conclusion

The shock to Glasgow's self-confidence, administered by the collapse of the City of Glasgow Bank
in 1878, to some extent marks off the period
covered by this chapter. But the resulting pause in
economic activity and building was short-lived,
and the recovery was led by the new industry of
shipbuilding. Leiper, for instance, who, following
the bank crash, had moved away to Paris to study
painting, was attracted back home to Scotland in
1880 by a commission to design the lavish interiors
of the royal yacht *Livadia*, a floating palace being
built for the Russian Tsar by John Elder & Co. in
Govan. A fresh building boom, albeit of a more
brittle and assertive kind, would soon return. The
legacy of Thomson and of Glasgow monumental
classicism was now being redefined and revitalised
in readiness for that opportunity.

Chapter 7

1880–1914

The Search for Order

'There had never been an age when the life of the individual was more governed by the practical necessities of the day . . . and therefore never before was the architect's problem, if varied, more easy of enunciation.'

J. J. Burnet, 1892 [1]

'. . . the ideal life in the ideal old, traditional "un-hurrying" Scotland.'

R. S. Lorimer, 1897 [2]

'The only true modern individual art . . . is produced by an emotion.'

C. R. Mackintosh, 1902 [3]

Introduction

The years covered by this chapter represented a turning point in the fortunes of *laissez-faire*, imperialist society. Scotland was still one of the richest countries in the world, having exploited imperial expansion through home-directed, export-orientated industrialisation, and mass emigration. As in the mid-century period, this vast power was expressed, at home, through both commercial might and private riches, and through a continuing consolidation of urban development. In 1901, 40 per cent of the population lived in Glasgow and the surrounding Clydeside towns. But by now, there were growing signs of a break-up of support for this extroverted conception of the nation. Among the intelligentsia, there was an increasingly comprehensive revulsion against what were seen as the physical and social consequences of *laissez-faire* – above all, against the industrial city in its own right. And among the workers there were the beginnings of collective organisation along class lines. In both cases, liberalism was rejected for new social solidarities, along with demands for state-sponsored change. With religion increasingly sidelined as a social force, the great competition between the two materialist philosophies of capitalism and socialism now began rising to a crescendo.

The variegated activity and wealth of the period continued to sustain a bewildering range of building programmes. Some stemmed from capitalist activity, others from the growing demands for social action. With a few exceptions, such as the multi-storey office block, no building type was actually invented in this period, but most were refined or radically modified. Some types became less important: for example, the country houses of the landed classes entered a gradual but, in the event, terminal decline in their importance within new architecture. On the whole, the nineteenth-century hierarchy of building types, with the great urban public building at its apex, was reaffirmed. Let us first briefly glance at some of the key building types of these years, and significant examples of each – while avoiding undue repetition in the account of architectural trends which will come later.

First, the monuments of capitalist enterprise. The main lubricants of Scotland's imperial economy – the banks, the shipping companies and the railways – were by now linked by a web of ownerships and directorships to the core heavy industries, especially in the west. The two decades

311

of recovery following the City of Glasgow bank crash saw a new star, the shipbuilding industry, eclipse the old giants in prestige. By 1900, up to half the world's new shipping tonnage (including luxury liners) was Clyde-built, creating a huge concentration of design and technical-services skills in the Glasgow area. For a number of architects, such as James Miller, some of their most sumptuous works were to be found afloat. For example, Alexander McInnes Gardner, working in Miller's office, designed the interiors of the *Lusitania* in 1906–7.

On land, the capitalistic confidence of the age was most proudly expressed in the ornate banks and commercial buildings of city centres. We will discuss in detail, later, the way in which the pressure of land values and site scarcity in central Glasgow, from the 1880s, led – as in the United States – to the evolution of a new type of tall commercial building, and a new type of verticalised monumentality. A more prosaic, but even more central building programme within Scottish capitalism was that of the big railway companies, especially the Caledonian and the North British. Where mid-nineteenth-century architects had sometimes tried to give expression to iron construction, now utilitarian engineering structures of often daring design, such as the vast, double-cantilever Forth Bridge (1882–90, Sir John Fowler and Sir Benjamin Baker), were rigidly segregated from 'architecture' [7.1]. At Edinburgh Waverley Station (extended from 1892 by engineers Cunningham, Blyth & Westland), the normal relationship was reversed because of the sunken site: the domed classical booking hall and office building was placed inside a broad train-shed. In the Caledonian Railway, the design of stations was the province of the forceful chief engineers George Graham and Donald A. Matheson, the latter thinking nothing of a study tour of the USA (1903) while researching the remodelling of Glasgow Central Station; while for most architectural work, from 1888, the Caledonian engineers turned to James Miller, who rose rapidly from a company draughtsman to head a thriving private practice. Alongside his showpieces, such as the *Lusitania* interiors or the 1901 Glasgow exhibition, the backbone of Miller's pre-war practice remained railway jobs: station frontages,

tenements, office blocks, hotels. He extended Glasgow's Central Hotel (1900–8) while Matheson was enlarging the station behind it (1899–06); Wemyss Bay Station (1903–4) had a circular glazed booking hall and ramp behind a gay towered facade. Miller's hotel projects included Turnberry and Peebles Hydropathic (1904–5), and Gleneagles (from 1913, planned in outline by him).

Alongside these variegated efforts of continuing *laissez-faire* enterprise, other building tasks were driven by the social and health problems caused by explosive urbanisation. The Christian social reformism which had been so prominent earlier in the century now atrophied, and was supplanted by a range of secular frameworks, including philanthropic action, direct central government intervention and, above all, municipal programmes. The workings of secular philanthropy reached a climax in the initiatives of the Dunfermline-born American steelmaster Andrew Carnegie. As part of an evolving gospel of global philanthropy and pacifism, he endowed a series of public libraries, beginning with Dunfermline in 1881, and later founded (with a $10 million endowment) the Carnegie Trust for the Universities of Scotland, which financed a range of projects culminating in the Marischal College extension, Aberdeen (by A. Marshall Mackenzie, 1893–8) [cf. 7.65].

Central Government involvement, through the newly instituted (1885) Scottish Office, remained, during this period, largely a matter of supervision of services provided by separate boards. For instance, the Board of Lunacy attempted to develop a national system of mental welfare, overseeing the building of a range of new pauper asylums on the dispersed 'colony' plan, including Crichton Royal Hospital extension, Dumfries (A. G. Sydney Mitchell, 1898–1914), Kingseat (A. Marshall Mackenzie, opened 1904) and Bangour (Hippolyte Blanc, 1898–1906). Board provision of schools remained locally organised, the main challenge in this period being the rapidly growing demand for higher-grade education. One of Edinburgh's first free secondary schools, Boroughmuir, opened in 1904, but enrolment expanded so rapidly that a completely new and larger Boroughmuir School soon had to be built, at Viewforth (1911–14) [cf. 7.20]. Edinburgh school architecture, overseen by architects Robert Wilson

7.1 Forth Bridge (Sir J. Fowler and Sir B. Baker, 1882–90), view of northern cantilever.

(in the 1880s and 1890s) and J. A. Carfrae, developed along consistent classical lines, while Glasgow and the surrounding burghs employed a great diversity of architects, including C. R. Mackintosh. In Dundee, a series of notable Art Nouveau schools was designed after 1900 by Board architect J. H. Langlands, with W. G. Lamond. For urban elementary schools, the most common plan was a compact block around a central hall. The fragmented patronage of hospital-building continued: architectural solutions varied from high-density patterns (for example T. G. Abercrombie's Royal Alexandra Infirmary, Paisley, 1896–1900, or James Miller's Glasgow Royal Infirmary rebuilding, 1907–14, following a 1901 competition) to looser pavilion plans for infectious diseases hospitals on the outskirts (for example Thomson & Sandilands' Stobhill, 1901–4).

The most rapidly growing strand of secular social intervention, and a powerful expression of local diversity and identity, was the activity of municipal government. After 1894, the Town Councils of the four cities (Glasgow, Edinburgh, Aberdeen, Dundee) were designated city corporations, responsible for all local government and police functions in their areas, and taking over other public organisations such as City Improvement Trusts. The cities, and the rather less powerful large burghs, consolidated their role as

centres of order and improvement, while successive Burgh Police Acts encouraged others to come up to their standard, and the pattern was extended to rural areas by the County Councils (set up by 1889). While Edinburgh was the centre of national institutions, the unchallenged focus of municipal endeavour was Glasgow Corporation. Where the most headlong phase of the city's development earlier in the century had been privately led, the more orderly 1880s and 1890s were, to the ratepayer administration directing Glasgow's programme of 'municipal socialism', the golden years of confidence. A vast array of services – ranging from water supply to street lighting – were celebrated in lavish publications. Like the British Empire, Glasgow surged forwards and, through successive boundary extensions and municipal service projections (such as tram routes), outwards. The city's pride in its new, highly structured progress was symbolised in its new Municipal Buildings, built in 1883–8 to the designs of William Young [7.2]. The superimposition of local, national and British symbolism was evident even at the 1883 foundation ceremony, where 600,000 spectators watched a trades march by skilled workers in the city's heavy industries; a civic-masonic procession marched through areas recently cleared by the City Improvement Trust to converge on George

7.2 Glasgow Municipal Buildings (Young, 1883–8).

Square, ringed by temporary triumphal arches. The city's civil progress, according to the commemorative book, was symbolised by the very fact that, in contrast to the old tolbooths of smaller burghs, this new complex was its fourth townhouse in living memory. [4] The completed building's entrance facade featured a triumphal Arch of Constantine surmounted by a 'Jubilee' pediment depicting Queen Victoria receiving homage from the empire. In other centres, Glasgow's civic spirit was echoed in grandiloquent classical projects for municipal buildings: for example, at Govan (1897–1901, by Thomson & Sandilands) or Hamilton (1906–14, by Alexander Cullen; extended 1928). The culmination of these schemes was the unbuilt 1911 proposal of Dundee's City Engineer and Architect, James Thomson, for a huge, domed Civic Centre as the centrepiece of a reconstructed city centre on axial 'City Beautiful' lines.

From around 1900, this confident climate of urban progress was undermined by industrial competition and trade depression, which prompted moves towards collective solidarity among skilled workers. The scope of action of existing co-operative mechanisms was expanded – as displayed in the huge classical warehouses of the Scottish Co-operative Wholesale Society in Morrison Street, Glasgow, designed by Bruce & Hay (1886–95) and James Ferrigan (1919–33). Increasingly, radicalised and overtly socialist mechanisms of mass action became more prominent, and attention focused more closely on what was now seen as the key arena of social action: working-class housing. Up to now, this had been accepted by all as an area of small-capitalist provision; official intervention, even at the grand scale of City Improvement, had taken the form of regulation or correction. Now, the growth of anti-landlordism of a bitterness unparalleled in Europe led to calls – especially by socialist groups seeking local political power – for large-scale municipal housing provision. Among the intelligentsia, the new and more pessimistic views of the city would be associated with even more sweeping prescriptions, concerned not just with urban housing reform but with schemes for population reordering or dispersal beyond city boundaries.

While municipal action was able to oppose *laissez-faire* with ideals of community based on locality and, increasingly, social class solidarity, the social mechanism which was most closely associated with the turn-of-the-century and early twentieth-century quest for a more orderly alternative to *laissez-faire* was that of the nation as a whole. Architecturally, as complexes such as the Vienna Ring testified, this period still upheld the hierarchical primacy of the monumental state building. In Scotland, the beginnings of administrative devolution from London (with the creation of the Scottish Office) prompted proposals for the building of government headquarters in Edinburgh, but not, at that stage, actual construction. In this period, direct government building was confined to more everyday areas such as post offices (where William T. Oldrieve's staff maintained a 'national' preference for a Scots Renaissance style), although Rowand Anderson's elaborate Scottish National Portrait Gallery, opened 1889, was partly the result of state patronage [cf. 7.31, 7.63].

The building type which highlighted most sharply the redefinition of the nation in more collective terms, was the national or international exhibition. Imperial Scotland saw five such events before 1914: two in Edinburgh (1886 and 1908) and three in Glasgow (1888, 1901 and 1911). At first, there was a combination of iron halls with temporary facades in lightly eclectic classical styles, to convey an air of gaiety. This exoticism increased steadily from J. J. Burnet's 1886 classicism to Sellars's striped, minaretted Saracenic palace in 1888 (an exhibition which symbolised the city's new cultural confidence), and the encrusted Mexican Spanish of 1901 [7.3]. But in the 1911 Glasgow Exhibition (designed by R. J. Walker), a different element became dominant. In previous exhibitions, alongside colourful colonial 'villages' and foreign pavilions (such as Fedor Shekhtel's brightly painted 'neo-Russian' style group in 1901), there had been the beginnings of historical reconstructions and tableaux vivants from Scotland's past. In 1911, the entire exhibition (which was dedicated to the Scottish patrimony) was designed in a unified and sober style inspired by Scottish Renaissance architecture [cf. 7.33]. This was the start of the idea of exhibitions as collective ideological projections of the unified nation, rather than as cosmopolitan trade bazaars.

7.3 The 1901 Glasgow Exhibition: (above) Industrial Hall (by James Miller); (below) 'Russian Village', by Fedor Shekhtel.

'Artistic Simplicity' and Discipline in Architecture

If the building types of the period seemed unprecedentedly diverse, the corresponding architectural solutions were, at first sight, even more varied. A broad pattern was, however, discernible. The years from around 1880 in Scotland, as elsewhere in Europe, saw a growing rejection of picturesque complexity and mass-produced ornament, and an increase in calls for greater orderliness – a variegated ideal expressed in terms such as 'artistic', 'refinement' and (most frequently) 'simplicity'. As we saw in Chapter 6, Free Renaissance and other highly decorated buildings continued to be built in relatively low-status contexts until the 1900s. But to younger architects, the endless ornamental subdivisions of buildings such as the North British Hotel seemed tasteless and crude, compared with the complex variety of new 'simplicities' now on offer.

Within secular architecture, this new thinking was channelled into two main groupings, each with its own set of architectural values, and (taking advantage of the 1889 relaxation of government restrictions within design education) each aspiring to set up its own matching educational system. The first grouping, concentrated in the west, sought not to reject the eclectic modernity seen in cosmopolitan Second Empire classicism, but to reshape and even heighten it. This was to be done through a practical professionalism and rationalism, and an avid exploitation of technology. The Glasgow classical tradition of Thomson and Wilson would be reinvigorated with elements drawn from the overseas classical world of the Beaux-Arts, and especially from the country which was now coming to symbolise modernity in all its aspects: the United States. Pre-eminent here, in a constellation of talent, was J. J. Burnet. On the other hand, in the east, a fresh movement was unleashed by Rowand Anderson. Its advocates, headed by the 1900s by Robert S. Lorimer, rejected the minutely subdivided, hierarchical stylistic eclecticisms of the mid-nineteenth century, and called for a more intuitive or emotionalistic individualism, inspired directly by what they believed to be the lost golden age of the Scottish Renaissance. They sought order not in

cosmopolitanism but in its opposite, the 'national'. Here they rejected Scotch Baronial as a model, for its lack of moral fervour, but continued elements of its formal vocabulary. This tendency, although concentrated in the east, also spawned a brilliant western offshoot in the 'Glasgow Style' of C. R. Mackintosh and his circle.

This split between the Beaux-Arts' western 'practical' advocates and the eastern upholders of 'artistic' wholeness continued into the interwar years, and even beyond. But in reality, both had much in common, notably a rejection of codified styles and a continuing reliance on elements of broad typological eclecticism. Despite numerous major differences in emphasis, both would generally design villas in 'domestic' styles, public buildings in relatively classical and monumental styles. Nor was their rupture from what went before as sharp as polemic often asserted. In contrast to, say, Germany or England, mass-produced decoration had not percolated down to the meanest buildings, and so there was less need to affect a trenchant primitivism or academicism. The underlying common ground between the Burnet and Anderson groupings was seen, for instance, in the career of the prominent Beaux-Arts-educated Glasgow architect A. N. Paterson, who built domestic-revival villas as well as two sophisticated classical blocks in central Glasgow, [cf. 5.29, 7.14] and regularly attended the visits and activities of the Edinburgh Architectural Association. After the turn of the century, and especially as war approached, both sides increasingly converged around a common agenda of sober discipline, whose main ingredients were a general resurgence of classicism and a preoccupation with the 'national'.

'The Poet of Modern Necessity': J. J. Burnet and the Classicism of Modernity [5]

The advocates of reinvigorated cosmopolitan classicism, concentrated in Glasgow and the west, sought to restore visual dignity and an architectural order crowned by the great public building, while increasing architecture's rationalistic responsiveness to the 'practical necessities' of modern life. [6] The tendency of Glasgow's new, intense urban developments to jumble up the traditional hierarchy of the city was to be countered by adapting classicism so as to create new types of public monument. As Honeyman put it in 1882, 'The exigency of art in the present day seems to be the classic treatment of entirely new arrangements and new modes of construction, suited to the requirements of the age, and securing the greatest amount of convenience, comfort and security which the means at our disposal can yield, untrammelled by the precedents of the past.' [7] The grand old Scottish neo-classical tradition, in its combination of antique stateliness with the intuitive aesthetic of the Picturesque and the Sublime, was hardly tailor-made for this task. But there were now systematic attempts in Glasgow to rejuvenate it with something that more plausibly was: the architectural philosophy taught at the École des Beaux-Arts in Paris.

In the late nineteenth century, the architectural culture of the Beaux-Arts was at the height of its international influence, which was now spreading across the anglophone world. Ever since the École's mid-century absorption of the Gothic rationalism of Viollet-le-Duc, what it taught was no longer stylistic classicism, but a systematic rationalist way of dealing with projects, based on the primacy of programme and plan over elevations: in the words of Burnet, 'the essentials'. From the satisfaction of this inner logic, architects could develop 'individuality' and 'artistic possibilities'. [8] And they could stay in step with the demands of contemporary life. Burnet in 1892 declared that the architect must be both a 'master builder', versed in 'the science of building', and a 'poet of modern necessity'. [9] Within this system, architectural change was incremental, rather than revolutionary. However, by the 1870s and 1880s – the point at which Scotland became involved – Beaux-Arts architects were beginning to argue that contemporary demands, especially in the field of public and urban buildings, required a more monumental, dynamic architecture, incorporating, if possible, boldly scaled, integral sculpture: what we, today, might label a more 'Baroque' approach.

The expressions of this tendency varied in different countries. In Scotland, it took the form of a Beaux-Arts development of the formal legacy of

the Thomson and Wilson era, emphasising the latter's practical modernity rather than the former's impassioned utopianism. As we noted in Chapter 6, the key figure in making this connection possible was Sellars: his public buildings and institutions, such as St Andrew's Halls and the New Club (which he described as 'modern French'), [10] had exploited the elements of Baroque massiveness in Thomson's work [cf. 6.60, 6.62]. He encouraged talented pupils to attend the École; one of them, John Keppie, recalled of Sellars that his 'greatest power was as a monumental architect; that is to say, a designer of public buildings or institutions. . . a thoroughly nineteenth-century architect'. [11] The development of the Glasgow Beaux-Arts connection is told in detail by Walker in *St Andrews Studies*, 1991. [12] A series of talented designers pursued this educational route: J. J. Burnet (in 1875–7), J. A. Campbell, A. N. Paterson, Henbest Capper and Keppie all attended the Atelier Pascal. At the same time, Beaux-Arts ideas infiltrated teaching at Glasgow School of Art (from 1887) and the Glasgow and West of Scotland Technical College (from 1892). In 1904, after a deputation to Paris led by Burnet and W. Forrest Salmon, Eugene Bourdon was nominated to report on reform of architectural education in Glasgow, and, following a merger of departments, was appointed first Professor of Architecture at the School of Art.

Besides this interaction between the Thomson and Wilson legacy and the Beaux-Arts, other tendencies were pointing towards a revitalisation and redefinition of monumental classicism, both in the west and the east. Even within the free Renaissance of the 1880s and 1890s, the tendency was towards more massive compositions, sometimes including tall towers or other forcefully architectonic elements. The competition particulars for Glasgow Municipal Buildings, for instance, demanded a 'classic style . . . treated in a broad and dignified rather than in a florid manner', [13] although Young's successful design (built in 1883–8), looked backwards (to Thomson, especially) as much as forwards [cf. 7.2]. Its sumptuous interior, with two vast staircases clad in alabaster and marble, conformed more to the older nineteenth-century taste for all-over decoration: in Young's own words, 'tier upon tier of pillars, arches and cornices – a truly palatial . . . splendour'. [14] Young's masterpiece sparked off a succession of more clearly 'Baroque' civic projects, such as Miller's Clydebank Municipal Buildings (1900–02), with blocked surrounds, high roof, and austere tower; or Alexander Cullen's Hamilton Municipal Buildings, with its paired towers. In Edinburgh, the Baroque tendencies of the earlier classical work of Bryce were developed on an Adam-like visionary scale, and combined with some Baronial elements, in Scott & Williamson's plan for commercial developments flanking the rebuilt North Bridge (1896): these tall gabled blocks and huge substructures provided a new romantic gateway to the Old Town [7.4]. Individual sites in this scheme were built up by various architects: Mitchell & Wilson, Hamilton Beattie, and, above all, Dunn & Findlay, whose titanic Scotsman Buildings outcrop (1899–1902) combined Baroque massing with Scots Renaissance detailing.

These efforts were paralleled in the Baroque/ Baronial monumentality of some of Norman Shaw's contemporary designs in England, such as New Scotland Yard, London (1887), or Chesters (1890–4). The influential work of Shaw, a 'London Scot' and former Burn pupil who falls outwith the direct scope of this account (as he built nothing in Scotland), provided many striking parallels to contemporary Scottish developments.

However, the leader of the impulse towards Baroque monumentality, J. J. Burnet, was a Beaux-Arts and Glasgow man [7.5]. Like Mitchell – his only rival in confident eclecticism and range of work – he had enjoyed a head-start, in this case as the son of a prominent architect (John Burnet Senior). But he was bold enough to choose a Paris training, in Pascal's atelier – the centre of the École's anglophone diaspora. In 1877 he returned to join his father's practice. At first, he developed an austere, overtly French classicism

7.4 North Bridge rebuilding scheme, Edinburgh (planned 1896 by J. N. Scott & J. A. Williamson). On the right, *Scotsman* buildings by Dunn & Findlay (1899-1902); on the left, block by W. Hamilton Beattie (1898).

7.5 J. J. Burnet, photograph by Annan, *c*.1900.

the most complicated Northern Renaissance efforts of others, while Drumsheugh Baths, Edinburgh (first built 1882, rebuilt 1892–3) was Moorish in style. And, as we will see, there were equally forceful interventions in the domestic and ecclesiastical fields. But it was in dense urban building that there came, in 1891, the first of the successive breakthroughs which were to mark out Burnet and Campbell as Scotland's leading 'poets of modern necessity' [7.6]. This was the Athenaeum Theatre, which introduced a new, verticalised intensity to Glasgow street architecture: in 1892, Burnet demanded that 'the modern architect' must aspire to 'the grandeur and nobler qualities of master building'. [16] The individual sources of the Athenaeum Theatre design were easily traceable: vertically gridded tower from Wilson's Free Church College, aedicule-crowned gable from Shaw, and arch-framed bay window from Central Station. These elements were combined into an asymmetrical, dynamic unity suggestive of Thomson's churches.

7.6 Athenaeum Theatre, Buchanan Street, Glasgow (Burnet and Campbell, 1891); on the left, A. N. Paterson's Liberal Club (1907–9).

in a succession of lavish projects. The first was the Royal Glasgow Fine Art Institution of 1878–9, in which, Burnet later recalled, 'the severe and refined Greek' was 'blended with the full flowing lines of the Renaissance in order to get a full share of breadth and dignity'. Then followed his 'restrained and simple' entries [15] for the 1880–3 Glasgow Municipal Buildings competition, his Clyde Trust Building (1882–6, and extended in 1905–8 with corner dome and Trust Hall), the Edinburgh Exhibition buildings (1886); and the Athenaeum (1887), with its arched facade.

In 1886, Burnet was joined in partnership by another, no less talented Pascal pupil, J. A. Campbell. From this point, their urban work took on a new vigour, rejecting the calm horizontality of designs such as the Fine Art Institute for a freer and bolder articulation. Stylistically, there was a typically late nineteenth-century Beaux-Arts eclectic opportunism: in some cases, such as Charing Cross Mansions, 1891 (a large complex of tenements and business chambers), they outdid

This Baroque dynamism was to be of most influence in the exploitation, and ennobling, of another, completely new building type: the multi-storey office block. Here we encounter the most significant of the late nineteenth-century trans-formations of Beaux-Arts classicism: the new admiration for America. At the 1893 World's Columbian Exposition at Chicago, the United States began to emerge as the new symbolic home of Western modernity – a 'home' which would exert a mesmeric fascination on the imaginations of European architects for the next three-quarters of a century. But 'America' meant different things in different European countries. In Scotland, it was above all the modern Beaux-Arts grouping who were influenced by American architecture, and especially by the arresting image of the skyscraper block. From the 1870s, as in some American cities, rising land values and site scarcity in central Glasgow had prompted more intense exploitation of the narrow, early nineteenth-century house-plots. During the mid and late 1890s, helped by advances in building technology and the new availability of power for lifts (especially with the building of Port Dundas Power Station from 1897 – an example of municipal support for *laissez-faire* development), there was a rapid spread of tall office blocks: for instance Alex Petrie's St Enoch Square block (1895) or James Thomson's Pearl Insurance (1896–7). These early examples kept to the formula of profuse added decoration, but soon, under the influence of the Atheneum Theatre, there were attempts at more sweepingly modulated designs, often employing deep red sandstone. As in American office blocks, the key attributes were vertical distortion from horizontal Renaissance proportions, and the contrasting of expanses of sheer surface with concentrated sculpture and emphatic crowning features. But where the Americans moved quickly to steel frames, with accompanying flatness and gridlike expression, full steel framing did not become prevalent in Glasgow until after 1905. As a result, the highly architectonic formula of the Athenaeum Theatre was very influential.

The most striking realisations of this neo-Baroque skyscraper pattern were, predictably, by Burnet and Campbell themselves, especially following the dissolution of their partnership in 1897. Burnet, invigorated by a visit to America the previous year, launched into a series of designs which combined a Chicago-like verticality, in symmetrical groups of bay windows, with a Thomsonian arrangement of flanking pylons and eaves colonnade, and integrated sculpture by artists such as Albert Hodge or Phyllis Archibald. Key examples included Atlantic Chambers (1899–1900) and Waterloo Chambers (1898–1900) – both dumb-bell plan blocks – and, in Edinburgh, the Professional and Civil Service Supply Association in George Street (1903–7) [7.7]. In 1900, the *Glasgow Herald* praised 'the fine sense of ensemble' and 'bold, almost masterful treatment' of his work, but chided him for a 'lack of consider-ation as to detail in places'. A confident and at times brash grandeur also informed Burnet's small-scale city buildings, such as the Savings Bank of Glasgow banking hall (1894–1900), with its deep, channelled masonry and facades flanked by sculptured aedicules: Burnet had just returned from a second visit to Italy when he carried out this commission [7.8]. J. A. Campbell's post-1897 designs, if less lively and variegated, were if any-thing even more powerful than Burnet's. They generally featured an integral mass with vertical patterning in the Athenaeum Theatre manner. Arguably his masterpiece was the vast masonry-built block at 163 Hope Street (1902–3): its sheer walls punched with unadorned windows and crowned by a deep loggia, this awesome structure combined fortress-like grandeur with sculptural sophistication [7.9]. The more overtly classical Edinburgh Life Assurance block, Glasgow (1904–6), expressed a soaring verticality through giant Orders clasped between towers, while, as we will see later, Campbell's Queen Victoria Memorial School, Dunblane (1907–8), translated this pattern into Scots Renaissance form [cf. 7.32].

By the turn of the century, the new multi-storey office style was being widely imitated. One of the most startling realisations stemmed from the partnership of Salmon & Son & Gillespie (now consisting of James Salmon II and J. Gaff Gillespie). The transition from ornate Northern Renaissance is seen in a massive 1897 block, Mercantile Chambers, a complex, gabled com-position combined with tall, Campbell /Burnet-like bay windows. Two years later, this worthy

7.7 Waterloo Chambers, Glasgow (J. J. Burnet, 1898–1900), *c.*1900 drawing.

7.8 A group of buildings in Ingram Street/Glassford Street, Glasgow, by John Burnet Senior and J. J. Burnet. The Glasgow Savings Bank headquarters was built by John Burnet Senior in 1866; in 1894–1900, it was heightened by one storey and reconstructed by J. J. Burnet, who at the same time added the banking hall at centre of the picture (sculpture by G. J. Frampton). On the right, the former Union Bank (facade 1876-9 by J. Burnet).

7.9 163 Hope Street, Glasgow (J. A. Campbell, 1902–3).

but restless design was followed by a much more idiosyncratic achievement, the ten-storey St Vincent Chambers (1899), which strained the compressed verticality of skyscraper-Baroque to its limit [7.10]. Its main novelty lay not in the tall bay windows, nor in the busily variegated facade and skyline, nor even in the Art Nouveau sculpture and ironwork, but in the maximisation of window size, giving the building the appearance of a rippling wall of glass. Other architects merged verticalising neo-Baroque and a continuing Free Renaissance detail, with results sometimes powerful, sometimes slightly bombastic. Notable examples included the cavernous Parish Council Chambers (1900–2) by Thomson and Sandilands, Miller's Caledonian Chambers, Union Street

(1901), a seven-storey block with jutting upper balcony and huge flanking aedicules; Burnet & Boston's large Baroque block at 140 St Vincent Street (1898) and turreted angle block at St George's Mansions (1900); James Chalmers's 64 Waterloo Street (1898–1900), its corner tower decorated with solomonic-columned aedicules; and Keppie's Parkhead Savings Bank (1908). In other towns, we may note Gabriel Andrew's block at Portland Street, Kilmarnock (1905), and Brown and Watt's Aberdeen Central Bakery (1900). The area in which these innovations in office architecture interacted most subtly with everyday turn-of-the-century building was that of speculative built tenement housing. If tenement bay windows' insistent, giant-order rhythm – popular

7.10 St Vincent Street, Glasgow: On the left, St Vincent Chambers (Salmon & Son & Gillespie, 1899–1902); on the right, 140–142 St Vincent Street (Burnet & Boston, 1898–1900).

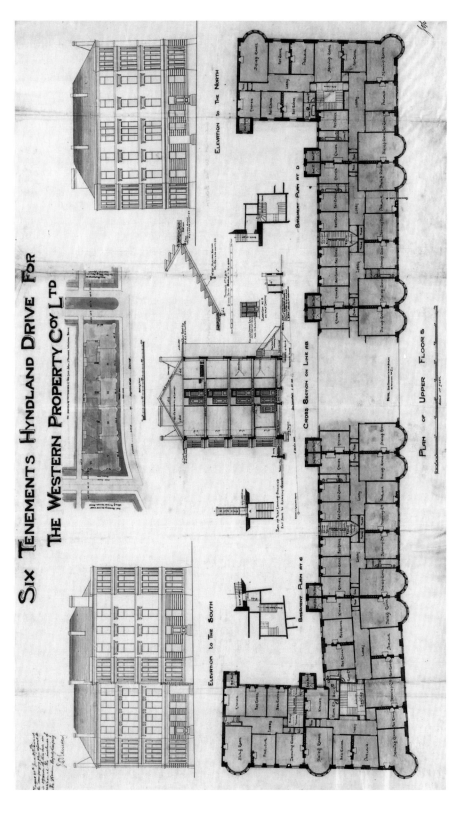

7.11 Architect John Short's 1898 plans and elevations for middle-class tenements in Hyndland Drive, Glasgow: the dwellings are of 5–7 rooms with internal bathrooms, and the facade treatment is still relatively faithful to neo-classical norms (for example retaining channelling, and architraves).

since the early 1880s – had helped pave the way for skyscraper Baroque, the compliment was now repaid in the massed building, around Glasgow, of two-roomed flats with bathrooms, by developers like Sir John Mactaggart. Windows became simple holes, bay windows were sliced off at the cornice-line, and there was a change from additive to integral ornament: a prominent example is John Nisbet's Springhill Gardens, Shawlands (1904), with its clustered, attenuated bay windows [7.11, 7.12; cf. C.7].

Around the turn of the century, a second phase began in the search for classical order: the replacement of the forceful Baroque by more reposeful tendencies. In German-speaking and Scandinavian countries, this classical revival took the form of an elemental geometry and revival of 'national' neo-classicism. By contrast, the dominant trend in Scotland, especially in Glasgow – just as in France and America – was first to combine modernity with images of antique stateliness, and then, after around 1910, to turn to a pared-down architecture of mass. Appropriately, it was Burnet, returning part of the way to his 1880 Greek/Renaissance phase, who led the Scottish

7.12 Tenements built in 1915–17 in Kitchener Street, Dalmuir, for Beardmore shipyard workers, by the company's property arm (the Dalmuir & West of Scotland Estates Company). The blocks have a plain and massive treatment, with flat roofs for wartime economy.

contribution to both phases of this more orderly cosmopolitan classicism. His key achievement in the first phase – the architecture of revived classical grandeur – was built outside Scotland: the King Edward Galleries of the British Museum, London (1905–14), with their giant Greek Ionic colonnade, neo-classically modest centre, low Baroque doorpiece, and McKim-like Grecian interior [7.13]. At home in Glasgow, Burnet's classicism became progressively calmer, yet no less grandiose, as in the Elder Library and Hospital (1901) or the Clyde Trust corner block (1905–8). Even more soberly Beaux-Arts public buildings were designed by others: for instance, Watson Salmond & Gray's City Chambers extension (1913–23), with triumphal arches spanning John Street. In the ecclesiastical field, the work of the Belgian-born architect C. J. Menart also showed an up-to-date Beaux-Arts tendency towards simpler classicism, with some Burnetian and Thomsonian touches. His most important work, St Aloysius's Church, Glasgow (1908–10), combined a tall tower with a temple-front perched on a colonnade, while Sacred Heart Church (1912) was simpler, with prominent lunettes. In response to the introduction of regular steel frames around 1907–1912, which made asymmetrical or heavily modulated facades relatively expensive, the Beaux-Arts commercial style became more austere and rectilinear. A key turning point was Campbell pupil A. D. Hislop's Phoenix Assurance Building, Glasgow (1912–13), with granite Doric-columned base in the manner of McKim, Mead & White and plain, flat upper storeys; Miller's designs for the Anchor Building (1905–7) and Cranston's Picture House (1914–16) were similar to this. More original solutions were devised by A. N. Paterson. His National Bank of Scotland, St Enoch Square (1906–8), with its massive sculptured figures by Phyllis Archibald, was a pioneer in the incorporation of a bank into a full-scale multi-storey office block, while his Liberal Club (1907–9) offset its multi-storey scale with delicately shallow, metal-framed bay windows [7.14].

Alongside this regularisation of mainstream Beaux-Arts classicism another, more novel response to steel-framed commercial building – which would last into the 1920s and 1930s – was being worked out by the now separately practising

7.13 King Edward Galleries of the British Museum, London (J. J. Burnet, 1905–14).

Burnet and Campbell. The outline of buildings was squared off, openings became plain, punched-in holes, and there was a geometrising, linearising or elimination of surface ornament. This was the beginning of the second phase of the return to classical order: the architecture of stereometric mass. As always in this period in the west, the influence of Thomson was not far beneath the surface. In two transitional Burnet works – McGeoch, in Glasgow (1905), and Forsyth, in Edinburgh (1906) – gridded facades are clasped within overall Baroque compositions [7.15]. McGeoch, slightly reminiscent of David Hamilton's Cleland Building in its crushed-together corner pylons, and provided with oversize sculpture by Phyllis Bone, showed a greater dynamism typical of the west. From 1910–11, however, Burnet's designs became steadily more austere. In two relatively utilitarian commercial buildings, the Kodak Building, London (1910), and the Wallace Scott Institute, Cathcart (1913), the main facade comprises a simplified grid-colonnade, flanked at Wallace Scott by massive pylons and at Kodak by slashed vertical openings crowned by a huge cavetto cornice. In the Alhambra Theatre (1911), the debt to Thomson was made clearer [7.16]. This cubic design was punched with vertical slits linked by a deep, canopied eaves colonnade, and surmounted by token oriental domes. Inside were canopies with sparing Louis XVI decoration. While Burnet built on Thomson's legacy, Campbell's last works developed a linearised

7.14 Sculpture by Phyllis Archibald on the front facade of A. N. Paterson's 22–24 St Enoch Square, Glasgow (1906–8).

7.16 Alhambra Theatre, Glasgow (Burnet, 1911), 1969 view.

verticality recalling Wilson's Free Church College [cf. 6.4], and the contemporary experiments of J. J. Joass, working in England. At 122–128 St Vincent Street (1904–6), this took a vigorous Baroque form, while at Northern Insurance (1908–9) Campbell fronted the steel-framed structure by a more compressed, abstractly detailed facade [7.17]. Just after the war, Burnet recalled these new emphases, so different from the thrusting modernity of the 1890s. He asserted that a monumental public building should be 'so simple in its conception that it appears a perfect harmony, created without effort, a simple and beautiful monument to the integrity and purpose of the generation in which it was built'. [17]

Turn-of-the-Century Classicism in Edinburgh and the East

7.15 McGeoch Building, Glasgow (Burnet, 1905), 1969 view.

While the turn towards classical order took the form of a dramatic modernity in the west, where Glasgow's commercial prosperity acted as a hothouse for innovation and change, the changes in the east were less abrupt, and reflected in many cases a northern European interest in 'national' classicism. Except in some verticalised developments in Edinburgh's Princes Street, commercial pressures were weaker and land values lower, making it easier for developers to acquire adjacent house-plots. And the weight of neo-classical

7.17 Northern Insurance Building, Glasgow (J. A. Campbell, 1908–9). On the extreme left is James Miller's Union Bank of 1924–7.

tradition seemed heavier. We encountered the scholarly Renaissance classicism of Anderson's 1874 Medical School design Chapter 6. When Anderson proposed a strictly eighteenth-century-style design for the Imperial Institute, London (1887) – a design rejected as impossibly formal in the context of the then extreme individualism of English architecture – he was doing little more than Burnet, seventeen years later at the British Museum, in marking the status of a great public building through monumental classicism.

But in Edinburgh, unlike Glasgow, that formula, with its traditional hierarchy of building-type status, had never been comprehensively over-hauled. Nor had there ever been a general rejection of Renaissance proportions (in, for example, window spacing). As the original neo-classical impulse began to peter out in the east, and

throughout the heyday of busy Northern Renaissance, a general continuity was maintained, for example, between Bryce's later palazzi and Anderson's Conservative Club (1881–4), or between Bryce's St George's Free Church and its massive campanile added by Anderson (1880–2) [cf. 6.38]. There was similar continuity in Aberdeen, in the flat classical facades of A. Marshall Mackenzie (Harbour Offices, 1883–5, and Trinity Free Church, 1891). In Dundee, the free classicism of the Improvement Act's new commercial streets, built 1876–92 under the direction of William Mackison (Burgh Engineer), shaded into such projects as Peddie & Browne's Royal Bank (1899), a palazzo with giant Ionic arcade, or Niven & Wigglesworth's Baroque office block of 1902 for the *Courier* newspaper (extended in 1960 with a 'skyscraper' in virtually the same style).

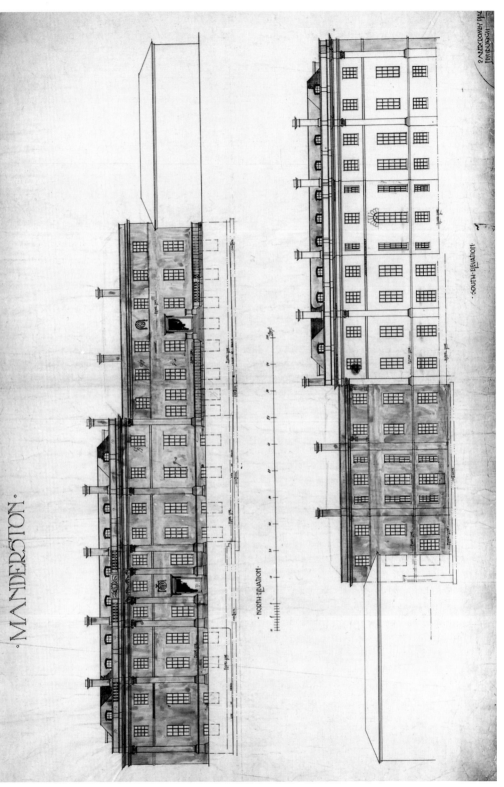

· MANDERSTON ·

· NORTH ELEVATION ·

· SOUTH ELEVATION ·

7.18 John Kinross's 1902 drawings for new 'Adams' style north and south elevations at Manderston House.

Soon, this continuation of tendencies inherited from the eighteenth century in the east began to shade into their conscious revival. The 1880s, height of the Northern Renaissance revolt against neo-classical austerity, also saw the reinvigoration of the romantic cult of Classical Edinburgh: in 1885, Gowans praised 'the harmony and propriety of Edinburgh street architecture'.

And it saw the beginnings of the attacks, which would last until the 1960s, against the now highly variegated appearance of Princes Street; by the mid-1900s, civic campaigns against advertisements and 'incongruity' were under way. (18) In 1890, G. Baldwin Brown, first professor of Fine Art at Edinburgh University, hailed the eighteenth century New Town terraces as 'priceless architectural treasures' which must be preserved. (19) The spearhead of this movement was a Robert Adam revival (known, in contemporary parlance, as the 'Adams' style) in the field of interior decoration. This formed part of an international trend which by 1900–10 had begun to reject late nineteenth-century interiors as dark and cluttered, and to substitute a whiteness – often still rich and elaborate – inspired by each country's own particular classical variants of the late eighteenth and early nineteenth centuries. The main 'Adams' movement in Scotland began with schemes such as Wright & Mansfield's work at Haddo House

(1880). A more scholarly stage was reached in Sir James Miller's commission of John Kinross from 1891 to remodel the showy neo-Renaissance eclecticism of Manderston into an 'Adams'/Louis XVI showpiece: the architectural decoration was by Scott Morton [7.18]. It was extended into the beginnings of a New Town Revival in 1904, when the 4th Marquess of Bute, encouraged by Baldwin Brown, bought 5 Charlotte Square. Employing the Anderson-trained architect Balfour Paul, and Scott Morton as decorator, he inserted a sumptuous suite of 'Adams' decoration. William Young's remodelling and re-creation (in 1891) of the original Adam design of Gosford House included 'Adams' decoration, but this sat alongside more dominant elements, such as the colossal pink alabaster entrance hall and staircase, which belonged to the earlier Baroque phase of decoration exemplified by Young's Glasgow work [7.19; cf. 4.4, 4.5].

External architectural evocations of the eighteenth century in the east began more gradually. An early example was Anderson's addition of a tall dome in 1886–7 to Robert Adam's main university facade [cf. 4.22]. Shaw, at this time, was busy introducing a more monumental classicism to England, based on seventeenth and eighteenth century precedent – notably at the Kinross-like Bryanston (1889–93) [cf. 3.15]. During the 1890s,

7.19 Gosford House, Marble Hall as rebuilt by William Young in 1891.

this neo-eighteenth-century trend closely paralleled, and moderated, Edinburgh's dominant neo-Baroque. The key architect here was J. Dick Peddie, partner of Washington Browne – who had already, in such works as Maisondieu Church, Brechin (1891), begun a move towards a more sober classicism. In 1897–1901, Peddie & Browne designed the Standard Life Assurance office in George Street, a neo-classical block of normal New Town height. Also restrained and pedimented was their Bank of Scotland branch in High Street, Ayr (1901); for the Edinburgh Life Assurance Company on a corner site in the capital, Peddie designed (1908–9) a colonnaded, domed, but somewhat static composition. In some cases, a high roof and emphatic Orders gave an air of Beaux-Arts authority: for instance, at the Caledonian Hotel (1898–1902), or, in 1906, at the Edinburgh College of Art (headed by the École-trained Frank Worthington Simon).

From about 1900, the capital saw a whole range of amalgams of neo-Baroque and eighteenth-century revivalism. For instance J. Mackintyre Henry's Midlothian County Buildings (1904), and A. Hunter Crawford's Freemasons Hall (1910–12, replacing an earlier hall by Bryce) combined Baroque density of detail (for example blocked pilasters, sculpture) with generally reposeful overall proportions: the *Glasgow Herald* praised Henry's 'dignified. . . Georgian Renaissance' design for its 'simplicity, directness and good proportion'. [20] Even more horizontal and calm were R. S. Lorimer's New Library, St Andrews (1907–8), and Rowand Anderson & Paul's university buildings in Dundee (1907) – in the latter case, quoting also specific stylistic features of late seventeenth-century Scottish classicism. Even narrow commercial blocks in Edinburgh, such as Dunn & Findlay's Victoria Chambers, Frederick Street (1903), avoided Glasgow-style verticalised dynamism. The new tendencies were echoed by progressive, middle-of-the-road Edinburgh architects such as the redoubtable T. P. Marwick, whose commercial work after around 1880–90 left Northern Renaissance behind: in 1914, he designed the Bread Street Co-operative headquarters in a slightly, attenuated classical manner with Roman Doric colonnade and slim corner dome. And by 1910, there was, as in Glasgow, an increasing tendency of cubic austerity evocative of neo-classicism. J. Arnott and J. Inch Morrison's Charlotte Chapel (1908) was a massive block with vertically-grouped fenestration, while Browne's YMCA, St Andrew Street (1914–15), was severe and colonnaded. In 1912, J. A. Dunn told the Edinburgh Architectural Association that Greek classicism had now returned to favour: the Edinburgh classical tradition of Adam, Playfair and Bryce was 'hard to beat', and young architects should study their work. [21]

After 1900, Edinburgh also witnessed a resurgence of post-Renaissance classical inspiration in its institutional buildings, especially in the individualistic designs of its School Board architect, J. A. Carfrae. Drawing on the wide range of Scottish Renaissance precedent now available for different tasks, he developed the tradition of heavy, rock-faced classicism already established in the police stations and swimming pools of the City Architect, R. H. Morham, from the mid-1890s, and the schools of his own predecessor, Robert Wilson. Carfrae's major projects ranged from the Baroque of Leith Academy Annexe (1903) to the massive Byzantine-Roman rhetoric of Boroughmuir High School (1911–14), a domineering outcrop with giant Ionic columns and harl on a two-storey rock-faced base [7.20]. For smaller-scaled projects, Carfrae chose more modest 'originals'. His Tollcross School (1911–13) combined Pinkie-like lines of chimneys and James Smith-like ogival-roofed pavilions with the monumental touch of rock-faced masonry; the school was designed to appear like a multi-phase lesser country house, incorporating a 'tower' at the centre rear [cf. C. 11]. A heavy, rather exotic classicism was also found in the last work of Sydney Mitchell (with his partner E. A. O. Auldjo Jamieson): the United Free Church headquarters in George Street (1911), a massive (originally symmetrical) palazzo, recalling Rowand Anderson precedents in its high roof and eaves colonnade but also, in its stubby Greek Doric columns and round arches, hinting at a Mycenean archaism [7.21].

The grandest realisations of the eastern classical revival were not located in the capital at all, but in Dundee. There the City Council embarked on a civic reconstruction plan of Beaux-Arts comprehensiveness and fifty-year timescale, prepared in

7.20 Boroughmuir School, Edinburgh (Carfrae, 1911–14).

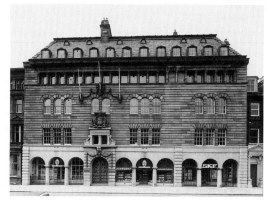

7.21 United Free Church headquarters, Edinburgh, 1967 view. Mitchell's 1911 block was symmetrical; the east extension was added in 1932–3 by E. A. O. Auldjo Jamieson & J. A. Arnott.

two stages by the new City Architect and Engineer, James Thomson (Central Improvement Scheme, 1910; Town Planning Report, 1918). Thomson's proposals, whose huge scale anticipated the city's colossal public housing drive later in the century, included the wholesale demolition of slums, the laying-out of parkway roads and garden suburbs,

and the building of classical libraries on landmark corner sites. Its centrepiece was the completion of Mackison's city centre redevelopment scheme on spacious, axial lines, including a 1911 proposal to build a domed Civic Centre. As eventually built, the scheme's focus was the Caird Hall, a public hall of Roman austerity designed by Thomson and begun in 1914, with the assistance of a £100,000 donation by city industrialist Sir James Caird. A giant colonnade was later gifted by Caird's sister: the Hall was completed in 1922, and the flanking civic buildings (by Burnet, modified by J. MacLellan Brown) in 1933.

Rowand Anderson and the Architecture of 'Tradition'

So far in this chapter, we have dealt with the attempt to create a new 'simplicity' or order largely within the existing rules of classical architecture, either through creating a more unified and dynamic overall effect, as in the skyscraper-Baroque, or through a more straightforward revival of neo-classical stateliness. But where Burnet saw the architect's problem as 'easy of enunciation', the architects we shall deal with now demanded a far more ambitious approach – an ideology, even – which would challenge the chaos not only of *laissez-faire* architecture but also of *laissez-faire* society. To them, contemporary 'modern' classicism, no less than mid-nineteenth century secular architecture (classical and Baronial alike), was the coarse product of a materialistic society, which demanded comprehensive reform.

The complexity of this task was short-circuited by simplifying discussion into a range of polarisations between the disharmonies of the present, and the utopian wholeness of a past golden age, which it was the architect's task to revive. In contrast to Thomson's utopianism, the ideals of these architects were secular rather than religious, and linked to a rejection of key aspects of modern urban society. The handmade was championed against the mass-produced, the natural against the artificial, the old town or the country against the industrial city, architectural 'truth' against architectural logic, 'sanity' and 'refined simplicity' against 'vulgar display'. [22] The established hierarchy of building status was up-ended, and attention lavished not on the monumental public building but on 'the home': the task was to ennoble not office blocks, but the 'ordinary' dwellings of middle-class or working-class people. Above all, overt modernity was rejected for 'tradition', by which was meant the pre-industrial golden age of the Scottish Renaissance: in the words of Robert Lorimer, in 1897, 'the ideal life in the ideal old, traditional "un-hurrying" Scotland'. [23] This was the first and most vigorous flowering of the Scottish architectural movement of Traditionalism, whose efforts to reform or contain aggressive modernity with appeals to a deeper coherence or a national community would endure, in various forms, until the 1950s, and even beyond.

Within such a broad movement, there were bound to be many paradoxes and conflicts. For instance, it violently rejected the cosmopolitan, the Franco-American, and the universal in favour of the particular and the 'national', basing itself on what were now thought to be the architectural and social characteristics of the Scottish Renaissance.

Yet it was itself related to a wider international movement, which originally stemmed from English critics of *laissez-faire* society and its architecture (notably Pugin, Ruskin and Morris), but by the late nineteenth century had spread throughout Europe and North America. And it drew its inspiration from the same, Scottish Renaissance, buildings as had the nineteenth-century movement – Baronial – that it most vehemently criticised. In some of its aspects, it favoured an aggressive individualism, in others a *Gesamtkunstwerk* (unity of the arts) shaped by collaboration between architects and craftspeople. It demanded an old-style 'simplicity'. Yet it was in some ways very 'modern' and complex, not least in its concern with the personality [24] of individual 'artists' such as Lorimer or Mackintosh – who skilfully exploited the new international medium of architectural periodicals to spread their fame [cf. 7.24, 7.40]. In 1889, Washington Browne noted that 'the personal identity of the artist with his work, of the producer with the thing produced, is a special characteristic of modern life and thought'. [25] This concept of the autonomy of form, pioneered a century earlier in the aesthetic of the Picturesque and the Sublime, was potentially contradicted by Traditionalism's equally 'modern' emphasis on the moral, social or national context; only after 1918 would it resolve that conflict by coming down on the side of collective values.

Despite the unprecedented aspects of this new ideology, its first champion was someone already familiar to us in these pages: Rowand Anderson [7.22]. The greatest of Anderson's achievements as the 'Nestor of Scottish architects' [26] in the late nineteenth century, was, arguably, his establishment of the Traditionalist Movement. The dominant role of this Episcopal stalwart, freemason, and member of the Royal Company of Archers reminds us that the at times anti-establishment, folk or bohemian image of equivalent movements in other countries (like the Arts and Crafts in England and America or National Romanticism in Scandinavia) was only partially echoed in Scotland. Anderson could, for example, combine criticism of 'the blighting influence of machinery, and capitalists using it to produce the false and untrue for . . . profit' with defence of 'free trade in art, as in everything else.' [27]

7.22 Sir Rowand Anderson, early twentieth-century photograph.

Before dealing with Anderson's architectural contribution to the new movement, we must first touch on his ideological and organisational innovations. The wide influence he exerted in the east through his practice continued: some of the most influential turn-of-the-century eastern architects, such as Mitchell, Lorimer or Kinross, were Anderson pupils. Equally important was his attempt to augment this by organising a new system of formal architectural education, to complement and rival the Beaux-Arts system taking shape in the west. Just as contemporary Catalan architects sought to develop a new 'national' architecture based on direct study of old buildings, so Anderson's new Edinburgh School of Applied Art (founded 1892) set out to establish an integrated system of recording and education, including (from 1895) the National Art Survey of Scotland, on the scientific analogy of anatomical drawing. But the polarisation against Glasgow cosmopolitanism was not all it seemed: despite his dislike of academicism on the French model, Anderson appointed a Beaux-Arts professor, Frank Worthington Simon, to his School. From 1887 onwards, study of Scottish Renaissance architecture was assisted by the publication of MacGibbon and Ross's five-volume inventory of that period's secular architecture. By now, the

study of old buildings was becoming linked with initiatives for their preservation: Kinross's restoration of the chapel range and gatehouse at Falkland for the 3rd Marquess of Bute (1887) was backed up by primary research into the Lord Treasurer's and Master of Work's Accounts [cf. 1.12]. Non-coercive state intervention in preservation (concentrated at first on prehistoric remains) began with the 1882 Ancient Monuments Act, and, following pressure by Baldwin Brown, the foundation of the Royal Commission on Ancient Monuments in 1908 and a second Ancient Monuments Act in 1913.

What were the architectural consequences of Anderson's new thinking? First of all, the new ideas broke sharply from the classical hierarchy of building types. Where the latter valued most highly the great public building, and its associated qualities of stately grandeur, here the focus of attention was the ordinary 'home'. In Scotland, in contrast to its equivalents in most other countries, the 'home' was defined so as to embrace not only the middle-class villa and artisan cottage, but also the collective housing and 'community' of the old burgh. The initial efforts of Anderson and others were concerned with the bourgeois house, where they rapidly became bound up with the new 'aesthetic' tendencies we noted in Chapter 6, in the work of designers such as Cottier or Stevenson. Beginning in English-speaking countries on either side of the Atlantic, the attempts to design a more 'artistic' and 'comfortable' dwelling – something more informal than the stodgy classical house, but more tasteful than the spiky picturesque villa – became popular, in many countries, from the 1880s onwards. The work of Norman Shaw was especially influential, in devising a picturesque style with half-timbered highlights. In many places, the result was a straightforward translation into local materials of this so-called Old English style. Although the most spectacular examples, such as Paul Schultze-Naumburg's Schloss Cecilienhof (1913–16), were overseas, Scotland saw specimens such as Leiper's Brantwoode, Helensburgh (1895, George Coutts's 1 Rubislaw Den North, Aberdeen (1909), or A. Marshall Mackenzie's Mar Lodge (1895). That style's light-hearted connotations also associated it with entertainment buildings, seaside hotels and shops: for example T. L.

Watson's Royal Marine Hotel, Hunters Quay (1888), or Hamilton-Paterson & Rhind's flamboyant showroom enlargement at 9 Randolph Place, Edinburgh (1901–2).

But in Scotland, as in most other countries, the mainstream of what critic James Nicoll, in 1908, dubbed 'the cult of the house' [28] grafted the new ideas on to existing patterns. This involved, on the one hand, the exploitation of 'artistic' interior design, and on the other an adaptation, and fundamental transformation, of Scotch Baronial into a new 'Scots Renaissance' style. The main principles of the new movement were enunciated by Anderson. Traditionalists' ideology of a lost golden age made it essential to reject the idea of a continuous Scottish 'classic tradition': here they diverged from the eighteenth-century revivalists we noted above. While acknowledging that Playfair and other neo-classicists had designed 'some of our finest buildings', Anderson criticised neo-classical streets for their 'dreary monotony', and Grecian public buildings as 'mere abstract pieces of design . . . screens to mask what is behind'. [29] 'Classic' was, by definition, not 'national'. But the main present-day target was Baronial, which Anderson, in two papers of 1889 and 1901, attacked as a false combination of excessive modernity (in its large plate-glass windows) and vulgar picturesqueness ('sham castles'). Correspondingly, the eighteenth-

and nineteenth-century anti-classical interpretation of the Scottish Renaissance was pushed to an extreme, and augmented by an element of moralising rationalism common to all European 'national romantic' movements of this era. Anderson followed Billings in arguing that the houses of the fifteenth, sixteenth and seventeenth centuries were not designed for any conscious visual effect: 'everything is built for the purpose of keeping out intruders'. But the results of this were praised for a new reason – that of social morality. In polarised terms, the Scottish Renaissance was acclaimed as 'true' rather than 'false' art, 'produced as in nature': here we recall Anderson's earlier involvement with Episcopal ecclesiological architecture. It displayed 'natural dignity, not artificial picturesqueness', and 'functional truth'. And for this reason, it was 'thoroughly national in character'. [30] As David McGibbon put it in 1889, Scottish architecture up to the seventeenth century was 'peculiarly and markedly national'. [31]

The polarisation against Scotch Baronial, so sharp in Anderson's rhetoric, was less clear in his architectural designs. His most influential domestic project, as noted by McKinstry, was built as early as 1879–82: his own villa in Colinton, 'Allermuir' [7.23]. Its basic elements were derived directly from the smaller-scale, cheaper

7.23 'Allermuir', Colinton (R. Rowand Anderson, 1879–82); photograph of *c*.1900, showing Anderson playing golf in his garden.

Baronial houses we encountered in Chapter 6, with their sash-and-case windows and rubble walling, and their absence of ornamental excrescences: for instance, Bryce's Stronvar (1850) and Shambellie (1856) [cf. 6.32]. In more recent designs such as Wardrop's Kinnordy (1879), the later Scottish Renaissance of seventeenth-century houses such as Pinkie was being openly evoked. Anderson now proceeded to apply this plainer variant of Baronial to the design of an avant-garde 'artistic' villa. Built of pinkish, rock-faced rubble, the impression conveyed by Allermuir was one of heavy sobriety, shorn of skyline trimmings and sharp edges. There was a bay window, crowned not by a corbelled gable but by a piended roof; it was set asymmetrically below a big crowstepped gable. The quotation of Pinkie was ironic, given Seton's own seventeenth-century Stoic affectations of 'cottage'-like modesty [cf. 2.21].

Internally, the 'comfort' of the 'artistic' house resulted not only from the avoidance of even and bright daylighting, and from the studiedly plain, bulky panelling and woodwork, but also from another factor. Where Scott Morton had boasted that the new, sumptuously eclectic interior of 25 Learmonth Terrace had been executed entirely by Scots tradesmen, the 'national' and 'artistic' character of the interior of Allermuir was dominated instead by the collecting of 'antiques', including pre-industrial, archaic-looking furniture and other items (such as tapestries and china), both from Scotland and from certain other countries. A party of Edinburgh Architectural Association visitors to Pinkie in 1883 had admired the interior, especially the 'antique moveables', including old china, [32] and Anderson rapidly made Allermuir the home of a formidable blue china collection. This approach, as we saw in Chapter 5, stemmed from Scott's work at Abbotsford, and had more recently been elaborated in Patrick Allan Fraser's interiors at Hospitalfield [cf. 5.48]. The most immediate influence on it was the new Aesthetic Movement contributed to by Cottier, but perfected in England and America; this drew inspiration eclectically both from the Middle Ages and from Japan. The new type of room avoided the 'clutter' of modern-looking ornament and furniture, and was furnished either with actual antiques or with new pieces that looked like antiques. The latter

were increasingly provided by the 'Edinburgh School' – a generation of craftsmen and women trained at Anderson's School of Applied Art from the 1890s – and snapped up by firms such as Scott Morton, Whytock & Reid, and Thomas Hadden, who specialised in fitting out and furnishing 'artistic' interiors.

Despite previous efforts such as Leiper's own plain gabled house in Helensburgh (Terpersie, 1871), or his Coll-Earn, Auchterarder (1869), Allermuir immediately became the most influential exemplar of the 'artistic' villa in the new Scots Renaissance style. The reason for this was chiefly the impact made by Anderson's drawings for it at the Royal Scottish Academy in 1880. One reviewer noted that they 'show all the artist, and none of the speculator who ministers to popular taste'; the house, he said, had banished Baronial's 'gaping oriels filled with plate glass' in favour of darker apartments. [33] The avoidance of big windows and machine ornament was also more archaeologically accurate – but, as we saw with Anderson's conception of 'functional' design for defence, historical accuracy was exploited selectively by Traditionalists.

During the 1880s and early 1890s, a growing number of key architects in the east embraced the ideal of the 'artistic' bourgeois villa. In 1886, for example, Kinross built a bright-red sandstone house, with bellcast roof, at 1 Cluny Gardens, Edinburgh. By the turn of the century, there was a wealth of mature examples – heirs to the elaboration and logic of planning of their larger predecessors in the age of Burn and Bryce (for example in their segregation of public and private, or their embrace of domestic technology) but more compact, lacking the mid-nineteenth century's extended wings and corridors [cf. 5.34]. Continuity with the past was also maintained by the general Scottish aversion to the living-halls and open-planning tendencies of America and England. There is no space here to explore at length the many local variants. The movement should be seen in the context of the continuing growth of middle-class suburbs, fed by railway branches. The principal villa work of eastern architects of national status, such as Mitchell, Kinross, Browne and Peddie, D. & F. Jerdan, or Deas, is found in outer-suburban Edinburgh and in exclusive, rail-accessible towns such as North Berwick. In other eastern and northern centres, there was no shortage of designers skilled in informal villa design: for instance, A. Marshall Mackenzie and George Coutts in Aberdeen, C. G. Soutar and Thoms & Wilkie in Dundee, W. L. Carruthers in Inverness, W. R. Davidson in Nairn, William Kerr in Alloa. In the west, with its equivalent villa suburbs in Glasgow, and commuter settlements such as Kilmacolm and Troon (Southwood), the architectural position was somewhat different: we will return shortly to the Scots Renaissance domestic work of Burnet and Campbell, as well as others such as Leiper, Paterson, Clifford, Salmon, and J. A. Morris (of Ayr). The influence of 'artistic' ideas was also seen in the design of country houses; building by landowners continued during this period, although at a reduced (and declining) level compared to previous decades.

By the turn of the century, the most articulate and successful exponent of the 'cult of the house' in the east was Robert S. Lorimer [7.24]. He had previously worked as pupil or assistant to architects such as Hew Wardrop, Maclaren and Anderson himself. An astute self-publicist, Lorimer applied the new approach not only to new projects, in a series of plain, harled villas beginning with the gabled The Grange, North Berwick (1893), but also in restorations of old houses, beginning with Earlshall in 1890–4 and culminating with Balmanno in 1916 [7.25]; the Lorimer family's childhood home, Kellie Castle, had already been cautiously restored in 1878 by Lorimer's father, to the designs of John Currie of Elie. Savage's book chronicles the record of Lorimer's personal ideas and reactions, contained in the letters to his friend R. S. Dods. His own work, Lorimer declared, was founded on a reaction against 'the ordinary rush of things'. The Glasgow commercial work of architects such as Burnet and Campbell, in its open embrace of urban modernity, was anathema to him: 'You never saw such vulgar stuff, or such hurriedly thought out stuff . . . they have to be rushed up . . . all the floors were the same height' [cf. 7.7, 7.10]. Such 'modern buildings' were 'crowded with unsuitable, meaningless ornaments', and their architects 'get in a very big way' but soon 'go to utter seed'. [34] Like Anderson, he

7.24 R. S. Lorimer, early twentieth-century photograph.

rejected the concept of a continuous Scottish classical tradition, disparaging the New Town and referring to himself as a 'Gothic' man. Being a 'Goth' involved rejecting 'classic' regularity for a philosophy of 'no repeats'. Architects in the east who embraced sumptuous classicism at the turn of the century, were also suspect: Lorimer disparaged Kinross's 'rich and nouveau-riche Louis Quinzery filth'. [35] By contrast with Burnet's prosaic definition of the architect's task, Lorimer's definition was more vague and complex. The architect had to act as a conduit which would allow a building's essence to emerge. 'The old thing, simplicity' meant the ability 'to leave things alone in detail'. The only solution was to design buildings in 'my sort of way so they don't fall down', which involved 'setting definite limitations to yourself'. [36]

According to Lorimer, a house must evoke a unified image of exterior (including garden) and interior (including antiques) – an image grounded in what were thought to be the social values of the Scottish Renaissance golden age, and especially of Bruce's era of Restoration classicism. The aristocratic connotations of this ideal would serve both to ennoble designs for bourgeois clients, and

7.25 Earlshall, Fife, bird's-eye view of Lorimer's rebuilding scheme, drawn by John Begg *c.*1893, and exhibited at the Royal Scottish Academy in 1896. The garden was executed in a modified form.

maintain an appropriate decorum in houses for landowners. Lorimer eulogised Balcaskie as 'the ideal of what a Scotch gentleman's home ought to be . . . dignified and yet liveable, spacious, lofty rooms, lovely plastered ceilings, where the "great parquetted, sparely furnished room of many windows" looks out on to a garden . . . that is an intentional and deliberate piece of careful design'. Unlike the 'naked tameness' of a house standing on a lawn, the walled garden was a 'sanctuary', a 'chamber roofed by heaven'. The demand for unity also applied to individual rooms: 'When you go into a room first it ought to give you a sort of total impression . . . of colour or light and shade, or of charm and lucid order.' (37) The same ethical-rationalistic principles applied to the associated crafts. Lorimer's preferred collaborators were people like the artist Phoebe Traquair: 'so sane, such a lover of simplicity, and . . . the simplest things of nature . . . without a trace of self consciousness!' (38) In furniture, the task was to avoid 'imitation' of period styles, and 'ask yourself what is the thing for – make it the most beautiful shape . . . to show its utmost beauty of grain and texture.' (39) At Earlshall, commissioned by the art collector, R. W. R. Mackenzie, Lorimer employed a local joiner to make archaic-looking furniture, and copied Kinross's reconstructed Falkland screen. But after that, travelling on the Continent with his friend, the millionaire collector William Burrell, he developed an eclectic approach to interior design. His restored or new houses contained actual antiques and tapestries (as at Balmanno or Formakin), or, for non-collector clients, package-deal interiors of imitation antiques. He remodelled his own New Town house, 54 Melville Street (in 1903), expunging the early nineteenth century through refenestration, seventeenth-century-style panelling and tapestries. In 1901, Lorimer described his ideal drawing room in robust Traditionalist language. Furniture would be of 'the simplest form. . . warm in colour'. China must be confined to 'some good big things, and simple . . . very few nick nacks lying about . . . not much on the walls . . . no feeling of the curiosity shop'. The room should be used informally by 'people forming themselves into groups at the various sofas' and 'should really look as if it was used'. The ideal, in short, was 'perfect fitness'. (40)

'Scotch' Monumentality: Harl and Rubble

While the first phase of the movement in house architecture pioneered by Anderson insisted on a demure reticence, there was a parallel trend, especially in the west, which treated the Scots Renaissance in a rougher or more assertively monumental manner, in the design of both houses and public buildings. The years when this movement reached its climax were the years of most fervent Scots commitment to a bellicose imperialism: the ending of the siege of Mafeking in May 1900, for instance, prompted mass celebrations on the streets of all four cities, and even in Crieff an effigy of President Kruger was burned in James Square.

The first signs of this new, more monumental Traditionalism came with the return to favour of harling from the 1880s. Up to the late nineteenth century, the use of harling on domestic buildings had previously been a sign of economy or low status. But by the time of James Nicoll's illustrated survey of 1908, *Domestic Architecture in Scotland*, the position had changed. He scorned the 'stodgy respectability' of late nineteenth-century villas built in local freestone. The best way to get 'more individuality and more sanity in our modern houses' was through brighter colours, and above all through harling, which was used in 70 per cent of the buildings he illustrated, and which had the great advantage, Nicoll noted, that it could be used in 'any locality'. The beginning of this revival in the status of harling was a largely non-urban phenomenon. Wardrop, Anderson & Browne's extensions to Tilliefour (1885–6, Lorimer was site architect) were low, plain and crowstepped, with small-paned windows – as was Anderson's Queens Hall, Charlestown (1887). James M. Maclaren, a Glasgow-trained architect based in London, built several projects for harled buildings in rural Perthshire: the Glenlyon farm buildings (1889–91) and the gabled, neo-Romanesque Aberfeldy Town Hall (1889–90) – in which, also, the influence of H. H. Richardson was very marked [7.26]. The harled primitivism of Maclaren and his successors, Dunn & Watson, was creatively developed by a number of designers. For example, in 1892, Mitchell & Wilson built a harled villa with massive

7.26 Aberfeldy Town Hall (James M. Maclaren, 1889–90). For comparison with H. H. Richardson's work, see for example North Easton Town Hall, published 1883 in the *British Architect*.

7.27 Barnbougle Castle, unexecuted scheme by Sydney Mitchell & Wilson for rebuilding in the style of Linlithgow Palace, 1889.

curvilinear gables at 2 South Lauder Road, Edinburgh; we will deal later with the even more notable contributions of Lorimer and Mackintosh. Maclaren's style was copied in a more literal manner in several works by other London-based or English Arts and Crafts designers – for instance R. W. Schultz's Scoulag Lodge, Bute (1898) and W. Lethaby's Melsetter (1898–1900).

The other monumentalising interpretation of Scots Renaissance involved the use of rough, especially rock-faced rubble. Like harling, this had been a utilitarian method during the mid-nineteenth century, associated especially with industrial and rural structures, as well as some churches. But the 1880s extended its scope not only to middle-class villas like Allermuir but also to prestigious public buildings and country houses. As in Germany during those years, rubble building allowed Traditionalists to become involved in the designing of stone-built monumental projects, particularly those associated with Scottish imperial themes, while remaining true to their image of archaic roughness. In this area, too, the influence of both Maclaren and Richardson was felt: Maclaren's Stirling High School (1887–8) perched a heavy stone tower and lower wing on a sharply sloping site.

The first association between rock-faced plasticity and imperial Scots symbolism had been several decades earlier, in the National Wallace Monument [cf. 6.34]. But that was a largely isolated setpiece. It was only in the late 1880s, when the wide acceptance of British 'manifest destiny' further inflated the established concept of the nation as an 'imperial partner', that this association began to be consistently made. Its first architectural manifestation in this period was the most startling: an 1889 proposal for the enlargement of Barnbougle Castle into an expanded version of Linlithgow Palace, complete with heightened towers and Stirling Great Hall bay windows [7.27; cf. 1.7, 4.11]. The architect for this unrealised scheme was Sydney Mitchell, and the client was the 5th Earl of Rosebery, later Prime Minister (1894–5) and one of the most ardent imperialist spokesmen during the Boer War. During those years, Mitchell & Wilson built a whole series of rubble palace-houses, laden with Stewart imperial imagery: Sauchieburn (1889–90); Duntreath (1889, an enlargement with courtyard and twin-turreted, towered entrance range); and the five-storey block of Glenborrodale (1898–1902). An earlier and more domestic version, but with crowstepped gables, was Mitchell's reconstruction of Leithen Lodge, Innerleithen, in 1885–7. He and Wilson also built Edinburgh University Students' Union (1887–8) as a palace-block with Holyrood-type towers.

Across the whole range of domestic architecture, down to medium-sized works, the years around the turn of the century saw an increasing attention to the theatrical potential of Scots Renaissance. This almost amounted to a selective revival of Scotch Baronial, avoiding the latter's hard-edged, large-windowed precision and small-

scale added ornament – although a group of four houses by Kinross at Mortonhall Road, Edinburgh (1898), including the architect's own house, went so far as to resurrect Brycean corbelled-out gables. The towered rhetoric of Mitchell & Wilson was reflected in work such as Thoms & Wilkie's twin-towered Kinpurnie Castle (1908–11), J. N. Scott and A. Lorne Campbell's Grange, Linlithgow (1904–9), and in the rubble and harled block of Niven & Wigglesworth's Kincardine (1894–1906), with its opulent Baroque porch. By 1908, Nicoll's _Domestic Architecture_ was able to show, alongside the plainer, harled houses and 'Old English' villas, a full range of designs in what he referred to as the 'Scottish national style'.

During the same decade, even Lorimer soon grew impatient with the demure quietness of his early houses and restorations. In an unrealised rebuilding scheme for Newark Castle (1898), he boasted of 'my great vista'. [41] And in projects at Rowallan (1902) and Ardkinglas (1905–1907), he developed a more monumental manner of bare rubble walls, archaic classicising detail and rounded, integral massing: he referred to this as his 'Scotch' style. The plans of these houses, with their first-floor principal apartments, were equally intended to evoke the Scots Renaissance. The tension between monumental assertion and Traditionalist restraint reached an extreme at Formakin (1912–14), built for a rich connoisseur

and horticulturalist, the Paisley stockbroker John A. Holms [7.28]. An austere, almost primitive exterior, with punched-in apertures and thick-jointed rubble – 'the purest Scotch I've ever done', Lorimer asserted [42] – was combined with a meticulous gradualness of construction, reminiscent of Lorimer's larger tower-house restorations (for example Dunderave, from 1911). Formakin's internal climax was a first-floor great chamber built to display a set of fifteenth-century tapestries. Elsewhere, Lorimer interpreted the Scots Renaissance more aggressively in his unbuilt triumphal arch project (1911) for the King Edward Memorial, Edinburgh – some of whose characteristics, such as the Stirling-type archway,

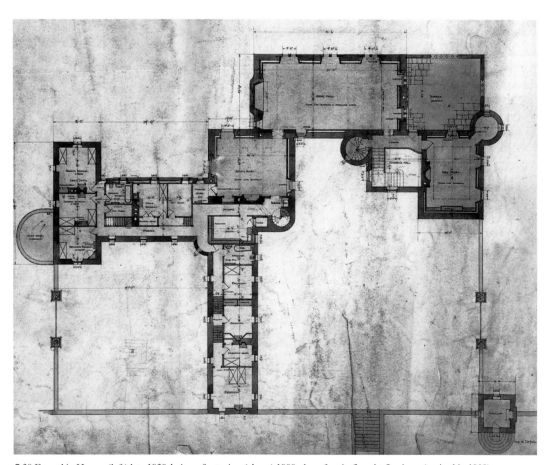

7.28 Formakin House: (left) late 1920s' view of exterior; (above) 1908 plan of main floor by Lorimer (revised in 1910).

were eventually realised in the Scottish National War Memorial project after the war [cf. 8.1, 8.2, 8.3, C.3].

So far, our discussion of the 'cult of the house' and its offshoots has overwhelmingly focused on the east. In the west, the morally charged utopian ideas of Traditionalism never took general hold – although it was reflected in some notable instances, such as A. N. Paterson's own house, the low, turreted Longcroft, Helensburgh (1901), with its many craftsmanlike interior features. J. J. Stevenson, writing from London in 1880, attacked the 'wild' Baronialism of the Wallace Monument [cf. 6.34]. [43] But the reaction of most architects in the west away from Baronial, towards more 'artistic' Scots Renaissance houses, took a more scenographic form – equivalent to the skyscraper-Baroque of Burnet & Campbell's city-centre work, and, even, to some aspects of Baronial itself. Already, the work of Leiper from the 1870s had seen a trend away from the bristling François Ier detail of Cairndhu (1871, with its lavish Aesthetic interiors) towards a heavier style: at Coll-Earn (1869–70), Dalmore (1873), Kinlochmoidart (1883) and the harled Auchenbothie (1898) [7.29]. One writer in 1898 argued that at Dalmore

7.29 Dalmore, Helensburgh (Leiper, 1873): 1993 view.

> may be found the work of the mature artist, able to seize and reproduce the spirit of the old work, its picturesque skyline, combined with the dignified simplicity of wall-spaces, while at the same time adapting it without loss of effect to modern require-ments in matters of ample light and a liberal use of bow-windows, a very different thing to the lover of Scottish architecture from the affectation of crow-steps and meaningless turrets. [44]

Leiper's innovations in house design were developed by Burnet & Campbell, who devised a Scots Renaissance style imbued with a Baroque panache. They designed a series of works of country house scale which began with the enlargement of Auchterarder House (in 1886–7), continued with Baronald (1889–91) and Garmoyle (1890), and culminated in Burnet's grandiose rebuilding of John Douglas's Finlaystone for a Clyde shipowner (1898–1903, with stair hall dominated by two giant Roman Doric columns). At the harled Fairnilee (1904–6), Burnet replaced Lorimer, who had refused to alter an existing

sixteenth-century castle on the site. There was also a period, around 1890, when Burnet & Campbell were influenced by American trends, including the work of Richardson and the Shingle Style. The sweeping breadth of the latter was reflected in a series of projects, including Corrienessan (1886, by Burnet) and the unbuilt Clyde Yacht Club-house design of 1889. After 1900, some villa designs in the west exaggerated the element of rubble archaism: for instance C. R. Mackintosh's Mosside, Kilmacolm (1906), with heavy walls dotted with arched openings; and J. Ednie's 11 Whittingehame Drive, Glasgow (1907), with rubbly gable and Art Nouveau detailing.

From the 1890s, this relatively exuberant and monumental Scots Renaissance style was extended to other secular building types by architects in the west. Burnet and Campbell, for example, designed the Glasgow Western Infirmary Pathology Building (1894), Alloa Baths (1895), and Campbeltown Library and Museum (1897–8, by Burnet alone), while the main facade of H. & D. Barclay's Jordanhill College, Glasgow (1913–22), echoed the west front of St Machar's Cathedral in a simplified form. In 1896–1900, T. G. Abercrombie built Paisley's Royal Alexandra Infirmary in the form of a keep with wings. During the 1880s and 1890s, rubble massiveness also spread to municipal buildings. Following the precedent of Sellars's Couper Institute (1887), H. E. Clifford's Pollokshields Burgh Hall (1888–90) [7.30] and Burnet & Campbell's Ewing Gilmour Institute (1888–91), all of which combined towers and seventeenth-/eighteenth-century townhouse-style wings into asymmetrical 'multi-period' ensembles – Anderson inflated his plain, crowstepped classical style into this more imposing mode at Pollokshaws Burgh Buildings (1895–8) and at the complex Pearce Institute, Govan (1892–1906) [cf. C.10]. From 1904 to 1914, under the aegis of Principal Architect W. T. Oldrieve (a former Baldwin Brown pupil), government buildings across the whole country became a redoubt of the new monumental variant of Scots Renaissance. Oldrieve's post-offices are usually asymmetrical compositions, often with a large crowstepped gable, but occasionally more ambitious, as at the drum-towered Aberdeen Head Post Office of 1907 [7.31]. In 1912, he prepared abortive designs for government offices on Calton Hill in a towered imperial Stewart style.

In 1901, a new edition of Billings was published. Anderson wrote the introduction, which repeated his contrast between the 'sham castles' of Baronial and the supposedly unselfconscious 'functional

truth' of the Renaissance originals, which were to be prototypes for the new 'national architecture'. The most grandiose Imperial Scots Renaissance design for a social institution was a school for soldiers' children – Queen Victoria Memorial School, Dunblane (1907–8) – built to commemorate the monarch and Scottish soldiers killed in the Boer War; its designer was J. A. Campbell [7.32]. It combined crowstepped gables with Thomsonian gridded fenestration on the main frontage; the chapel had a St Monans-like spire and King's College window.

The preoccupation with the imperial variant of Scots Renaissance came to a climax in 1911. This was the year of the Scottish Exhibition of National History, Art and Industry, in Glasgow, designed by R. J. Walker (assistant to Miller in 1901) [7.33]. Here, History displaced Industry: the chief aim was to finance a chair of Scottish History at Glasgow University. The 'fantastic . . . bizarre' classicism of previous exhibitions was banished in favour of 'thick-set, broad-shouldered . . . essentially Scottish' buildings inspired by Stewart palaces, as well as an 'Auld Toun', and a Highland settlement group, the 'humble, realistic' *An Clachan*, designed by Dr Colin Sinclair. [45] The years after 1910 also saw the climax of another

7.30 Pollokshields Burgh Hall (H. E. Clifford, 1888–90).

7.31 Aberdeen Head Post Office (completed 1907; W. T. Oldrieve, government Principal Architect; drawings by J. Cumming Wyness).

7.32 Queen Victoria Memorial School, Dunblane (by J. A. Campbell), view after completion in 1908.

The Fine Arts Building.

7.33 Scottish Exhibition of National History, Art and Industry, Kelvingrove, Glasgow, 1911 (by R. J. Walker), contemporary view of the Fine Arts Building.

grandiose fashion, namely the 'restoration' of fantasy castles in rock-faced rubble. Already a similar tendency, driven by imperial nationalism, had flourished in Germany, where Kaiser Wilhelm II commissioned Bodo Ebhardt to reconstruct Hohkönigsburg, Alsace (1899–1908). The fashion for exposed rubble in restoration, already visible in the stripping of harl from Brodie in the 1870s, had taken on a more assertive edge by the time of Lorimer's Newark proposals of 1898. By then, the remodelling of Edinburgh Castle from a Georgian barracks to a focus of Scots imperialist symbolism, first prefigured in Colonel Moody's 1859 project, was under way [cf. 6.35]. From 1886, many of its structures were subjected to a Baronialising reconstruction by Hippolyte Blanc. Soon Lorimer, alongside his continuing conservative restorations (such as Balmanno), began a fashion for the radical stripping-out of Baronial features in favour of a rougher rubble finish: for instance, at Lennoxlove (1912–14). From now on the phase of castle re-creation began in earnest. Already in 1883 Andrew Kerr had reroofed Doune Castle for the Earl of Moray, and in 1897–1902, Schultz had rebuilt the

ruined Wester Kames Tower for the 3rd Marquess of Bute. Now a series of larger schemes started: for example, Burnet's Duart (1911–16), or Dean (a prolonged campaign of 30 years, from 1905, by the 8th Lord Howard, to the designs of Ingram & Brown, and J. S. Richardson). The most ambitious was Major John MacRae-Gilstrap's £250,000 scheme to convert Eilean Donan Castle (from 1913–32) from a ruined stump to a huge, block-like complex, in rubble inside and out, designed by Edinburgh architect George Mackie Watson (a former Anderson assistant) [7.34; cf. C.14].

The Imperial Scots Renaissance, in its original form of 'manifest-destiny' confidence, ended with World War I. Before that, there were already hints of a revised conception of national identity, in terms of an 'essence' under threat, which was to be typical of the interwar years. In 1911, the winning of Edinburgh's Usher Hall competition by the classical design of an English architect (J. Stockdale Harrison) led to an outcry that 'national' qualities were being suffocated. However, there was a continuing echo of imperialism in the 'Château Style' used for early twentieth-century state

7.34 Eilean Donan Castle, as rebuilt and expanded 1913-32 (G. M. Watson), including war memorial in foreground.

buildings in Canada – at the same time as an outpost of the 'cult of the house' was established at McGill University, Montréal, by a succession of professors from Edinburgh: Henbest Capper (from 1896–1907), the Lorimer-trained P. E. Nobbs (1907–12), and Ramsay Traquair (from 1912).

'Old Edinburgh': The Rise of Social Traditionalism

In contrast to the sometimes hectoring assertiveness of turn-of-the-century 'Scotch' architecture, another contemporary variant of Traditionalism pursued large scale and monumentality for a completely different purpose: the 'artistic' reform of working-class housing, and of the city as a whole, in the belief that one source of golden-age Scottish harmony had been the collective values of burgh community. Here the doctrine of the ennoblement of the ordinary home, applied by Anderson, Lorimer and the others chiefly to bourgeois villas, was for the first time tentatively extended into the field of working-class dwellings. In contrast to the earlier rationalistic debates in Glasgow about tenemental versus

cottage reform solutions, the romantic turn-of-the-century attempt to encompass tenement dwellings within the scope of the ideal of the 'artistic house' was largely an Edinburgh matter – although, in Glasgow, a Baronial railway village had been designed by Heiton at Springburn in 1863, and there were later essays by Burnet at Cathedral Court (1891–2) and Greenhead Court (1897–9), for the Glasgow Workmen's Dwellings Company, and by Burnet, Boston & Carruthers for Scots Renaissance tenements flanking the High Street (1901–3).

The focus of this emergent tendency of 'artistic' social housing, during the 1880–1914 period, was the 'Old Edinburgh' movement: an admiration of the dilapidated Old Town of Edinburgh, inspired by the writings of Scott and Robert Louis Stevenson. Just as with the 'Tenement Revival' of the later twentieth century, the characteristics previously most reviled now became the subject of utopian admiration: a 'very metropolis of squalor, yet likewise of Romance'. This new movement defined itself by opposition chiefly to the classicism of the 'regular and utilitarian modern New Town': [46] in 1889 the Marquess of Lorne attacked 'facades which look as if they were all punched out of grey paper with one machine'. [47] However, as we noted above, there was already the beginning of a revival in the public esteem of the New Town. Robert Louis Stevenson extended the growing artistic prestige of the Old Town to embrace the New: 'The two re-act in a picturesque sense, and the one is the making of the other'; in site and layout, 'how much description would apply commonly to either'. He put forward a new *bête noire*: the 'deformity' and 'monstrosity' of suburban villa development. [48]

In the field of new architecture, the Old Edinburgh concept sprang into life almost fully formed in 1883, in what was probably the most remarkable of Sydney Mitchell's prolific works: Well Court, Edinburgh – a complex of working-class tenements commissioned by *Scotsman* publisher J. R. Findlay [7.35]. Well Court was a microcosm of advanced architectural ideas about housing reform: a sanitary slum redevelopment of emphatically 'artistic' character, taking the form not of scattered cottages but of a dense block, with communal facilities, arranged around a garden courtyard. Its picturesque grouping, steep roofs and small windows (designed to be viewed at its most dramatic from Findlay's own, Mitchell-designed house across the Water of Leith) seemed to resemble old Germanic walled cities rather than Old Edinburgh, and, more immediately, recalled some work of Richard Norman Shaw (for example the Bradford Exchange proposal of 1864). But it also incorporated, ready for transmission onward into twentieth-century social housing design, centuries-old features of Scots tenement architecture, such as paired windows. Mitchell's developing style became more specific to Old Edinburgh in the display of that name at the 1886 Edinburgh International Exhibition [7.36, 7.37]. The notion of a replica old city to recall the national past, pioneered only thirteen years earlier at the Vienna world's fair, and expanded later in the 1911 Glasgow Exhibition, was here carried through with Mitchell's usual confidence. In 1885, he had already restored the Mercat Cross in the real High Street. Now he designed a microcosm of the High Street in earlier days, containing recreations - slightly miniaturised, and peopled with authentically clad actors – of the vanished Old Town landmarks recently celebrated in

Stevenson's novels. The spiny skyline of Mitchell's miniature city was bizarrely embedded in the rear section of Burnet's overall glazed roof.

These scenographic images of urban community seemed to anticipate the doctrine of enclosed, 'artistic' townscape propagated in Vienna from 1889 by Camillo Sitte. But the most important immediate effect of the 1886 display was the deep impression it made on the man who would actually begin the revitalisation of Old Edinburgh: the socio-biologist and pioneering city planner Patrick Geddes. There is no space here for any general account of Geddes's vast and variegated activity, nor even of his attempts to describe cities and their regions through techniques of systematic social and spatial analysis – an approach, symbolised by his remodelling of the Castlehill Outlook Tower, which would ultimately bear fruit not only in Scotland but across the world. What concerns us here is his decisive intervention in the urban Traditionalist movement in Edinburgh. Already in 1883, for reasons of patriotism and civic pride, and inspired by Scott and Stevenson's romanticism and, doubtless, by the building of Well Court, Geddes had decided to try to revive the eighteenth-century 'Golden Age' of Edinburgh University and Old Town. Seeking to integrate art and science, he saw the Old Town, in its present slum-ridden state, as a diseased organism which could be regenerated. He thought it essential that this should be done by spatial means – through an actual physical recuperation of the Old Town fabric. In this, he was motivated not by socialist desire to abolish poverty, but by the cultural aim of reviving the capital's glory, by infusing the Old Town with academic community life. In support of this aim, he took to an extreme the Andersonian language of golden-age harmony, adding to it a declamatory 'organic' rhetoric which anticipated some of the Traditionalist catch-phrases of the 1930s. Old Edinburgh was to experience a 'rebirth', a 'renewed harmony', a 'reunion of Democracy and Culture', a 'still deeper sign of . . . Renascence', 'a rebuilding of analysis into synthesis, an integration of the narrow window of the individual outlook for the open tower which overlooks college and city'. [49]

After some attempts (from 1884) at tackling the problem collaboratively, through agencies such as

7.35 Well Court, Edinburgh (Mitchell, 1883) 1880s' perspectives and plan.

In the Court

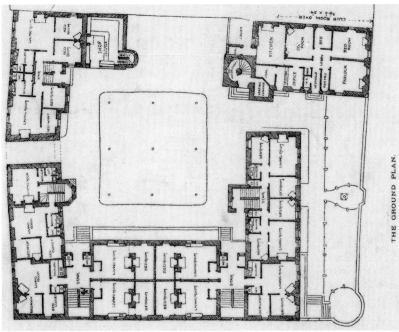

THE GROUND PLAN.

CLUB ROOM OVER
36·6 × 24

SHOP

KITCHEN

PARLOUR

BED
ROOM

BED

7.36 'Old Edinburgh' section of 1886 Edinburgh Exhibition (Mitchell), view of street and 'Netherbow Port' exhibit.

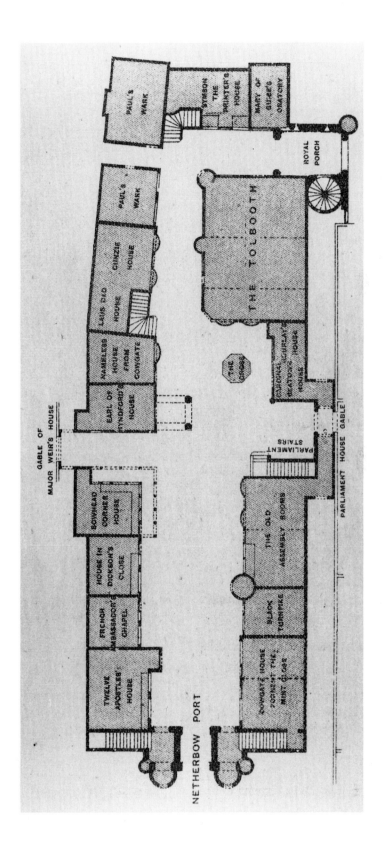

7.37 Plan of 'Old Edinburgh' section of 1886 exhibition.

the Edinburgh Social Union, Geddes set out to carry through this plan himself, along with a few key helpers, such as his future son-in-law Frank Mears. Drawing on his lifelong love of property speculation, he began to buy decayed tenements and undeveloped sites, and commenced a rolling programme of 'conservative surgery', designed to revitalise the Old Town as a 'university city'. The City Improvement Acts' sweeping demolitions and remodelling he branded 'civic ruin': 'We shall not get art . . . by piling up colossal rabbit hutches'. [50] Some blocks Geddes improved as working-class dwellings. Here the aim was less housing reform than to remedy the 'artistic ineptitude' of the working class: 'What we want is Centres of Life'. [51] Others were converted to university halls. The reconditioned blocks were ornamented with picturesque timber outshots, and interspersed with 'reclaimed' garden spaces. In his journal, *Evergreen*, Geddes likened (1895) the 'renascent

capital' to a 'phoenix' rising: it would once again become 'one of the European powers of culture'.

Geddes's most spectacular building achievement was the Ramsay Gardens development overlooking the Castle Esplanade [7.38]. Here he employed Henbest Capper (from 1892) and Sydney Mitchell (from 1893) to expand existing buildings, including Allan Ramsay's villa, into a soaring, turret-encrusted fantasy. The dramatic style of Well Court (which Geddes identified in 1889 as the 'best modern addition' to the 'old city') was adapted in harl with stone dressings [cf. 7.35]. Ramsay Garden contained a mixture of university halls and large flats (including Geddes's own) intended for collegiate living by students and intellectuals. Also included in the project, as a counter to Anderson's pragmatic, history-based design course at his new Edinburgh School, was the establishment of an Old Edinburgh School of Art, which harnessed the capital's burgeoning

7.38 Ramsay Garden, Edinburgh, view of section designed by Sydney Mitchell (1892–4).

school of Celtic symbolist designers and mural painters, such as Phoebe Traquair (then executing her renowned mural scheme at Anderson's Catholic Apostolic Church) and John Duncan [cf. 7.52]. In 1894, Geddes described Ramsay Garden as 'not indeed, happily, a New, but a renewed Old Town'. (52)

Geddes's activities in Old Edinburgh closely paralleled the turn-of-the-century concept of 'artistic' urban regeneration popular in several continental countries – for example, in the philosophy of 'diridamento' practised in Rome from *c.*1913 by that city's 'Artistic Association'. In these countries, inner urban rehabilitation was usually seen in parallel to a radically different regenerative policy: the building of low-density garden suburbs or garden cities outside the urban area. In Germany especially, 1890s reformists began to see historic urban conservation as part of a comprehensive system of land regulation and reordering that would ensure the abolition of 'barracks-tenements' and the regeneration of rural areas through mass colonisation. In Scotland, the folk or peasant romanticism which informed Central European efforts was lacking. But the simple harled style of Maclaren's Glenlyon buildings was taken up by Lorimer from 1893, in the design of small bohemian villas in the Edinburgh suburb of Colinton. Around 1900, this 'Colinton Manner' (as Lorimer called it) and the growing middle-class predilection for the single-storey bungalow began to merge: for instance, in G. Fordyce's 'The Chalet', 4 Anderson Drive, Aberdeen (1902), where rock-faced granite was combined with a low and massive grouping. What is of more importance here is the application of the 'artistic' simple cottage style to low-density working-class housing. The later 1890s saw numerous small initiatives: by Lorimer, for instance, an unrealised project for cottages at Inveralmond (1899), and, in 1900–2, an artisans' group at Colinton ('Rustic Cottages'); or by Peddie, in 1895–6, a harled miners' terrace of flats, with exaggeratedly simplified Baroque doorcases, at Philpingstone Terrace, Bo'ness. From 1902, Geddes himself commenced a terraced garden-suburb development at Roseburn Cliff. But these small initiatives were hardly different from Gowans's Rosebank Cottages of 1854. The impulse

towards large-scale garden city development in Scotland, as in Germany, only began in earnest in the mid-1900s, ushering in an ascendancy of over twenty years in housing debates. The focus of this campaign was the pressure for a workers' garden city at the new military base at Rosyth, built by the government as part of the pre-war naval race with Germany. By 1909, the progress of English and German garden city construction had not only won the support of the rising Labour Party, but had convinced even Geddes that the main thrust of sanitary working-class housebuilding must be in the form of garden city cottages. Rosyth, built from 1914, and a Clydeside equivalent at Westerton (1912–15) would serve as training-grounds for a generation of Scots garden suburb architects, such as A. H. Mottram (Rosyth) and J. A.W. Grant (Westerton). Chapters 8 and 9 will trace the fluctuating fortunes of this strategy of working-class population dispersal.

Linked with ideas of dispersal in social housing and of images of the cottage-like 'home' were developments in health planning. We noted above the tendency in some hospitals towards more spread-out layouts – for instance, at Thomson & Sandilands' Stobhill (1901–4) or A. B. McDonald's Ruchill (1895–1900), both with rows of pavilions and central tower. Bridge of Weir Orphan Colony, built by William Quarrier after 1876, had followed a similar pattern. In asylums, the new colony plan of dispersed pavilions reflected a desire both for more specialised categorisation of patients and also, in the words of John Sibbald, a Commissioner for Lunacy (1897), for an atmosphere of 'private houses . . . ' of having a home not of inordinate size'. (53) Pioneering examples were built by Sydney Mitchell: his father was a Depute Commissioner to the Board of Lunacy. In complexes such as New Craig House, Edinburgh (from 1897) and Crichton Royal Hospital extension, Dumfries (from 1897), the dispersed layouts and informal architectural detail were offset by a delight in monumental massing: New Craig House, a colony for the wealthy insane, was Mitchell's *tour de force*, comprising four detached residential 'villas' and a palatial central services building, 375 feet in length, containing an arched hall of great splendour [7.39]. There was a similar hybrid plan at Thomson & Sandilands' Gartloch

7.39 New Craig House, Royal Edinburgh Asylum (Mitchell, from 1889): (above) central building; (right) *c*.1900 view of hall.

(1890–7), a symmetrical, towered Baronial composition with some dispersed annexes. A full-blown colony plan emerged at Bangour, West Lothian, designed by Hippolyte Blanc (competition win 1898, completed 1906).

'The Soul that Lies Beneath': The Architecture of C. R. Mackintosh

One of the key elements in the architectural reaction against capitalist society and eclectic mainstream architecture was an urge towards artistic individualism – an urge that, in Scotland, stemmed ultimately from the romanticism of Robert Adam. This tendency took its most extreme form in the 'Glasgow Style' pioneered by 'The Four': the designers Margaret and Frances Macdonald, and the two architects they later married, Charles Rennie Mackintosh and Herbert MacNair. The focus of this account is the architectural achievement of Mackintosh, in which some of the social-utopian elements of Traditionalism, notably a stress on the 'national', were combined with an avant-garde insistence on 'emotion' as the basis of art. In view of the extensive, and still growing literature on Mackintosh, there is only space here to offer a brief summary [7.40].

The central thrust of the Glasgow Style was its development of one aspect of the 'artistic house' – the ideal of interior *Gesamtkunstwerk* – to an unequalled intensity and refinement, guaranteed (in contradiction to mainstream Traditionalist ideas) not by delegation but by personal control and execution. Mackintosh's acquaintance, Hermann Muthesius, wrote in 1904 that 'The central aim. . . is the room as work of art, as a unified organic whole, embracing colour, form and

atmosphere. Starting from this notion, they develop not only the room but the whole house.' [(54)] It was his intense focus on architecture as an all-embracing art – an intensity backed, during the heyday of his career, by an indefatigable capacity for work – which set Mackintosh apart from the longer, but more diffuse careers of the other turn-of-the-century 'giants': Anderson, Burnet and Lorimer. In discussing the Glasgow Style, therefore, we will deal first with the interiors, then the exteriors, of the group's early years and 'high' turn-of-century period. Finally, we will trace the beginnings (from *c*.1905) of their partial reconciliation, and that of Traditionalism in general, with mainstream classical architecture.

The roots of the Glasgow Style of artistic interior lay, first, in the work of Whistler and of the Aesthetic Movement, which had reacted against heavily loaded decoration by insisting on a new refinement in interior design. By the 1890s, the Glasgow School of painters had established an international reputation for a style verging on Celtic symbolism, an approach increasingly reflected in Francis Newbery's liberal regime at the Glasgow School of Art, and also seen in the appointment as Dean of Architecture in 1894 of W. J. Anderson – whose own design at Napier House, Govan (1898–9) fused a Linlithgow-like massiveness with flowing Art Nouveau detail. The rise of Celtic symbolism was also seen in the 1890s' work of Edinburgh designers such as Phoebe Traquair and John Duncan. Of Mackintosh's education and early work (from 1890) as assistant to Honeyman & Keppie, we need only note his remarkable draughtsmanship and eclectic facility of design, at home alike in Free Renaissance and Beaux-Arts or Thomson-like classicism. On the one hand, he showed respect for the Glasgow classical tradition, as transmitted by Sellars, Honeyman and J. J. Burnet. On the other, he felt an excitement at the Eastern exoticism of Byzantine or Venetian mosaics: like the young Bertram Goodhue, Mackintosh was greatly influenced by the mystical writings of Lethaby. From around 1892, these threads were pulled together, when his own architectonic sensibility became allied with the neo-occult symbolism and mysticism of the Macdonald sisters, and the Glasgow Style of interior emerged.

7.40 C. R. Mackintosh, 1914 portrait by F. H. Newbery, showing the architect holding the plans for the Glasgow School of Art.

In common with Lorimer – whose work he admired – Mackintosh insisted on unity and background plainness, in opposition to mainstream eclectic 'clutter'. Nor did his practical planning or disposition of domestic layouts significantly diverge from the long-established tradition inherited from Burn and Bryce. His key difference from mainstream Traditionalism lay in the degree of intensity of the aesthetic visualisation of interiors. In contrast to Lorimer, whose spacious rooms, dotted with antiques and tapestries, seemed episodic, almost casual by comparison, Mackintosh began by creating a background of highly charged neutrality, of sweeping, elemental forms – 'a spacious, grandiose, almost mystical repose' (H. Muthesius), [55] in which sombre and brilliantly lit rooms were carefully contrasted. Against this background were set limited areas of intense decoration, such as symbolist gesso panels by Margaret Macdonald, light fittings or stencilled friezes. The picture was completed by the precise, but not symmetrical placing of furniture made by the artists themselves. The crucial series of domestic interiors began in 1899–1900: the remodelling of the Dunglass Castle drawing room, and of Mackintosh and Macdonald's house at 120 Mains Street, Glasgow (now Blythswood Street), and the building of Windyhill, Kilmacolm. Then, in 1902–4, followed Hill House, Helensburgh, for the publisher W. Blackie [7.41]. Along with these ran a notable series of tearoom interiors for Kate Cranston. At Buchanan Street (1896) and Argyle Street (1897), Mackintosh contributed, respectively, murals and furniture to an overall scheme by George Walton. At Ingram Street (1901) he and Macdonald were for the first time in charge of the remodelling, which included a staircase and white dining room. And at the Willow Tea Rooms (1903) – where he also designed the facade – their interiors included a flowing sequence of dark and light spaces on the ground floor, and culminated in the jewel-like Room de Luxe, its focal point a gesso panel by Macdonald. The climax of their interior work was their entry in a 1901 competition in the *Zeitschrift für Innendekoration* for a '*Haus eines Kunstfreundes*' [7.42]. Here Mackintosh theatrically exaggerated the traditional division between dark 'masculine' and light 'feminine' rooms. In the ruthlessly axial dining room design, a pale ceiling and floor contrasted with the gravity of vertically gridded, dark-stained wall-panels, inset with decorative rectangles. In the similarly proportioned music room, a light grey background, with sparing, asymmetrically placed furniture was offset by bright splashes of red and blue, by large symbolist panels, and by an ornate piano with baldacchino at one end.

This design, published in 1901 by Alexander Koch (and, from 1988, built in Glasgow: see Chapter 9), leads us to touch briefly on Mackintosh's continental activity. The dependence of his work on the intense and individualistic expression of 'emotion' through abstracted forms led him into contacts with the German-speaking architectural world, where the rejection of mass-produced eclectic ornament was bound up with a new concept of the expression of 'feeling' through 'form' and 'space' – destined to be one of the key elements in the complex formulas of the twentieth-century Modern Movement. This was the first and only time that Scotland joined in with the 'avant-garde', which was such a powerful motor of advanced continental design from the 1890s to the 1930s, but which hardly touched the anglophone countries. Beginning with an 1898 article in *Dekorative Kunst* and culminating in triumphant displays by 'The Four' at the 1900 Vienna Secession and 1902 Turin International Exhibitions, Mackintosh spent several years collaborating with Secessionist designers such as Hoffmann in international endeavours to evolve a new, intensely 'artistic' type of interior design. This affinity with the Germans and Austrians was underlined in a key lecture of 1902, 'Seemliness'. Here Mackintosh identified the central values of 'the artist' as 'emotion', 'soul' and 'spirit'. 'Tradition and authority' were to be rejected for 'individuality, freedom of thought and personal expression', 'the soul that lies beneath', and 'the hushed reserve that is always felt in nature'. 'Modern individual art', with its 'hallucinating character', was 'like an escape into the mountain air from the stagnant vapours of a morass.' [56] One can hardly imagine even Lorimer, far less Burnet, writing in those terms.

But these uncompromising formulations were chiefly applicable to Mackintosh's interiors. In his external architecture, other values far more closely related to mainstream Traditionalism came into play. Above all, there was a stress on the 'national', 'a feeling that has grown with our growth'. Architecture, he said in 1892, 'should be less cosmopolitan and rather more national'. He rejected monumental Grecian classicism ('as cold and lifeless as the cheek of a dead Chinaman') and Burnetian skyscraper-Baroque (in Ruskinian terms, for its 'want of apparent strength'); industrial structures such as railway bridges were

dismissed as 'almost unavoidably obnoxious'. The only true model could be the Scottish Renaissance, which he praised, in Andersonian 'functional' terms, for its 'decorating constructing' (that is, decorated construction). [57]

How was Mackintosh's admiration for this 'national' past expressed in his built architecture? In his first works for Honeyman & Keppie, a Scots Renaissance with Baroque elements – not dissimilar to the contemporary work of Burnet – was offset by emphatic touches of personal individuality, notably the sinuously corbelled-out angle tower of the *Glasgow Herald* building (1893–4) [7.44]. The beginning of the mature phase of his architecture was heralded in 1896 by the award to the firm of the Glasgow Art School commission – largely secured

by the influence of his friend and patron Fra Newbery [cf. 7.40]. Mackintosh's design was built in two stages (completed 1909), and is located on a steeply sloping site like MacLaren's Stirling High School, whose drama it in some ways echoes. It features, in the same way as his interiors, a studied contrast between austerely plain background and intense decorative highlights. The plan is an elongated letter 'E', with north-facing main facade and three wings falling to the rear, in a composition which seems to recall the main front of Fyvie [7.43]. The regularity of the front facade's large studio windows is offset by asymmetrical elements, including an entrance bay with juxtaposed elements of forceful stone geometry and concentrated detail. The east side facade is of rubble, studded with small

7.41 Hill House, Helensburgh (Mackintosh, 1902–4): (left) 1904 view of hall; (above) 1904 exterior view.

windows and mannered details, while the harled rear (south) wall forms, as completed, a towering, roughly symmetrical grouping.

Other turn-of-the-century public and commercial commissions were treated with an austere, even harsh originality: the soaring, bay-windowed *Daily Record* building (1900); Scotland Street School (1902–6), its twin stairtowers combining an evocation of the Earl's Palace, Kirkwall, with bold fenestration; and his unbuilt designs for massive, battered structures at the 1901 Glasgow Exhibition [7.45]. The Willow Tearooms facade (1903–4) featured a more refined austerity, with sweeping first-floor window fronting the Room de Luxe. Mackintosh's domestic architecture, like that of his Secession friends, sought inspiration in the rendered severity and geometry of pre-industrial dwellings. But where the Viennese or Germans tended to look towards 'folk' houses or Mediterranean vernacular, Mackintosh's designs for Windyhill and Hill House (and for unbuilt projects such as the Artist's Cottage and Town House, 1900) drew directly on harled Scottish Renaissance domestic architecture, as well as on the recent work of MacLaren and Voysey [cf. 7.41]. At Hill House, for the first time Portland cement render rather than harling was used. The

culmination of this aesthetic, outside as much as inside, was the *Haus eines Kunstfreundes* design: here, the near-symmetry and horizontality seemed to evoke the seventeenth century laird's house as a model [cf. 7.42].

Although the individualism of Mackintosh's secular architecture – almost by definition – inspired no 'school', a number of other disparate Art Nouveau tendencies can be traced. Salmon & Son & Gillespie, at the time of St Vincent Chambers, designed two banks (Glasgow Savings Bank, Anderston, 1899–1900, and British Linen Bank, Govan, 1897–1900), with emphatic Art Nouveau-like sculpture, and a house at 12 University Gardens (1900), with rich interiors. Also noteworthy, in its attempt to combine harled austerity with asymmetry, was H. & D. Barclay's recast frontage for the Argyle Street Tearooms (1897); although this was hardly as daring as Mackintosh's later Willow Tearooms facade, it did introduce a large expanse of harling into a city centre context. Outside Glasgow, there was a cluster of examples in Dundee, including board schools by W. G. Lamond (assistant to School Board architect J. H. Langlands), notably Stobswell of 1906, St Joseph's (1905–6) and Eastern School, Broughty Ferry (1911); the

DER·WETTBEWERB·FÜR·EIN·HERRSCHAFTLICHES·WOHNHAUS·EINES·KUNST·FREUNDES   7

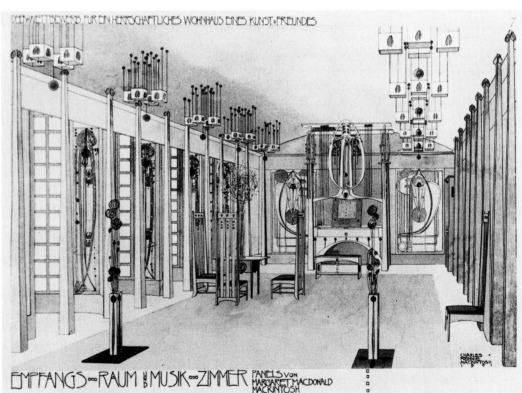

EMPFANGS ··· RAUM ¦ MUSIK ··· ZIMMER PANELS VON
MARGARET MACDONALD
MACKINTOSH

CHARLES
RENNIE
MACKINTOSH

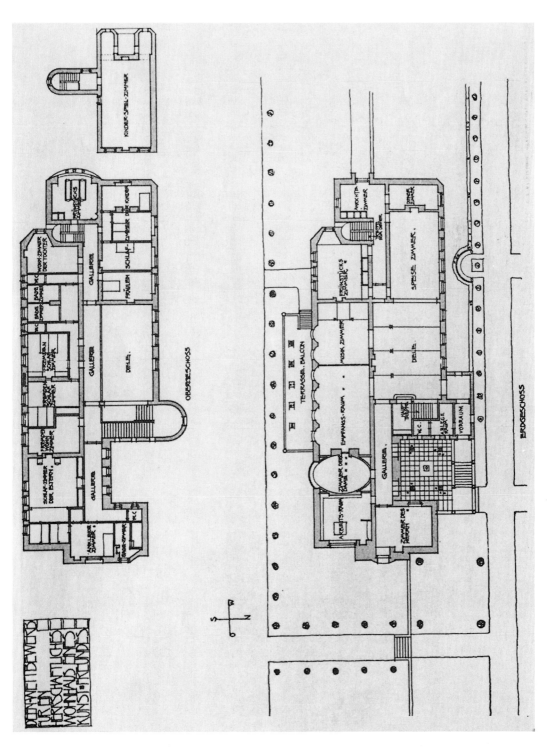

7.42 C. R. Mackintosh, *Haus eines Kunstfreundes* project, 1901: (opposite above) design for exterior; (opposite below) design for music room; (above) plans.

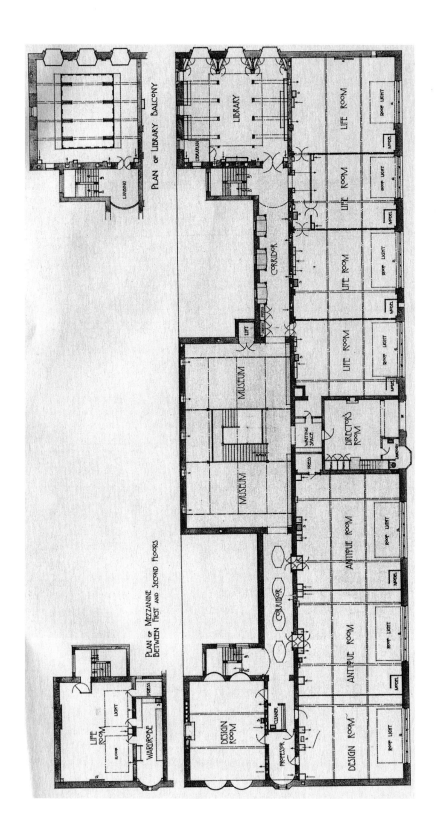

7.43 Glasgow School of Art (1896–1910), 1910 plan by Mackintosh, with north at bottom.

7.44 *Glasgow Herald* building (1893–4), 1965 photograph. In the left foreground is Burnet, Boston & Carruthers's Gordon Chambers, 1903–4.

curvilinear campaniles added earlier by T. M. Cappon (again to Lamond's designs) to St Mary's Forebank Church (1900); and the multi-stage rebuilding of Ballumbie House from 1902 by James Findlay, in a roughcast, geometrical style imitating Mackintosh, but with more crowded Baronial detail and rock-faced dressings [7.46].

Aspects of Mackintosh's 'artistic' interiors were presaged in George Walton's work before his move to England in 1897. Other major interiors included Salmon's remodelling of the palatial 22 Park Circus (1897–9), and W. D. MacLennan's Bull Inn, Paisley (1900).

7.45 Scotland Street School, Glasgow (Mackintosh, 1902).

7.46 Ballumbie House, Dundee (J. Findlay, from 1902).

The Return to Classicism in Domestic Architecture and the Glasgow Style

The early/mid-1900s saw not only a search for 'order' within the mainstream classicism of public buildings (by Burnet, and others), but the beginnings of a reintegration of Art Nouveau and Traditionalism with that mainstream. While the Glasgow Style increasingly tended towards an archaic-looking classicism, the quest of architects such as Lorimer for a wholesome, pre-industrial past began to move away from its anti-classical or Gothic interpretation of the Scottish Renaissance, and instead to evoke the classicism of the time just before industrialisation: the late seventeenth and early eighteenth centuries. This trend included a fresh burst of interest in the formal Scots garden; one was included by Lorimer at Earlshall in 1893 [cf. 7.25]. There was also a growing Traditionalist liking for classical interiors. Like the German 'Biedermeier' revival of those years, and in contrast to the 'Adams' revival discussed earlier in this chapter – for example, at Kinross's Manderston (from 1891) - this focused on less grandiose examples: we noted above Lorimer's attack on Kinross's opulence [cf. 7.18]. Lorimer paralleled Mackintosh's 'cult of the white drawing room', for example in the flowing white interiors of Rowallan (from 1902), at Hyndford, North Berwick (1903), and (from 1915) in the remodelling of Dunrobin in an eighteenth-century eclectic style; a Kinross equivalent was Ardtornish (1908). But in contrast to Mackintosh's intensity, Lorimer simply extended the scope of antique-collecting and furnishing into the eighteenth century, making backgrounds rather lighter and more neutral. At Balmanno, for instance, he designed a floor plan for Whytock & Reid to supply imitation antiques. The sources of his furniture designs ranged increasingly widely across Europe, including provincial (not high Parisian) French Rococo. This classicising tendency soon spread to Traditionalist exteriors. Following Mitchell's example at South Lauder Road in 1892, Lorimer's houses from the late 1890s increasingly sported seventeenth-century-type shaped gables, and arched loggias. From the 1900s, there was growing symmetry, and a reassertion of 'Renaissance' horizontality of proportion. In his remodelling of Wemyss Hall (1905–7) to display the eighteenth-century French furniture collection of a jute baron, Frederick Sharp, Lorimer provided a symmetrical front with low piended roofs, overlooking terracing; his other classical remodellings included Midfield and Marchmont, both 1914 [7.47]. A similar piended-roof symmetry was found at Peddie's Blervie House, Moray (1909–10).

By the turn of the century, this move towards classical order was paralleled, within the Glasgow Style. The years after 1902 were a time when the impetus of Art Nouveau fell away across Europe. Now, designers such as Salmon and Gillespie or

7.47 Wemyss Hall, Fife, view of Lorimer's new garden front, seen *c.*1907.

Mackintosh converged, in some respects, with the increasingly austere work of the Glasgow classical/Beaux-Arts mainstream. We saw above, for example, the plain, harled symmetry of J. A. Campbell at Queen Victoria School, Dunblane (1907–8) [cf. 7.32]. In the late work of Salmon and Gillespie, the closeness of ideals to the elemental classicism of contemporary Traditionalism was also clear. In a key paper by Salmon in 1908, there was much Anderson-like rhetoric of 'sane and sensible' design and aversion to added ornament, and an anti-cosmopolitan insistence that 'each nation should do as much as possible to preserve its distinctive character'. But Salmon went further. Architecture was above all else 'engineering': 'Copy nothing. Obey no-one'. The only real beauty now lay in 'grandeur . . . great planes of monotone . . . vast and enormous plain masses'. Plain tenements could be beautiful: 'A great, long, crowded street, with houses all along both sides, is a fine thing'. Here we catch a strong whiff of the interwar years' predilection for the architecture of unadorned 'mass'. [58]

The best way to build this 'national' Sublime architecture, Salmon asserted, was by exploiting the new technique of reinforced concrete. Seeking to develop a Glasgow office skyscraper style inspired not by America but by 'the old rough-cast castle' [59] of the Scottish Renaissance, he and Gillespie left behind their earlier window-wall architecture for a more massive-looking solution, employing, ironically, very thin concrete walls [7.48]. In 1904–7, they designed and built Lion Chambers, a tall block of lawyers' offices employing experimental (Hennebique) concrete frame and panel construction, to allow maximum accommodation on a tiny site: the building measured 90 feet high, but only 33 by 46 feet in area. The main designer was probably Gillespie. Its sheer facades were plain and rendered, with some integral panels of relief decoration, but were crowned by a corbelled outcrop with tall pediments. This startling attempt to devise an 'artistic' type of high office block, with overtones of cultural nationalism, echoed (although not in style) the earlier work of Sullivan in America. Salmon and Gillespie's chamfered, gabled house The Pantiles, Kilmacolm (1907, now 'Nether Knockbuckle') compressed the style of Lion

Chambers to a two-storey scale. The culmination of this tendency in their work was their 1907 design for Stirling Municipal Buildings, where a Lion Chambers-like tower crowned by big pediments is incorporated into a grandiose imperial Baronial composition - here, stone-built - with a colonnade flanked by massive turrets [7.49]. Their unsuccessful design for London County Hall (1907) was a symmetrical composition with huge pediments flanking a heavy Baroque tower: 'a rhythmical repetition of large architectural chords binding together the richer motifs, all of which are expressive of actualities'. [60]

The later projects of Mackintosh also reflected this wider trend towards discipline – although he did not follow the Germans' fusion of ideas of 'soul' and the 'national' into an ordered ideology of

7.48 Lion Chambers, Glasgow (Salmon & Son & Gillespie, 1904–7); view of *c.*1910.

7.49 Stirling Municipal Buildings (1907), view of the completed portion of Salmon & Son & Gillespie's design.

'national will'. Already in 1901, the front facade of his *Haus eines Kunstfreundes* design displayed an insistent regularity. In an elevation for an undated Country House (probably *c.*1905–10) he envisaged complete symmetry, with flat-topped, vertically-windowed towers flanking a low central section with tall windows. And in a 1915 project for his friend Geddes, for a symmetrical block of shops and offices (unbuilt) in India, Burnet-like features such as a tall glazed ground floor, and eaves colonnade, are combined with concentrations of incised, linear decoration. But other late projects, such as the Cloister Room and China Tea Room at Ingram Street (1910–11) and the remodelling of 78 Derngate, Northampton (1916), seemed to look beyond the search for classical 'order' towards the, by then, growing continental upheaval of expressionistic fragmentation and cubistic geometry. The break from the irregular or Gothic interpretation of the Scottish Renaissance was not quite so clear in Mackintosh's final built masterpiece, the west wing of the Glasgow Art School (1905–9); this well-known design can only be summarised here [7.50]. Like the contemporary work of Campbell or Joass, the exterior modelling was dominated by linear verticality. Its gabled west facade featured three tall, flat-topped oriel projections fronting the Library; the south facade (flush with the building line) contrasted with this, its complex pattern of recessed windows and voids, with small calculated elements of irregularity, recalling the sculptural decoration around the main east facade gateway at Linlithgow. Internally, the Library – perhaps Mackintosh's most renowned interior – exploited the Glasgow shipfitting skills of prefabricated timber assembly to create a complex grid of galleries and supports, decorated with notched and geometrical patterns

7.50 Glasgow School of Art west wing
(Mackintosh, 1905–9).

[7.51]. For a detailed description, the reader
should consult J. Macaulay's 1993 book on the
School of Art. Other Glasgow School/Art
Nouveau designers also moved towards a greater
formality at this time. J. Gibb Morton's Howard
Street warehouse of 1903 was symmetrical around
a central circular tower and flanking buttresses.
And J. H. Langlands (with Lamond) designed the
Dundee College of Technology (1907) as an
assertively Baroque composition. We should also
note here one highly individualistic essay in
commercial architecture by Romanesque church
specialist Peter McGregor Chalmers: Neptune
House, Glasgow 1906, whose grid-like facades and
semicircular windows resembled much contemporary commercial architecture in Germany.

7.51 Glasgow School of Art west wing, library interior.

'The Renascence of Worship': Ecclesiastical and Neo-Medieval Architecture [61]

The search for 'order' in the secular field, and the Traditionalists' evolution of a new secular utopianism, was matched in religious architecture (and also in secular buildings in medieval styles) by a number of striking developments. Within Presbyterian architecture, the gradual atrophying of the Churches' social role, in favour of secular agencies such as the municipalities, was accompanied by a new liturgical movement to heighten the devotional and ceremonial element of worship – a trend whose beginnings we traced in Chapter 6. This was seen in the foundation of the Church of Scotland Service Society (1865), the Scottish Church Society (1892), and equivalent societies in the UP Church (1883) and Free Church (1891), and in the proselytising activities of key individuals such as the minister of Govan Parish Church, Revd. John Macleod, or Dr John Hunter, minister of Trinity Congregational Church, Glasgow. This essentially neo-Catholic liturgical movement was part of an international tendency within Protestantism, which had already passed its climax in England and Germany, but was still gathering force in the United States. In Scotland, it provoked vigilant counter-campaigns, such as that of Revd. Jacob Primmer, to keep 'symbolism' out of church interiors. Architecturally, the problem its advocates faced was to retain the essential characteristics of a *Predigtkirche* within a more medieval plan and devotional atmosphere, and to envisage the church as a comprehensive complex, including halls, and the like. In 1881, architect William Hay advised that, to compete with Catholicism, 'we should make our artillery as efficient as that of our opponents by pulling down our barns of churches', or improving them 'with the aid of the sculptor and painter, as well as the glass stainer'. A 'more effective architectural character' could be got by 'removal of galleries, addition of session halls, and introduction of organs'. [62] In 1888, Professor Blackie compared Pilkington's solution to the preaching-auditorium plan at Barclay Church to 'a congregation of elephants, rhinoceroses and hippopotamuses with their snouts in a manger and their posteriors turned to the golf players in the links' [cf. 6.46]. [63] Some architects were more cautious. Honeyman, in 1884, questioned the acoustical efficiency of cruciform plans: 'The more comfortable form of auditorium was something in the form of a modern theatre.' [64] The new Presbyterian ceremonial movement represented, in some ways, a convergence with Roman Catholic trends, where the populist emulation of Protestant evangelical and extra-church activities from the 1880s was producing large, hall-like churches with ancillary suites of buildings. Glasgow examples of the prolific designs of Pugin & Pugin include the rebuilt St Francis, Gorbals (1878–95, with Friary) or St Alphonsus, London Road (1905).

In resolving the question of how to make Presbyterian churches more 'worshipful', while the 1870s had seen some innovations such as the introduction of arcades and clerestories, the decisive steps were taken in the 1880s by Rowand Anderson. His and others' earlier work for the Episcopal Church had essentially relied on English Gothic Revival attitudes of Puginian 'truthfulness' and ecclesiological 'correctness'; but his response to this new Presbyterian liturgical campaign was different. He took the multi-cellular medieval nave/transept/chancel plan and converted it into a hall-like pattern, by widening the nave (which could be galleried) to the combined width of chancel and flanking aisles. This layout pioneered at his Edinburgh church for the ritualistic Catholic Apostolic Church (1873–94, subsequently decorated with brilliantly coloured murals by Phoebe Traquair), was first built for Presbyterian worship at Macleod's (new) Govan Old Parish Church (designed 1882, built 1884–8), and was then taken up by J. J. Burnet at the Dunblane-fronted Barony Church (1886–90) [7.52]. Its use also immediately spread to the Free Church.

The large volumes available in these grandiose new Protestant design solutions were increasingly exploited through the building of 'cathedral'-like commissions. The Catholic Apostolic Church had been neo-Romanesque in style, and Hippolyte Blanc's rebuilding of St Cuthbert's, Edinburgh (1892–5), had been lavish Baroque. Now, more generally, neo-Gothic was employed – a Gothic which, developing the tendencies of the 1870s, avoided the heavy forms and spiky profiles of the mid-century in favour of a greater contrast

7.52 Catholic Apostolic Church, Edinburgh (Anderson, 1873–94).

between bare walls and rich detail. The most lavish commissions of the age were commissioned by magnates: for example, Coats Memorial Church, Paisley (a competition-win by Hippolyte Blanc, 1886–94), with its sumptuously marbled sanctuary-baptistery and crown steeple [7.53]; or Clark Memorial Church, Largs (1890–2, by T. G. Abercrombie, with windows by renowned Glasgow artist Stephen Adam), its tall steeple modelled on Leiper's Camphill and on Burnet's unsuccessful Coats Church design [cf. 6.48]. Sydney Mitchell secured large commissions, including the Memorial Church at Crichton Royal Hospital (1890–7), and Dean Free Church, Edinburgh (1888), while Leiper built his self-proclaimed Franco-Scottish St Columba, Kilmacolm (1901–3). An Episcopal equivalent to these churches was St Bride's, Hyndland, designed in 1903 by the English architect G. F. Bodley and completed in 1916 (with tower) by H. O. Tarbolton.

However, the most emphatic example of ecclesiastical lavishness and Traditionalist crafts collaboration during the pre-war years was motivated less by religious 'worshipfulness' than by imperial Scottish patriotism. This was Lorimer's Thistle Chapel, built in 1909–11 as a permanent home for the ceremonial Order of the Thistle, whose rituals now symbolised the allegiance of the Scots nobility to the British imperial monarchy. The chapel, built as an annexe to St Giles in Edinburgh, is of tiny area but great height, and its interior is of a Rosslyn-like elaboration [7.54]. A continuous range of densely canopied stalls, carved by William and Alexander Clow with countless variations of detail, is surmounted by a soaring vault congested with ribs and bosses. All stonework was carved by Joseph Hayes and his assistants, some from models by Louis Deuchars. Stuart Matthew, who oversaw the completion of the decorative scheme, wrote in his comprehensive guidebook (1988) that the chapel expresses 'the very essence of Gothic . . . an emphasis of the vertical which gives a sense of reaching upwards beyond material confines'. [65] A direct link with the closely comparable work of Cram, Goodhue & Ferguson in the USA was established by James Taylor Thomson [cf. 8.14]. He left Lorimer's office in 1912 to spend eight years with the New York firm, where he was responsible for much of the 'Lorimerian' feeling of Goodhue's woodwork. Later, Thomson returned to Scotland, and built St John's Renfield Church, Glasgow, in 1927–31.

Running alongside this 'worshipful' lavishness was a far more direct reflection of the current secular trend towards archaic monumentality. This took hold in smaller and cheaper churches, where it was pioneered in a series of designs by Burnet and Campbell, beginning with Burnet's St Molios, Arran (1886), and culminating in such examples as the Gardner Memorial Church, Brechin (1896–1900) and the Maclaren Memorial Church, Stenhousemuir (1897) [7.55]. In all these cases, a squat tower was juxtaposed with a low wing containing the broad auditorium of the church; styles varied from Romanesque to Gothic with

Scots fifteenth-century detailing. As with Burnet's classical urban architecture, the influence of Campbell Douglas & Sellars's designs (as in their broach-spired, round-arched Dysart church of 1872–4) is discernible here. Other architects developed this ground-hugging rustic style, employing various forms of steeple. James Chalmers designed Scotstoun West Parish Church in 1905–6 with a low tower. H. E. Clifford's St Michael Carntyne (1902), W. G. Rowan's St Margaret Tollcross (1900–2), and Sydney Mitchell's St John's Free Church, Port Ellen (1898) and Gullane United Free (UF) Church (1908) all had broach spires – in the Gullane case, of gargantuan breadth and heaviness – and swept-down roofs [7.56]. Mitchell's Cockenzie UF church (1904) had a saddleback tower.

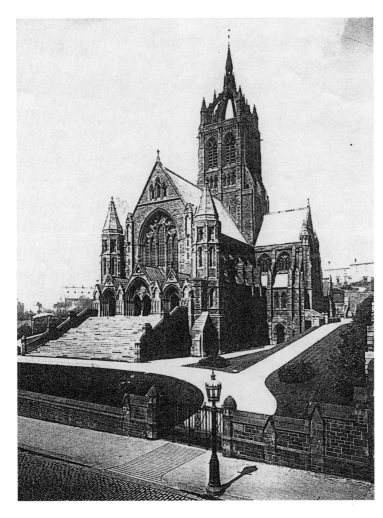

7.53 Coats Memorial Church, Paisley (Blanc, 1886–94), 1894 view.

7.54 Thistle Chapel, St Giles Cathedral (Lorimer, 1909–11), view when newly completed.

7.55 St Molios's Church, Arran (J. J. Burnet, 1886), 1909 view.

7.56 St Peter's UF Church, Gullane (Mitchell, 1908).

After the turn of the century, as in the USA, the urge towards rectilinearity found one outlet in a turn towards English Perpendicular Gothic. Built examples included Mackintosh's Queens Cross Church (1897), Miller's St Andrew's East (1903–4, cubic towers linked by an arch), Abercrombie's rubble Wallneuk Church, Paisley (1913–15) and J. T. Walford's St John Evangelist, Portobello (1903–6). The prosaic Perpendicular body of W. D. MacLennan's St George's UF Church, Paisley (1905) gives no hint of the fantastic bulbous crown steeple (doubtless influenced by Mackintosh's *Glasgow Herald* tower) that was originally intended [cf. 7.43]. And of course, had it been built, Mackintosh's Liverpool Cathedral design (1903) would have brought this tendency to a climax, fully matching the monumentality of Cram, Goodhue & Ferguson masterpieces such as West Point Academy (from 1903). The application to neo-Gothic of the Thomson tradition of tall colonnaded steeples (already seen in Pirie & Clyne's work) continued: for example H. & D. Barclay's Lamlash Parish Church (1886) and J. G. Fairley's linear-patterned tower at St Andrew, Bathgate (1904).

But a greater impetus towards a more austere ecclesiastical architecture which would still preserve the new devotional atmosphere came from neo-Romanesque (or, as it was still normally called at the time, 'Norman') architecture. It would be misleading to speak of a revival of Romanesque,

since the work of several Glasgow architects had maintained a great continuity with mid-nineteenth-century Romanesque. For example, W. G. Rowan of McKissack & Rowan had designed Strathbungo Parish Church (1886–7), whose soaring crown steeple showed a keen appreciation of the revived Romanesque element in fifteenth-century Scots church architecture, and the powerfully Richardsonian, quadrangular-towered (St Ninian's) Wynd (1888) [7.57]. Following the precedent of Campbell Douglas & Sellars, this Glasgow neo-Romanesque tradition was merged with early Christian elements by Peter Macgregor Chalmers, in churches like Kirn (1906–7), Carriden (1908), St Nicholas, Prestwick (1908, rigidly symmetrical with tall, austere tower), and St Leonard's, Dunfermline (1903–4), with tall Brechin-style round tower [7.58]. Chalmers was described in an obituary of 1923 by J. J. Waddell as a reincarnation of 'a Scots medieval architect'. [66] Lorimer's St Peter's, Morningside (from 1906), commissioned by the flamboyant Fr John Gray, was, Lorimer told his friend Dods, 'to be in the upstanding and primitive manner' [7.59]. [67] Its rubble exterior with low-pitched, pantiled roofs and campanile, and starkly arched interior of white-painted brick, conveyed a mixture of Romanesque solidity and Mediterranean vernacular.

In two stocky town churches of 1911 by Anderson pupil Ramsay Traquair (Christian Scientist Church, Edinburgh) and Lorimer pupil

Reginald Fairlie (Our Lady of the Assumption, Troon), the fifteenth-century Scots neo-Romanesque tradition was evoked [7.60]. By that time, a more general revival of Scottish ecclesiastical forms was well under-way. Crown steeples had been increasingly popular since the mid-1880s, as at Coats and Strathbungo [cf. 7.53];

they were particularly favoured by J. J. Stevenson (St Leonard's, Perth, 1885; Nathaniel Stevenson Memorial Free Church, Glasgow, 1898–1902; and Peter Memorial Church, Stirling, 1901). Other examples included McKissack & Rowan's Craigmailen Free Church, Bo'ness (1883) and William Young's Peebles Parish Church (1885–7).

7.57 Wynd Church, Glasgow (McKissack & Rowan, 1888); in the background, late-nineteenth-century tenements of Crown Street.

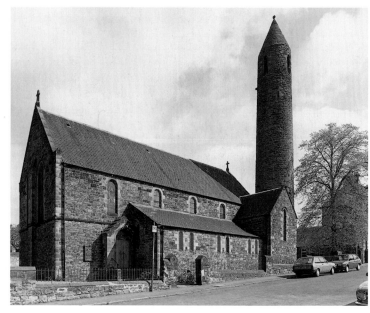

7.58 St Leonard's Church, Dunfermline (Chalmers, 1903–4).

Other fifteenth-century precedents were exploited by A. M. Mackenzie at Lowson Memorial Church, Forfar, 1912 (like Campbell's Dunblane chapel, based on St Monans) [cf. 7.32]; in Sydney Mitchell's recasting of the squat Chirnside Parish Church (1906); and in Fairlie's designs (1914) for St Benedict's Abbey, Fort Augustus. More delicate Episcopal interpretations of Scottish late-medieval architecture were designed by Ninian Comper, notably St Margaret's, Braemar (1895–1907), while an idiosyncratic compendium of medieval sources was built by the amateur architect Walter Douglas Campbell at St Conan's Church, Loch Awe (1881–6, extended from 1906). The Romanesque revival also benefited from a neo-Byzantine tributary. This began with Anderson's St Sophia, Galston (1885/6) and Schultz's Edinburgh RC Archepiscopal Chapel (1904–7); and it culminated in Mitchell's sumptuously remodelled St

7.59 St Peter's RC Church, Edinburgh (by Lorimer, 1906; nave completed 1928–9), view of *c*.1930.

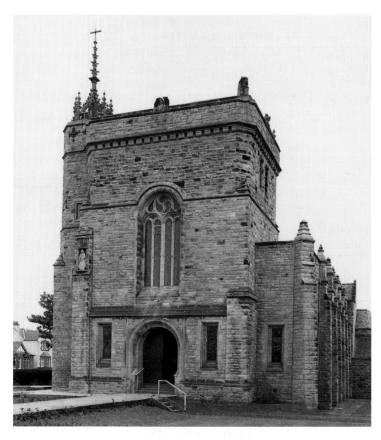

7.60 Our Lady of the Assumption RC Church, Troon (Fairlie, 1911).

Cuthbert's Church, Colinton (1907–8), and H. F. Kerr's Dalziel North UF Church, Motherwell (1915), with its domed auditorium and tall Thomsonian tower [7.61].

Mention of St Sophia and the Archepiscopal Chapel leads us to a brief consideration of the architectural activity of their patron – John Patrick, 3rd Marquess of Bute. Bute, as an eccentric aristocratic palace-builder fuelled by enormous industrial wealth, was the late nineteenth-century equivalent of the 10th Duke of Hamilton. It was perhaps a sign of the growing uncertainties of 'Imperial Scotland', however, that Bute was motivated not by Napoleonic grandiosity but by religious mysticism, and that his buildings rejected classical monumentality for a romantic medievalism. Readers seeking a more general account of Bute's tempestuous life, including his early conversion to Roman Catholicism and his subsequent astrological and psychic forays, should consult Hunter Blair's biography. Bute's building activities, paradoxically, had relatively limited bearing on religious architecture. Although his detestation of Anglican erastianism sometimes led him to draw romantic parallels between Catholicism and the militant Presbyterianism of the Covenanters, there is no evidence that he was involved in the movement to introduce Catholic ritual to the Scottish Protestant churches. In the field of secular architecture, the strength of the

classical tradition limited the impact of his medievalism to a few buildings – but buildings of great individual importance. When, in 1878, Bute came to rebuild his own house, Mount Stuart, after a fire, his medievalising impulse naturally led him to commission Anderson, who drew on his own studies of secular medieval architecture in southern France and northern Italy. The result was very different from the fantasy-castles built for Bute in Wales by W. Burges: a rectangular palazzo block, with sheer, unbroken walls as at the contemporary Glasgow Central Station, and an eaves gallery and bellcast roof evocative of Antwerp Town Hall [7.62]. Mystical and astrological decoration was reserved for the interior, including the focal space of 'a vast hall, gleaming with light . . . lined with rarest marbles, pavonazzetto, emperor's red, and pink-flushed alabaster' [68] Yet at the same time, the house was fitted with the latest technology; it was the first in Scotland lit by electricity. Various additions culminated in 1897–1902 in the chapel, with Spanish Gothic lantern tower.

Anderson brought the main themes of the Mount Stuart principal block to maturity at the Scottish National Portrait Gallery and National Museum, built in 1884–9 [7.63]. Largely financed through anonymous donations (totalling £50,000) from J. R. Findlay, the realisation of the Gallery was the climax of a long campaign for the building of a national pantheon. The design of Anderson,

7.61 Dalziel North UF Church, Motherwell (H. F. Kerr, 1915), photographed when new.

7.62 Mount Stuart, Bute (Anderson, rebuilt 1878–1902), 1880s' view, before lowering of tower and addition of eaves gallery and chapel.

here acting in his capacity as architect to the Board of Manufactures (as the government were shouldering half of the cost), repeated the rectangular block shape of Mount Stuart, but added corner spires (originally intended as round turrets) and contrasted the ornate central entrance bay with a vast expanse of bare upper walling. Findlay encouraged the Board to provide an extensive decorative scheme – an intention which accorded well with Anderson's concern to foster the building crafts. The scheme included nationally symbolic external and internal sculpture, and, in the central hall, a cycle of historical murals by William Hole (painted from 1895). Evoking as it did the Doge's Palace, Anderson's design reconciled medievalism with classical gravity and symmetry, and thus upheld the hierarchical primacy of the great public building. Such a combination of palazzo architecture and symbolic decoration was a well-established tradition within turn-of-the-century Northern European and American public buildings of national status: one can cite, for instance, Martin Nyrop's contemporary Copenhagen Town Hall (1892), or, slightly later and on a much larger scale, Ragnar Östberg's Stockholm Town Hall (from 1909) with its monumental Golden Hall. In the Edinburgh context, the use of this style, and of red rubble, allowed a contrast with New Town plainness without a total rupture from monumental stone classicism.

The Portrait Gallery's arresting secular-Gothic redness was immediately taken up and elaborated by Leiper (perhaps under the influence of Sellars's Glasgow exhibition designs the previous year) in the spectacular Venetian facade of the Templeton Carpet Factory, Glasgow (1889) [7.64]. Otherwise, the secular use of medieval styles remained uncommon. Examples such as Browne's Redferns, Edinburgh (1891), or Baird & Thomson's Schaw Hospital, Bearsden (1895), attract attention by their very rarity. The most significant of these isolated cases was one of Scotland's greatest nineteenth-century secular works: A. Marshall Mackenzie's extension to Marischal College, Aberdeen (1893–6, with new Greyfriars Church, 1903). Its Perpendicular style was inherited from Simpson's existing collegiate group, which Mackenzie extended both outwards (including the new Mitchell Hall) and upwards (in the 260-feet-high Mitchell Memorial Tower) [7.65]. The soaring tower and the crystalline intricacy of the new Broad Street facade departed radically from Simpson's horizontality, and paralleled the American trend towards a skyscraper-Perpendicular style for collegiate buildings. The icy hardness of Mackenzie's building was not only a culmination of his otherwise mainly classical career, but also an exalted climax to Aberdeen granite building, which was then enjoying its heyday. In his history of the city's granite industry (1949), W. Diack boasted that Marischal College was (after the Escorial) the world's second largest granite building; it was 'a testimony to the superb durability of our Aberdeenshire granite, and the

7.63 Scottish National Portrait Gallery (Anderson, 1884–9): (left) exterior photograph; (below) view of central hall.

7.64 Templeton Carpet Factory. Leiper's 1889 facade is at centre and left; on the right is a wing of 1936 by George Boswell.

7.65 Marischal College Extension, Aberdeen (A. M. Mackenzie, 1893–1906), view of Mitchell Hall and Memorial Tower.

pride of our silver city by the sea'. [69] Mackenzie designed a smaller and plainer Perpendicular institutional group at Scott's Hospital, Huntly, in 1901.

Conclusion

It is appropriate to end this chapter by returning, yet again, to Anderson [cf. 7.22]. For the revival of 'order' he helped orchestrate culminated in 1917, with the founding, through the force of his own personality, of the Institute of Scottish Architects (which was renamed in 1922 the Incorporation of Architects in Scotland; and in 1929 assumed its present title, the Royal Incorporation of Architects in Scotland). We have seen how the turn-of-the-century architectural trend towards sobriety and dignity, and the ever-increasing emphasis on the 'national', seemed to run hand in hand. During the half-century after 1918, this disciplining of the built environment by the Scottish nation would assume a more and more concentrated form, as the people's attention turned inwards rather than outwards. Architecture and building would increasingly become an arena for the action of the State, undertaking initiatives of modernisation determined by 'social needs', 'standards' and 'planning'. For that future, Scottish architects were now organising themselves on a national and professional basis.

Chapter 8

1914–1960

'By the People, for the People': The Traditionalist and Modernist Visions

'The new Government building is a conception worthy of its dominating position on the Scottish "Acropolis". . . Here is proof that architecture in our country, so long trammelled with traditional ornament and lacking in original thought, is again vibrant with imagination and in step with the progression of a great (or transitional) age.'

Thomas Tait, 1934 [cf. 8.10] [1]

'. . . a new sharp sense of the national past of Scotland, not as the board for an antiquary's game or a pageant of the romantic and picturesque, but as something real, and important to the present.'

Agnes Mure Mackenzie, 1941 [2]

'For the first time since the fifth century BC, public architecture has become popular architecture – in the strict sense, by the people, for the people.'

Robert Matthew, 1952 [3]

'. . . the objective interpretation of social and technological progress into building.'

Frank Arneil Walker, 1960 [4]

Introduction

In the decades covered by this chapter, the turn-of-century reaction against nineteenth-century eclecticism towards a more socially and visually ordered architectural expression accelerated, with public agencies playing a growing role as patrons. Especially after the mid-1920s, the luxuriantly diverse traditions of 1880–1914 began to coalesce into two formulae: Traditional and Modern. These seemed in many ways to be opposed, but had in common a new ideological and moral intensity, focused on the reconstruction of the nation as a whole. Eventually, in the 1950s, fuelled by the collectivism of another, less disorientating war, the Modernist recipe would triumph – but its ascendancy would prove short-lived.

Towards a 'Social' Architecture: 1920s–1930s

The loss of life and economic cost of World War I dealt a savage blow to Imperial Scotland's confident sense of national identity and material progress. After a brief post-war boom in 1918–20, cost-cutting measures disarticulated the country's export-orientated economy. Yet by comparison with the economic and political chaos in many other parts of Europe, Scotland remained relatively stable, and attempts were made to compensate for these setbacks, by the creation of a state-sponsored 'commonweal' of internal social reform. This rested ultimately on the new structures of mass democracy, but more immediately on a huge expansion of administrative devolution through Scottish Office boards and departments, motivated by the philosophy of 'planning'. Especially strenuous efforts were made in the field of housing, where skilled workers, exploiting wartime conditions, had forced the government in 1915 to cripple the private-rented sector with rent controls. An influential 1917 Royal Commission report (the Ballantyne Report) had argued that Scotland suffered an especially bad 'housing problem' which could only be cured by direct state intervention. From 1919 onwards a new structure of direct municipal housing provision, supervised by the Scottish Board of Health (SBH: later the Department of Health for Scotland, or DHS), began to emerge.

During the 1930s, the system of devolved government social administration gained strength, especially under Walter Elliot, Secretary of State in 1936–8; in 1939, the Scottish Office moved to its newly built headquarters, St Andrew's House [cf. 8.10]. Planned social intervention was paralleled by the growth of planned economic corporatism, to combat the 1930s' slump. Although a 10 per cent fall in building costs during the early 1930s was followed by a modest economic revival in the east, deepening depression in the west prompted the beginning of an industrial strategy, in the Scottish Industrial Estates programme. The growth of Labour, and working-class, municipal political power – taking in 40 per cent of the population in 1935, compared to 5 per cent in 1931 – also had its own economic effect, in constructing networks of patronage. After Labour's 1933 victory in Glasgow, ratepayer political power sharply declined, and large spending programmes, sustained by government grants and local property taxes, began: the focus of these efforts was mass housing provision.

These changes had a marked material impact on architecture and its patronage. The exuberant individualism of the turn-of-the-century patrons seemed to have vanished without trace. In 1920, the 4th Marquess of Bute, son of the builder of Mount Stuart, advertised the house for sale 'conditional to its complete demolition and removal by the purchaser . . . suitable for re-erection as a Hotel Hydro, Restaurant, Casino, Public Building, Etc' [cf. 7.62]. [5] We will explore below in greater detail the 4th Marquess's own

very different architectural ideology, of social nationalism. The 1920s' retrenchment meant less money for the Scottish economy, and also, at first, less confidence, especially on Clydeside: postwar architecture resumed on a less assertive note than at the turn of the century. For instance, economic pressures slashed the number of stonemasons from 10,000 in 1914 to virtually none in 1939, and reinforced the tendency towards use of cheaper materials, especially harled brickwork. And the 1930s depression, in fostering a range of public building programmes, marked a watershed in private practices' monopoly of prestige in the profession; public organisations began to attract able young architects. In this respect, the municipal innovations of Edinburgh in the eighteenth and Glasgow in the nineteenth century, as patrons of urban modernisation, now began to bear fruit nationally, as public networks of patronage, including design, were built up – for instance within Glasgow Corporation, or in the government work of John Wilson (architect to SBH/DHS) [L.2].

It is more difficult to pin down any exact relationship between the economic and political difficulties of those years and Scottish architectural *ideas* of the time. As in some other ex-combatant countries, such as the USA, England or France, there was an emphasis on stability immediately after the war, followed by a measured questing for 'modernity' in the 1930s. The brief turn-of-the-century links with continental avant-garde groups were not resumed. The course of innovation was relatively gradual, and marked particularly by changing definitions of, and an interaction between, two labels: Traditional, and Modern. We should carefully distinguish between Modernism, or the Modern Movement, as an architectural movement which was adopted in Scotland from the 1930s, and the wider movement of cultural and economic modernity, which had been developing in Scotland since the eighteenth-century explosion in 'improvement'.

In some respects, the 1920s saw the maturing of the pre-war attempts to restore architectural 'order', after the eclectic variety of the late nineteenth century, in a new form which did not depend on degree of ornament or precise stylistic differentiation. The new, wider national mood of introversion and avoidance of imperial bluster was reflected, within the newly consolidated architectural profession, in an overpowering concern to document and reinforce 'tradition'. The outlets for this included Incorporation of Architects-run annual prizes, the IAS *Quarterly* journal (*QIAS*), and other pub-lications such as the National Art Survey. All this was in sharp contrast to the exuberant ferment of the 1920s' 'Renaissance' in Scottish literature. During the 1920s, the conflict between the two competing interpretations of 'national tradition' (classical continuity and Traditionalist golden age) abated to some extent. From 1924, the *QIAS* began a series, 'Great Architects of the Past', whose subjects spanned the late seventeenth, eighteenth and early nineteenth centuries, and in 1923, Burnet wrote to the Incorporation suggesting that its headquarters should be ornamented with plaster busts of 'Bryce, Burn, Hamilton, Greek Thomson and other Scottish architects of distinction'. [6] In that year, the style stipulated for the Rowand Anderson Medal competition (subject: a boys' college) was 'classic, as practised in Scotland from the period of Sir William Bruce to Alexander Thomson': the winning design, a massive cubic grouping with explicit Thomson-like touches, was by L. G. Farquhar. [7]

This ideological emphasis on the unifying force of 'tradition' was matched, in architectural practice, by a consensus, throughout secular archi-tecture, on a broadly astylar classical appearance. But there was an increasing reluctance, among architects of all persuasions, to describe buildings in terms of particular styles. Instead, a more abstract or metaphoric language, with terms such as 'mass' or 'sculpture', was used. There were still sharp divergences, which in some ways perpetuated the pre-war division between the Beaux-Arts and Andersonian schools. The latter, at first dominated by Lorimer, continued its domestic (and ecclesiastical) preoccupations and its archaic classicism, and began to elaborate its framework of golden-age Scottish 'essence' into an increasingly vehement rhetoric of nationality, with new overtones of resistance to threat. By contrast, the Beaux-Arts grouping, as cosmopolitan and transatlantic as ever, and led by the reinvigorated firm of Burnet, Tait & Lorne, continued to put greatest emphasis on the design of great public buildings – now including big office blocks. They continued their affiliation to 'American' modern-ity, which they saw as a matter of advanced construction and services, clad in a stripped-down classical architecture of 'mass composition'. During the later 1920s and early 1930s, the Andersonian preoccupation with 'national tradition' and intuitive architecture seemed backward-looking in comparison with this Beaux-Arts modernity, which flexibly changed its focus from the commercial preoccupations of the 1920s to the social programmes and new popular building types of the 1930s. This versatile modernised classicism, which we sometimes call today Art Deco, culminated in Scotland at the 1938 Glasgow Empire Exhibition.

The Inter-War Lorimer School

During these years, the main concern of the heirs of Anderson was to consolidate and, to an extent, to merge the tendencies we traced in Chapter 7: the 'cult of the house', social housing reform, archaic monumentality, and neo-Romanesque church architecture. Just as before, the basic inspiration was Scottish Renaissance classicism, retaining the plasticity of rubble and harl, and elements of asymmetry. It was said that James V's architecture had featured 'the classic feeling appearing alongside a rough and bold flavour of Scottish character'. Key words included 'reserved' and 'sane'. [8]

Perhaps in response to the withering of Imperial Scotland and its forceful external solidarities, the previous ideal of a national style now took on a sharper edge. For the first time, explicit and critical comparisons were made with English architecture. In 1928, Lorimer, addressing the IAS convention as President, criticised the awarding of commissions to English designers. After his death, his disciples elevated him to the status of a patriotic standard-bearer. One of his favourite craftsmen, Douglas Strachan, recalled a 'Napoleonic . . . portentiousness', [9] and John Begg in 1932 hailed him as a saviour and rescuer of 'the Scottish tradition' as 'a living modern body'. [10] Traditionalist criticism of 'classic' archi-tecture as 'English' sometimes became explicit. In 1929, Lorimer's pupil Leslie Grahame Thomson asserted that he had 'rejected the classic styles – perhaps unconsciously defending the northern ethos from the domination of an alien and southern philosophy in stone'. [11] Thomson defined Lorimer's architecture as 'sane modernism': 'the true Scots tradition – I do not mean tripe à la Bryce, overloaded with mullions, plate glass, stringcourses and useless turrets – but that sane line of work refounded and continuously practised by the late Sir Robert Lorimer'. [12]

Despite the nation's new, 'home'-centred mood, the interwar era's most important individual work was a great public monument to imperial warfare: Lorimer's Scottish National War Memorial, built in 1924–7 [8.1, 8.2, 8.3]. Following much debate, it had been decided that the national tribute to the war dead should take the form of a memorial hall, converted from an eighteenth-century barracks building within Edinburgh Castle. Drawing on pre-war ecclesiastical precedents such as Fairlie's Troon church, Lorimer converted the barracks into a sumptuous nave-like space (the Hall of Honour) of Scots Renaissance character, with tall octagonal columns, round-headed windows and a Falkland Palace-like bay arrangement (including paired roundels); attached at the centre was the Shrine, a neo-Romanesque apse with Gothic vaulting and separately articulated roofline [cf. 1.14, 7.60, C.15].

For a movement such as Traditionalism, which was greatly concerned with concepts of national solidarity, a war memorial was the supreme challenge, and Lorimer brought to bear – in a building which was itself of small dimensions - all the monumentalising tendencies of the turn of the century. But the latter were muffled by the contemplative, less bellicose attitudes of the post-war years. The result was a temple of martial 'sacrifice' exceeding even the work of Thomson in emotional intensity. The building is of such importance that it is worth discussing its governing ideas in some detail. The first key element was Imperial Scotland's liking for archaic rubble heaviness. This predominated externally: the rough severity of the barracks, sitting on the bare castle rock, was accentuated by a cavernous portal of Stirling Palace pattern, closely based on Lorimer's unsuccessful King Edward Memorial design of 1911: he said that the Memorial should

'look as if it was a hundred years old' [cf. 1.15]. The effect of burly primitivism was reinforced by the (in Lorimer's words) 'bold and rather heavy type of detail', [13] and by some of the sculpture, notably the attenuated figure by Percy Portsmouth, 'The Survival of the Spirit', set deep in the shadows of the portal. Inside, imperialist pomp vanished, and another Andersonian principle – *Gesamtkunstwerk* – predominated. Where Late Traditionalism, in the 1930s and 1950s, would express its disciplined interpretation of the 'national' through a geometrical austerity, here a profusion of figurative and heraldic memorials to individual military units, including fan-shaped weapon displays, was required. This provided a field day for Edinburgh School designers, craftsmen and women, including Pilkington Jackson (who designed most of the architectural ornaments). The building's monumentality and lavish craft decoration can equally be seen in the context of the Renascence of Worship campaign. The non-denominational Memorial, crowded with quasi-funerary monuments, provided an opportunity, normally denied to Presbyterians, for an interior laden with quasi-religious symbolism. The very absence of a tradition of Presbyterian art allowed, in this special case, great freedom of symbolic depiction.

The tragic emotionalism of the Memorial reaches its climax in the apse-like Shrine. Here the primeval castle rock pushes through into the building, supporting a steel casket, guarded by angels, which contains the names of the 100,000 dead. Above soars a suspended statue (designed by Alice Meredith Williams and carved by the Clow brothers) of the Archangel Michael [cf. C.15]. The central panel of Douglas Strachan's encircling stained-glass windows, depicting Christ rising free from the cross, hints at the 'resurrection' of the warrior-martyrs. As a monument to a double loss – of the dead soldiers, and of the 'imperial nation' as a whole – the Memorial was accorded unqualified and enduring reverence, both by the public, and by the architectural profession. John Begg, for instance, wrote of the 'perfect rightness of its expression'. [14] The number of visitors, or 'pilgrims' as they were often called in the 1920s, was so great that the rough rock on the Shrine floor was worn smooth within a few years.

8.1 Scottish National War Memorial, Edinburgh Castle (Lorimer, 1924–7), external view just after completion. The former barracks comprises the main body of the building, and the Shrine is the higher wing.

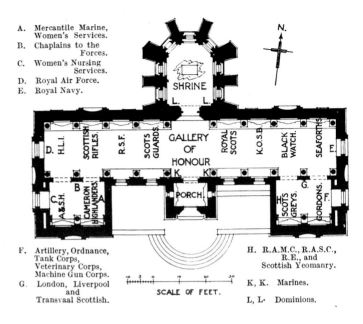

A. Mercantile Marine, Women's Services.
B. Chaplains to the Forces.
C. Women's Nursing Services.
D. Royal Air Force.
E. Royal Navy.

F. Artillery, Ordnance, Tank Corps, Veterinary Corps, Machine Gun Corps.
G. London, Liverpool and Transvaal Scottish.

H. R.A.M.C., R.A.S.C., R.E., and Scottish Yeomanry.

K, K. Marines.

L, L· Dominions.

SCALE OF FEET.

8.2 Plan of Memorial.

Exhausted, perhaps, by this supreme effort, the Lorimer school's other work in the field of public architecture was of a more modest character. Among war memorials, some followed a mercat-cross pattern stemming from J. G. T. Murray and J. A. Minty's 1912 Wallace Memorial at Elderslie. Galashiels Town Council's monument took the more assertive form of an extension block of municipal offices by Lorimer (1924), incorporating a squat, corbelled-out memorial tower and arch-way. At Eilean Donan, a war memorial was added, appropriately in jagged rubble [cf. 7.34, C.14]. Otherwise, the tradition of public buildings with high pitched roofs, crowstepped gables and asymmetrical classical facades continued in a low-key manner. Typical were William Williamson's Tayside Institute, Newburgh (1923), or Frank Mears and Carus-Wilson's Lucy Sanderson Homes, Galashiels, a colony-plan institution in rubble with ogee-roofed clock tower (completed 1934). To one such as Mears, the 'mass composition' of interwar Beaux-Arts public buildings was anathema. Writing in *QIAS* of the 1925 Rowand Anderson Medal entries, he complained that students had 'overloaded' their designs with 'unnecessary masses of plain masonry . . . extravagant attic walls . . . great unnecessary blocks on each side of the main entrance'. [15]

The focus of these designers' efforts remained, firmly, on domestic architecture. Here, through economic circumstances, the scale of building had now markedly shrunk. Some architects, especially in the west (such as A. Mair or J. & J. A. Carrick of Ayr), continued to uphold half-timbered and other 'English' styles. But the mainstream continued to build on an archaic Lorimerian classicism, with an increasing proliferation of shaped gables, Renaissance arcades, and splay plan-forms. Elements such as these are seen, for instance, in Fairlie's Kilmany (1914–19), St Nicholas Boarding House, St Andrews (1932), and Baro House, Gifford (1939); in Orphoot, Whiting & Bryce's enlargement to Haystoun House, Peebles (1924–5); in William Kerr's Cochrane Hotel, Alva (1929); and in J. Jerdan's The White House, Gullane (1933). The most indefatigable advocate of the splay plan was Leslie Grahame Thomson: for instance, at a villa in Easter Belmont Road (1932), 'The Pantiles' hotel, West Linton (1937–9), and the Isobel Fraser Home, Inverness (1936).

The builders of large-scale speculative housing, such as J. A. Mactaggart in Glasgow or James Miller & Partners Ltd in Edinburgh, maintained a rather more eclectic manner. Although the private sector still built occasional groups of tenements (such as the Dean Property Investment

8.3 Interior view of Memorial just after completion, looking into south-east wing.

Company's development at Comely Bank, Edinburgh, built 1938/46 to Stewart Kaye's designs), [cf. 6.31] the falling cost of land and the wider availability of motor transport encouraged the dominance of a new solution – the bungalow [8.4]. This distributed single-storey dwellings in separated rather than stacked form, while still preserving the massive and monumental aesthetic of the tenement block. Private building was at its strongest in Edinburgh, because of the Corporation's eager exploitation of subsidy powers and its dislike of municipal housing. And the capital also developed the most marked local tradition of bungalow architecture, combining a Lorimer-like harled or stone severity with other elements, such as Baronial window-mullions and chamfering and, often, a classical symmetry. Street layouts were generally curved and picturesque. Elsewhere, there were slightly different patterns: in Aberdeen (home of the colourful councillor-builder T. Scott Sutherland) there was more use of external timber, and in Glasgow much building of two-storey flats in terraces. While the *Scotsman*, in March 1935, hailed 'the bungalow era', Traditionalist architects mostly disapproved. Hierarchically extending the logic which had condemned Baronial complication in country houses, they demanded an even simpler treatment for small dwellings: Robert Hurd condemned 'chatty, perky' bungalows. [16]

Some scope for these ideas, in private building, was provided in the standard plans used from 1921 by the Board of Agriculture for subsidised self-built houses in crofting areas. The main field for

8.4 4 Davidson Road, Edinburgh, bungalow built in 1935-6 in a speculative private development by James Miller & Partners Ltd (builders and contractors).

architect-designed mass housing, however, was now no longer in the private sphere, but, instead, in the emergent field of public social housing. Architecturally, this tenurial revolution seemed to be bound up with the radical change in building materials. Despite calls, especially in the east, to continue with stone, harled brickwork became standard; but the shortage of bricklayers also led to increasing reliance on concrete blockwork building. There were also experiments with steel houses and (in the Highlands and Islands) with mass concrete construction. But there were implications for dwelling types. As in most European countries, state intervention in housing was combined with imposition of hygienic standards, especially through density reduction and promotion of cottage garden-suburbs. But high cost and tenant opposition soon led to revived large-scale building of smaller flats, in two-storey 'four in a block' units, or three-storey tenements. This compromise solution of lower-density flats, based on long-established private patterns in smaller burghs, had already emerged in the first completed post-war municipal scheme, Logie in Dundee, built 1919–20 under James Thomson's direction [8.5].

The reversion to flatted types was also influenced by architectural reaction against the first municipal schemes. Some opposition simply stemmed from suspicion of salaried local-authority designers: *QIAS* in 1922 blasted Glasgow's Mosspark houses as 'devil's spawn . . . domiciliary abortions'. [17] But once programmes were established, they assured much work for Traditionalist architects such as J. A. W. Grant. In rural areas and small burghs, longstanding relationships began. Sinclair Macdonald & Son of Thurso, for example, established a network of contacts and work across Caithness and Orkney. More persistent was an architectural dislike of the scattered form of the new suburbs; a campaign spread for a 'tenement revival'. This was begun by Ebenezer MacRae, Edinburgh City Architect (from 1925), who in 1927 criticised building of cottages in towns. The main impetus was provided by Lorimer himself, as *IAS* President. In a combative address to the 1928 *IAS* Convention, he launched a blistering attack against municipalities' cottage schemes: if they went on 'building the

8.5 Logie municipal housing scheme, Dundee, designed by James Thomson, City Architect and Engineer, 1919–20: (above) view of typical 'four-in-a-block' two-storey flats; (below) view of commemorative plaque.

ON 27TH MAY 1920 SIR WILLIAM DON, K.B.E.,
LORD PROVOST AND LORD LIEUTENANT OF DUNDEE,
FORMALLY OPENED THE DWELLING HOUSES
ERECTED UNDER THE LOGIE SCHEME
FOR THE HOUSING OF THE WORKING CLASSES,
THE FIRST SOD ON THE SITE HAVING BEEN TURNED BY
SIR GEORGE McGRAE, D.S.O.,
VICE-PRESIDENT OF THE LOCAL GOVERNMENT BOARD FOR SCOTLAND,
ON 4TH JULY 1919,
THIS HOUSING SCHEME BEING THE FIRST IN SCOTLAND
TO BE PROCEEDED WITH BY A LOCAL AUTHORITY
IN PARTNERSHIP WITH THE STATE.

little villa type of houses until the crack of doom', they would never 'solve the problem of clearing the slums'. Arguing that anti-flat 'prejudice' had been 'greatly overdone', he called for rehabilitation of Old Town tenements, and the building of 'a considerable proportion of large blocks of flats' in outer-suburban schemes. [18]

The Architecture of 'Mass': Burnet, Tait and the Beaux-Arts Legacy

While 1920s' Traditionalism was largely concerned to consolidate pre-war trends, developments in the parallel Beaux-Arts tradition at first glance seemed equally conservative. In many European countries, around World War I, architects looked back to the neo-classicism of a century before – in Germany to Schinkel, in Denmark to Hansen, or in England through 'neo-Georgian'. For Scotland, the focus of attention was more recent: Alexander Thomson. The pre-war architecture of Burnet and others had revived Thomsonian features such as eaves colonnades. The 1920s and, especially, the early 1930s saw an accentuation of this tendency, accompanied by an outpouring of eulogies to Thomson. For instance, in 1933 Ninian Johnston wrote that he occupied 'a place among the master builders of the world. The spirit of his work pervades Scottish Art and Architecture, for he was of the aristocracy of race, of mind and of heart'. The subject set the following year for the Alexander Thomson Travelling Studentship was 'a National Memorial to Alexander Thomson', to be 'strictly monumental in conception and . . . simple in its detail'. [19] The first prize was won by W. N. W. Ramsay's design, crowned by a looming cornice; the runner-up, T. Warnett Kennedy, proposed a sheer wall surmounted by a columned pavilion.

But this interwar cult of Thomson should not be attributed solely to conservatism or hankering for neo-classical tradition. What made his inspiration so powerful at this time in the west was not his utopian emotionalism but almost the reverse: the way in which his work seemed to anticipate, and chime in with, contemporary international conceptions of architectural modernity held among architects of the Beaux-Arts tradition, but also

among some others opposed to it, such as (in the USA) Bertram G. Goodhue. This notion of modernity was associated with a modification to classical, regular forms, by visualising a building as a single, malleable mass, with vertical or horizontal distortions of Renaissance proportions. Along-side this, there was a continuation of the pre-war move (associated with steel framing) away from articulation through the Orders and additive detail towards astylar, stereometric, cornice-less blocks with punched-in openings. Key Scottish Beaux-Arts phrases of the period included 'mass', 'strength', 'refinement' and 'sculpturesque'. [20] The concept of 'sculpture' was central to this architecture of mass. Carved sculptural ornament was reduced from additive groups to integral panels, and the whole building was now envisaged as a giant sculpture: T. S. Tait referred to the terraced south facade of St Andrew's House as 'one fine piece of sculpture work'. [21] This was combined with an emphasis on repetitive, geometrical, often exotic detail of a kind already seen in Mackintosh's work of the 1910s, and at the 1925 Paris Decorative Arts Exposition.

In such a context, the relevance of Thomson was obvious. In 1930, David S. Paterson described St Vincent Street Church as 'a composition of masses, almost reminiscent of the zoning of Modern American buildings'. [22] [cf. 6.40] Built evocations of this spirit included John Arthur's Marr College (1919), or P. Waterhouse's Younger Graduation Hall, St Andrews (1923–9). More unexpected was the 1923 scheme (unbuilt) by Frank Mears for a 'Civic Museum and Outlook Tower for an American City': a skyscraper crowned with Thomson-like temple and steeple. Mears described it to Geddes as 'a skyscraper in a somewhat American Imperial style – you will probably not like it'. [23] The most powerful built example came, predictably, from Burnet's firm, where the tendencies seen in embryo in Wallace Scott and Alhambra Theatre reached an early post-war climax in Adelaide House, a large commercial block in London (1920–5). We should bear in mind that, although Burnet's main office was located in the British capital, his practice was chiefly concerned with carrying forwards the developing Scottish/Beaux-Arts world-outlook. Adelaide House marked the emergence of a new force in his office, Thomas S. Tait. Tait, who had worked with Burnet for several years from 1903 as personal assistant, rejoined him (after a short stay in the USA) as partner in 1919. Educated at John Neilson's Institution and (under Bourdon) at Glasgow School of Art, and initially apprenticed to James Donald – formerly Thomson's chief draughtsman – Tait naturally accentuated the Thomsonian leanings of the office. In his successive sketches for Adelaide House, the evolution from ornate, columnar Baroque to Thomson-like mass composition can be traced. The final design was a heightened echo of Egyptian Halls, made asymmetrical with a huge corner pylon, and treated with incised detail of Beaux-Arts vigour [8.6,; cf. 6.8]. Crowned with a massive, concave cornice, the building was originally also to have had an attic. The French writer, Maurice Casteels, claimed in 1931 that at Adelaide House, 'the monumental quality is retained with an almost religious fanaticism'. [24]

In a way, Adelaide House is a little misleading as a landmark building, because this cubic neo-Thomson style would only become pervasive in the 1930s. But it does bring us to the key area of 1920s Beaux-Arts prestige-building in Scotland: that of sumptuous commercial complexes. The interwar years were the time when Europe followed the established American trend towards designing office blocks not as plot slices featuring front and back facades only, but as partly or wholly freestanding buildings with two or more formal facades, and preferably covering one or more whole street blocks. In the process, the architectural status of the office block was raised to that of a major public building, further complicating the Beaux-Arts hierarchy. This tendency was eagerly taken up by the builders of the new, big inter-war Glasgow office blocks and their architects, who exploited the city centre's gridiron plan and built as high as the firemaster would allow. The weathervane of the shift in patronage and architectural status was James Miller. He moved smoothly from his eclectic Caledonian Railway pre-war work to the post-war design of massive, steel-framed office blocks, developed by his chief draughtsman and designer, Richard Gunn (who, like Tait, had worked in the USA until 1918). In his

8.6 Adelaide House, London (Burnet & Partners, 1920–5), drawing by T. S. Tait of scheme as built (except for attic), from *Academy Architecture*, 1921.

8.7 Scottish Legal Life Assurance Society headquarters, Glasgow (Wylie, 1927–31).

8.8 North British and Mercantile Building, St Vincent Street, Glasgow (Burnet, 1926–9).

work, and that of others, the massive, Thomsonian tendencies of Adelaide House were not at first taken up during the 1920s. Instead, a verticalised palazzo-like format was used. The prototype was the first major Scottish building to adopt the US principle of a ground-floor bank with offices above: Miller's Union Bank headquarters, St Vincent Street (1924–7), a scheme pushed through by the bank's chairman, Norman Hird. Another major palazzo block was A. Balfour and Stewart's Bank of Scotland Chambers, 93 St Vincent Street, 1924–6, with six-storey pilasters and Greek detail. The culmination of the commercial Beaux-Arts phase of 1920s' Glasgow was Wylie, Wright & Wylie's Scottish Legal Life Assurance Society headquarters (1927–31), a commission won by Wylie in competition [8.7]. The steel-framed front facade echoed the Burnet tradition in its general arrangement of flanking pylons, central colonnade and deep-set eaves windows. The company's commemorative brochure highlighted three attributes of the block: first, 'Renaissance' dignity; second, gigantic size; third, the 'thoroughly modern' and 'futuristic' technology of this 'Robotised building'. [25] A variant of the office-palazzo which was less thrustingly 'modern', but also prophetic of late 1930s' classical austerity, was devised by Burnet himself in one of his most sophisticated late works, 200 St Vincent Street (1926–9): a neo-classical cube with big cornice and punched-in windows above an arched colonnade of paired columns and statues [8.8]. In Edinburgh, the first office building in this style was Alfred G. Lochhead's Cleghorn block (1924–5), with vertically grouped windows.

If office blocks now counted as great public buildings, what of conventional public monuments themselves? There was no loss of grandiose aspiration. Burnet himself was a key member of the international commission for the new League of Nations building in Geneva. They organised an abortive competition (1927), and finally designed the building themselves. In the Beaux-Arts outlook, the public remained segregated from the utilitarian. Tait's colossal granite rubble pylons for Sydney Harbour Bridge (1924–32), evoking an arcuated Roman grandeur, were coupled with an engineering design for the bridge trusses by Dorman Long. Other public buildings of a

generally Beaux-Arts character included A. Graham Henderson's Glasgow Cross remodelling scheme (1922–32, including some offices) and J. Steel Maitland's Russell Institute, Paisley, 1926–7. In the east, a plainer neo-classical tendency continued, as in A. M. Mackenzie & Son's War Memorial and Cowdray Hall, Aberdeen, 1923–5.

From around 1930, the full elements of Thomson-like mass composition became increasingly widespread within Scottish monumental architecture, as part of a further emphasis of the American interpretation of Beaux-Arts. In the design of major commercial buildings, cornices were shaved off, and cubic, flat-roofed design became the norm. Examples included Miller's Commercial Bank, Bothwell Street, Glasgow (1934) [8.9]; or in Edinburgh, T. P. Marwick & Son's National Bank of Scotland, 11 George Street (1936). The climax of this tendency, however, was in the more conventional Beaux-Arts arena of a major governmental complex: the new Edinburgh centre of devolved Scottish state administration,

8.9 Commercial Bank of Scotland, Bothwell Street, Glasgow (Miller, 1934): architects' drawing of south facade.

8.10 St Andrew's House, Edinburgh (Burnet, Tait & Lorne, 1936–9): (above) night view of south facade in 1946; (left) 1939 view of Secretary of State's room.

St Andrew's House, designed by Tait and built in 1936–9 [8.10]. A dramatic site, on the edge of Calton Hill, was exploited with a pyramidal, terraced composition; the north (entrance) facade was dominated by a massive central block with sculpture-crowned piers. The building, although small by comparison with the stepped American commercial and public complexes designed in the wake of the 1916 New York zoning law, was invested with a similar monumental power. The year 1930 had seen an organisational transformation of Burnet's main practice: Tait now effectively took charge, and Francis Lorne was taken on as partner. Lorne completed the Americanisation of the office's staffing and practices. For a detailed account of this episode, readers should consult Walker's *St Andrew's House*. One of Lorne's key appointments was that of his brother-in-law, L. Gordon Farquhar, as office administrator. Since his 1924 Rowand Anderson Medal win, Farquhar had worked with US skyscraper specialist Raymond Hood. In 1934, Tait described the St Andrew's House proposal in terms similar to contemporary US rhetoric: 'The design is simple and sculpturesque rather than decorative, but carried out with that strength and refinement expressive of present-day sentiments . . . A direct scientific approach . . . beauty, dignity, and refined simplicity.' [26]

Beaux-Arts Modernity and Social Building

If governmental and commercial complexes occupied the summit of the Beaux-Arts hierarchy, they were increasingly joined there, during the 1930s, by social building projects. These, during the Depression, became a prominent and prestigious element within public architecture, where they reinforced the Beaux-Arts pre-occupation with classical modernity. The proportion of social building within total output reached a peak in 1931, and again after 1935. Architects such as E. G. Wylie slipped easily from the rationalistic planning of office palazzi to that of social buildings, dedicated to ideals such as hygienic openness, penetration of light and air, and provision for the 'needs' of the 'community'.

Architectural expression was to some extent shaped by the density of any particular development. Concentrated groups tended towards simplified classicism, while lower, dispersed layouts tended to employ steep-roofed 'domestic' styles, or a more assertively modern combination of mass composition and horizontal metal-framed windows.

School-building around 1930 saw numerous variations of plans featuring long corridor wings, in compact or sprawling form: in Glasgow, there was Wylie's cross-shaped, red-brick Hillhead High (1928–31) and Keppie & Henderson's Cloberhill Elementary (1929–32); in Dundee, Thoms & Wilkie's twin-courtyard Harris Academy (1926–8) and Maclaren Soutar Salmond's Logie (1927); and in Edinburgh, there was J. M. Johnston's Wardie Elementary (1931–2). After 1936, the raising of the school-leaving age prompted a new burst of building. Reid & Forbes designed a succession of large schools, including Edinburgh's Craigmillar Intermediate (1936) and Kelso High (1936), as well as small village schools such as Chirnside (1937). In hospital planning, the emphasis on fresh air, sunlight and dispersed layouts remained strong, especially in the treatment of tuberculosis. Burnet, Tait & Lorne's Paisley Infectious Diseases Hospital (from 1933) employed parallel blocks, while James Miller & Son's Auxiliary Hospital and Convalescent Home, Canniesburn (1935–8) comprised a single group with wings: both were flat-roofed. Auldjo Jamieson & Arnott's single-storey Astley Ainslie Hospital (1925–39) had harled walls and steep tiled roofs. But on urban sites, new American-inspired concepts of controlling the spread of infection by technology rather than cross-ventilation prompted a planning trend back towards concentration on steel-framed multi-storey blocks. This trend was presaged in Tait's design for a Royal Masonic Hospital (1930–3), in the British capital: a symmetrical, steel-framed, brick-clad group whose lavish financing allowed Tait to indulge his Beaux-Arts fondness for internal service-engineering. In his Glasgow Dental Hospital of 1926–31, Wylie echoed the Burnet formula of pylons flanking a framed facade, while Edinburgh Royal Infirmary's ambitious fund-raising drive (from 1929) allowed the construction of two large new blocks in 1935–9: a multi-storey nurses' home and a maternity hospital (designed by the Infirmary's Master of Works, Thomas W. Turnbull, with some help from Miller). These stepped, symmetrical blocks were to be faced in concrete blockwork, but, after a protracted dispute in 1935, the Meadows facade of the maternity hospital was built in ashlar. In other areas, low-density plans still prevailed. In asylums, the colony plan reached an interwar climax in E. G. Wylie's plans for the Lennox Castle Mental Defectives Institution. Built on a spectacular hillside site by Glasgow Corporation Public Assistance Committee in 1931–6, Wylie's dispersed, yet monumental layout featured steep-roofed, red-brick pavilions in axial groups. These were serviced by an extensive underground services ducting network, and large community and assembly buildings. A similar pattern was reflected in building programmes which combined capitalistic and social aspects, such as the series of planned industrial estates designed by Wylie after his 1937 appointment as Senior Co-ordinating Architect to Scottish Industrial Estates Ltd: Hillington (from 1937), and Carfin and Larkhall (from 1938). Pit-head baths built by the Miners' Welfare Committee throughout the 1930s (architect F. Frizzel) included the monumental Polkemmet (1934) and the circular Arniston (1933), while rationalised farming production was symbolised by Arnott & Morrison's Fenton Barns, East Lothian (1938–40), with its big glazed, curved staircase.

This Beaux-Arts institutional modernity of the 1930s continued, in some fields, after World War II. For example, early post-war factories on industrial estates, such as Beard, Bennett & Wilkins's Dundee NCR and Timex factories (both designed 1946) perpetuated the single-storey, brick, banded-window asymmetry of their 1930s' predecessors; and Wylie ensured consistency in the developments under his oversight. In some urban social buildings, a Taitian brick manner continued to predominate. Examples included Thomas S. Cordiner's Notre Dame School, Glasgow (designed 1939, built 1949–53), its symmetrical main facade dominated by a squat tower with pitched roof and cross finial; or the same architect's Lourdes School (1951–7), with enormously long window-bands across its south facade.

Popular Eclecticism and the Architecture of Entertainment

In parallel with its association with the sober social architecture of the 1930s, Beaux-Arts modernity was able to demonstrate its eclectic versatility by satisfying another, completely different demand: the beginnings of a light-hearted architecture of leisure, catering mostly for the rising incomes of those in work. Here, too, there was a powerful American influence, transmitted through the medium of the cinema, where the drama and glamour of US popular culture struck a deep popular chord, especially in Glasgow. The cinema boom had begun as early as 1910: the Green's Playhouse cinema and dance hall complex, built in 1925–7 with 4,400 seats, was then the largest in Europe. By 1928 the city had 96 cinemas, by 1938 114. In Glasgow, a higher proportion of citizens than anywhere else in the world (except Chicago) went regularly to the cinema. This was also a national phenomenon: many of the smallest burghs acquired their own picture houses.

In such a context, the gravity of mass composition was inappropriate: what was needed was an architecture of facades and interiors, an imagery of fantasy and exoticism. During the 1920s, the existing tradition of exhibition architecture and Clydeside shipfitting prefabrication had been exploited in the building of exotically decorated classical cinemas. In the 1930s, this was replaced by a new, American variant of entertainment design, originating chiefly in skyscraper architecture. It borrowed much of the machine-age imagery of 1920s' avant-garde continental Modernism. Materials such as stainless steel, glass, vitriolite, or features such as Mendelsohn's sweeping corner windows, rhetorical asymmetries and vertical punctuations, made their first appearance in Scotland in this popularised context. Tait, as competition assessor, had in 1934 awarded a major commission in England (Bexhill Entertainment Hall) to Mendelsohn and Chermayeff. These continental-derived elements, along with well-established details from the 1920s such as triangular and zig-zag patterns, were applied to otherwise massive and symmetrical buildings. The image of bright, commercialised modernity was accentuated at night, by the external use of coloured neon lighting.

These innovations were spread across Scotland largely by a specialised group of designers of cinemas and entertainment buildings, some from a Beaux-Arts background: for instance, in Glasgow, Lennox & McMath, James McKissack, John Fairweather & Son; in Edinburgh, T. Bowhill Gibson; and in Kingussie, Alexander Cattanach, designer of countless small rural cinemas in the north. In Aberdeen, T. Scott Sutherland, in addition to his many other private and public roles, was also, predictably, the owner and architect of a cinema development company. In Ayrshire, James Houston, a former Glasgow School of Art lecturer, designed the Radio Cinema, Kilbirnie (1937, with 'radio mast' facade) and the Viking Cinema, Largs (1939, with 'longship' facade), as well as the nautically-detailed 'Moorings' café in Largs (1936). By the decade's end, this eclecticism was giving way to more unified and flowing designs influenced by the 'streamform' of American designers such as Loewy and Bel Geddes: for example, at McNair & Elder's Lyceum, Govan (1937–8), with its plain, horizontal side facades and finned, curved angle; or T. Bowhill Gibson's County Cinema, Portobello (1939), with rounded fin-towers and blue synthetic stone facing.

This cinema-led, popularised modernity soon spread to other building types. In 1937–8, for instance, the architect/developer William Beresford Inglis, designer of the Spanish Colonial-style Toledo Cinema, Muirend (1933), set out to introduce the 'colours and lines of the cinema' to Glasgow hotel-building. [27] His eight-storey Beresford Hotel in Sauchiehall Street light-heartedly echoed the symmetrical Art Deco massiveness of the contemporary Glasgow Empire Exhibition. The late 1930s also witnessed a boom in such building types as ice rinks, or cafés and bars (the latter rejecting nineteenth-century ornateness for a chrome/machine imagery). Even municipalities joined in the consumer and entertainment drive, with projects such as Edinburgh Corporation's Portobello Swimming Pool (designed by Edinburgh City Engineer W. A. Macartney and, when new in 1936, one of the largest in Europe); the asymmetrical Rothesay Pavilion, with its dramatically projecting circular

wing (1936, by J. & J. A. Carrick); or Glasgow Corporation's Gas Department showroom at 522 Sauchiehall Street (1935, A McInnes Gardner), with huge, chunky facade lettering. There were a handful of large private apartment blocks in this style (in Glasgow, Kelvin Court of 1937–8 by J. N. Fatkin; in Edinburgh, Napier House of 1934 by John Jerdan, Ravelston Garden of 1935–7 by Neil & Hurd, and Learmonth Court of 1937 by Stewart Kaye), and a considerable number of smaller, flat-roofed villas with metal-framed windows, imitating Tait's pioneering project of flat-roofed houses at Silver End, England (1927–30). In some industrial projects, too, a relatively showy image of 'modernity' was aimed at: for instance, the India Tyre Factory at Inchinnan (1929–30) by US designers Wallis, Gilbert & Partners, George Boswell's multi-coloured extensions of 1934 and 1936 to Leiper's Templeton factory, or O. Williams's vitrolite and glass *Daily Express* building, Glasgow (1936). The most spectacular example of commercial 'modernity' was in Edinburgh: the 1937 extension by T. W. Marwick (designer E. J. McManus) to the St Cuthbert's Co-operative Association store at Bread Street. The store's ashlar side piers and parapet act as a frame for a single vast window, cantilevered out from a grid of thick reinforced-concrete members, through which are visible open sales and showroom floors. Its design closely resembles the White Swan Store in Prague (1937–9) by Josef Hrubý and Josef Kittrich [8.11].

During the Depression years, the optimism of this popularised conception of modernity struck a chord not only with the general public and with commercial architects, but also with some younger designers who would later rise to elevated status. In 1934, Ninian Johnston of Glasgow School of Architecture castigated the 'anti-modernist' views of a colleague: 'Does he not envy me my naked body glistening in the water and the sunlight, clean, fresh, invigorating, rhythmic, alive, gloriously white and shining silver?' [28] Increasingly, youthful innovation was shared between the Beaux-Arts world of Glasgow and Edinburgh College of Art. Stimulated by an intake of new lecturers, especially Joe Gleave (winner of the 1928–31 competition for the colossal Columbus Memorial Lighthouse in the

8.11 St Cuthbert's Co-operative store, Bread Street, Edinburgh (Marwick, 1937), 1939 view.

Dominican Republic, built 1939–92) [8.12], Edinburgh's individualistic Anderson tradition experienced a reinvigoration, inspired not by collectivist Beaux-Arts modernity, but by continental Modern architecture. It should be emphasised that, during the 1930s, the latter was simply used as a fresh source of stylistic motifs, for eclectic use alongside others. This was also the context of stylistically more-or-less Modernist works already mentioned, such as the Glasgow *Daily Express* building or the Edinburgh Bread Street Co-operative store. There was no attempt to embrace international Modernism, as an ideology, until the end of the decade. To young Edinburgh designers, the Continental Modern Movement, like the cinema to the general public, provided an image of escape from the by now dreary and decayed legacy of Imperial Scotland. The young Alan Reiach recalled that the capital in the 1920s was 'like a permanent wet Sunday . . . I felt liberated by Modernism'; and in the 1930s, 'one had the constant expectation of an architectural revolution which was just about to start'. [29] Rhetoric such as Reiach's 1935 call for the jettisoning of architecture's 'useless trappings – the mouldings, the cornices and the baskets of fruit and flowers', should be seen in the light of this combination of generalised aspirations of 'modernity' with a continuing stylistic eclecticism.

8.12 View of Joseph Gleave, *c*.1931, with a model of his competition-winning design for the Columbus Memorial Lighthouse, Dominican Republic (built 1939–92).

The central figure in this playfully eclectic phase of youthful Edinburgh design was Basil Spence [cf. 8.14]. Even when a student at the College of Art, Spence's drawings of old buildings already exhibited the scenographic verve which was to characterise his mature work; he was, however, awarded poor marks for building construction. In 1933, after graduation, he and another College graduate, William Kininmonth, joined A. F. Balfour Paul in Rowand Anderson's old firm, Rowand Anderson & Balfour Paul. Paul had perpetuated a restrained, Lorimer-like classicism in works such as his Edinburgh University Chemistry Building of 1920–4; or the restorations at Pollok House for Sir John Stirling Maxwell. The new partners brought a Sydney Mitchell-like vivacity and eclecticism to the practice. Kininmonth recalled that 'we rather prided ourselves on being able to work in any style'. [30] Early works by the two new partners (some on their own account) included boxy Art Deco villas at Dick Place (1933, Kininmonth's own house) and Easter Belmont Road (1935); a Lorimerian villa by Spence at 6 Castlelaw Road (1932); a concrete garage at Causewayside, Edinburgh (1933); a painted cottage-terrace at Dunbar, with big arched entrances (1934–5); various shops and exhibition pavilions; and, finally, two Lorimerian country houses, the demure Quothquan (1937–8), and the spectacular Broughton Place (1935–8), a massive tower house in some respects recalling Formakin, with decorative stonework by Hew Lorimer [8.13].

The 1938 Glasgow Empire Exhibition

The Scottish Beaux-Arts interpretation of modernity reached its climax at the end of our period, in the Glasgow Empire Exhibition (or 'Empirex') of 1938. Driven forward by shipbuilding magnate Sir James Lithgow, the exhibition repackaged the radial relationship between Scottish industry and the British Empire within a framework not of imperialist *laissez-faire* but of corporatist modernisation. As the exhibition was nationally symbolic, yet had to be built rapidly, Tait was the obvious choice as architect. Typically, his response was based on the values of Taylorism: scientific management and technical efficiency. While retaining overall control, he organised a group of younger architects from west and east to design most of the buildings [8.14]. Exploiting the Glasgow dry-assembly tradition, he devised a system of standard unit construction, comprising asbestos sheeting on metal or timber frames. The complex took precisely the fourteen months scheduled to build: for instance, the Palace of Industries West, a vast exhibition hall incorporating over 900 tons of structural steel, was erected by twelve men in ten weeks.

8.13 Broughton Place (Rowand Anderson & Balfour Paul, 1935–8), view of *c*.1938-9.

8.14 Drawing (1938) of the designers of the Glasgow Empire Exhibition. Clockwise: Thomas Tait (ringed), T. W. Marwick; Margaret Brodie, Launcelot Ross, Esme Gordon, Gordon Tait; Jack Coia, J. Taylor Thomson, A. D. Bryce, Basil Spence (with dogs).

An assessment of the Exhibition's architecture should begin in the context of the succession of major national and international expositions staged in the 1930s: especially Chicago (1933), Paris (1937) and New York (1939). The most immediate link was in Tait's office: Farquhar had worked with Raymond Hood at the Chicago event. But Glasgow had key features in common with all of them: a monumental, axial layout; buildings of relatively uniform design with elements of stylistic Modernism, painted in bright and co-ordinated colours; and (in contrast to the trade-bazaar atmosphere of many previous expositions) a concentration on national ideological projection [8.15]. Where Paris projected a more traditional, classical monumentality, and New York a futuristic

image of 'Democracity', Glasgow stood midway between the two, combining a quiet, Beaux-Arts layout with technically innovative construction. These attributes were offset by a degree of theatrical gaiety indebted to the devices of cinema design, with coloured surfaces and sculpture by day, and vivid lighting and cascades by night. The psychological aim was to create public 'optimism': in Tait's words, to 'prevent any feeling of drabness, solemnity or sadness . . . to get into the minds of the people that life is not so solemn . . . by judicious use of colour, to achieve a spirit of happiness and life'. The architecture itself was quite plain: most pavilions were low, flat-roofed, generally with rectangular plans. Tait explained that 'with asbestos sheets, everything must be kept very

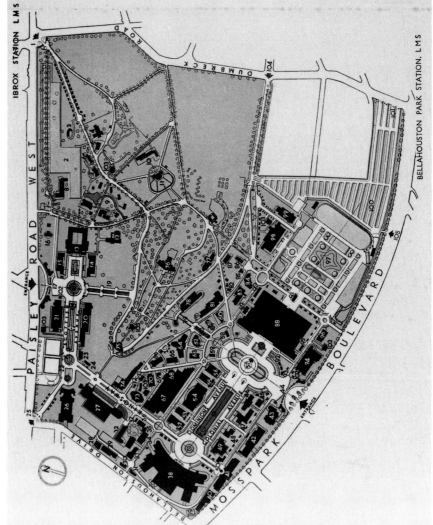

8.15 Plan of Empire Exhibition from official guidebook.

simple, relying only on the shape and masses of the building to produce the effect desired'. [31] There were a few exceptions, such as Basil Spence's ICI pavilion, which reproduced a popular motif from the 1925 Paris and 1933 Chicago exhibitions: a ring of three pylons, here linked with curved bars and with Whalen sculptures and water-display [8.16].

But popular Modernism's emphasis on asymmetrical 'dynamism' also required a vertical accent, to offset the horizontal, massive main exhibition grouping [8.17]. This accent, designed by Tait himself (in collaboration with Launcelot Ross and the engineer James Mearns), was the 300-feet-high Tower of Empire, a symbolic observation tower rising from a restaurant building at the summit of Bellahouston Park. Anchored in a 3,500-ton block of concrete, the Tower was built of the same system as the other buildings: steel-framing covered in corrugated sheeting (here, asbestos-coated steel). It comprised a stepped-back, symmetrical body topped by a fin and slim vane, offset by horizontal, projecting balconies near the top, and painted in a striking variant of national colours: silver, with turquoise fin and slashes of blue running down its face. Tait commented that it was 'Very dramatic, and certainly very sensational. No-one can say that we copied it from anywhere.' [32] Transatlantic comparisons are, however, inevitable: for example, with the stepped, symmetrical forms of the Rockefeller Center, or of some John Storrs sculpture; the transverse balconies were probably inspired by Mallet-Stevens's Tourism Pavilion at the 1925 Paris Exposition (visited by Tait). Next to the Tower, in complete contrast, was Dr Colin

8.16 Imperial Chemical Industries pavilion at the Empire Exhibition, by Basil Spence; sculpture by T. Whalen.

8.17 Tower of Empire, by T. S. Tait with Launcelot Ross and engineer James Mearns, May 1938 view.

Sinclair's An Clachan. This was a repeat of the 1911 display, but now with the declared purpose of promoting the modernisation of the Highlands.

The end of 'Empirex' marked a change in public climate. A recovery of confidence seemed to be under way, both in Glasgow and across the whole nation. Lord Provost Patrick Dollan pronounced that 'the exhibition has taught us all a finer and more colourful way of living, and that it is possible in Glasgow to educate and enjoy ourselves without drabness and greyness'. [33] And Agnes Muir Mackenzie asserted that 'the dowdiness which had sodden two generations of Scottish national life was drying out, and the moribund country was cocking her bonnet again'. [34]

Late 1930s to 1960: The Era of Planning

By the late 1930s, a new, state-based national identity was in course of construction, whose dynamic momentum was provided not by imperial and industrial expansion, but by disciplined social reconstruction at home. Although, as late as 1939, the economist J. A. Bowie could still take issue with 'the greatly cherished Scottish belief that liberty consisted in frustrating Government', [35] such a statement, by the next decade, would become almost incomprehensible.

In the built environment, the leitmotiv of this new collectivist conception of the nation was 'planning'. In Scotland, this was, as we have seen, an idea with a long and variegated pedigree, stretching back through Geddesian conservative surgery and Glasgow city improvement, to the new towns of the eighteenth century and earlier. Now, however, it acquired a new ideological intensity, encapsulating as it did all the main aspects of the 20th century's concept of the social nation. From the mid-1930s, there was a crescendo of calls for co-ordinated national reconstruction, and this time the actual experience of war reinforced, rather than undermined, the prewar efforts. In 1941, William Power wrote that 'national planning is no longer a Utopian fantasy. It is an urgent and admitted necessity, to which the State has implicitly pledged itself'. [36] Following principles first enunciated by the wartime Secretary of State (1941–5) Tom Johnston, the Scottish Office was to co-ordinate a programme of social and industrial regeneration, which would balance the needs of the industrial Lowlands for modernisation with those of the Highlands for the stemming of depopulation. The nineteenth-century *laissez-faire*, imperial image of the nation had reached the nadir of its reputation. The task, Alan Reiach and Robert Hurd wrote in 1941, was now to destroy the 'chaos and ugliness' created by the nineteenth century: 'Here is a challenge which we meet joyfully. Here is a new Scotland to be built.' [37]

On the whole, the early post-war initiatives led by the Scottish Office concentrated on the areas where its power was already established: social policy and physical infrastructure. Vast public programmes of building, of houses, schools, whole new towns, were undertaken. Each was overseen by its own balance of professional experts and politicians, and central and local forces, but all were united by the ideal of planning. There was to be planned social provision, planned regional development through the building of new towns in the Lowlands, and a planned revitalisation of the Highlands through a huge hydro-electric programme [cf. 8.24]. In the most emotive arena of mass social provision, housing – with its intimate link to demographic and industrial policy – the drive towards planned state provision was now so strong and diverse that competing solutions could flourish: the municipal (focused on Glasgow Corporation), and the 'regional'. Overall, many thought planning and the building of state-socialist welfarism were the same thing. In 1947, Secretary of State Joseph Westwood defined planning as the 'national housekeeping of the common people'; the Secretary of State was 'Scotland's Planning Minister'. (38)

The relationship between architecture and the building of the Scottish welfare state from the late 1930s to the late 1950s was quite complex. The previously prominent Beaux-Arts tendency became less important. Its conception of order, in terms of an internationalist and classicising rationalism, began to seem passive and complacent. And all its visual elements were being called into question – mass composition as ponderous and heavy, and popular Streamform as vulgar and commercialised. What was now sought was a dynamic and teleological discipline, directed towards urgent goals. Debates became increasingly polarised into two rival formulae: the Modern (or Modernist) and the Traditional. The Moderns emphasised progress, often with overtones of socialism, and the Traditionalists emphasised the nation. Both, however, relied on a kind of state-co-ordinated modernity which radically modified the ideas of their predecessors. The new breed of Modernists rejected Taitian sculpture-architecture as debased stylism, and demanded thoroughgoing new 'community planning' based on international Modernist principles. The new generation of Traditionalists, rejecting the establishment patriotism of the Anderson generation, called for a different sort of community, looking to the future but rooted firmly in concepts of the national past.

There were many overlaps: for instance, just as Thomson had been the Beaux-Arts idol, both the new Modernists and Traditionalists, from the mid-1930s, began to venerate the very recent memory of C. R. Mackintosh. (39) Broadly speaking, the reinvigorated Traditionalism was dominant in the late 1930s; the position was fluid in the 1940s and early 1950s; but from the mid-1950s, there was a successful attempt, led by Robert Matthew, to introduce an institutionalised version of Modern architecture, tailor-made for public patronage. By 1960, a wider confidence that the nation was at last imposing collective discipline on its built environment seemed to be reflected in this new architectural order, whose internal consistency and all-encompassing scope brought to a climax trends that had been gathering pace since the turn of the century.

'A National Awakening': The New Traditionalism and Public Architecture, 1930s–1950s (40)

As the 1930s progressed, Scotland, like many other Depression-hit European countries, witnessed an upsurge in ideologies of national cohesion, and of calls for new, implicitly anti-capitalist recipes of folk solidarity. At first, there was concentration on the threat to the Scottish 'essence': John Buchan claimed in 1932 that 'we are losing some of the best of our race stock by migration', and Ian C. Hannah's *The Story of Scotland in Stone* complained that 'the wide river of Scottish culture has for many days flowed in a course that has been well-nigh Jewish in its cosmopolitanism, almost rudderless in its direction'. (41) But increasingly, this was replaced by heady talk of 'rebirth', and an outpouring of popularised publications. In 1941, for instance, Agnes Mure Mackenzie wrote of 'a new vision, a new sense of Scotland': 'the bare trees are flushing with rising sap'; 'we have Scotland's future history to shape'; she called for 're-settlement on the land' and 'the enlistment of labour battalions of unemployed for a war on bracken'. (42) In opposition to socialist class politics, there was an insistence on a classless national community – accentuated by conviction of the 'organic' cohesion of Scotland in comparison with England's 'caste-ridden society'. [43] Culturally, the central force in this movement was the Saltire Society, founded in 1936 by several academics at Glasgow University.

In architecture, these new ideas prompted the emergence of a new generation of aggressively modernising Traditionalists. Prominent was a new hostility to cosmopolitanism, and the drawing of a sharp contrast between avant-garde 'flashy, international' continental modernism and the concept of a 'wholesome' or 'national' Scottish modernism: 'a sound modern tradition'. [44] Sir John Stirling Maxwell, patron of Rowand Anderson and Balfour Paul at Pollok, dismissed Taitian Art Deco as 'ignoring the traditions of our race', and warned that while 'artistic clients will want Craigievar with a few Corbusier corners thrown in', architecture must 'recover its national character . . . imparting a wholesome Scots reserve and vigour even to buildings designed to meet the latest demand in the most up-to-date materials . . . the only traditions worth following are those of one's own country'. [45] Leslie Grahame Thomson went further, blasting 'rabbit-hutch' flat-roofed Continental modernism as 'sheer bunkum . . . an international mess of pottage'. [46]

As to the architectural form of this 'national character', while it was still held that the sixteenth and seventeenth centuries were the 'most national', [47] the Andersonian and Lorimerian reliance on Scots Renaissance style, based on antiquarian research, was criticised as 'harking back to old forms'. Instead, there was a reliance on more imprecise, emotional formulae with ethical overtones. The concept of 'antisyzygy' popularised by G. Gregory Smith and Hugh MacDiarmid in the 1920s' Scottish (literary) Renaissance allowed almost anything to be embraced within the unique Scottish 'essence'. Robert Hurd asked in 1938: 'of what does this essential traditional spirit consist? I would say bold simplicity threaded by an odd streak of vanity.' It was this which would inspire the new 'national' modernism, whose chief 'herald' had been Mackintosh. [48] Other words such as 'functional' and 'organic' were sometimes used instead of 'modern'. [49] Ian Lindsay, one of the most prominent of this new grouping of designers, noted in 1935 that, in old tower houses, 'turrets . . . are not crudely stuck on the corners

but grow out, and form an organic part of the building . . . simplicity and functionalism is not modern'. [50]

Where previously the Scots Renaissance style, with varying emphases, had been applied to all building types, now there was a marked differentiation, aimed at establishing distinctions between honorific buildings and more utilitarian types. For public buildings, a flat-faced monumental classicism free of mass emphases was favoured. Construction was not an issue here: both this and Taitian classicism were equally suited to steel-framing. For larger churches, too, there was a new tendency of roomy classicism. For domestic buildings, including smaller churches, an elemental, harled simplicity, with massive, steep roofs, was preferred – a tendency interrelated with the newly powerful conservation movement, focused both on Old Edinburgh and on small burgh collective architecture. These two recipes of 1930s' and 1940s' Traditionalism – public classicism and domestic primitivism – were closely paralleled, along with their accompanying anti-cosmopolitan rhetoric, in many other countries. And, just as elsewhere in Europe, their power would be undermined in the late 1940s and 1950s by greater acceptance of the state-socialist model of national reconstruction.

In major public buildings, the new tendency towards classical rectangularity was presaged by Mervyn Noad's competition winning entry for Prestwick Municipal Offices and Public Baths (1933, unbuilt), a group of symmetrical, austere, flat-roofed parapeted buildings with vertical or horizontally banded windows. For Noad, [51] 'good design' consisted of 'good proportion, careful arrangement of solids and voids, coupled with simple though beautiful materials'. By the mid-1930s, student projects manifested a growing taste for sober, horizontal groupings set in open space, with often attenuated external detail, such as slender window surrounds – although neo-Thomson pyramidal elements also often persisted. In the 1938 Rowand Anderson prize competition (subject: law courts), the winning design by Catherine M. H. Henderson (Glasgow), a severe block with arched front, was praised by the assessor, W. W. Friskin, as 'imposing, if somewhat merciless'. [52] The year before, Friskin had complained that entries were polarised between modernist 'emotionalists' copying Gropius and Corbusier, and classical 'Roman geese, goose-stepping in unison, honking into emptiness'. [53]

The two most important urban projects of this movement – the National Library of Scotland (NLS), by Reginald Fairlie, and Kirkcaldy Town House, by Carr and Howard – were both commenced in 1937 but only finished after the war. The NLS presents a striking contrast to its 'sculpturesque' near-contemporary, St Andrew's House [8.18; cf. 8.10]. Perched on a substructure stretching down many storeys to the Cowgate, the upper portion of the building is a large, plain rectangular block, with severe, low-relief main facade to George IV Bridge, ornamented with suitably attenuated statues by Hew Lorimer. Kirkcaldy Town House was designed by two very young architects, but shows the same characteristics as Fairlie's design – flat roofline, rectangular profile, and delicate, somewhat linear detail – in addition to neo-classical window-spacing and an asymmetrical main facade with spindly belfry steeple [8.19]. David Carr's commentary of 1937 to this competition-winning design makes clear that the Traditionalist concepts of folk community were just as important in classical public architecture as in domestic building:

> Scottish towns have very strongly rooted characters; they are entities; most of the towns-people are descendants of the original founders. . . These inborn characteristics should not be ignored . . . styles of architecture suitable for other lands and places, should they conflict with the sensibilities of the people, would be unsuited to form the basis of the design for the civic centre of this community. [54]

Other distinguished urban realisations of Traditionalist classicism – mostly in the East – included the massive Graeco-Italian cube of Oldrieve, Bell & Paterson's Edinburgh Savings Bank (1939); [8.20] the slightly more florid Commercial Bank, Union Street, Aberdeen, by Jenkins & Marr (1936), with its huge Corinthian columns; the flat facade, with incised colonnade, of Miller's Nairn headquarters at Kirkcaldy (1938); the low-relief, neo-classical-windowed, but still asymmetrical Jay's store, Princes Street (1938–9, by T. P. Marwick & Son); and the sheer, polished corner block by Leslie Grahame Thomson and F. J. Connell for the Caledonian Insurance Company (1938–40). In the west, several projects of 1938 by Basil Spence, including a Kilsyth experimental school for the Scottish Council for Art and Industry (built after the war in altered form), and a villa for steel magnate John Colville (Gribloch, near Kippen), showed a marked drift away from his previous eclecticism towards a neo-classical horizontality and calmness, combined with asymmetrical elements.

After the war, in urban buildings in the east, this severe, usually astylar classicism was widely continued. W. N. W. Ramsay's competition-winning design for Edinburgh University Medical School (competition 1951, only the west part was built), the first element in the university's redevelopment of George Square, was envisaged by the architect and the assessor (A. G. R. Mackenzie) as 'entirely in harmony' with the eighteenth-century buildings. To echo the latter, Ramsay envisaged his new buildings as 'an essay in recessed and projected surfaces of varying materials'. [55] His competition win for Glasgow University Arts Building (1953) was similar but asymmetrical. An austere classicism persisted in many commercial buildings: for instance, in T. P. Marwick & Son's Sun Alliance building, Edinburgh (1954–5), and the Royal Exchange Assurance block, Dundee, 1955–8, by John Needham of Gauldie, Hardie, Wright & Needham. This stone-faced style was developed in the 1960s by Esme Gordon of Gordon & Dey in Edinburgh's George Street electricity offices (1960–4, with 1930s-style integral sculpture by Whalen) and Scottish Life Assurance Company offices (1960). Gordon also designed additions at Moray House College of Education: a gymnasium block built as late as 1968–70 had an attenuated portico.

Of the architects who carried on an interwar-style eclecticism into the 1950s, the most versatile and subtle was Spence's former partner, W. H. Kininmonth (of Rowand Anderson, Kininmonth & Paul). His public buildings continued a late 1930s formality, avoiding overbearing scale. A fondness for 'open approaches classical scale of order and balance . . . play of form and light . . . direct and simple plan' [56] was displayed in the Pollock Halls university residences in Edinburgh

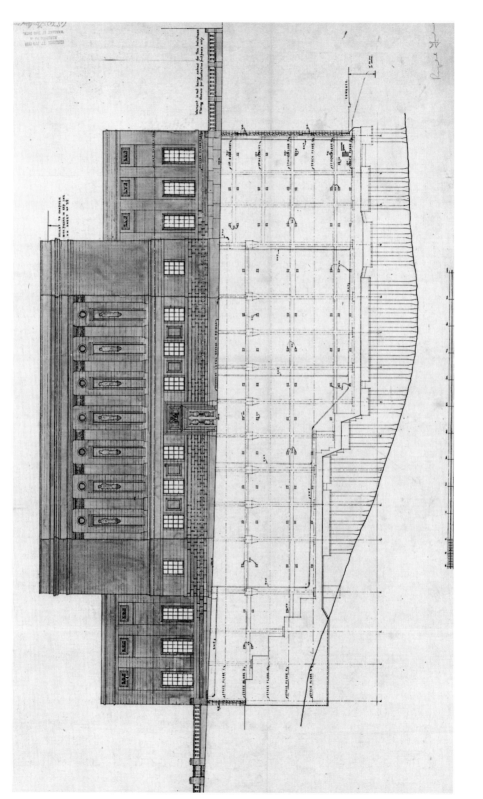

8.18 National Library of Scotland (Fairlie, 1937–55), 1937 drawing showing front facade and stack floors below George IV Bridge level.

8.19 Kirkcaldy Town House (Carr and Howard, 1937–56), 1937 competition perspective.

8.20 Edinburgh Savings Bank (Oldrieve, Bell & Paterson, 1939), 1939 perspective by C. A. Farey.

(1952–9). This symmetrical group, with its thin lantern towers, had as an axial focus a dining hall with arched concrete colonnade of simplified Quattrocento character [8.21]. For a university examination block in Chambers Street, opposite Old College (1954), Kininmonth chose a more vertical, monumental classicism, including a central arched window, inspired by an eighteenth-century predecessor on the same site. Kininmonth saw the design as 'a triumphal arch through which all students pass to success or failure'. [57] Yet at just the same time a very different project of his was under construction in the west: the extravagantly cantilevered concrete skeleton of the Renfrew Airport Terminal (1953–4), whose main roof was supported by a soaring bowstring arch. Asked by the Ministry of Aviation to create a building with a strong image of modernity, Kininmonth (and his project architect Michael Laird) had avoided the 'purely functional' and preferred 'aesthetics' to 'utility'. He himself used the contrast between Renfrew and Chambers Street to illustrate his own eclectic principles:

> one is an airport, built in an open field . . . while the other is a University building filling a gap site, in a stone street of classical architecture, built of rock . . . Architecture is a microcosm within the greater macrocosm of nature which it faithfully reflects in all its forms, whether we call those forms classicism, romanticism or merely functionalism. [58]

That this philosophy was still active, within not only private architecture but also much state architecture, is illustrated by the range of major projects designed by Stewart Sim, Senior Architect to the Ministry of Works in Scotland. For government administrative complexes (some designed before the war and built after), he used reinforced-concrete frame construction clad in a massive, simplified classicism. Noteworthy

8.21 Pollock Halls, University of Edinburgh (Rowand Anderson, Kininmonth & Paul, 1952–9), photograph (signed by W. H. Kininmonth) of dining hall when newly completed.

8.22 Carstairs State Institution (Sim, 1956–8), 1957 view of complex.

examples included the colonnaded Greyfriars House in Aberdeen (1953), the taller Montrose House, Glasgow, with its rounded, finned corner (1951–3), and Fountainbridge Telephone Exchange, Edinburgh (1948–50), whose asymmetrical grouping of a curved office wing and pilastered apparatus block projected 'a feeling of openness' while expressing 'in a modern way . . . the dignity of a Government undertaking'. [59] Sim's most important work was Carstairs State Institution, a high-security national mental hospital built in 1956–8 on a colony-type axial plan, its Lorimerian ward blocks dominated by monumental shaped gables and buttresses [8.22, 8.23].

The post-war culmination of state-sponsored classical monumentalism was located in the more emotively resonant context of the Highlands. Johnston's success in setting up the North of Scotland Hydro-Electric Board in 1943 unleashed an outpouring of hope, that at last the Highland 'problem' could be finally resolved, by state initiative [8.24]. The Board's mighty engineering works – which began with the buttress dam at Loch Sloy (from 1946), and culminated in the deep underground machine hall of the Cruachan pumped-storage scheme (1960–5), for which 330,000 cubic yards of rock had to be blasted out, made a tremendous impression on many

8.23 Carstairs State Institution, 1957 view of entrance to one of the ward blocks.

architects tending towards Modernism. In 1952, Basil Spence declared that the dams recalled 'the magnificence of Roman architecture'. [60] But in the hierarchical world of Traditionalism, it was rather the power stations which were exalted as

noble works of architecture. They would, it was hoped, serve as a catalyst both for monumental design and for a state-sponsored attempt to revive the use of facing stone. In the first big schemes, Sloy (1946–50) and Tummel-Garry (1947–53), H. O. Tarbolton, as the Board's architectural adviser, designed power stations in a flat, cubic style similar to Fairlie's National Library [cf. 8.18]. Sloy was built in granite-aggregate blockwork, while the massive Pitlochry, integrated with a dam and bridge, was faced in granite, and prominently adorned with the Board's coat of arms and motto, *Neart nan Gleann* (Power of the Glens). After Tarbolton's death in 1947, Mears chaired the Board's Amenity Committee; the next series of stations was commissioned from James Shearer and Annand. Shearer became the most forceful

designer-propagandist of Hydro architecture, and a vehement opponent of cosmopolitan Modernism's 'glassy, shadowless and somewhat flighty architecture'. His stations for the Affric project were squat, cubic and detailed in simplified classical fashion: at the largest, Fasnakyle (1946–52), Hew Lorimer sculpted low-relief panels of 'Celtic legends'. In an attempt to revive a 'commonsense practice of the past', when buildings were 'seemly, and at home with their settings', [61] Shearer used locally quarried rubble for the stations, and built a 'model Highland village' of stone-built staff houses at Cannich [62] – the first of several such schemes. In his next series of stations, at Conon Valley (1951–6), he continued his struggle for an 'appropriate sense of rugged strength' and 'massive simplicity'; one station, Achanalt (1951–5),

NEART NAN GLEANN

Strength of the Glens

THE motto of the North of Scotland Hydro-Electric Board has a wider meaning than the strength of concrete and steel typified by the buttresses of the Loch Sloy Dam. It signifies the great water power resources that are being harnessed in the Highlands and their importance to the future of our country.

From the turbulent waters of the glens new strength is flowing to serve the people of the north, to bring comforts and facilities to croft, clachan, and city, to ease labour of farm, hotel, and workshop, and to speed the wheels of industry. More power, too, is being made available for the industrial belt of Central Scotland.

More and more power from future hydro-electric schemes will be ready to serve new ideas, initiative, and enterprise. This is a task worthy of the traditions of Scots pioneers . . . a heritage for future generations.

NORTH OF SCOTLAND HYDRO-ELECTRIC BOARD

8.24 Traditionalist architecture and rhetoric of the North of Scotland Hydro-Electric Board: (left) Fasnakyle Power Station (Shearer, 1946–52), late 1950s' view; (above) advertisement in G. Scott-Moncrieff, *Living Traditions of Scotland*, 1951, p. 77.

was built 'hard against a great vertical cliff'. [63] Other Traditionalist architects became involved in the programme, such as Robert Hurd & Partners (Aigas and Kilmorack, 1958–63) or Ian G. Lindsay (Loch Gair); while Leslie Grahame Thomson drew up abortive plans in 1949 for a vast Hydro Board headquarters complex at Pitlochry in a towered Lorimerian manner.

A separate element within the honorific, or public Traditionalism of these decades was a new classicising tendency in church design. In the 1920s, within the Protestant churches, the impetus of the neo-Catholic movement had faded, although isolated Gothic prestige commissions continued, such as L. G. Thomson's own Reid Memorial Church, Edinburgh, of 1929–33, or J. Taylor Thomson's St John Renfield Church, Glasgow, of 1927–31. The mainstream was now a plain, massive neo-Romanesque (or, less often, neo-Gothic), stemming ultimately from the smaller churches of Burnet [cf. 7.55]. Protestant examples of this style, which continued through the 1930s, included H. O. Tarbolton's Bangour Village Church (1924–30) and St Salvador, Saughton (1939–42, Gothic); and L. G. Thomson's stumpy, rubble Fairmilehead Church (1937) [8.25]. Roman Catholic examples included Reginald Fairlie's prolific output, culminating in the block-towered Immaculate Conception Church, Fort William (1933–4); and the jaggedly idiosyncratic brick Romanesque of Archibald Macpherson (for example St Matthew, Rosewell, finished 1926). As the 1930s opened, the reunification of the Church of Scotland the previous year had, at a stroke, removed much of the need for new Presbyterian church-building. Now, the main concern was in renovating nineteenth-century churches to make them more 'worshipful'. [64] By this was meant the toning-down of extremes of preaching-hall or ritualistic furnishings, and the replacement of dark varnish by white or neutral colour schemes. The Calvinistic aversion to ornate decoration remained strong in some quarters. Leslie Grahame Thomson scorned 'the muck of rococo pulpits and monuments which clutter the churches of Belgium'. [65] For new churches, ideas of modernity were of peripheral significance: Frank Mears's 1931 call for a 'Clydeside Church' of stainless steel to express Presbyterian 'austerity'

8.25 St Salvador's Episcopal Church, Saughton, Edinburgh (Tarbolton, 1939–42).

went unanswered. Rather, the chief new tendency of 1930s' church design was a move towards classicism. The judges of the 1934 Incorporation Prize (subject: a country church) noted that 'from Edinburgh came collegiate chapels in the Renaissance. Glasgow contributed small classical churches, with here and there a flavour of the vernacular; while both types came from Aberdeen and Dundee'. [66] Although there were isolated large classical Protestant commissions in the 1930s, such as Oldrieve, Bell & Paterson's Bristo Baptist Church, Edinburgh (1933–5, with big Cape Dutch gable), the most striking realisations of this new trend were in the Roman Catholic Church, where since Pope Pius X (1903–14) a movement towards centralised, worshipper-centred plans had been emerging. This would culminate in the 1960s, in the work of Pope John XXIII and the Second Vatican Council, but already by the 1930s a move towards basilican plans was under-way across northern Europe.

The key innovator who popularised these tendencies in Scotland was Giacomo Antonio (Jack) Coia [cf. 8.14]. Taught at Glasgow School of Art by Professors Gourlay and McGibbon, Coia had trained in a wide range of Glasgow offices, including those of J. Gaff Gillespie, A. N. Paterson, and A. D. Hislop. The deaths of Gillespie and William Kidd had left him sole heir to their practice (renamed Gillespie, Kidd & Coia). He now took up with vigour, in the west, the brick style of Catholic church architecture previously pioneered in the east in the work of Macpherson, along with the classicising tendencies evident in Fairlie's refacing of St Patrick's, Cowgate, with a triumphal arch facade in 1928–9. Coia's first church, St Anne's, Dennistoun (1931), exploited engineering skills in Beaux-Arts fashion, to obtain, rather as in cinema designs, a broad, centralised space, flanked by narrow arcades rather than aisles. Its monumental facade was red-brick, classical, and hard-edged in the Beaux-Arts manner, with Byzantine elements. Subsequent commissions – St Patrick, Greenock (1934–5), St Columba,

Maryhill (1937), and St Columbkille, Rutherglen (1934–40) – adopted a more linear plan [8.26]. St Patrick's was the most striking of these, with its tall, gabled facade, sloping side walls offset by pilastered dormers, and circular columned pavilion as a visual link to the integral church house. The building had a profusion of carving of an Early Christian or Byzantine character by Archibald Dawson, head of sculpture at Glasgow School of Art. Coia's 1930s' churches began the trend of selective use of details indebted to Mackintosh. Later in the decade Coia took into partnership the most talented of his former pupils, T. Warnett Kennedy. The two commissions designed by Kennedy – the temporary, open-roofed Catholic chapel at the Empire Exhibition (fronted by a Mackintosh-like grid of metalwork), and St Peter in Chains Church, Ardrossan (both 1938) – were influenced by the 'abstract compositions' of contemporary Swedish architecture; [67] both had austere walls and towers.

After the war, Roman Catholic churches, especially in the west, continued their pre-

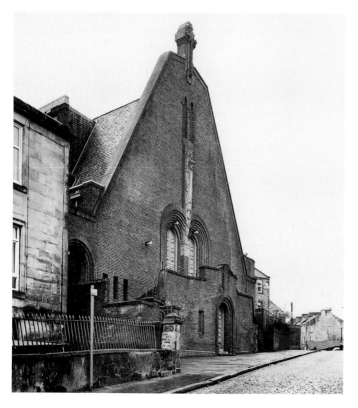

8.26 St Patrick's RC Church, Greenock (Gillespie, Kidd & Coia, 1934–5), 1993 view, including sculpture by Archibald Dawson.

occupation with hierarchical dignity, with brick monumentality outside and marble within: these large structures made liberal use of reinforced concrete elements. Some architects, such as Alexander McAnally & Partners, still employed neo-Romanesque. McAnally's most prominent work was the massive, towered St Teresa of Lisieux, Glasgow (1956–60). Coia's larger churches of the 1940s and early 1950s often featured triangular 'Gothic' elements. The largest and most powerful was St Lawrence, Greenock (1951–4), a stepped group sited on a St Vincent Street-like substructure, with dramatically lit interior. The 'triangular' theme, representing the Holy Trinity, was carried to an obsessive extreme at Cordiner's Immaculate Conception Church, Maryhill (1955–6), a concrete A-frame structure with swept-down roof and mosaic-faced entrance front. An even larger 1950s' religious project grounded in 'traditional' honorific imagery – in the context, however, not of Scottish Catholicism but of the Church of England – was Basil Spence's winning design in the 1951 competition for a new Anglican

Cathedral at Coventry (built 1954–62). Here Spence put to new use his theatrical skills, putting aside his exhibition modernity for a grave, stone-faced monumentality: 'I saw the Cathedral as a great hunk of rock standing for permanence.' (68) He designed a hall of slightly tapering plan, with zigzag walls of sandstone and (internally) concrete, and a structurally separate roof of shell structures supported by slender columns intended to evoke English Perpendicular architecture. There was a subordinate axis between the circular Chapel of Unity, on one side, and the font, a rough boulder from Bethlehem. The design, like Lorimer's Scottish National War Memorial, was dominated by a concern that 'the new building should grow from the old', and by a celebration of wartime 'sacrifice' through profuse, symbolic *Gesamtkunstwerk*. A tall glass window and overhanging external canopy attempted to integrate the ruins of the old cathedral within the sequence of spaces, and, like Edinburgh, there was a dominant sculpture of St Michael slaying the Devil. Following his Coventry win, Spence moved

8.27 Colinton Mains Church, Edinburgh (Lindsay, 1954).

permanently to England in 1953, but continued to take on work in Scotland, through an increasingly autonomous grouping of partners based in Edinburgh (set up in 1951 as a separate practice: Basil Spence, Glover and Ferguson).

In contrast to these grandiosely ceremonial solutions, the Kirk's 1950s' building drive in existing suburbs and new housing schemes took a more self-effacing form, sometimes close to Traditionalist domestic architecture. Many noteworthy new parish churches were built in or near Edinburgh: Kininmonth's Drylaw, a geometrical, rendered group with swept-down pitched roofs (1956–7, job architect J. E. A. Baikie); Ian G. Lindsay & Partners' Livingston Station and Colinton Mains (1949 and 1954), evoking the pyramidal-towered eighteenth-century Caithness parish churches later praised in Lindsay's *The Scottish Parish Kirk;* and Leslie Grahame MacDougall's circular-towered Longstone (1954) [8.27]. A larger work by MacDougall was the rendered, green-roofed Christ Church Dunollie, Oban (1954–7). Basil Spence, in a small parish church of this later period, Clermiston (1957–9), enlivened a modest hall with a tall skeletal bell tower on one side, and provided theatrical lighting through holes in the gable wall: the church was the axial focus of a garden suburb (1952–61) by J. A. W. Grant.

Social Traditionalism and Burgh Preservation

Where the urban utopianism of Geddes and others, at the turn of the century, had been largely the concern of an 'artistic' intelligentsia, the rising populist collectivism of the late 1930s ascribed much wider importance to the ordinary dwelling, and to the ideal of social community. This was a key arena for the clash between socialist Modernism and organic Traditionalism. The latter's new tendencies of the late 1930s, just as in the Anderson and Lorimer years, closely bound together the design of new dwellings, and the liking for old groups of houses. A much sharper oppositional spur was now present, in the form of municipal housing schemes, whose sanitary openness Traditionalists saw as alienating

and fragmenting. In contrast to these, small burghs were idealised as 'organisms', whose buildings also shared in the classless folk community: 'the big rubs shoulders with the small, and all stand in a warm and friendly neighbourliness'. [69] Eventually, in the late 1940s and 1950s, the growing prestige of planned state socialism and of international Modernism would undermine such rhetoric.

In new architectural design during the 1930s, two tendencies stemmed from these ideas. The first formed part of the typical northern European interwar search for a 'national' pattern of small detached rural or suburban cottage, with steep roof and the utmost 'simplicity of statement'; [70] it was bound up with *Heimatschutz* rural protection movements and, in Scotland, the ongoing architectural polemic against 'fussy' bungalows. In 1932, L. G. Thomson and Mears produced standard rural cottage designs of 'unobtrusive uniformity', not dissimilar to council houses, for the Association for the Preservation of Rural Scotland. [71] In 1935, Mears's future partner, H. A. Rendel Govan, commenting on Robert H. Matthew's steep-gabled winning design for another cottage competition by the Edinburgh Architectural Association (EAA), argued that 'while the plan is essentially modern and functional, the elevations are composed entirely of inherent house forms, and are the true development of local traditions to suit modern planning' [8.28]. By contrast, the 'machine-form house' of continental Modernism was 'inimical to family life'. [72] Similarly steep-roofed, with shutters, was Kininmonth's double villa at 40–42 Dick Place, Edinburgh (1934) and Ian Carnegie's small house at Ratho, 1937. The second branch of 1930s' Traditionalist housing design was concerned with dwellings in linked groups, and had connotations of small-burgh rather than rural community. This movement also fed off anti-bungalow and anti-sprawl polemic, and formed the main focus of Saltire Society endeavours in housing. It continued the Geddesian emphasis on enclosed rather than open space, and thus implicitly opposed the open planning of continental Modernist urbanism – although some of its champions, such as J. Steel Maitland in Renfrew, introduced elements of continental detailing. In

1937, the Saltire Society initiated its annual Good Design in Housing awards scheme: the 1937 and 1938 awards went to picturesque cottage schemes by Joseph Weekes (architect to Dunbarton County Council) at Milton and J. A. W. Grant at Westquarter. These endeavours spurred new debates about the definition of the national 'essence': for instance, over the colouring of harl. Some, such as W. Schomberg Scott, Grant, or Noad, advocated colour washes as part of the 'bright and cheery . . . traditions of Scottish architecture', while others, such as Sir W.

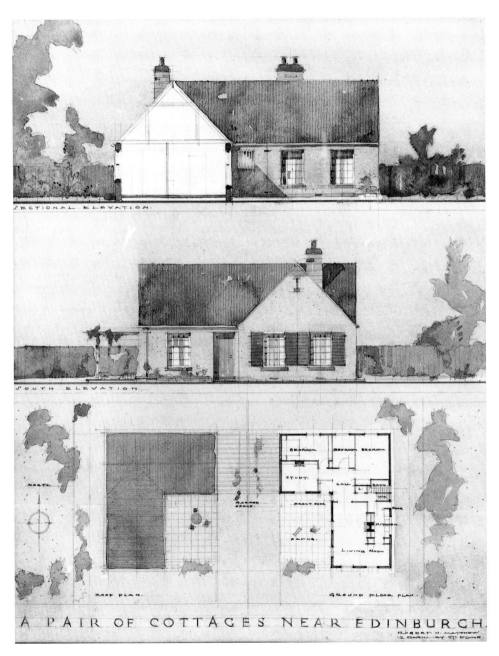

8.28 'Vernacular'-inspired design (1930s): winning design by Robert H. Matthew for Edinburgh Architectural Association cottage competition, 1935.

Alexander, insisted that white harl was the only authentic 'Scottish tradition'. [73]

Just as in the time of Mitchell and Geddes, the design of new housing inspired by the picturesque groups of the past naturally linked up with the aim of preserving those old groups – and there were the first hints of the way in which, by the 1970s, old buildings would come to take precedence over new. The EAA stand at the 1937 Building Exhibition, entitled 'Housing Old and New', combined photographs of old Scots houses and new flats on the Continent. Geddes's advocacy of 'conservation of the historic heritage' [74] was progressively developed into the beginnings of state-sponsored 'listing', by a series of innovators. The first of these was Frank Mears – Geddes's collaborator and (from 1915) son-in-law. Apprenticed to Hippolyte Blanc, Mears had worked with R. Weir Schultz and Sydney Mitchell, and then with Traquair. After establishing his own practice in 1910, Mears worked with Geddes on the design for a Hebrew University in Jerusalem (partly built, 1919–29). Back home in Edinburgh, Mears implemented the Geddesian philosophy of conservation in a series of restoration schemes: Huntly House, 1927–32 (for Edinburgh Corporation); the David Livingstone Memorial Buildings, Blantyre (1927); Gladstone's Land, Edinburgh, 1934–5. From 1936, as consultant to Stirling Town Council, Mears began the regeneration of the historic Broad Street area, a scheme carried through into the 1960s by his later partners H. A. Rendel Govan and R. J. Naismith; since 1927 the Thistle Property Trust had already been reconditioning old houses in Stirling.

In the 1930s, burgh preservation activity accelerated. In 1931, the National Trust for Scotland (NTS) was founded, and soon extended its work from landscape to buildings conservation; the Gladstone's Land scheme was sponsored by the NTS. The new 1930s' architectural rhetoric of nationality concerned itself with the question of the Edinburgh Old Town. In 1935 Sir Ian Colquhoun pointed to its houses as 'monuments of the Scottish race' and opposed its conversion into a 'mummified' tourist precinct. A vocal advocate of these views, and close ally of Mears, was the young architect and Saltire Society council member Robert Hurd. In 1930, he identified NTS

schemes as a 'bulwark' against the 'provincialisation' of Scotland. [75] The demands of DHS's 1930 Housing Act for active slum-clearance soon shifted conservation anxiety from the well-trodden closes of Old Edinburgh to the smaller burghs. The focus of concern was Fife, where the NTS was already (in 1932) beginning its restoration of Culross [cf. 2.32]. Some Fife burghs, such as Crail, deliberately avoided demolishing their older houses, but others began clearance with relish. By the mid-1930s, conservationist alarm was growing: in 1937, Stirling-Maxwell described small burgh houses as 'smaller houses . . . in which the bulk of the Scots race has been reared . . . precious records of the national life'. [76] But the most significant boost to this campaign – as well as one of the clearest manifestos of Traditionalist opposition to socialism, broadly defined – came in 1936 with the publication of a polemical pamphlet, *A Plea for Scotland's Architectural Heritage*, by Scotland's premier interwar preserver: the 4th Marquess of Bute.

It was perhaps a sign of the decline of the direct power and wealth of the aristocracy, by comparison even with the era of his father, that the 4th Marquess's architectural crusade was concerned not with the building of country houses but with the preserving of groups of small burgh dwellings. And it was also significant that he pursued his cause not by personal expenditure but by proselytising and persuasion. In his 1936 pamphlet Bute, who was already privately promoting the preservation of the burgh of Falkland, made a head-on attack against municipal slum-clearance. These 'unintelligent . . . new Government settlements' represented a 'complete decay of national spirit', and an attack on the real interest of the working classes. For it was only the 'working man' who truly appreciated these 'archives of stone' of 'our country'. Bute at once began a campaign to pressurise DHS to offset the effects of slum-clearance, by inventorising old burgh houses as a preliminary to their preservation and reconditioning. Although it was an ambitious task to persuade a government department to endorse a project calculated to undermine one of its own main policies, he succeeded in convincing DHS Secretary Highton to agree to a burgh survey under NTS auspices. He then engaged the young

Ian G. Lindsay (who had worked with the National Trust at Culross and Dunkeld), to carry out the survey. Over the next two years, 92 burghs and 1,047 buildings were inventorised, using a categorisation system (A, B, C) derived from an Amsterdam municipal inventory. This national survey inspired various local initiatives such as the founding of the St Andrews Preservation Trust in 1938 under the influence of Annabel Kidston, Ronald Cant and others. To complement these efforts, the Scottish National Buildings Record was set up in 1941, under Bute (as chairman) and Scott-Moncrieff (as secretary). Its aim, in Scott-Moncrieff's words, was above all to record the 'modest homes of the people'. [77]

After the war, although the growing public acceptance of state socialism diminished the ideological base of social Traditionalism, the tradition of conservative surgery continued in a range of setpiece burgh schemes. Robert Hurd

remained a key figure. He had risen in the 1940s to such posts as Saltire Society president and design award chairman, Hydro Board amenity panel member, and planning consultant for Lewis and Ross & Cromarty. He devoted much energy to rural questions: his Kyle of Lochalsh primary school (1959–60), cradled in a rock outcrop, was plain and rendered with big pitched roofs. Hurd's promotion of 'organically sound . . . healthy community life' increasingly concentrated on the continued reconstruction and improvement of Edinburgh's Royal Mile. The 'repopulation of the Old Town . . . drawn from all classes' could help counter the 'sanitary isolation' of housing schemes like Craigmillar. [78] His most renowned scheme focused on a severely run-down area at the Canongate Tolbooth, in which he proposed selective redevelopment around retained architectural setpieces [8.29, 8.30]. The programme comprised Tolbooth Area (1953–8), Morocco

8.29 Mid-1960s' view of Robert Hurd & Partners' Chessels Court scheme, Canongate, Edinburgh (1958–66).

8.30 Photograph (1954) of the architects and workforce of Robert Hurd and Partners' Tolbooth Area redevelopment, Canongate. Seated at front, Ian Begg (left) and Robert Hurd (right).

Land (1956–7) and Chessel's Court (1958–66): the project architect was Ian Begg. Redevelopment must preserve enclosure: 'the couthy, intimate quality of the street'. [79] Broken rooflines and levels would avoid repetitive fenestration: there would be bright colours, pantiled roofs, balconies and arcading – 'an old feature treated with modern simplicity and restraint'. The new buildings would not be 'reproductions', but a 'twentieth-century development of Scottish burgh architecture'. [80]

During the 1950s, the gradual atrophying of Traditionalism as a movement of new architecture was matched by the evolution of preservation into a separate movement in its own right. Increasingly, Ian Lindsay became a leader of that grouping. He continued to organise improvement schemes in the old burghs, both through the new medium of National Trust for Scotland's new 'Little Houses' programme, in burghs such as Dunkeld, and through local authority-promoted schemes such as Inveraray, where his firm undertook a complete scheme of housing reconstruction and visual homogenisation (1958–63), creating the unified white-and-black image that we take for granted today [cf. 2.32]. In 1953, Lindsay explained that the National Trust aimed 'not to encumber the land with museums but to give the people of Scotland civilised decent homes of character and beauty'. [81] Lindsay now began to modify earlier Lorimerian orthodoxies: for example in 1952 he severely castigated restorations that stripped off harling, making old buildings look like a 'vertical rock garden'. [82]

But it was in itself a mark of the post-war growth in state power within architecture, that Lindsay made his greatest impact – between 1945 and his death in 1966 – in the field of government 'listing'. Here he became DHS's part-time Chief Investigator of Historic Buildings, charged with expanding the pre-war Bute lists into a nationwide inventory. This listing programme achieved nationwide coverage by 1967. Initially, part-time investigators were used, including people such as Weekes (Glasgow), Reiach (East Lothian and Edinburgh) and A. G. R. Mackenzie (the North-East). At first, there was a continuing stress on small burgh architecture: under Mackenzie's influence, Lindsay introduced area ('group') listing of lesser burgh houses. Soon, however, the growing influence of art history began to change the emphasis towards listing the works of named architects. And there was a forward shift in the centre of gravity of preservationism. Just as in 1930 Edinburgh Corporation had issued a preservation order for Charlotte Square, and in 1927–30 the IAS, the Cockburn Association and Edinburgh Corporation had campaigned against the demolition of Bryce's Sheriff Courthouse (1863–8), now in 1948 Lindsay's listing guidelines argued that 'we may not like revival "baronial", but future generations may'. [83] Moves to give the lists statutory force began, experimentally, with Dunblane (1957), but Lindsay undermined his own authority by raising Edinburgh's George Square to Category A status in 1959, when it was clear that the university's redevelopment was likely to proceed [cf. 8.48]. After the George Square demolitions in 1960 (proposals for which had prompted, in 1956, the formation of the Scottish Georgian Society as a protest group), a series of defeats culminated in William Ross's 1967 decision to allow demolition of the Life Association building, Princes Street [cf. 6.19]. Even at that late date, nobody yet suspected that 'conservation' would emerge, within five years, as perhaps the most prominent force within Scottish architecture.

'Needs' and 'Standards': Modernist Research and Propaganda

Where the new Traditionalists answered the demand for disciplined reconstruction by invoking national community, other young architects pointed instead to the sweeping rationalist and socialist utopianism of the continental Modern Movement as the best way to rebuild the nation.

This new tendency developed equally in the west and in the east. In the west, the old life was gradually going out of the Beaux-Arts tradition during the 1930s: one commentator in 1933 observed that Glasgow School work now had 'less direction' – it was 'noticeable that a modern note has entered many of the designs'. [84] And as the decade went on, many younger Glasgow designers began to demand a different sort of modernity from what they saw as the commercialisation offered by Art Deco and the Beaux-Arts. Their teachers were figures such as the charismatic Coia, who cultivated a new kind of dashing, artistic image at odds with the disciplined teamwork of the Burnet tradition – while retaining a Beaux-Arts engineering 'hardness' in design [cf. 8.14]. Warnett Kennedy recalled his first day working in Coia's office, 'when the boss blew in and, planting his elbow on the mantelshelf of the drawing office, raved about the "mother of all the arts – architecture!" Never had I experienced such a torrent of love for design in all its aspects, and my own imagination instantly lit up like a lamp!' [85] In a 1938 lecture, Kennedy summed up the younger Glasgow Moderns' charge against popularised modernity. [86] He listed 'what is *not* modern architecture. It is not slick drawing on paper with black ink and stencilled lettering. It is not the

ability to copy Mendelsohn's north point. It is not something white or long and horizontal. It is not corner windows and glass brick walls. It is not flat roofs instead of pitched, and iron ladders running up the sides of houses.' True modern architecture, he declared, was 'an organic understanding of the needs of a new problem, and their solution in the simplest terms'.

Here we arrive at the point where younger Scottish designers began, for the first time, to affiliate themselves to the ideas of the international Modern Movement, rather than (as with Kininmonth, Spence and the cinema designers) just eclectically appropriating its stylistic motifs. At the heart of mainstream continental Modernism was the rationalistic notion that it was possible actually to solve social problems through a new kind of design approach, in which scientific research and definition of 'needs' would be integrated with visual form. Continental Modernists, since the 1920s, had referred to this ideology by the name 'Functionalism': it need hardly be emphasised that our use of this word in the present account does not imply endorsement of its claims, or of its system of values. Previous movements, such as the Beaux-Arts or Andersonian Traditionalism, had tried to fuse aesthetic with social or rationalist aims, but Modern Functionalism made this integration more hard-hitting, by binding it into a simple, unidirectional logic, which governed both its ends and its means. Its overall task was seen as facilitating the march of Progress, in both material betterment and the social development of Community. Some architects made more specific links. In 1960, for instance, Frank Arneil Walker wrote that 'both the international socialist movement and the modern architectural movement . . . are expressions in different fields of the new scientific outlook on life . . . each provides its respective rational response to the socio-economic situation created by capitalism'; the aim of Modern architecture was 'the objective interpretation of social and technological progress into building'. [87] That was not a definition to which any Traditionalist architect, however 'modern', could have subscribed. This progress was to be achieved by a rational, linear process, in which universal 'standards', defined by research into the needs of a newly defined group in architecture – the users, or occupants of buildings – would be embodied in mass provision for all. In their visual expression, the anti-hierarchical implications of these ideas of universal standards became an ennobling factor; the traditional use of ornament and symmetry to denote degree of stateliness was given up in favour of the free disposition of unadorned shapes in open space. However, this Modernist concern with abstract masses and with 'space' brings up a complication: that there existed always at the same time, within the Modern Movement, a potential counter-trend against Functionalism – an emphasis on 'pure form', in opposition to everyday practical considerations. This, however, would only reassert itself significantly during the 1960s.

In contrast to the Traditionalist evocations of old burgh community, this new and full-blooded Modernism responded to the cry for national reconstruction by focusing directly on the nation's decayed industrial heartland, and proposing its replacement by new, planned communities. In accordance with formulas evolved during the previous decade by the International Congresses of Modern Architecture (CIAM) – the chief forum of the continental Modern Movement – the new patterns emphasised provision 'for all' of dwellings with all mod. cons., set in residential areas segregated from industrial and other functions, and provided with open space, sunlight and integrated social facilities: these new communities might even be in separate planned towns. While all those demands might equally have been satisfied by the established Garden City formula, there was also a new integrated visual conception of sheer, un-adorned buildings arranged in free, open patterns, sometimes incorporating high towers to provide a degree of monumentality. The high tower, as a Modern-building form, derived its original status from the symbolic impact of the American skyscraper, but this had been modified by the ideas of continental Functionalism: Walter Gropius advocated the building of tall slab blocks aligned in parallel (*Zeilenbau*), claiming that this would maximise sunlight, and open space between.

Within Scotland, these demands, by linking spatial openness and urban monumentality, cut across the existing debate between the Garden City and tenement revival advocates. Where in

1932 MacRae still recoiled from the 'almost brutal . . . nakedness' of the Continent's 'extreme modernism' [88] an accommodation with the latter was signalled in two key DHS-sponsored reports – a Report on Working-Class Housing on the Continent (1935: the Highton Report) and a Report of the Scottish Architectural Advisory Committee (1937). This change was concerned not with internal facilities, space or hygiene, where Scotland was still seen as far ahead, but with socio-architectural matters. Here it was the very hygienic superiority of Scottish public housing that condemned it: its schemes of segregated blocks were, DHS Architect John Wilson suggested, conceived not in terms of 'community planning', but 'merely as units of accommodation unrelated to their environment'. [89] As an interim compromise, the DHS encouraged municipalities to build more unified and open-planned schemes of tenements. Examples included the 'monumental, axial' layout of MacRae's rubble-and-harl ranges at Piershill (1937–8); [90] the grandiose classicism of Port Glasgow Town Council's tenement projects, such as the axial Carnegie scheme (1937–9); or Aberdeen City Architect Albert Gardner's curved, metal-windowed courtyard group at Rosemount Square (from 1938) [8.31]. There were overlaps with Traditionalist ideas: Hurd, asserting a Scottish 'love of democracy and the free mixing between the people of the different classes', demanded a new 'light and fresh and open' conception of the tenement. [91]

But a more radical break, within State architecture, was soon charted by the most illustrious of that talented 1930s generation of Edinburgh College of Art graduates: Robert H. Matthew [8.32]. Matthew studied at the college from 1926 to 1930, qualified in 1931, and spent three years in his father's office, Lorimer & Matthew, where he designed the travertine-clad reconstruction of 8 Picardy Place (1934–5). From then on, he diverged from the eclectic individualism of Kininmonth, Spence and others, towards the new career of public-authority architect and planner. Systematically pursuing this course, he would eventually outstrip all his contemporaries in national and international influence. During a two-year postgraduate course (1933–5) at Edinburgh College of Art, where Mears encouraged

8.31 Port Glasgow Town Council's Carnegie housing scheme (1937–9), designed with help from DHS in the layout.

him to pursue research in town and country planning, Matthew began to formulate his own Modernist philosophy of 'solving, architecturally, the most difficult of social problems'. [92] Reared as he was in the Lorimer school, he took his conception of collaborative public architecture not from the Burnet/American business-efficiency ethos, but from the socially orientated sobriety of some European interwar architects, such as Paul Bonatz. For the would-be young international Modernist in the 1930s, the first and foremost duty was to address the housing problem, and Matthew plunged into this with relish. In a prize-winning project of 1935 for urban redevelopment, he proposed not tenement-height blocks, but *Zeilenbau* slabs of ten storeys, with internal mod cons (including central heating, to eliminate coal fires) and 'community' facilities such as nursery schools and health centre. Citing Gropius, he asserted that 'great advantages lie in building upwards'. [93] On the basis of this research, Matthew was engaged by the DHS in 1936 as an assistant architect.

The advocacy of Modern design in housing grew in strength after the passing of a new Act in 1938, providing much higher subsidies linked to building costs, with the aim of sparking off large-scale central redevelopment using tenements. This Act, hailed by Warnett Kennedy as likely to bring about a 'social revolution', was linked by reformists to a range of initiatives. Pursuit of 'good design' [94]

of furniture and fittings was linked to the drive for Modern housing. Rationalist design of mod. cons. would satisfy both the scientific ideals of Modern Functionalism and the continuing pre-occupation with hygiene in working-class housing. This strategy was followed by the Scottish Council for Art and Industry, who built two sharply contrasting model dwellings at the Empire Exhibition. Spence designed a 'Modern Country House' in close conformity to the Traditionalist 'Vernacular' movement discussed above: it was

8.32 Robert Matthew (on the right: then President of the International Union of Architects) seen in 1963 with Alan Reiach in Brasilia, attending an IUA meeting.

plain and rendered, with high pitched roof. Mervyn Noad's 'Model Flats' comprised a specimen floor of a Modern block, with a built-in balcony for pram, an entrance hall rather than a close, built-in furniture and a 'planned' kitchen [8.33].

The war's centralised planning and mass-production chimed in with Modernism's central tenets, and the state-socialism that followed emboldened its advocates. The 1940s saw a move from avant-garde advocacy to preparations for actual implementation, through the agency of public authorities. Scottish housing output, in the 1950s, would be dominated by public authorities (municipal and Scottish Special (Areas) Housing Association) to an extent far exceeding that of any other developed country, East or West. Even in the 1960s nearly 80 per cent of output was publicly built (compared to, for example, 3 per cent in West Germany or 0.3 per cent in Belgium). Although

post-war Modernism, internationally, combined democratising tendencies with an international super-élite of architects and canonical works, the emphasis in Scotland, in the wake of the organisational efforts of the war, was on the 'social'. Modernism praised above all the public office organised on 'the group method, under first-class leaders, where the most junior member becomes part of a team, seeing the job or jobs through from start to finish . . . a sense of responsibility can immediately be given' [cf. L.2]. (95)

In the researching and definition of rationalist standards under the aegis of the state, Robert Matthew's methodical steadiness rapidly propelled him to dominance. He rose to become DHS Deputy Chief Architect in 1943 – charged with building up a planning division – and, in January 1945, Chief Architect and Planning Officer. Matthew's characteristic way of working was by delegation

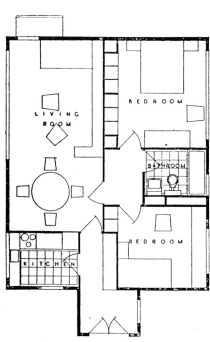

Plan A. Illustrating a modern flat, the planning of which eliminates the lobby as an essential feature (para. 79).

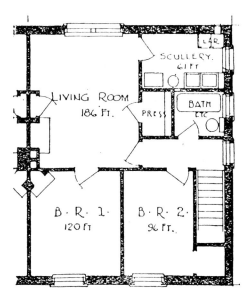

Plan B. This plan—selected from a brochure of plans issued to local authorities before the war—has many of the faults noted in this chapter. To mention only the most obvious defects—it is impossible to sit comfortably round the living-room fire; the five doors opening into the living-room leave no space for furniture; the direct alignment of bedroom-window, door, and living-room window creates a through draught in both rooms.

8.33 Illustration from the 1944 Westwood Report (*Planning Our New Homes*), showing 'modern' and old-fashioned flat plans.

and encouragement. He developed this method in his longstanding collaborative relationship with Alan Reiach. During the war, he arranged Reiach's appointment to the department (in 1940), and used his research as a way of advancing the cause of Modernist housing and planning, in projects such as the Scottish Housing Advisory Committee's official prescription of Modern housing standards (the Westwood Report, or *Planning our New Homes*: published 1944), and the 'community planning' chapter of the Clyde Valley Regional Plan [cf. 8.33, 8.39].

Under Robert Gardner Medwin and T. A. Jeffryes, Matthew's successors (from 1946) as Chief Architect, this structure of research and development was expanded. They established the Westwood Report's standards of modernity as local-authority norms for 'general-needs' or 'family' dwellings, and researched the needs of 'special groups', such as elderly or single people. Materials shortages also made research into space-saving plans a high priority. This research philosophy was extended to the health field by DHS architects such as Justin Blanco White or John Ogilvie. For example, the Department designed and built (in 1951–3) the country's first health centre, at Sighthill, Edinburgh: an informal group ranged around a garden courtyard, whose boldly coloured interior, with soaring concrete staircase, was intended to banish any 'chill institutional atmosphere'. [96] The second DHS health centre was a prototype for a country town, at Stranraer (1954–5). John Holt, Regional Architect to the South-Eastern Regional Hospital Board, built up a similar team: their first project was a Radio-therapeutic Institute at Edinburgh's Western General Hospital (1952–4), with dramatic egg-shaped operating theatre. J. L. Gleave (at that stage, a partner in Keppie, Henderson & Gleave) carried out extensive planning and constructional research when designing the modular, pre-cast concrete Vale of Leven Hospital – the first new post-war hospital built by the Scottish national health service (1952–5) [8.34].

Having established standards, Functionalism's linear logic demanded that ways then be worked out to implement them 'for all'. If the housing drive was to be, in Kennedy's words, a 'social revolution', then the first requirement was for

much higher output. The virtual disappearance of stonemasons by 1939, along with the shortage of bricklayers, meant that this would require large-scale innovation in construction. The Scottish Special (Areas) Housing Association (SSHA), set up in 1937 by the government as the brainchild of Walter Elliot, was intended to supplement local authorities by 'strategic' building in economic development areas, employing so-called 'non-traditional' construction. Wilson and, later, Matthew co-ordinated its work, through the researches of the SSHA's panel of young architects – for example that of Sam Bunton into no-fines (*in situ* large-aggregate) construction; or Carr & Howard into timber building. A striking, mono-pitch roofed group of SSHA timber houses was built at Forth by Kininmonth and Spence in 1939; examples by Carr included a batch at Polbeth (1938). Outside the housing field, the Empire Exhibition powerfully stimulated the idea of programme-led prefabrication.

After the war, the materials crisis worsened – with stockpiles of millions of Belgian bricks imported by towns such as Clydebank – and there was a new rhetorical urgency. One critic in 1942 asserted that 'THE method to build decent houses quickly in Scotland can be summed up in one word – PREFABRICATION. The Little Eric method of brick by brick just won't do. Houses in sections straight from the factory are the houses to meet the emergency . . . a great army of attack on one of the worst Scottish evils.' [97] The first phase of non-traditional building concentrated on prefabrication of one- and two-storey dwellings: temporary aluminium bungalows produced by retooled aircraft factories (the 'prefabs'), and permanent houses which usually depended on varieties of concrete construction. By 1947, the non-traditional proportion of total Scottish permanent housing output had reached two-thirds. Out of 204,000 public dwellings completed between 1945 and 1954, 100,000 were non-traditional. Matthew was closely involved with this campaign: in 1945 he designed type plans for the building of 3,500 cottages using prefabricated timber sections made in Sweden, and travelled there – on a blacked-out wartime night flight from Leuchars – to organise shipment of the required parts. In 1949 he commented that 'we

8.34 Vale of Leven Hospital, Alexandria (Keppie, Henderson & Gleave, 1952–5), mid-1950s' view when newly completed.

8.35 The 'prefab' and its successors: 1950 cartoon by Robert Matthew (under pseudonym 'J. F. McCosh'). Matthew's caption reads: 'I may be old-fashioned, but there's a lot to be said for the jolly old traditional pre-fab'.

are still suffering from a sense of shock at the sight of an aluminium prefabricated house trundling along the highway, and we are bewildered and sometimes angered by their appearance'; standardised, mass produced housing, if not handled sensitively, could be 'a deadly curse' [8.35]. [98] No such doubts were harboured by one influential member of the SSHA's panel of architects in the west, Sam Bunton, who established himself during the war as a co-ordinating figure in prefabricated

social building. He orchestrated the joint research carried out by the DHS and the Scottish Building Group (a contractors' consortium set up in 1946), as well as acting as private consultant architect for various non-traditional methods, such as Orlit or Blackburn. In 1953, he claimed new techniques would allow the nation's housing output to be trebled to 90,000 'without the addition of a single man to the labour force': 'Timber and brick is a prehistoric method of building, and it is preposterous to think to-day in terms of a unit used in the times of the Pharaohs'. [99] Constructional fashions in housing, schools and other programmes shifted with bewildering speed: from mass concrete to aluminium and pre-cast concrete, then on to blockwork crosswall building and gypsum panels. Bunton was always in the forefront, bombarding the DHS with proposals for new 'systems' denoted by slogans or acronyms. For example, he became obsessed with the architectural use of plastics in the late 1940s, and commissioned Warnett Kennedy to undertake research. But while these programmes made a major contribution to output, by well-researched constructional methods, their utilitarian appearance was attacked by many architects as old-fashioned and incompletely Modern.

In sharp comparison with these urgent and somewhat improvised efforts, the Modernists' concern for 'community design' assumed its most sweeping, strategic form in the call for integration of architecture with town and regional planning. The notion that entire cities or regions must be reshaped in accordance with a rational definition of human needs was, in Scotland, ultimately inspired by Geddes's social Darwinism, as transmitted by Mears through his teaching at Edinburgh College of Art and his town planning schemes for local authorities under the 1932 Planning Act. John Wilson was also active, pleading in 1933 that 'Scotland must plan or disintegrate'. [100] These town-planning campaigns were paralleled by the economic and political ideas of a faction led by J. A. Bowie, Principal of the School of Economics and Commerce in Dundee. They advocated application of Geddesian regional planning, combined with state intervention in the Tennessee Valley manner, to encourage the reconstruction of the industrial Central Belt, and of the Highlands, as part of a strategy of Scottish devolution.

Where Geddes had been concerned with Edinburgh, the focus of his successors' campaigns soon moved westwards. More and more attention was devoted to debating the 'Glasgow problem' and arguing that it should be tackled by a combination of Modern redevelopment and satellite Garden City communities. In 1935, Stirling Maxwell attacked the spread of Glasgow, and Warnett Kennedy ceaselessly pressurised the Corporation to build a satellite town and appoint a City Architect to ensure Modern design in its housing. Before the war, the rhetoric had authoritarian overtones: planning critic William Power argued in 1938 that Glasgow needed a 'Housing Dictator' inspired by the 'admirable social polity' of Germany. After 1939, the emphasis shifted to language of 'strategic planning': Garden City advocate Jean Mann argued that 'under enemy fire, the soldiers scatter'. [101] In the late 1930s and 1940s, Matthew made the interrelation of housing and planning a special crusade: he organised a town planning exhibition in 1937 at the Royal Scottish Academy and, within the DHS, set up an integrated structure of architecture and planning, including a planning division. As he later put it: 'We must judge this period of intense public building activity – activity unparalleled in our civic history – in terms of Civic Architecture, or Town Planning.' [102] The first steps to draw up and begin to implement a town plan on Modern

lines were taken by Sam Bunton, following two devastating bombing raids on Clydebank on 13 and 14 March 1941. Exploiting personal contacts with Tom Johnston and John Wilson (then still DHS Chief Architect), he was appointed Reconstruction Architect and town-planner, and drew up a rebuilding plan for the entire burgh on CIAM neighbourhood principles, with parallel *Zeilenbau* layout of housing to maximise sunlight. In 1943, Johnston opened an exhibition of this plan. By 1944 an entire district (Whitecrook North) was under construction, with over 500 dwellings already completed: Bunton was also the architect for this housing. The DHS hoped that the 1947 Town and Country Planning (Scotland) Act, which compelled all municipalities to prepare a town plan, would spread the Clydebank example across the country.

However, the advocates of regional planning believed that their formula, by overriding administrative boundaries and linking town and country, would offer an even more potent route to Modernity for all. In 1943 Patrick Abercrombie and Matthew were asked by Johnston to prepare a regional plan for the entire Clyde Valley, taking in both Glasgow and the areas in which satellite towns might be established. Drawing on his DHS experience, Matthew brought in a range of designers and other professions, including the planner Robert Grieve, and Alan Reiach. The latter wrote a detailed case study of community planning, covering the Vale of Leven, and a chapter (number 9) linking this with 'The Vernacular Tradition'; we will return later to Reiach's conception of the 'Vernacular' [cf. 8.38]. Overall, the Clyde Valley planners envisaged an incredibly ambitious reordering of population and industry in the region – a strategy laid out in 1946 in legislation and an interim report. Dense Glasgow would be thinned out and 'overspilled' into planned new towns, by declaring much of its suburban building land as Green Belt, and thus diverting new building of houses away from the City. In 1947, the first new town, East Kilbride, was designated. In effect, this amounted to an official government endorsement of the pressure-group ideas of the late 1930s.

Where the work of designers such as Matthew or Bunton was laying the research foundations for post-war public architecture and planning, the general public was meantime becoming acquainted with Modern ideas and imagery through the ephemeral, but far more vivid medium of public exhibitions. Here a dominant role was naturally claimed by Basil Spence, who now established himself as a specialist exhibition architect by adopting a brash and forceful Modernity. Despite his new embrace of the language of 'honesty' and 'function', his basic instincts and talents of pictorial eclecticism were undiminished. Alongside a number of less important shows (for example 'Enterprise Scotland' or 'Britain Can Make It'), Spence's two key exhibitions were the Sea and Ships pavilion at the 1951 South Bank Exhibition in London, and the Exhibition of Industrial Power in Glasgow during the same year. Sea and Ships was a large building comprising a steel framework with aluminium cladding, but Spence laid open most of one side, to expose the sterns of a line of cut-away ships, evoking the drama of a shipyard. The Glasgow exhibition, a series of enclosed spaces constructed within the Kelvin Hall, was a matter largely of interior design. This, Spence explained, [103] demanded both a sense of theatre and an intuitive grasp of the psychology of the visitor. His central principle – inspired, he claimed, by the Acropolis at Athens – was to play asymmetry, essential for intermediate 'lead-on' vistas, against symmetry and grandeur in the main setpieces. The exhibition, dominated by the dual theme of coal and water, comprised an entrance hall, with a deafening water cascade on one side, and, on the other, Thomas Whalen's 'Coal Cliff', a looming, concave relief of black-painted plaster. From this led two sequences of spaces, with tableau-vivant effects to bring the visitor 'right into the story' as 'an actor': there was a sodden 'coal swamp', and a 'coal mine' with four tons of coal strewn underfoot to show 'the horrors of mining a hundred years ago'. The climax of the exhibition was a Hall of the Future, dedicated to the promise of atomic power: it was dominated by a giant cone, emitting million-volt flashes. A similarly theatrical air informed some of Spence's architectural commissions during those years, such as Duncanrig Secondary School, East Kilbride (1953), with its central spine and projecting glazed 'space ship' classrooms, or the

massive, rubble-gabled hall block added to his pre-war design for Kilsyth Academy, when eventually completed in 1953. [104] Others, such as the stone-faced Glasgow University Natural Philosophy Department (1947–51), perpetuated elements of late 1930s' Traditionalist regularity, although now in asymmetrical form.

Post-War Small-Burgh and 'Vernacular' Community Planning

After the war, the polarisation between national Traditionalism and international Modernity began to break down. The hegemony of the planned welfare state within Scotland, and the international ascendancy of the Modern Movement, were both increasingly acknowledged. Some, such as Steel Maitland, called themselves 'unrepentant traditionalists', [105] but on the whole there was an implicit acceptance of Modernism's claims that elements such as ornament, or symmetry, or Andersonian antiquarian study, were obsolete and beyond recall. That polemical weathervane of Traditionalist opinion, Leslie Grahame Thomson (renamed MacDougall in 1953), conceded in 1955 that 'the battle is won and modernism is accepted as the order of the day . . . structure, clean lines, new materials have all been allowed to have their say.' This, however, must be a Modernism of 'spirit', not just of 'mechanics'. [106] For the 1950s, the uneasy tension between the two movements was exemplified by the fact that, at the same time as Spence's 1951 Industrial Power exhibition in Glasgow, an extensive 'Living Traditions' exhibition of Scottish crafts and design was mounted at the Royal Scottish Museum in Edinburgh, with an accompanying book by George Scott-Moncrieff.

The gradual accommodation to Modernism after the war was especially clear in planning and housing, where Traditionalist solutions were proposed which would be just as comprehensive and up-to-date as Modern Functionalism, but which would supplement the latter's concept of planned Community with their own ideal of classless solidarity. Hurd, in 1942, attacked the new-town protagonists for their 'ruthless attitude towards the older burghs'. [107] We have already dealt, above, with post-war Traditionalists' most ambitious initiative of planning in the broadest sense – the Hydro programme – which they assigned to the different architectural category of the monumental public building. In the field of community design, their utopian inspiration was not the city with all its problems, but a composite ideal of rural wholeness and small-burgh community. In Scott-Moncrieff's words, 'The place of the country cottage, or the farms and their steadings, the little groups of houses that form villages, in our mind's-eye picture of our country, is a very big one.' While Matthew's team were charting the remodelling of Clydeside and the planting of new towns, in the east a team under [Sir] Frank Mears was working out a different recipe, published in 1948 as the Central and South East Scotland Plan. They proposed to accommodate the planned expansion of the coal industry in the east, and arrest Borders depopulation, not by building new towns but by nucleated development of small burghs and villages. Echoing Geddes, Mears argued for the restoration of 'vitality. . . in the outlying valleys, the "root tips" of our national life, the sources of our finest traditions of independence and initiative'. [108]

Despite the rural imagery invoked by its ideology, this community-building utopia had to confront as its main challenge the problems of urban housing, social building and reconstruction. We saw above that some perpetuated fairly straightforwardly the conservative surgery and preservation ideas of the 1890s-1930s. Elsewhere, there were attempts to design infill or new developments in a more openly 'contemporary' manner, often termed 'Vernacular': the first widespread architectural use of the latter word. It was here that the greatest overlaps with Modernism occurred. The concept of Vernacular was fed by the ideas of younger Traditionalists of the 1930s, such as Lindsay, and those intent on a more 'national' Modernism, such as Reiach and even Matthew. It held that a Scottish essence, ignored by nineteenth-century architectural eclecticism, had been preserved both in the work of Mackintosh and in the unforced simplicity of 'lesser' or Vernacular buildings, especially country cottages and steadings. In the continuing battle between the City Beautiful/CIAM tradition of open or

monumental space and Camillo Sitte's ideas of artistic enclosure, it generally championed the latter [8.36].

The shift towards more Modern ideas in small-burgh infill schemes began at Basil Spence's picturesque fishermen's housing scheme at Dunbar (1949–52), with its rubble and harl walling, metal windows and forestair-like concrete balconies [8.37]; there followed Spence's plainer Annfield, Newhaven (1957) and his more rhetorical arched concrete and rubble group in the Canongate, Edinburgh (1966–8). A key role in fostering this tendency was played by the Saltire Society housing awards, revived in the late 1940s at DHS instigation. The 1951 award went to Spence's Dunbar housing, which Hurd (as Saltire Secretary) praised as 'an enrichment of the tradition of Scottish burgh housing . . . houses of purely modern Scottish character' which gave 'an inspiring lead' to other burghs. [109] Younger architects responded to this challenge. The Glasgow-trained H. Anthony Wheeler, for example, emerged as a dominant force in the rich field of Fife burgh redevelopments. A long series of schemes in the 1950s and 1960s (latterly in partnership with Frank Sproson) included Leslie (The Bowery, 1953–6), Burntisland (from 1955), Lochgelly (from 1957–64) and the multi-stage Dysart redevelopment (from 1958). To Wheeler, the 'difficult' sites in small burghs were an 'opportunity' for 'original and exciting' designs at higher density. These contrasted spatial enclosure with Modernist openness and 'drama', and juxtaposed old buildings, retained as focal points, with sharp geometry and even flat roofs. Unlike Hurd, Wheeler saw variegated colours as 'dangerous': 'grey concrete and texture' was preferable, and features such as balconies should be used not as decoration but to get 'a very strong, pure pattern to the elevation.' His ideal was 'mixed-type schemes, conceived as three-dimensional compositions, in which every aspect is planned . . . by one man or team'. [110] Robert Matthew designed the Barshare scheme, Cumnock (1957–61), in a similar manner, with big pitched roofs and plain render. Other architects established themselves as regional specialists in small-burgh housing. In Shetland, R. & B. Moira of Edinburgh designed a notable series of small schemes in

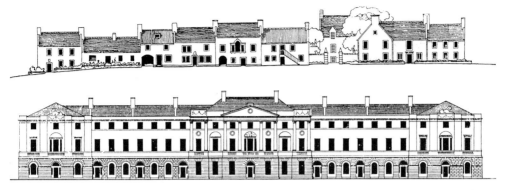

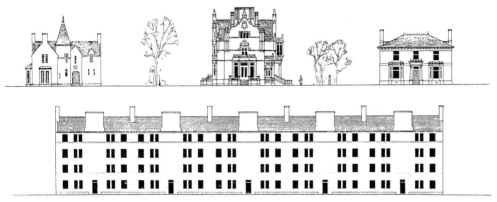

eighteenth century

nineteenth century

twentieth century

Trend of Scottish domestic architecture

8.36 Illustration from Sir F. C. Mears, *Regional Plan for Central and South East Scotland*, 1948, p. 148. The accompanying text asserted that the pictures 'show well the relationship between past or passing native tradition and the alien substitutes which threaten to reduce the Scottish house to the level of a ready-made box enlivened by traces of chromium and plastic'.

8.37 Perspective (1952) by Basil
Spence of his Dunbar housing
schemes: the 1934–5 terrace is in
the middle, and the other small
groups (with balconies) were added
in 1949–52.

Lerwick's Lanes area, including Heddell's Park
and Annsbrae (1956–9), Leog (1958–60),
Greenfield (from 1963) and Kveldsro (1965)
[8.38]. These turned once run–down backland sites
into pedestrianised 'precincts' where 'each house
had its own identity and was not merely an
anonymous dwelling in a large scheme.' [111] A
different way of infusing old-burgh revitalisation
with Modern principles was pioneered by Frank P.
Tindall, East Lothian's County Planning Officer
from 1950–75. He and his architect wife, Mary,
had previously worked as social researchers in
Berthold Lubetkin's avant-garde team at
Haddington, Tindall engineered a town-centre
campaign of improvement, spearheaded by a
repainting scheme (co-ordinated by Eric Hall, and
completed 1962). He linked this with a Modernist
community-building drive for urban/industrial
growth, including Glasgow overspill: 'There's no
difference between development and conservation.
It was a precondition for conservation, that you
first had to get new people into the town, to give
it new social characteristics.' [112]

The dissemination of the concept of Vernacular
was the achievement, above all, of Alan Reiach.

[cf. 8.32] After the war, he became a popular
lecturer (1947–54) at Edinburgh College of Art,
and member of the Saltire housing award panel.
Reiach's most influential contributions were
contained in a series of publications of the 1940s.
His views shaped the Westwood Report's
argument that Modern community planning could
be reconciled with 'the best Scottish traditions in
domestic architecture': interwar low-density
schemes and extreme Modern *Zeilenbau* solutions
were both condemned [8.39]. [113] In the Clyde
Valley Plan, Reiach's Vale of Leven study argued
that Modernist neighbourhood units separated
by greenery could be woven into run-down
industrial towns; a series of drawings, including
startlingly coloured elevations of eighteenth-
century cottages, accompanied his essay calling for
'harmony' in community planning. These ideas
were expressed most forcefully in his polemical
book written with Hurd, *Building Scotland* (1941).
Arguing through oppositions of 'good' and 'bad'
photographs in the manner of Paul Schultze-
Naumburg, they advocated a revival in new
architecture of the 'homely and spacious' values
embodied in old buildings: 'Tradition is the pool
of a nation's continuous experience'. But *Building*

8.38 Leog housing development, Lerwick, Shetland (R. & B. Moira, 1958-60): view when newly completed, looking out across Bressay Sound.

Scotland was no tract of folk-community: it lavished equal praise on the 'courage' of 'superbly bold and sincere' Modernist buildings such as Aalto's Paimio sanatorium, and new flats in Stockholm and Copenhagen.

Reiach diverged most sharply from the Traditionalists in his ebulliently internationalist outlook. And it was to Scandinavia, above all, that he was drawn. That was hardly unusual in the late 1940s, when Scandinavian social building, carried on almost irrespective of the war, exerted a pervasive influence throughout Europe. Scandinavia meant different things to different countries. In Scotland, as in Germany and the Netherlands, Scandinavia was viewed as a beacon of wholesome Modern provision 'for all': in 1952, A. N. Doak praised Swedish social housing's 'unanimity of aim', 'homogeneous outlook' and 'standardised . . . elements': these were 'milestones in the social development of Sweden'. [114] It was the architecture not of Sweden but of Denmark that struck the deepest resonances with Reiach and many other Scots architects of the 1940s and early 1950s – as demonstrated in the incessant exchange visits and cultural events during those years. In the east, with its Anderson-Lorimer legacy, the Danes' preoccupation with quiet, practical comfort, and with the 'natural' fusion of innovation and tradition, struck a particular chord. In Reiach's first major commission, the Edinburgh and East of Scotland

Agricultural College, designed 1949–50 (with Ralph Cowan) and built 1954–60, the debt to buildings such as Aarhus University is obvious: a combination of large scale, asymmetrical plainness and pitched roofs.

Among Reiach's early post-war jobs, one, although small, was very influential because of its location: a local shopping centre, café and flats at Whitemoss, East Kilbride (from 1949, architect-in-charge was T. R. Spaven). East Kilbride was the place where the DHS and new town architects were first able to begin implementing the community planning patterns proposed in Reiach's Vale of Leven study. The Whitemoss group, with its sweeping roofs, white render and brilliantly coloured details, showed that their solutions would be shaped by Danish-style informal Modernity [8.40]. By 1952, with 500 dwellings completed, East Kilbride had begun to dominate the Saltire Housing Awards. Another departure from older garden-suburb concepts, under Scandinavian influence, concerned dwellings' surroundings. Exploiting an apparent wave of working-class apathy towards gardening, Modern designers rejected private gardens as a community-building device, and advocated communal landscaping, green and flowing in places like East Kilbride, and harder and enclosed in small burghs. This was in effect a new type of *Gesamtkunstwerk* tailored to social mass building: in B. L. C. Moira's words, the 'design, as one entity, of a building and

1

THESE sketches give an impression of some of the possibilities in design, grouping and layout envisaged in the Report.
1. Terraced cottages of simple design grouped with three-storey modern flats give variety of architectural composition.
2. Single-storey rural cottages of traditional design.

2

8.39 Illustrations by Alan Reiach from the 1944 Westwood Report (*Planning Our New Homes*), showing 'modern' and 'traditional' designs.

8.40 Flats and shops by Alan Reiach at Whitemoss, East Kilbride(from 1949).

the outdoor space, great or small, which is to be used with the building'. [115]

The overlap between Modern and older values seen in architecturally elevated form at East Kilbride and the burgh redevelopments was echoed in a more mundane way in the 1950s' huge output of municipal housing up and down the country. The basic amenities that were now standard in all new urban dwellings – hot and cold water, fixed bath, inside WC, segregation of internal functions – had been widespread in middle-class homes long before the Modernist era, and some had first been introduced in the great houses and palaces of nobles and kings centuries earlier [cf. 8.33]. The more elaborate provisions demanded by International Modernism, such as central heating or collective refuse-disposal, were, by the mid-1950s, still largely confined to a few experimental high blocks: Crathie Drive (1949–52) and Moss Heights (1950–3) in Glasgow, Westfield Court (1949–51) and Queensferry Road (1953–5: by Leslie Grahame MacDougall) in Edinburgh; Melbourne Avenue (1953) in Clydebank; Valley Gardens (from 1954) in Kirkcaldy; and the SSHA's Toryglen, Glasgow (from 1955: 'no-fines' blocks designed in consultation with Dr Ludwig Kresse of Stuttgart). All of these blocks were of rather old-fashioned, bulky appearance. Nor could the appearance and layout of the great mass of 1950s' housing – 'family' dwellings in cottages or tenements, on generally garden-suburb street-

plans – be described as fully Modern. In 1944, at DHS instigation, the RIAS had prepared 38 standard housing plan types, later much used by smaller burghs and rural authorities: these comprised only one- and two-storey blocks, mostly cottages with pitched roofs. Some burghs, such as Dumfries, led a campaign to revive stone building: in 1956 an indirect subsidy was instituted by the DHS. In the field of philanthropic housing, J. A. W. Grant's Salvesen Gardens, Edinburgh (1948), differed little from his pre-1914 Westerton designs, while Robert Matthew's brother Stuart designed the Thistle Foundation settlement in Edinburgh (from 1947) in the form of rows of steep-roofed cottages. In Glasgow, the vast tenemental schemes of the 1950s, Castlemilk, Drumchapel and Easterhouse, were conservative in appearance, with almost no landscaping. Yet their house types themselves differed little from East Kilbride: Frank Scott, the new town's Chief Architect from 1952, had previously occupied the same post in Glasgow's Housing Department, and 18,000 dwellings had been built in the city since 1945 to his designs (as well as numerous pre-war houses). Standard four-storey Glasgow blocks, in a relatively affluent area (Fyvie Avenue), were given a Saltire award for 1951 and praised for their 'low-pitched roofs of pantiles . . . balcony access . . . and a variety of light, cheerful colours' [L.2]. [116]

Robert Matthew and the Victory of the Modern Movement

Although much routine Traditionalist building continued throughout the decade, 1953 would prove, in retrospect, the decisive turning point in the fortunes of the Modern Movement in Scotland. This was the year that Robert Matthew, returning home after a period as Architect to the London County Council (1946–53), began in earnest a campaign to press home a fully-fledged international Modernism, by binding private practice and academia to its aims of planned social provision [cf. 8.32]. He took up two senior academic posts, including a new personal Chair of Architecture at Edinburgh University; and he embarked on private practice in Edinburgh (from 1956, in a partnership with Stirrat Johnson-Marshall: Robert Matthew, Johnson-Marshall & Partners, or 'RMJM').

Matthew's international status ensured that the Modernist view rapidly became the establishment view, and began to shape the actual implementation of post-war Scottish reconstruction. However, his own interpretation of Modern Movement ideology, like Reiach's, was quite complex, and overlapped in some ways with the 'national' concerns of late Traditionalism. Upholding the Modernist refusal of building-type hierarchies, he denied there was any 'fundamental difference between the design of . . . a bridge and the design of an auditorium . . . surely they are simply structures, and surely they are all equally architecture, and all must be judged by the same standards of stability, convenience and aesthetic value'. [117] His views represented an extreme, within Modernism, of the 'contextual' rather than 'formal' view: the essence of architecture was 'the systematic analysis of people's needs'. [118] But alongside this, he called for a Modern 'National Movement' in Scotland, an evocation in 'contemporary work' of 'the strong and almost unique character of Braid Scots in architecture'. Matthew reconciled these two poles by the ideal of the 'organic'. Citing Frank Lloyd Wright, Matthew claimed that the end of the 'Gothic' or medieval period had opened up a 'vast gulf' between architecture and 'the people'. The antithesis to this golden age was not the 'Renaissance' classicism reviled by the Lorimerians; this, he believed, had added 'a new dignity to cities'. It was, rather, in the 1920s and 1930s that 'Scottish architecture . . . reached its lowest point . . . an atmosphere that was stone dead'. [119] Continuity with 'Gothic' had been maintained by 'the humbler buildings of society – cottages, farms, windmills and minor industrial structures' whose 'rugged and strong . . . quality' could inspire the integration of architecture and engineering. [120] Here he agreed with the Traditionalists in calling for the revival of stone building, but in rationalistic terms as Scotland's 'basic building material'. [121] As the son of Lorimer's partner, he loved not ashlar but, above all, rock-faced rubble. From the mid-1950s Matthew, and like-minded designers, began putting into practice these ideas. The first step was research; in the late 1950s, he built up a research section, as part of his work, to establish a post-graduate architecture department at Edinburgh University. He claimed in 1959 that the housing drive had so far provided much 'clinical material' but little 'objective study'. [122] And in 1954 he sent his Departmental Registrar, Patrick Nuttgens, to the north-east to research Vernacular architecture – which he now defined to include planned villages.

When it came to the large-scale realisation of Modernism, all building types were now expressed in forms which, outwardly, conformed to Modern abstraction: added decoration was banished, as was literal imitation of past forms. But in other ways there was continuity and diversity. For example, this new international style acted as an umbrella for subtle regional differences. The east followed Matthew into a more craft-like Modernity, with Andersonian overtones, while the west showed more structural, plastic boldness: a key example of the latter was Alexander Buchanan Campbell's audacious Dollan Baths, East Kilbride (1964–8), with its 324-feet-wide parabolic arched concrete roof planted on massive diagonal struts [8.41]. There was greater complexity than before in the relation between building tasks and architectural solutions, further obscuring the honorific demarcation between elevated and mundane. We saw above the way in which an enclosed-space, or Vernacular, Modernism was used by designers

8.45 Rothes Colliery, Thornton (1957), view of car circulation hall.

eventually, stigmatised subject of massed multi-storey housing and 'comprehensive' redevelopment. By contrast, projects with a public or cultural element – such as university buildings – were dealt with in an individualised manner and were disposed as landmarks. Matthew's initial design (1955) for New Zealand House, London, envisaged a dynamically massed tower with a tall fin punching up one side, and flowing spaces inside [8.46]. Although a lower and plainer version was substituted under planning pressure, its features were echoed in later Matthew designs. For instance, his Queen's College Dundee tower (1958–61) added a vertical punctuation in a 'modern idiom' [128] to Perth Road, idiosyncratically faced (for a high block) in rubble and

timber [8.47]. His George Square redevelopment for Edinburgh University inherited a high block from an earlier Spence proposal of 1955: as built, the 15-storey Arts Tower (1960–3) was clad in black slate and polished ashlar [8.48, 8.49].

Other designers soon took up the same theme. Of all major Modernist statements across the country, perhaps the proudest was a local-authority office: Lanark County Buildings, Hamilton, the headquarters of Scotland's largest county authority, and designed by its County Architect, D. G. Bannerman (1959–64) [8.50]. The 17-storey, glass-walled office tower, and adjoining circular council chamber and raised plaza, was closely affiliated to the Brasilia/UNO pattern of the ceremonial, monumental slab block. Alluding to the abstract spatial play of CIAM-style Modernism, its designers described the asymmetrical group as a 'three-element composition', whose 'strictly formal' forecourt would 'lead the eye' from the council chamber to the 'severe angularity' of the tower's 'gigantic back-cloth'. [129] Other prestige towers included the multi-stage Aberdeen Municipal Buildings project (by City Architect George McI. Keith), with a tall block built from 1965, and Wylie Shanks & Underwood's Glasgow city-centre project of 1960–4 for twin Stow Colleges of Building and Printing, and of Distributive Trades: slab blocks of Brasilia-like plasticity, with boldly modelled roof structures, travertine–clad gables, and vitriolite/glass curtain walls which, 'like a great looking glass, reflect the scudding clouds' so that 'the wall is abolished'. [130]

The arresting impact of Modernist open planning was not the exhaustive preserve of prestigious tower groups, but was applied across the entire range of social and commercial types. In building for education, for example, a typical solution in the east was RMJM's Firrhill High

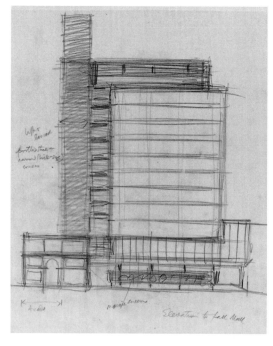

8.46 New Zealand House, London, preliminary design of 1955 by Robert Matthew.

8.47 Queens College, Dundee (RMJM, 1958–61), contemporary perspective by RMJM of new frontage building and tower.

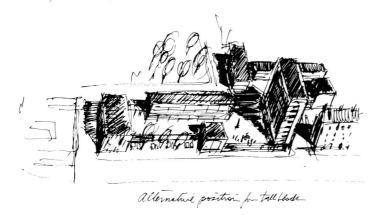

University of Edinburgh · Arts Faculty · George Square

Alternative position for tall block

8.48 University of Edinburgh Arts Faculty buildings, including Arts Tower (1960-3, by Robert Matthew/ RMJM), 1958 preliminary sketch by Matthew.

8.49 Arts Tower (David Hume Tower).

8.50 Lanark County Buildings, Hamilton (County Architect, 1959–64).

School, Edinburgh (from 1957) – a loosely asymmetrical group, with timber cladding and accents in rubble walling, punctuated by a five-storey classroom block – whereas in the west, slightly later (1964–6), Glasgow Corporation architects designed the Smithycroft Secondary School in the striking form of two concentric circles with an administrative wing. In the commercial field, the years around 1960 saw, for the first time, large-scale building of Modern office blocks. Some were freestanding towers: the tallest was Arthur Swift & Partners' St Andrew's House, Glasgow (1961–4). More frequent was a street-line infill pattern. Some of the most sophisticated examples of this type were found around St Andrew Square, Edinburgh. Michael Laird & Partners' Standard Life Extension Phase 1 (1964, with RMJM) was a green and grey glass curtain-walled block, while the marble walling, regular fenestration and black base of Basil Spence, Glover & Ferguson's first Scottish Widows building (1962) evoked the New Town classical tradition. In a rural setting, solutions were more restrained: Alan Reiach's Veterinary Field Station, Roslin (1962), featured elegant two-storey ranges of concrete frame with timber curtain walling.

Conclusion

Among Scottish architects, there was around 1960 a general feeling of optimism that the welfare state standards defined in the 1940s were now, in substantial areas, at last being provided for all, and through the medium of Modern architecture. There was even some exhilaration: in 1964 John

Holt noted that 'in Glasgow there is a tremendous sense of achievement, and on all sides new buildings reach towards the sky'. Jack Coia called for more young people to become architects: 'We must encourage them to help in tackling the new Scotland as a crusade'. [131] Matthew was more cautious. In 1960, he claimed that Scotland was not yet a front-rank participant in international Modernism, but it was 'plucking up courage to knock at the door': a number of 'world standard' projects were now being realised, especially within public architecture. [132] The picture in the early 1960s seemed on the whole to be one of co-ordinated Progress. Architects were contributing to the 'crusade' of the 'new Scotland' not by defending a 'national essence', but by participating in an international architectural movement, of a consistency and discipline that had not been witnessed since the age of neo-classicism a century and a half before. However, as with all attempts to impose order on architecture since the eighteenth-century dethroning of Antiquity's authority, this triumph of the Modern Movement was to prove short-lived, especially in the area which was its central concern: 'community planning'.

Chapter 9

1960 to the Present Day

The Crisis of Modernity

'The Ville Radieuse . . . here was logic, but logic carried to the brink of insanity. Does anyone really believe that one can create a live city from diagrams showing density, daylighting, smoke dispersal, zoning and traffic circulation? . . . We have to *create* in our existing cities an image or images which reflect the character of that city, not merely to try to make the city function efficiently as a mechanism to live and work in.'

John L. Paterson, 1957 [1]

'. . . the logic of a central infrastructure of highways and walkways, layers and ledges promising shelter, warmth and family freedom.'

Geoffrey Copcutt, on Cumbernauld Town Centre, 1995 [2]

'. . . a nation of enterprise, that has pulled itself back from the brink and is now, hungrily, contemplating the next step.'

RIAS, *Review of Scottish Architecture*, 1992 [3]

Introduction

The years between World War I and 1960 had seen a drawing together of diverse threads into an increasingly tight and disciplined recipe, under the banner of the Modern Movement. This architectural order reflected a wider societal and national cohesion, a sense of battling against successive external crises, whether of war, of economic slump, or of urban chaos and squalor. Now, in contrast, we enter a prolonged internal crisis – in the opinion of some, a terminal crisis – within this wider vision of ordered modernity; a gradual rejection of discipline and of state-led authority, a reaction which stemmed from affluence and from the very success of the material aims of 'national reconstruction'. This crisis of cultural modernity would be marked by calls for greater diversity and social responsiveness, and, in architecture by a crescendo of attacks on Functionalist and other Modernist ideologies. Yet there would be no challenge to the central ideological and social elements of the wider modernity of architecture over the previous century, namely: the utopian concern that architecture should reflect, and foster, local and national 'community'; the equally idealistic emphasis on the intuitive shaping of 'form'; and the accelerating division of labour within architecture, by which each phase rejects its predecessor as crude or mechanistic, and puts forward antidotes (such as 'user participation') which demand ever more complex groupings and relationships.

The 1960s: 'Late' Modernism and the Breakdown of Discipline

The 1960s saw the beginning of the final decline of traditional heavy industry, but also the gradual building-up of a new, diversified industrial and financial base. Where in the mid-1950s, bad infrastructure and a structurally weak economy had been concealed by an economic boom, the situation by 1980 would be the reverse. Even by 1960, there was an increasing perception of prosperity across most parts of Scotland – although the brief recession of 1957–9 kept the old memories of unemployment in people's minds. This new climate led to calls for a redefinition of the planned welfare state in terms not of war-like campaigns against emergency conditions or post-industrial squalor, but of the management of growth and affluence. What was demanded was not fewer experts, but larger numbers of more sophisticated experts. In this decade, the post-war social modernisation initiatives rose to their climax: in housing, of course, with annual targets rising to 50,000 under the dynamic Labour housing Minister, Jesse Dickson Mabon; in education, with the introduction of comprehensive schools and a doubling in higher education student numbers to 33,000 over the decade; and – a new emphasis – in road-building, to cater for the explosive growth in vehicle ownership.

For the planners, this was a time of burgeoning confidence. Following the recommendations of the Toothill Report of 1961, most infrastructural functions within government were in 1962 gathered into a single department, the Scottish Development Department (SDD), with the aim of fostering employment growth through social infrastructure spending. Under Sir Douglas Haddow, SDD and (from 1964) the Scottish Office's Regional Development Division co-ordinated a succession of official plans: for instance, the 'Central Scotland Programme', 1963 (which promoted economic 'growth areas'); and the national 'Plan for Scotland', 1966. In 1965, a new optimism about the Highlands led to the establishment of a development agency with industrial investment powers: the Highlands and Islands Development Board. An accelerated road-building drive was a key part of the SDD's planned modernisation of communications. Its showpiece was the Forth Road Bridge (1958–64, Mott Hay & Anderson/Sir G. Scott), a design admired, internationally, as a harbinger of a new era of lightness and slenderness in spun-cable suspension bridge design, hitherto dominated by solid, monolithic structures such as Verrazano-Narrows (1964). [9.1] This golden age of planning would only come to an end with economic troubles from 1966 onwards. In 1963, Percy Johnson-Marshall hailed planning as a 'nation-building activity' in which, 'after a period of reaction from planning, Scotland is now forging ahead'. [4]

Among architects, this new climate of affluence, and its demands for planned growth, proved to be both a stimulant and a destabilising force. In the area of 'community design', the old identity of interest with the planners began to dissolve, and was replaced by new and complex patterns. The end of the 1950s saw an increasing emphasis among Modern architects on the redevelopment and reshaping of existing towns, rather than regional planning and new settlements elsewhere. This was the first stage in the move back from all-encompassing 1940s' utopianism to the Postmodern concern to 'regenerate the City'. But unlike the latter's emphasis on small-scale 'interventions' and conservation, the 1950s' CIAM urbanist formula envisaged large-scale remodelling: the key term was 'comprehensive'. This formula was exemplified in the 1958 International City Planning Competition 'Hauptstadt Berlin', which Robert Matthew entered along with Michael Laird, Patrick Nuttgens and John L. Paterson: their (unsuccessful) design envisaged a vast podium across the Friedrichstrasse area, with clusters of high blocks rising from it; there was to be an extensive grade-separated road system and much greenery. The actual application of these concepts to the reconstruction of industrial, urban Scotland was prompted not by bombing (as Scotland was one of the least war-damaged of combatant nations), but two new demands: the political and public cry for slum-clearance from the mid-1950s, and the rise in private vehicle ownership from around 1960.

As early as 1955, the Unionist housing minister, J. Nixon Browne, proclaimed that most local authorities had 'broken the back of their housing problem'; effort must shift to redevelopment of 'Scotland's greatest shame, the slums.' [5] The first burgh to embark on a planned Modern redevelopment drive was Paisley, which, in 1944, charted out a self-contained strategy: peripheral house-building followed by decanting, clearance and rebuilding of central sites. Its Development Plan, prepared by the powerful Burgh Engineer, J. A. McGregor, was the first in the country to be approved (1953). By 1955, redevelopment of the first area (George Street/Canal Street) was under way. This new scheme, with its smokeless district heating, would help banish nineteenth-century

9.1 Forth Road Bridge (Mott, May & Anderson, 1958–64), view of deck erection in June 1963.

grime from Paisley. However, its housing was laid out not in open *Zeilenbau* fashion, but in a more formal manner. Low flats in render and reused rubble were set around landscaped courtyards, with a 15-storey tower as a punctuation at one end. [6]

The centrality of Glasgow within the housing-planning question ensured that the greatest attention in 1950s' redevelopment debates would be claimed by its schemes. Here, there was an attempt to maintain the link with regional planning and overspill: planning was still part of the department of the City Architect, Archibald Jury. His planners, led by R. E. Nicoll, proposed (from 1957) to channel slum-clearance into a planning-led framework of 29 'Comprehensive Development Areas' (CDAs), much of whose population would be overspilled from Glasgow. The most prestigious of these, Hutchesontown/Gorbals, was allocated to a range of designers. One site (Area A, 1956) was rebuilt by Jury's planners using four-storey maisonettes which echoed the scale of the existing tenements. Area B was allocated to Matthew (1958–64, with I. Arnott and J. L. Paterson); Area C to Spence (1960–6, with

Charles Robertson); and Area D (1961–8) to the SSHA, under its new Chief Technical Officer, Harold Buteux. We will discuss Spence's unconventional solution later. Matthew designed a rectilinear grid of 18-storey towers and lower blocks; in CIAM style, these were laid out on a north-south axis (to optimise sunlight) in disregard of existing street alignments. Its towers (originally designed for the Leith Fort competition in Edinburgh, 1957) were planned by Ian Arnott with a staggered cross section inspired by a J. R. Bakema project.

In the early 1960s, the demand to accommodate present and projected increases in motor traffic added a new element to the Glasgow CDA proposals: the threading of an Inner Ring Road motorway through the innermost belt of clearance areas. Under engineers Scott Wilson Kirkpatrick and consultant architect W. Holford, the North and West Flanks of the road were put in hand in 1965, including a high-level Clyde crossing [9.2]. Glasgow's mid-1960s' combination of area redevelopment, new tower blocks and road schemes seemed to promise a full-scale realisation in

9.2 Glasgow Inner Ring Road, perspective from 1965 *Glasgow Highway Plan* showing Charing Cross section of West Flank – depressed in cutting for amenity reasons.

Scotland of the CIAM pattern of urbanism, with its concomitant ideals of social and material Progress. In 1966, RIAS President Douglas W. N. Calder warned the faint-hearted that

> vast areas of renewal are essential; the demands of the motor vehicle and the need to segregate it from pedestrians will change the whole civic pattern, and building by industrialised means will bring a rate of growth such as will be difficult to control without thwarting legitimate demands for expansion. More than ever it is essential for architects to think big and to think fast. [7]

But by then, even as the Modern 'comprehensive' prescription was at last being implemented, there were the first forebodings of crisis. The first blow did not threaten the internal coherence of the new Modernist design establishment, as it came from a source that the latter could unite in condemning, but it struck at Modernism's prestige by undermining the architectural respectability of its supreme symbol: the tower block. When Scottish Functionalism came – as it had to, given its unidirectional argumentation – to the stage of mass propagation of the 'standards' its pioneers had established, its ideas and forms passed into the control of other groups, who used them in ways which conflicted with key tenets of Modernism. From 1961, the Glasgow planners' CDA formula was directly challenged by municipal housing interests opposed to overspill. Led by David Gibson, an idealistic councillor set on a personal crusade to raze the slums and 'give the people homes', [8] the Housing Committee began to build tower blocks in a manner diametrically opposed to the 'comprehensive' pattern: on gap sites, as and when they came up, and mostly not even in the CDAs. The culmination of this campaign was a colossal group of steel-framed tower and slab blocks designed by Sam Bunton and built by the City's direct labour organisation at Red Road, Balornock (1962–9), but many big blocks were also designed as 'package deals' by the architects of contractors such as Wimpey or Crudens: for instance, Crudens's ten 20-storey slab blocks at Sighthill (1963–9), arranged in relentless *Zeilenbau* fashion [9.3]. Anybody in Gibson's way was pushed aside: even Matthew was deposed in 1963 from two sites, at Springburn and Royston (be-

cause he had pressed for comprehensive development of a wider area), and Reema package-deal blocks were built on the foundations started for his scheme.

By this means, successive dramatic production records were broken. In February 1968, Secretary of State William Ross opened the 'millionth new house' in Scotland since 1918 (in an SSHA slab block at Wyndford), and two months later, Prime Minister Wilson opened the '150,000th Glasgow council house' (in a point block at Springburn). But what many Modern designers now began to say was that these enormous programmes of high blocks were not properly 'Modern' at all. The criticisms were not the same as those levelled at the mass-produced non-traditional cottages of the 1940s, or at the interwar housing schemes by Highton in 1935: the tower blocks *looked* Modern. And their massed building maximised the propagation not only of the basic sanitary facilities, but of more advanced Modern amenities: central heating, lifts and communal waste disposal collection. Where Postmodern critics in the 1980s would disparage the 'tabula rasa planning' and 'architects arrogance' of these towers, it was precisely their conflict with 'comprehensive planning', and the fact that they were mostly designed by low-status contractors' architects, which damned them in the eyes of their Modern detractors. In Edinburgh, an equivalent controversy was stirred up by a 1962 proposal to build 25-storey municipal tower blocks in Holyrood Park; the Planning Committee commissioned Lord Holford to produce a High Buildings Policy (published in interim form in 1966) to restrain tower-building.

These attacks showed that, despite Matthew's insistence that bridges and auditoria were 'all equally architecture', [9] there was in reality a complex hierarchy of elevated and mundane design within the Modern Movement. Soon, however, younger architects began a deeper questioning, not just of the 'debasement' of Modern architecture, but of its fundamental definitions. In 1958, John L. Paterson, the job architect for Matthew's Hutchesontown blocks, opposed the 'rigidity' of the scheme's 45-degree angle to surrounding roads, 'set against the grain of the city'; but Matthew insisted on the paramountcy of daylight orientation, and the towers stayed the

9.3 Red Road development, Glasgow
(Bunton, 1962–9), seen under construction, 1966.

way they were. [10] The Glasgow architect A. N. Doak, in 1960, attacked the 'clinical sterility' of much new architecture, and, in 1964, announced that 'the fight is no longer for modern architecture, but for good architecture'. [11]

What alternatives to orthodox Modernism were on offer? First of all, any overt pursuit of the 'national' or of Traditionalist ideas seemed, for the moment, deeply unfashionable – a paradoxical fact, given that these were the years when the national reshaping of the Scottish physical environment reached its height. The new architectural tendencies which responded to the changing social and economic climate of the 1960s, should above all be seen in an international context. But this context was one in which International Modernism, at the moment of its triumph across the Western world, was beginning to fragment. Two critiques of CIAM had emerged in the 1950s. In Europe, socio-architectural critics

such as the Team 10 group or the English 'New Brutalists' scorned CIAM's view of community, branding it mechanical, and called for more sophisticated reflections of social reality. Equally importantly, the American paradigm of modernity had reorientated itself, turning from the imagery of mass production to that of sophisticated consumption, and from the East Coast and the Midwest to California. Alongside these was a third tendency, on both sides of the Atlantic, led by architects such as Corbusier and Kahn: a revival of the strand in Modernism which idealised pure 'form'. After the last CIAM congress at Dubrovnik in 1958, the International Modern Movement was consigned to history. Henceforth, Modernism, internationally speaking, became a matter of pluralist tendencies, each developing and heightening what were previously claimed to be integrated strands: the socio-architectural, the rationalistic, the formal or 'poetic'.

The Architecture of Social Complexity

The first of these elements of Scottish Late Modernism – the socio-architectural – was the most ambitious in its attempt to question, and restructure, CIAM ideals. If Functionalism's ideology of urban redevelopment had claimed to create community through new patterns marshalled in a 'comprehensive' manner, this fresh phase aspired to a greater socio-visual complexity, in which the new would be balanced with the existing. There were two ways of arriving at this balance. One was through a radical aestheticisation of the everyday. Here the articles of the young John L. Paterson (from 1957) led the way. He attacked CIAM-style segregation of functions as 'logic carried to the brink of insanity'; both the 'horizontal city' (garden city) and the 'vertical city' (Ville Radieuse) had failed. Instead 'we have to create in our existing cities an image or images which reflect that character of that city'. Sources of inspiration might include Skid Row, neon advertising, speculative bungalows, or the casualness of youth culture: 'another society, another direction'. [12] When working with RMJM as job architect for Hutchesontown 'B', Paterson unsuccessfully suggested that the tower blocks' elevations should be faced with broken bottles, as a symbol of the 'social reality' of the Gorbals. [13] The other way of acknowledging existing patterns within new community planning was to evoke the old, or traditional, but (in contrast to both Traditionalism and the conservation rhetoric of the 1970s) to do so in Modern form. In 1957, Ninian Johnston praised the Gorbals's 'uncompromising cliffs of classical tenements' and pleaded that the 'local spirit . . . must be carefully preserved while the buildings are being demolished'. [14] And the following year, Michael Laird attacked the 'rampant piles of concrete' of freestanding tower blocks: 'A close-knit and varied network of housing types is in the best of Scottish traditions . . . a real culture which was nurtured in these more vernacular housing developments. We should remember the wynds, the closes, the back greens, and the "stair heids", and ponder awhile on the lonely isolation of point blocks in perhaps too spacious swards.' [15]

By the early 1960s, a range of new conceptions of community planning was being realised in built projects. In the field of housing, the emphasis was on rejection of open-plan layouts and high blocks in favour of lower, but equally dense patterns. Appropriately for an 'architecture of affluence', the new guiding principles were worked out not within public architecture, but in microcosm form, in the design of small private houses in the late 1950s. Here, by comparison with the more spartan early postwar years, as seen for instance at Spence's 'The Cottage', Longniddry, 1952 – with its big sloping rubble chimney, but separately articulated rooms – central heating and greater wealth now fuelled demands for freer planning, and for a more sensuous Modernism. In 1960 Frank Tindall called for house designs 'to suit our less formal, more interdependent way of life . . . people stimulated by modern magazines want houses properly related to the sunshine, with privacy and quiet, and an aesthetic derived not from the past but from the modern materials themselves'. [16] There was admiration for the richness of contemporary American houses, and for the more austere Modernism of north European architects such as Aalto. In 1958 Reiach advocated more innovative speculative dwellings, such as 'patio' houses and building in squares. [17]

The most consistent series of innovative small houses was produced by Peter Womersley. He had previously (1952–4) designed a house for a relative in Northern England, 'Farnley Hey', with an innovative narrow, open-plan layout on a steep wooded site, and use of timber and other natural materials. His main series of timber-framed houses commenced in 1955, and used one-storey, rectangular plans laid out on the Miesian principle of the subdivision of 'simple open volume, derived from the plan'. 'High Sunderland', 1956–7, built for the textile designer Bernat Klein, was planned around two courtyards, with an open interior arranged around 'natural visual obstacles', and featuring vivid contrasts of colour and materials. The most dramatic of this series was Port Murray, Maidens (1960–3), perched on a cliff: 'simple in overall shape, strongly geometric both inside and out'. [18]

Other architects also embarked on the same course at around the same time. In 1955, the young partnership of Morris & Steedman launched into house design, fired by the idealistic hope that they could help 'rethink how to live in this country today', by devising 'a specifically Scottish house, which would fit into the landscape'. It was a sign of the changed cultural climate that this search for the 'national' took its inspiration predominantly from the opulent houses of Neutra, Johnson and other post-war American Modernists – which Morris and Steedman were able to visit during a scholarship in the USA in the mid 1950s. These small houses might, they hoped, act as a 'marker' for wider trends. Their first commission, the Tomlinson house ('Avisfield'), Edinburgh, was built at a cost of only £4,500 in 1956–7. It was constructed of stone and painted brick, with a rubble walled courtyard garden, interpenetrating flat roofs, and open-plan interior focused on a massive rubble fireplace: 'flowing, yet interrupted space – always a hidden area or an "escape" '. In sharp contrast, their second commission, the Wilson house, Lasswade, 1958–9, was a extroverted 'promenade house', dramatically cantilevered out over a rolling landscape. [19] Later commissions brought other solutions, including the austere rectilinearity of the Sillitto house, Edinburgh (1960), with fully glazed first-floor living accommodation, and the stark spiral of the Snodgrass house, Silverburn (1964) [9.4]. Other architects pursued a similar path: Ian Arnott's own house at Gifford (1963) and Reiach's own house at Winton Loan, Edinburgh (1962–4), both combined single-aspect planning with openness on their garden side; in the west, Jack Holmes's 'Lyford', Strathblane (1957–8), was a split-level house located atop a crag.

The ideas pioneered in these private commissions were soon extended into the field of public housing, in the form of dense, low layouts, sometimes described in a metaphoric manner, using terms such as 'cluster' or 'carpet'. Sociological reinforcement was provided by the research and development frameworks set up by Matthew – which also, of course, helped create new, more complex user-centred discourses to occupy the growing numbers of young graduates. In 1959, his Edinburgh University department established a Housing Research Unit, including a sociologist. Its research concentrated on the following four areas: 'A sociological study of the factors which turn a group of dwellings into a community'; 'a similar study of the dwelling itself, and of the factors which make a house into a home'; access arrangements; and construction. [20] Its first building scheme was a group of 45 patio houses at Prestonpans, built 1962, and then (after extended user-studies) published 1966. The Unit also carried out a study of a similar scheme at Ardler, Dundee (built 1963–5): the latter's architects, Baxter, Clark & Paul, went on to build further courtyard developments at Blairgowrie, Peterhead and Keith, in the late 1960s.

9.4 Snodgrass house, Silverburn (Morris & Steedman, 1964), when newly completed.

9.5 Leith Fort redevelopment, Edinburgh (Shaw-Stewart, Baikie & Perry, 1960–6), view of point blocks.

At around the same time, other similar schemes were being built by private architects. The competition-winning entry by the newly graduated architects Shaw-Stewart, Baikie & Perry for Edinburgh's Leith Fort redevelopment competition (1957, built 1960–6) included point blocks (with Kahn-like service towers and industrial-aesthetic cladding) at one end of the site, in combination with a dense grouping of patio houses and a deck-access block (with access by pedestrian ways, or decks, set into the blocks) [9.5]. In 1964, Gillespie, Kidd & Coia designed an old people's complex at Round Riding Road, Dumbarton, as a one-storey broken wall of dwellings around a landscaped courtyard. John Paterson's scheme of 1958 for individual courtyard houses dotted across the edge of a city remained unbuilt. [21]

The most coherent and internationally renowned realisation of these new low, dense patterns of community design was achieved by a public authority, charged with developing one of the new centres of Scottish planning for affluence: Cumbernauld New Town Development Corporation. Cumbernauld's planning, as a whole,

reacted against the fairly low density and separate residential units of East Kilbride. Its initial town plan, drawn up by L. Hugh Wilson, Chief Architect and Planning Officer (until 1962, thereafter D. R. Leaker) envisaged a compact urban mass clustered around a hilltop town centre. Already, in 1960, Matthew identified Cumbernauld's planning conception as 'an immensely valuable tonic' to Scottish Modernism as a whole: when it was realised, 'the pulse will really begin to beat'. [22] The designers within its Development Corporation laid out Cumbernauld's housing as a low, relatively homogeneous 'carpet'. The building types – terraced cottages and low flats – were not dissimilar to East Kilbride, but there were denser layouts and harder landscaping [cf. C.13]. On the town's steep northwest escarpment, facing the backdrop of the Campsie Fells, there were rows of cottages with steep roofs and outshots – perhaps evoking the imagery of nearby nineteenth-century mining rows – and agglomerations of flat-roofed, split-level houses such as Seafar 2 (1961–3). Around these, the Corporation's landscape architect, Bill

Gillespie, wove a new belt of forest, designed to evoke the 'flowing, natural' settings of housing in Finland or Norway. [23] On the flatter south-east flank, there were grid layouts of long, flat-roofed rows. Early groups of flats were in slabs, or Y-plan blocks inspired by Gröndal in Stockholm (for example Kildrum 5, 1959–61). And the entire mixture was punctuated by the landmarks of 'Bison' tower blocks, built from 1964. Most of these schemes were designed by the Corporation architects, but some private firms were involved: for instance Wheeler & Sproson laid out Abronhill 4 (1968–70) in a more monumental manner, with a grand pedestrian axis. Elsewhere, and later, there was a shift towards the Vernacular forms of the 1970s, with steeper monopitch roofs: for instance, at Wheeler & Sproson's later stages of Dysart (for example. Phase 2, 1963–5) and Blackburn Town Centre, 1968 (with pedestrian mall, monopitch roofs, stark white harling); or in the vertically clustered forms of Baxter Clark & Paul's St Peter's Street, Peterhead (1968–71).

The field of primary-school design also saw a research and development-led trend towards lowness and compact flexibility. The educationalist advocacy of group teaching and more child-centred activities, and the continuing demand for economy in planning, encouraged a move towards more compressed, open plans, using the same social metaphors as in housing. The experimental Kirkhill Primary School, Broxburn (1968–9), designed by Lane, Bremner & Garnett with a joint team of the Scottish Education Department (SED) and West Lothian County Council, was divided into three 'clusters', with 'home bases' for the children. The rejection of finger-planned sanitary airiness was taken to an extreme in Gillespie, Kidd & Coia's dense, dark Kildrum Primary School, Cumbernauld (1960–2).

'An Open Citadel': The Megastructural Ideal [24]

At the same time as these variegated, but low-key reactions away from segregated planning and tower blocks, 1960s' Late Modernism witnessed another, more monumental evocation of the new ideas of social complexity: the Megastructure, an artificial landscape governed by communication, in which flexible uses and traffic functions would be juxtaposed within a single envelope. In this pattern, too, a decisive role was played by Cumbernauld New Town – in this case, by its internationally renowned Town Centre [9.6; cf. C.12].

Phase 1 of the Centre (designed from 1959, built 1963–7) was entrusted to Geoffrey Copcutt, a flamboyant and often controversial designer. He conceived the Centre as a linear, stepped, multi-function structure, with vehicle routes (including a fast divided highway) slicing through its centre, and pedestrian access ways crossing at right angles: 'a nine-level package accommodating most of the commercial, civic, cultural and recreational uses for a population of 70,000, elevated over a vehicular system linked to radials a mile apart'. It was to have been sheltered from the hilltop winds by 'curved and stepped terraces of apartments and earthworks arranged at the Glasgow portal'; these were never built. [25] Boldly rising through the main concrete structure, a separate row of columns supported a range of penthouses sailing over the top – an image inspired, perhaps, by Rudolph Schindler's Lovell Beach House, Los Angeles (1922–6). Copcutt's concept was carried forward on a heady wave of socio-rationalist investigations: he recalls that

> by day we engaged rowdy academics on a 100-towns retail-social study, and spent weekends recording the wind regime and sampling test bores. In between we debated income and spending patterns, projected travel modes, deliveries and solid waste values, juggled structural grids to match parking volumes, mitigated Venturi effects and correlated tenant, corner shop and sub-centre distribution to match the first phase. And all the while, like a jeweller fashioning precious metal, I hammered the cross-sections and shaped landscape, to forge an urban morphology. [26]

In 1963, Copcutt described the Centre's daring design using a Futurist rhetoric of technological consumerism. It would be

> a single citadel-like structure nearly half a mile long . . . a drive-in town centre . . . a vast terminal facility . . . All decks are perforated and interpenetrating . . . all planes are inhabited both above and below until the final statement is made by long terraces of penthouses. The basic structure of parallel linked frames

9.6 Cumbernauld Town Centre, Phase One (Copcutt, 1963–7): (above) 1964 drawing of bus station and through–motorway; (below) 1963 view of model of Centre as built, with the main structure, crowned by the range of penthouses, on the left, and the car park access road on the right.

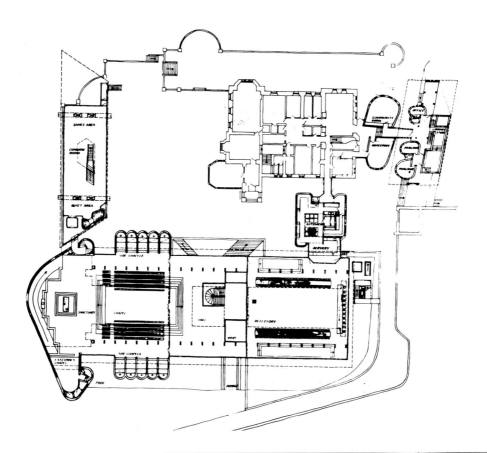

9.7 St Peter's College, Cardross (Gillespie, Kidd & Coia, 1959–66): (above) site plan, with the original nineteenth-century house at top right and the main accommodation and chapel block at the bottom; (right) 1966 view of chapel looking towards sanctuary, with accommodation ranges tiered above.

9.8 Students' residences (Andrew Melville Hall), University of St Andrews (J. Stirling, 1964–7): (left) original site plan of whole project and perspective of Phase I by James Stirling; (above) detail of Phase I.

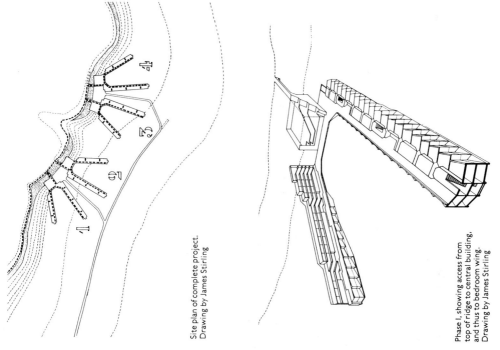

Site plan of complete project.
Drawing by James Stirling

Phase I, showing access from
top of ridge to central building,
and thus to bedroom wing.
Drawing by James Stirling

9.9 Hutchesontown/Part Gorbals CDA Area 'C', Glasgow (Spence, 1960–6): (above) 1965 view of one of 20-storey slab blocks; (right) 1962 view of main supporting columns beneath blocks, under construction.

creating a linear core within the scheme is able to accept . . . erupting forms, a variety of furnishings and a kaleidoscope of advertising.

Copcutt speculated that should pedestrian-based shopping become obsolete 'in the extreme future', then 'the centre could become a gigantic vending machine through which the motorized user drives to return revictualled'. Phase I was hailed by international Modern Movement historian Reyner Banham as 'the canonical megastructure'. [27] And the entire town was internationally acclaimed as a landmark in 'community planning'. In 1967, for instance, the American Institute of Architects awarded it the prestigious R. S. Reynolds Memorial Award for Community Architecture, preferring it to Tapiola (Finland) and Stockholm, as 'the most significant current contribution to the art and science of urban design in the Western world'. Cumbernauld, they proclaimed, was 'designed for the millennium': 'the dreams of the 1920s and

1930s are being built on a hill near Glasgow'. [28]

While Cumbernauld Town Centre was a spectacular 'one-off', others began to employ similar ideas as a basis for consistent building programmes. Gillespie, Kidd & Coia, rejuvenated after the war by younger Modernists (notably Isi Metzstein, who started in 1945 as an apprentice, and Andrew MacMillan, who joined in 1954), embarked from 1958 on a series of educational commissions based on a sectional planning concept. Reacting away from older school layouts with long corridors and wings (in response to the government's demand for economy in circulation space), this new, more intense pattern comprised double-banked teaching or residential accommodation around communal spaces in the centre. The series comprised Simshill Secondary School (1956–63) and Our Lady and St Francis School, Glasgow (1958–64), with cantilevered upper floors; Our Lady's High School, Cumbernauld (1963–4); and Cumbernauld Technical College (1972–5).

The most significant of Gillespie, Kidd & Coia's sectional buildings was St Peter's Seminary at Cardross (1959–66, project architect Isi Metzstein), a courtyard complex on an abruptly steep site (like Corbusier's La Tourette, 1953–60) with an existing nineteenth-century Baronial house as the focus [9.7]. The two main elements were a stepped-section accommodation block with a chapel and refectory below ranges of study-bedrooms, and a library and lecture block jutting out over woodland. The section-planned form set out to express community, by 'associating large spaces and small spaces within a linear building of many repeating cells'. 'Every floor is a memorable space . . . identical forms demean people.' To describe these large and complicated structures, the firm increasingly adopted an exalted, metaphoric socio-architectural language: for instance, student residences at Hull were described in 1968 as an 'inhabited wall'. [29]

In educational designs by other architects, elements of megastructural agglomeration began to appear: for instance, in the sectional, curved Craigmount High School (Alison & Hutchison

& Partners, 1968–70), and in Rowand Anderson, Kininmonth & Paul's clustering of cubic shapes around courtyards at Mary Erskine School, Edinburgh (1964–7, designed by Kininmonth and William Leslie). James Stirling's harshly crystalline university residences complex at St Andrews (1964–7), with its wide internal 'decks' radiating outwards from a social core, inventively developed some of the community patterns and metaphors being devised at that time by the English New Brutalist movement [9.8]. In the civic field, Hutchison, Locke & Monk's competition-winning design for Paisley Civic Centre (1964, partly built 1966–71) was an irregular linear grouping with 'civic concourse' below: the assessors praised its 'grandeur of urban space'. The most visually stylish of all Scottish images of urban agglomeration – if at the border-line of the strict definition of megastructure – was Basil Spence's design for Area 'C' of the Hutchesontown redevelopment in Glasgow (built 1960–6, project architect Charles Robertson, dynamited 1993) [9.9]. He grouped the 400 dwellings required into a line of 20-storey towers, which were in turn marshalled into two long slab blocks by the linking device of 'garden slabs' on alternate floors, each intended to provide sheltered open space for the adjacent four dwellings: it was these that gave the project its megastructural aspect. Spence originally wanted to support the spectacular, cliff-like blocks on a line of single centrally placed struts, but after engineering warnings the simpler method of slanting, paired columns was adopted.

In the capital, the idea of megastructure was developed in a more fragmentary way. In 1962, Percy Johnson-Marshall, who for a time acted as planning consultant for RMJM projects, proposed the extension of Edinburgh University's George Square scheme into a multi-level, decked redevelopment of much of the South Side [9.10]. Of the 20-year, four-phase plan, described by Johnson-Marshall in Geddes-like rhetoric as a 'University-Within-the-City' or a 'new New Town', [30] only the first stage, directly adjacent to Matthew's tower in George Square, was even partly implemented. Set apart from the surrounding streets by podiums and decks, this included RMJM's jutting concrete George Square Theatre and linear, four-storey faculty buildings (both

9.10 Decked redevelopment scheme designed by Percy Johnson-Marshall for University of Edinburgh Comprehensive Development Area, 1962: illustration from 1962 University booklet, showing Nicolson Street from south and Old College in distance. None of the new structures shown in this perspective was built.

1964–7), and Basil Spence, Glover & Ferguson's University Library (1965–7, designed by Andrew Merrylees). An even more ingenious idea was devised by the Princes Street Panel (whose members, by 1966, were Kininmonth, Reiach and David Wishart) for the capital's most renowned boulevard. It was to be gradually converted into a megastructure, by including a first-floor walkway in all new developments: we should here recall that Abercrombie & Plumstead's 1949 plan for Edinburgh had proposed the building of a two-level highway beneath Princes Street. The Panel formula was abandoned in the 1970s, with only isolated sites rebuilt: one distinguished example was Reiach's New Club redevelopment (1966–9, in association with Stuart Renton), with sumptuous new interiors.

While projects such as Cumbernauld Town Centre principally conceived of the megastructure as a vehicle for socio-architectural flexibility, the subsequent spread of the idea simplified it into a new urban monumentalism. A varied group of megastructures, for instance, was built in Glasgow's city-centre Anderston Cross CDA. The Anderston Industrial Zone (Holmes & Partners, 1965–9) was built for displaced industry: a decked mass of concrete and brick, containing factories above warehouses and car parks. Offices and a bus station were housed in the Anderston Commercial Centre (R. Siefert, 1967–73), while Heron House (Derek Stephenson & Partners, 1967–71) comprised an office tower and substructures, embracing Thomson's St Vincent Street Church. Much later, 1976 saw the completion of the first phase of the new centre of Irvine (by the New Town's architects), an elevated commercial complex spanning a river.

It was only in the 1970s, and in a programme outside the bounds of conventional architecture – the construction of permanent platforms for North Sea oil production – that the most extreme futurist possibilities of the megastructure concept were realised. Oil platforms developed both the community and the technological frame/infill elements of megastructure utopianism in a startlingly literal fashion. The largest and most daring of all the fixed installations of this programme was the Ninian Central Platform, an artificial island constructed 125 km east of Unst, in 200-metre-

deep water, to serve as the production hub of the Ninian oilfield. Designed in 1975 by Chevron Ltd (Aberdeen) and Doris (France), the 590,000 tonne, 236-metre-high structure was assembled in Loch Kishorn (with deck built by McDermott of Ardersier) and floated into position in 1978. It comprised a massive circular concrete base and shaft, containing a reservoir for oil and gas, and supporting an above-water superstructure into which a complex assortment of prefabricated or pre-assembled accommodation and deck units was slotted.

1960s' Rationalism: An Architecture of Precision

The technological daring of the North Sea platforms brings us to the second main element of 1960s' Late Modernism: a rationalist, or scientific paradigm. This did not, on the whole, challenge Functionalism's claimed integration of visual, social and technical elements and its faith in the optimum solution, but instead tried to refine its rationalistic elements, both in the design of buildings, and in the building process. These ideas took different forms in the design of individual public buildings and of serial building programmes.

In the field of public architecture, there was an emphasis on precise, understated construction, preferably not in wet but in dry construction, whether in panel or skeleton form. The most audacious example of the latter was Edinburgh Royal Botanic Garden's new Plant Exhibition Houses, built in 1965–7 to the designs of Ministry of Public Building and Works Scotland (team leader George A. H . Pearce, in consultation with the engineer L. R. Creasy) [9.11]. In 1961, Dr E. E. Kemp, Curator of the Garden, had called for a new building to replace decrepit old exhibition houses, and stipulated that its structure must not intrude into the interior. The designers evolved an externally suspended steel structure of tetrahedron space frames. Inside, in place of rows of plant-pots, flowing multi-level environments were constructed – a relationship of frame and infill which partly realised some earlier avant-garde megastructure visions. [31]

9.11 View (1967) of newly completed Plant Exhibition Houses at Royal Botanic Garden, Edinburgh.

The architecture of rationalist economy in large public complexes was developed especially within RMJM's Edinburgh head office, where it became linked with a more general 1960s' updating of Matthew's philosophy by Tom Spaven, John Richards and other colleagues. They were motivated by a faith in 'the inevitability and desirability of progress. Inventions, once made, could not be de-invented. Art had gone through a revolution since Mondrian and Stravinsky which could not be ignored. All the lines of all the graphs were going up: population, health, the economy, and expectations of an egalitarian and well-ordered society.' [32] Richards respected Functionalist claims to have integrated beauty with utility and solidity, but distanced the formal expression of that claim from Matthew's often scenographic massing of high blocks, towards a more restrained architecture of low ranges faced in precise dry-cladding: 'buildings you could put up in clean overalls, rather than grubbing around on a muddy building site'. [33] The first to be built was the initial phase of the new University of Stirling. Stirling (developed 1966–73) was not only the first new university built in Scotland for 400 years,

but a project strongly symbolic of the community-building aspirations of Modernism, as well as a key part of the Central Scottish regional development plan. The planning of Phase 1 was dictated by both the construction requirement for speed (planning and building within eighteen months) and the university's interdisciplinary philosophy of academic community. These pointed to a lightweight, all-purpose building (with steel frame, concrete floors and prefabricated timber wall panels).

This second-generation development of Matthew's Modernist ideology evolved further at the Central (or Royal Commonwealth) Pool in the capital, designed 1965–7 and built 1967–70 (partner in charge, John Richards. [9.12]. The General Manager of the Corporation's Baths & Laundries Department, Jack Black, had the simple, yet Modern idea of reorientating his baths from cleansing to recreation and safety: a new system of pools across the city, headed by a new Central pool, would ensure that every child in Edinburgh could learn how to swim. Richards's response to the simplicity of that programme was to seek a correspondingly spare, uncluttered

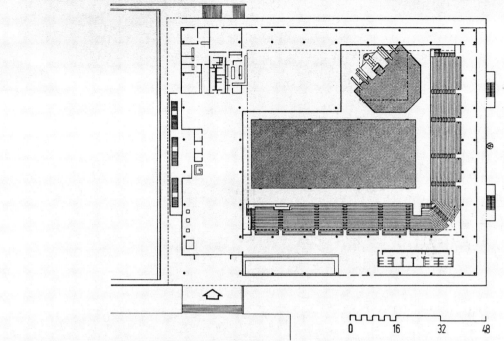

Plan at entrance-hall level, showing main pool in centre and diving pool at top right

```
0          16          32          48
```

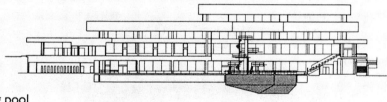

Section through diving pool

9.12 Central (Royal Commonwealth) Pool, Edinburgh (RMJM, 1967–70): (above) RMJM drawings of plan and section; (below) 1967 perspective of interior.

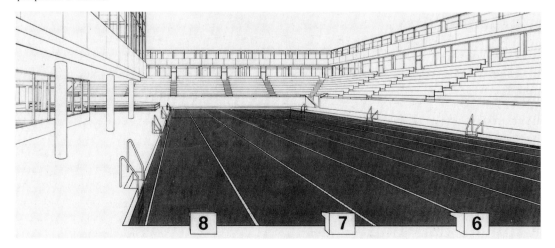

architectural 'form': 'If the programme was beautiful, all you had to do was reveal it; to open it up like a flower. You actually had to strip away the "architecture" – we called it "noise". Economy of expression was our aim.' [34] The practical problems of swimming pool design – heat loss, condensation and glare – were tackled by enclosing the main pool hall with other spaces, including a vast roof service zone. A sloping site was exploited to provide a ground-level entrance at the top, with the pool hall at an angle below. This minimised apparent bulk from the street while maximising the spatial drama inside. [35]

These were rather high-status, individualised projects. Late Modernist rationalism really took off in the field of serial building. In particular, the hospital-building drive combined elements of megastructural architecture with concepts of scientific organisation of building use, and integrated user-research. The post-war decades witnessed the supercession of the old orthodoxy of control of infection in open pavilions, by the American concept of compact, highly serviced blocks subdivided into smaller, more private rooms. This coincided with a trend, begun by Vale of Leven, towards more open-ended hospital planning. A government-sponsored programme of architectural research in the 1960s associated this movement with a striking Modernist image: the multi-storey slab block of 'racetrack' wards, with services in the middle and small ward rooms running around in a loop. Following tentative experiments in the early 1950s, the first fully-fledged racetrack multi-storey block in Scotland was built by Gillespie, Kidd & Coia at Bellshill Maternity Hospital (1959–62). The type was then subjected to user study in an experimental prototype block built in 1963–6 at Falkirk Royal Hospital, designed jointly by Keppie, Henderson & Partners and a Scottish Home & Health Department study team (comprising a nurse, doctor and architect). Having established appropriate standards, the Department then began a big multi-storey building drive. This included new suburban developments, at Gartnavel General Hospital, Glasgow, 1968–73, by Keppie, Henderson & Partners; Aberdeen Royal Infirmary, Forresterhill, from 1964, by C. C. Wright (Chief Regional Architect of North Eastern Regional

Hospital Board); and Inverclyde Royal Hospital, Greenock, 1977–9, by Boswell, Mitchell & Johnston. And it included megastructural city-centre redevelopments, at Glasgow's Western Infirmary, 1965–74, by Keppie, Henderson & Partners; at Glasgow Royal Infirmary, 1971–82 by Spence, Glover & Ferguson; and, after twenty years of discussion, at Edinburgh Royal Infirmary Phase 1, 1975–81, by RMJM. The climax of the hospital-building drive presaged a major change of course: RMJM's protracted, research-led design of Ninewells Hospital in Dundee (from 1961, completed 1974), Scotland's first new teaching hospital this century. Here the freestanding multi-storey slab was abandoned for a low, dense complex disposed around service spines and courtyards, and strung out along a sloping site: the contours were exploited to achieve a megastructure-like, yet horizontal, separation of traffic and functions.

The complex dedicated most singlemindedly to ideas of rational building use was the computerised Inland Revenue headquarters, 'Centre 1' at East Kilbride – the prototype for a series of tax centres which was never, in the event, built. Completed in 1968 to the designs of R. Stevenson of Ministry of Public Building and Works (Edinburgh), this comprised a 19-storey tower containing allocation units and lower wings for the processing of data: the heart of the complex was a huge ICT 1904 computer, fed by punched card and magnetic tape, which contained records of all 2 million employees and employers in Scotland. The Centre was seen not merely as a machine for 'mass production' of data, but also as a community. Its carefully integrated social and sports facilities embodied 'new ideas on how people may work together'. [36]

The 1960s also saw an insistent rationalist concern with the process *of* building. Spurred on by the power in design which contractors had accumulated in system building, it distinguished between 'open' and 'closed' systems. The former was based on standard components which an architect could marshal at will. The latter was a cut and dried formula exemplified by the contractor's package-deal tower block. In practice, this campaign to assert leadership over mass building in the 1960s through open systems proved impracticable. The usual compromise that public architects settled on was either to design their own system, or to get a design-minded contractor to adapt one to their requirements. One of the most unusual projects of industrialised housing was a large pro- gramme in Tripoli organised by Matthew and Spaven, from the late 1960s, for the Libyan Arab Republic National Housing Corporation.

'Poetry' and 'Form' in Late Modernism

The tendency towards visual monumentality in patterns such as Megastructure, and the concern of Richards to strip away 'noise' from an inner architectural essence, both hinted at a renewed concern with the 'form' of architecture. This tendency was accentuated further by some architects of the late 1950s and early 1960s, who assigned a strictly subordinate role to Function- alism's professed preoccupation with integration of beauty with utility and solidity, and instead emphasised individualistic formal expression – more strongly than at any time since the turn- of-the-century work of Mackintosh. Abroad, Corbusier had already launched into a trend of more personalised Modernism: in obituaries of 1966, Alan Reiach claimed there was 'a connection between the lyricism and poetic vision his work displays and the fervent idealism of youth in Scotland today', [37] while Metzstein panegyrised his late work's 'monumentality without rhetoric . . . permeated by love of reality, fertilised by intuition and experience and unconfined by narrow tech- nology'. [38] Equally influential was the work of Louis I. Kahn; in Scotland his rejection of ration- alist, programme-based design in favour of the symbolism of form, and his doctrine of 'served and servant spaces', were echoed in William Whitfield's Glasgow University Library (1965–81) [9.13]. This project's bristling, towered shape was intended to mask the bulk of the 'warehouse for books' required by the librarian, while answering the call of J. L. Gleave, the university's planning consultant, for a monumental landmark to crown the new extension area; but it was also inspired by Whitfield's love of the massive castles and forbidding military imagery of his native Northumberland. [39]

The most consistent Scottish champion of 'formal' architecture in the 1960s was Peter Womersley. Putting his timber house style behind him, Womersley began a series of public buildings in a refined yet forceful manner. This was backed up by an explicit pursuit of intuitive form, even of the building as 'a piece of sculpture'. In 1969, he identified 'the heart as the birthplace of any good architecture'; post-war affluence now allowed utility and structure to be dealt with by consul- tants, leaving the architect free to achieve 'sheer unadulterated Delight, as Wright did for me many years ago with Falling Water'. Architecture could not 'be created from standard details'. His 1960s' buildings were bound together by an overall aesthetic of geometric, concrete monumentality. In common with his earlier houses was their 'basically Miesian' principle of 'subtractive architecture': in most cases, Joseph Blackburn was project archi- tect. Key commissions included the massive first phase of Roxburgh County Buildings, with tower (1966–8); a studio for Bernat Klein at High Sunderland (1969–72) with open-plan interior, externally articulated by deep, horizontally projecting edge beams [9.14]; and the Fairydean stadium, Galashiels (1963–5, with Ove Arup), a daring composition based on triangular beams, with a canopy base appearing to rest on a sharply pointed edge. Most complex was the Nuffield Transplantation Surgery Unit at the Western General Hospital – a commission steered in his direction by John Holt. The Unit (designed 1963, built 1965–8) comprises a low, corbelled-out ward unit with jutting stairtower, lobby and office wing [9.15]. The planning of the ward block combined visual interpenetration with medical requirements for isolation and sterility. Later 'sculptural' concrete works included Monklands Leisure Centre, Coatbridge, and Dingleton Hospital Boiler House, Melrose (both 1977). But by then, Womersley's designs had pointed in a new direction, to- wards 'additive' rather than 'subtractive' archi- tecture. [40] The clustered, harled, rounded forms of his Edenside Group Practice Surgery, Kelso (1967), can also be seen as a precursor of the Vernacular forms of the 1970s [9.16].

Rowand Anderson, Kininmonth & Paul were also undergoing a Late Modernist formal trans- formation, under the influence of younger design- ers who had entered the practice in the 1950s, such as William G. Leslie and Thomas H. Duncan. First completed of these new buildings, which

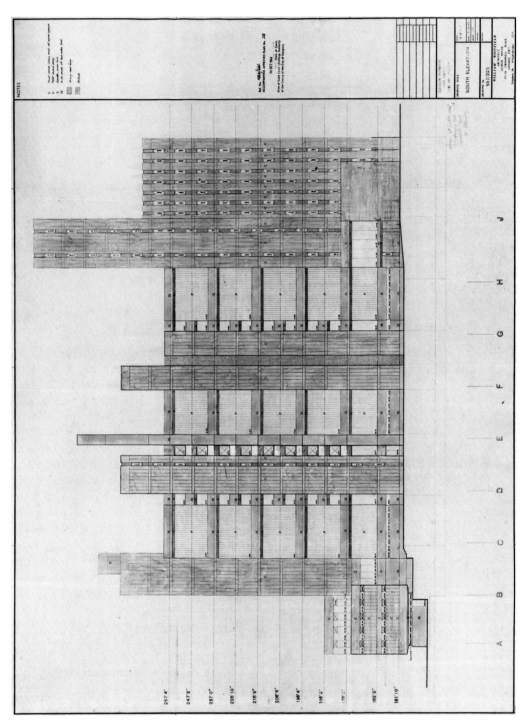

9.13 Glasgow University Library (Whitfield, 1965–81), south elevation, 1964.

9.14 Bernat Klein studio, High Sunderland (Womersley, 1969–72), 1974 photograph.

focused on the dramatic juxtaposition of solids and voids, was Edinburgh University's Student Union extension (1962–4, by Kininmonth himself), a tall annexe with bold rectangular windows, conical-headed, slightly classical internal columns and circular rooflights, built of boardmarked concrete. A more costly and refined expression was given to this aesthetic in the staged redevelopment of an L-shaped headquarters site in St Andrew Square by Scottish Provident (1961–9, by Leslie) [9.17]. The main facade featured patterns of smooth granite-clad solids and sheer glazed voids, of horizontal and vertical: the composition was crowned by a glass-topped staircase tower (now altered).

Alongside the efforts of Womersley and others in these secular buildings, others exploited the more obvious potential for 'poetic' design in religious architecture. Here was a striking parallel to the secular redefinition of community in the 1960s – and expressed in even more novel and forceful forms. In this decade, the long, twentieth-century trend towards worshipper-centred plans reached its climax, especially in the Roman Catholic Church, where the innovations of Pope John XXIII and the Second Vatican Council

emphasised closer clergy-congregation relations. Among architects, there was a demand to express these trends through more unified, monumental forms. Within the Kirk, this could develop naturally out of the domestic plainness of 1950s hall-churches. Reiach's Kildrum Parish Church, Cumbernauld (completed 1962), manifested a flat-roofed, well-lit clarity, with linear, unambiguous circulation routes, and steel-framing clad in timber and brick: its single rhetorical touch was a tall bell tower. Or, there was, for both Protestant and Catholic churches, the well-established Modernist precedent of Expressionism to fall back on: the breaking-down of rectangular plans into curved, faceted or agglomerated forms. In the east, Spence's Mortonhall Crematorium, Edinburgh (1964–7), was a jagged cluster of chapels with smooth-faced blockwork: the main chapel had a backlit interior. The hyperbolic paraboloid roof of Wheeler & Sproson's Boghall Church, Bathgate (1965) evoked a Beaux-Arts structural daring. And Rowand Anderson, Kininmonth & Paul's younger designers produced two striking works for the Church of Scotland in 1964–6: Brucefield, Whitburn (by Thomas Duncan), with a wide roof

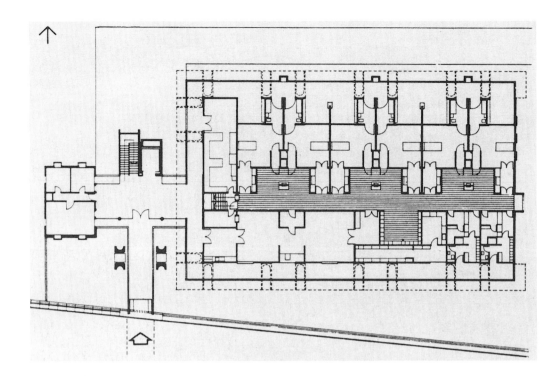

9.15 Nuffield Transplantation Surgery Unit, Western General Hospital, Edinburgh (Womersley, 1965–8): (above) plan showing (left–right) main administration building, entrance hall with stair and lift tower, and ward-unit; (right) 1968 view of main entrance from disposal corridor.

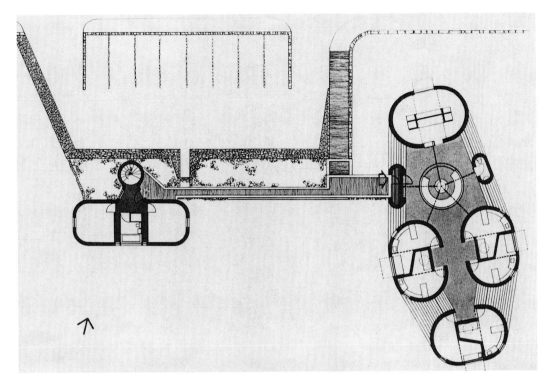

9.16 Group Practice Consulting Rooms, Kelso (Womersley, 1967), plan.

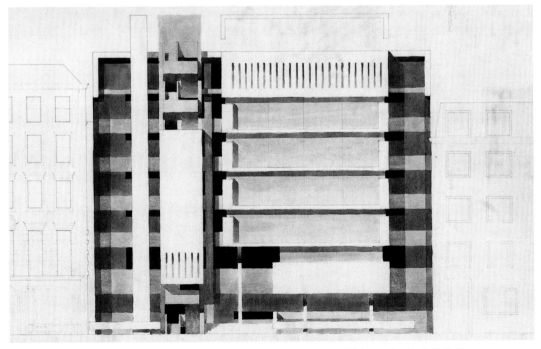

9.17 Scottish Provident Institution headquarters, Edinburgh (Rowand Anderson, Kininmonth & Paul, 1961–9).

broken by dramatic convex and concave extrusions; and Craigsbank, Edinburgh (by William Leslie), a harled block with geometrical incisions and low, concave bell tower.

In the Roman Catholic Church, the most important steps towards a more fluid or expressionistic way of designing were taken in the late 1950s by Coia's firm. While continuing to build hierarchically decorated basilicas for well-established parishes, Coia's team experimented with innovations for low-cost churches in new housing areas. A decisive break, prior to the main liturgical changes in the Church, came with St Paul's Church in Glenrothes New Town (1956–7: architect in charge, Andrew MacMillan). Responding to a commission from a priest, Father Grace, who had decidedly avant-garde ideas, a wedge-shaped church built of white painted common brick was built, with the aim of 'creating an image of a church' with 'monumental presence'. [41] All the ingredients of the later 'Coia style' were there, such as 'sectional' top-lighting (through a tall roof projection) and sweeping walls with small windows; the focal point was a dramatic, jagged metal cross by the sculptor Benno Schotz. At the consecration ceremony, Archbishop Gray's anxiously-awaited verdict was positive. Coia phoned Schotz and announced, 'We have broken through with a modern building and a modern Cross.' [42]

From about 1960, all Gillespie, Kidd & Coia's churches were designed in this Late Modernist manner. At first, some large commissions retained a rectangular plan. St Bride's, East Kilbride (1963–4), contained a single windowless space, lit through timber spars in the roof, and entered by a slit-like entrance door in a curved embrasure [9.18]. Externally, at the request of the R. C. Archdiocese, the apparent scale of the 'castle-like' structure was maximised by a high parapet, and a tall campanile intended to 'signal the presence of a strange but important building in this new town'; the campanile has since been demolished. [43] By the mid-1960s, all their new churches had adopted centralised, non-rectangular plans, reflecting the new liturgical emphases with seating ranged round the altar. Their expressionistic formalism 'carved building out of solids', in contrast to Womersley's 'subtractive' treatment and Richards's 'post-Cubist modelling' of space. [44] Sacred Heart Church, Cumbernauld (1964), was an impassive block mystically lit through dark coloured windows; Our Lady of Good Counsel, Dennistoun (1965), had a splayed plan and slanted ceiling; while St Benedict Drumchapel (1965–7, demolished) had a prow-like roof supported on curved, laminated timber members. The daring of these designs inspired other innovative essays in Catholic church design. Richard J. McCarron's Our Lady of Sorrows, South Uist (1964–5), reflected liturgy and exposed maritime climate in a massively compact form and deeply recessed windows. A large mosaic over the entrance was designed by David Harding (later Town Artist to Glenrothes in the 1970s). The concern of architects such as Gillespie, Kidd & Coia or Womersley with artistic form and personality, and their description of their work using an elevated, metaphoric rhetoric, anticipated aspects of the architecture of the 1990s. Coia spoke of the practice's search for 'a collective personality': 'the art needs to come first'. [45] But their repudiation of the orthodox Modernist claims that beauty was inseparable from solidity and utility was not without consequent difficulty: the Roman Catholic Church later demolished some of Coia's most daring designs, including St Benedict's Drumchapel and the tower of St Bride's, citing structural or maintenance problems.

Before we pass to the period of the crisis of the Modern Movement, let us briefly summarise its general impact – an impact which only became apparent once the crisis was well under way, from the late 1960s and 1970s. The last tower block of flats, after all (Jasmine Place, Aberdeen), was completed as late as 1985. The 19th century had seen an even more radical transformation of the built environment, but only elevated building types had fallen within the scope of architects. It was against that period that Modern architects defined themselves, in their claims to have ennobled the design of everyday, mass building through an integration of the artistic with the social and the technical – although Late Modernism began to see that supposed integration in much more complex, even problematic terms. Quantitatively, what had been done seemed formidable. Modernism not only aspired to rebuild the nation, but actually succeeded, in key areas

9.18 St Bride's Church, East Kilbride (Gillespie, Kidd & Coia, 1963–4), mid-1960s interior photograph.

such as the provision of self-contained homes with modern amenities – in other words, social privatisation – and the sweeping-away of the decayed urban legacy of the nineteenth century. This reconstruction, carried out in the name of the whole people through collective state agencies, had taken the form of an architecture within which the passionate concern for the 'national' and for 'Scottish tradition' seemed for the time being to have become quiescent. How would the next generation of architects, who, thanks to these efforts, no longer faced all-consuming problems such as the 'slums', come to terms with this legacy? Designers of the 1970s and 1980s did so in a very simple way – by outright rejection.

The 1970s: Modernity Rejected

The post-1968 years saw a steady undermining of the mid-century Scottish consensus between Capitalism and Socialism in support of corporatist welfare state provision. The reconstruction drive was still in full swing, but the authority of planning and professional experts now steadily declined, under the pressure of radical critiques and of the growth of privatised, mobile domestic life. This breakdown in state-led discipline occurred in most Western countries – in some cases much more dramatically than in Scotland. Here, it was at first supported by the same political consensus that had underpinned the building of the welfare state. For instance, it was a Labour Government Green Paper in 1977 which heralded the break-up of local-authority monopoly housing. Alongside these social and economic trends, the crisis of Modern architecture grew more intense. While it was a highly variegated movement, all its branches had in common an overall acceptance of material progress through the New. In some countries, such as the Netherlands or Finland, the 1970s merely reduced the teleological forcefulness of this ideology without renouncing it altogether, and augmented Modern forms with 'traditional' patterns. In Scotland both the ideology and the forms of Modernism were called into question. Many labelled the entire Modernist ideal of Progress, through mass provision of new buildings, naïve or oppressive: spirit of the age was challenged by spirit of place.

The strength of this reaction was epitomised in the way in which that central Modernist socio-psychological ideal, Community, was turned on its head. It was seen no longer as something created for users by design of new buildings, but as something to be protected against new development by the action of residents or users. All previous providers – designers and politicians alike – were rejected by a new alliance of some users and some designers: in 1969 Andrew Gilmour of the Edinburgh University Architecture Research Unit argued that housing standards 'had been imposed for the "good of the people" and have absolute priority, yet many are expressed in a most arbitrary manner. They are concerned with matters of public health, safety and morals, but have not resulted from demands from the users, whose satisfaction is more consciously concerned with convenience.' [46] Where Functionalism had been disparaged in the 1960s as 'monotonous, dull and boring', [47] now the Late Modern attempts to reflect social complexity were mocked as a kind of dishonesty: in 1974 Edwin Johnston contrasted a Copcutt perspective with a dreary photo of a child in the rain, in front of Cumbernauld Town Centre: a 'glamorous gift wrapper' versus 'the disillusion of reality . . . bleak and perhaps hostile . . . the product as experienced by the inhabitants of Cumbernauld' [cf. 9.6]. [48] Megastructure became a symbol not of flexibility but of mechanistic crudity: the building of Ian Burke & Martin's St James Centre (1964–70), containing a car park, hotel, shopping centre and

offices, was vehemently opposed by Edinburgh's growing conservation movement. In 1966, A. G. Jury's plans for a megastructural 'Cultural Centre' in Buchanan Street were attacked by a panel of architects (Coia, Reiach, Walter Underwood and Ninian Johnston) as too 'grandiose' and lacking in 'openness and nobility'. [49] The 1969 'Skeffington Report' promised a new harmony through 'participation' in planning. But the next year, Lindsay Mackie dismissed the idea that participation would be a way of smoothing away objections to the experts: instead, it would expose to debate the 'irreconcilables' in planning. [50]

The Ascendancy of Conservation

Under Modernism, the mainstream of Progress and the New had been balanced, even buttressed, by attempts to address context and to respond to 'traditional' patterns; but old buildings, and preservation, nevertheless remained peripheral. The 1970s were the first and, perhaps, only decade in which the central driving force in Scottish architecture was not new buildings of any kind, but preserved old ones. This was the decade of reaction, the decade of ascendancy of the Conservation Movement. Conservation's ascendancy was presented, within its own mythology, as a victory in a battle. But we could equally well attribute it to the success (within its own terms) of Modernist reconstruction, leaving a gap to be filled at the heart of community planning: not so much a May 1968-style overthrow, as a displacement, of Authority. Indeed, one element within it was a reinvigoration of the Traditionalist movement for conservation of ordinary homes, and opposition to state housing schemes: by the 1980s, the string of conservation titles held by the grandson of the 4th Marquess of Bute (chairman of the National Trust and of the National Museum, and president of the Alexander Thomson Society) showed the real power which now resided in Heritage.

The administrative foundation of the conservation victory was laid, in the 1970s, by the transformation of Ian Lindsay's lists into an apparatus of State control, ironically under the aegis of the Scottish *Development* Department. After uncertain fortunes following Lindsay's death in 1966, a change of government and administrators in 1970 brought in new and sympathetic faces, especially George Younger as junior minister in charge of the SDD. The 1969 and 1972 Town and Country Planning Acts gave force to statutory listing; controls were tightened by the SDD and local authorities, and advertisement of demolition applications exposed them to public criticism. The years 1970 also saw a resumption of the oversight role played by Lindsay up to his death in 1966, but in an unexpected form: Robert Matthew was appointed conservation adviser to the Secretary of State. That Matthew – son of Lorimer's partner, pioneer of Scottish Modernism, and part-redeveloper of George Square – could now emerge as 'Scotland's first conservation supremo', was another startling demonstration of the recurrent continuities in Scottish architecture. He called for full implementation of the 1969 Act, for a crash expansion of school and university teaching of the 'environment', and for involvement of 'the community' in conservation. One must avoid a 'museum attitude', and use 'imagination to link up the best of the past with the things of the present'. [51] He began to intervene in individual cases: in 1971 he signed a petition against demolition of Haymarket Station for an office tower, and in 1974 he stepped in to block demolition of Mackintosh's Martyrs School, reminding the Secretary of State that 'we are surely past the stage when a unique part of this country's most valuable architectural heritage has to disappear on account of urban road works'. [52]

Robert Matthew's most important contribution to the growing Conservation Movement, as a new arena of national cultural power, was his drive for preservation of the Edinburgh New Town – securing for posterity the unified conception first charted by his namesake, Robert Adam, two centuries earlier at Charlotte Square [cf. 4.18, 5.17, 5.20]. As early as 1967, the New Town bicentenary celebrations had begun to stir public concern about its condition. The centrepiece exhibition, 'Two Hundred Summers in a City', was designed by John L. Paterson, who transferred his concept of 'environmental theatre' from Modernist design to the evocation of a 'poetical impression' of Edinburgh's past. He warned that unless the New Town was protected, 'the alternative is the prospect of a visual celebration in 2067 entitled

"One Hundred Winters in a Wasteland" '. [53] The practical answer to such pleas came from Matthew, who now turned his formula of programme-formulation and delegation from area redevelopment to area conservation. In 1967, partly in response to the passing of the Civic Amenities Act (which provided for preservation of groups of buildings through conservation areas), but also as an offshoot of the Late Modernist preoccupation with fostering variegated 'urbanity', the Scottish Civic Trust was founded. At an initial meeting, Matthew pressed on his fellow trustees the idea that 'we must do something about the New Town of Edinburgh', and thereafter per-suaded the EAA to carry out a condition survey of the entire area. [54] The costed findings and recommendations, which emphasised the need for regular maintenance, were presented at a special international conference in June 1970. By December of that year a permanent organisation, the Edinburgh New Town Conservation Com-mittee (ENTCC), was being set up, jointly financed by the Government and Edinburgh Corporation, and run by eighteen members representing the Corporation, Historic Buildings Council, amenity societies; Matthew was a member in his capacity as Secretary of State's conservation adviser. The ENTCC's first director, from 1972, was Desmond Hodges.

Conceived in a period of rapid architectural transition, the ENTCC project pointed in several directions. Being concerned with an area – larger than virtually all others in Europe – of formal classical buildings, it dovetailed both with the official listing process and the declaration of conservation areas. But it also acknowledged the Bute ideology of social Traditionalism: at Matthew's instigation, its efforts were at first concentrated on the 'tattered fringe' of slum tene-ments in areas such as Stockbridge. The ENTCC, conceived and pushed through by the former leader of Scottish Modernism, was a supreme achievement of the apparatus of consensual administration which had formed around the Modernist concept of community planning. But it also contained within it elements of more explicit anti-Modernism. In 1971, John H. Reid, a key figure in the EAA's New Town survey, pointed to a 'social revolution . . . children in revolt' . . .

'people' were dissatisfied with the planning process. And in 1977, Hodges attacked Modern architecture as 'puritanical'. By 1985, Colin McWilliam could remark, about the ENTCC's office in a converted New Town shop, that 'the most important architectural development in Edinburgh since the war is located at 13A Dundas Street'. [55] Matthew's new conservation role was cut short by his death in 1975. After that, professional leadership in state conservation passed to a new (from 1976) Principal Inspector of Historic Buildings, David Walker. He vigorously projected art-historical research and listing, including a large resurvey programme, into the field of nineteenth- and early twentieth-century architecture. These official developments were matched by a growth in the power of voluntary bodies, and a proliferation of specialist conservation architects, especially in Edinburgh: Robert Hurd & Partners was joined by such new practices as Simpson & Brown, and Benjamin Tindall Architects.

If the capital's revival of the social conservation tradition was to some extent an elite matter, in the west a different story was unfolding, which took up the Bute ideology of the ordinary home in a novel way, augmenting it with post-1968 opposition to authority. Previously, various attempts to shift social housing provision towards improvement of private property had all foundered on the rock of anti-landlordism, and early conservationist definitions of Glasgow the 'Victorian City' had, on the whole, excluded 'the slums'. By the mid-1960s, the progress of the housing drive began to change the position. On the recommendation of the 1967 Cullingworth Report, the 1969 Housing Act introduced new grants and incentives. But it was still assumed that top-down provision would prevail: the new Housing Treatment Areas could include improvement as well as demolition, but would be run by local authorities using compulsory purchase powers. Only after Glasgow Corporation's attempted use of compulsory purchase powers for two prototype schemes (Old Swan and Oatlands) was blocked by occupiers, did a new and powerful formula emerge: rehabilitation by local, 'community-based' housing associations. This new formula was hit upon by 'ASSIST', a group of former Strathclyde

University architecture students (of whom the most prominent was Raymond Young) who inspired and helped organise, on participatory lines, a tenement improvement scheme at Taransay Street Treatment Area, Govan (from 1971). The new pattern pioneered by ASSIST at Taransay Street was made the basis of the 1974 Housing Act; by the early 1980s, with the aid of over thirty local housing associations and 90 per cent grants, the city was absorbing half of all Scottish housing improvements expenditure [9.19, 9.20].

This 'rehab' programme, in its concern with large-scale provision of basic amenities, resembled the Modernist preoccupation with output, but its devolved control renounced provision by experts. And its success, in turn, helped stigmatise Modernist housing, by then itself in some places sliding into disrepair. Eventually, Tenement turned from a byword for dystopia to utopia. And this had a wider impact beyond housing. In the words of John Gilbert of ASSIST in 1992: 'Glasgow's regeneration can be traced to the rise of tenement rehab in the early 1970s.' [56] Here, anti-authority radicalism would shade into capitalist 'enterprise', and the emergence of new, more complex subprofessions of design.

Vernacular in the 1970s

If conservation was the lead tendency in 1970s' architecture, what was the effect of this on new buildings? Increasingly, there were attempts to mark off new buildings from mainstream Modernism, without, as yet, resorting to overt historical and added ornamental elements. Some architects adopted strong colours and chunky shapes inspired by Pop Architecture, especially in interior design work. Examples included Edwin Johnston & Nicholas Groves-Raines's 1971 Landmark Visitor Centre, Stirling; the orange-brown colour scheme of the rebuilt Glasgow Underground; or at a smaller scale, the Brian Drumm hairdresser's shop at George Street, Edinburgh. Michael Laird's Kings Buildings Centre chimney, Edinburgh University (1970), comprised converging massive steel tubes. For large, freestanding groups, Late Modernist devices sought to reduce apparent bulk, as in the stepped sections of Michael Laird & Partners' Royal

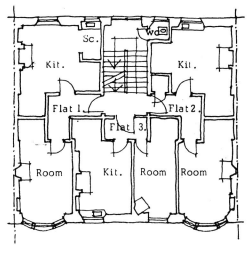

Fig. 1.1
PLAN AS EXISTING
3 Flats each of 2 apts.
sharing common wc on stairs.
No bathrooms, no hot water supply

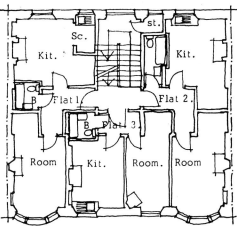

IMPROVED PLAN
3 Flats retained.
Bathrooms in each flat,
new kitchen sinks,
re-wiring, window repairs, etc.

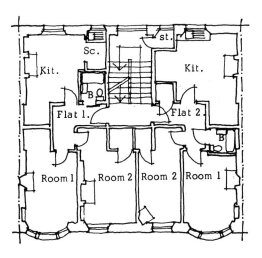

ALTERNATIVE IMPROVED PLAN
2 Flats each of 3 apts.
Centre flat split.
Other improvements as above

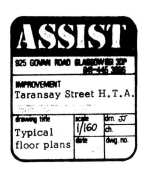

ASSIST
925 GOVAN ROAD GLASGOW G51 3DP
041-445 3866

IMPROVEMENT
Taransay Street H.T.A.

drawing title	scale 1/160	drn. JJ
		ch.
Typical floor plans	date	dwg. no.

9.19 Plans of Taransay Street Housing Treatment Area, Glasgow (from 1971), by ASSIST (drawing by Jim Johnson).

9.20 View (1976) of participants in a community-based Glasgow rehabilitation scheme (Annandale Street, Govanhill). The block is a typical four-storey working-class tenement built around 1890, containing mostly two-room houses. Standing third from right is Raymond Young, originally the driving force in ASSIST.

Bank Computer Centre, Edinburgh (1978), or James Parr's much later General Accident headquarters at Pitheavlis, near Perth (1986); the brown solar glass polygons of Basil Spence, Glover & Ferguson's Scottish Widows Fund headquarters, 1972–6; or the glazed oriel windows of King Main

& Ellison's Scottish Amicable Life Assurance, Glasgow (1973–6). In Aberdeen, the Town House Extension (1975, by City Architect Tom Watson) attempted to remain 'in keeping' with granite [cf. 6.36]. In Edinburgh, there was a fashion for juxtaposition of curtain walling and an old facade – a trend presaged by the stone piers and horizontal window-bands of the Standard Life Phase 2 extension, St Andrew Square (by Michael Laird in association with Robert Matthew, 1968). Such juxtapositions included Spence, Glover & Ferguson's Royal Bank, West End (1976) or the rebuilding of Anderson's Conservative Club as a department store (1978–82) by Simpson and Brown (with Ketley, Goold & Clark). More extreme were the decisions to build the National Gallery extension underground, with a single strip window to the open air, and the concealment of the diagonally planned Waverley Market shopping centre (Building Design Partnership, 1982–4) under a street-level terrace, marked only by three spike-like finials.

An easier way for architects to distance themselves from mainstream Modernism was to look back to the Vernacular architecture built in the 1950s and 1960s by architects such as Wheeler & Sproson. In 1974, Colin McWilliam hailed the 'simple vernacular' as 'the most deeply relevant tradition' in Scottish architecture. [57] By the 1970s, this tendency had merged with the dense, low patterns seen at Cumbernauld New Town. Vernacular was developed by Irvine New Town Development Corporation's architects in a range of contexts. These included new housing sites (for example Bourtreehill, 1973–80); infill in the old town (for example Montgomerie Street, 1984); and other building types, such as the geometrical Beach Park Maintenance Depot (1981), with its shell-like plan. In the researches of the Scottish Local Authorities Special Housing (SLASH) Group, new emphases on rehabilitation and low-rise design were combined with Late Modernist rationalist initiatives. Even into the 1980s, small-burgh housing continued to be a redoubt of Vernacular. There is no better place to trace its further evolution than the variegated sequence of Baxter Clark & Paul's burgh redevelopments, beginning with the abstract Modernist forms of the 1970s (for example Castle Street, Fraserburgh,

1976–8), through a high-point of overtly histori-cising, strongly coloured picturesque in the early 1980s (for example Harbourlea, East Green, Anstruther, completed 1981), to a simpler harled whiteness at the end of the 1980s (for example Dorward Gardens, Montrose, completed 1989) – a progression which almost brings us full circle to the ideas of Reiach in the 1940s. But alongside this consistent evolution, others, by the beginning of the 1980s, began to question the use of Vernacular in urban contexts. In 1982 Charles McKean blasted the loss of urban 'monumentality' caused by 'Neukery . . . a transitory, neo-vernacular fishing-village imagery' which has 'now started to invade our major cities'. [58] Among many urban designers, the word 'Vernacular' now started to acquire strongly pejorative overtones.

On the whole, rural architecture remained a fairly rich area for Vernacular designs in the 1980s and early 1990s: there was a continuous grumble of concern about kit houses, and polemic against the 'suburbanisation' of the Highlands (by writers such as Alastair Alldridge of Skye) resulting in a 1992 rural house design competition, 'Fields of Vision', sponsored by the RIAS and others. [59] Generally, there was a wide variety of formal solutions for rural house types, including a turf-roofed timber house by Ian and Marjorie Apple-ton in Perthshire, 1986, or a circular house at Avielochan (1993–4) by Roddy Langmuir. A single-storey rural house built by Brian McClymont at Lamington, Easter Ross (1993), reacted against Vernacular materials with lightweight steel fram-ing and aluminium cladding. Oil revenue financed a vigorous drive of Vernacular social building on the Shetland Isles. Housing, for example, ranged from dispersed rural layouts (for example at Brae, 1975–6, by Miller Construction) to dense Lerwick infills (for example Richard Gibson's John Jamieson's Closs, Hill Lane, 1982). Later, there were ground-hugging recreation centres, some with boat-like curved wooden roofs (South Mainland and Scalloway, 1991–3, by Faulkner Browns). The most dramatic formal solution in the Shetland social building drive was Gibson's Hamnavoe School, 1980, with its stepped plan and range of curved shelters.

Although Vernacular was, almost by definition, not a style of big public buildings, there was one major exception: the Burrell Collection, won by Barry Gasson, John Meunier & Brit Andreson in a 1971 competition and completed in 1983. The brief distanced the building from the rebuilding chaos and grandeur of Modernist Glasgow. It was to be 'a collection in a park, not in a city' . . . 'not an institution but rather a home, in scale and sympathy with the collection and the environment of the park'. [60] The focus of Gasson's design was not the exterior, which was of unassertive stone and glass, but the internal courtyard and the reconstructed Hutton Castle Rooms next to it. Around this was a Late Modern perimeter plan, linking variegated spaces designed to create a sense of *genius loci* for individual pieces. A more in-tensely modelled Vernacular public building was John L. Paterson's Visitor Centre at Carrbridge (1969–70) – a timber-clad grouping with rounded overtones of Pop Architecture, commanding a heavily landscaped vista, including an artificial lochan; internally, Paterson created a unified series of exhibition and interpretative spaces.

The 1980s: Postmodernism

During the 1980s, the renewed decline of traditional heavy industry and the rise of new and more diversified industries brought to fruition, at last, the basic modernisation demand of the regional planners; yet there was no revival in the fortunes of central planning as an ideology. Controversy over how this decline of state-socialist discipline should be managed provoked a growing instability in the external political consensus between Scotland and England, while the growth of European federalism fuelled the demands for secession from Britain. Here as throughout Europe, there was a seemingly inexorable turn towards market-led social and economic policies, but this was combined in Scotland with a veneration for symbols of the post-1918 'commonweal' of the social nation. As Mrs Thatcher put it, 'The balance sheet of Thatcherism in Scotland is a lopsided one: economically positive but politically negative'. [61]

Where the 1970s were the years of reaction and respite, the 1980s saw a revival in the prestige of new building – but in a new patronage context. For the first time, there was a sharp move away from state-sponsored construction programmes. In architecture, Scotland participated avidly in a new and vigorous international movement – Postmodernism. This was, as its name suggests, still basically defined by the continuing criticisms of the Modern Movement: here the 1970s acted as incubator for the 1980s. But these reactive elements were subsumed within a new, heady climate shaped both by post-1968 radicalism and by anti-corporatist market ideas. Here, new socio-economic developments excluded from Scottish political discourse by association with Thatcherite English nationalism could find open expression. But just as the allegiance of Scottish society to an ideology of social cohesion survived the 1980s' swing against the corporate state, so too the twentieth-century Scottish architectural conception of the social nation would survive the crisis of the Modern Movement.

It was a sign of the revolutionary change in the climate of architecture, compared with the orderly, establishment rationalism of Matthew's world, that the pivotal figure in 1980s' Scottish architecture was not himself an architect, and that his background was in late 1960s, anti-Modernist radicalism – in agitation against motorway-building and the 'destruction of the soul' of Glasgow through clearance. [62] Charles McKean, Secretary of the RIAS between 1979 and 1995, was the driving force in the movement for a polycentric and less deferential architectural culture, which would discard the old statist consensus in favour of a combination of democratisation and commercialisation. He built up the previously dormant RIAS as the focus for a new 'self respect among Scottish architects', [63] by a blitzkrieg of initiatives: introduction of a range of professional services; expansion of the annual Convention into a major international event; publications such as the illustrated area *Guides*, launched in 1984; and high-profile RIAS participation in events such as the 1988 Glasgow Garden Festival. A range of RIAS-run international competitions and a plethora of commercially-sponsored awards and competitions was instituted. In 1985, the Royal Institute of British Architects finally renounced its claim that the RIAS was a 'regional' branch. Alongside his RIAS activities, McKean maintained a constant campaign of personal proselytising through individual publications, broadcasts and lectures on his own interests in architecture: his Scottish Thirties project, for example, opened the door, more generally, to the revaluation of the Modern Movement in Scotland.

The first and most obvious effect on architecture of this new, invigorating climate, with its overtones of populist anti-elitism, was the reinstatement of buildings' appearance as a separately discussed, often dominant factor. All Modernists had at least paid lip-service to the integration of the three Vitruvian qualities – beauty, solidity and utility. Now there was a growing emphasis on decoration, eclectic appearance and facades: a 'relaxation to permit greater expression or richness'. [64] In 1987, the RIAS proclaimed 'the stirring of a new Scots architecture. The first element that strikes is the colour, accompanied by picturesque shapes: no more grey monoliths . . . massing, roofscape, craftsmanship and applied art seem set to make a comeback'. [65] In 1982 McKean advocated 'the addition of architecture': architects were 'no longer . . . sneered at if they put a bit of pleasure into a building'. [66] The new concern with 'style' did not amount to a revival of 'styles', in the nineteenth-century sense of precise recipes; instead, there was a looser eclecticism.

The revival of aesthetic concerns and of decoration under Postmodernism was an international phenomenon. Alongside it, the rise of Postmodernism had also unleashed a renewed concern for the 'national', dormant during the 1960s. This took place in a radically changed cultural context, compared with the preceding era of explicit concern for national identity in architecture – the interwar period. The decline in the prestige of the centralised state had undermined Modernism, but also made impossible any return to old-fashioned Traditionalism, with its messianic calls for a disciplined 'national awakening'. The new ideology of the 'national' was an extrovert and diverse impulse, powering a wide range of architectural ideas and solutions: as with the ever wider scope of conservation, no period was now privileged as a golden age or seen as a threatened essence. In place of the latter, McKean identified an open-ended series of 'revival cycles' since the 18th century, which had acted as a counterweight to internationalist tendencies in

Scottish architecture: the fifth of these cycles was now, the 1980s. [67] In 1987, he wrote that 'a new Scotland is in the making. Out of unemployment . . . out of strength comes sweetness . . . the stirrings of a new Scots architecture. The challenge is to produce an architecture at once richly Scottish *and* international.' [68]

What were the visual manifestations of Scottish Postmodernism, as actually built? The first and most prominent was of a strongly international character: a resurgence of classicism. This could only be an altered return, a 'return to Ithaca' rather than a simple reversion to the pre-Modernist situation, when even Art Deco architects were steeped in classical training. [69] Loss of continuity of expertise would have to be made up in other ways, such as through individualistic touches. Internationally, two broad interpretations emerged: an attempt to integrate classicism within an urbanism of enclosed space, and an emphasis on the eclectic classical treatment of individual monuments – often with ironical or whimsical details. We will deal later with the Scottish response to Postmodern urbanism; but let us glance, first, at the new patterns of classicising eclecticism. In Glasgow, for instance, 1981 saw two contrasting works by a new and dynamic practice, Elder & Cannon: the D. & D. Warehouse, Centre Street, with jaunty brickwork and pediment detail, and the Bank of Pakistan in Sauchiehall Street, a remodelling of the Art Deco gas showroom of 1935 in a severe neo-Art Deco manner, with blank facade of diamond-shaped stone slabs on a veined green marble base, and sombre, columned interior. For public buildings, an alternative tendency stressed a more stately, columned appearance. The chief example was the Sheriff Court of Glasgow (Keppie, Henderson & Partners, 1980–6), whose sombre, stone-faced exterior exuded 'a timeless quality. . . of materials that have withstood the test of centuries. . . A powerful but restrained building, projecting its authority unobtrusively from the emerging landscape into the still lifeless Gorbals.' [70] The building's commemorative brochure highlighted its combination of 'timeless' classicism on the outside, high technology inside: the same rhetoric as at Wylie's Scottish Legal Life building sixty years earlier. Other variants on this theme were the Royal Concert Hall (Sir

L. Martin/RMJM, 1987–90) and – in brick – the Royal Scottish Academy of Music and Drama (Sir L. Martin/William Nimmo & Partners, 1982–7).

The new Postmodern classicism found a more cautious welcome in the capital: in 1985, McWilliam protested that it 'has no place in a city like Edinburgh, where classicism is not yet a joke' (although he himself had, in 1977, suggested the National Gallery extension should be in a Schinkel classical style). [71] The conservation-dictated policy of building exact copies of original patterns in New Town redevelopments was expanded in the 1980s. But soon this austere philosophy was combined with outbreaks of US-style Postmodernism: RMJM's design for the Scottish Gallery of Modern Art (1982–4) restored the neo-Grecian shell of Burn's John Watson's Hospital, but inside chose to 'parody' it with 'ephemeral, light relief' classical detail in bright colours. [72] The new facade and interior of Trotters' optician shop by Simpson & Brown (1985) combined Postmodern irony in such details as the spectacle-like capitals, with heavyweight scholarship: a measured survey of buildings in Ostia was carried out first by job architect Mehdad Saniee [9.21]. [73] A variant of Postmodern classicism, which took Edinburgh reverence for context to an extreme, was the new Scottish Life Assurance head office in Henderson Row (1991–2, by Alan Fiddes of Kennedy

9.21 Trotters' shop, George Street, Edinburgh (Simpson & Brown, 1985).

Partnership): here, a fragment of an 1886 tramway depot by North British Hotel architect Hamilton Beattie was carefully made the centrepiece of, and inspiration for, a mountainous, neo-Second Empire confection. And Hurd Rolland refaced the Modernist Old Course Hotel, St Andrews in a 'classic Edwardian Railway Hotel image' (completed 1990). [74] The 1988 Glasgow Garden Festival contained a microcosm of Postmodern solutions, ranging from Strathclyde Regional Council Architects' colonnaded Roman Garden Pavilion and N. Groves-Raines's Egypto-classical Historic Gardens Pavilion, to Walter Underwood & Partners' evocation of historic Glasgow landmarks in skeleton form. Before long, the new approach filtered into speculative office-building, reflecting the planning-led spread of stone or blockwork cladding (for example Baron Bercott's 100 West George Street, Glasgow, 1988; or the capital's vastly inflated Lothian Road developments of the mid-1990s by Michael Laird and Cochrane McGregor). A culmination of Postmodernism in office-block design was Covell

Matthews's bristling, spired Edinburgh House, St Andrew Square (1993).

While these classical interpretations stemmed chiefly from international elements within Postmodernism, a revival of 'national' ideology was also influential in the revitalised world of visual architecture. Two individual strands, or tendencies stood out above all others in the 1980s: the 'neo-Baronial' of Ian Begg, and the Mackintosh-inspired designs chiefly pioneered by Gillespie, Kidd & Coia. Begg's work, following his retiral from Robert Hurd & Partners in 1983, comprised few, but enormously prominent buildings. These revived the modernising Traditionalism of Hurd's 1930s' propaganda and 1950s' Hydro designs (on which the young Begg had worked), but with an architectonic verve reminiscent of the imperial rubble monumentality of *c.*1910. The grandest of these projects was the Scandic Crown Hotel (1988–9), situated in one of the most prominent sites in the Edinburgh Old Town [9.22]. This was treated as a picturesque composition in the Sydney Mitchell Old

9.22 Scandic Crown Hotel, Edinburgh (Begg, 1988–9).

Edinburgh manner, with the addition of a massive Holyrood-style tower as a corner feature: like Matthew's Queens College Dundee tower of 1958, rubble was here used to clad a reinforced-concrete multi-storey structure. Begg described the Scandic Crown as 'bold and gutsy . . . robust . . . a positive statement of renewal'. [75] Similar in appearance was the Cathedral Square Visitors' Centre, Glasgow (1990–3). The third of this series of key buildings was located not in a historic urban core but in a spectacular Highland setting: Begg's own house, Ravens' Craig, Plockton (1987–9), a five-storey tower of harled blockwork, rising from a massive ground-floor arched vault and crowned with an Old Edinburgh-style timber gable [9.23]. The architect described the genesis of this 'huge statement in the landscape': 'The idea was to see if I could build something modern, meeting all building regulations, using modern materials, and yet get a feeling inside that this was a protecting structure, achieve that very strong sense of enclosure.' His architectural philosophy

9.23 Ian Begg seen in front of Ravens' Craig, Plockton, 1995.

emphasised the shift from Traditionalist defence of a threatened 'essence' to a new optimism: 'I've tried to make statements, not of where we are, but restatements of roots and memory, and more than that . . . of connecting points for people to see and realise, this is Scotland. We know this is Scotland and we can push on forward.' [76] The architectural influence of these powerful buildings was indirect, in helping legitimise a pictorial massing for large urban complexes, such as Yeoman McAllister's Old Edinburgh-style design for High Green, Dean Village (1990–1, right opposite Mitchell's Well Court).

The second 'national' variant of Scottish Postmodernism – the Mackintosh Revival – was, by contrast, a runaway success across the country. Even under Modernism, Mackintosh had assumed a deified status among cognoscenti: McWilliam, for example, wrote in 1966 of 'the master who is beyond style, about whom there is something which simply defies explanation or criticism'. [77] But it was only in the 1970s, when an anti-Modernist yearning for decoration was combined with residually Modernist diffidence about launching into classicism, that his real 'revival' started – especially after 1973, when the Mackintosh Society was founded in Glasgow, and Alison and Cassina's Milan Triennale Exhibition launched Mackintosh on his posthumous global career as a 'contemporary designer' of reproduction furniture. Architecturally, this was no indiscriminate revival. It was not curvilinear early Mackintosh but late, rectilinear Mackintosh, the Mackintosh of the Chinese Room grids and the Art School west wing, that was revived.

The element in this revival which concerns us here was a new, Postmodern type of architecture inspired by the spatial play of Mackintosh, and using his motifs in new ways – for instance, by exploiting decorative lattices, originally internal, as external motifs or in fenestration. Ironically, the key building in this process was located not in Glasgow or Scotland, but in southern England: Gillespie, Kidd & Coia's Robinson College, Cambridge (competition win 1974, built 1977–80). Here the section-based 'community' design of Cardross was developed into a highly complex perimeter-plan pattern of outer wall and internal street: 'more a fragment of the city than . . . a

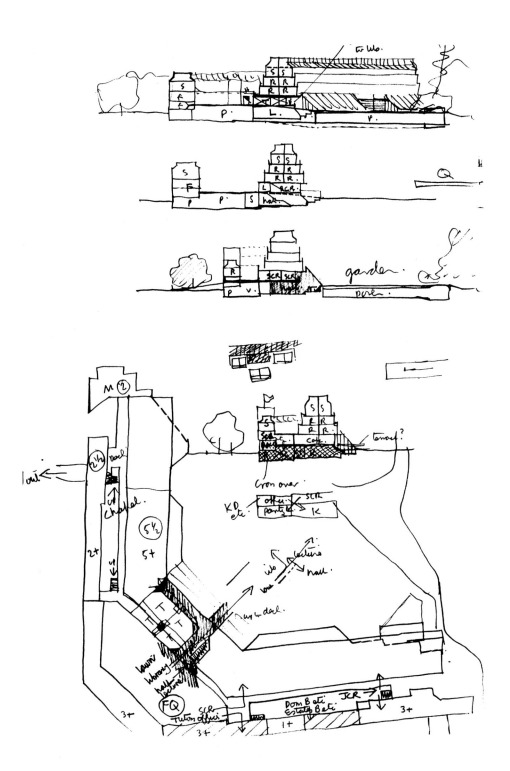

9.24 Robinson College, Cambridge, England (Gillespie, Kidd & Coia; competition win 1974, built 1977–80), drawing by Andrew MacMillan, *c.*1974, showing proposed sectional arrangement.

college' [9.24]. [78] The local English brick building tradition was carried throughout the college with monumental singlemindedness, reminiscent of the massive plasticity of Mackintosh and Aalto. Outer walls were punctuated by lattice windows and stepped openings, while grid decoration was ubiquitous inside. Robinson College's evocation of the 'spirit' of Mackintosh reached its climax in the library, a large space containing a freestanding, three-storey timber structure, whose dramatic juxtaposition with full-height windows recalled the Glasgow Art School library.

The formal and planning complexity of Robinson College was the climax of Gillespie, Kidd & Coia's forty-year long development of the legacy of Mackintosh. However, the college's chief impact back home was at a stylistic level. It is no exaggeration to say that it substantially altered the architectural vocabulary of Scotland in the early 1980s, acting as one of the chief vehicles for the triumph of the visual and of decoration: by 1985, it could be said that there was a 'Post-Coia . . . "style" ', in which the debt to Mackintosh became clearer with successive stages of popularisation. [79] Visible everywhere was a combination of chunky but plain external massing, lattice patterns inside and out, and stepped windows. The early 1980s in Edinburgh witnessed two sophisticated projects with Mackintosh overtones of bulky, geometrical massing and gridded fenestration. The first was the new Distillers headquarters by RMJM (1981–4), a stone-clad group in heavy landscaping, generally low but with erupting latticed staircase windows. More demonstrative was Andrew Merrylees's National Library Causewayside Building (1985–7, extended 1993–4), planned like Glasgow University Library with perimeter services but expressing these extrusions in a more abrupt, prismatic manner, with gridded towers – a 'rich, dynamic' pattern intended to evoke Expressionist architecture and 'traditional Scots forms' [9.25]. [80] Smaller examples of the same tendency included: Tollcross Fire Station, Edinburgh (1986, by Lothian Regional Council Architectural Services); St John Ogilvy Church, Irvine (Douglas Niven & Gerard Connolly, 1982); and Nicoll Russell Studios' TSB St Andrews Branch (1988) [9.26]. A more monumental Mackintosh Revival of grids and square patterns dominated the interior of Keppie Henderson's Sheriff Court of Glasgow and Strathkelvin, with its atrium and twenty-one courts.

The further popularisation of this Mackintosh influence on new Postmodern buildings was supported by a second architectural trend: the recreation of actual Mackintosh designs. This began with Whitfield Partners' reassembly of the interiors of Mackintosh's house, 78 Southpark Avenue (demolished 1963) within the structure of the new Hunterian Museum (completed 1982). Reconstructed elements of the dwelling, including

9.25 National Library of Scotland Causewayside Building, Edinburgh (Andrew Merrylees 1985-7, extended 1993-4), 1995 view, showing second phase in foreground.

9.26 Tollcross Fire Station, Edinburgh (Lothian Regional Council, 1986).

a front-door half a storey up in the air, were surrealistically embedded in Whitfield's Late Modernist concrete facades. In 1988, engineer and Mackintosh enthusiast Graham Roxburgh commissioned Andrew MacMillan to build the 1901 *Haus eines Kunstfreundes* design in Bellahouston Park: this, he declared, was 'not pastiche, it is building to Mackintosh's design for the first time, creating, not recreating, a masterpiece'. [81] Then followed the building of the 'Artist's Cottage' design near Inverness in 1987–92 by architect R. H. Macintyre for Dr P. Tovell. By 1990, the Mackintosh Revival was increasingly confined to commercial schemes: it became an identifiable, populist 'style'. Examples include Cowie Torry & Partners' Alloway Street Clydesdale Bank, Ayr (1987); Leach Rhodes Walker's Kirkstane House, Glasgow (completed 1991); the reconstructed 'Boots Corner', Glasgow (1991, Duffy Coleman Anderson); and GRM Kennedy's Lord Todd public house and Strathclyde University residences (1982–92). Ubiquitous in shop-fronts and commercialised interior design, it was caricatured by younger architects as 'Mockintosh': Mark Cousins denounced it in 1990 as 'myopic . . . slavish imitation'. [82]

'The City': 1980s' Urbanism

So far, we have examined Postmodernism in terms of its greatest novelty – the revival of visual and decorative elements. At first glance, the

renunciation of Modernism's ideal of a fully integrated Vitruvian triad – utility, strength and beauty – also seemed to have banished that prime Modernist socio-psychological and rationalist aim: community design. Yet behind the reinvigorated formal facade, socio-psychological concerns were just as pressing as before. What had disappeared was, on the one hand, Traditionalism's idealisation of the rural, and, on the other, Modernism's aspiration to overarching reconstruction, especially through the Geddesian regional planning framework and mass housing across the country. This rejection of comprehensive or regional planning was symbolised in the new importance ascribed to one key arena: 'The City' – a change which was dramatically heralded in 1976 when the seventh New Town, Stonehouse, was abruptly cancelled and its resources were redirected into 'GEAR' (Glasgow Eastern Area Renewal), a huge assault against urban dereliction in Glasgow.

In some ways, this Postmodern concept of The City perpetuated the Modernist aim of fostering community by tackling existing socially and visually pathological elements, and providing new buildings. But unlike Modernism, there was a new assumption that these activities should be grounded in the patterns and substance of the 'traditional', pre-1914 city – whose essence was interpreted as one of complex, *ad hoc* agglomeration. The key word of this Postmodern urbanism was 'regeneration'. One of the country's most prestigious architectural awards by the early 1990s was the RIAS/Scottish Enterprise 'Regeneration Design Award'. And the chief icon of regeneration was none other than the previous bogeyman: the tenement. The tenement rehabilitation and stonecleaning drive which had begun tentatively in the early 1970s was, by the early 1980s, venerated as the source of the new urban regeneration. Correspondingly, the pathological element within the city, the target of regeneration, was now identified as the Modernist redevelopment. Disregarding the tendency towards complex mixed use in Cumbernauld-style Late Modernism, all Modernist solutions were now branded the opposite to the 'traditional city'. They were *tabula rasa* rather than cumulative, 'inhuman' in scale rather than piecemeal and 'human', segregatory rather than mixed and integrated, imposed from above rather than generated from below. They had inflicted wounds needing to be healed, an emptiness requiring 'reoccupation'. [83] The increasing ecological stigmatisation of the private car enabled urban motorways to be condemned along with Modernist buildings.

The therapy to tackle this malady was based on a prescription first presented by Paolo Portoghesi, Aldo Rossi and other theorists at the 1980 Venice Biennale, and, of course, fundamentally informed by the anti-Modernist writing of Jane Jacobs in the 1960s. This turned on its head the chief demand, and boast, of Modernism: to bring new material standards to all through comprehensive design and planning. Instead, there was emphasis on piecemeal interventions and mixed uses, following patterns and context established by existing old buildings, and reflecting 'the city in its contradictory and even chaotic essence'. Any co-ordination should take the more personalised form of 'master-planning'. In reaction against orthodox Functionalist urbanism's downplaying of the autonomy of the visual, there was a renewed reverence for Sitte's conception of the artistic street-picture. Here, the 1970s' conservationist movements of the ENTCC and tenement rehabilitation, and the vernacular movement of new architecture, lay behind the new architecture of the 1980s. In economic terms, there was a shift to emphasis on wealth creation rather than distribution, and a rejection of prescriptive

planning in favour of politicised debate – a framework embraced easily both by ex-'rehab' radicals, and ex-corporatist organisations such as the Scottish Development Agency.

These ideas shaped the design of both individual buildings and city areas. In the first case, buildings were increasingly treated as variegated microcosms of Community, with blurring of institutional characteristics – although the planning within individual complexes was essentially a continuation of Late Modernism's fascination with complex spatial and social arrangements. Within traditional social building types such as schools and health buildings, there was emphasis on 'flexibility' and integration of the outside 'community': Comhairle nan Eilean's Sgoil Lionacleit (completed 1991) 'hums with activity from 9 in the morning to 9 at night'. [84] Lothian Regional Council's new Leith Academy (opened 1991, designed by the Region's own architects, project architect was Laura Ross) mixed social and commercial imagery in its 'street grid . . . planned like a shopping centre' with a 'glazed main street, warm and sunny, with extensive planting, seats, a street cafe, displays, festooned with hanging banners which indicate graphically the wares on offer'. [85] In the design of hospitals, the trend away from racetrack slab blocks continued: SBT Keppie's low, hipped-roofed Ayr Hospital (completed 1992) combined 'the welcoming character and scale of a cottage hospital with the overtones of a hotel'. [86] Taking the reassuring connotations of domestic and 'village' to an extreme, but with a tension between 'integration into the community' and privacy, there was a boom in the building of special-needs hospices and care centres. One of the most complex realisations was Nicoll Russell's White Top Centre, Dundee (1992–4), an informally massed brick and rubble group with 'landscape threaded through the building' and a 'rich mixture of multisensory experiences'; it 'might be said to fall somewhere between a school, a kindergarten, a community centre, a house and a specialised clinic'. [87]

The same blurring tendencies affected traditional cultural and recreational building types. Nicoll Russell Studios' Dundee Repertory Theatre (1979–82), a massive blockwork-built cube, was punched with openings to 'exude welcome', [88] including a big glazed cantilevered staircase sailing up into the first floor. Sports complexes, especially swimming pools, changed again in character from municipal recreation to commercial entertainment, in step with a change in architectural fashion to externally-styled shed-like structures with highly variegated interiors. Here the implication was, if anything, that of introversion rather than the reverse: we are reminded of Spence's early post-war exhibition work. The pioneer was the externally plain Magnum Centre, Irvine (Development Corporation architects, 1976); in the later 1980s, the English firm Faulkner Browns, after their success at Perth Leisure Centre (1986–8), went on to design a whole succession of pools and leisure centres, including the Hamilton Water Palace (1993–5) and an oil-financed programme on the Shetland Islands in 1985–93. The Monklands Time Capsule, Coatbridge (1991, Limbrick Grayshon Associates) comprised a swimming pool and recreation centre whose shed-like building was fronted by futuristic pinnacles, and contained a themed clutter of model dinosaurs, rocks, old industrial artefacts, a 'space satellite', profuse greenery and rubble walls. A more striking contrast to the sober abstraction of the Commonwealth Pool could hardly be imagined. In shopping centres, too, the tendency was one of introversion, through the development and modification of the originally Modernist megastructural pattern of Cumbernauld, by the introduction of devices such as toplit central atriums.

The most fundamental implications of Postmodern urbanism were for the city as a whole. If the orderly rationalism of national, regional or city planning had now been abandoned, its replacement, here as throughout Europe, was a new stress on competition between individual cities, through the medium of privately and publicly sponsored cultural projects. Within each city, the emphasis was now on the mixed, piecemeal, and private-led rather than on the comprehensive and state-directed. The result was a growing competition between Edinburgh and Glasgow – a contest in which the latter, throughout the 1980s and 1990s, was consistently victorious, with a string of propaganda coups ranging from Dr Michael Kelly's 'Glasgow's Miles Better' campaign to the award of the 1988 Garden Festival and 1990 European City of Culture designation. The fullest ideological exposition of Glasgow's turnaround from corporatist to 'enterprise' city, and of the resulting assertive architectural 'renaissance', was provided, during the 1990 Festival, by the 'Glasgow's Glasgow' exhibition, co-ordinated by Douglas Clelland of Clelland Associates, and executed by a range of Glasgow architects. It provided a microcosm of Glasgow Postmodern urbanism in its location (in formerly derelict vaults under Central Station), in its selfconsciously chaotic collage-like presentation, and in its capitalistic repackaging of a Geddes slogan: 'The place, the people, the sparks of innovation'. Integral to the message, too, was a polemical portrayal of Modernist Glasgow as 'barbaric . . . a new place with all meaning removed'. [89]

The built manifestations of Glasgow's Postmodern urbanist revolution divided into three, radially ordered categories, concerned respectively with the city centre, the old tenemental suburbs and the outer housing schemes. The first initiative was a capitalist-led drive to 'regenerate' the city centre, focused on the down-at-heel area of eighteenth- and nineteenth-century commercial buildings east of Buchanan Street, whose mixture of warehouses, offices and public buildings seemed a tailor-made base for Postmodernist mixed-use interventions. Dubbed the 'Merchant City' by McKean in the mid-1970s, the area was included in the Central Conservation Area in 1976. From 1980, large-scale investment poured in, spurred by the SDA's City Centre Project. The guiding philosophy was that of accentuating the existing 'mixed' character by a combination of new building and rehabilitation, pushing it upmarket by introducing groups of higher-income dwellings. By 1990, 1,143 houses had been built or converted in the area. A conscious policy of piecemeal development was pursued, with different architects assigned individual sites, or groups of scattered sites; and there was a stress on enhancing the existing street-grid, with its perimeter plans and internal courtyards. In both respects there was a marked resemblance to West-Berlin's IBA regeneration project (1984–9), with its fixation on the image of the *Hinterhof* (rear courtyard), and the associated socio-architectural conception of worlds of life hidden behind an impervious facade. Douglas Clelland himself made a noteworthy intervention in the IBA: his block at Friedrichstrasse 10 (planned and built 1983–91) masked with external austerity a complex interior of mixed uses and spatial ingenuity.

This capitalistic formula of central-area regeneration was spearheaded by a new breed of architect-developers. Most venturesome was the Kantel Development Company, founded in 1980 by Andy Doolan and Andy Burrell, and divided into two separate businesses (Kantel and Burrell) in 1985. Kantel's most complex achievement was Ingram Square (1984–9), a Merchant City street-block regeneration comprising ten separate sites, in a mixture of rebuilding behind facades or new buildings – the largest new building being a Postmodern classical corner block with a tower. The aim of Ingram Square, whose architectural design was the work of Elder & Cannon, was to create a microcosm of the essence of the Merchant City: a new kind of urban intensification, intended to turn banal courtyards into art. Another architect -entrepreneur who focused on historic buildings was Nicholas Groves Raines. After a number of early works in Edinburgh (including a startling brick apartment block at Cameron Crescent, 1982–3), he established his own development company, Steinhus, and began a series of historic building conversions in Glasgow, including the Babbity Bowster bar/restaurant (1984–5), and the Spiers Wharf regeneration scheme (conceived 1984, built from 1988, later stages completed 1993 by James Cunning Young). More overtly Postmodern was the early work of McGurn, Logan Duncan & Opfer, including the Pelican Blonde café, Sauchiehall Street (1985), or Glassford Court (1985), a vivid red-brick pile crowned with jazzy geometrical features. Hugh Martin & Partners contributed the Princes Square development (1985–7), which filled a down-at-heel city-centre courtyard with a rampantly eclectic atrium, crammed with sinuous metalwork and other glittering decoration. The architects' aim was 'to create the feeling of a conservatory in a characterful old house'. [90]

The climax of the Merchant City programme in the 1980s was represented by two contrasting commercial redevelopments. The St Enoch Centre, 1985–9, designed by Reiach & Hall with GMW Partnership, attempted to evoke the panache of Glasgow's engineering tradition, as represented by buildings such as the Kibble Palace or the People's Palace. This vast development comprises a huge L-shaped lean-to glazed roof bearing against a seven-storey multi-storey car park, with a separate structure of shops inside. The effect was the opposite of the prevalent trend of introverted atria. Here, incredibly for such a 'high-tech'-looking building, it was possible to rely exclusively on passive energy systems. Outwardly more conservative was the Italian Centre, which combined elements of variegated Postmodern urbanism with new, harder-edged ideas. The architects, Page & Park, had first emerged as urbanist designers with the remodelling of the Glasgow Cathedral precinct (1984–91) to create a 'civic space'. [91] At the Italian Centre (designed 1988, completed 1992, extension 1993–4), a street-block of old warehouses was converted into a mixed courtyard development modelled, according to the architects, 'on the Italian palazzo form, where external restraint is set against a visually exciting and vibrant courtyard' [9.27]. [92] Inevitably, a comparison suggests itself with that pioneering Postmodern scheme, Charles Moore's Piazza d'Italia, New Orleans (1976–9) – also a new and boldly decorated courtyard converted from old buildings. Page & Park's design, however, showed growing discontent with the easy, ironic pluralism represented by Moore's project. The facades of its first phase combined architectural austerity with a jagged metal sculptural scheme by Jack Sloan, and statuary by the militant neo-classicist Alexander Stoddart. On the 1993–4 extension (a new building), neo-classical architecture was overlaid with fasces and busts by Stoddart, and crowned by an intimidating scheme of metalwork by Sloan, including punching spears and swirling patterns of thistles.

The move to private-sector interventions in the centre of Glasgow was matched by a similarly variegated pattern in the socially orientated regeneration of 19th-century working-class housing areas. The tendency towards tenurial diversity, begun by the 1977 Green Paper, culminated in 1989 with the creation of a new central agency, Scottish Homes, which merged the SSHA with the

9.27 Italian Centre, Glasgow (Page &
Park, 1988-92; extended 1993–4),
drawing of courtyard, *c*.1989.

Housing Corporation Scotland: its declared policy aim was 'community regeneration'. By the late 1980s, Glasgow's community-based housing associations – 'the Medicis of Maryhill' – [93] had virtually completed the improvement of nineteenth-century tenements, and now shifted their attention to energetic new building on cleared sites. Here, under the influence of 'rehab', there was a return to building tenements along street frontages. This neo-tenement style had been presaged as early as 1970, in a late Modernist redevelopment by Glasgow Corporation: Woodside CDA Phase 3, designed by Nori Toffolo of Boswell, Mitchell & Johnston. This 5/8-storey group broke from the open spatial patterns of Modernism towards a layout of squares: 'traditional' elements such as oriel windows sat alongside the exaggerated curves and extrusions of Pop Architecture. It also used bright red brick – a tendency which was avidly developed in the 1980s, when English brick companies sponsored numerous Scottish design awards in an attempt to make brick architecturally respectable. Modernism's polarisation between 'bright, new' and 'old, grey' was inverted by Postmodernism. The first

category now included new brick and stone-cleaned nineteenth-century tenements, while the second now consisted of council schemes: 'Twenty years ago, housing was considered as a matter of units of habitation to be completed as fast as possible. Nowadays, different priorities prevail. Our great cities are being knitted together with patches of colourful new tenements between restored examples of the old.' [94] But, even in 1979, there were already counter-warnings that these small-scale, picturesque brick developments risked 'suburbanising the city'. [95]

While the burgeoning housing associations switched from rehabilitation to new building, the public-housing sector did the reverse. The abolition of shortages and tenement-slums, along with council house sales and management difficulties, led to a situation in which many peripheral housing schemes (according to a 1990 Scottish Homes report) had 'moved from solution to problem status within two decades'. Some architects, continuing the tradition of grand rhetorical prescriptions, responded simply by defining 'The City' so as to exclude these schemes: Andrew MacMillan, as late as 1995, advocated 'demolishing the whole of Easterhouse and bringing the people back into the city'. [96] But this position was already undermined by the claims of residents that the peripheral schemes had generated the same 'community in adversity' as had the old tenements. Indeed, the 1980s had already seen a variety of 'community' based regeneration initiatives, beginning with Easterhouse's Calvay Street. As Jim Meldrum of Reidvale Housing Association put it, 'They're the same people, Glaswegians, living further out, but facing the same problems. Housing schemes are as integral a part of Glasgow as is the city centre.' [97] Such projects echoed the ideas of Oscar Newman in trying to create private or 'defensible' space, coupled with management and maintenance reforms. These reforms were expressed, architecturally, through bright colours and variegated, often Postmodern classical details. Their aim was to break up schemes' homogeneity by giving 'identity' to groups of dwellings, and, in the case of tower blocks, to reduce 'apparent scale'. [98] In 1994, Glasgow District Council architects boasted that at Springburn, 'oppressive linear blocks have been converted into bright, safe, freestanding tenemental blocks' – once again demonstrating the startling reversal in the connotations of the word 'tenement'. [99] Within previously uniform, Modernist schemes, rehabilitation sometimes brought a visual divergence, with low-rise blocks assuming a vernacular appearance (with render rather than brick), but tower blocks recast in a bolder manner, with geometrical colour patterns or Postmodern classicism. Coloured overcladding of Glasgow towers began in 1982 at Red Road [cf. 9.3]. By 1990, Gibson's mass Modernist icons, alongside stone-cleaned tenements, had been turned into Postmodern standard-bearers of the 'Glasgow's Miles Better' public-relations gospel.

In the late 1980s and early 1990s, for a time the impetus of regeneration moved away from Glasgow: in Dundee, for example, large-scale remodelling and privatisation was undertaken at peripheral schemes, notably Whitfield. In Edinburgh, the early 1990s saw an attempt to move away from Postmodern piecemeal urbanism towards a more grandiose vision akin to France's *grands projets* – but still drawing chiefly on private capital for its resources. The main driving force

was a powerful councillor, George Kerevan: he branded the 1970s and 1980s 'directionless' years dominated by conservation, and embarked on a massive building drive, focused above all on major cultural institutions. Writing in 1994, he set out his governing principles. First, the building of 'axes' to rediscover Edinburgh's 'Cartesian sense of order'. Then 'personality': he blasted the Postmodern mixed-use idea as a 'porridge' of mixed uses, and called instead for higher density and differentiated 'character' between city neighbourhoods. Finally, 'meaning': citing the work of Stoddart, he called for monumental sculpture 'to engender a sense of common citizenship in a shared space'. [100] What was actually built in Edinburgh at this time was, however, more varied than Kerevan's rhetoric suggested. Some large public monuments in the centre were of Postmodern classical appearance. For instance, Campbell & Arnott's Saltire Court (1989–91), a

9.28 Great Mosque of Edinburgh, elevation drawing by Basil al-Bayati, 1988.

mixed-use complex combining offices with theatre and café, featured a concave, symmetrical main facade with central curved pediment and Burnet-like corner turrets: McKean acclaimed it as 'a majestic, palace-fronted, symmetrical block'. [101] Terry Farrell's International Conference Centre (1993–5) parodied Ledoux with a vast, squat rotunda. But elsewhere there were other patterns. The Iraqi/English architect Basil al-Bayati's Great Mosque of Edinburgh, planned from 1988, attempted to synthesise its Islamic function with a four-towered walled enclosure evocative of 'Scottish castles' [9.28]. [102] And there persisted a tendency of piecemeal, Geddes-like Old Town redevelopment: realisations included Michael Calthrop and A. Campbell Mars's social housing block in the Grassmarket (1984), Rob Hunter's rendered, mixed-use courtyard scheme at Buchanan Court (1991–2), and John C. Hope's masterplan (from 1993) for the redevelopment of a brewery site to the south of Canongate, which set out to 'reinstate' a linear Old Town pattern of 'small, tight urban spaces' and mixed uses, without recourse to 'pastiche forms'. [103]

The 1990s: Return to Idealism?

As we have seen, Postmodernism had barely been established, during the 1980s, when there were attempts to qualify or depart from it. But by the early 1990s, a wider rejection of its ideas was under way. Encouraged by the spread of its decorative principles to the least prestigious building types, such as supermarkets or speculative villas, the label Postmodern had become narrowed to associations of sybaritic eclecticism and doctrinaire market ideology, and there were demands for a return to greater idealism in design. There was a growing unease about the 1980s' regeneration of Glasgow, a feeling that it had been driven by a capitalist concern with 'image'. The rejection of Taitian Art Deco modernity in the late 1930s had been followed both by a reinvigorated Traditionalism and a more radical Modernism. Now, the long crisis of cultural modernity had left the position more complicated. Traditionalism was already a well-worked seam, while any renewed Modernism – like Postmodern Classicism – could only be a 'return to Ithaca', as the previous Modernist faith

in such ideas as mass provision, or designed solutions to social problems, or the availability of unlimited cheap energy, could hardly be revived. The most crucial question concerned the significance of the 'Late' Modernism of the 1960s. Were the latter's attacks on the linear, materialist argumentation of Functionalism symptoms of the exhaustion and impending demise of the Modern Movement, and, with it, all architectural conceptions of Progress? Or were the demands of the 1960s for greater social and visual complexity, and formal richness, in fact signals of a cathartic crisis of renewal, within which the conservationist ascendancy and Postmodernism would prove to be merely transient episodes?

The first explorations of this issue came from former Late Modernists – from the heirs of Matthew and Coia. As early as 1985, John Richards praised the 'vigour' of 1950s Modernism. [104] At the 1988 RIAS Convention and in his 1990 Playfair lecture, Isi Metzstein attacked the 'polyfilla and plywood language of Postmodernism':

> We are in a post-optimistic phase, so that much architectural theory looks backwards with love of the old and in fear of the new; we now value continuity, decentralisation, restoration, rehab and recycling. We practise conservation, nostalgia and pluralism. We doubt and fear the future. That is hardly a basis for an exciting, encouraging and forward-looking architecture . . . The search for a modern credible Scottish urban architecture must go on. (105)

By 1989, the theme was taken up by younger designers: Davis Duncan Partnership, describing their Carrick Quay scheme of steel-balconied apartment blocks overlooking the Clyde, stated flatly that 'there is no place here for the panoply of applied decoration exhibited by the Postmodern. The building is unashamedly modern, expressing the spirit of a society in the 1990s with . . . a healthy respect for the past'. [106]

With this rejection of Postmodernism as 'applied decoration', we witness a return to one of the places where 'Late' Modernism left off – to an emphasis on the 'form' of buildings, both as an ideal or abstract quality, and as an expression of socio-psychological values. There was also a resurgence of the intense turn-of-the-century conception of artistic individualism: David Page argued that 'in the end, it's each person's soul that drives them – we're all engaged in this struggle to create form'. [107] Now, however, these qualities of form were seen as residing equally in new buildings and in the existing city as a whole. This 'heritage' now even included the Modern Movement: in 1993, for example, the Lanark County Buildings tower block (completed 1964) was listed by Historic Scotland at Category 'A'. [cf. 8.50] A Scottish branch of the international Modernist heritage group DOCOMOMO (Documentation and Conservation of the Modern Movement) formulated a historical interpretation of Modernism in explicitly national terms, arguing the centrality within the Scottish Modern Movement of mass social building. At the group's 1992 conference, 'Visions Revisited', David Page claimed that in Scotland – unlike countries such as Finland – there had been a systematic Postmodern denigration of the recent past, with the result that 'our Modern history is censored by neglect'. [108] The dissolution of the Traditionalist concept of a national golden age in the far past was now complete. Any attempts to argue for an 'essence' were now couched in non-time-specific terms. In 1995, Frank Arneil Walker spoke of a 'syntax' or a 'language of national form' which could unite Scottish buildings of all different periods and styles. [109]

What actual architectural realisations resulted from this growing reassessment of the Modern Movement? The first point that must be emphasised is that, despite the 1980s' rhetoric of rejection, that decade had in fact seen, at a more everyday architectural level, a considerable continuity of essentially Modernist design. Many office blocks were still designed as abstract masses of curtain walling, although often in a more theatrical or dynamic manner than would have been acceptable in the 1960s: prominent examples are Holmes Partnership's 100 Bothwell Street, Glasgow (from 1987), with 'powerful vertical sculptural' cluster of towers; [110] or SBT Keppie's Eagle Building, Glasgow (completed 1992), with Alexander Kirkland's arcaded 1854 facade incorporated like a postage-stamp inside the front lobby. Engineering design had also bypassed Postmodernism, in projects such as road bridges: a striking example was Ove Arup &

Partners' 276-metre-long Kylesku Bridge, 1984.

It is difficult to determine whether these late offshoots of the original Modern Movement led directly into the new tendencies of the 1990s. By the end of the 1980s some younger designers, working within major Edinburgh practices with roots in the Modernist period, were developing for major public or commercial commissions a sleek, refined manner evocative of the RMJM projects of John Richards and his colleagues, but embodying greater 'sensuousness'. [111] RMJM's own designs exemplified this image: for example, the reposeful 'parkland campus' design [112] for Motorola's Bathgate plant (first stage finished 1991), or the Victoria Quay Scottish Office headquarters (1993–5), whose colonnaded, symmetrical facades combined Modernist overtones with evocations of St Andrew's House, and whose full natural ventilation was trumpeted as a major advance for 'sustainable' design. [113] Within Reiach & Hall, the years after completion of the St Enoch Centre saw the emergence as principal designer of Neil Gillespie, who emphasised a trend towards a disciplined corporate aesthetic. A 1993 brochure stressed the firm's 'continuously evolving heritage', and its continuity with Reiach's own Nordic inclinations: 'northern quality of light . . . clear and economical expression . . . through a process of refinement'. Their design for an office block at 10 George Street (1993) aimed, according to Gillespie, both to give 'vigorous and honest expression' to 'steel frame and stone cladding', and to 'engage . . . the spirit of the Georgian condition' [9.29]. [114] Law & Dunbar-Nasmith's Edinburgh Festival Theatre (1992–4) dramatically juxtaposed a preserved 1920s' classical auditorium and a concave glass frontage. Some younger architects in the west interpreted this revitalised Modernist aesthetic in a more forceful manner. Two notable small projects in a 'unifying architectural language of clean lines and crisp edges' [115] were completed in 1993 by McNeish Design Partnership of Motherwell: Challenge House, Glasgow, a mixed-use commercial/residential block which exploited its prominent situation by the Inner Ring Road with a dynamic, wedge-like plan and aluminium cladding; and an extension to Bothwell Evangelical Church, with circular, flat-roofed sanctuary and glazed, steel-framed

9.29 10 George Street, Edinburgh (Reiach & Hall, 1993), main elevation.

lobby. More spectacular was Richard Horden's competition-winning design (1992) for a revolving Glasgow Millennium Tower in St Enoch Square.

To challenge Postmodern urbanism in its heartlands – inner 'regeneration' and social housing – different, more complex forms would be needed. The growing economic impact of car-accessible peripheral developments lent urgency to the drive for 'regeneration'. The Postmodern principles of piecemeal intervention, and of respect for old buildings and patterns, were subtly modified rather than rejected. There was a changed approach to design of new elements within this framework – a new belief in contrast rather than conformity to old neighbours, and a move away from imitative styling to more abstract or monumental appearance. Sometimes these new elements reflected the international movement of Deconstructivism, which combined the ruptured aesthetic of some 1920s' Russian Constructivist projects with a Postmodern philosophy of contradiction and discontinuity: but these reflections were highly diluted, as any whole-hearted assault on the self-containedness and enclosure of building forms would be impracticable in Scotland's temperate and changeable climate. Instead, the inspiration of Modernism, and the renewed intensity of 'form', led Scottish architects in other directions.

Most typical, in these confrontations of new and old, were projects for conversion of historic public buildings. In the west, the work of Page &

Park, following the Italian Centre, increasingly tended in this direction. Their 1994–5 remodelling of David Hamilton's Port Glasgow Town Buildings (1815) restored the main structure while converting the formerly blank rear wall into a dramatic and spatially complex new facade; a 1995 project for a cinema museum in Coatbridge proposed to envelop completely John Stephen's Gartsherrie School in an overall glazed box-structure; and a 1996 competition win for the conversion of Glasgow's General Post Office into a new National Gallery of Scottish Art inserted boldly monumental interiors into the classical outer shell. In Edinburgh, a proposed extension of the Royal Museum of Scotland to house the Scottish collections was the subject of an RIAS international competition. In 1991 (after attempted interference by Prince Charles had been rebuffed by the museum trustees), the commission was awarded to Gordon Benson and Alan Forsyth [9.30]. Their design, built from 1996, combined cladding in ashlar with a bold, slightly deconstructive massing of diagonals and incisions; at the corner was a round tower intended to echo the Half Moon Battery of the Castle. The assertive urbanism of the exterior, and the microcosm-like plan and section – topped by a cantilevered roof garden of Scottish flora – showed how far the 1990s had departed from the the 1970s coyness of the Burrell.

The new formula of boldly juxtaposed old and new forms was also reflected in smaller projects

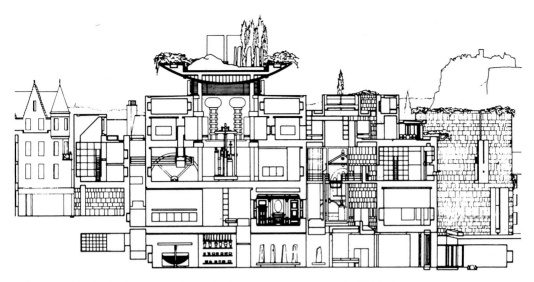

9.30 Museum of Scotland, Edinburgh, section by Gordon Benson and Alan Forsyth, 1991; built from 1996.

in the capital. Richard Murphy carried out a series of carefully detailed, structurally emphatic interventions which set out to engage internal with external space, confronting new and old: inspirations, according to Murphy, ranged from De Stijl to the alteration projects of Carlo Scarpa. In 1992–3, he remodelled the Fruitmarket Gallery with an opened-up ground floor and a new 'industrial roofscape': his aim was 'to sub-vert conventional gallery tenets, so the space is an inclusive, partly transparent box that engages with its surroundings'. A later project was the redevelopment of an infill site in the New Town (Dublin Street Lane North, from 1995) with a group of timber-clad, steel-framed flats, including small towers with wave-form aluminium roofs. [116] The concern to devise new curved or broken-pitch roof sections, straining to avoid the 'tyranny' of the ordinary pitched roof without reverting to Modernist flat roofs, was typical of this period. [117] At a smaller scale still, Ewen & Fiona McLachlan's 1988–91 recasting of a Marchmont tenement flat broke down its rectangular layout with angled 'deflections', and set up sharp oppositions of form and colour. [118]

This meticulous approach of contrasted old and new, however appropriate in 'historic' contexts, inevitably seemed less relevant as an alternative within that other key area of Scottish urbanism: the building, and rehabilitation, of social housing. The late 1980s and 1990s saw the beginnings, especially in Glasgow, of a shift in regeneration efforts away from the Merchant City to the task of reviving collective or civic dignity in social housing. These attempts in no way rejected the new framework of diversified tenure established in the Postmodern years, but instead vigorously built on the power and *esprit de corps* of community housing associations. Architecturally, the fading appeal of Postmodernism was reflected in a decline in the picturesque use of brick in high-status housing design. In 1991, Scottish brickmaker Charles Wemyss, after energetically trying to foster a 'Scottish' brick style by com-missioning an innovative range of Mackintosh-like house types from Roger Emmerson (1990), ruefully concluded that there seemed no way of throwing off 'the old adages of utilitarian, incompatible and English'. [119] Although its use was attacked by some critics such as Murray McNaught, many neo-tenement architects still remained faithful to brick, arguing that it was 'in keeping' with nineteenth-century stonework: in 1992, for instance, ASSIST described their newly completed Anderson Street development in Partick as 'a "new tenement", contemporary yet in contextual harmony'. [120] But, on the whole, the material was slipping back down-market, where it was enjoying a vast new popularity with suburban speculative house-builders.

In the search for an alternative to brick Post-modernism in new tenement design, a significant precedent was set in 1984 by the '21st Century Tenement' competition, sponsored by Maryhill Housing Association and RIAS. The winning design, by Ken MacRae, was built (with McGurn, Logan, Duncan & Opfer) in 1984–8 at Stratford Street, Maryhill [9.31]. Its Thomson-like convex facade of smooth-faced blockwork fronted an ingenious split-level section, which combined nineteenth-century-height storeys at the front with lower rooms at the back – allowing big living rooms and mixed sizes of flats. By the late 1980s and early 1990s, many Glasgow projects showed concern for greater scale and dignity, and facing in stone or stone-like treatments. Elder & Cannon's Duke Street block (1992) for Reidvale Housing Association also had split-level sections, with a severe front facade and a boldly complex rear elevation of 'grander, more volumetric' living rooms: it was built of beige brick laid in patterns to simulate channelled ashlar. [121] Simister Monaghan's Byres Road corner block for Hillhead Housing Association (completed 1994) was fully stone-clad, and combined a heavy classicism with a recessed, glazed corner drum [9.32].

In the east, where brick had made less of an impact in the 1980s, there were also now moves towards more monumental tenement architecture. In Dundee, Page & Park's Sinderins housing

9.31 Stratford Street housing development, Glasgow (McGurn, Logan, Duncan & Opfer, with Ken MacRae, 1984–8), the winning entry in the RIAS/Maryhill Housing Association '21st Century Tenement' competition.

9.32 Byres Road/University Avenue housing, Glasgow (Simister Monaghan, 1991–4).

project (1986) comprised a sharply modelled, four-storey group in two-tone blockwork. In the capital, new projects echoed the flush facades of pre-1914 Edinburgh and Leith tenements. N. Groves-Raines had, as early as 1979, designed a group of flats (Moncrieff Terrace) which juxtaposed solid blockwork and timber balconies cut into the wall surface. Also in blockwork, Reiach & Hall's Yeaman Place scheme (1988) echoed the 'monolithic nature' of the street through 'static dignified blocks', [122] as did several schemes for new Edinburgh tenement blocks, designed by Arcade Architects in the early 1990s. In small burghs, some projects retained the irregularity of Vernacular, but combined it with a new theatrical element of panache: on a prominent corner site in Crieff, Nicoll Russell built a complex agglomeration of towered flats in blockwork and render (1990–2), intended to 'reflect Crieff's heritage without vernacular reproduction' and to 'appear almost to grow out of the existing fabric'. [123]

These attempts to create a more elevated architecture of social housing were still mostly designed on a piecemeal basis. But by the early '90s, there was an increasing appetite for co-ordinated housing design, and, even, for area planning. The revival of interest in Modernist idealism did not, however, imply any return to Modern ideals of mass provision controlled by experts. Private-sector or 'partnership' initiatives continued to spread their scope: 1994 saw the foundation of the Glasgow Regeneration Fund, set up with public/private support to 'nurture . . . the Scottish entrepreneurial spirit' in 'deprived areas'. [124] At the same time, 'community participation' remained unshaken as an ideal: and so, especially in Glasgow, its procedures were adapted to the new and more forceful climate. Located on the site of former Modernist blocks in Hutchesontown were two new developments which offered the prospect of a fresh, co-ordinated approach to social housing design. First off the mark was the Crown Street Project, headed by Mike Galloway. Inspired (Galloway claimed) by the Berlin IBA, its plan, published in 1992, attempted to combine urbanist stress on tenements and street-grids, and on the collective 'bustle of city life', with acknowledgement of the popular push for privatised living space. Where Spence's 20-storey slab blocks had combined self-contained Modern dwellings with romantic evocations of tenement back-greens,

9.33 Crown Street, Glasgow, design by Page & Park (drawing by Suzanne Ewing), 1995.

Galloway's 'rethink of the tenement concept' ruled out communal back areas as a 'legacy of the ash heap and the outside privy', and insisted on private gardens [cf. 9.9]. There must be a 'public and private face', families 'want to be part of an urban community while retaining the right to be themselves'. The days of 'monolithic' council schemes were gone: Crown Street's 'integrated community' would include a high proportion of owner-occupied dwellings. [125]

Although Crown Street's sinuous street plan, and the first blocks built, seemed suburban, rather than urban in character, more monumental designs were soon proposed there [9.33]. The adjoining area (Gorbals East) saw pressure by the New Gorbals Housing Association for more co-ordinated design: a master plan by Page & Park set out (1994), with residents' support, a range of unified ensembles. At its centre was Moffat Gardens (a 'garden square development'), incorporating a 'dialogue' between designs by Page & Park, Simister Monaghan, and a group by Elder & Cannon with a forceful Modernist tower [9.34].

Fraser Stewart of the New Gorbals H. A. spoke of Gorbals East as an 'organic and participative process' which would provide a 'model of good practice in urban regeneration for the future'. [126] Page hailed the 'new confidence' of the housing-association movement, which made possible new 'questions of leadership: being a provider, but also a patron'. [127] In peripheral housing schemes such as Castlemilk, some residents also began to criticise Postmodern restyling as a mere 'image change', and demanded more 'radical', 'dynamic and modern' solutions, in reflection of a 'growing design consciousness and self-confidence in the community'. [128] By 1995, this new philosophy was spreading beyond Clydeside. Ewen & Fiona McLachlan's competition-winning development at South Gyle, Edinburgh (1995–6), for instance, was designed as a perimeter-planned layout of variegated dwelling-types (with area of 'wetland' at the centre), to show that even low-density outer-suburban housing could be given a social and visual 'focus' [9.35].

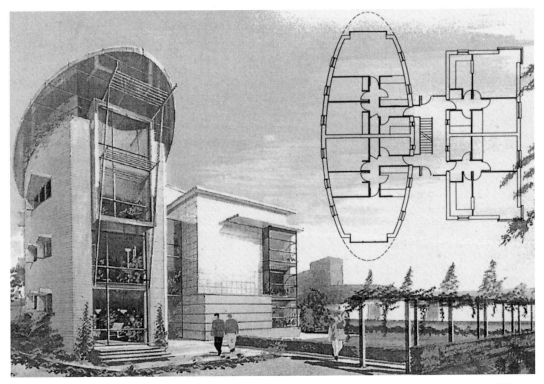

9.34 Moffat Street Gardens, Gorbals, Glasgow, ground-floor plan and perspective of proposed Elder & Cannon block, 1994.

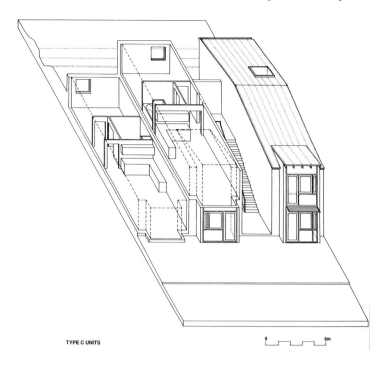

TYPE C UNITS

0 ⌐_⌐_⌐ 5m

9.35 Gyle housing project, Edinburgh, 1995 drawing by E. & F. McLachlan, showing specimen house types.

Conclusion

The 1990s saw Scottish architecture at a point of transition, which in some ways resembled the previous turn-of-the-century in its rejection of a phase of brash eclecticism, and its search for renewed idealism and order. The persistent twentieth-century identification of the nation's architecture with values and images of the 'social' seemed strong again, and there was much discussion of how to channel this energy into 'form'. Unlike the 1930s and 1950s, the Modernist faith in materialistic Progress, and in state-directed discipline, was no longer available as a simple answer. But Modernism's confidence and optimism had not vanished: the revived concern for the 'national' was now orientated towards planning for a diverse, outward-looking future, rather than guarding a threatened 'essence' of the past. McKean wrote in 1992 that 'Scottish architects are European and cosmopolitan in outlook . . . and eager to lead the country in another cultural revival comparable to that which took place a hundred years ago'. [129]

Conclusion

'Architecture is the work of nations . . .'

C. R. Mackintosh, c.1891–3 [1]

'. . . the manifold and tangled elements of Heritage and Burden from the Past.'

Patrick Geddes, 1923 [2]

C.1 Monumentality and modernity: front facade detail of Alexander Thomson's Egyptian Halls (1871–3).

In this final section, we come to the two most basic questions which arise from this study. What underlying patterns and continuities within Scottish architecture have emerged? And what relationship is there between those architectural patterns and the wider issues of present-day Scottish culture?

The Grand Themes of Scottish Architecture: Monumentality and Modernity

Throughout Chapters 5-9, one of the most persistent themes was the effort, on the part of architects and critics, to define 'national' characteristics in

503

architecture. Even in earlier periods, there was a foretaste of this approach – for example, in the 1424 description of castellation as 'the manner of the kingdom of Scotland'. [3] But the search for the 'national' became much more insistent from the early nineteenth century. At first, the focus was one set of specific forms in the past – castellated architecture – followed, in the early twentieth century, by a shift to broader, more abstract qualities with ethical or utopian overtones. Finally, the 1980s brought a further redefinition, which discarded the driving ideas of national discipline or historical destiny in favour of freer, more open-ended conceptions of Scottish architectural identity, built on the broad foundations of Heritage. Our own historical account of the development of this architecture naturally conforms to the present-day concern with broad currents or qualities rather than specific or formal essences. Our definitions of the principal themes of Scottish architecture have emphasised the diverse and fluctuating relationships between forms and wider cultural influences, and have set those relationships in the context of international comparisons. It is for these reasons of complexity and ambiguity that the word 'national', throughout this book, has mostly been used in inverted commas.

Despite all these complexities and qualifications, what finally emerged from our account *was*, in fact, a striking continuity within Scottish architecture, a continuity which spanned several centuries and which resulted from an interaction between the material aspects of architecture, the cultural development of the nation as a whole, and the interpretation of both these by designers. This dynamic process was dominated by two variegated

C.2 Marischal College Extension and Greyfriars Church, Aberdeen (1893–1906, by A. M. Mackenzie).

yet persistent ideas – formal 'monumentality' and cultural 'modernity' – whose conjunction left Scotland's architecture strongly distinct from the patterns of other countries, especially its neighbours in north-west Europe. Monumentality in architecture arose from an emphasis on the quality of enduring, masonry-built solidity, whether in substance or as an image, and by a wide variety of means. It was not just a matter of size: small buildings could also be monumental. The drive for modernity, on the other hand, stemmed from an eagerness for radical change and openness to the outside world, which drove Scottish society to transform itself repeatedly and radically – changing from the hierarchical structures of religion and feudalism, to the expansiveness of imperialist capitalism and the class-stratified discipline of mass society. The architecture which resulted from the dual influence of monumentality and modernity fused the unprecedented building programmes of industrial and social revolution with an imagery of timeless, material strength. This was done in a way that was unique, and yet was also set firmly within the 'Western' mainstream. In a country at the centre of a global empire and at the 'border' of Europe and America, there could be no '*Sarmatyzm*', no equivalent of the debates in countries such as Poland, Hungary, even Germany, about whether they formed part of the 'West' at all. [4]

Eventually, the late twentieth century saw a fundamental challenge to these dynamic patterns. Both the wider process of cultural and social modernity and the more restricted, twentieth-century architectural phenomenon of 'Modernism' or the 'Modern Movement' (a difference in definition explored in Chapter 8) simultaneously went into crisis. In their place, new patterns, such as the Heritage movement, emerged, which challenged modernity's driving force of faith in Progress.

How did monumentality first become established as a prominent theme within Scottish architecture? The first explanations are essentially topographical, concerned with the adoption of stone as the main material for formal or permanent architecture. Well before the Renaissance, the free availability of building stone had already begun to influence building patterns; this was also the time when resources of building timber began to dry up. The precise links between developments in building materials and in architectural form are unclear. What is certain, however, is that by the beginning of the period covered in this account, in the late fifteenth century, the use of massive masonry construction, and of an aesthetic of heavy walls and small windows, was well established in Scotland not just out of necessity, but as a matter of cultural preference. Larger churches often used facing stone, while other buildings, including the castles and palaces of the rich, were usually of harled rubble. This pattern differed from the remainder of north-west Europe, where framed or brick construction was common. In some ways, it was more akin to patterns in the Mediterranean.

The contribution of the Renaissance to this established pattern of stone monumentality was to superimpose on it a more systematic and international system of ideas and forms – a system which we, today, call 'classicism'. From around 1500, classicism gradually took hold as the most versatile expression of Scottish monumentality; it enjoyed a period of special dominance between the late seventeenth and the early twentieth centuries. The classicism of the sixteenth, seventeenth and early eighteenth century, however, was based on ideas unfamiliar to our post-eighteenth-century eyes, at both a Scottish and an international level. There was a combination of a single authoritative ideal – the classical Antique, as represented in texts such as Vitruvius – with a natural, unstructured diversity in its expression across Europe, flowing across borders. This was especially true of the 'Northern Renaissance', to which Scotland generally adhered, although at first her close religious links to Rome also provided a more direct route of interaction with early Renaissance ideas in Italy. In the Northern Renaissance, the precisely formulaic or canonical element of classicism seemed to be restricted to the addition of ornament to long-established forms of the country or area concerned. In Scotland, as shown by Seton's contrasting houses at Fyvie and Pinkie, images or motifs of classical antiquity were used alongside seemingly nostalgic castellated forms with genealogical or Arthurian overtones. Although there was no concept of exact styles, as in later centuries, there was a bewildering variety of symbolic motifs or forms.

C.3 'The Palice of Honour': main
east gateway of Linlithgow Palace,
1995 photograph.

Gradually, this first phase of the Scottish
Renaissance, with its free mixture of the
cosmopolitan and the nostalgic, was displaced by
an adherence to more literal classicism, which
involved increased use of the Orders to articulate
overall design. Following the Reformation, which
established the primacy of secular patronage in
Scottish architecture, the now well-established
tradition of stone monumentality was reinforced
by the gradual spread of ashlar construction into
secular building. This was still a time of wide
and spontaneous geographical diversity in architecture, and Scotland's emerging monumental
classicism differed markedly from the classicisms
of nearby countries such as England and the
Netherlands – for instance, in matters such as
window-to-wall proportions. Of course, there was
an even sharper contrast between the relatively
severe, architectonic patterns of north-west
Europe as a whole, and the sculptural complexities
of the Baroque and Rococo of central and southern
Europe.

    This period also saw the first traces of a more
self-consciously historical or archaeological
attitude both to the classicism of antiquity, and
to the buildings of the Scottish past. And, in the
work of figures such as Mar, Clerk of Penicuik
or William Adam, there were attempts – which

transcended the sharp political differences of the years around 1700 – to link these intellectual developments with the beginnings of the most vigorous phase in Scotland's drive for agricultural and industrial 'improvement'.

It was in the mid- and late eighteenth century that there began that revolutionary social and cultural rupture, out of which modern society would emerge. [5] The great adventure of modernity was an international development, in which the anglophone nations flanking the Atlantic, including Scotland, played a leading role. In the first rush of modernisation, driven by uncompromisingly *laissez-faire* private endeavours, Scottish entrepreneurs were in the forefront, both in agricultural and industrial improvement and in British imperialism. And Scotland, through contributions such as the work of Scott, also helped shape the next phase, in the late nineteenth and twentieth centuries, when rampant capitalist individualism was gradually replaced by a more disciplined modernity emphasising the 'community' of the whole nation.

Architecturally, the spread of modernity in society had its most clearly definable effects in building patronage and professional organisation. In the wake of the Reformation, churches were replaced by country houses at the top of the architectural hierarchy; for a time the initiative oscillated between landed patronage and attempts (especially after 1660) at royal reassertion on the absolutist model. Gradually, Scottish architecture's social structure broadened from the landed patronage of the seventeenth and eighteenth centuries (in which women played a powerful role) to the vast complexity of nineteenth-century middle-class and institutional building, and the inclusion of some of the working class in the patronage of twentieth-century public bureaucracies and user-participation groups. There was also a widening of the social scope of previously élite architectural features: we witnessed earlier the popularisation of the concept of segregation and specialisation in dwelling-plans, from palaces to middle-class villas and, ultimately, working-class housing. But at all stages, architecture stayed an 'Establishment' matter. The most important projects were always built by the ruling classes, however broadly defined.

In tandem with these developments, the status of architects changed from one of dependence on the values of the landed élite to one of autonomous professionalism and (often in the twentieth century) salaried or official status; however, some elements of the latter were already in evidence as early as the sixteenth and early seventeenth centuries, in the activity of the royal masters of work. The shift away from the aristocrat-designer to the middle-class professional had the effect of bolstering male domination in design: it was not until 1914 that Scotland's first woman architect, Edith M. Burnet Hughes, began practice. The nineteenth and twentieth centuries also saw a lasting accentuation of the concept of the architect as an individual artistic personality, an idea that had been introduced by the Italian Renaissance and was first popularised in Scotland in the case of Bruce.

The late eighteenth- and early nineteenth-century beginning of large-scale improvement and urbanisation was also the time when the characteristic bipolar (west–east) geography of modern Lowland Scottish culture – including architectural patronage – began to emerge, in place of the previously more dispersed distribution of patronage epicentres. The vigorous transatlantic and imperial-oriented capitalism of the west was matched by the romanticism and institutional gravity of the east; foremost among the other regions was the granite north-east. The strength of this diverse, urban-centred pattern of Lowland culture was accentuated by the comprehensive scope of improvement in the countryside, which left the Lowlands without the peasants and folk traditions common on the Continent. There still, of course, remained different 'ethnological regions' in the Lowlands, but material culture, including building patterns, was increasingly monopolised by post-improvement modernity. [6]

What was the reaction of Scotland's monumental architecture, from the late eighteenth century, to the nation's new and ferociously 'enterprising' temper? There was no single, simple response, but instead three, broadly overlapping trends: first, an eclectic classicism, for both setpiece buildings and mass urban expansion; second, a romantic search for 'national' qualities in architecture; and third, in the twentieth century, the Modern Movement's

C.4 The triumphal gateway to Robert Adam's University of Edinburgh building (from 1789).

uncompromising architecture of Progress and the New. All were marked off from what went before by the new awareness of History: the late eighteenth century, after all, was the 'historical Age' and Scotland was the 'historical Nation'. [7] From now on, the unselfconscious aspects of continuity within Scottish monumental architecture would be overlaid by the historically based, highly conscious choices made by designers [C.4].

Eclectic Classicism and the Modern City

The first of these three responses, the transformation of classicism in accordance with the new ideas of romantic individualism and eclecticism, was in a way the most straightforward. Here, the attributes of stone monumentality were retained, but modified. Already, the earlier eighteenth-century Scots classicism of Mar and Adam had developed a rich diversity in its expressions of the antique. There was no prescriptive orthodoxy, no equivalent, for instance, to the rule of Palladianism in England. From the late eighteenth century, this diversity became more extreme and

calculatedly 'historical'. In secular architecture, a variety of precise classical styles emerged, many either astylar or divergent from the 'correct' Graeco-Roman Orders. And the unitary classical utopia was replaced by a range of competing utopias and individualistic aesthetic concepts reflecting the growing complexity of urban, industrial society, with its proliferation of building types and its unprecedented increase in the sheer quantity, and social scope, of new 'architecture'. Despite the new, self-conscious attitude to history and to styles, this eclectic classicism remained faithful, with modifications, to the distinctive elements of Scottish monumental stone architecture.

At one extreme, some designers, in their designs for the public and commercial institutions of the Scottish capitalist city, stressed the individualism and driving force of the architect as artist. This trend gathered force in the work of Robert Adam, Stark, and Playfair father and son; and it reached a climax in the work of Alexander Thomson. With very few exceptions, Thomson avoided using forms that directly evoked the Scottish past, yet his personal blend of cosmopolitan eclecticism and

Calvinist emotionalism was not found, and could hardly have been found, in any other country. A different interpretation of Scottish classical monumentality was brought to bear on the task of building segregated living-areas for the urban bourgeoisie and (later) the skilled workforce. The monumental romanticism of the Edinburgh New Town, although mostly composed out of classical Grecian forms, nevertheless proved to be one of the most world-renowned and inimitable achievements of Scottish city-design. And a similar uncompromising monumentality applied to the residential development of Aberdeen, or Glasgow and its suburbs, whether in the individualistic yet contextual housing designs of Thomson, or in the uniform facades of ordinary late nineteenth-century tenements [C.5, C.6].

It was the down-playing of architectural individuality in these everyday tenement facades – built by countless small speculators under feuing or Dean of Guild controls – which most underlined the role of materials and construction in maintaining the visual continuity of masonry-monumentality. Yet it was in construction that revolutionary but unseen changes, driven by economic factors, were taking place in the nineteenth century. The new cheapness of machine-cut ashlar, timber and cast or wrought iron allowed the old massive, additive, load-bearing rubble techniques to be replaced by hybrid patterns. In

C.5 Granite City: view of Union Street, Aberdeen, *c.*1878. On the right: Archibald Simpson's Assembly Rooms.

C.6 Thomsonian eclecticism in the North-East: granite-built houses of the 1880s in Hamilton Place, Aberdeen, designed by Pirie & Clyne.

buildings such as Thomson's commercial blocks, the *substance* of solid stone building was replaced by an *image* of monumentality. Behind the surface, elements of framed building proliferated. On the surface, there was a growing refinement of facing stonework – a trend which culminated in the nine-teenth-century creation of Aberdeen as a homoge-neous 'Granite City'. In city layouts, too, there was unobtrusive, but far-reaching change: the old burgage plots' dense, small-windowed layouts were replaced by an opposite concern with space and ventilation. In its new love of openness, as in its combination of a quasi-industrial production process with highly finished, unified facades, Scottish tenement-building contrasted with the slower, denser and less specialised patterns of the Continent. The only other country with a similar approach in housing production and unified design, industrial England, differed sharply in its use of brick and low-rise terrace houses. Scotland was the only country in the world where the facade presented by the pre–1914 mass capitalist city was an ashlar wall [C.7, C.8].

At the end of the century, the swing in opinion against free-enterprise led to modifications, but no revolution, within eclectic classicism. The more cosmopolitan designers, such as Burnet, Campbell and Tait, attempted to reinvigorate it with new elements. These included Beaux-Arts rationality, along with bolder patterns, such as skyscraper-Baroque, which were inspired by the architecture of that new home of Western modernity, the United States. By that stage, some classical architects (especially in the east) were beginning to point to a continuous Scottish 'classic tradition' since the late seventeenth

C.7 Houses for shipyard workers under construction in 1902 in George Street, Whiteinch, by the speculative builders P. W. and A. Lightbody, to the designs of John McRae of Oran Street, Maryhill: (a) Rear facade of block, including the head of the building firm, William Lightbody, standing on the wooden ramp; (b) delivery of window-mullions.

C.8 The 'inhabited wall': 22 Bank Street, Greenock (tenement block built *c*.1890).

century. Of course, architects such as Bruce or Smith would hardly have recognised the designs of two hundred years later, such as St Andrew's House or the 1938 Empire Exhibition, as great-grandchildren of their own work. Yet to the historian, judging in retrospect, the movement of classical monumentality does seem a strikingly long-lasting and coherent 'endeavour to realise the idea of eternity' (as Thomson put it), [8] in an era of incessant change in Scottish society.

The Quest for a 'National' Architecture

Prominent among the new utopias and ideas of the late eighteenth century onwards was the histori-cally inspired concept that the nation itself could be a source of artistic creativity, and could even provide an alternative to the old authority of universal classicism. Corresponding to this was an insistence that styles should express 'national' characteristics. In the rise of French absolutist

classicism to international status in the seven-teenth century, and in its debate between 'ancients' and 'moderns', the anti-cosmopolitan concept of the architecture of nations had already been foreshadowed. But in the Romantic era of the late eighteenth and early nineteenth century, the Scotland of Ossian, Robert Adam and Sir Walter Scott surged into the forefront of a far more explicit and unambiguous international fashion for the 'national' ideal. For example, Adam Menelaws's Cottage Palace at Peterhof, an Abbotsford-inspired retreat built in 1826–9 for Scott's admirer, Tsar Nicholas, was stuffed with neo-medieval emblems of Russian nationalism and references to the 1828–9 'holy war' with Turkey. [9]

Within Scotland, while Adam's castles implicitly conveyed a romantic image of Scottish national identity, the first explicit architectural evocation of that ideal was classical: the movement of neo-Grecian architecture in romantic or

C.9 'Second Empire' Baronial: David Bryce's Fettes College, Edinburgh (1864–70).

Sublime settings. Soon, this was rejected as insufficiently 'national' and lacking in picturesque romance, especially as the completeness of improvement and modernity in the Lowlands had shifted the focus of patriotic imagery to the Highlands. Gradually, the 'national' acquired *anti*-classical overtones; the Scottish Renaissance, despite its own elements of classicism, was identified as its 'essential' period; and Scotch Baronial emerged as a new, secular, non-Gothic 'national' style. But this break from monumentality and modernity was less real than it seemed. Baronial had much in common with classical eclecticism in its insistence on high-finish facing stone and other up-to-date trappings, such as plate-glass windows. A building such as Peddie & Kinnear's new Aberdeen Town House, with its expanses of precisely cut granite, represented a level of stereotomic refinement which would have amazed the builders of the harled Scottish Renaissance castles. And indeed, the high-roofed Franco-Baronial style of Bryce can perhaps best be understood as a sophisticated Scottish variant of international Second Empire classicism [C.9].

In contrast to the relative internationalism of Baronial, in the hands of the late-nineteenth and eary-twentieth-century Traditionalist architects the movement of 'national' architecture began to adopt an antagonistic position towards some aspects of modern, capitalist society. There was an ethically based rejection of *laissez-faire* values and specific stylistic formulae (including Baronial), and, instead, a utopian insistence on the 'community' of the 'essential' nation as the central organising principle. Traditionalists denied there was any grand Scottish classical tradition stretching to the present. In a development of the Ossian–Scott idealisation of a pre-improvement or Jacobite past, the only valid classicism was now seen as that of the age of Bruce: everything else was branded as too modern, and inimical to national community.

As to what was actually built by Traditionalism, the position was much less polarised than this rhetoric suggested [C.10, C.11]. Stylistically, there was a good deal of continuity within the movement, in the use of semi-Baronial forms of Scottish Renaissance inspiration, until at least the 1930s. These were increasingly expressed in a new and freer manner. Under Anderson, Lorimer and Hurd, as well as other architects more usually associated with classicism, such as Burnet, this simplified Baronial, often using harling rather than stone facing (which had become debased, in Traditionalists' eyes, by its mass-production on low-status classical buildings), was systematically developed for secular architecture, and especially for the design of the 'home'. It was, emphatically, secular rather than religious architecture that attracted these 'national' endeavours. There was a tacit consensus that neo-Gothic and neo-Romanesque church architecture was a less emo-

C.10 Social Traditionalism: Rowand Anderson's Pearce Institute, Govan (1892–1906).

C.11 Emergence of the public
architect: Tollcross School
(1911–13, by J. A. Carfrae of
Edinburgh School Board).

tionally resonant vehicle. Thus, Traditionalism's
'cult of the house' perpetuated into the twentieth
century, and reinvigorated, one of the key
continuities within post-Renaissance Scottish
architecture – the greater prestige assigned to
secular buildings than to religious ones.

Paradoxically, Traditionalism also included, in
the work of Mackintosh and the Glasgow Style,
Scotland's only equivalent to the Continental
avant-garde. Mackintosh contributed to the
undermining of the remaining authority of
classicism, through his heightened psychological-
symbolic emphasis on individually created 'form'.
This heyday of Scotland's architectural avant-
garde was short-lived: in contrast to some other
countries, it ended around 1910. Overall, Scottish
Traditionalism emphasised anti-cosmopolitanism
rather than the reverse, especially between the
wars; but it lacked the kind of driving, dominating
chauvinism characteristic of continental fascist
architectural ideologies of the interwar years.

Mass Modernity and Architectural Modernism

Eventually, as we saw in Chapter 8, both
Traditionalism and classicism, swamped by the
mid-twentieth-century's pace of change, gave way
to their new rival, the Modern Movement. The
latter represented a different sort of order from
Traditionalism, one which maintained classical
eclecticism's concern to express the progress of
modern civilisation and deal with new mass

building programmes, but combined this with
unprecedentedly abstract forms and a new,
collective utopianism specifically directed towards
social ideals and state initiative. The twenty years
following 1945 saw the most furious burst of
modernisation in the Scottish built environment
since the mid-nineteenth century, now within
the framework of ordered 'planning'. This was
overseen by a partnership between a new devolved
government administration with cross-party
support and a socialist-led reinvigoration of
municipal power, spearheaded by Glasgow.

Modernism raises different, but equally acute
problems of evaluation compared with those of
'national' architecture. Rather than too many
definitions of nationality, it presented almost
none. This was a quintessentially international
movement, which reached Scotland relatively late,
in the 1930s, and which was generally attuned to
socialism, rather than nationalism. Post-1945
Modern architecture, in its ascendancy, almost
resembled the early eighteenth century formula of
unitary utopia and natural, international diversity.
Therefore Scotland's own vast post-war drive of
reconstruction through Modernist architecture
and planning, despite its highly co-ordinated,
national organisation, avoided any explicit
architectural references to the 'national'.

Modernism was also the movement which most
emphasised innovation and breaks from tradition.
It attempted to arrive at formulas and standards
tailor-made to the twentieth century's organised,
disciplined interpretation of cultural modernity.

Yet even here there were striking elements of continuity with previous periods of Scottish architecture. In the area of constructional techniques, for example, the virtual collapse of the economics of stone building (at least, in the urbanised Lowlands) was followed by the transformation, rather than the abolition, of the image of the masonry wall. Certainly, there had been sensational departures from the latter formula even in the 1930s, notably the vast glass sheet of Marwick's Edinburgh Co-operative building. From the 1950s, the headline-grabbing Modernist landmarks of tower blocks broadcast a new, verticalised type of monumentality, based on frame construction and (in the west) a continuation of the Beaux-Arts rationalist philosophy. Even more avant-garde was the almost anarchic design and construction of Cumbernauld town centre [C.12]. But within the great mass of the new programmes of state-led modernity, such as social housing, masonry walling mostly continued to prevail, in the form of harled brickwork or concrete blockwork; and these were treated with the same appearance of massive solidity as before [C.13].

There was also a great deal of continuity with the pre-Modernist era in general attitudes to the ordering of the urban environment. Where nineteenth-century urbanisation had cleared away the old, rustic, thatched buildings of the pre-industrial era from towns, it was mid-twentieth-century Modernist redevelopment that went on to sweep away the *ad-hoc* structures of the industrial era – the countless brick sheds or corrugated-iron

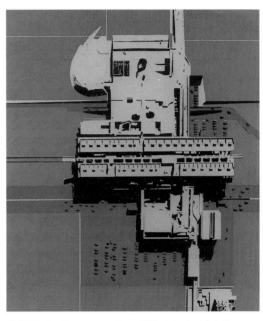

C.12 Modernist avant-gardism: 1964 view of model of Cumbernauld Town Centre (1963–7).

C.13 Late Modern, 'traditional' or 'vernacular'? Split-level dwellings designed by Cumbernauld New Town Development Corporation's architects at the Seafar housing area, seen newly completed in 1962.

workshops, often built in brick or wood, that had sprung up at the interstices of nineteenth-century urban development. The image of the Scottish city as a place of homogeneous, monumental 'greyness' – by comparison with other Western countries – was only fully achieved in the 1960s.

Modernism's overt novelty and international-ism, and its emphasis on the ennobling of mass building, also concealed some significant overlaps with Traditionalist architecture. This was especially true in the east, where the Modernist utopian researches of Reiach and Matthew drew on the social concerns of Geddes in the 1890s, and even the 1930s' social ideology of Bute or Hurd. Some of these continuities even outlasted mid-century Modern architecture itself. Robert Matthew himself personally linked the conservation movement of the 1970s with the Modernism of the 1950s, and, even further back, with Lorimerian Traditionalism. And in Glasgow and the west, concepts of social conservation were taken up and reformulated with even greater energy in the 1970s. In a way, the emphasis on social concerns, especially those of the ordinary home, has been *the* most enduring theme of Scottish architecture from the late nineteenth century to the present day.

The End of 'Progress'?

The years from the late 1960s, as we saw in Chapter 9, brought a challenge to all these patterns, in the form of a growing disenchantment with Progress (especially in its twentieth-century socialist or nationalist form of state-led planning) and with grand narratives of history. At the same time, there was also change afoot in the affiliations of the Scottish nation. Some began to reject the old pattern of cultural autonomy within an expansion-ist and modernising Britain, in favour of a new external affiliation with 'Europe'. Glasgow, for instance, became in 1990 the sixth European city designated under the European Union's annual programme of 'Cultural Capitals of Europe'.

This loss of the old certainties naturally affected architecture. The immediate impact was obvious: a deep, possibly terminal crisis in the Modern Movement. But the longer-term consequences were unclear. Some, in the 1980s, put forward

alternatives such as decorative Postmodernism or elements of classicism. Others, in the 1990s, called for a selective revitalisation of aspects of Modernism, ranging from social idealism to a Mackintosh-like ideal of artistic individualism and abstract form (which had been developed throughout the Modernist ascendancy, particular-ly by Gillespie, Kidd and Coia). Everything, now, seemed much more open and free; there was no universal prescription.

The repudiation of the history-driven dynamic of modernity was reflected above all in the new status of Heritage. Although the absolute domi-nation of the Conservation Movement in the 1970s was short-lived, from then on the most important factor in architecture, including bold new 'interventions', seemed to be the totality of what existed already. What mattered especially in buildings, far more than before, was their material solidity and potential longevity – their ability to adapt to new tasks and to transcend their original purposes and ideological contexts. Across Europe in general, previous architectural 'movements', including some earlier twentieth-century atti-tudes to old buildings, had often been associated with aggressive confrontations between rival nations or socio-political ideologies. But now the cumulative, all-inclusive principles of Heritage offered a way to actually help reconcile historical or geographical conflict.

However varied the architectural responses were to this cultural upheaval, one thing was clear: there would be no diminution of the Scottish concern with the image of enduring monumentality. To begin with, the natural affinity between that image and the concern of Heritage with preservation and re-use was obvious. And even in new building, despite the sudden prolifer-ation of brick boxes in speculative housing, the same appeared to apply – for instance, in the advocacy of the 'traditional street' or the revived use of stone facing in city buildings. By the late twentieth century, Scottish architectural monu-mentality seemed to have distanced itself, to some extent, from its centuries-long relationship with progress-based modernity.

Contemporary Architectural History and Heritage: National and European

We conclude with a more immediate question. What relationship is there between the concerns of this account – as a historical description of the development of today's architectural heritage – and the wider issues of contemporary Scottish culture?

As we noted above, the increasingly confident reformulations and assertions of Scottish cultural values during the 1980s and 1990s have been coupled with a new element of European cultural nationalism, which reflected the growing power of economic and political federalism, and the decline of old-style unitary nationalism across western and central Europe. The writing of history, naturally, was not exempt from this wider shift in climate towards a combination of Scottish and European nationalism; the 1980s and 90s saw an accelerating scramble to reassess and remould concepts of the nation's architectural past. 'Euro-Scottish' credentials were attributed as a matter of course to all the most revered figures within that heritage, such as Mackintosh and Geddes, and to others as well. Anderson, for instance, was described by McKean as 'a man of European predilections, tastes and stature'. [10] Other elements of the Scottish heritage faced more critical reappraisal: in 1991, Frank A. Walker pointed to the 'middle-class Unionism' of some turn-of-the-century villa patrons, while in 1994 Charles McKean took the battle between 'European' and 'British' back much further, arguing of eighteenth-century Edinburgh that 'once upon a time there was a great European city which lost confidence in its own greatness. It lost confidence in itself, when it stopped wanting to be European and started wanting to be British.' [11]

More importantly for our purposes here, the new ideas were also applied to the evaluation of historical accounts themselves. McKean went so far as to argue that Scotland was

'a country suffering from an advanced case of amnesia. There are few books on the history of Scottish architecture that can be safely recommended as a general introduction to what was built. That is because, for the past 300 years,

Scottish architecture has been interpreted as a difficult provincial manifestation of English or British architecture'. [12]

Our own account, although conforming in general to the present-day norm of 'European' affiliation, has in fact suggested a rather different picture of the status and self-esteem of Scottish architecture during those past centuries. Protected by the ring-fence of British imperial security, it was able to evolve with freedom and confidence. Even during the age of greatest turbulence in the establishment of the new British order, the workings of Scottish cultural power and autonomy in architecture were unmistakable: for example, of the roughly seven hundred large country house commissions (including major alterations) between 1707 and 1840, only forty were given to English architects. And later, English designers and critics tended either to ignore Scottish architecture or to treat it with polite deference: Burnet's move to London in 1905, for example, was one consequence of a turn-of-the-century admiration for French and Scottish classicism among some English architects. [13]

C.14 Imperial Scotland: Eilean Donan Castle war memorial.

Despite occasional exceptions, such as the controversies surrounding Sir G. G. Scott's Glasgow University commission or the 1891 Glasgow Art Gallery Competition, the beginning of harsher words on the subject of Scottish-English architectural relations was a comparatively recent phenomenon, coinciding with the gradual decline in British power and cohesion after 1918. As early as 1928, the IAS convention saw an altercation between Lorimer, who criticised as 'unpatriotic' the employment of English designers in Scotland, and the visiting RIBA president, Walter Tapper, who described Lorimer's argument as 'rubbish', and contended that 'the great thing was, to get good work'. [14] More recently, historians began to join in these debates. On the Scottish side, we noted above the rejection of British affiliations by McKean and F. A. Walker. Correspondingly, among some English historians, a new, more competitive nationalism began to assert itself. While Sir John Summerson's *Architecture in Britain 1530 to 1830* (first published 1953) confined itself to elegant gibes against the 'quaintly barbaric richness' and 'sheer sullen gloom' of Scottish classicism, a harsher tone emerged in Giles Worsley's *Classical Architecture in Britain: The Heroic Age* (1995). Although he cautioned that Scottish architectural history was 'a minefield of nationalist passions', Worsley's own account of the advance of 'British Palladianism' was itself dominated by triumphal nationalism; he branded Irish, Scottish and American classicism as 'essentially provincial' or 'peripheral' reflections of English themes. [15]

Potentially, there is an inconsistency between this kind of nationalistic historiography and the more orderly type of cross-cultural relationships implicit in the 'European' ideal of many present-day Scottish architects and historians. After all, the anti-hierarchical, competitive emphasis on the 'national' first emerged in the eighteenth and nineteenth centuries in reaction *against* the canonical or universal frameworks of Renaissance-derived classical architecture. If the history of Scottish architecture were to become swamped in chauvinistic rhetoric, then any measured evaluation of its achievements in an international context – one of the main aims of this book – would be extremely difficult. In reality, however,

there seems little risk of that happening, not only because of the general decline in nationalist animosities across western Europe, but also because in Scotland, as in most other parts of north-west Europe, architecture has never been subject to violent politicisation, and there is no likelihood that it (or its historiography) ever will be.

To illustrate the point, it is worth recalling the ferocious rhetoric that characterised art-historical relations earlier this century between some other European countries – for example, between Germany and Poland. As early as 1917, on the German side, a guidebook to the Marienburg Castle wrote menacingly of the 'fight for the cultural work of the Teutonic Knights for the Ostmark', and in 1944 – the year in which German troops dynamited Warsaw's Royal Castle – Breslau historians extolled Silesian art and architecture as a 'gangway of attack' for the 'forces of German form'. [16] In response, the restoration of the Warsaw Old Town was described by the director of the Polish National Museum, as 'the last victorious act in the fight with the enemy . . . the finishing touch of our unbending struggle with enemy violence'. [17] One of the most striking aspects of Scottish architectural history is the very absence of these kinds of violently political engagements. Consistent themes have been pursued, and a cumulative heritage built up, *alongside* radical political changes, such as the Jacobite–Hanoverian wars of the early eighteenth century. By contrast with their counterparts in, for instance, Germany or Russia, Scotland's architectural historians will never face the need for reconciliation or pacification of some aspect of their heritage which symbolises internal tyranny, or 'anti-European' external aggression against neighbours.

Conclusion

In this book, we have traced the measured way in which Scottish architecture was able to respond, and contribute, to wider international movements – including the changing concepts of national identity in architecture – while maintaining its own monumental integrity. The first two centuries covered by this book were a time of invasions and conflicts, and some of the masterworks of the Renaissance years, such as Linlithgow, still lie in (carefully preserved) ruins. But the great mass of our nation's architecture, as it exists today, is the result of a continuity of peaceful development by Scottish architects and patrons, working in accordance with principles, ideals and building programmes determined within this country: including even the Scottish National War Memorial itself, 'built by Scottish brains, Scottish hands, and Scottish money'. [18]

At times, as in nineteenth- and twentieth-century Glasgow, this process involved dramatic transformations, but the energy for these architectural struggles was the product of, and in turn fuelled, wider emotions within the nation. These included the urges to urbanise and to 'improve', and, later, the crusade against social injustice. Time and time again, we have witnessed

C.15 The Shrine, Scottish National War Memorial, Edinburgh (1924–7), late 1920s photograph. The suspended statue of the Archangel Michael was designed by Alice Meredith Williams and carved by the Clow brothers.

not only the shaping of architecture *by* social, political, economic, and religious changes, but also the invigorating impact of architecture *on* those movements, through its monumental and enduring presence. And in today's prevailing climate of building re-use, architecture's ability to accommodate changing meanings, as the most durable and abstract of the visual arts, seems more relevant than ever. Scottish architecture, including the heritage described in this book, is a vital and unfinished story.

Bibliography and Notes

General Introduction

As this book is chiefly a synthesis and interpretation of existing published material, rather than a work of research based on primary sources, there is no conventional apparatus of footnotes. Instead, the notes focus on two limited categories of material – direct quotations and help received – while chapter bibliographies are used to cover other background information. Full title references are contained in the General Bibliography (Part C); the summary citations in the Chapter Bibliographies (Part A) and the Notes (Part B) cross-refer to the full references in Part C.

All three parts draw mainly on secondary published sources, chiefly books and periodical articles. Owing to the scale of the task, we have not attempted to make a general survey of periodicals, books and newspapers. The following is a brief summary of the available material.

Architectural Journals

Scotland has not, so far, enjoyed a fully-fledged architectural press. The only architectural periodicals have been *Prospect* (formerly also the IAS/RIAS *Quarterly*; published from 1922) and shorter-lived efforts such as the *Scottish Architect and Builders' Journal* (published 1938–9 by T. Warnett Kennedy). There is also limited coverage of Scottish architecture in English periodicals such as the *Architects' Journal*, the *Builder* and *Country Life*.

Other Periodicals and Newspapers

A wide range of evidence is contained in Scottish periodicals indirectly concerned with architecture. Key examples include the *Innes Review* (from 1950; on Catholic history); the *Proceedings of the Society of Antiquaries of Scotland* (from 1851; on archaeology); and the *Scottish Historical Review* (from 1903; on mainstream history). A vast amount of information is also contained in national and local newspapers. The most important are: (in Aberdeen) the *Press and Journal* (from 1845; formerly the *North of Scotland Gazette/Aberdeen Free Press/Aberdeen Daily Journal*); (in Dundee) the *Courier* (from 1861; formerly the

Dundee Courier and Advertiser); (in Edinburgh) the *Scotsman* (from 1817; formerly also the *Daily Scotsman*); and (in Glasgow) the *Herald* (from 1789; formerly the *Glasgow Herald/Glasgow Advertiser*).

Serials and Miscellaneous Publications

The three most important series specifically devoted to architecture are the RCAHMS *Inventories*, the *Buildings of Scotland* volumes and the RIAS *Illustrated Architectural Guides*: titles published to date are listed in full at the end of Part C. Of more indirect importance are the volumes of the *Statistical Account* (21 volumes, 1791–8), the *New Statistical Account* (15 volumes, 1834–45) and the *Third Statistical Account* (from 1951). Other published sources concerning architecture, not listed here systematically, include guidebooks to individual buildings, especially those of Historic Scotland and the National Trust for Scotland. Various publications contain compilations of primary source material; examples pertaining to the early part of our period are listed in R. Fawcett, *Scottish Architecture from the Accession of the Stewarts to the Reformation*, 1994, pp. 366–7. The papers of selected practices are listed in R. Bailey, *Scottish Architects' Papers*, 1996. The most comprehensive guide to source material on urban history of all periods is D. Moody's *Scottish Towns: A Guide for Local Historians*, 1992, pp. 135–73. Other compendiums of more general historical source information are G. Donaldson and R. S. Morpeth's *Dictionary of Scottish History*, 1977, and I. Donnachie and G. Hewitt's *Companion to Scottish History*, 1989.

Abbreviations Used in the Bibliography

JSAH	*Journal of the Society of Architectural Historians*
NMRS	National Monuments Record of Scotland
PSAS	*Proceedings of the Society of Antiquaries of Scotland*
Q(R)IAS	*Quarterly* of the (Royal) Incorporation of Architects in Scotland
(R)IAS	(Royal) Incorporation of Architects in Scotland

Part A: Chapter Bibliographies

This section comprises a list of the author names of the most important source-books for the text; these abbreviated names cross-refer to the full citations in Part C. The list begins with works relevant to the whole book or to several chapters. These are followed by individual chapter lists, each sub-categorised into works concerning the historical and architectural background, and (from Chapter 3 onwards) works pertaining to individual architects.

General

Bailey; Buildings of Scotland; Colvin 2, 3; Craig; Cummings and Devine; Davis; Devine; Dunbar 4; Ellis and Cuff; Fenton and Walker; Gomme and Walker; Gordon; Gow 9; Gow and Rowan; G. Hay; Hitchcock; Hume; Lynch 2, 3; Macmillan; Macmillan Encyclopedia; National Library of Scotland; Paul; RCAHMS 1, 2; P. Reed; RIAS 6; P. H. Scott; Vitruvius; Wagner; Walker 8; Worsdall.

Chapter 1

Historical Background
(including royal patronage)

Bawcutt; Baxter; A. Brown; J. M. Brown; Dalyell; Donaldson; Fradenburg; Hamer; D. Hay; Hume Brown; Kidd; Lythe; Macdougall 1, 2; MacQueen; Mason; Sanderson; Stephens; Warrack.

Architecture/Building/Design

Billings; I. Campbell 1, 2; Dickson and Balfour Paul; Dunbar 1, 5, 6; Fawcett 1, 2, 3; Ferguson; Howard 1; Jamieson; MacGibbon and Ross 1, 2; MacIvor; McKean 3, 4; Paton; RIAS 2; J. S. Richardson; Stell 2, 4, 5, 6; Zeune.

Chapter 2

Historical Background
(including royal patronage)

K. M. Brown; Donaldson; Laing; Lee; Lynch 1; MacRoberts; Mason; Sanderson; Seton 1, 2; Stevenson; Warrack.

Architecture/Building/Design

Apted; Bath; Billings; Bryce and Roberts; Cavers (Slezer); Fawcett 1, 2; Hannay and Robertson; Hart; Howard 1; Imrie and Dunbar; MacGibbon and Ross 1, 2; MacIvor; McKean 7; Murray; Mylne 1, 2; Paton; RIAS 2; Slade 2; Somerville; Stell 2, 3, 5; Wood 2; Zeune.

Chapter 3

Historical Background
(including royal patronage)

Campbell and Skinner; Colley; Donaldson; Ouston; Philipson and Mitchison; Warrack.

Architecture/Building/Design

Barnard & Clark; I. Brown 1; C. Campbell; Cavers (Slezer); Clough; Colvin 1, 3; Cruft; Dingwall; Dunbar 3, 7; Gow and Rowan; Holloway; Innes-Smith; Jones; Kuyper; Lindsay and Cosh; Louw; Lowrey 3; Macaulay 1, 3; Macky; Nuttgens 2; Palladio; Pérouse de Montclos; Piggott; Pryke 1, 2; Society of Architectural Historians; Spink; Stell 1; Tabraham and Grove; Tait 2; *Vitruvius Scoticus*; Wood 1, 2.

Architects

ADAM (WILLIAM): Cosh; Gifford; Gow 7; Rowan 3, 5; Simpson; *Vitruvius Scoticus*. BRUCE: Dunbar 2, 3; Howard 2; Lowrey 2; Rowan 3; Scottish Arts Council. CAMPBELL (COLEN): Campbell; Goodfellow; Stutchbury. DOUGLAS: Gow 5. EDWARD: Lowrey. GIBBS Friedman 1; Little; Roberts. MAR: Friedman 2; Stewart 1, 2, 3, 4. SMITH: Dunbar and Cornforth 6; James Smith Anniversary Committee; Roberts.

Chapter 4

Historical Background

Campbell and Skinner; Devine and Jackson; Mitchison; Philipson and Mitchison.

Architecture/Building/Design: General

Brogden; Colvin 3; Donnachie and Hewitt; Gow 1; Howard and Kuznetsov; Kames; Kauffman; Lindsay and Cosh; Macaulay 1, 3; Markus 1, 2; Nuttgens 2; Perouse de Montclos; Rosenau; Saumarez Smith; Shvidkovski 1; Tait 2; D. M. Walker 8; Wood 2; Youngson.

Architects

ADAM (ROBERT AND JAMES): R. Adam; R. and J. Adam; Beard; Bolton; I. Brown 2, 3; N. M. Cameron 2; Emerson; Fleming 1, 2, 3, 4; A. G. Fraser; King; MacInnes; Rowan 1, 4, 5; Sanderson; Stillman; Tait 1, 4, 5; F. A. Walker 3. BYRES: Slade 2. CAMERON: Rae; Salmon; Shvidkovski 2. CHAMBERS: Chambers; Harris. CRAIG: Cruft and Fraser; Lewis and Lowrey.

Chapter 5

Historical Background
Anderson; Brown and Fry; Cleland; Daiches; Devine and Jackson; Durie; Grant; MacUre; Sweeney.

Architecture/Building/Design: General
Allen; Billings; Bindman and Reimann; Britton; Colvin 2; Crook; Durand; Gow 1, 6; Howard and Kuznetsov; Macaulay 1; Markus 1, 2; Maxwell Scott; J Reed; Wainwright 1, 2; D. M. Walker 8; Wood 2; Youngson.

Architects
BURN: D. M. Walker 4, 6. GILLESPIE GRAHAM: Macaulay 2. HAMILTON (DAVID): MacKechnie; Tait 5; Watters 2. HAMILTON (THOMAS) Fisher; Rock. KEMP: Bonnar. PLAYFAIR (W. H.): A G Fraser; Gow 2, 4, 8; Gow and Clifford. ROBERTSON (W.): Beaton. SIMPSON: Aberdeen Civic Society; Higgs.

Chapter 6

Historical Background
Brown and Fry; Checkland; Fraser and Morris; Lynch 3; Sweeney.

Architecture/Building/Design: General
Chisholm; Corporation of Glasgow 1; Dixon and Muthesius; Edwards 1, 2; Frew 2; Gowans; Hardie; W. Payne; P. Reed; Ruskin; D. M. Walker 8; Watson; Wood 2; Worsdall.

Architects
BRYCE: Allan; Fiddes and Rowan; Rowan 2; D. M. Walker 5. BURN: D. M. Walker 4, 6. GOWANS: McAra.HAMILTON (DAVID): Mackechnie. PILKINGTON: Jeffery. RHIND: Gow 3. THOMSON (ALEXANDER): McFadzean; Stamp and McKinstry. WILSON: Sinclair; Thomson.

Chapter 7

Historical Background
Checkland; Fraser and Morris; Scott and Hughes.

Architecture/Building/Design: General
Architectural Heritage; H. Begg; Chisholm; Cohen; Corporation of Glasgow 1; Cumming 1; Cumming and Caplan; Drexler; Edwards 1, 2; Hunter Blair; P. and J. Kinchin; MacGibbon and Ross 1; National Association for the Advancement of Art; Nicoll; H. Richardson 1; D. M. Walker 8, 9; F. A. Walker 2; Worsdall.

Architects
ANDERSON: McKinstry 1, 2; Smailes. BROWNE: Mays 2.

BURNET AND CAMPBELL: D. M. Walker 1, 9, 11. FAIRLIE: Nuttgens 1. GEDDES: Edinburgh Review; Grieve; Johnston; Meller; Scottish Geographical Magazine. KERR: Swan. KINROSS: Mays 1. LEIPER: Green. LORIMER: Macbeth; S. R. Matthew; H. Richardson 2; Savage. MACKINTOSH: Brett; Eadie; Howarth; Kaplan; Macaulay 5, 6; Macleod; Neat; Pevsner; P Robertson; D. M.Walker 2. MACLAREN: Royal Institute of British Architects. MILLER: Sloan 1, 2. MITCHELL: Dunlop. NOBBS: Wagg. PATERSON: Riches. SALMON AND GILLESPIE: Cusack; D. M. Walker 3; F. A. Walker 1. SCHULTZ: Stamp. TRAQUAIR: Cumming 2. YOUNG: Young.

Chapter 8

Historical Background
Bowie; Devine and Findlay; Dickson and Treble; Gibson; Harvie 1; London Scots; Mackenzie; Scott and Hughes; Ward.

Architecture/Building/Design: General
Architects' Journal 2; Cohen; Hurd 1; McKean 1; Ockman; P. L. Payne; Reiach and Hurd; *Scottish Architect and Builders' Journal.*

Town and Country Planning
Abercrombie and Matthew; Abercrombie and Plumstead; R. Bruce; Dobson Chapman and Riley; Grieve; Mann; Mears; Osborn and Whittick; Smith and Wannop.

Housing
T. Begg; Corporation of Glasgow 2; Department of Health for Scotland 1, 2, 3; Frew 1; Glendinning and Muthesius; Jury; Scottish Housing Advisory Committee; Scottish Office Building Directorate.

Conservation
G. Bruce; Bute; Hannah; Horsey; Hurd 2; Kelsall and Harris; Lindsay 1, 2; NMRS; Pittaway; Scott-Moncrieff 1, 2, 3; Stirling-Maxwell; D. M. Walker 10.

Architects
BURNET, TAIT & LORNE(including 1938 Glasgow Empire Exhibition): J. N. Baxter; Sir J. Burnet & Partners; Crampsey; Fox; Gold; P. and J. Kinchin; *1938 Exhibition Official Guide*; D. M. Walker 7. FAIRLIE: Nuttgens 2. GILLESPIE, KIDD & COIA: *Mac Journal*; Rogerson. HOUSTON: N. M. Cameron. KERR: Swan. KININMONTH: Pentreath. LORIMER: I. Hay; Scottish National War Memorial; Weaver. MATTHEW (R. H. AND RMJM: *Architects' Journal* 1; Richards 1; Spaven. MEARS: Purves. MILLER: Sloan 1, 2. REIACH: Reiach and Hurd.

SPENCE: L. Campbell 1, 2, 3; Edwards 3; MacGregor.
STEEL MAITLAND: Hamilton.

Chapter 9

Historical Background
Devine and Findlay; Dickson and Treble; Gibson; Glasgow City Council; Glasgow's Glasgow; Harvie 1, 2; Lynch 3; Patterson; Scottish Council (Development and Industry).

Architecture/Building/Design: General
Architect and Building News; *Architects' Journal* 2; Ellis and Cuff; Finch and Melvin; Gilbert and Flint; Glendinning and Muthesius; Inland Revenue; Keating 1, 2; Kemp; McKean 2, 6; Matthew, Reid and Lindsay; Ockman; RIAS 1, 3, 4, 5; D. S. Robertson; Scott & Wilson, Kirkpatrick & Partners; Scottish Development Department 1, 2, 3, 4, 5; Scottish Home and Health Department; Walker 10; Willis.

Architects
ASSIST: Hook. CUMBERNAULD NEW TOWN DEVELOPMENT CORPORATION: Architectural Design; Banham. GASSON (et al.): Marks et al. GILLESPIE, KIDD & COIA: *Architects' Journal* 3; *Mac Journal*; Rogerson; Watters 1. MATTHEW (R. H.) and RMJM: Richards 1, 2; University of Edinburgh. MORRIS & STEEDMAN: Macintosh. WOMERSLEY: *RIBA Journal*.

Part B: Notes

These notes, which refer to the superscript numbers in the main text, are largely concerned with direct quotations (in which a secondary source is in many cases cited) and acknowledgements of help received. In the case of authors cited without title, and journal names cited without date, please refer to the full citation in Part C. Owing to space constraints, these notes are in summary form.

Chapter 1

(1) Macdougall 1, p. 98.
(2) Bawcutt, p. 93.
(3) A. Brown, p. 43.
(4) 'fredome': Mason, p. 56.
(5) Mason, p. 56.
(6) Mason, p. 59.
(7) I. Campbell 1; Fawcett 3.
(8) 'Architecture of mass': letter from C. McKean, 1995.
(9) I. Campbell 1, p. 5 ('in more alpinatum' interpreted as 'albainn').
(10) Bawcutt, p. 92.
(11) Macdougall 1, p. 98.
(12) Lynch 2, p. 145.
(13) Hume Brown, p. 41; J. W. Baxter, p. 176.
(14) 'Arthuris-Sete': J. Grant, *Cassell's Old and New Edinburgh* 2, 1882, p. 305.
(15) Mason, p. 60.
(16) A. M. Mackenzie (ed.), *Scottish Pageant*, 1946, p. 119.
(17) G. Eyre-Todd (ed.), *Scottish Poetry of the 16th Century*, 1892 (1971 reprint), p. 160.
(18) Palace: I. Campbell 1, p. 12.
(19) *Palatium ad modum castri*: I. Campbell 1, p. 314.
(20) Pavia: I. Campbell 1, p. 318.
(21) Bawcutt, p. 133.
(22) Bawcutt, p. 93.
(23) 'Battaling': RCAHMS, *Midlothian and West Lothian*, 1929, p. 225.
(24) King's House: Fawcett 3, p. 317.
(25) Dickson and Balfour Paul 2, pp. 23, 213, 216.
(26) Jamieson.
(27) Hamer, p. 75.
(28) 1481 and 1535 acts: Zeune, pp. 114 and 134; 1528 act: Fawcett 3, p. 237.
(29) 'Sub-department': Lynch 2, p. 155.
(30) A. J. G. Mackay (ed.), *The Historie and Cronicles of Scotland*, 1899, p. 339.
(31) I. Campbell 2, p. 1.
(32) Finnart: McKean 3.

(33) McKean 4.
(34) 'Best and mest plesand': C Rogers, *History of the Chapel Royal of Scotland*, 1882, p. lxxxvi.
(35) 'Haldis . . .': A. Murray, 'Financing the Royal Household', in I. Cowan and D. Shaw (eds), *The Renaissance and Reformation in Scotland*, 1983, p. 58. 'Palice': PSAS, 1940–1, p. 185.
(36) J. Major, *A History of Greater Britain* (1892edn), cited by G. Stell in J. M. Brown, 1977, p. 164.
(37) Hume Brown, p. 47.
(38) S. Cruden, *The Scottish Castle*, 1981, p. 141.
(39) Mackay, *Historie and Cronicles*, pp. 336–8.
(40) Names of houses: Zeune, pp. 95–101.
(41) 'Foirwerk': Howard 1, p. 218.
(42) Information from C. McKean.
(43) 'Mansio cum aula': Zeune, p. 25.

Chapter 2

(1) Hume Brown, pp. 111, 139.
(2) Laing, p. 64.
(3) Lynch 1.
(4) M. Pittock, *The Myth of the Jacobite Clans*, 1995, p. 90.
(5) Howard 1.
(6) 'Darsy': Howard 1, p. 188.
(7) Warrack, p. 99.
(8) Stevenson, p. 26.
(9) Denmark: information from Charles McKean.
(10) Colvin 2, 1978 edn, p. 862.
(11) 1618 and 1636: Hume Brown, pp. 111 and 139.
(12) Imrie and Dunbar, p. 269.
(13) M. Lynch, 'Scottish Culture in its Historical Perspective', in P. H. Scott, p. 17.
(14) *Black Book of Taymouth*, 1855, p. 77.
(15) Lithgow: Hume Brown, p. 299.
(16) Bryce and Roberts.
(17) R. Maitland, *The History of the House of Seytoun to the Year 1559*, 1829, p. 63, cited in Bath.
(18) Bishop Leslie 1578: Howard 1, p. 48.
(19) Laing, pp. 67, 65–6, 68, 63–5, 64.
(20) Howard 1, p. 48.
(21) Seton north-east quarter: Stevenson, p. 29. 'New wark': I. A. G. Shepherd, *Exploring Scotland's Heritage: Grampian*, 1986, p. 85.
(22) Slade 1, p. 154.
(23) Balfour: Fawcett 3, p. 261.
(24) 'Sumptuous and glorious palace': D. Calderwood, *The History of the Kirk of Scotland*, 1842–9, vii, p. 153.
(25) Imrie and Dunbar, p. lxix.

(26) Hume Brown, p. 133.

(27) 'Most sweit garden': 1668 description by Lauder in D. Crawford (ed.), *Journals of Sir John Lauder*, 1900, p. 189.

(28) Bath, pp. 79–108.

(29) A. M. Mackenzie (ed.), *Scottish Pageant 1513–1625*, 1948, p. 47.

(30) Hume Brown, p. 93.

(31) Hume Brown, p. 219.

(32) A. M. Mackenzie (ed.), *Scottish Pageant 1625–1707*, 1949, p. 18.

(33) RCAHMS, *Tolbooths and Town Houses*, draft introduction, 1995, p. 47.

(34) 'Paterne and prescript': Howard 1, p. 137.

(35) Denmark: information from C. McKean. Jorevin de Rocheford: Hume Brown, p. 222.

(36) Hume Brown, p. 223.

(37) MacGibbon and Ross 1, vol. 4, 1892, p. 161.

Chapter 3

(1) Fleming 2, p. 331.

(2) Cited Lowrey 2, p. 3.

(3) Gifford, p. 6.

(4) p. 128.

(5) Pérouse de Montclos, p. 242.

(6) J. G. Fyfe (ed.), *Scottish Diaries & Memoirs 1550–1746*, Stirling 1928, p. 181.

(7) MacGibbon and Ross 1, vol. 2, p. 64.

(8) 'Skandalous': Macaulay 3, p. 48.

(9) E.g. Earl of Lauderdale on Thirlestane as 'Castle' in 1671: C. A. Strang, *Borders & Berwick*, 1994, p. 191.

(10) National Library of Scotland, p. 8.

(11) 'Everie man . . .': Macaulay 3, p. 48. 'No man . . .': Howard 1, p. 53. 'Inflam'd . . .': Scottish Historical Society, *The Book of Record*, 1890, p. 41. 'My Great Hall', 'Tho' it be an old house . . .': R. Innes Smith, p. 27.

(12) Brunstane: Macaulay 3, p. 12.

(13) Dunbar 3, p. 208.

(14) 'Pavillions': R. K. Marshall, 'Scarce a Finer Seat in Scotland', in Gow and Rowan, p. 36.

(15) NMRS reference DFD/58/3.

(16) Macaulay 4, p. 19.

(17) Dunbar and Cornforth.

(18) Lowrey 2, p. 3.

(19) Clough, p. 75.

(20) Gallery House, 1677 contract: J. G. Dunbar and K. Davies (eds), 'Some Late Seventeenth-Century Building Contracts', *Miscellany of the Scottish History Society* 11, 1890.

(21) Macaulay 3, p. 14.

(22) N. M. Cameron 3, p. 367.

(23) Macaulay 3, p. 19.

(24) Cited in Lowrey 2, p. 3.

(25) 'True ancient simple taste': Friedman 2, p. 108.

(26) 'Upon suspition': H. Fenwick, *Architect Royal*, 1970, p. 78. Edward's instructions: Lowrey 1, p. 19.

(27) Stewart 3, p. 8.

(28) All quotations, National Library of Scotland, pp. 10 and 70.

(29) Stewart 3, p. 13.

(30) Stewart 3, p. 44.

(31) Stewart 3, p. 66.

(32) Colvin 2, p. 296.

(33) Stewart 3, p. 21; Friedman 2, pp. 115 and 112.

(34) Friedman 2, p. 106.

(35) Stewart 3, Friedman 2.

(36) Friedman 2, p. 113.

(37) Friedman 2, p. 106.

(38) Friedman 2, p. 107.

(39) Stewart 3, p. 9.

(40) Stewart 3, p. 35.

(41) Gifford, p. 129.

(42) J. Gibbs, *A Book of Architecture*, 1728, pp. 2–3.

(43) Colvin 2, p. 182.

(44) 'Temple Beauties': National Library of Scotland, p. 31.

(45) Barnard and Clark (introduction by H. Colvin and chapter by J. Clark).

(46) J. G. Dunbar, 'The Building of Yester House', *Transactions of the East Lothian Antiquarian and Field Naturalists' Society* 13, 1972.

(47) Clerk: Spink, p. 32. Blair: *Country Life*, 4 November 1949, p. 1, 366.

(48) Gow 5, p. 4.

(49) Macaulay 3, p. 87.

(50) H. Hamilton (ed.), *Selections from the Monymusk Papers*, 1945, p. 78.

(51) Macaulay 3, pp. 92–3.

(52) Macaulay 3, p. 80.

(53) Gifford, p. 81.

(54) Hadrian's Wall: information from J. Lowrey. 'Classicks': Macaulay 3, p. 63.

(55) Gifford, p. 81.

(56) Gifford, p. 83.

(57) Gifford, p. 83.

(58) Mackenzie: H. H. Wood (ed.), *James Watson's Choice Collection of Comic and Serious Scots Poems*, vol. 1, 1977. Clerk: Spink, p. 33; Piggott, pp. 112 and 115.

(59) Colvin 3, p. 99.

(60) Gifford, p. 90.

(61) 'Like a touer': J. M. Gray (ed.), *Memoirs of the Life of Sir John Clerk of Penicuik*, 1892, p. 115.

(62) 'Landscap': Macaulay 3, p. 62. Tivoli: Spink, p. 35.
(63) Macaulay 3, pp. 101–2.
(64) Colvin 1, p. 18.
(65) J. Gifford, 'William Adam and the Historians', *Architectural Heritage* 1, 1990, p. 1.
(66) W. R. M. Kay, *Architectural Heritage* 1, 1990, p. 50.
(67) Gifford, p. 20.
(68) J. Lowrey (review), *Architectural Heritage* 1, 1990, p. 118.
(69) Macaulay 3, p. 77.
(70) Decker: Rowan 5, pp. 18–20.
(71) 'Great Plan': Lowrey 3.
(72) Information from F. Jamieson.
(73) Macaulay 3, p. 77.
(74) 'Enterprising': Kay, p. 50.
(75) Macaulay 3, p. 165.
(76) Gow 5, p. 4.
(77) Macaulay 3, p. 130.
(78) Tait 2.
(79) Dingwall, p. 133.
(80) Dingwall, p. 138.
(81) RCAHMS, *The City of Edinburgh*, 1951, p. 160.
(82) Macky, p. 81.
(83) Tabraham and Grove, p. 12. Covert Jacobite: J. Clark, 'Lord Burlington is here', in Barnard and Clark.
(84) RCAHMS, *Tolbooths and Town Houses* manuscript.
(85) Colvin 2, p. 530.
(86) Scottish Arts Council, p. 12.

Chapter 4
(1) Letter from D. Hume to W Strahan (1770): J. Greig (ed.), *Letters of David Hume*, 2, 1932, p.230.
(2) R. and J. Adam, vol. 1, pt 4, 1776 (1975 edn, p. 54).
(3) Quotation from James Thomson's poem, 'Prospect of Britain': James Craig's Edinburgh New Town engraved plan of 1768.
(4) Youngson, p. 26.
(5) Colvin 2, p. 47.
(6) A. T. Milne (ed.), *The Correspondence of Jeremy Bentham* 4, 1981, p. 310.
(7) Letter from D. Hume to W. Strahan (1770): J. Greig (ed.), *Letters of David Hume*, 2, 1932, p. 230.
(8) National Library of Scotland, p. 66.
(9) I. Brown 3, pp. 10 and 11.
(10) National Library of Scotland, p. 30.
(11) Saumarez Smith, p. 216.
(12) Tait 5, p. 136.
(13) Cited by I. G. Brown in Gow and Rowan, p. 16.

(14) Sanderson 2, p. 58; M. H. B. Sanderson, 'Trivial Pursuit?', *Architectural Heritage* 4, 1993, pp. 70–1; I. G. Brown 3, p. 11; Saumarez Smith, p. 216.
(15) R. and J. Adam, vol. 1, pt 4, 1776 (1975 edn, p. 54).
(16) R. and J. Adam, vol. 1, pt 1, 1773 (1975 edn, p. 48).
(17) R. and J. Adam, vol. 1, pt 1, 1773 (1975 edn, p. 47).
(18) R. and J. Adam, vol. 1, pt 1, 1773 (1975 edn, p. 46).
(19) R. and J. Adam, vol. 1, pt 1, 1773 (1975 edn, p. 46).
(20) R. and J. Adam, vol.1, pt 1, 1773 (1975 edn, p. 45, 47).
(21) I. Brown 3, p. 49.
(22) Adams on Kedleston: R. and J. Adam, vol. 1, pt 1, 1773 (1975 edn, p. 46). 'Excessively and ridiculously bad': Worsley, p. 248. 'Noble and elegant . . .': R. and J. Adam, vol. 1, pt 1, 1773 (1975 edn, p. 48).
(23) R. and J. Adam, vol.1, part 1, 1773 (1975 edn, p. 49).
(24) R. and J. Adam, vol. 2, 1779 (1975 edn, p. 61).
(25) R. and J. Adam, vol. 1, part 1, 1773 (1975 edn, p. 45).
(26) R. Adam on Spalato 1764: cited in Macaulay 3, p. 152.
(27) Sanderson 2, p. 44.
(28) Colvin 2, p. 181.
(29) G. Donaldson and R. S. Morpeth, *A Dictionary of Scottish History*, 1988, p. 148.
(30) Macaulay 3, p. 181.
(31) D. M. Walker and C. McWilliam, *Country Life*, 28 January 1971.
(32) Fleming 4.
(33) Sanderson 2, p. 88.
(34) Sanderson 2, p. 91.
(35) R. Emerson, cited in J. Thomas, *Midlothian*, 1995, p. 37; Emerson, p. 166.
(36) J. Thomas, *Midlothian*, 1995, p. 37.
(37) Bruce: J. Grant, *Old and New Edinburgh*, 1882, p. 336. Friedman 2, p. 109.
(38) Cruft and Fraser, p. 49.
(39) Letter from D. Hume to W. Strahan (1770): J. Greig (ed.), *Letters of David Hume* 2, 1932, p. 230.
(40) Information from J. Lowrey and J. Hume.
(41) Youngson, pp. 113 and 116.
(42) C. Byrom, 'The Pleasure Grounds of Edinburgh New Town', *Garden History*, Summer 1995, p. 67.

(43)   Colvin 2 (1995 edn), p. 487.
(44)   National Library of Scotland, p. 36.
(45)   Sanderson 2, p. 114; National Library of Scotland, p. 39; National Library NS 3431 FF214-5.
(46)   National Library of Scotland, p. 39; National Library MS 3108-F41.
(47)   Scottish Record Office GD 18 4961/37, letter from Mary Drysdale.
(48)   Shetland Archive, Lerwick Dean of Guild files, memo 13 March 1908 from J. M. Aitken, contractor, to Town Clerk.

Chapter 5
(1)   G. d'Eichthal, *A French Sociologist looks at Britain*, 1977, p. 74. Scott: Wainwright, p. 14.
(2)   S. J. Brown, *Thomas Chalmers and the Godly Commonwealth in Scotland*, 1982, p. 30.
(3)   Wainwright, p. 14.
(4)   Pérouse de Montclos, p. 399.
(5)   J. Gifford, C. McWilliam and D. M. Walker, *Edinburgh*, 1984, p. 437.
(6)   Colvin 2, p. 46.
(7)   Markus 2, p. 136.
(8)   RCAHMS, *Dundee on Record*, 1992, p. 21.
(9)   Colvin 2, p. 776.
(10)   Gow 2, p. 46.
(11)   'Patient study': Gow 4, pp. 1, 3. 'Nothing good': Colvin 3, p. 645.
(12)   Gow 2, p. 46.
(13)   Cited in F. A. Walker, 'National Romanticism', in Gordon, p. 127.
(14)   F. A. Walker, 'National Romanticism', in Gordon, p. 129.
(15)   Gow 2, p. 46.
(16)   Gow 2.
(17)   Gifford et al., Edinburgh, p. 406.
(18)   Stark quotations: Youngson, p. 151. Playfair 'tame monotony', Youngson, p. 154. Playfair 'new Town': Colvin 3, p. 646.
(19)   Gow 9, p. 52; Gow and Clifford, p. 47. Moray Place houses, I. R. Gow, 'The Northern Athenian House', *Scottish Local History*, June 1995.
(20)   Rock, p. 17.
(21)   Gow 2, p. 45.
(22)   Gow and Clifford.
(23)   *Journal of the Society of Artists*, 16 December 1846.
(24)   Gow and Clifford, p. 22.
(25)   Cited in Gow 2, p. 54.
(26)   Devine and Jackson, p. 10.
(27)   Devine and Jackson, p. 10.

(28)   S. J. Brown, *Thomas Chalmers*, 1982, title page.
(29)   L. Smith, *Northern Sketches of Glasgow*, 1809: cited by J. Kinchin in Stamp and McKinstry.
(30)   D. Bindmann and G. Riemann (eds), *K. F. Schinkel, 'The English Journey'*, New Haven, 1993, pp. 150, 174, 197.
(31)   M. Walker, *Chatelherault Country Park*, 1989.
(32)   Tait 3.
(33)   Tait 3, p. 395.
(34)   Cited in I. R. Gow, 'David Hamilton and Hamilton Palace', in Mackechnie.
(35)   D. Walker 'Burn and Bryce', in Fiddes and Rowan.
(36)   Gow 8, p. 81.
(37)   C .McKean, *The District of Moray*, 1987, p. 51.
(38)   J. Rock, 'Relugas and the Dick Lauder Family', in Gow and Rowan, p. 274.
(39)   Colvin 2, 1995 edn, p. 320.
(40)   *A Sketch of a Tour in the Highlands of Scotland*, 1819.
(41)   'Norman': Watters 2, p. 60.
(42)   Walker 4.
(43)   Gow 4, p. 4.
(44)   Gow 8.
(45)   NMRS, GD121, Box101, vol. XXI, 127.
(46)   National Library of Scotland, p. 56.
(47)   S. Nenadic, in Devine and Jackson.
(48)   Lord Cockburn 1852, cited in J. G. Fyfe (ed.), *Scottish Diaries and Memoirs 1746–1843*, p. 420.
(49)   Gifford et al., *Edinburgh*, p. 40.
(50)   F. Worsdall, *The City that Disappeared*, 1981, p. 81.
(51)   D. M. Walker 8.
(52)   Rock, p. 58.
(53)   Sir W. Scott, *The Letters of Malachi Malagrowther*, 1826 (1981 edn), p. 143.
(54)   R. Emerson, cited in J. Thomas, *Midlothian*, 1995, p. 37.
(55)   National Library of Scotland, p. 55.
(56)   National Library of Scotland, p. 76.
(57)   National Library of Scotland, p. 76, Scott 1816: Wainwright 1, p. 14. See also Wainwright 2.
(58)   Gow 9, p. 42.
(59)   Gow 9, p. 40.
(60)   Gow 9, p. 42.
(61)   Howard and Kuznetsov; K. Kretkowska, 'Scotland in the Life of the Polish Country Estate', in T. C. Smout (ed.), *Scotland and Europe*, 1986, p. 183.
(62)   J. F. Methven, *An Appreciation of the Life and Work of G. M. Kemp*, 1988, p. 16.
(63)   Bonnar, pp. 108 and 128.

Chapter 6

(1) Cited by C .McKean, 'In Search of Purity', in Stamp and McKinstry.
(2) *Building Chronicle*, 1 January 1854, cited in McKean, 'In Search of Purity'.
(3) Cited in *London Review of Books*, 6 April 1995.
(4) *Building Chronicle*, 9 November 1854, cited in McKean, 'In Search of Purity'.
(5) Thomson, p. 8.
(6) D. M. Watters, in Sinclair.
(7) *Building Chronicle*, April 1857, p. 185, cited in C. McKean, 'In Search of Purity'.
(8) Eternity: 2nd Haldane Lecture.
(9) *Alexander Thomson Society Newsletter*, May 1995, pp. 4–5, and December 1995, p. 10.
(10) 2nd/4th Haldane Lectures.
(11) 2nd Haldane Lecture.
(12) 3rd Haldane Lecture.
(13) 4th Haldane Lecture.
(14) Alexander Thomson, *Enquiry into the Appropriateness of the Gothic Style for the University of Glasgow*, 1866.
(15) R. Macleod, *Style and Society*, 1971, p. 72.
(16) 1st Haldane Lecture.
(17) 2nd, 1st and 2nd Haldane Lectures.
(18) 1st Haldane Lecture; Thomson, *Enquiry*; Stamp and McKinstry, p. 65.
(19) *British Architect* 2, 1874, p. 51.
(20) Cited in J. M. McKean, *AA Files*, 1985.
(21) 1st Haldane Lecture.
(22) Edwards 2.
(23) Sweeney, p. 330.
(24) *Building Chronicle*, 1 January 1855, cited in C. McKean, 'In Search of Purity'.
(25) E. Williamson, A. Riches and M. Higgs, *Glasgow*, 1990, p. 599.
(26) D. Thomson, text p. 7.
(27) Gow 9.
(28) Harmonic proportion: 1993 lecture by I. R. Gow at RCAHMS.
(29) McAra, p. 13.
(30) Ruskin; Lord Cockburn, *Memorials of his Time*, 1856.
(31) A. Macpherson (ed.), *Report of a Committee of the Working Classes of Edinburgh*, 1860.
(32) Billings, vol. 1; 1853 Act, cited by F. A. Walker in Gordon, p. 149.
(33) F. A. Walker in Gordon, p. 151.
(34) National Association for the Advancement of Art, p. 182.
(35) Billings, vol. 3 (Kilravock).
(36) National Library of Scotland, p. 79.
(37) R. Kerr, *The Gentleman's House*, 1864, p. 57.

(38) Balfour: J. Gifford, *Highland and Islands*, 1992, p. 360.
(39) Billings, vol. 4 (Udny).
(40) *Building Chronicle*, 9 November 1854, cited in C. McKean, 'In Search of Purity'.
(41) Wilson: D. Thomson, p. 2.
(42) F. Worsdall, *The City that Disappeared*, 1981, p. 85.
(43) *Building Chronicle*, 1 April 1856, cited in C. McKean, 'In Search of Purity'.
(44) J. Fleming (1916): cited in McFadzean, p. 97.
(45) 'Quiet and massive': J. F. O'Gorman, *Three American Architects*, Chicago 1991, p. 37.
(46) Drummond, p. 83.
(47) Drummond, p. 88.
(48) 'Beauty of holiness' and general developments in mid-nineteenth-century Episcopal church architecture: information from Tristram Clarke.
(49) National Library of Scotland, p. 74.
(50) D. Thomson, p. 9.
(51) A. Thomson, *Enquiry*.
(52) Cited by F. A. Walker in Gordon, p. 142.
(53) Cumming 2, p. 16.
(54) *British Architect*, 21 December 1883.
(55) E. Hardie, *A Short History of . . . W. Scott Morton & Co.*, MSS 1976 (NMRS).
(56) *British Architect*, 4 March 1894.
(57) *British Architect* 14, 1880, p. 16; 18, 1882.

Chapter 7

(1) *British Architect*, 1 April 1892, p. 225.
(2) Savage, p. 20.
(3) Mackintosh, 'Seemliness' lecture, cited in P. Robertson.
(4) *Description of . . . Laying the Foundation Stone of the Municipal Buildings*, 1885, p. 1.
(5) *British Architect*, 1 April 1892, p. 225.
(6) *British Architect*, 1 April 1892, p. 225.
(7) *British Architect* 17, 1882, p. 181.
(8) *RIBA Journal*, 26 June 1920.
(9) *British Architect*, 1 April 1892, p. 225.
(10) D. M. Walker 9, p. 27.
(11) *Scottish Arts Review* 1, 1889, p. 192.
(12) D. M. Walker 9.
(13) *British Architect* 16, 1881, p. 377.
(14) Young, p. 25.
(15) *RIBA Journal*, 26 June 1920; *British Architect* 18, 1882, p. 427.
(16) *British Architect*, 1 April 1892, p. 225.
(17) G. Stamp, *Perspectives*, July 1994, p. 44.
(18) Gowans: *British Architect*, 25 September 1885.
(19) *Edinburgh Architectural Association Transactions*, 1890, 'Incongruity': Address by J. H. A.

Macdonald to Edinburgh Architectural
Association, 4 November 1907, p. 101.

(20) *Glasgow Herald*, 17 April 1900.

(21) *British Architect*, 10 May 1912.

(22) R. S. Lorimer, 1894: cited in Savage, p. 113.

(23) R. S. Lorimer, 1897: cited in Savage, p. 20.

(24) Anderson: *British Architect*, 6 December 1907.

(25) *Scottish Arts Review* 1, 1889.

(26) H. Muthesius, *The English House*, 1979 edn,
p. 61.

(27) *British Architect*, 6 December 1907. National
Association for the Advancement of Art, p. 363.

(28) Nicoll.

(29) *British Architect*, 25 November 1892.

(30) National Association for the Advancement of
Art, pp. 149–54; foreword to Billings, 1901 edn.

(31) National Association for the Advancement of
Art, p. 155.

(32) *British Architect*, 27 April 1883.

(33) *British Architect*, 5 March 1880, p. 112.

(34) Savage, pp. 20 and 92; *British Architect*,
20 April 1900.

(35) Savage, pp. 65 and 83; Macbeth.

(36) Savage, pp. 51 (on 1897), 115, 92.

(37) 'Sanctuary': *Architectural Review*, November
1899. 'When you go into a room': Lorimer,
1897, cited in Savage, p. 51.

(38) Savage, p. 20 (on 1890s).

(39) Savage, p. 70.

(40) Savage, pp. 130–1.

(41) Savage, p. 22.

(42) Savage, p. 115.

(43) J. J. Stevenson, *House Architecture*, 1880, p. 377.

(44) *Builders' Journal*, 12 January 1898, p. 487.

(45) *Glasgow News* book of views of 1911 exhibition
(NMRS).

(46) *Scottish Geographical Magazine*.

(47) National Association for the Advancement of
Art, p. 20.

(48) R. L. Stevenson, *Edinburgh: Picturesque Notes*,
1903 edn, pp. 13, 70, 78.

(49) *Evergreen*, Spring 1895; National Association
for the Advancement of Art, p. 307.

(50) National Association for the Advancement of
Art, p. 301.

(51) National Association for the Advancement of
Art, p. 307.

(52) Johnston.

(53) Richardson 1.

(54) H. Muthesius, *The English House*, 1979 edn,
p. 51.

(55) H. Muthesius, *The English House*, p. 52.

(56) Mackintosh, 'Seemliness': P. Robertson.

(57) Mackintosh, 1892 lecture: P. Robertson.

(58) *Builders' Journal and . . . Engineer*, 25 March
1908.

(59) Cusack, p. 200.

(60) *British Architect*, 25 October 1907.

(61) Drummond, p. 88.

(62) *British Architect*, 1881, p. 664.

(63) *British Architect*, 1888, p. 151.

(64) *British Architect*, 29 August 1884.

(65) 'Essence of Gothic': S. R. Matthew, *The Knights
and Chapel of the Thistle*, Edinburgh 1988, p. 25.

(66) QIAS 7, 1923.

(67) Savage, p. 99.

(68) G. Stamp (ed.), *Mount Stuart*, 1995.

(69) W. Diack, *The Rise and Progress of the Granite
Industry in Aberdeen*, 1949, p. iii.

Chapter 8

(1) Tait, cited in D. M. Walker 7, p. 51.

(2) Mackenzie, p. 376.

(3) Matthew: QRIAS, August 1952.

(4) F. A. Walker, *Prospect* 19, 1960.

(5) Stamp, *Mount Stuart*, p. 9.

(6) QIAS 8, 1923.

(7) QIAS 8, 1923; QIAS 11, 1924.

(8) Henry R. Kerr, *Edinburgh Architectural
Association Transactions* 10, 1933; Stirling-
Maxwell, p. 205; QRIAS 38, 1932.

(9) Savage, p. 150.

(10) QRIAS 40, 1932.

(11) QRIAS 31, 1929.

(12) QRIAS 38, 1932.

(13) Savage, pp. 149 and 148.

(14) QRIAS 51, 1935.

(15) QIAS 14, 1925.

(16) Hurd 2, p. 6.

(17) QIAS 2, 1922, p. 19.

(18) QIAS 26, 1928.

(19) Johnston: QRIAS 43, 1933; Strictly monumental': QRIAS 48, 1934–5.

(20) QRIAS, April 1939, p. 6; D. M. Walker 7, p. 39.

(21) D. M. Walker 7, p. 39.

(22) QRIAS 33, 1930, p. 19.

(23) National Library of Scotland, acc. 11024, 1994.

(24) M. Casteels, *The New Style*, Paris 1931, p. 45.

(25) United Publishing Company, *Scottish Legal Life
Assurance Society*, n.d.

(26) Walker 7, p. 39; see also note 1.

(27) McKean 1, p. 85.

(28) QRIAS 47, 1934, p. 52.

(29) NMRS, notes of 1991 interview by N. M.
Cameron; RIAS, reply sheet to 'Scottish
Thirties' survey, 1984.

(30) RIAS, reply sheet to 'Scottish Thirties' survey, 1984.
(31) *QRIAS* 60, 1939, pp. 5–14.
(32) *QRIAS* 60, 1939, p. 11.
(33) Crampsey, p. 153.
(34) Mackenzie, p. 388.
(35) Bowie, p. 154.
(36) W. Power, in Mann.
(37) Reiach and Hurd.
(38) *QRIAS*, November 1947.
(39) For example, J. J. Waddell and J Begg in *QRIAS* 43, 1933, and *The Builder,* 7 July 1933, p. 8.
(40) Bute.
(41) J. Buchan, in 1932: T. Gallagher, *Glasgow, the Uneasy Peace,* 1987, p. 145; Hannah, p. 3.
(42) Mackenzie, pp. 3, 386, 380, 383.
(43) Interview by M. Glendinning with R. Cant, 1991.
(44) J. Steel Maitland, *QRIAS,* August 1952; R. Hurd, *QRIAS,* July 1939, pp. 11–17; R. Hurd, in London Scots Self-Government Committee.
(45) *QRIAS* 51, 1935.
(46) *QRIAS* 38, 1932.
(47) Hurd 1, p. 120.
(48) Craig, vol. 4, pp. 59, 120; Hurd 1, pp. 120–3.
(49) G. Scott-Moncrieff, *The Scotsman,* 18 December 1936.
(50) *QRIAS* 49, 1935.
(51) *QRIAS* 44, 1933, p. 42.
(52) *QRIAS* 56, 1938.
(53) *QRIAS* 54, 1937.
(54) (D. Carr) *Royal Burgh of Kirkcaldy, Proposed New Municipal Buildings, Report by 'Prodo'*: NMRS MS221-1.
(55) *The Builder,* 9 February 1951.
(56) *The Builder,* 26 May 1961, p. 991.
(57) Pentreath, p. 106.
(58) *The Builder,* 7 January 1955.
(59) *The Builder,* 20 June 1952.
(60) *The Builder,* 5 December 1952.
(61) The Scotsman, *The New Scotland,* 1958; *The Builder,* 30 November 1956.
(62) *The Builder,* 31 October 1952.
(63) *The Builder,* 4 May 1956.
(64) Drummond, p. 325.
(65) *QRIAS* 38, 1932.
(66) *QRIAS* 47, 1934.
(67) Letter from Warnett Kennedy to M. Glendinning, 1994. Mackintosh-like iron-work: information from D. Watters.
(68) L. Campbell 1, p. xiv.
(69) W. Jack, *QRIAS* 65, 1946.
(70) Interview by M. Glendinning with Stuart R. Matthew, 1995.
(71) *QRIAS* 39, 1932.
(72) *QRIAS* 50, 1935, p. 28.
(73) *QRIAS* 44, 1933; 52, 1936; 62, 1939.
(74) *Scottish Geographical Magazine.*
(75) Colquhoun: *Scotsman,* 30 March 1935. R. Hurd, *Scotland Under Trust,* 1939, p. xiii.
(76) Stirling-Maxwell, p. 210.
(77) G. Scott-Moncrieff, *The Buildings of Scotland,* 1944.
(78) London Scots Self-Government Committee; Town Planning Institute, *Report of St Andrews Summer School,* 1941; *The Builder,* 15 February 1952.
(79) Hurd speech, 1955: National Trust for Scotland, *Newsletter* 14, April 1956, p. 11. *Edinburgh Architectural Association Yearbook* 3, 1959.
(80) *The Builder,* 1 August 1952, 7 December 1951, 20 June 1952, 15 February 1952.
(81) *QRIAS,* February 1953.
(82) *The Builder,* 12 December 1952.
(83) Department of Health for Scotland, *Notes for Guidance of Investigators,* 1948 (text by I. G. Lindsay).
(84) *QRIAS* 45, 1933, p. 47.
(85) Letter from Warnett Kennedy, 1994.
(86) *QRIAS* 57, 1938.
(87) F. A. Walker, *Prospect* 19, 1960.
(88) Frew 1, p. 81.
(89) J. Wilson, *Scotsman,* 14 March 1935, p. 6.
(90) *Official Architect,* September 1941.
(91) *Scotsman,* 17 February 1938; see also Hurd on 'appallingly low' standard of council house design: *(Edinburgh) Evening News,* 29 June 1939.
(92) Matthew: foreword to A. W. Cleeve Barr, *Public Authority Housing,* 1958.
(93) *RIBA Journal,* 22 February 1936, p. 398.
(94) *Scottish Architect and Builder's Journal,* November 1938.
(95) R. H. Matthew, *The Builder,* 8 February 1952.
(96) *The Lancet,* 23 May 1953.
(97) Norrie Fraser, in London Scots Self-Government Committee, p. 2.
(98) *Glasgow Herald,* 11 April 1949: lecture by Matthew to Saltire Society in Ayr, April 1949.
(99) *The Builder,* 3 April 1953.
(100) *QRIAS* 42, 1933.
(101) Power: *Town and Country Planning,* April 1938. 'Soldiers scatter': *Scottish Architect and Builders' Journal,* July 1939, p. 18.
(102) *QRIAS,* August 1952.
(103) Spence on 'honesty': *The Builder,* 22 June 1956. Spence on Kelvin Hall exhibition: *QRIAS* 85, 1951.

(104) *Prospect*, August 1956.

(105) *QRIAS*, August 1952.

(106) 'Mechanics': *QRIAS*, May 1955. 'Spirit': *QRIAS* 67, 1947. Leslie G. MacDougall on self as 'Traditionalist': *QRIAS* 97, 1954.

(107) R. Hurd, in London Scots Self-Government Committee, p. 66.

(108) *Journal of the Town Planning Institute*, 1948.

(109) *QRIAS*, August 1952.

(110) Royal Fine Art Commission for Scotland, 'Minds Meeting' seminar, 1993: lecture by Wheeler. *Scottish Field*, April 1967.

(111) Shetland Archive, Heddell's Park file: letter 3 January 1957 from R. Moira to Lerwick Town Clerk.

(112) Interview by M. Glendinning with Frank Tindall, 1993; also *Scotsman*, 21 January 1960.

(113) Scottish Housing Advisory Committee.

(114) A. N. Doak, *QRIAS,* November 1952. Germany, K. Kaspar, *New German Architecture*, 1956, p. xii.

(115) *Prospect*, August 1956.

(116) *QRIAS* 89, 1952.

(117) *The Builder*, 13 November 1953.

(118) 'Systematic analysis': interview by M. Glendinning with Professor P. Nuttgens, 1995.

(119) R. H. Matthew, lecture in Dundee, 20 February 1960 (Matthew papers, Keith Marischal).

(120) *The Builder*, 4 December 1953.

(121) *QRIAS*, February 1954.

(122) *Architects' Journal*, 15 January 1959.

(123) *Prospect*, February 1956.

(124) 'Grand Piranesi composition', *Prospect* 8, Winter 1957, p. 20.

(125) Spaven.

(126) J. McKechnie, M. Macgregor, *A Short History of the Scottish Coal Mining Industry*, 1958.

(127) *Scottish Building and Civil Engineering Yearbook*, 1963.

(128) *The Builder*, 4 July 1958.

(129) *Prospect* 19, 1960.

(130) A. M. Doak, in *Prospect* 14, 1959.

(131) *The Builder*, 28 May 1965.

(132) R. H. Matthew, lecture in Dundee, 20 February 1960 (Matthew papers, Keith Marischal).

Chapter 9

(1) John L. Paterson, *Prospect* 8, 1957.

(2) G. Copcutt, 1995 manuscript paper (courtesy of Derek Lyddon).

(3) RIAS 4.

(4) *Scottish Building and Civil Engineering Yearbook*, 1963.

(5) *The Builder*, 7 October 1955.

(6) J . A. McGregor, *Prospect* 7, 1957.

(7) *Edinburgh Architectural Association Yearbook*, 1966.

(8) Glendinning and Muthesius, p. 220.

(9) *The Builder*, 13 November 1953.

(10) Interview by M. Glendinning with J. L. Paterson, 1987.

(11) *Prospect* 14, 1959. A. N. Doak: *Glasgow Institute of Architects Yearbook*, 1964.

(12) *Prospect* 8, 1957; and 10, 1958.

(13) Interview by M. Glendinning with J. L. Paterson, 1987.

(14) *Prospect* 5, 1957.

(15) *Architects' Journal*, 12 June 1958.

(16) *Weekly Scotsman*, 21 January 1960.

(17) The Scotsman, *The New Scotland*, 1958.

(18) *RIBA Journal*.

(19) Royal Fine Art Commission, 'Minds Meeting', seminar by R. Steedman, 1993.

(20) *Architects' Journal*, 15 December 1959; *The Builder*, 26 February 1960.

(21) *Prospect* 12, 1958.

(22) R. H. Matthew, lecture in Dundee, February 1960 (Matthew papers, Keith Marischal).

(23) Royal Fine Art Commission, 'Minds Meeting', seminar by B. Gillespie, 17 August 1995.

(24) 'Open citadel': G. Copcutt, 1995 manuscript paper.

(25) G. Copcutt, 1995 manuscript paper.

(26) G. Copcutt, 1995 manuscript paper.

(27) *Architectural Design*; Banham, p. 105.

(28) *American Institute of Architects Journal*.

(29) 'Associating': Royal Fine Art Commission, 'Minds Meeting', seminar by I. Metzstein, 1993. 'Every floor': A. MacMillan, lecture to Twentieth Century Society, Glasgow, 1994. *Building*, 6 September 1968.

(30) *The Builder*, 31 July 1964; *University of Edinburgh Comprehensive Development Area*.

(31) Kemp: cited in DOCOMOMO Register fiche by D. Whitham, 1994.

(32) John Richards, *EAA Review*, 1985.

(33) Royal Fine Art Commission, 'Minds Meeting', seminar by J. Richards, 1993.

(34) Seminar by J. Richards, 1993.

(35) Account by J. Richards, cited in DOCOMOMO fiche by D. Whitham, 1994.

(36) Inland Revenue.

(37) *Edinburgh Architectural Association Yearbook*, 1966.

(38) *Glasgow Institute of Architects Yearbook*, 1966.

(39) Royal Fine Art Commission, 'Minds Meeting',

seminar by W. Whitfield, 1993.

(40) All Womersley quotations: *RIBA Journal*, May 1969.

(41) Royal Fine Art Commission, 'Minds Meeting', seminar by I. Metzstein, 15 August 1995.

(42) B. Schotz, *Bronze in my Blood*, 1981.

(43) Royal Fine Art Commission, 'Minds Meeting', seminar by I. Metzstein, 15 August 1995.

(44) Interview by M. Glendinning with J. Richards, 1995.

(45) *Building Design*, May 1973; *Building*, 27 June 1969.

(46) *Building*, 17 January 1969.

(47) A. Doak, *Glasgow Institute of Architects Yearbook*, 1966.

(48) *Edinburgh Architectural Association Yearbook*, 1974.

(49) Letter from four architects to Glasgow Corporation Town Clerk, 16 June 1966 (information from Alistair MacDonald, Glasgow District Council Planning Department).

(50) *Scotsman*, February 1970.

(51) *Scotsman*, 28 November 1970.

(52) Letter from Matthew to Secretary of State, 14 February 1974 (Matthew papers, Keith Marischal).

(53) *Edinburgh Architectural Association Yearbook*, 1968, pp. 101–2; *Building*, 25 August 1967.

(54) Matthew, Reid and Lindsay, preface.

(55) Reid: *Edinburgh Architectural Association Yearbook*, 1971. Hodges: *Edinburgh Architectural Association Yearbook*, 1977. Colin McWilliam, lecture to Architectural Heritage Society of Scotland, 10 December 1985.

(56) J. Gilbert and A. Flint, *The Tenement Handbook*, 1992.

(57) *The Architect*, May 1974.

(58) *Scottish Review*, August 1982.

(59) D. Jarman (ed.), *Fields of Vision*, 1993.

(60) Marks et al., p. 16.

(61) *Sunday Times Scotland*, 10 October 1993, p. 3.

(62) Interview with C. McKean, 1995.

(63) Letter from C. McKean to M. Glendinning, 1995.

(64) Letter from C. McKean to M. Glendinning, 1995.

(65) RIAS 1.

(66) *Scottish Review*, August 1982.

(67) McKean 2; *Scotsman*, 19 April 1993, p. 11.

(68) RIAS 1, p. 1.

(69) P. Portoghesi, *Postmodern*, New York 1983, p. 31.

(70) Scottish Courts Administration, *Sheriff Court of Glasgow and Strathkelvin*, 1986.

(71) Colin McWilliam, lecture to Architectural Heritage Society, 10 December 1985.

(72) *Edinburgh Architectural Association Review*, 1985.

(73) *Prospect*, Summer 1985.

(74) RIAS 3, p. 101.

(75) *Prospect*, Summer 1988 and Spring 1990.

(76) *Scotsman*, 11 April 1994.

(77) C. McWilliam, *Scotsman*, 26 May 1966.

(78) B. Carter in *Architects' Journal*, 5 August 1981.

(79) *Prospect*, Summer 1985.

(80) *Prospect* 32, Winter 1987–8; RIAS 1.

(81) *Glasgow Herald*, 11 February 1989.

(82) *Prospect*, Summer 1990; *Glasgow Herald*, 11 February 1989.

(83) McKean, in RIAS 3.

(84) Prospect 43, 1991.

(85) Prospect 44, 1991.

(86) RIAS 4.

(87) *Architects' Journal*, 4 August 1994.

(88) RIAS 1, p. 4.

(89) Glasgow's Glasgow, p. 9.

(90) RIAS 3, p. 127.

(91) RIAS4.

(92) *Prospect* 46, 1992; Brochure *'The Italian Centre'*, c.1993.

(93) Charles McKean, letter 1995.

(94) RIAS 1.

(95) A. MacMillan, *Scottish Review*, August 1979.

(96) *Glasgow Herald*, 22 March 1995.

(97) Lecture at RIAS Convention, Glasgow 1995.

(98) RIAS 4: pp. 109, 113.

(99) Glasgow District Council, DARS headquarters, June 1994 publicity board for Springburn Area B rebuilding.

(100) *Prospect* 51, 1994.

(101) C. McKean, *Scotland on Sunday*, 9 October 1988.

(102) Basil Al-Bayati, *Basil Al-Bayati*, 1988, p. 231.

(103) Royal Fine Art Commission, 'Minds Meeting', seminar by J. C. Hope, 11 August 1994.

(104) *Edinburgh Architectural Association Review*, 1985.

(105) *Prospect*, Summer 1988; *Prospect*, Summer 1990 (suppl.).

(106) *Prospect*, Autumn 1989.

(107) Interview by M. Glendinning with D. Page, 1995.

(108) Also see *Prospect* 48, 1992.

(109) Lecture, RIAS Convention, 1995.

(110) RIAS 3.

(111) Interview by M. Glendinning with J. Richards, 1995.

(112) RIAS 4.

(113) *Scotsman*, 27 September 1993.

(114) *Architects' Journal*, 20 January 1993; *Prospect*, Winter 1995.
(115) *Prospect*, Winter 1995.
(116) RIBA Journal, November 1994.
(117) 'Tyranny': interview by M. Glendinning with D. Page, 1995.
(118) S. O'Toole, *Tales from Two Cities*, Dublin 1994.
(119) *Prospect* 42, 1990.
(120) RIAS 4.
(121) *Architects' Journal*, 9 February 1994.
(122) RIAS 3.
(123) *Prospect*, Winter 1995.
(124) *Scotsman*, 17 January 1995.
(125) Royal Fine Art Commission for Scotland, 1994 Festival exhibition: caption.
(126) Fraser Stewart, *Prospect*, Spring 1995.
(127) *Citizen 99*, vol. i, 1995, p. 3.
(128) K. Dougan, *Prospect*, Spring 1995.
(129) RIAS 4.

Conclusion
(1) P. Robertson, p. 180.
(2) P. Geddes, *Dramatisations of History*, 1923, p. iv.
(3) S. Cruden, *The Scottish Castle*, 1981, p. 141.
(4) Sarmatyzm: Muthesius, p. 43. Aesthetic of masonry monumentality: we are indebted to Charles McKean for discussions/correspondence on this subject; see also A. MacMillan, 'Stone Age', and I. Metzstein, 'After the Stone Age', *Prospect* 40, Summer 1990 (Supplement)
(5) Rupture, modern society: Wagner, p. 3.
(6) Stell 7, p. 159.
(7) J. Greig (ed.), *Letters of David Hume*, vol. 2, 1932, p. 230.
(8) Thomson, 2nd Haldane Lecture, 1874.
(9) Holy war: J. Howard and S. Kuznetsov, p. 40.
(10) McKean 5, p. 229.
(11) F. A. Walker: J. Frew and D. Jones (eds), *Scotland and Europe*, 1991, p. 56. 'Great European city': McKean lecture at RIAS Convention, 6 May 1994.
(12) 'Amnesia': McKean 6, p. 77.
(13) See also *National Association for the Advancement of Art*, p. 299.
(14) *QIAS* 26, 1928.
(15) J. Summerson, *Architecture in Britain 1530–1830* (1970 edn.), pp. 377 and 509 (most recent edition was 1993); Worsley, pp. 153, 160.
(16) Muthesius, pp.11 and 12.
(17) National Trust for Historic Preservation, *Historic Preservation Today*, Charlottesville, 1966.
(18) I. Hay, p. 15.

Part C: General Bibliography

Introduction

This list contains detailed citations of all titles included in Part A, and of those mentioned frequently in Part B. The books are listed in full, with three exceptions: some titles are abbreviated, and page numbers of articles are omitted, as is the place of publication in the case of books published in Scotland or England. Authors are listed in alphabetical order, and multiple entries by individual authors are grouped chronologically and numbered. At the end of the main list, the volumes so far published in the three chief topographical series of architectural books (the RIAS *Illustrated Architectural Guides*, the RCAHMS Inventories and the *Buildings of Scotland* volumes) are listed in area order.

P. Abercrombie and R. Matthew, *The Clyde Valley Regional Plan* 1946, 1949

P. Abercrombie and D. Plumstead, *A Civic Survey and Plan for Edinburgh*, 1949

Aberdeen Civic Society, *Archibald Simpson*, 1978

R. Adam, *Ruins of the Palace of . . . Spalatro, in Dalmatia*, 1764

R. and J. Adam, *Works in Architecture of Robert & James Adam*, 3 vols, 1773–1822 (vol. 1, 5 parts, issued 1773–8; vol. 2, 1779; vol. 3, 1822; all reissued and edited by R. Oresko, 1975)

M. J. Allan, *Hamilton Mausoleum* (Dissertation, Scott Sutherland School of Architecture, Aberdeen), 1976

N. Allen (ed.), *Scottish Pioneers of the Greek Revival*, 1984

American Institute of Architects Journal, July 1967

J. Anderson, *Sir Walter Scott and History*, 1981

M. R. Apted, *Painted Ceilings of Scotland*, 1966

Architect and Building News, 6 May 1964 (N. Taylor)

1. *Architects' Journal*, 5 July 1956 (Turnhouse)

2. *Architects' Journal*, 6 May 1964 (W. S. Gauldie)

3. *Architects' Journal*, 5 August 1981 (Robinson College)

Architectural Design, May 1963 (especially article by G. Copcutt)

Architectural Heritage 3, 1992 (J. Lowrey (ed.), *The Age of Mackintosh*); see also separate article references.

R. Bailey, *Scottish Architects' Papers*, 1996

R. Banham, *Megastructure*, 1976

T. Barnard and J. Clark (eds), *Lord Burlington*, 1995

M. Bath, 'Alexander Seton's Painted Gallery', in L. Gent (ed.), *Albion's Classicism*, New Haven 1995

P. J. Bawcutt (ed.), *The Shorter Poems of Gavin Douglas*, 1967

J. N. Baxter, *Thirties Society Journal*, 1984 ('Empirex')

J. W. Baxter, *William Dunbar*, 1952

G. Beard, *The Work of Robert Adam*, 1978

W. Beaton, *William Robertson*, 1984

H. Begg (ed.), *100 Years Town Planning in Dundee*, 1992 (chapter 2)

T. Begg, *Fifty Special Years*, 1987

R. W. Billings, *The Baronial and Ecclesiastical Antiquities of Scotland*, 4 vols, 1845–52

A. Bolton, *The Architecture of Robert and James Adam*, 2 vols, 1922

T. Bonnar, *Biographical Sketch of George Meikle Kemp*, 1892

J. A. Bowie, *The Future of Scotland*, 1939

D. Brett, *Charles Rennie Mackintosh*, 1992

J. Britton, *Modern Athens!*, 1829

W. Brogden (ed.), *The Neo-Classical Town*, 1996

A. Brown, *The Renaissance*, 1988

1. I. Brown, 'Critick in Antiquity: Sir John Clerk of Penicuik', *Antiquity* 51, 1977

2. I. Brown, 'David Hume's Tomb', *PSAS* 121, 1991

3. I. Brown, *Monumental Reputation*, 1992

J. M. Brown (ed.), *Scottish Society in the Fifteenth Century*, 1977

K. M. Brown, 'The Scottish Aristocracy, Anglicisation and the Court', *Historical Journal*, 1993

S. J. Brown and M. Fry (eds), *Scotland in the Age of the Disruption*, 1993

G. Bruce, *'To Foster and Enrich': The First Fifty Years of the Saltire Society*, 1986

R. Bruce, First Planning Report, 1945, and Second Planning Report, 1946

D. Bryce and A. Roberts, '*Post Reformation Catholic Houses of North-East Scotland*', *PSAS* 123, 1993

Buildings of Scotland series: (see Bibl. p. 542)

Sir J Burnet & Partners, *The Architectural Work of Sir J. Burnet & Partners*, 1930

Lord Bute, *A Plea for Scotland's Architectural Heritage*, 1936

1. N. M. Cameron, *Scotsman*, 16 October 1989

2. N. M. Cameron, 'Adam and "Gothick" at Yester Chapel', *Architectural Heritage* 4, 1993

3. N. M. Cameron, 'St Rule's Church, St Andrews', *PSAS*, 124, 1994

C. Campbell and others, *Vitruvius Britannicus*, 3 vols, 1715-25

1. I. Campbell, 'A Romanesque Revival and the Early Renaissance in Scotland', *JSAH*, September 1995

2. I. Campbell, 'Linlithgow's "Princely Palace" and its Influence in Europe', *Architectural Heritage*, 1995

1. L. Campbell (ed.), *To Build a Cathedral*, 1987

2. L. Campbell, *RIBA Journal*, April 1993

3. L. Campbell, *Coventry Cathedral*, 1996

R. H. Campbell, A. S. Skinner, *The Origins and Nature of the Scottish Enlightenment*, 1982

K. Cavers, *A Vision of Scotland: The Nation observed by John Slezer*, 1993

Sir W. Chambers, *A Treatise on Civil Architecture*, 1759

O. & S. Checkland, *Industry and Ethos*, 1989

S. Chisholm, 'The History . . . of the Glasgow City Improvement Trust', *Proceedings of the Philosophical Society of Glasgow* 27, 1895-6

J. Cleland, *Annals of Glasgow*, 1816

M. H. Clough, *Two Houses*, 1990

J.-L. Cohen, *Scenes of the World to Come*, Paris 1995

L. Colley, *Britons*, New Haven 1993

1. H. Colvin, 'A Scottish Origin for English Palladianism?', *Architectural History* 17, 1974

2. H. Colvin, 'The Beginnings of the Architectural Profession in Scotland', *Architectural History* 29, 1986

3. H. Colvin, *A Biographical Dictionary of British Architects 1660-1840*, 1995 edn

1. Corporation of Glasgow, *Municipal Glasgow*, 1914

2. Corporation of Glasgow, Housing Department, *Review of Operations*, 1947

M. Cosh, 'The Adam Family and Arniston', *Architectural History* 27, 1984

C. Craig (general ed.), *The History of Scottish Literature*, 4 vols, 1987–8

R. Crampsey, *The Empire Exhibition of 1938*, 1988

J. M. Crook, 'The New Square Style', in Gow and Rowan

K. Cruft, 'The Enigma of Woodhall House', *Architectural History* 27, 1984

K. Cruft and A. Fraser (eds), *James Craig*, 1995

1. E. Cumming, *Arts and Crafts in Edinburgh*, 1985

2. E. Cumming, *Phoebe Anna Traquair*, 1993

E. S. Cumming and W. Caplan, *The Arts and Crafts Movement*, 1991

A. J. G. Cummings and T. M. Devine, *Industry, Business and Society in Scotland since 1707*, 1994

P. Cusack, 'Lion Chambers', *Architectural History* 28, 1985

D. Daiches, *Sir Walter Scott and His World*, 1971

J. G. Dalyell (ed.), *The Chronicles of Scotland*, 1814

M. Davis, *The Castles and Mansions of Ayrshire*, 1991

1. Department of Health for Scotland, *Working-Class Housing on the Continent*, 1935

2. Department of Health for Scotland, *Report of the Scottish Architectural Advisory Committee*, 1937

3. Department of Health for Scotland, *Housing Handbook* (especially Part I 'Housing Layout', revised 1958, and Part III 'House Design', 1950–6)

T. Devine (ed.), *Scottish Elites*, 1994

T. Devine and R. J. Findlay (eds), *Scotland in the 20th Century*, 1996

T. Devine and G. Jackson (eds), *Glasgow* 1, 1995

A. Dickson and J. N. H. Treble (eds), *People and Society in Scotland* iii, 1992

T. Dickson and J. Balfour Paul (eds), *Accounts of the Lord High Treasurer of Scotland*, 1877–1916

C. Dingwall, 'Gardens in the Wild', *Garden History*, Winter 1994

R. Dixon and S. Muthesius, *Victorian Architecture*, 1978

W. Dobson Chapman and C. F. Riley, *Granite City*, 1952

G. Donaldson, *Scotland, James V–James VII*, 1987 edn

I. Donnachie and G. Hewitt, *Historic New Lanark*, 1993

A. Drexler (ed.), *The Architecture of the École des Beaux-Arts*, 1977

A. L. Drummond, *The Church Architecture of Protestantism*, 1934

1. J. G. Dunbar, 'The Palace of Holyroodhouse', *Archaeological Journal* 120, 1963

2. J. G. Dunbar, 'Kinross House', in H. Colvin and J. Harris (eds), *The Country Seat*, 1970

3. J. G. Dunbar, 'The Building Activities of the Duke and Duchess of Lauderdale', *Archaeological Journal* 132, 1975

4. J. G. Dunbar, *The Architecture of Scotland*, 1978 edn

5. J. G. Dunbar, 'Some Aspects of the Planning of Scottish Royal Palaces in the Sixteenth Century', *Architectural History* 27, 1984

6. J. G. Dunbar, 'Some sixteenth-century French Parallels for the Palace of Falkland', *Review of Scottish Culture* 7, 1991

7. J. G. Dunbar, 'Two Late Seventeenth-Century Designs for Kinnaird Castle', in Gow and Rowan

J. G. Dunbar and J Cornforth, 'Dalkeith House, Lothian', *Country Life*, 19 April and 26 April 1984

J. C. and A. H. Dunlop, *The Book of Old Edinburgh*, 1886

J.-N.-L. Durand, *Recueil et Parallèle des Edifices Anciens et Modernes*, Paris 1800

A. Durie, 'Tourism in Victorian Scotland', *Scottish Economic and Social History* 12, 1992

W. Eadie, *Movements of Modernity*, 1990

Edinburgh Review, Summer 1992

1. B. Edwards, 'The Glasgow Improvement Scheme', *Planning History* 12:3, 1990

2. B. Edwards, 'Urban Reform in Glasgow', *Planning History* 13:1, 1991

3. B. Edwards, *Basil Spence 1907–1976*, 1995

R. Ellis and D. Cuff (eds), *Architects' People*, New York 1989, chapters 11–13

R. Emerson, 'Robert Adam and John Clerk of Eldin', in Gow and Rowan

1. R. Fawcett, *Edinburgh Castle*, 1986

2. R. Fawcett, *The Abbey and Palace of Dunfermline*, 1990

3. R. Fawcett, *Scottish Architecture from the Accession of the Stewarts to the Reformation*, 1994

A. Fenton and B. Walker, *The Rural Architecture of Scotland*, 1981

J. Ferguson, *Linlithgow Palace*, 1901

V. Fiddes and A. Rowan, *David Bryce*, 1976

P. Finch and J. Melvin (eds), *The Glasgow Tower*, 1993

I. Fisher, 'Thomas Hamilton', in N. Allen (ed.), *Scottish Pioneers of the Greek Revival*, 1984

1. J. Fleming, 'An Adam Miscellany', *Architectural Review*, February 1958

2. J. Fleming, *Robert Adam and his Circle*, 1962

3. J. Fleming, 'Robert Adam's Castle Style', *Country Life* 143, 1968

4. J. Fleming, ' "A Retrospective View" by John Clerk of Eldin', in J. Summerson (ed.), *Concerning Architecture*, 1968

T. N. Fox, *Thirties Society Journal*, 1987 (Lorne)

L. A. Fradenburg, *City, Marriage, Tournament*, Madison (Wis.), 1991

A. G. Fraser, *The Building of Old College*, 1989

W. H. Fraser and R. J. Morris (eds), *People and Society in Scotland*, vol. 2, 1990

1. J. Frew, 'Ebenezer MacRae and Reformed Tenement Design', in J. Frew and D. Jones (eds), *Scotland and Europe*, 1991

2. J. Frew (ed.), *Building for a New Age*, 1984

1. T. Friedman, *James Gibbs*, 1984

2. T. Friedman, 'A Palace Worthy of the Grandeur of the King', *Architectural History* 29, 1986

J. S. Gibson, *The Thistle and the Crown*, 1985

J. Gifford, *William Adam*, 1989

J. Gilbert and A. Flint, *The Tenement Handbook*, 1992

Glasgow City Council, *The 1990 Story*, 1992

Glasgow's Glasgow, *The Words and the Stones*, 1990

M. Glendinning and S. Muthesius, *Tower Block: Modern Public Housing in England, Scotland, Wales and Northern Ireland*, 1994

S. Gold, *Thirties Society Journal*, 1982 (Masonic Hospital)

A. Gomme and D. M. Walker, *Architecture of Glasgow*, 1968

G. Goodfellow, 'Colen Campbell's Shawfield Mansion', *JSAH* 23, 1964

G. Gordon (ed.), *Perspectives of the Scottish City*, 1985

1. I. R. Gow, *The Edinburgh Villa* (thesis, Cambridge University), 1975

2. I. R. Gow, 'William Henry Playfair', in N. Allen (ed.), *Scottish Pioneers of the Greek Revival*, 1984

3. I. R. Gow, 'David Rhind', in K. Downes (ed.), *The Architectural Outsiders*, 1985

4. I. R. Gow, William Henry Playfair (RIAS exhibition text), 1988.

5. I. R. Gow, John Douglas (NMRS exhibition text), 1989

6. I. R. Gow, 'The Northern Athenian Room', *Review of Scottish Culture* 5, 1989

7. I. R. Gow, 'William Adam, Planner of Genius', *Architectural Heritage* 1, 1990

8. I. R. Gow, 'William Henry Playfair's Design for a "Roman Villa" at Lurgan', *Architectural Heritage* 2, 1991

9. I. R. Gow, *The Scottish Interior*, 1992

I. R. Gow and T. Clifford, *The National Gallery of Scotland*, 1988

I. R. Gow and A. Rowan (eds), *Scottish Country Houses*, 1995

Sir J. Gowans, *Model Dwelling Houses*, 1886

J. Grant, *Old and New Edinburgh*, 3 vols, n.d.

S. T. Green, 'William Leiper's Houses in Helensburgh', *Architectural Heritage* 3, 1992

R. Grieve, *Grieve on Geddes*, 1990

D. Hamer (ed.), *The Works of Sir D. Lindsay of the Mount*, 1931

L. Hamilton, *Scottish Georgian Society Annual Report*, 1983

I. G. Hannah, *The Story of Scotland in Stone*, 1934

R. K. Hannay and C. P. H. Watson, 'The Building of the Parliament House', *Book of the Old Edinburgh Club* 13, 1924

E. Hardie, *A Short History of . . . Scott Morton and Tynecastle Co.*, 1976 (NMRS)

J. Harris, *Sir William Chambers*, 1970

V. Hart, *Art and Magic in the Court of the Stuarts*, 1994

1. C. Harvie, *No Gods and Precious Few Heroes*, 1981

2. C. Harvie, *Fools' Gold*, 1994

D. Hay, 'Scotland and the Italian Renaissance', in I. B. Cowan and D. Shaw (eds), *The Renaissance and Reformation in Scotland*, 1983

G. Hay, *The Architecture of Scottish Post-Reformation Churches*, 1957

I. Hay, *Their Name Liveth*, 1931

M. Higgs, 'Archibald Simpson', in N. Allen (ed.), *Scottish Pioneers of the Greek Revival*, 1984

H.-R. Hitchcock, *Architecture: Nineteenth and Twentieth Centuries*, 1958

J. Holloway, *The Norie Family*, 1994

M. Hook, 'Project ASSIST', *Architects' Journal*, 10 January 1973

M. G. Horsey, *Journal of the Architectural Heritage Society of Scotland*, 1987

1. D. Howard, *Scottish Architecture: Reformation to Restoration*, 1995

2. D. Howard, 'Sir William Bruce's Design for Hopetoun House', in Gow and Rowan

J. Howard and S. Kuznetsov, 'Scottish Architects in Tsarist Russia', *History Today*, February 1996

T. Howarth, *Charles Rennie Mackintosh and the Modern Movement*, 1952

J. R. Hume, 'Engineering and Technology', in P. H. Scott (ed.), *Scotland: A Concise Cultural History*, 1993

P. Hume Brown, *Early Travellers in Scotland*, 1978 edn

D. Hunter Blair, *John Patrick, Third Marquess of Bute*, 1921

1. R. Hurd, 'Design for To-Day', in J. R. Allan (ed.), *Scotland 1938*, 1938

2. R. Hurd, *The Face of Modern Edinburgh*, 1939

J. Imrie and J. G. Dunbar, *Accounts of the Masters of Works* 2, 1982

Inland Revenue, *An Introduction to Centre 1*, 1968

R. Innes-Smith, *Glamis Castle*, 1993

James Smith Anniversary Committee, *Minerva's Flame*, 1995

F. Jamieson, 'The Royal Gardens of the Palace of Holyroodhouse', *Garden History*, Summer 1994

T. M. Jeffery, *The Life and Works of F. T. Pilkington* (thesis, Newcastle University), 1976

M. Johnston, *Architectural Heritage Society of Scotland Journal*, 1989

D. Jones, 'A Seventeenth Century Inventory of Furnishings at Kinnaird Castle', in J. Frew and D. Jones (eds), *Aspects of Scottish Classicism*, 1989

A. G. Jury, *Glasgow's Housing Centenary*, 1966

Lord Kames, *Elements of Criticism*, 2 vols, 1769

W. Kaplan (ed.), *Charles Rennie Mackintosh*, New York, 1996

E. Kauffmann, *Architecture in the Age of Reason*, Cambridge (Mass.), 1955

1. M. Keating, *The Designation of Cumbernauld New Town*, 1986

2. M. Keating, *The City that Refused to Die*, 1988

M. Kelsall and S. Harris, *A Future for the Past*, 1961

E. E. Kemp, *Royal Botanical Garden 1946–70: The New Plant Houses*, 1992

C. Kidd, 'The Canon of Patriotic Landmarks in Scottish History', *Scotlands* 1, 1994

P. and J. Kinchin, *Glasgow's Great Exhibitions*, 1988

D. King, *The Complete Works of Robert and James Adam*, 1991

W. Kuyper, *Dutch Classicist Architecture*, Delft, 1980

D. Laing (ed.), *Correspondence of Sir Robert Kerr*, 2 vols, 1875

M. Lee, 'King James's Popish Chancellor', in I. B. Cowan and D. Shaw (eds), *The Renaissance and Reformation in Scotland*, 1983

A. Lewis and J. Lowrey, 'James Craig', *Architectural Heritage*, 1995

1. I. G. Lindsay, *Georgian Edinburgh*, 1948

2. I. G. Lindsay, *The Scottish Parish Kirk*, 1960

I. G. Lindsay and M. Cosh, *Inveraray and the Dukes of Argyll*, 1973

B. Little, *The Life and Work of James Gibbs*, 1955

London Scots Self-Government Committee, *The New Scotland*, 1942

H. J. Louw, 'The Origin of the Sash-Window', *Architectural History* 26, 1983

1. J. Lowrey, '*A Man of Excellent Parts*', 1987

2. J. Lowrey, 'Bruce and his Circle at Craigiehall', in J. Frew and D. Jones (eds), *Aspects of Scottish Classicism*, 1989

3. J. Lowrey, 'Development of the Formal Landscape at Hamilton Palace', in J. Frew and D. Jones (eds), *Aspects of Scottish Classicism*, 1989

1. M. Lynch, 'Queen Mary's Triumph', *Scottish Historical Review*, 1990

2. M. Lynch, *Scotland: A New History*, 1991

3. M. Lynch (ed.), *Scotland 1850–1979*, 1993

S. G. E Lythe, *The Economy of Scotland in its European Setting*, 1960

Mac Journal 1, 1994 (J. Macaulay and C. Hermansen (eds)

D. McAra, *Sir James Gowans*, 1975

1. J. Macaulay, *The Gothic Revival 1745–1845*, 1975

2. J. Macaulay, 'The Architectural Collaboration between J. Gillespie Graham and A. W. N. Pugin', *Architectural History* 27, 1984

3. J. Macaulay, *The Classical Country House in Scotland*, 1987

4. J. Macaulay, 'The Seventeenth Century Genesis of Hamilton Palace', in J. Frew and D. Jones (eds), *Aspects of Scottish Classicism*, 1989

5. J. Macaulay, *Glasgow School of Art*, 1993

6. J. Macaulay, *Hill House*, 1994

L. Macbeth, 'The Nuremberg Twist and the Amsterdam Swing', in J. Frew and D. Jones (eds), *Scotland and Europe*, 1991

1. N. MacDougall, *James III*, 1982

2. N. MacDougall, *James IV*, 1989

R. McFadzean, *The Life and Work of Alexander Thomson*, 1979

1. D. MacGibbon and T. Ross, *The Castellated and Domestic Architecture of Scotland*, 5 vols, 1887–92

2. D. MacGibbon and T. Ross, *The Ecclesiastical Architecture of Scotland*, 3 vols, 1896–7

C. MacGregor, 'Gribloch', *Architectural Heritage* 5, 1995

R. MacInnes, 'Robert Adam's Public Buildings', *Architectural Heritage* 4, 1995

S. A. F. Macintosh, *The Private Houses of Morris & Steedman* (thesis, Mackintosh School of Architecture, Glasgow), 1995

I. MacIvor, *Edinburgh Castle*, 1993

1. C. McKean, *The Scottish Thirties*, 1987

2. C. McKean, 'Local Roots and the Revival Cycle', *Royal Society of Arts Journal*, January 1987

3. C. McKean, 'Finnart's Platt', *Architectural Heritage* 2, 1991

4. C. McKean, 'Hamilton of Finnart', *History Today*, January 1993

5. C. McKean, 'The Scottishness of Scottish Architecture', in P. H. Scott (ed.), *Scotland: A Concise Cultural History*, 1993

6. C. McKean, 'The Scottishness of Scottish Architecture', in J. Fladmark (ed.), *Heritage*, 1993

7. C. McKean, 'The Wrychtishousis', in *Book of the Old Edinburgh Club* 3, 1994

A. MacKechnie (ed.), *David Hamilton, Architect*, 1993

A. M. Mackenzie, *Scotland in Modern Times*, 1941

1. S. McKinstry, *Rowand Anderson*, 1991

2. S. McKinstry, 'Light from Languedoc', in J. Frew and D. Jones (eds), *Scotland and Europe*, 1991

J. Macky, *A Journey through Scotland*, 1723

R. Macleod, *Charles Rennie Mackintosh*, 1968

Macmillan Encyclopedia of Architects, New York 1982

D. Macmillan, *Scottish Art, 1460–1990*, 1990

J. MacQueen (ed.), *Humanism in Renaissance Scotland*, 1990

D. MacRoberts, 'Material Destruction caused by the Scottish Reformation', *Innes Review* 10, 1959

J. MacUre, *A View of the City of Glasgow*, 1830

J. Mann (ed.), *Rebuilding Scotland*, 1941

R. Marks, R. Scott, B. Gasson, J. Thomson, P. Vainker, *The Burrell Collection*, 1983

1. T. A. Markus (ed.), *Order in Space and Society*, 1982

2. T. A. Markus, *Buildings and Power*, 1993

R. Mason, 'Chivalry and Kingship', in R. Mason and N. MacDougall (eds), *People and Power in Scotland*, 1992

R. H. Matthew, J. Reid, M. Lindsay (eds), *The Conservation of Georgian Edinburgh*, 1972

S. R. Matthew, *The Knights and Chapel of . . . the Thistle*, 1988

W. Maxwell Scott, *Abbotsford*, 1982

1. D. Mays, *The Life and Works of John Kinross* (Ph.D. St Andrews), 1989

2. D. Mays, 'A Profile of Sir George Washington Browne', *Architectural Heritage* 3, 1992

F. Mears, *A Regional Survey and Plan for Central and South-East Scotland*, 1949

H. Meller, *Patrick Geddes*, 1990

R. Mitchison, 'Patriotism and National Identity in Eighteenth-Century Scotland', in T. W. Moody (ed.), *Nationality and the Pursuit of National Independence*, 1978

D. Murray, *Memories of the Old College of Glasgow*, 1927

S. Muthesius, *Art, Architecture and Design in Poland*, Königstein/Taunus, 1994

1. R. S. Mylne, *The Master Masons to the Crown of Scotland*, 1893

2. R. S. Mylne, '*The Masters of Work to the Crown of Scotland*', PSAS 30, 1896

National Association for the Advancement of Art, Edinburgh Meeting, *Transactions*, 1890 (sections by Gowans, Anderson, MacGibbon, Bonnar, Geddes)

National Library of Scotland, *Scottish Architects at Home and Abroad*, 1978

T. Neat, *Part Seen, Part Imagined*, 1994

J. Nicoll (ed.), *Domestic Architecture in Scotland*, 1908

1938 Exhibition Official Guide, 1938

NMRS, Ian Lindsay cuttings books and Fairlie/Bute correspondence files

1. P. Nuttgens, *Reginald Fairlie*, 1959

2. P. Nuttgens, 'Regional Planning in Eighteenth-Century Scotland', *Prospect* 17, 1960

J. Ockman, *Architecture Culture 1943–1968*, 1993

F. J. Osborn and A. Whittick, *New Towns*, 1977

H. Ouston, 'York in Edinburgh', in J. Dwyer, R.A. Mason and A. Murdoch (eds), *New Perspectives of the Politics and Culture of Early Modern Scotland*, 1982

A. Palladio, *The Four Books of Architecture*, 1965 edn (reprint of 1738 Isaac Ware edition)

L. Paterson, *The Autonomy of Modern Scotland*, 1994

H. M. Paton (ed.), *Accounts of the Masters of Works* 1, 1957

J. B. Paul, *The Scots Peerage*, 9 vols, 1904–14

P. L. Payne, *The Hydro*, 1988

W. Payne/National Galleries of Scotland, *Hospitalfield*, 1990

B. T. Pentreath, 'Classical Modernism in Fifties Edinburgh', *Architectural Heritage* 5, 1995

J.-M. Pérouse de Montclos, *Histoire de l'architecture française: de la Renaissance à la Révolution*, Paris 1989

N. Pevsner, *Studies in Art, Architecture and Design* 2, 1968

N. T. Philipson and R Mitchison (eds), *Scotland in the Age of Improvement*, 1970

S. Piggott, 'Sir John Clerk and "The Country Seat"', in H. Colvin and J. Harris (eds), *The Country Seat*, 1970

C. Pittaway, 'A National Awakening', 1993

1. S. Pryke, 'Francis Brodie', in J. Frew and D. Jones (eds), *Aspects of Scottish Classicism*, 1989

2. S. Pryke, 'Hopetoun House', *Country Life*, 10 August 1995

G. A. S. Purves, *An Introduction to the Work of Sir F. Mears* (Heriot-Watt Research Paper 4), 1983

I. Rae, *Charles Cameron*, 1971

1. RCAHMS, *Inventories*: see p.542.

2. RCAHMS, *National Monuments Record of Scotland Jubilee: A Guide to the Collections*, 1991

J. Reed, *Sir Walter Scott: Landscape and Locality*, 1980

P. Reed, *Glasgow: The Forming of a City*, 1993

A. Reiach and R. Hurd, *Building Scotland*, 1941/1944

1. RIAS, *Scottish Architecture in the Nineteen-Eighties*, 1987

2. RIAS, *The Architecture of the Scottish Renaissance*, 1990

3. RIAS, *RIAS Jubilee Souvenir 1840–1990*, 1990

4. RIAS, *RIAS Review of Scottish Architecture 1992*, 1992

5. RIAS, *RIAS Review of Scottish Architecture 1994*, 1994

6. RIAS *Illustrated Architectural Guides*: see p. 542.

RIBA Journal, May 1969

1. J. Richards, *Sir Robert Matthew and His Work*, 1984 (lecture text)

2. J. Richards, *Edinburgh Architectural Association Transactions*, 1985

1. H. Richardson, 'A Continental Solution to the Planning of Lunatic Asylums 1900–1940', in J. Frew and D. Jones (eds), *Scotland and Europe*, 1991

2. H. Richardson, 'Lorimer's Castle Restorations', *Architectural Heritage* 3, 1992

J. S. Richardson, 'Sixteenth and Seventeenth Century Mural Decoration at the House of Kinneil', *PSAS*, 1940–1

A. Riches, 'The Architect's House and the Search for a 'National Style', in Gow and Rowan

A. Roberts, 'James Smith and James Gibbs', *Architectural Heritage* 2, 1991

D. S. Robertson, 'Scottish Home Improvement Policy', *Urban Studies*, 1992

P. Robertson (ed.), *Charles Rennie Mackintosh: The Architectural Papers*, 1990

J. Rock, *Thomas Hamilton, Architect*, 1984

R. W. K. Rogerson, *Jack Coia*, 1986

H. Rosenau, *The Ideal City in Its Architectural Evolution*, 1959

1. A. Rowan, 'After the Adelphi', *Royal Society of Arts Journal* 122, 1974

2. A. Rowan, *The Creation of Shambellie*, 1982

3. A. Rowan, 'The Building of Hopetoun', *Architectural History* 27, 1984

4. A. Rowan, *Catalogue of Architectural Drawings in the Victoria and Albert Museum: Robert Adam*, 1988

5. A. Rowan, 'William Adam's Library', *Architectural Heritage* 1, 1990

Royal Institute of British Architects, *James MacLaren*, 1990

J. Ruskin, *Lectures on Architecture and Painting Delivered at Edinburgh*, 1854

F. Salmon, 'Charles Cameron and Nero's *Domus Aurea*', *Architectural History* 36, 1993

1. M. H. B. Sanderson, *Scottish Rural Society in the Sixteenth Century*, 1982

2. M. H. B. Sanderson, *Robert Adam and Scotland*, 1992

C. Saumarez Smith, *Eighteenth Century Decoration*, 1993

P. Savage, *Lorimer and the Edinburgh Craft Designers*, 1980

R. Saville (ed.), *The Economic Development of Modern Scotland*, 1985

K. F. Schinkel, *Reise nach England, Schottland und Paris im Jahre 1826*, Munich 1986 (English edn: D. Bindmann and G. Riemann (eds), '*The English Journey*', New Haven 1993)

Scott & Wilson, Kirkpatrick & Partners, *Report on a Highway Plan for Glasgow*, 1965

J. Scott and M. Hughes, *The Anatomy of Scottish Capital*, 1980

P. H. Scott (ed.), *Scotland: A Concise Cultural History*, 1993

Scottish Architect and Builders' Journal, published 1938–9 (RIAS Library)

Scottish Arts Council, *Sir William Bruce*, 1970 (introduction by J. G. Dunbar)

Scottish Council (Development & Industry), *Inquiry into the Scottish Economy*, 1961 (Toothill Report)

1. Scottish Development Department, *Annual Reports* (from 1963)

2. Scottish Development Department, *Central Scotland: A Programme for Development and Growth*, 1963

3. Scottish Development Department/Scottish Housing Advisory Committee, *Scotland's Older Houses*, 1967

4. Scottish Development Department, *The Older Houses in Scotland*, 1968

5. Scottish Development Department, *Housing: A Consultative Document*, 1977 (Cd 6852)

Scottish Geographical Magazine, September/October 1919

Scottish Home and Health Department, *The Falkirk Ward*, 1966

Scottish Housing Advisory Committee, *Planning Our New Homes*, 1944 (Westwood Report)

Scottish Legal Life Assurance Society (brochure), n.d.

Scottish National War Memorial, 1932

Scottish Office Building Directorate, *A Guide to Non-Traditional Housing in Scotland*, 1987

1. G. Scott-Moncrieff, 'The Old Houses', in J. R. Allan (ed.), *Scotland 1938*, 1938

2. G. Scott-Moncrieff, *Living Traditions of Scotland*, 1951

3. G. Scott-Moncrieff, *Scotland's Dowry*, 1956

1. G. Seton (ed.), *Memoir of Alexander Seton*, 1882

2. G. Seton, *A History of the Family of Seton*, 1896

1. D. Shvidkovski, 'Classical Edinburgh and Russian Town Planning . . . the Role of William Hastie', *Architectural Heritage* 2, 1991

2. D. Shvidkovski, *The Empress and the Architect*, 1996

J. Simpson, 'An Account of the Reconstruction of William Adam's Design for Gladney House', in Gow and Rowan

F. Sinclair (ed.), *Charles Wilson Architect*, 1995

1. H. G. Slade, 'Fyvie Castle', *Château Gaillard* 12, 1984

2. H. G. Slade, 'James Byres of Tonley', *Architectural Heritage* 2, 1991

1. A. Sloan, 'James Miller', *Architectural Heritage* 3, 1992

2. A. Sloan, *James Miller*, 1993

H. Smailes, *A Portrait Gallery for Scotland*, 1985

R. Smith and U. Wannop (eds), *Strategic Planning in Action*, 1985

Society of Architectural Historians of Great Britain, *Classicism in Scotland 1670–1748* (1983 conference)

A. R. Somerville, 'The Ancient Sundials of Scotland', *PSAS*, 1987

T. Spaven/RMJM, *The Early Years*, 1975

W. Spink, 'Sir John Clerk of Penicuik', in P. Willis (ed.), *Furor Hortensis*, 1974

G. Stamp, *Robert Weir Schultz*, 1981

G. Stamp and S. McKinstry (eds), *Greek Thomson*, 1994

1. G. P. Stell, 'Highland Garrisons 1717–23', *Post-Medieval Archaeology* 7, 1973

2. G. P. Stell, 'Scottish Burgh Houses 1560–1707', in A. T. Simpson and S. Stevenson (eds), *Town Houses and Structures in Medieval Scotland*, 1980

3. G. P. Stell, 'The Earliest Tolbooths', *PSAS*, 1981

4. G. P. Stell, 'The Scottish Medieval Castle', in K. J. Stringer (ed.), *Essays on the Nobility of Medieval Scotland*, 1985

5. G. P. Stell, 'Urban Buildings', in M. Lynch, M. Spearman and G. Stell (eds), *The Scottish Medieval Town*, 1988

6. G. P. Stell, 'Kings, Nobles and Buildings of the Later Middle Ages', in G. G. Simpson (ed.), *Scotland and Scandinavia*, 1990

7. G. P. Stell, 'Towards an Atlas of Scottish Vernacular Building', in H. Cheape (ed.), *Tools and Traditions*, 1993

J. Stephens, *The Italian Renaissance*, 1990

D. Stevenson, *The Origins of Freemasonry*, 1988

1. M. C. H. Stewart, *Lord Mar's House 'A'* (manuscript in NMRS), 1986

2. M. C. H. Stewart, 'An Exiled Jacobite's Architectural Activities', *Journal of the Architectural Heritage Society of Scotland*, 1987

3. M. C. H. Stewart, *Lord Mar's Plans, 1700–32* (M.Litt. thesis, University of Glasgow), 1988

4. M. C. H. Stewart, 'Lord Mar's Garden at Alloa', in J. Frew and D. Jones (eds), *Aspects of Scottish Classicism*, 1989

D. Stillman, *The Decorative Work of Robert Adam*, 1973

Sir J. Stirling-Maxwell, *Shrines and Homes of Scotland*, 1937

H. E. Stutchbury, *The Architecture of Colen Campbell*, 1967

A. M. Swan, 'William Kerr', *Architectural Heritage* 3, 1992

I. E. Sweeney, *The Municipal Administration of Glasgow* (Ph.D., Strathclyde University), 1990

C. Tabraham and D. Grove, *Fortress Scotland and the Jacobites*, 1995

1. A. A. Tait, 'The Picturesque Drawings of Robert Adam', *Master Drawings* 9, 1971

2. A. A. Tait, *The Landscape Garden in Scotland*, 1980

3. A. A. Tait, 'The Duke of Hamilton's Palace', *Burlington Magazine*, 1983

4. A. A. Tait, 'Reading the Ruins', *Architectural History* 27, 1984

5. A. A. Tait, *Robert Adam: Drawings and Imagination*, 1993

D. Thomson, *The Works of the Late Charles Wilson*, Glasgow Philosophical Society, Architectural section, paper 13 March 1882 (NMRS)

University of Edinburgh Comprehensive Development Area, 1962 (text by Percy Johnson-Marshall)

Vitruvius, *The Ten Books on Architecture*, trans. by M. H. Morgan, New York, 1960 ed

Vitruvius Scoticus, c.1812 (reprint, ed. J Simpson, 1980)

S. Wagg, *Percy Erskine Nobbs*, Kingston, 1982

P. Wagner, *A Sociology of Modernity*, 1994

1. C. Wainwright, 'Walter Scott and the Furnishing of Abbotsford', *The Connoisseur*, 1977

2. C. Wainwright, *The Romantic Interior*, New Haven, 1989

1. D. M. Walker, 'Sir John James Burnet', in A. Service (ed.), *Edwardian Architecture and Its Origins*, 1975

2. D. M. Walker, 'Charles Rennie Mackintosh' in A. Service (ed.), *Edwardian Architecture and Its Origins*, 1975

3. D. M. Walker, 'The Partnership of James Salmon and John Gaff Gillespie', in A. Service (ed.), *Edwardian Architecture and its Origins*, 1975

4. D. M. Walker, 'William Burn', in J. Fawcett (ed.), *Seven Victorian Architects*, 1976
5. D. M. Walker, 'David Bryce', *Country Life*, 28 October 1976
6. D. M. Walker, 'William Burn', in N. Allen (ed.), *Scottish Pioneers of the Greek Revival*, 1984
7. D. M. Walker, *St Andrew's House*, 1989
8. D. M. Walker, 'The Rhind Lectures: A Synopsis', PSAS 121, 1991
9. D. M. Walker, 'Scotland and Paris 1874–1887', in J. Frew and D. Jones (eds), *Scotland and Europe*, 1991
10. D. M. Walker, 'Listing in Scotland', *Transactions of the Ancient Monuments Society* 38, 1994
11. D. M. Walker, 'The Country House, Larger Villas and Related Hotel Designs of Sir John James Burnet', in Gow and Rowan
1. F. A. Walker, 'Six Villas by James Salmon', *Architectural History* 25, 1982
2. F. A. Walker, 'The Significance of the Folk House', in J. Frew and D. Jones (eds), *Scotland and Europe*, 1991
3. F. A. Walker, 'Robert Adam at Walkinshaw', in I. Gow and A. Rowan (eds), *Scottish Country Houses*, 1995
S. V. Ward, *The Geography of Interwar Britain*, 1988
J. Warrack, *Domestic Life in Scotland 1488-1688*, 1920
M. Watson, *Jute and Flax Mills in Dundee*, 1990
1. D. M. Watters, *St Peter's College, Report for DOCOMOMO Scottish National Group*, 1994
2. D. M. Watters, 'David Hamilton's Lennox Castle', *Architectural Heritage*, 1995
L. Weaver, *The Scottish National War Memorial*, 1927
P. Willis, *New Architecture in Scotland*, 1977
F. Worsdall, *The Glasgow Tenement*, 1989
1. M. Wood, 'All the Statelie Buildings', *Book of the Old Edinburgh Club*, 1942
2. M. Wood, 'Survey of the Development of Edinburgh', *Book of the Old Edinburgh Club*, 1974
G. Worsley, *Classical Architecture in Britain*, 1995
W. Young, *The Municipal Buildings, Glasgow*, 1890
A. J. Youngson, *The Making of Classical Edinburgh*, 1975
J. Zeune, *The Last Scottish Castles*, Buch am Erlbach (Germany), 1992

RCAHMS *Inventories*

Argyll, 7 vols., 1971–92
Berwick, revised 1915
Caithness, 1911
Dumfries, 1920
East Lothian, 1924
(City of) Edinburgh, 1951
Fife, Kinross and Clackmannan, 1933
Kirkcudbright, 1914
Midlothian and West Lothian, 1929
Orkney, 1946
Outer Isles, 1928
Peebles, 1967
Roxburgh, 1956
Selkirk, 1957
Shetland, 1946
Stirlingshire, 2 vols, 1963
Sutherland, 1911
Wigtown, 1911

Buildings of Scotland Series

Dumfries and Galloway: by J. Gifford, 1996
Edinburgh: by J. Gifford, C. McWilliam and D. M. Walker, 1984
Fife: by J. Gifford, 1988
Glasgow: by E. Williamson, A. Riches and M. Higgs, 1990
Highland and Islands: by J. Gifford, 1992
Lothian (except Edinburgh): by C. McWilliam, 1978

RIAS *Illustrated Architectural Guides*

Aberdeen: by W. A. Brogden, 1988 edn
Ayrshire & Arran: by R. Close, 1992
Banff & Buchan: by C. McKean, 1990
Borders & Berwick: by C. A. Strang, 1994
Central Glasgow: by C. McKean, D. M. Walker and F. A. Walker, 1989
Clackmannan & the Ochils: by A. Swan, 1987
Dundee: by C. McKean and D. M. Walker, 1993 edn
Edinburgh: by C. McKean, 1992 edn
Fife: by G. Pride, 1990
Gordon: by I. Shepherd, 1994
Midlothian: by J. Thomas, 1995
Monklands: by A. Peden, 1992
Moray: by C. McKean, 1987
North Clyde Estuary: by F. A. Walker and F. Sinclair, 1992
Orkney: by L. Burgher, 1991
Ross & Cromarty: by E. Beaton, 1992
Shetland: by M. Finnie, 1990
South Clyde Estuary: by F. A. Walker, 1986
Stirling & the Trossachs: by C. McKean, 1985
Sutherland: by E. Beaton, 1995
West Lothian: by R. Jaques and C. McKean, 1994

Glossary

This selective glossary contains specialist architectural terms found in the text, as well as key historical terms possibly unfamiliar to non-Scottish readers. This is not a comprehensive architectural glossary; examples of the latter include those in the *Buildings of Scotland* volumes (for instance, in *Dumfries and Galloway*, 1996, pp. 575–602). Definitions of particular architectural styles are provided at the appropriate points in the text. Cross-references are provided in the few cases of sharp divergence between Scottish and English or American equivalents (abbreviated Engl. or Am.). Dates in brackets refer to period of currency of usage, in cases where this is ambiguous; alternative usages not found in the text are excluded here.

aedicule opening with columnar classical surround and entablature

aisle (a) projecting wing of a church; (b) side passage of a building

all' antica (of sixteenth/seventeenth-century ornament) see: grotesque

anta rectangular-section Order at end of colonnade

antiquity era of Western and Mediterranean civilisation preceding the Middle Ages

apartment (a) in seventeenth–nineteenth centuries: linked group of rooms in dwellings of the rich; (b) in nineteenth–twentieth centuries: an individual room, excluding kitchen, in a working- or middle-class house

apse semi-circular or polygonal extension of room or church

arabesque see: grotesque

architrave lowest level of a classical entablature

arris sharp edge at junction of two surfaces

ashlar squared, dressed, regular stone masonry

astragals (a) glazing bars; (b) circular-section moulding

astylar classical elevation without columns

atrium Postmodern plan-form with glazed-over central courtyard

axis imaginary centre line of an architectural design

baldacchino tent-like canopy with supporting columns

banded rustication horizontally-recessed rustication

bartizan corbelled turret at top of building

basilica plan rectangular plan with nave, aisles and apse battered with sloping-back walling

bay (a) repetitive facade unit; (b) projecting unit of facade

bay window externally projecting window

bellcast roof concave double-pitch roof

blockwork masonry of precast concrete blocks

boss projection, usually covering vault ribs' intersection

broach spire spire with square base and octagonal-section top

buckle quoins quoins featuring projecting and recessed rounded motifs

bungalow single-storey (sometimes with attic) detached twentieth-century middle-class house

burgage plot property holding of medieval burgess: narrow plot at right angles to street

burgh pre-1975 municipality or formally constituted town

burgh of barony burgh founded and dominated by landowner

buttress reinforcing mass of masonry placed against a wall

campanile freestanding tower (especially of church)

canted tilted (usually on plan)

cantilever horizontal projection supported by balancing element behind a fulcrum

capital enriched upper section of column or pilaster

caponier stone-roofed firing gallery

caryatids female figures used in place of columns

castellated battlemented or with bartizans

cast iron iron shaped by moulding process

chamfer diagonally cut-away edge

chancel ceremonial wing of Latin cross church plan

circus circular-plan range of dwellings

classical Greek and Roman antiquity, and its legacy and evocations, including those in architecture

clerestory windowed wall rising above an adjoining roof

close access passage, especially in tenement block

coffering decoration of ceiling with inset panels

collegiate church   church endowed with college of priests

colonnade   regular range of columns

colony plan   lunatic asylum planned in dispersed pavilions

conservation area   local authority-controlled heritage zone

conservative surgery   area improvement doctrine of Patrick Geddes

console   ornamental bracket

corbel   projection supporting feature above

cottage   (a) small dwelling of rural character; (b) in early twentieth century, small non-flatted dwelling with garden

cottage orné   rustic

course   layer of building blocks

Covenanter   supporter of 1638 National Covenant; opponent of post-1660 state religious policy

crosswall   construction using regularly-spaced front-back walls to perform load-bearing function (also known as box frame)

crown spire   crown-shaped openwork spire formed of converging arches

crowstepped gable   gable with stepped sides

cupola   (a) glazed dome over stairwell; (b) domed turret

curtain walling   in Modernist architecture, a non-loadbearing wall fronting framed structure

curvilinear gable   gable-head with several curves at the sides

dado   lower part of wall

(Lord) **Dean of Guild**   pre-1975 urban official who superintended building standards

deck-access   Modernist housing with interconneced access balconies

Diocletian window   see: thermal window

Disruption   1843 split in Kirk over issue of erastianism

district heating   heating of area of housing from one plant

distyle   two-columned (portico)

dormer window   window projecting from roof

double-depth   house-plan two rooms in depth

dressed stone   masonry worked to a smooth finish

dressings   dressed stones used as highlights (for example around a window)

eaves   overhanging edge of roof

eclecticism (synthetic)   style composed of elements selected from different sources

eclecticism (typological)   use of different styles for different building types

engaged   column partly attached to wall or pier

entablature   classical member resting on columns

Episcopalians   champions of more ceremonial and hierarchical Protestantism, within the Kirk before 1689, and as a non-established church afterwards

erastianism   doctrine of state control of church

Evangelicals   in early nineteenth century: expansionist, missionary faction within Kirk: prominent in Disruption

feu   landholding (including buildings) granted in perpetuity

finial   ornamental crowning feature

fluting   series of parallel vertical grooves, especially on a column

forestair   external stair

forework   front building

four-in-a-block   detached two-storey block of four flats

frieze   high-level horizontal band, often ornamented

geometrical staircase   stair with open well, cantilevered from stairwell walls

Gesamtkunstwerk   collaborative work by different types of artist

giant order   classical order two or more storeys high

great apartment   stately group of rooms for use by landed family or guests

Greek cross   right-angled cross with four equal arms

grotesque   classical decoration of fantastic character.

halsgraben   defensive ditch

harling   wet-dash roughcast

Heimatschutz   German movement of national cultural conservation

hexastyle   six-columned (portico)

hôtel   urban dwelling of the rich (especially in France), often with walled forecourt

improvement   especially in eighteenth century: agricultural and industrial/urban modernisation

ingleneuk   hearth recess, often expressed externally

ingo   inward plane of opening (Am./Engl.: reveal)

Jacobite   post-1689 supporter of exiled Stuarts

jamb   (a) wing or extension of building; (b) vertical side of an opening

kirk   church

The Kirk   the post-Reformation Church of Scotland

kit house   late twentieth-century prefabricated house, often rural

laird   landowner

laird's aisle   aisle added to church for laird's use

laminated   layered construction

lancet   thin pointed window

Latin cross   cross with one long and three short arms

lintel   horizontal member spanning opening

listed building   architectural monument classified by State

lists   State register of classified architectural

monuments

lobby hallway in smaller dwelling

lochan small loch

loggia colonnaded or open gallery, or walkway

lunette semi-circular window

machicolation corbelled gallery around castellated house

maisonnette two-storey dwelling in block of flats

mansard roof convex double-pitch roof (Am.: gambrel roof)

masonry wall construction in blocks (stone, concrete or brick)

megastructure covered-in multi-use building

mercat cross column at centre of market area in old burgh

mezzanine intermediate, or subordinate storey

monopitch roof single-pitch sloping roof

mullion vertical member dividing window lights

multi-storey block block over five storeys in height (especially in State housing)

nave main congregation space in Latin cross or bicameral church plan

neighbourhood (unit) housing and 'community' area in 1940s planning ideology

New Town new town built as part of regional planning movement

no-fines in-situ large-aggregate construction

octostyle eight-columned (portico)

ogee double or 'S' curve

Order classical arrangement of column and structurally related elements

oriel bay window starting above ground level

overspill regional planning concept of population decentralisation from cities

palazzo building in style of Italian Renaissance urban palace: massive rectangular form, heavy cornice

panopticon radial prison plan allowing supervision from focal point

pantile curved S-section roof tile

parterre geometrical Renaissance garden layout

patio house single-storey dwelling incorporating private courtyard

pavilion (a) detached specialised or temporary structure; (b) projecting, accented unit in a facade

pediment formalised temple-like classical gable

pend passage spanning entire depth of building

perimeter plan pattern of residential area with buildings in strip around perimeter

peristyle classical colonnade all around a building

perron double (two-arm) forestair

piano nobile principal floor of Renaissance or later house, usually one storey above ground level

piazza (seventeenth/eighteenth-century Scottish use) ground-level arcade

piend(ed) roof roof with sloped ends (Am./Engl.: hip roof)

pier massive blocklike loadbearing column or wall section

pilaster rectangular-section engaged column

pilastrade range of pilasters

pinnacle tapering finial

point block Modernist tower block with compact plan

police urban system of public regulation

polychromy multi-coloured decoration or stonework

polyhedral (sundial) geometrical faceted design

porte-cochère porch incorporating carriageway

portico classical porch with detached columns

prefab temporary aluminium 1940s dwelling

Presbyterianism Calvinist Protestantism

press cupboard

pylon tower-like gateway; solid, high structure (especially, supporting cables)

quarter one side of quadrangular or courtyard complex

quoins dressed stones at angle of building

racetrack ward hospital plan with central services ringed by ward-rooms

rock-faced masonry blocks with rugged facing

rubble stonework of irregular size and shape

rustication masonry with deeply recessed joints or textured surface

saddleback tower tower with gabled roof

saltire diagonal cross, as used on Scottish national flag **sash window** vertically sliding, counterweighted window (Am.: double-hung window)

scale and platt staircase staircase with parallel flights and half-landings

scheme twentieth-century local-authority housing development (Am: project; Engl.: estate)

sheriff court local law-court dealing with lesser offences

slab block Modernist tower block with elongated plan

splay plan symmetrical 'V' plan

state apartment elaborate group of rooms for use of royal or socially elevated guests

steading group of farm buildings

steeple tower, especially of tolbooth or church

strap-work sixteenth/seventeenth century decoration resembling scrolled leather patterns

Taylorism doctrine of scientific management

tenement (a) original usage: plot of land; (b) present-day usage: older block of flats (Am.: apartment building)

terrace   row of houses, or tenements, of unified design

tetrastyle   four-columned (portico)

thermal window   semi-circular window with two to four mullions

tolbooth   burgh headquarters building containing clock, council-chamber and prison

tower block   Modernist multi-storey housing block

tower house   compact type of stone-built castellated dwelling

town house   (a) tolbooth; (b) urban house of landowner

tracery   decoration within an arch or opening

transepts   side wings of Latin-cross church plan

triglyph   stylised beam-endings in Doric frieze

triumphal arch   massive columnar Roman-inspired archway, usually with central and flanking openings, and either freestanding or applied to facade

turnpike staircase   circular stair around central newel

tympanum   triangular or segmental area framed by an arch or pediment

unionist   supporter of political union between Scotland and England (and/or between those two countries and Ireland)

vault   (a) arched ceiling (especially stone ceiling of church); (b) burial aisle

Venetian window   tripartite classical window with raised arch at centre

villa   (a) since Roman times, a country or suburban retreat for the wealthy; (b) since the nineteenth century, a mass-built small suburban dwelling

wainscoting   wood-panelled dado

Whig   in early eighteenth century, Hanoverian government supporter

wrought iron   iron shaped by hammering process

yet(t)   gate

Zeilenbau   Modernist arrangement of slab buildings strictly in parallel

zoning   spatial segregation of urban functions by town-planning regulation

List of Architects and Building Designers

L.1 *The private architect*: bust of David Bryce, by George McCallum, 1866.

Purpose, Scope and General Arrangement

This is a summary list of selected works by Scottish architects and building designers, including 'London Scots' and other expatriates; and of works in Scotland by designers from other countries. It takes the form of an alphabetical index of the names of designers/design organisations and a selection of their works (unrealised projects are not included).

It should be emphasised at the outset that, in contrast to detailed, primary research-based projects such as Colvin's *Dictionary*, or Prof. David Walker's forthcoming dictionary of Scottish architects, this index is, essentially, a summary list derived from the published or publicly available researches of others. The balance and accuracy of the index are thus directly dependent on the (high) standards of those secondary sources.

The most important sources used were: the Historic Scotland lists (available in the National Monuments Record of Scotland); the research notes on individual architects compiled by Prof. David Walker (copy lodged in NMRS); the 1995 edition of Colvin's *Dictionary*; the volumes published so far in the Buildings of Scotland and RIAS Illustrated Guide series; the revised edition (1987) of Gomme and Walker's *Architecture of Glasgow*; Rebecca Bailey's *Scottish Architects' Papers* (1996); and J R Hume's three *Industrial Archaeology of Scotland/Glasgow* volumes (1974–7). During the process of compilation of the list, additional help was received from David Walker (who read several drafts and made many corrections and suggestions); John Hume (especially on engineering works and Episcopal churches); and Fiona Sinclair (on Dunbartonshire buildings). We also received information from the

Saltire Society (on past housing award winners) and from various present-day architectural practices and public authorities. If any errors or significant omissions have escaped our checking process, we would be grateful to learn of these (through the publishers) from readers.

By comparison with the main text of the book, this list avoids any intensive or exclusive focus on works of 'high architecture'. To be sure, virtually all buildings mentioned in the text are also included in this index, and the works of architects of national or international significance, as well as buildings of formal architectural merit, are dealt with in particular detail. But we have also cast the net of selection somewhat wider, in three significant respects.

First, we have tried to reflect sheer quantity of 'architectural' output, and variety of building tasks (two of the key themes in the text), as much as 'quality': the work of organiser-architects such as James Thomson or James Miller is more prominent in our list than that of innovators who built relatively little, such as Lord Mar or William Stark. In a few cases of the most prolific output (such as those of William Burn or Thomas Telford), reference is made to fuller lists in other publications. The relative lack of scholarly research on post-1945 architecture, and on twentieth-century institutional architecture in general, has made it difficult to apply this principle properly to those areas: by comparison with the large nineteenth-century private practices, both twentieth-century architecture and the public architect are somewhat under-represented in this index.

Second, the social scope of 'design' has been defined slightly more widely, for instance by including selected works of engineering (for which the three Hume volumes are basic sources), and building projects of large size and social or economic significance (as distinct from 'architectural merit'). Key architectural conservation or restoration schemes are also included. However, this list is *not* a general index of building: structures not designed by named designers or organisations, but built piecemeal or in an anonymous or low-status manner (for example, the mass of rural housing, nineteenth-century tenements, shops, or small agricultural and industrial buildings) are generally excluded. This distinction highlights still further the relative under-representation of the Modernist era in this index. For those years were, arguably, the time when co-ordinated design (rather than piecemeal or vernacular building) aspired to its widest scope, ranging from the layout of a kitchen to the 'planning' of a whole region or country. Clearly, more research is urgently needed into the work of the many institutions concerned with architectural design after 1945.

Third, we have aimed at a rather wider geographical scope than that of the main text. While the latter (especially in Chapters 5–9) was dominated by the work and concerns of national–status designers in Edinburgh and Glasgow, this list, by contrast, includes a selection of local practices, and buildings from a wide spread of towns across the country.

Guidelines for Individual Entries

Names of Designers

The entries fall into the two main categories of private and public practices. With the former, lack of space and of research time has precluded any comprehensive and consistent listing of the shifting names or dates of partnerships, or of the identities of individual partners and designers within practices: readers seeking a cross-referenced inventory of practices should consult Bailey's *Scottish Architects' Papers*, or the indexes in recent Buildings of Scotland volumes. In this index, we have followed an empirical approach: minor practice changes are aggregated together, and named designers or partners are specified only where prominently known or otherwise significant. With public offices, the names of chief officers during relevant years, especially city architects, have in some cases been listed, for reference purposes; this does not imply direct involvement in individual designs. For the same reasons as with private practices, namely lack of space and of research time, names of individual project designers in public offices are only specified where easily obtainable (for instance, in the case of Irvine DC). Dates of the formation or abolition of public organisations (for example, local authorities) are not generally included. During the nineteenth century, while some official architects (such as John Carrick in Glasgow) worked full time, most (such as John Smith or David Cousin) also enjoyed a private status; the latter are indexed under their own names.

Immediately following the names of architects or practices, supplementary information is listed. In the case of deceased designers, dates of birth and death are included where known. Engineers and certain other professional categories are identified by abbreviations. The square brackets following designers' names and dates of birth/death are used for two purposes. In the case of non-Scottish designers (where their nationality is known), the brackets contain country-abbreviations; and the designers' names are also asterisked. In the case of Scottish designers, the brackets contain the location of their practice, where readily obtainable. Branch offices are not listed; successive principal offices in different locations, during the period covering works cited, are listed in chronological order (separated by commas). Practice names are not included for designers before *c.*1750, as their work was generally of an itinerant nature; court designers worked throughout the east central region, especially at the royal palaces. Practice locations are not included in the case of urban authorities (for example, town councils or school boards).

Works in other countries by Scottish designers are listed more selectively than buildings within Scotland (by Scottish or non-Scottish designers); the most selective treatment of all has been applied to those Scottish or Scottish-trained architects who built nothing at all in Scotland (for instance, Richard Norman Shaw).

Names of Buildings

Where known, the original name is used; only the most important or well-known name changes are included. There is no space in this index to provide systematic information on subsequent changes to the buildings cited, but those known to the authors to have been *completely* demolished are marked with a dagger; we are indebted to Prof. Walker for help in identifying these. City names are used to refer both to locations within contemporary municipal boundaries, and to those outside but later incorporated; examples include pre-1891 buildings in Pollokshields, pre-1912 buildings in Govan or Partick, or pre-1920 buildings in Leith. Town locations are not given in the case of buildings erected by town/city authorities. Buildings in other countries (by Scottish designers) are indicated by bracketed country-abbreviations, except in the most obvious or frequent cases (for example, London).

Dates

The form of each date is determined by its source. Where the latter is sufficiently specific, precise abbreviations (p, b, s, f) are used: see 'Abbreviations: Date', on this page.

Abbreviations

Designer Name

A:	Aberdeen
attr:	attributed
b:	(designer date) birth
d:	death
D:	Dundee
e:	engineer
E:	Edinburgh
G:	Glasgow
m:	mason
(R)MOW:	(royal) master of work(s) or surveyor general (up to early nineteenth century)

Building/Project Name (abbreviations not used in some formal titles)

A:	Aberdeen
a/a:	alterations or additions (except restoration schemes; see below)
br:	bridge
Cong:	Congregational
D:	Dundee
E:	Edinburgh
Epis:	Episcopal
G:	Glasgow
hs:	houses/housing/housing scheme
part:	partial section of a street
RC:	Roman Catholic
restr:	restoration/conservation scheme
UF:	United Free
UP:	United Presbyterian

Self-explanatory abbreviations: Av, Cas, Cath, Ch, Coll, Ho, Hosp, La, Pk, Pl, Rd, Sch, Sq, St, Sta, Terr. Some country houses and villas are listed under name only (without abbreviation 'Ho').

Date

b:	(building date) built
compl:	completed by/completion of
d/u:	precise date unknown
f:	finish of construction
p:	plans drawn up/approved
s:	start of construction

Symbols

*	designer both non–Scottish and based outwith Scotland (country indicated by abbreviation in square brackets)
†	building known to the authors to have been demolished.

ABERCROMBIE, Charles [of E]
Union St general plan, A, p1800; Golden Sq area, A, p1807

ABERCROMBIE, Thomas Graham (1862–1926) [of Paisley]
From 1921, in partnership with J Steel Maitland; post–1926 works, see J S Maitland.
Clark Memorial Ch, Largs, 1890–2 (with W Kerr); Broadlie, Dalry, 1891; Army Drill Hall, Paisley, 1896; Royal Alexandra Infirmary, Paisley, 1896–1900; Paisley Technical Coll, 1898; Hunterhill Ho, Paisley, *c.*1900; Crosbie, Paisley, 1903; Causeyside (part) hs, Paisley, 1903–6; Renfrew District Asylum, Paisley, f1909; Bird in the Hand public ho, Johnstone, *c.*1910; Union Bank,

Renfrew, *c*.1910; Nethercommon Carpet Works, Paisley, 1912; Wallneuk Ch, Paisley, 1913–15; Victory Baths, Renfrew, 1921; Anchor Recreation Club, Paisley, 1924–5; Little Croft, Paisley, 1924–36 (by Maitland)

ABERDEEN CORPORATION/DISTRICT COUNCIL
City Architects from 1924: A B Gardner, 1924–54; George McI Keith, 1954–70; Tom Watson, 1970–5; Ian Ferguson, 1975–89; Tom Steele, 1989–96. Works of pre–1924 postholders listed under their own names.
Woodend Municipal Hospital Nurses' Home, *c*.1936; Bon Accord Baths, 1937; Aberdeen Crematorium, 1937; Rosemount Sq, 1938–46; Provost Skene's Ho restr, s1951; Ashgrove VIII hs, s1959; Municipal Buildings, Broad St, p1962, s1965; Hazlehead hs, s1962; Gallowgate redevelopment, 1964–6; Castlehill redevelopment, s1966; Canal St/Jute St hs, 1972–4; Town Ho Extension, 1975; Jasmine Pl multi–storey sheltered hs, 1983–5

ABERNETHY, James & CO. [of A] (e)
Tongland Br, 1864; Cambus o' May Br, 1905; Invercauld Br, 1924

ADAM, James (1732–94) [of London, E]
See also R Adam.
Cullen Ho gateway, 1767; Shire and Town Hall, Hertford (Engl), 1767–9

ADAM, John (1721–92) [of E and Blair Adam]
Some buildings jointly with Robert Adam.
Banff Cas, *c*.1749–50; Hopetoun Ho compl, 1750–4; Inveraray new town works (including hotel and town house), s1751; Merchant Exchange, E, S1753; Castle Grant a/a, 1753; Yester chapel a/a, *c*. 1753; William Adam mausoleum, Greyfriars Churchyard, E, 1753; †Milton Ho, E, 1754–8; Arniston Ho compl, 1754–8; Dumfries Ho, 1754–9; †Hawkhill Villa, 1757; Douglas Cas, 1757–61; Moffat Ho, 1761–7; Banff Tolbooth Steeple, 1764–7

ADAM, Robert (1728–92) [of London, E]
Pre–1758 work listed under John Adam; some works in this list jointly with James Adam; works built after 1792 largely by James Adam.
Scottish works: 7 Queen St, E, *c*.1770; Mellerstain, *c*. 1770–8; Caldwell Ho, 1771–3; Register Ho, E, p1771, s1774; Wedderburn Cas, 1771–5; Letterfourie, 1773; †Bellevue, E, 1774; †Langside Ho, G, 1777 (attr); Culzean Cas, s1777, a/a, s1785; David Hume Monument, E, 1777; Auchencruive tea–house, 1778; Queensberry Monument, Dumfries, 1780; Oxenfoord Cas a/a, 1780–2; Megginch Cas a/a, *c*.1780–90; Dalquharran Cas, s1782; †Jerviston Ho, 1782; Pitfour Cas (attr), *c*.1785; †Dalquharran rustic hut, *c*.1785; Sunnyside, Liberton, 1785–8; Kirkdale Ho, 1787–8;

†Barholm Ho, 1788; Edinburgh University Coll, s1789; Newliston Ho, 1789–91; Archerfield Ho a/a, *c*.1790; Lauderdale Ho, Dunbar, a/a, 1790; Glencarse Ho, 1790; Caisteal Gorach, Tulloch Cas, 1790; Seton Cas, 1790; Airthrey Cas, s1790; Johnstone Mausoleum, Westerkirk, *c*.1790; Balavil Ho, *c*. 1790–6; Charlotte Sq, E, p1791, s1792; Trades' Hall, G, 1791–4 (refaced J Keppie, 1927); †Bridewell Prison, E, 1791–5; St George's Episcopal Chapel, E, 1792; Dalkeith Palace Br, 1792; †Walkinshaw Ho, 1792; Stobs Cas, 1792–3; †Balbardie Ho, 1792–3; †Infirmary, G, 1792–4; †Mauldslie Cas, 1792–6; Gosford Ho, 1792–1803; †Professors' Lodgings, High St, G, s1793; Tron Kirk, G, rebuilt 1793–4; Assembly Rooms, G, s1796 (largely †; portico resited 1893).
Principal English works: Harewood Ho a/a, 1759–71; Kedleston Hall a/a, s1761; Syon Ho a/a, s1762; Osterley Pk a/a, s1763; Luton Pk, 1766–74; Kenwood a/a, 1767–9; †Adelphi Buildings, London, 1768–71; †Northumberland Ho a/a, 1770–5; 20 St James Sq, London, 1771–4; †Derby Ho, London, a/a, 1773–4; Home Ho, London, 1773–6; Portland Pl, London, s1774; Fitzroy Sq, London, 1790–4

ADAM, William (1689–1748)
Makerstoun Ho, *c*.1715; Hopetoun Ho a/a, s1721; Floors Cas a/a, 1721–6; Dalmahoy Ho, fl725; Craigdarroch Ho, 1726–9; Arniston Ho, 1726–33; Somerville Ho (The Drum), 1726–34; Hamilton Palace landscaping, 'Great Plan', 1728; Hamilton Parish Ch, 1729–32; Yester Ho a/a, 1730; House of Dun, s1730 (with Lord Mar); Robert Gordon's Hosp, A, 1730–2; Cumbernauld Ho, 1731; †Dundee Town Ho, 1731–4; Chatelherault, 1731–*c*.1742; Haddo Ho, 1732–5; †Glasgow University Library, 1732–45; Tay Br, Aberfeldy, 1733–5; Taymouth Cas a/a, *c*.1733/42; †Orphans' Hosp, E, 1734; Mansion Ho, Earl of Hopetoun's mines, Leadhills (attr), 1734–40; Sanquhar Tolbooth, 1735–7; Duff Ho, 1735–40; Murdostoun Cas, *c*.1735–40; Brunstane Ho a/a, 1735–44; †George Watson's Hosp, E, 1738; Eglinton Garden Temple, *c*.1738; Tinwald Ho, 1738–40; Minto Ho, Roxburghshire, a/a, *c*.1738–43; Minto Ho, E, 1738–43; Royal Infirmary, E, 1738–48; Torrance Ho a/a, *c*.1740; Gartmore Ho, 1740–5; †Buchanan Ho, 1741; Haddington Town Ho, 1742–5

* AHRENDS, BURTON & KORALEK [Engl]
Cummins Engine Co. Ltd factory, Shotts, 1975–83

AITKEN, George Shaw (1836–1921) [of D, E]
In Dundee 1873–81; partner of James MacLaren, 1873–7.
Queen St Ch, Broughty Ferry, D, 1876; Calcutta Buildings, D, 1877; Ryehill Ch, D, 1878; Northwood, Broughty Ferry, D, 1880; Lady Stair's Ho, E, restr, 1893–7

* AL–BAYATI, Basil [Engl/Iraq]
Great Mosque, E, p1988

ALEXANDER, Sir Anthony (d.1637) (R)MOW
Argyll Lodging, Stirling, a/a, 1632 (attr); Alexander (later Bowie) Aisle, Holy Rude Kirk, Stirling, 1630s

ALISON, James Pearson (*c.*1862–1932) [of Hawick]
From 1959, practice renamed Aitken & Turnbull.
Hawick Cong Ch, 1893; Victoria Hotel, Hawick, 1893; Wilton UP Ch, Hawick, 1894; North Bridge St, Hawick, 1899–1900; Jedburgh Public Hall, 1901; St Dunstan's Pk, Melrose, 1966–8; Croft St hs, Galashiels, 1968–76; Liddesdale Rd hs, Hawick, 1972–4; Howegate restr, Hawick, 1978–85; Edenside Ct hs, Kelso, 1985–7; Peebles Old Town restr, 1990

ALISON & HUTCHISON & PARTNERS [of E]
Grangepans Redevelopment, Bo'ness, 1958–9; Napier Coll, E, 1961; Couper St hs, Leith, E, 1961–3; Paisley Coll of Technology, 1962–3; Windyknowe Primary Sch, Bathgate, 1963; Scottish Woollen Technical Coll, Galashiels, 1963–5; Cables Wynd hs, Leith, E, 1963–6; Tolbooth Wynd hs, Leith, E, 1964–6; Mingle hs, Bo'ness, 1967; St Andrew's RC Ch, Livingston, 1968; Craigmount High Sch, E, 1968–70; Cardonald Coll, G, 1968–72; Princess Alexandra Eye Pavilion, E, 1971

ALLAN, Alexander [of E]
Comely Bank Av hs, E, 1898

ALLAN, J A Ogg (1869–1955) [of A]
Robert Gordon's Institute annexe, A, 1920; Tullos Sch, A, 1939; Cummings Pk Sch, A, 1953 (by Allan, Ross & Allan)

ALLAN, W (d.1945) **& FRISKIN, William Wallace** (b.1889) [of D]
St Mary's Sch, D, 1926; Rockwell Central Sch, D, 1929–30); Saints Peter and Paul RC Sch, D, 1929–30; UF Ch, Caird Av, D, 1931; St Joseph's Sch, D, 1933–4; St Mungo's RC Ch, Alloa, f1961

ALSTON, W [of G] (e)
Engineer-in-Chief to Clyde Navigation Trust.
Meadowside Granary, G, 1911–13 (compl 1967)

ANDERSON, J Macvicar (1835–1915) [of London]
Bowhill Ho a/a, 1874–6; †Alloway, Doonside Ho and gates, 1884–9; Inverlochy Cas a/a, 1889–92

ANDERSON, Sir Robert Rowand (1834–1921) [of E]
Partnerships: Anderson & (G W) Browne, 1881–4; Wardrop, Anderson & Browne, 1884–5; (H M) Wardrop & Anderson, 1886–99; Anderson, Simon & Crawford, 1899–1902; Anderson (Rowand) & Paul, 1904–36; Anderson (Rowand), Paul & Partners, 1936–45; Anderson (Rowand), Kininmonth & Paul, 1945–76;
Rowand Anderson Partnership, post–1976; post–1904 work: see separate entries.
Christ Church Epis Ch, Falkirk, 1863–4; St Michael and All Saints Epis Ch, E, 1865–78; St Andrew's Epis Ch, St Andrews, 1867–9; St Vigeans Parish Ch, restr, 1871; St Augustine's Epis Ch, Dumbarton, 1873; Catholic Apostolic Ch, E, 1873–94; Stockbridge, †West Fountainbridge and †Causewayside Schs, E, 1874–6; Iona Abbey restr, 1874–6; West Primary Sch, Linktown, 1874–80; Edinburgh University Extension Buildings, 1874–88; Jedburgh Abbey restr, 1875; Holy Trinity Epis Ch, Stirling, 1875–6; St James the Great Epis Ch, Stonehaven, 1875–7 (compl with A Clyne, 1883–1906); St Bride's Ch, Douglas, restr, 1878; Mount Stuart a/a (first phase), 1878–86; Torduff, Colinton, E, 1879; St John's Epis Ch, Forfar, 1879–81; Allermuir, Colinton, E, 1879–82 (for himself); North Berwick Parish Ch, 1879–82; Nile Grove, E, *c.*1880 (and other Braid Estate hs, 1880–4) (by Browne); lodge and sanatorium, Fettes Coll, E, s1880; St George's Free Ch, E, steeple, 1880–2; Conservative Club, E, 1881–4; Govan Old Parish Ch, p1882, b1884–8; Caledonian Railway offices (later hotel), Central Sta, G, 1882–4; Normand Hall, Dysart, 1883–5; Hermitage Terr, E, 1884–7; Glencorse Parish Ch, 1884–8; Scottish National Portrait Gallery and National Museum, 1884–9; St James's Epis Ch, Inverleith, E, p1885; St Sophia's Ch, Galston, 1885–6; Ardgowan Estate office, Greenock, 1886; Edinburgh University College, dome, 1886–7; Queen's Hall, Charlestown, 1887; 1–11 Inverleith Pl, E, 1887; St Cuthbert's Epis Ch, Colinton, E, 1888–9; 3–13 Braid Rd, E, 1889–90; Dunblane Cath restr, 1889–93; St Paul's Ch, Greenock, 1890; King's Coll Chapel, A, restr, 1890–1; South Morningside Ch, E, 1890–2; Pollok Ho, G, a/a, 1890–1908 (with A Balfour Paul); Pearce Institute, Govan, 1892/1902–6; 4–6 Barnshot Rd, Colinton, 1895–6; Pollokshaws Burgh Buildings, 1895–8; Glencoe Ho, 1896; McEwan Hall, E, 1897; Mount Stuart chapel, 1897–1902; Paisley Abbey restr, 1898–1907; †Inchinnan Ch, 1899–1904

ANDERSON, William J (1863–1900) [of G]
Balmory, Sherbrooke Av, G, *c.*1893; Orient Ho, Cowcaddens, G, 1893; Napier Ho, Govan, G, 1898–9

ANDERSON (ROWAND) & BALFOUR PAUL/ANDERSON (ROWAND), PAUL & PARTNERS [of E]
See also R R Anderson; A F B Paul; B U Spence. From 1933/4, most design work was by William Kininmonth and Basil Spence, who also ran informal partnership of Kininmonth and Spence.
5 Charlotte Sq, E, a/a, s1904 (by Balfour Paul); Harmeny Ho, Balerno, 1906; Dundee University

buildings, 1907; St George's Sch, E, 1911–14; Edinburgh University Chemistry Building, 1920–4; 6 Castlelaw Rd, E, 1932 (by Spence); Causewayside garage, E, 1933; 46a Dick Place, E, 1933 (by Kininmonth; his own house); 40–2 Dick Place, E, 1934; Dunbar fishermen's cottages, 1934–5; 4 and 11 Easter Belmont Rd, E, 1934/5; Broughton Pl, 1935–8; Edinburgh Dental Hosp, 1936 (by Paul and Spence); Quothquan Lodge, 1937–8; Pearl Assurance Building extension, E, 1937–9 (by Spence); Gribloch, 1938; †Scottish Pavilions, ICI Pavilion and 'Modern Country House', 1938 Glasgow Empire Exhibition (by Spence); Kilsyth Academy, s1938, compl 1948–53 (by Spence); Forth timber hs for SSHA, 1939

ANDERSON (ROWAND), KININMONTH & PAUL [of E]

Design work by Kininmonth and later partners (Ian C Gordon, Thomas Duncan, William G Leslie, Richard Ewing, A Somerville).
Pollock Halls, E, 1952–9; Renfrew Airport Terminal, 1953–4; University Examination Halls, E, 1954; Drylaw Parish Ch, E, 1956–7; Castlehill hs, Forres, 1956–8; Elgin Town Hall, f1961; Scottish Provident offices, E, 1961–9; Edinburgh University Student Union extension, 1962–4; Muirhouse Phase II (Martello Ct), E, 1962–4; James Gillespie's High Sch, E, 1962–4; Linlithgow West Port hs, 1963; Philiphaugh, 1964; Brucefield Ch, Whitburn, 1964–6; Craigsbank Parish Ch, E, 1964–6; Mary Erskine Sch, E, 1964–7; Linlithgow CDA, 1967–9

ANDREW, Gabriel (1851–1933) [of Kilmarnock]

Later, in partnership with William Newlands.
Croft St whisky bonds, Kilmarnock, 1897; Co-operative Buildings, Newmilns, 1900; Co-operative Buildings, Galston, 1901; Kilmarnock Equitable Co-operative Society, Portland St, Kilmarnock, 1905

ANGUS, George (1792–1845) [of E]

Kettle Parish Ch, 1831–2; Kinross West Ch, 1832; Dundee Public Seminaries, p1832; Tulliallan Ch, Kincardine-on-Forth, 1832–3; Dundee Sheriff Ct, s1833; Reform St, D, s1834; Watt Institution, D, 1838–9

ARCADE ARCHITECTS [of E]

Hutchesontown Area D rehab masterplan, G, 1988–90; Spilmersford Mill Ho, Pencaitland, 1990; 10 Hunter Sq restr, E, 1993; 8 Lyne St hs, E, 1993–4; 28 Dickson St hs, E, 1993–4; Coltbridge Millside hs, E, 1994–5

ARCHIMEDIA [of E]

†Broom Milk Bar, Glasgow Garden Festival, 1988; 10 Hillpark Rd a/a, E, 1992

ARGYLL COUNTY COUNCIL [of Dunoon]

Dunbeg Village hs, Oban, 1957–61 (County Architect, W R Tocher); Kilmory Ho a/a, 1980–2 (by Argyll and Bute District Council).

* ARKWRIGHT, Sir Richard (1732–1792) [Engl]

Bell Mill, Stanley Mills, 1786–7

ARNOTT, J E

See Campbell & Arnott.

ARNOTT, James Alexander (1871–1950) & MORRISON, J Inch (d.1944) [of E]

Charlotte Chapel, E, 1908; Pleasance Trust, E, 1925–38 (by Morrison); Fenton Barns, 1938–40 (by Morrison)

ARROL, Sir William, LTD [of G] (e)

Harland & Wolff Scotstoun Works, G, c.1907; Travelling Crane, Glen Shipyard, Port Glasgow, 1974 (by Arrol-Jucho PMB)

ARTHUR, John M [of G]

Marr Coll, Troon, 1919; Students Union, Glasgow University, 1929 (with Alan MacNaughtan)

* ARUP, Ove & PARTNERS [Engl] (e)

Scottish offices opened from 1960 (in Edinburgh, Glasgow, Dundee, Aberdeen).
Kessock Br, 1982 (with Ove Arup); Kylesku Br, 1984

ASSIST [of G]

Taransay St Treatment Area hs restr, Govan, G, s1971 (and numerous later community rehab schemes); Briggait Centre, G, a/a, 1983–6; West End Park St hs, G, 1988–9; Kerr St hs, G, 1991–2; Anderson St hs, G, f1992; Carnarvon St hs, G, 1992–3; Murano St student hs, G, 1992–3; Hutchesontown D hs a/a, G, s1993; Achamore Rd hs, G, 1993–4

* ATKINSON, William (c.1773–1839) [Engl]

Scone Palace a/a, 1803–12; Rossie Priory, 1807–15; Tulliallan Cas, 1817–20; Abbotsford, 1817–23 (with Sir Walter Scott); Taymouth Cas a/a, 1818–25; Canonbie Parish Ch, 1821–2

AYTOUN, W (d. c.1643) (m)

George Foulis of Ravelston monument, Greyfriars Churchyard, E, 1636; Innes Ho, 1640–53

BACHOP, Tobias (d.1710) (m)

25 Kirkgate, Alloa, 1695; Dumfries Town Hall, s1705 (with W Moffat)

BAIRD, Hugh (e)

Edinburgh & Glasgow Union Canal, 1818–22

BAIRD, John (I) (1798–1859) [of G]

†Greyfriars United Secession Ch, G, 1821;

†Wellington Ch, G, 1823; †Anderston Old Parish Ch, G, 1839; Somerset Pl, G, 1840; Cairnhill Ho, Airdrie, 1841; †Erskine UP Ch, G, 1842; St Peter's Epis Ch, Kirkcaldy, 1844; Claremont Terr, G, 1847; Woodlands Terr, G, 1849–50; 64 Buchanan St, G, 1851; 27–59 James Watt St, G, 1854 (later a/a 1870, 1910–12, 1932); Ury Ho, 1855; Gardner's warehouse, G, 1855–6

BAIRD, John (I) & THOMSON, James [of G]
In partnership from 1856. Entry includes works of James Thomson, and (after 1900) of J B & W A Thomson.
Dowanhill feuing plan, G, 1858; Crown Circus, G, 1858; Provincial Insurance Building, West George St, G, 1859–60 (heightened *c.*1900); 217–21 Argyle St, G, 1863; Govan Combination Poorhouse (Southern General Hosp), G, 1867–72; Belhaven Terr, G, 1868–9; Prince's Terr, G, 1868–72; Belhaven Terr West, G, 1870–4; Crown Gardens, G, 1873–4; Strathbungo –Queens Park Ch, G, 1873–5; Crown Terr, G, 1873–80; 101–3 St Vincent St, G, 1876; Kirklee Gardens, G, 1877–8; 150–4 West George St, G, 1878; Garnethill Public Sch, 1878 (extended 1886 by W F McGibbon); †Grand Hotel, G, 1882; Queen's Gardens, G, 1882–93; 1–9 Devonshire Terr, G, *c.*1883; Belmont Cas, Meigle, 1885; Standard Buildings, Hope St, G, 1890 (a/a 1909); MacKirdy Mon, Glasgow Necropolis, 1891; Schaw Hosp, Bearsden, 1895; Pearl Assurance office, G, 1896–7; Stewart & Macdonald workshop block, G, 1897–8; Connal's Building, West George St, G, 1898; Liverpool, London & Globe Assurance Buildings, G, 1899–1901; Dumbarton Municipal Buildings, 1900; St Vincent Chambers, Buchanan St, G, 1902

* BAKER, Sir Benjamin (e) [Engl]
See Sir J Fowler.

BALDIE, Robert (d.1890) [of G]
Carron Iron Works offices and foundry, 1875–6; Pollokshields Established Ch, G, 1878; †Kelvingrove UP Ch, G, 1879; Glasgow Maternity Hosp, G, 1880–1; Carluke Town Hall, 1884

BALFOUR, Andrew (1863–1948) [of G]
St Columba's Ch, Largs, 1891–3 (by Steele & Balfour); Langside Sch, G, 1904–6; Bank of Scotland Chambers, St Vincent St, G, 1924–6 (by Balfour & Stewart)

BARBOUR, James (1835–1912) [of Dumfries]
From 1896, with John McL Bowie (b.1871).
Castle Douglas Town Hall, 1862–3; Maxwelltown West Ch, 1865–6; Waterbeck Ch, 1868–9; Kirkpatrick Irongray Parish Ch a/a, 1872–3; County Police Barracks, Dumfries, 1876; New Abbey Parish Ch, 1876–7; 24–36 Buccleuch St, Dumfries, 1877; Closeburn Ch and Sch, 1878; Troqueer Ch, 1886; Cowhill Estate Creamery, 1922

BARCLAY, Hugh (1828–92) and David (1846–1917) [of G]
Prior to D Barclay's partnership, known as Barclay & Watt.
†Colosseum Building, G, 1856–7; †Ewing Place Ch, G, 1858; 7–15 Partickhill Rd, G, 1874; 53–63 Peel St, G, 1875; Glasgow Academy, 1878; Melville St Sch, 1878–9; Abbotsford Sch, G, f1879; Greenock Municipal Buildings, 1881–9; Pollokshields Secondary Sch, G, 1882; †Rutland Cres Sch, G, 1883; Hillhead High School, G, 1883; Jean St Sch, Port Glasgow, 1883–4; St George's in the Fields Ch, G, 1885–6; Lamlash Parish Ch, Arran, 1886; Govanhill Sch, G, 1886–7; Clune Park Sch, Port Glasgow, 1887; Blacklock & McArthur Warehouse, G, 1888; Fairfield Sch, G, 1891; Cumming & Smith warehouse, Sauchiehall St, G, 1891–5; Central Thread Agency, G, 1891–1901; Coats Thread Agency, G, 1891–1901; Lorne St Sch, G, 1892; Mount Florida Sch, G, 1895; Millport Burgh Chambers, 1895; Cunninghame Ch, G, 1897; 106–14 Argyle Street, Miss Cranston's Tearooms, G, 1897; Dowanhill St, Downside Rd, G, 1898–1907; St Leonard's Sch, Dunfermline, 1900–2; Albert Rd Academy, G, 1901; Royal Coll of Science and Technology, G, 1901–5; 11–24 Kensington Gate, G, 1902–3; Leverndale Hosp (Hawkhead Asylum) a/a, G, 1903–5; Grange Sch, Bo'ness, 1906; Coatbridge Higher Grade Sch, 1908–10; Jordanhill Coll, G, 1913–22

BARCLAY, Thomas [of Balbirnie]
Falkland Town Hall, 1800

* BARLOW, W H & SON [Engl] (e)
Second Tay Br, 1887

BAXTER, John, the elder (d. *c.*1770) [of E]
†Hawkhead Ho, *c.*1738; Galloway Ho, 1740–5; Mayshade Ho, 1753

BAXTER, John, the younger (d.1798) [of E]
Mortonhall Ho, *c.*1769; †Gordon Cas a/a, 1769–82; Cowgate Chapel, E, 1771–4; Kenmore Br, 1774; Fochabers new town, s1776; Balbirnie Ho a/a, 1777–82; Peterhead Town Ho, 1788; Merchant Company Hall, E, 1788–90; Bellie Ch, Fochabers, 1795–7

BAXTER, David, CLARK, John S & PAUL, James [of D]
Practice formed 1959; in succession to Johnston & Baxter, q.v.
Ardler patio hs, D, 1963–5; Little Nursery hs, Montrose, 1964–6; Ferguson Pk hs, Blairgowrie, 1965–70; Ilderton hs, Banchory, 1966–8; School Rd hs, Keith, 1967–9; East St hs, St Monans, 1968–70; Royal

Hosp for Sick Children, G, 1968–71; St Peter's St hs, Peterhead, 1968–71; Matthew Building, Duncan of Jordanstone Coll, D, 1969–74; Claben Ltd offices, A, 1973; Strathmore hs, D, 1972–4; Penny La hs, Nairn, 1976–8; Castle St hs, Fraserburgh, 1976–8; Harbourlea hs, Anstruther, 1977–81 (and a/a 1991); Whinnieknowe Gardens hs, Nairn, 1978–80; Paisley District General Hosp, 1978–85; Upper Dens redevelopment, D, 1981–8; Clydesdale Bank, Longman Estate, Inverness, 1983; Caithness General Hosp, Wick, 1983–6; Lindsay Court, Dundee Technology Pk, 1985; Dorward Gardens, Montrose, 1988–9; Seafield Pl, Portsoy, hs, 1990

* BEARD, BENNETT & WILKINS [Engl]
NCR Factory, D, s1946; Timex Factory, D, 1947

BEATTIE, W Hamilton (1840–98) [of E]
Braid Hills Hotel, E, 1886; Grand Hotel, Lerwick, 1886–7; Jenners Store, E, 1893–5; North British (Balmoral) Hotel, E, 1896–1902; Carlton Hotel, E, 1898

BEATTIE, George & SON (W H Beattie) [of E]
See also W H Beattie.
Royal Bank Stationery Warehouse, West Register St, E, 1864; City Poorhouse, Craiglockhart, E, 1867–9

* BECKETT, Sir Martyn [Engl]
Callernish Ho, North Uist, 1962

BEGG, Ian [of E and Plockton]
Pre-1983 work: see R Hurd. From 1985, in partnership with Raymond Muszynski.
Hopetoun Ho restr, s1985; Ravens' Craig, Plockton, 1987–9 (for himself); Scandic Crown Hotel, High St, E, 1988–9; Paxton Ho restr, 1988–91; Cathedral Sq Visitor Centre (St Mungo Museum), G, 1990–3; Caberfeidh, Skye, 1991; Cawdor Estate a/a, 1993; Priorwood Garden Shop, Melrose, 1993–4; Gosford Ho restr, 1993–4

BEGG, James [of E]
1–5 Gayfield Pl, E, s1790

BEGG, John (1866–1937) [of Johannesburg, Bombay, E]
Agricultural Coll, Poona (India), 1902; Bombay General Post Office (India), 1903–9; Institute of Scottish Architects headquarters, 15 Rutland Sq, E, a/a, 1922–3; 57–9 Upper Craigs, Stirling, 1935

BEL, George (m)
Midmar Cas, 1570–5

BEL, John (m)
Craigievar Cas (compl), 1610–26; Castle Fraser a/a, 1617–18

BELL, Eric S [of Stirling]
Drip Rd hs, Stirling, p1920; Boys' Club, Stirling, 1929

BELL, Jonathan Anderson (c.1809–65) [of E]
Valleyfield Mill Sch, Penicuik, 1823; Beeslack Ho, 1855–7

BELL, Samuel (1739–1813) [of D]
St Andrew's Ch, D, 1772; †Trades Hall, D, 1776; †English Chapel (Union Hall), D, 1783; Forfar Parish Ch, 1790–1 (compl Patrick Brown)

BELL, William [of E]
Secession Ch, Great Junction St, Leith, E, 1824–5

BENSON, Gordon & FORSYTH, Alan
[of London]
National Museum of Scotland, E, s1996

BERCOTT, Baron [of G]
Sandyhills House multi–storey hs, G, 1964–9; Falkirk Municipal Buildings, f1965; Whitehill Sch, G, 1973–9; 100 West George St, G, 1988

* BERNHARDT, Karl [Ger]
North British Diesel Engine Works, G, 1912–13 (with J Galt)

* BERU, Sherab Palden [Tib]
Kagyu Samye Ling Tibetan Centre, Davington, 1979–88

* BILLINGS, Robert W (1813–74) [Engl]
Gosford west lodge, 1854; 115–37 Ingram St, G, 1854–6; King's Old Building, Stirling Cas restr, 1857; Dalzell Ho a/a, s1859; Castle Wemyss a/a, s1860

BINNIE, Thomas (1792–1867) [of G]
Monteith Row, G, s1812

BINNIE, William Bryce (b.1885/6)
Memorial to the Missing, Nieuwport (Belg), f1928

BISSET, L [of Golspie]
Golspie Drill Hall, 1892; Dunrobin Sta, 1902; Golspie UF Ch, 1905–6

BLACK, James (d.1841) [of D]
Dundee Town's Architect, 1833–41.
Arbroath Public Library (originally Academy), 1821; †St George's Ch, D, 1824–5; South Commercial St layout, D, 1828; 1–4 Somerville Pl, D, 1830

BLACK, Robert (c.1800–69) **& SALMON** [of G]
See also J Salmon senior.
†Mechanics' Institute, G, 1831 (by Black); †City of Glasgow Bank, G, 1838 (by Black); Adelaide Pl, G, s1839 (by Black); Barony Ch, Ardrossan, 1844; St Mark's Free Ch, G, 1848; †St Matthew's Free Ch, Bath St, G, 1849; 65–81 Miller St, G, 1849–50

BLANC, Hippolyte (1844–1917) [of E]
Christ Church Epis Ch, E, 1875–8; Mayfield Free Ch, 1876–80; St Margaret's Epis Ch, Easter Rd, E, 1879–80; Marchmont Rd east side hs, E, 1880; St James's Epis Ch, Paisley, 1880; Greenbank UF Ch, Greenock, 1882; Bruntsfield Pl hs (part), E, 1882; St Luke's Free Ch, West Ferry, 1884; Edinburgh Cas a/a, s1886; Coats Memorial Ch, Paisley, 1886–94; New Cafe (Edinburgh Cafe), 70 Princes St, E, 1886–98; Perth Middle Ch, 1887; St Matthew's Ch, Morningside, E, 1889–90; Ferguslie Pk, Paisley, 1890; St Leonard's Epis Ch, Lasswade, 1890; All Souls Ch, Invergowrie, 1891; Morningside Free Ch, E, 1892; St Cuthbert's Ch, E, a/a, 1892–5; Troon Old Parish Ch, 1894; Edinburgh District Asylum, Bangour, 1898–1906

* BLORE, Edward (1787–1879) [Engl]
Corehouse, 1824–7

BLYTH & BLYTH [of E] (e)
Partnership details: from 1848 to 1854, Benjamin Hall Blyth (1819–66); 1854–67, Blyth & Blyth; 1867–86, Blyth & Cunningham; 1886–93, Cunningham, Blyth & Westland; 1893–1913, Blyth & Westland; from 1913, Blyth & Blyth.
Avon Railway Viaduct, Chatelherault, 1865; Glasgow Central Sta (including Clyde rail br), 1876–9; Ayr New Br, 1877–9; Carlisle Citadel Sta (Engl), a/a, 1881; Victoria Br, A, 1881; Perth Sta a/a, 1884; Waverley Sta a/a and Mound outer tunnels, E, 1892; North Br, E, 1894–7; Glasgow Br, Jamaica St, 1896–9; New Dunglass Br, 1931–2

* BODLEY, George F (1827–1907) [Engl]
St Salvador's Epis Ch, D, 1865–75; St Bride's Epis Ch, Hyndland, G, p1903 (compl H O Tarbolton 1916)

BONNAR, Thomas (d.1847) [of E]
Edinburgh City Superintendent of Works, 1809–19.
Dundas St, E, s1807; Bellevue Cres, E, p1818; East Claremont St, E, s1824; Atholl Cres/Pl/Torphichen St, E, s1824/5

BORDERS REGIONAL COUNCIL, Department of Architectural Services [of Melrose]
D A S Henry, Director.
Broomlands Primary Sch, Kelso, 1980; Saltgreens Home, Eyemouth, 1989

BOSWELL, George (1879–1952) [of G]
From 1950: Boswell, Mitchell & Johnston.
Ciro shopfront, Buchanan St, G, 1926–7; Templeton Factory extensions, G, 1934 and 1936; Chirnside Sch, G, 1950; IBM factory, Spango Valley, s1952; Dunoon pavilion, s1956; Hutcheson's Boys Grammar Sch, G, 1957–60; Sacred Heart Sch, Cumbernauld, 1960; Seafar Primary Sch, Cumbernauld, 1962–3; Pollokshaws CDA Unit 2 hs, G, 1962–74 (with Concrete Scotland Ltd); Eastmuir Sch, G, f1963; Woodside CDA Area A hs, G, s1964, and Phase 3 hs, 1970; Borestone development, Bannockburn, Phase 2, s1966; Hamilton Teacher Training Coll and residences, f1969; Dumfries & Galloway Royal Infirmary, Dumfries, 1970–5; Inverclyde Royal Hosp, Greenock, 1977–9

BOUCH, Sir Thomas [of E] (e)
Balbirnie Viaduct, 1861; Leslie Viaduct, 1861; †(First) Tay Br, f1878

BOUCHER, James (1832–1906) **& COUSLAND, James** (c.1832–66) [of G]
Kemp's warehouse, G, 1853–4; †Renfield Free Ch, G, 1857; †35–7 St Andrew's Dr, G, 1858; 66–70 Gordon St, G, 1858; Tighnabruaich Parish Ch and manse, 1863; Kibble Palace, Coulport, 1863–6 (moved to Glasgow Botanic Gardens 1873); †St George's, Berkeley and Elderslie Streets, G, 1864; †St George's Free Ch, G, f1865; 1, 3, 4 Sydenham Rd, G, c.1865; Greenock Club, 1867–9; Redlands Ho, G, c.1871; 22 Park Circus, G, 1872–4; 20 St Enoch Sq, G, 1875; 79 West George St, G, 1875; 998 Great Western Rd, G, 1877; †Woodside Parish Ch, G, 1880

BOULTON, William [of A] (e)
Denburn and Rosemount Viaducts, A, 1886

BOYD, John
Tolbooth Steeple, G, 1625–7; †Library Ho (south-west tower) restr, Glasgow Cath, 1628

BOYS, David (MOW)
Ravenscraig Cas a/a and artillery defences, 1461–3 (attr, with H Merlzioun)

BOYS JARVIS PARTNERSHIP [of G]
Chivas Regal Building, Paisley, 1962–4 (by Lothian Barclay, Jarvis & Boys); Shambala, Gourock, 1968; Glenallachie Distillery, 1969 and 1975; Refuse Incineration Plant, Linwood, f1974; West Campbell St offices, G, 1986

BRASH, John (d.1848) [of G]
Strathblane Ch, 1803–4; Tollcross Relief Ch, 1805–6; Galston Old Ch, 1808–9; Riverside Ch, Dumbarton, 1811; Largs Parish Ch a/a, 1812; First Reformed Presbyterian Ch, G, 1819; Shotts Ch, 1820; Blythswood Sq, G, compl 1823–9 (attr, with W Burn, G Smith)

BRODIE, Margaret B [of Lochwinnoch]
†Women of the Empire Pavilion, 1938 Glasgow Empire Exhibition; St Martin's Ch, Port Glasgow, 1957–9; St Brendan's Ch, Rothesay, 1974; Laurieston-Gorbals Ch, G, 1974–80

BRODIE, William (d.1787) [of E]
Tweeddale Court hs, E, 1783

* **BROOKS, James** (1825–1901) [Engl]
St Modoc's Ch, Doune, 1877–8

BROUNHILL, John (m)
Gatehouse, Falkland Palace, fl541

BROWN, Alexander (d.1925) **& WATT, George**
(1853–1931) [of A]
Aberdeen Public Library, 1891–2; Holburn Free Ch, A,
1894; Beechgrove Free Ch, A, 1896–1900; 1–27
Rosemount Viaduct, A, 1897; 32 Rubislaw Den South,
A, 1897; 34 Rubislaw Den South, A, 1900; Aberdeen
Central Bakery, 1900; Ruthrieston West Ch, A, 1900–1;
Melville UF Ch, A, 1901–3; Infectious Diseases Hosp,
Stonehaven, 1902–3; Oldmill Poorhouse, A, 1902–7;
Torphins Ch, 1905; 25 Rubislaw Den North, A, 1909

BROWN, James (*c*.1729–1807) [of E]
Brown Sq, E, 1750s; George Sq, E, 1766–85;
Buccleuch Pl, E, 1779–92

BROWN, James (d.1878) **& CARRICK, John** [of G]
See also John Carrick.
†Old Corn Exchange, G, 1841; Sandyford Pl, G, 1842;
†Renfield St UP Ch, G, 1848 (by Brown); Kew Terr, G,
1849 (by Brown, with J T Rochead)

BROWN, Robert (1802–60) [of E]
Easter Coates estate plan, E, 1808 (including Coates
Cres, s1813, and Melville St, p1814); Brandon St, E,
1822; Hope Park Chapel, E, 1823; St Stephen St, E
(attr), s1824; Hope estate plans, E (especially
Haddington Pl), s1825

BROWN, Sir Samuel (1776–1852) [of London] (e)
Union Bridge, Hutton, 1820

BROWN, Thomas (*c*.1781–1850) [of E]
Edinburgh City Superintendent of Works, 1819–47.
Exchange Buildings, Leith, E, 1809–10; Nicolson Sq
Methodist Ch, E, 1815–16; Trinity Ho, Leith, E,
1816–18; Fettes Row, E, p1819, s1821; Royal Cres, E,
p1819, b1823–88; Cumberland St, E, p1822; Walker
Estate, E (Melville St, etc.), 1822–5; Inverleith Row/Pl
layout, E, 1823–6; St Mary's Ch, Bellevue Cres, E,
1824; Ingliston Ho, 1846

BROWN & WARDROP
See J M Wardrop.

BROWNE, Sir George Washington (1853–1939)
*See Sir R R Anderson; and Peddie & Washington
Browne.*

BROWNHILL, James (d. *c*.1728) (e)
James Court, E, 1723–7

BRUCE, Sir William (*c*.1630–1710) (R)MOW
Balcaskie a/a, 1668–74; Thirlestane a/a, s1670;
Lethington (Lennoxlove) a/a, 1670s (with J Slezer);
Holyroodhouse rebuilding, 1671–9; Panmure Ho gates,
1672; Brunstane a/a, 1672; Lauder Parish Ch, 1673;
†Dunkeld Ho, 1676–84; †Moncrieffe Ho, fl679;
Kinross Ho, 1679–93; †Edinburgh Exchange, 1680–1;
Craighall a/a, 1697–9; Hopetoun Ho, s1698, and a/a
s1702; Craigiehall House, 1698–1701; Harden
(Mertoun) Ho, 1703; Stirling Town Ho, 1703–4;
Abercorn aisle, 1707–8; †House of Nairne, *c*.1709–12
(compl A McGill)

BRUCE, Donald (*c*.1835–1919) **& HAY, E A B**
(1855–1934) [of G]
Scottish Co-operative Wholesale Society building,
Morrison St, G, 1886–95 (and adjoining block in
Wallace St, 1882 and 1892); 101–3 High St, G, 1892–4;
Meadowside Shipyard Offices, G, 1895; Kinning Park
Colour Works, G, *c*.1895 (attr); Partick Academy, G,
1903; Balshagray Public Sch, G, 1904; Our Lady and
St Margaret's Sch, G, 1910

BRUCE, J L & STURROCK, David Woodburn
(d.1934) [of G]
St John's Ch, Gourock, crown spire, 1877–8; St
Aloysius RC Ch, Springburn, G, a/a, 1881–2;
Bishopbriggs High Sch, fl896 (by Sturrock)

BRYCE, David (1803–76) [of E]
In partnership with W. Burn, q.v., 1841–50.
St Mark's Unitarian Ch, E, 1834–5; Coylton Ch, 1836;
Monkton Ch, 1837; Refuge Assurance Building, E,
1840; 15–19 George St, E, a/a, 1840; Seacliffe Ho a/a,
1841; Edinburgh & Leith Bank, E, 1841, a/a 1847;
Edinburgh Life Assurance (now Royal Society)
Building, E, 1843; Carradale Ho, 1844; Inchdairnie,
1845; †Western Bank and Exchange Bank of Scotland,
E, both 1846; Grange Cemetery layout, lodge, cata-
combs, E, 1846; British Linen Bank, E, 1846–51;
Balfour Cas, Shapinsay, Orkney, a/a, 1846–51;
Capenoch Ho, 1847–68; Tollcross, 1848; Hamilton
Palace Mausoleum, 1848; Portmore, 1850; Stronvar,
1850; Ormiston Hall, 1851; †Kimmerghame Ho, 1851;
†Hartrigge a/a, 1854; Kinnaird Cas a/a, s1854;
Dundee Royal Exchange, 1855; Inzievar, 1855–6;
Birkhill a/a, 1855–9; The Glen, Innerleithen,
1855–60; St Ninian's Epis Ch, Alyth, 1856; Hunter
Blair Monument, Craigengower Hill, 1856;
Shambellie, 1856; †Craigends, 1857–9; Cullen Ho a/a,
1858; Torosay Cas, Mull, 1858; †Belladrum a/a, 1858;
Assembly Hall, The Mound, E, 1858–9; †Eaglesham,
1859; †Fothringham, 1859; †Inverardoch, 1859; Keiss
Cas, 1859–62; †Langton Ho, 1862; †Edinburgh
Sheriff Courthouse, 1863–8; Castlemilk, s1864;
Ballikinrain, s1864; Fettes Coll, E, 1864–70; Bank of

Scotland head office, E, a/a, 1864–70; Allan Ramsay Monument base, E, 1865; Carnwath Ch, 1865–9; †Halleaths, 1866; St George's Free Ch, E, 1867–9; Post Office, College Green, Dublin (Irl), 1868; 112–14 West George St, G, 1868; †West Coates Ch, E, 1868–70; Castlecliffe, St Andrews, 1869; Warrender Estate feuing plan, E, 1869; Broadstone, 1869; Meikleour Ho a/a, 1869–70; Blair Cas a/a, 1869–76; Glenapp Cas, 1870; †Cortachy Cas a/a, 1870; Ellary Ho, 1871; St Giles St elevations, E, 1872; †New Gala Ho, 1872; Edinburgh Royal Infirmary, s1872 (compl J Bryce 1879); Logan Ho a/a, 1874; Union Bank, E, 1874 (compl J Bryce); St Mungo's Ch, Kettleholm, 1875–7; Lochmaben Town Hall a/a, 1876–7 (by D & J Bryce)

BRYCE, David, junior (1815–74) [of E]
†Star Hotel, E, 1861; City of Glasgow Bank (Merchants' Hall), E, 1865–6, compl T P Marwick, 1901

BRYCE, John (1805–51) [of G]
†Duke St Reformatory, G, *c*.1838; Queens Cres, G, 1840; 55–71 Ashley St, G, 1849; 4–26 Bothwell St, G, 1849–52 (with A Kirkland); Queens Terr, West Princes St, G, 1850

BRYCE, John (d.1922) [of E]
Leith Tower, Fyvie Cas, p1890

BRYCE, John [of G]
Later Glasgow Director of Housing, 1923–8.
Knightswood housing scheme, G, p1921

BRYDEN, Robert Alexander (1841–1906)
See Clarke & Bell.

BRYDON, John M (1840–1901) [of London]
Principal English works: Chelsea Vestry Hall, London, 1885–7; Government Buildings, London, 1898–1912

BUCHANAN, Robertson (e)
White and Black Cart Bridges, Inchinnan, 1809–12

BUILDING DESIGN PARTNERSHIP SCOTLAND [of G]
Wolfson Hall and Veterinary Sch, University of Glasgow Garscube Site, G, 1961–70; Waverley Market Centre, E, 1982–4; Atlantic Quay, G, 1988–90; Centre 1 relocation, East Kilbride, 1993–4; Lochside Court, Edinburgh Pk, E, 1994–6

BUNTON, Sam [of G]
Barrwood and Balmalloch hs schemes, Kilsyth, 1936–9; Lighting Department, Millbrae Rd, G, 1937–9; Hoggan Cres hs, Dunfermline, 1940; Clydebank reconstruction scheme, *c*.1943; Whitecrook neighbourhood, Clydebank, s1944; Melbourne Av hs, Clydebank, s1953; St Cuthbert's Sch, Hamilton,

1954–7; Tormusk Sch, G, 1957–8; Blairdardie South hs, G, 1960–5; Red Road hs, G, 1962–9

* BURGES, William (1827–81) [Engl]
Mount Stuart Oratory, 1873–8; St John's RC Ch, Cumnock, 1882

BURKE, Ian D, MARTIN, Hugh H & PARTNERS [of D]
See also Hugh Martin & Partners for later work.
Overgate redevelopment, D, s1961; Union building, University of Dundee, 1962–3; Belville St hs, Greenock, 1963–9; St James Centre and Government offices, E, 1964–70; Maxwelltown CDA hs, D, s1965; Motherwell town centre, 1967; new town centre, Greenock, 1968–76

BURN, James (d.1816) [of Haddington]
Aberdeen Bank, Castlegate, A, 1801–2; †Aberdeen Bridewell, 1809

BURN, Robert (1752–1815) [of E]
Hermitage of Braid, 1785; Picardy Pl, Union St, Forth St, Broughton St, E, p1800, b1804–10; Castle St, George St, Irvine St, Dumfries, p1806, b1820–30; Nelson Monument, E, 1807–14

BURN, William (1789–1870) [of E, London]
In partnership with D. Bryce, q.v., 1841–50.
North Leith Ch, s1813; Gallanach Ho, 1814; St John's Epis Ch, E, 1816–18; Greenock Custom Ho, 1816–19; Craigielands, 1817; Saltoun Hall, s1817; Edinburgh Assembly Rooms portico, 1818; Dundas Cas, 1818; Dunfermline Parish Ch, 1818–21; Blairquhan, 1820–4; Lothian Rd, Morrison St, Bread St, E, 1820–5; Dundas Monument, E, 1821; Dunfermline Abbey a/a, 1821; Camperdown Ho, p1821, b1824–6; Carstairs, 1822–4; Edinburgh Academy, 1822–4; Murray's Royal Asylum, Perth, 1822–7; †Riccarton a/a, 1823–7; Blythswood Sq, G, 1823–9 (attr, with J Brash and G Smith); Brodie, 1824; Henderson Row, Pitt St, Perth St, E, 1824–6; †Snaigow, 1824–7; John Watson's Hosp, 1825; Freeland, 1825–6; Kinnoul Parish Ch, 1826; †Garscube, 1826–7; Laurieston Cas a/a, 1827; Murray Royal Asylum, Perth, 1827–33; †Dupplin, 1828–32; †St Fort, 1829; Stenton Ch, 1829; Faskally Ho, 1829; Tyninghame a/a, 1829; †Milton Lockhart, 1829; St Giles High Ch, E, restr, 1829–33; United Associate Synod Ch, E, 1830–1 (by Bryce); St Peter's and St Andrew's Ch, Thurso, 1830–2; Auchmacoy, 1831; †Kilconquhar, 1831; Kirkcudbright Parish Ch, 1831–8; Auchterarder Ho, 1832; The Barony, 1832–3; Madras Coll, St Andrews, 1832–4; Dalkeith Ho conservatory, 1832–4; St Peter's Epis Ch, Peebles, 1833; Signet Library staircase, E, 1833; Ardanaseig Ho, 1833; †New Club, E, 1834; Kirkmichael Ho, 1834; Inverness Sheriff Court, 1834–5; Crichton Institution,

Dumfries, 1835–9 (compl W Moffat, 1867–71); Minigaff Parish Ch, 1836; Sutherland Monument, Golspie, 1836–8; Castle Menzies a/a, 1836–40; Tynron Ch, 1837; Invergowrie, 1837; Harlaxton Manor (Engl) a/a, from 1838; Penninghame Parish Ch, Newton Stewart, 1838; Royal Edinburgh Hosp, 1839; Morton Parish Ch, 1839–41; Falkland Ho, 1839–44; Whitehill, 1839–44; Preston Ho, 1840; West Ch, Dalkeith, 1840; Thirlestane Cas a/a, 1840–1; Portpatrick Parish Ch a/a, 1840–2; Stoke Rochford Ho (Engl), 1841; Bank of Scotland, D, 1842; Langholm Parish Ch, 1842–3; St Mary's Epis Chapel, Dalkeith, 1843–5; Town's Churches, D, 1843–7; Revesby Ho (Engl), 1844; Capenoch Ho, 1847–68; †Poltalloch Ho, 1849–53; Buchanan Ho, 1852–4; Balintore Cas, 1859–60; †Polmaise, 1863. For full list of works in Scotland and England, see Colvin, *Dictionary*, 1995 edn, pp. 183–92

BURNET, John, senior (1814–1901) [of G] Fitzroy Pl, G, 1847; 246–56 Bath St, G, *c*.1850; 61–3 Miller St, 1854; Elgin Pl Cong Ch, G, 1855–6; 1–3 Bridge St, G, 1857; Auchendennan, 1864–6; †Kilmahew Ho, 1865–8; Glasgow Savings Bank, Glassford St, G, 1866; Arden Ho, 1866–8; Clydesdale Bank, West George St, G, 1867; Arlington Baths Club, G, 1869–71; Clydesdale Bank, St Vincent Pl, G, 1871–4; †Glasgow Western Infirmary, 1871–7; Woodlands UP Ch, G, 1874–5; Glasgow Merchants' Ho, 1874–7 (extended 1907–9 by J J Burnet); Glasgow Stock Exchange, 1875; Cleveden Cres, G, 1876; Killean Ho, 1876 (compl J J Burnet 1877); Union Bank (Lanarkshire Ho), Ingram St, G, a/a, 1876–9

BURNET, Sir John James (1857–1938) [of G, London] *In partnership with J A Campbell 1886–97 as Burnet, Son & Campbell; all pre–1897 Campbell work included here. Post–1909 work of Burnet, Son & Dick (of G) abbreviated 'BSD'. Post–World War I work of Sir John Burnet & Partners (of London) abbreviated 'JBP'; post–1930 work of Burnet, Tait & Lorne (of London) abbreviated 'BTL': T S Tait was partner from 1919 and chief designer from early 1920s, and Lorne was partner from 1930. See also J A Campbell; N A Dick; T S Tait.* Royal Glasgow Fine Art Institution, 1878–9; Edinbarnet, 1881–2; Drumsheugh Baths, E, 1882, rebuilt 1892–3; Deanston Ho a/a, 1882–3; 2–10 University Gardens, G, 1882–4; Clyde Trust Building, G, 1882–6; Edinbarnet a/a, 1885–9; Shawlands Old Parish Ch, 1885–9 (by Campbell); Kilneiss Ho, 1886; †Edinburgh International Exhibition, 1886; St Molios's Ch, Arran, 1886; Corrienessan, 1886; Glasgow University Union, 1886 (and a/a 1893, 1908); Auchterarder Ho a/a, 1886–7; Barony Ch, G, 1886–90;

Athenaeum building, G, 1887; Ewing Gilmour Institute, Alexandria, 1888–91; Baronald, 1889–91; Garmoyle, Dumbarton, 1890; Charing Cross Mansions, G, 1891; Athenaeum Theatre, G, 1891; Cathedral Ct hs, G, 1891–2; Glasgow Western Infirmary Pathology Building, 1894; Dundas UP Ch, Grangemouth, 1894; Glasgow Stock Exchange extension, 1894; Campbeltown Cottage Hosp, 1894–6; Savings Bank of Glasgow, Glassford St, G, banking hall and main block heightening, 1894–1900; Alloa Baths, 1895; Hamilton Terr, Lamlash, *c*.1895; Killean Sch and estate hs, *c*.1895; Clydebank Riverside Sta, 1896; Kelvinside Sta, G, 1896; Albany Chambers, G, 1896–9; Gardner Memorial Ch, Brechin, 1896–1900; 66–70 Gordon St, G, a/a, 1896–1902; Carronvale Ho a/a, 1897; Maclaren Memorial Ch, Stenhousemuir, 1897; 'Rothmar', Craigdhu Mansions, Library and Museum, Campbeltown, 1897–8; †Greenhead Court hs, G, 1897–9; Royal Faculty of Physicians, G, interior a/a, 1898; Waterloo Chambers, G, 1898–1900; Finlaystone a/a, 1898–1903; Dalgorm, Lamlash, 1899; Atlantic Chambers, G, 1899–1900; 15–17 Hope St, G, *c*.1900; Botany and Engineering Buildings, University of Glasgow, 1900–1 (with J O Scott); Rutherglen Old Parish Ch, 1900–2; Broomhill Trinity Cong Ch, G, 1900–8; St Gerardine's Ch, Lossiemouth, 1901; Elder Library, 1901–3; Elder Cottage Hosp, G, 1901–4; Professional & Civil Service Supply Association, E, 1903–7; 14 University Gardens, G, fl904; Fairnilee, 1904–6; Union Bank, Lerwick, 1904–6; †McGeoch building, G, 1905; Clyde Trust extension, G, 1905–8; British Museum King Edward Galleries, London, 1905–14; Forsyth's store, E, 1906; St Philip's Epis Ch, E, 1908; General Buildings, Aldwych, London, 1909–11; Kodak Building, London, 1910; †Alhambra Theatre, G, 1911; Duart Cas restr, 1911–16; Wallace–Scott Tailoring Institute, G, 1913–22 (BSD); Memorial Chapel, University of Glasgow, p1913, b1923 (BSD; with J Taylor Thomson); Institute of Chemistry, London, 1914–15; Imperial War Graves Commission schemes, 1919–28, including cemeteries and memorials at Cape Helles, Lone Pine, Twelve Tree Copse, Gallipoli (Tur), Jerusalem (with Anning Bell and Gilbert Burges), †Port Tewfik (Egy); Adelaide Ho, London, 1920–5 (JBP); War Memorial, George Sq, G, 1921–4 (BSD); Zoology Building, University of Glasgow, 1922–3 (BSD); 2nd Ch of Christ Scientist, London, 1923–6 (JBP); City Sq, D (with J MacLellan Brown), p1923, fl933 (BSD); Sydney Harbour Br pylons (Aus), 1924–32 (JBP); Carliol Ho, Newcastle (Engl), 1926–7 (JBP); North British & Mercantile building, G, 1926–9 (BSD); Daily Telegraph building, London, 1927–9 (JBP); Lloyds Bank, Cornhill, London, 1927–9 (JBP); Silver End village hs (Engl),

1927–30 (JBP); Unilever building, London, 1929–32 (JBP); Royal Masonic Hosp, London, 1930–3 (BTL); Nurses' Home, Gartnavel Royal Hosp, G, 1931–7 (BSD); Paisley Infectious Diseases Hospital, s1933 (BTL); St Andrew's Ho, E, 1936–9 (BTL); Waterloo air terminal, London, 1953 (JBP)

BURNET, Frank (1848–1923) **& BOSTON, William J** (1861–1937) [of G]
Partnership formed 1889; previously, F Burnet alone. From 1901 to 1908, Burnet, Boston & Carruthers; from 1961, Frank Burnet, Bell & Partners.
540 tenements in Dalmarnock, Parkhead, Woodside, Queens Pk, Battlefield and Dennistoun, G, 1884–1906 (as developer-architects); 142 St Vincent St, G, 1898; Castle Chambers, G, 1898–1902; 116–28 Buchanan St, G, 1898–1902; St George's Mansions, G, 1900–1; CIT High Street hs, G, 1901–3; Gordon Chambers, Mitchell St, G, 1903–4; Scottish Amicable Building, St Vincent Pl, G, 1903–6; Fa'side Ho, Mearns, a/a, 1911; 91–3 West George St, G, 1911–13; Battlefield Rest, G, 1914–15; Greenock Central Area redevelopment scheme hs, s1954; National Water Sports Training Centre, Great Cumbrae, f1976; St Mary's Epis Ch, Port Glasgow, 1983–4

BURNET, SON & DICK
See J J Burnet.

BURNET, TAIT & LORNE
See J J Burnet; and T S Tait.

BUTTER, Charles and William [of E]
Gayfield Ho, E, before 1765

* BUTTERFIELD, William (1814–1900) [Engl]
St John's Sch, Jedburgh, 1844; Millport Epis Cath, 1849–51; St Ninian's Epis Cath, Perth (first section), 1849–51

BYRES, James (1734–1817) [of Rome, Tonley]
Aquhorthies Seminary, 1796–9

CAIRNCROSS, Hugh (d.1808) [of E]
Ardgowan Ho, Inverkip, 1797–1801; 12–32 Gayfield Sq, E, 1807

CALDWELL, Thomas (m)
Kelburn Cas a/a, *c*.1692–1700

CALTHROP, Michael & CAMPBELL MARS, A [of E]
Town Clerk's Office, North Berwick, f1975; Grassmarket hs, E, 1984

CALVERT, Edward (d.1914) [of E]
Tenements in Edinburgh: Warrender Pk Terr (part), 1878–81; 56–66 Marchmont Cres, 1881; Bruntsfield Pl

(part), 1887; 2–16 Marchmont Rd, 1890–1; Viewforth Sq, 1891

CAMERON, Charles (1743–1812) [of London, St Petersburg]
Principal works at Tsarskoye Selo (Rus): Sophia New Town, s1779; palace buildings and interiors (including Cold Baths and Cameron Gallery), 1779–87. Principal works at Pavlovsk (Rus): Palace of Grand Duke Paul, 1782–6; Temple of Friendship, *c*.1780

CAMERON, Duncan (d.1899) **& BURNETT, J Russell** (d.1921) [of Inverness]
Station Hotel, Nairn, 1896; †Foyers Aluminium Works, 1896 (attr); Upper Foyers hs, 1897; Glen Lochy Distillery, Fort William, 1898–1900; West Highland Hotel, Mallaig, 1898–1900; Highland Hotel, Strathpeffer, 1909–11

CAMPBELL, Alexander Buchanan [of G]
St Christopher's Ch, Pollok, G, 1961–2; St Teresa's Sch, G, 1961–3; Dollan Baths, East Kilbride, 1964–8; Garscadden Policies multi–storey hs, G, 1965–71

CAMPBELL, Colen (1679–1729)
In Scotland: Shawfield Mansion, G, 1712. Principal English works: Wanstead Ho, 1714–20; Stourhead, *c*.1720–4; Mereworth Cas, *c*.1720–5; Houghton Hall, 1722–35 (compl J Gibbs)

CAMPBELL, Dugal (d.1757)
Edinburgh Castle Governor's Ho, 1742

CAMPBELL, John A (1859–1909) [of G]
Pre–1897 work, see J J Burnet. Joined c.1909 by A D Hislop, q.v. for post–1909 work.
Dundas Ho, 160–8 Buchanan St, G, 1898; Dalskairth Ho a/a, 1899; 71–5 Robertson St, G, 1899; 71–5 Robertson La, G, 1899–1901; 7–23 Kirklee Rd, G (and other houses in Kirklee Rd, Redlands Rd, Mirrlees Drive), 1900–9; Todhill, Newton Mearns, 1901; 163 Hope St, G, 1902–3; Drumquhar, Blanefield, 1904; Ranfurly Cas Golf Clubhouse, Bridge of Weir, 1904–5; Edinburgh Life Assurance office, 122–8 St Vincent St, G, 1904–6; villas in Bridge of Weir (including Dundarroch, Homestead, Hermiston, Greendykes, Kincraig, Threeplands, Greenways and Inchgarvie), 1904–8; Southwood Ho, Troon, 1905; 50 Argyle St, G, 1905; South African War Memorial, Falkirk, 1905–6; Queen Victoria Memorial School, Dunblane, 1907–8; Northern Insurance office, G, 1908–9

CAMPBELL, Walter Douglas [of Lochawe]
St Conan's Church, Lochawe, 1881–6 and 1906

CAMPBELL, William D & ARNOTT, Ian [of Haddington, E]
Amisfield Mains development, Haddington, 1961;

Caird's Row hs, Musselburgh, 1962; Arnott house, Gifford, 1963; Mitchell's Close restr, Haddington, 1964–7; Kingsburgh Gardens hs, East Linton, 1980–2; Inverleith Pavilion, E, 1982–3; Edinburgh Solicitors Property Centre, 1985; Lammermuir Ho, Dunbar, 1985–6; Dunbar Parish Ch restr, 1987–91; Saltire Court, E, 1989–91; organ, St Giles Cath, E, 1991; masterplan for Edinburgh Pk, E, s1991 (with R Meier); Royal Hosp for Sick Children a/a, E, 1991–4

CAMPBELL DOUGLAS & MORRISON/ SELLARS/STEVENSON
See Douglas (Campbell) & Morrison; Douglas (Campbell) & Sellars; Douglas (Campbell) & Stevenson.

CAMPBELL DOUGLAS & PATERSON
For works by Paterson, see N Paterson.

CAPPER, Stewart Henbest (1860–1924)
[of E, Montréal, Manchester]
Wardrop's Court, E, 1892; Burns Land, E, 1892; Ramsay Garden (part), E, s1892; Riddell's Court, Lawnmarket, E, restr, 1893; Blackie Ho, Lawnmarket, E, restr, 1894; 35 Inverleith Terr, E, 1897; Whitworth Laboratory, Manchester (Engl), 1909

CAPPON, Thomas M (1864–1939) [of D]
1898–1904: with W G Lamond as assistant.
St Mary's Epis Ch, Newport–on–Tay, 1887; Vicarsford Cemetery Chapel, 1895–7; Ramsay Arms Hotel, Fettercairn, 1896–7; Brechin Drill Hall, 1897; St Patrick's Ch, D, 1897; St Mary's RC Ch, D, towers, 1900; Wishart Memorial Ch, D, 1901; Coll of Education (Scrymgeour Building, Dundee University), 1911–22

CARFRAE, John Alexander (1868–1947) [of E]
See also Edinburgh School Board.
18–20 Inverleith Pl, E, 1897

CARMICHAEL, E M
See Public Works (Office of Works).

CARNEGIE, Ian [of E]
Rushforth cottage, Ratho, 1937

CARR, David (1905–86) [of E]
Pre–war work with Mr Howard, post–war with Stuart R Matthew, and also (1955–64) with Stewart Todd. See also Carr & Matthew.
Kirkcaldy Town Ho, 1937–56; Polbeth SSHA timber hs, 1938

CARR & MATTHEW (Stuart R) [of E]
See also Lorimer & Matthew.
Strathyre cottage a/a, 1950; Royal Blind Asylum, E, a/a, 1950–6; Broomridge SSHA hs, Stirling, 1951–3; Meadowfield hs, E, 1952–7; Astley Ainslie Hosp, E,

a/a, 1953–9; St Andrews University Observatory, 1954; Duddingston Sch, E, 1954–6; Nairn St and Boquhanran Rd hs, Clydebank, 1959

CARRICK, John (1819–1900) [of G]
In partnership with J Brown 1839–54: see separate entry. Post–1844 official work for Glasgow Town Council: see separate entry.

CARRICK, James (1880–1940) & James A [of Ayr]
Cragburn Pavilion, Gourock, 1935–6; Rothesay Pavilion, 1936; Ayr racecourse buildings, 1963–71

CARRUTHERS, Frank J C [of Dumfries]
Lockerbie Town Hall, 1887–91; Dumfries Academy, 1895–7; Annan Academy, c.1896; Dryfesdale & Trinity Parish Ch, Lockerbie, 1896–8; Central Hotel, Annan, 1898; 74–8 High St, Annan, 1900; Queensberry Terr, Cummertrees, c.1900; Lochmaben Hosp, 1907–8

CARRUTHERS, William Laidlaw (d.1914)
[of Inverness]
Lethington, Inverness, 1892; 22–6 Crown Drive, Inverness, 1895

CARSEWELL, James (c.1833–97) [of G] (e)
Queen St Sta roof, G, 1878–80; Hyndland Sta, G, 1886

CARSWELL, James (1767–1856) & William (d.1852) [of G]
Candleriggs, west side, G, s1790

CATTANACH, Alexander (c.1857–1928)
[of Kingussie]
Meadowside Hosp, Kincraig, 1906; Duke of Gordon Hotel, Kingussie, 1906; Kingussie UF Ch, 1908–9; Aviemore hs, s1921; Perth Playhouse Cinema, p1933; Regal Cinema, Rothesay, 1937–8

CAULFEILD, Governor Edward (e)
Highland roads programme, 1746–67; Br of Orchy, c.1751; Old Invercauld Br, 1752

CHALMERS, James (d. c.1928) [of G]
Wright & Greig warehouse and offices, 64 Waterloo St, G, 1898–1900; St Peter's Epis Ch, G, 1899; All Saints Epis Ch, Jordanhill, G, 1904–10; Scotstoun West Parish Ch, G, 1905–6; Kirklands, Dunlop, a/a, 1910; The Homesteads, Stirling, c.1910

CHALMERS, Dr Peter MacGregor (1859–1922)
[of G]
Cardonald Parish Ch, G, 1888–9; St Margaret's Epis Ch, Newlands, p1895, b1908–35; †St Bride's Ch, Rosevale St, G, 1897; †St Kenneth's Ch, Govan, 1897–8; Keil Ch, Lochaline, 1898 (attr); Kilmore Ch, Mull, c.1900; Ardwell Ch, 1900–2; St Margaret's Ch, Polmadie, G, 1902; St Leonard's Ch, St Andrews, 1902–4; Iona Abbey restr, 1902–10; St Columba's Ch,

Craigleith, E, 1903; St Leonard's Ch, Dunfermline, 1903–4; Dennistoun Parish Ch, G, 1906; †Neptune Ho, Argyle St, G, 1906; Kirn Ch, 1906–7; Braes of Rannoch Parish Ch, 1907; St Cuthbert's Ch, Saltcoats, 1907; St Luke's Ch, Fettes, E, 1907–8; Holy Trinity Ch, St Andrews, a/a, 1907–9; Carriden Ch, 1908; St Nicholas's Ch, Prestwick, 1908; Paisley Abbey restr, 1909; Colvend Ch, 1910–11; St Anne's Ch, Corstorphine, E, 1912; Whiteinch-Jordanvale Parish Ch, G, 1912–13; Lady Glenorchy's Ch, E, 1912–13; Merrylea Holy Trinity Parish Ch, 1912–15; Urr Parish Ch, 1914–15; St Modan's Ch, Falkirk, 1914–15; Symington Parish Ch, 1919; Greyfriars Epis Ch, Kirkcudbright, a/a 1919

* CHAMBERS, Sir William (1723–96) [Engl/Scot; of London]
Scottish works: Duddingston Ho, 1763–8; 23–6 St Andrew Sq, E, 1770–2; Dundas Ho, E, 1771–4

CHESSER, John (1820–93) [of E]
Abbotsford Cres, Hope St, Howard Pl, St Andrews, p1847, b1860s–90s; Dean estate, E, plans for various streets, e.g. Buckingham Terr, E, s1860; Grosvenor Cres, E, 1869–71; Eglinton Cres, Glencairn Cres, Coates Gardens, E, 1871–9; Wester Coates Heriot Trust estate, E, plan 1872; Learmonth Terr, E, s1873; Belgrave Cres, E, s1874; Southfield, E, 1875

CHEVRON LTD (ABERDEEN) AND DORIS (FRANCE)
Ninian Central (oil) Platform, 1975–8

* CHIOCCHETTI, Domenico and others [Ital]
Italian Chapel, Orkney, 1942–4

CLACKMANNAN COUNTY COUNCIL
[of Alloa]
Main St hs, Tullibody, s1967 (County Architect, W H Henry)

CLARK, William [of G] (e)
Coplawhill tram depot and works, G, 1894–1912; Possilpark tram depot, G, 1900

CLARKE, William (c.1812–89) **& BELL, George** (1814–87) [of G]
From 1870s to 1890s, with R A Bryden; later, as Clarke, Bell & Craigie, with James Hoey Craigie (d.1930).
(City and) County Buildings, G, 1841–4 (compl 1871); †Anderston Free Ch, G, 1848; Granby Terr, Hillhead, G, 1856; Darlington Place Ch, Ayr, 1860; St Andrew's Ch, Girvan, 1870; Clyde Spinning Mill, G, 1871–5; Fish Market, G, 1872–3; Western Baths, G, 1873; Johnston Memorial Ch, Springburn, G, 1873; Dunoon Burgh Hall, 1873–4; Orphan Homes of Scotland, Bridge of Weir, s1876; Free (St John's) Ch, Dunoon, 1876–7; Avondale Old Parish Ch, 1879 (by Bryden);

Ayr Academy, 1880; Skibo Cas, 1880; Paisley Sheriff Court and County Buildings, 1885; 42–50 Gordon St, G, 1886; Bridge of Weir Hosp for Consumptives, 1894–1907 (by Bryden); †Bible Training Institute and YMCA Club, Bothwell St, G, 1895–8; Dunoon Pier, 1896; Lennox Joint Infectious Diseases Hosp, Milton of Campsie, 1897–8 (by Bryden); Ocean Chambers, G, 1899–1900 (by Bryden); Grosvenor Building, G, a/a (new upper storeys), 1907 (by Craigie); Justiciary Courthouses, G, a/a, 1910–13 (by Craigie); St Mary's Parish Ch, Kirkintilloch, 1912–14 (by Craigie)

CLELAND, James (1770–1840) [of G]
Glasgow Superintendent of Public Works, 1814–34.
†Nelson St Post Office, G, 1810; †Magdalen Asylum, G, 1812; †City Hall, G, s1817; †High Sch, G, 1820

CLELLAND, Douglas & ASSOCIATES
[of G, Berlin]
Friedrichstrasse 10, West–Berlin (Ger), 1983–91; †'Glasgow's Glasgow' exhibition, G, 1990

CLERK of Eldin, John (1728–1812) [of Lasswade]
†'Adam's Hut', Eldin Ho, c.1769–74 (attr); Lasswade Cottage, c.1781 (attr); †Lasswade Ch, 1791 (attr; possibly with R Adam)

CLERK of Penicuik, Sir James (1709–83)
[of Penicuik]
Penicuik Ho and stable block, 1761–9 (with John Baxter the elder); Hailes Ho, E, c.1765; Penicuik Ch, 1771 (attr); Rossdhu Ho, 1772–8 (with John Baxter the younger)

CLERK of Penicuik, Sir John, 1st baronet (d.1722)
Mausoleum, Penicuik Churchyard, 1683–4

CLERK of Penicuik, Sir John, 2nd baronet (1676–1755)
Cammo Park layout, 1710–26; Mavisbank Ho, 1723–6 (with W Adam)

CLIFFORD, Henry Edward (1852–1932) [of G]
Later works with Thomas Lunan.
Pollokshields Burgh Hall, G, 1888–90; Washington St Public Sch, G, 1890; Pollokshields-Titwood Ch, G, 1893–5 (moved to Pollok scheme 1951); 44–84 Terregles Av hs, G, 1895–6; Whitecraigs Ho, Eastwood, c.1898; Newlands South Ch and Hall, G, 1899–1907; Albion St/Ingram St workshop, G, 1900–6; Stoneleigh, Kelvinside, G, 1900–6; Elmvale Sch, G, 1901; St Michael's Carntyne, G, 1902; 17–57 Fotheringay Rd hs, G, c.1902; 145–95 Howard St warehouse, G, 1902–5; Victoria Infirmary a/a, G, 1902–6; 99 Springkell Av, G, 1903–4; Croftmohr Ho, Skelmorlie, 1904; Fraser Bros. clothing warehouse, Albion St, G, 1906; Shennanton, Kirkcowan, 1908; Crosbie, Troon, 1908; Battlefield West Ch, G, 1908–9;

Perth City Hall, 1909–14; Hyndland Public Sch, G, 1910; Education offices, 127–9 Bath St, G, 1910–11; †Dewar Whisky Bond, Perth, 1912; Monkton Hall, Troon, *c*.1912; Cathcart Old Parish Ch, G, s1914

CLYNE, Arthur (1852–1923)
See Pirie & Clyne.

COCKER, Philip, & PARTNERS
[of Grangemouth, E]
Kersiebank Av Shopping Centre, Grangemouth, 1960–2; Link hs, Polmont and Barnton, 1963–6; Cramond Green hs, E, 1965–7; Village 7, 8, 9 hs, Cumbernauld, 1967–9; Craigshill 6 hs, Livingston, 1967–9; West Mill, Dean Village, E, restr, 1971–3; Fair-a-Far hs, E, 1971–3; Keith St hs, G, 1977–81; Raemoir Rise hs, Banchory, 1979–81; Jamaica Mews hs, E, 1979–82; Cowcaddens St hs, G, 1979–82; Buccleuch St hs, E, 1980–2

* COCKERELL, Charles (1788–1863) [Engl]
National Monument, E, 1826–9 (with W H Playfair)

* COE, Henry E (1825–85) **and GOODWIN** [Engl]
†Farington Hall, D, 1853; Dundee Royal Infirmary, 1853–5; St Mary Magdalene Ch, D, 1854

COIA, Giacomo (Jack) Antonio (1898–1981)
See Gillespie, Kidd & Coia.

COLLIE, James (*c*.1805–*c*.1870) [of G]
Montrose Infirmary, 1836–9

COMHAIRLE NAN EILEAN (DEPARTMENT OF ARCHITECTURAL SERVICES) [of Stornoway]
Sgoil Lionacleit, f1991; Calanais Visitor Centre, 1994.

COMPER, Sir J Ninian (1864–1960) [of London]
St Margaret's Epis Ch and convent, A, a/a, 1887/1908; St Margaret's Epis Ch, Braemar, 1895–1907; St Cyprian's Ch, London, 1903; St Mary's Epis Ch, Kirriemuir, 1903–4; St Michael's Epis Ch, Inverness, 1904; St Mary's Ch, Wellingborough (Engl), 1904–31; National War Memorial, Cardiff (Wal), 1923–8; †St Andrew's and St George's Epis Ch, Rosyth, 1926; St John the Baptist Epis Ch, Rothiemurchus, 1928–31; St Andrew's Epis Ch, A, a/a, 1935–43

COMPREHENSIVE DESIGN [of E]
Scottish Nuclear head office, East Kilbride, 1990–2; Gyle Centre, E, 1993

COOPER CROMAR ASSOCIATES [of G]
1079 Sauchiehall St, 1330 Argyle St, G, 1990–2

COPCUTT, Geoffrey
See Cumbernauld New Town Development Corporation.

CORDINER, Thomas Smith (d.1965) [of G]
Later: Thomas Cordiner, Cunningham & Partners; Cunningham Glass Partnership.
Notre Dame Sch, G, p1939, b1949–53; Lourdes Sch, G, 1951–7; †Immaculate Conception Ch, Maryhill, G, 1955–6; †Kingsridge Secondary Sch, G, 1955–8 and 1967–9; St Margaret Mary's RC Ch, G, 1956–7; Our Lady and St George's RC Ch, G, 1957–9; Christ the King RC Ch, G, 1957–60; Linn Park Crematorium, G, f1962; St Stephen's RC Ch, Sighthill, G, 1970–2; Westhill Township, s1972; Oman projects (UAE), s1974

COUSIN, David (1809–78) [of E]
Includes official works as Edinburgh City Architect, 1847–78.
Old Kirk, Greenock, 1839–41; Cambuslang Old Parish Ch, 1839–41; Monteath Mausoleum, Glasgow Necropolis, 1842; Warriston Cemetery layout, E, 1842 (later enlarged J Dick Peddie); St Thomas's Epis Ch, E, 1842–3; Pilrig Free Ch, E, 1843; St Cuthbert's Free Ch, E, 1843; Dean Cemetery layout, E, 1845; Oban Free Ch, 1846; Newark Castle, Ayrshire, a/a, 1848–9; 7 Greenhill Gardens, E, 1849 (for himself); †Corn Exchange, E, 1849; The Grange layout plan, E, 1851; Dalkeith Corn Exchange, 1853; Reid Sch of Music, E, 1858; British Linen Bank, D, 1858; Free Church Coll, E, 1858–63; Tobermory Union Poorhouse; 1–19 Murrayfield Gardens, E, 1862; Argyll District Asylum, Lochgilphead, f1863; India Buildings, E, 1864; Chambers St facades, E, p1864; St Mary's St Improvement Act hs, E, s1869 (with J Lessels, R Morham, D Clunas); Blackfriars St Improvement Act hs, E, 1870–3 (with J Lessels, R Morham, D Clunas); High Street/Blackfriars St hs, E, 1873 (by R H Morham).

COUTTS, George [of A]
Fountainhall Rd, A, 1884–6; 28 Rubislaw Den South, A, 1895; 10–16 Crown St, A, 1899–1901; 90–4 Queens Rd, A, 1900; Glen o'Dee Hosp, Banchory, 1900–1; 88 Queens Rd, A, 1902; 1 Rubislaw Den North, A, 1909

COVELL, MATTHEWS & PARTNERS
[of London and E]
Originally established 1937 in London; from 1992, Scottish practice only.
McCance Building and David Livingstone Tower, Strathclyde University, G, 1962–8; Northern Co-operative, A, 1966–70; SDA Advance Factory, Dalmuir Industrial Estate, Clydebank, 1984; Glenfinlas St infill block, E, 1989; Edinburgh Ho, E, 1993

COWAN, James Linburn (*c*.1821–1905) [of G]
1512–28 Maryhill Rd, G, 1892; St Peter's Sch, Partick, G, 1898; 3–7 Lancaster Crescent, G, *c*.1898

COWIE, William (1867–1949) [of Ayr]
Later: Cowie & Torry, and Cowie, Torry & Partners.
9–15 Burns Statue Sq, Ayr, 1900 (with J & H V Eaglesham); Girvan Academy, p1938, b1948–55; Ayr Baths, 1970–2; Riverside Ho, Ayr, 1975; MacLaurin Art Gallery, Ayr, 1976; Girvan CDA, f1976; Blackfriars Walk, Ayr, f1976; Alloway St bank, Ayr, 1987

COX, George A [of D] (e)
High Mill, Camperdown Works, D, 1857–68 (with   P & J Carmichael); Cox's Stack, Camperdown Works, D, 1865–6 (with James MacLaren)

CRAIG, James (*c*.1744–95) [of E]
Edinburgh New Town first section, layout, p1766; 35 St Andrew Sq, E, 1769; St James Sq, E, p1773; †Physicians Hall, E, 1775–9; Observatory Ho, E, s1776; Blythswood layout (part), G, p1792–3

CRAIK, William (1703–98) [of Arbigland]
Arbigland Ho a/a, *c*.1753–5; Mossknowe Ho, 1767; Kirkbean Parish Ch, 1776

CRAWFORD, Alexander Hunter (1865–1945) [of E]
Freemasons Hall, E, 1910–12

CRAWFORD, Andrew Rennie & VEITCH [of G]
Cathcart Parish Council Chambers, G, 1907

CRAWFORD, J M (b.1854) [of Dumbarton, G]
St Mungo's Ch, Alexandria, 1894; Station Rd/College St hs, Dumbarton, 1898; Dumbarton Joint Fever Hosp, 1898–1901

CRERAR, W G & PARTNERS [of Oban, E]
Corran Halls, museum, library, Oban, f1964; Oban hs development, 1968–70; Fort William Swimming Pool, 1973; Dragonara Hotel, E, 1978; Tangusdale Hotel, Barra, 1978; Aonach Mor Ski Centre, 1990

CRICHTON, Richard (*c*.1771–1817) [of E]
Craig Ch, 1799; †Rossie Cas, *c*.1800; Gask Ho, s1801; †Abercairny Abbey, s1805; Gelston Cas, *c*.1805 (attr); Stirling Courthouse, 1806–11; †Dunglass Ho, 1807–11; Kincardine in Menteith Ch, 1814–16; Balbirnie Ho a/a, 1815–19

*** CRICKMER, Courtenay Melville** (1879–1971) [Engl]
St John's Epis Ch, Eastriggs, 1917; St Andrew's Ch, Gretna Green, 1917

CROMBIE, A B (1845–1904) [of Dumfries]
Rosefield Mills, Dumfries, 1885–9; Masonic Hall, Dumfries, 1889; Ewart Library, Dumfries, 1900–4; Kirkcudbright Academy, 1901

CROUCH & HOGG [of G] (e)
(Second) Bonhill Br, 1898; (second) Bonar Br, 1973; Kessock Br, 1982 (with O Arup)

CRUDENS LTD [of Musselburgh]
Chief Architect: George Bowie.
Sighthill hs, G, 1963–9; Ardler hs, D, 1964–6; Whitfield hs, D, s1967; Laurieston-Gorbals CDA hs, G, 1970–3

CULLEN, Alexander (1857–1911) [of Hamilton]
Entry also includes work of Cullen, Lochhead (James, 1870–1947) & Brown (William).
Clason Memorial Free Ch, Motherwell, 1892; Hamilton Police Sta, 1894; District Hosp, Motherwell, f1897; Brandon Chambers, Hamilton, 1898; Middle Ward District Offices, Hamilton, 1899; Parish Council offices, Hamilton, *c*.1900; Douglas Chambers, Hamilton, 1903; Omoa Poorhouse, Cleland, f1903; Hamilton Masonic Buildings, 1903; Templehall Buildings, Hamilton, 1904; Carnegie Library, Coatbridge, 1905; Dundyvan Ch, Coatbridge, 1905; Hamilton Municipal Buildings, 1906–14 and 1928; 116 Cadzow St, Hamilton, 1907; Methodist Ch, Hamilton, 1908; Gourock Central Senior Sch, 1908; Chapeltoun Ho, 1908–10; Hamilton Academy, 1910–13; Blackpool Library and Art Gallery (Engl), 1911; Nurses' Home, Hartwood Hosp, s1926; Lauder Hall, Strathaven, 1933–6; Hartwoodhill Hosp, *c*.1935; Law Hosp, f1939; Fire Brigade headquarters, Hamilton, f1955; British Steel Mess Rooms, Airdrie, 1970–1

CUMBERNAULD NEW TOWN DEVELOPMENT CORPORATION
Chief Architect and Planning Officer: L Hugh Wilson, 1956–62; Dudley R Leaker, 1962–70; G Kenneth Davie, 1970–1992.
Preliminary planning proposals, 1958; Park 1 hs, 1958; Blairlinn advance factories, 1959–61; Kildrum 5 hs, 1959–61; Town Centre, Phase 1, p1959, b1963–7 (Group Leader: Geoffrey Copcutt); Seafar 1 hs, 1960–3; Carbrain 1 and 2 hs, 1961–3; Seafar 2 hs, 1961–3; Park 4 hs, 1964–7; Abronhill 1 hs, 1964–7; Kildrum 22 hs, s1967; Town Centre Phase 2, s1968; Abronhill 3 hs, 1968–70; Westfield 5 hs, 1977–9; Balloch 1 hs, 1979–81

CUNNINGHAM, John (1799–1873) [of E]
County Hall, Greenlaw, 1829

CUNNINGHAM, BLYTH & WESTLAND
See Blyth & Blyth.

CUNNINGHAM, JACK, FISHER, PURDOM [of St Andrews]
Successor firm to J C Cunningham. Subsequently: Jack Fisher Partnership.
Buchanan Arts Building, University of St Andrews, 1962; Pluscarden Abbey restr, 1967–96; Scottish Fisheries Museum, Anstruther, restr 1968–70 (by W Murray Jack); West Shore redevelopment, St Monans,

1968–70; Fife Folk Museum, Ceres, restr 1969 (and a/a 1984, Hurd Rolland); South Court restr, St Andrews, 1971; The Maltings hs, St Monans, 1984

CURRIE, John (*c.*1840–1922) [of Elie]
Kellie Cas restr, 1878

* DANNATT, Trevor [Engl]
Pitcorthie Ho, 1967

DAVIDSON, W R (d.1946) [of London]
Linkside, Nairn, 1900; Broomholm, Nairn, 1903

* DAVIES, R Llewellyn [Engl]
Experimental hospital block, Larkfield, Greenock, 1953

DAVIS DUNCAN PARTNERSHIP [of G]
Robertsons Close hs, E, 1986–8; Carrick Quay Phase I, G, 1989–91; Fettes Village, E, 1990–2; Lenzie Union Ch, 1990–2; Compaq Factory, Erskine, 1990–2; Scion Ho, Stirling, Phase III, 1991–3; Riverside 2 Phases I and II, Govan, G, 1991–6; Craigs Ho, Stirling, 1992–3; South Clerk St hs, E, 1992–4; Bank of Scotland, Marketgait, D, 1992–6; Kincaids Court, Cowgate, E, 1994–5; Bank of Scotland, Paisley Cross, 1995–6

DEAS, Francis W (1862–1951) [of London]
Tofthill farm ho, 1904; Braehead, St Boswells, 1905; The Murrel, Aberdour, 1908 (for himself); Fyndynate Ho, Perthshire, 1909

DEPARTMENT OF HEALTH FOR SCOTLAND [of E]
Early post-war Chief Architects: Robert H Matthew, 1945–6; Robert Gardner-Medwin, 1947–52; T A Jeffryes, from 1952.
Swedish Timber hs, various sites, 1945–6 (designed by Matthew); Sighthill experimental hs, E, s1950 (with SSHA); Sighthill Health Centre, E, 1951–3; Toryglen space-saving cottages, G, f1952; Sighthill experimental flats, E, f1954; Stranraer Health Centre, 1954–5; experimental maisonettes, Muirhouse, E, 1956

* DEVEY, George (1820–86) [Engl]
Macharioch Ho a/a, 1874

DICK, Norman Aitken (1883–48) [of G]
See also J J Burnet.
Merchiston Castle Sch, E, 1929–31

DICK PEDDIE
See Peddie (Dick) & Washington Browne; Peddie (Dick) & Walker Todd.

DICKSON, Richard (1792–1857) and Robert (*c.*1794–1865) [of E]
Kilconquhar Ch, 1820–1; Gardner's Cres/Morrison St, E, 1822; †Millearne Ho, 1823–34; Leith Sheriff Court, E, 1827–8; Tron Kirk Steeple, E, 1828; Muirhouse, E, 1830–2; Bathgate Academy, 1831–3; St James's Epis Ch, Muthill, 1836; Collessie Parish Ch, 1838–9; Dr Bell's Sch, Leith, E, 1839; Dunimarle Cas a/a, 1840; Collessie Sch, 1846

*DIXON, Jeremy and JONES, Edward [Engl]
Tower Residences, Garthdee, A, 1992–3

DOUGLAS, Campbell (1828–1910) [of G]
Partnerships: with J J Stevenson 1860–70, J Sellars 1872–88, A Morrison ; c.1890–c.1901, A N Paterson 1903–7. See also Douglas (Campbell) & Morrison; Douglas (Campbell) & Sellars; Douglas (Campbell) & Stevenson; for work with A N Paterson, see separate Paterson entry.
Pre–1860 work: Alloway Ch, Ayr, 1857–8; Largs Academy, 1858; †Briggate Free Ch, G, 1859; †Hartfield, Cove, 1859; St John's Ch, Ardrossan, 1859

DOUGLAS, John (d. *c.*1778) [of E]
Ardmaddy Cas a/a, 1737 (attr); Lochnell Ho, 1737–9 (attr); Taymouth Cas a/a, 1743–50; Killin Ch, 1744; Archerfield Ho a/a, 1744–5; Fullarton Ho, 1745 (attr); Finlaystone Ho a/a, 1746–7; Campbeltown Town Ho, 1758–60

DOUGLAS (CAMPBELL) & MORRISON [of G]
Carnegie Library, Ayr, 1893; Discharged Prisoners' Aid Society, G, 1896; Sandeman Public Library, Perth, 1898; Port Dundas Warehouse, G, 1899

DOUGLAS (CAMPBELL) & SELLARS, James (1843–88) [of G]
Most design work was by Sellars; entry includes some independent Sellars commissions.
Stewart Memorial Fountain, G, 1872; Wesleyan Ch, Claremont St, G, 1872; Queens Park High Church, G, 1872–3; Free Church, Cowcaddens, G, 1872–3; Dysart Free Ch, 1872–4; †Keil Ho, Southend, 1872–5; St Andrew's Halls, G, 1873–7; Bank of Scotland Buildings, George Sq, G, 1874; Belmont–Hillhead Parish Ch, G, 1875–6 (Sellars competition win); St John's Free Ch, Cupar, 1875–8; Blackfriars Parish Ch, G, 1876–7; Belhaven UP Ch, 1876–7; Anderston Free Ch, G, 1876–8; Netherhall, Largs, 1876–92; Kelvinside Academy, G, 1877; Gilmorehill Ch, G, 1877; Tower Buildings, Buchanan St, G, *c.*1877; Mugdock Cas a/a, *c.*1877; †Milton Sch, G, 1877–8; †City of Glasgow Bank, Glassford St, G, 1878; Her Majesty's (Citizens) Theatre, G, 1878 (by Douglas); New Club, G, 1878; Ayr Municipal Buildings extension, 1878–81; Glasgow Herald office, Buchanan St, G, 1879; Finnieston Free Ch, G, 1879–80; Lambhill Cemetery gateway, G, 1881; 252–6 Paisley Rd West, G, 1882; Pathhead Hall, Kirkcaldy, 1882–4; Lochgoilhead Free Ch, 1883; Wylie & Lochhead store, G, 1883–5; Dispensary of Sick

Children's Hosp, G, 1884–8; Proudfoot Institute, Moffat, 1886; 137–9 Trongate, G, 1886–7; Couper Institute, G, 1887–8; †Speir School, Beith, 1887–8; †Glasgow Exhibition buildings, 1888; Anderson's College of Medicine, G, 1888 (compl by J Keppie); Victoria Infirmary, G, s1888

DOUGLAS (CAMPBELL) & STEVENSON [of G]
See also J J Stevenson.
†McDonald Mission Ch, Cowcaddens, G, 1861; Cupar Corn Exchange, 1861–2; Townhead & Blochairn Parish Ch, G, 1865–6; Cove Cas, 1867; Campbeltown Epis Ch, 1867; 31–9 St Vincent St, G, 1870–3 (later a/a by Burnet & Boston); Wylie & Lochhead stables and workshops, Kent Rd, G, 1870–3; †St Enoch's Free Ch, G, 1871

DREGHORN, Allan (1706–65) [of G]
†Town Hall, G, 1736–8 (with others); St Andrew's Parish Ch, G, 1737–59 (with Mungo Naismith, m); †Dreghorn Mansion, G, 1752 (for himself)

DUFF, Major Hugh Robert (1771–1832) [of Inverness]
Muirtown Ho, Inverness, 1800–34 (attr)

DUFF, Neil C (*c*.1861–1934) [of G]
Ruchill Parish Ch, G, 1903–5

DUGUID W, & SON [of Ballater]
Albert Memorial Hall, Ballater, 1875; Newkirk Parish Ch, 1876; Gordon Institute and Victoria Hall, Ballater, 1895

DUMFRIES AND GALLOWAY REGIONAL COUNCIL [of Dumfries]
The Barony a/a, 1984–9 (by P Nelson); Dumfries bypass bridges, 1988–90 (by Hugh Murray, e)

DUNBARTON COUNTY COUNCIL [of Dumbarton]
Joseph Weekes (d.1949), County Architect 1930–47.
Milton 2nd hs scheme (Whyte Corner), 1934; Kirkfield Place hs, Arrochar, 1938; Braehouse hs, Rhu, 1939; Hawcraigs and Freelands Place hs, Old Kilpatrick, 1938; Station Rd hs, Garelochhead, 1938; Ardenconnel Rd hs, Rhu, 1947; Clydebank High Sch, 1947

DUNDAS, Robert (e)
St Rollox Works, G, 1880s

DUNDEE SCHOOL BOARD (architect, J H Langlands)
Schools designed by W G Lamond: see separate Lamond entry.
Hawkhill Sch, 1892

DUNDEE TOWN COUNCIL/ CORPORATION/DISTRICT COUNCIL
City Architects: William Alexander, to 1904; James Thomson, 1904–24 (with assistance of his son Frank); Vernon Constable, 1924–30 (as senior architect in City Engineer's Department); James MacLellan Brown, 1930–44 (as senior architect in City Engineer's department) and 1944–51 (as City Architect); Robert Dron, 1951–63 and 1968–70; James Kidd, 1963–7; A Preston, 1970–5; R Carlisle, 1974–9; Ian Dunsire, 1979–91; Lindsay Davidson, from 1991. See also F Thomson.
Improvement Act central area redevelopment (outline plan by W Mackison, Burgh Engineer, with J Lessels; individual developments in Commercial St, Whitehall St and Crescent, etc., by various architects), p1872, b1876–1892; Dundee Infectious Diseases Hosp, 1887–90 (by Mackison); Blackness Library, 1904; Coldside Library, 1906–8; St Roque's Library, 1910; Ward Rd Library, 1911; Caird Hall, 1914–22; Logie hs, 1919–20; Craigiebank hs, p1919 (by A and H Thomson); 'Mystery House', 21 Glamis Rd, 1919; †Beechwood hs, f1938; Mid Craigie hs, s1938; Kirkton High Sch, s1959; Wellgate hs, 1972–4; Dryburgh sheltered hs, 1977–9; Watson St hs, 1981; Whitfield hs a/a, s1989

DUNN, James Bow (1861–1930) **& FINDLAY, James Leslie** (1868–1952) [of E]
Adam Smith and Beveridge Halls, Kirkcaldy, 1894–9; Home St hs, E (part), 1897; Abinger Gardens, E, 1898; Methodist Central Hall, Tollcross, E, 1899–1901; Scotsman building, E, 1899–1902; Fleming Cottage Hosp, Aberlour, f1900; Bruntsfield Pl hs, E (part), 1902; Dean Parish Ch, E, 1902–3; Queen's Club, Frederick St, E, 1903; Victoria Chambers, Frederick St, E, 1903; Glenfarg Ho, 1907–15 (by Dunn); Kirk o' Field, E, 1910–12; Jenners Depository, Saughtonhall, E, 1925; The Bield, Elgin, 1930

DUNN, William (1859–1934) **& WATSON, Robert** (d.1916) [of London]
Glenlyon Ho a/a, *c*.1890; Fortingall Inn, 1891; Scottish Provident Association, London, 1908

EAST KILBRIDE NEW TOWN DEVELOPMENT CORPORATION
Chief Architect and Planning Officer/Head of Architecture: Donald P Reay, 1947–51; F C Scott, 1952–65; J D Beaumont, 1965–70; R B Bryden, 1970–1; R W Colwell, 1971–7; T Fraser, 1977–83; J Barrie, 1983-94; K Synnot, 1994–5.
Markshill hs, Limekilns hs, and shops at Whitemoss, s1950; Murray 1st development hs, f1952; Town

Centre, p1954; Westwood II, Brouster Pl and Quebec Drive hs, f1955; Calderwood 14 hs, 1963–5

* EASTON, GIBB & SON LTD [Engl] (e)
Rosyth Naval dockyard, 1909–14

EDINBURGH SCHOOL BOARD
Robert Wilson, Architect to 1901, followed by J A Carfrae, 1901–20.
Marchmont Rd Sch, 1882; Milton Ho Sch, 1886; Sciennes Sch, 1889; South Morningside Sch, 1891; Bruntsfield Sch, 1893 (by Carfrae); Broughton Sch, 1897; Flora Stevenson Sch, 1899–1900 (by Carfrae); Boroughmuir Sch Annexe, 1902; Leith Academy Annexe, 1903; Tollcross Sch, 1911–13; Boroughmuir High Sch, 1911–14

EDINBURGH TOWN COUNCIL/ CORPORATION/DISTRICT COUNCIL
City Superintendents of Public Works: James Gordon, 1786–9; William Sibbald 1790–1809; John Paterson, 1809; Thomas Bonnar, 1809–18; Thomas Brown 1819–47. City Architects: David Cousin 1847–78; Robert H Morham, 1878–1908; James A Williamson, 1908–25; Ebenezer J MacRae, 1925–46; A G Forgie, 1946–53; Alexander Steele, 1955–72; Brian Annable, 1972–84. Post abolished in 1984. Works of pre–1878 postholders listed under own names.
City Chambers reconstruction, 1875–86 and 1898–1904; Dalry Baths, 1893–5; Electric Lighting Central Generating Sta, Dewar Place, 1894; City Infectious Diseases Hosp, 1896–1903; Glenogle Baths, 1897–1900; Lauriston Pl Fire Sta, 1897–1901; Portobello Public Baths, 1898; West End Police Sta, 1908–9; Grassmarket hs (new and restr), 1929; East Pilton hs scheme, 1930; Greyfriars Hotel, 1930; Craigmillar hs, 1930–8; Nurses' Home, Edinburgh District Asylum, Bangour, 1931; Canongate hs, 1931–3; standard police boxes, 1931–3; Heriot–Watt Coll Extension, 1932–5; †Portobello Power Sta, 1934 (by MacRae and W A Macartney, CE); †Portobello Bathing Pool, 1934–6 (by W A Macartney, CE); West Pilton hs, s1936 (by MacRae with Stewart Kaye; West Pilton Circus built from 1951); Piershill hs, 1937–8; Meadowbank Sports Centre, 1968; City Art Centre, 1979–80

EDINBURGH UNIVERSITY HOUSING/ARCHITECTURE RESEARCH UNIT
Patio hs, Inchview, Prestonpans, 1962; Park 3 West hs (West View), Cumbernauld, 1966–9; St Mary's St hs, Kirkcudbright, 1970–2

EDNIE, John (1876–1934) [of E, G]
11 Whittingehame Drive, G, 1907

EDWARD, Alexander (1651–1708)
Careston Cas a/a, 1702 (attr); Atholl Monument, Dunkeld, 1704; Brechin Cas a/a, p1704, f1711; Hamilton Palace landscaping plan, 1708

EDWARD, Charles (1816–90) [of D]
Partner of T S Robertson, q.v., from c.1867.
Arbroath Corn Exchange, 1855; Dundee Corn Exchange, 1858; Perth District Asylum, Murthly, f1864; Glengall Asylum, Ayr, 1868; Ogilvie Ch, D, 1876

ELDER & CANNON [of G]
D & D Warehouse, G, 1981; Bank of Pakistan, Sauchiehall St, G (a/a to Gas Showroom by A McI Gardner), 1981; Ch of the Holy Name, G, 1984–5; Ingram Sq redevelopment, G, 1984–9; Duke St and Sword St hs, G, 1992; Coplaw St and Langside Rd hs, G, 1993–4; Melville St hs, G, 1994–5; Kilmarnock Bus Sta, 1994–5; Brunswick St hotel, G, 1995; Wellpark Sch a/a, 1995–6

ELLIOT, Archibald (1760–1823) [of E, London]
Some items jointly with brother James (1770–1810).
†Dreghorn Cas a/a, c.1805; Dunfermline Guildhall, 1805; Stobo Cas, 1805–11; Loudoun Cas, 1806; Taymouth Cas main block, 1806–9 (interiors 1809–13); †Minto Ho a/a, 1809–14; Glenorchy Parish Ch, Dalmally, 1810 (by James); †Edinburgh New Prisons, 1815–17; Waterloo Pl and Regent Br, E, 1815–22; Waterloo Monument, Penielheugh, 1816; Callendar Ho Mausoleum, 1816; St Paul's and St George's Epis Ch, E, 1816–18; †County Hall, E, 1816–19; Newbyth Ho, 1817; Cockpen Parish Ch, 1818; †Paisley County Buildings, 1818–20; Rutland Pl/Sq, E, p1819, s1830; Revd James Hall's United Associate Synod Chapel (Broughton Ch), E, 1820–1; Jedburgh County Prison, 1820–3; Blair Atholl Parish Ch, 1823–5;

ELLIOT, Archibald, II (d.1843) [of E]
Royal Bank of Scotland, G, 1827

ELLIOT, William [of Kelso]
Teviot Br, 1795 (attr); Ladykirk Ho, 1797–9; Crailing Ho, 1801–3; Langholm Town Ho, 1811–13 (attr); Drumlanrig Cas a/a, 1813

ELLIS, Alexander (1836–1917) **& WILSON, Robert G** (1844–1931) [of A]
Pre–1869 work by Ellis alone; post–1896 work by Wilson alone.
St Mary's RC Cath, A, 1860 (spire 1877 by Wilson); St Mary's Epis Cath, A, 1862; St Magnus's Epis Ch, Lerwick, Shetland, 1864; Carden Pl UP Ch, A, 1880–2; Bon–Accord UF Ch, A, 1894–6; Esslemont & Mackintosh west block, A, 1897; 96 Queens Rd, A, 1898; New Coll, St Mary's Coll, Blairs, 1898–1902

(and a/a 1906); 6 Upperkirkgate, A, 1899; Station Hotel, A, 1901; 62 Rubislaw Den South, A, 1901; Clydesdale Bank, Marischal St, A, 1902; Angusfield Ho, A, 1904

EMMERSON, Roger
See Archimedia.

* EMMETT, J T (1828–98) [Engl]
New Independent Ch, Bath St, G, 1851; Sandyford Ch, G, 1854–6 (with J Honeyman)

EWAN, Robert [of G]
Crieff Hydropathic, 1867–8

* EWING, G T [of Crieff]
Drummond Cas a/a, 1878; Pitkellony Ho a/a, c.1880; Crieff Parish Ch, 1882

* FAIRBAIRN, Sir William & CO. [Engl] (e)
Findhorn Br, 1855; Dalguise Br, 1862–3 (with J Mitchell); Logierait Br, 1865

FAIRHURST, W A & PARTNERS [of G] (e)
Glasgow Inner Ring Rd, West Flank, s1965 (with W Holford, consultant architect); Kingston Br, G, f1970

FAIRLEY, James Graham (1846–1934) [of E]
Girls' High Sch, D, 1889 (with ex–partner Alexander McCulloch); Brechin Public Library, 1892; Kirkbrae Ho, Dean Br, E, a/a, 1892; Fountainhall Rd Ch, E, 1896–7; Linlithgow Academy, 1900; St David's UF Ch, Bathgate, 1904; Balbardie Sch, Bathgate, 1904

FAIRLEY, J McLellan
See Leadbetter & Fairley.

FAIRLIE, Reginald (1883–1952) [of E]
Entry includes work of Fairlie, Reid & Forbes, and Fairlie & Partners; see also Reid & Forbes.
St James's RC Ch, St Andrews, 1910; Our Lady of the Assumption RC Ch, Troon, 1911; St Benedict's Abbey, Fort Augustus, choir, 1914–7, and nave, 1949–56; Kilmany Ho, 1914–19; Northfield hs scheme, E, 1919; Methil Parish Ch, 1924–5; Kippen Ch a/a, 1924–6; Cuil-an-Duin, Logierait, 1925–7; St Adrian's Epis Ch, Gullane, 1927; American–Scottish War Memorial, E, 1928; St Patrick's RC Ch, Cowgate, E, a/a, 1928–9; †Lour Ho pavilions, 1929; Floors Cas lodges and gates, 1929; St Nicholas's Ho, St Andrews, 1932; Princess Margaret Rose Hosp, E, 1930–9; Immaculate Conception RC Ch, Fort William, 1933–4; National Library of Scotland, E, p1934–6, b1937–55; St Patrick's RC Ch, Mallaig, 1935; Immaculate Conception RC Ch, Jedburgh, 1937; Our Lady Star of the Sea RC Ch, Tayport, 1939; Baro Ho, 1939–55;

Cowal Power Sta, 1950; Ewing Building, Queens Coll, D, 1950–3; St Laurence's Ch, Drumchapel, G, 1954–7

FAIRWEATHER, John (1867–1942) **& SON** [of G]
†Green's Playhouse, G, 1925–7; Playhouse Theatre, E, 1927–9; †Green's Playhouse, D, 1934–6; British Linen Bank, Gallowgate, G, 1936

* FARRELL, Terry [Engl]
Edinburgh International Conference Centre (and area masterplan), 1993–5

* FATKIN, J N [Engl]
Kelvin Ct, G, 1937–8

* FAULKNER-BROWNS [Engl]
Perth Leisure Centre, 1986–8; Unst Leisure Centre, Yell Leisure Centre and North Mainland Swimming Pool, 1988; South Mainland and Scalloway leisure pools, Shetland, 1991–3; Hamilton Water Palace, 1993–5

FERRIGAN, James (c.1883–1947)
See Scottish Co-operative Wholesale Society.

FIFE COUNTY COUNCIL [of Cupar]
County Architect in late 1960s: John Fisher.
Mills Buildings development, Guardbridge, 1966–8; Dairsie Village Sch, 1970.

FINDLAY, James (d.1943) [of D]
Successor to J M Robertson (q.v.). Later Findlay, Stewart & Robbie. See also Robbie & Wellwood.
Ballumbie Ho, D, a/a, s1902; Medical Schools, University College, D, 1902; Abernyte Sch, 1906–9; Netherwood, D, 1924–33

FINNART, Sir James Hamilton of (d.1540) (R)MOW
Craignethan Cas, 1530s (attr); Cadzow Cas, c.1530 (attr); Linlithgow Palace a/a, s1534; Stirling Cas palace block, s1538.

FLETCHER, Thomas [of A]
Union Br, A, 1801–5 (with T Telford and James Burn); King St outline plan, A, 1803

FLOCKHART, William (c.1850–1915) [of London]
2 Palace Court, London, 1891; †Rosehaugh Ho, 1898–1903

* FOWKE, Captain Francis (1823–65) [Engl]
Royal Scottish Museum, E, 1860–1

* FOWLER, Sir John (1817–98) [Engl] (e)
†St Enoch Sta trainshed, G, 1876–9 (with James F Blair); Forth Br, 1882–90 (with Benjamin Baker)

FRANCHE, Thomas (m)
Br of Dee, A, c.1500–27 (with Alexander Galloway, MOW)

* **FRASER, J de Courcy** [Engl]
Lewis's store, G, 1932

FRASER, Patrick Allan (1813–90) [of Arbroath]
Hospitalfield, Arbroath, a/a, s1850; Blackcraig Ho and
lodge, Blairgowrie, 1856; Blackcraig Br, Blairgowrie,
1870; Western Cemetery Chapel, Arbroath, 1875–80

FRAZER, Major Andrew (d.1795) [of E]
Fort Charlotte, Lerwick, a/a, 1781; St Andrew and St
George's Ch, E, 1782–7; St Cuthbert's Ch, E, 1789–90
(attr)

FRAZER, George (c.1701–74) [of E]
Corstorphine Manse, E, 1768–9; Inverness High Ch,
1769–72

FREEBAIRN, Charles [of E]
Innerpeffray Library, 1758–62

FRISKIN, William Wallace (b.1889)
See Allan & Friskin.

FULTON, Jack, ASSOCIATES [of D]
Botanic Garden Visitor Centre, D, 1982

GARDNER, Albert V [of G]
Campbeltown Picture Ho, 1913; Orient Cinema, G,
1931–2

GARDNER, Alexander McInnes (d.1934) [of G]
See also J Miller.
Ship interiors from 1910 for Fairfield, Denny, etc.;
Clydebank Public Library, 1912; Electricity Board
Offices, Waterloo St, G, 1927; Gas Showroom,
Sauchiehall St, G, 1935

* **GARNER PRESTON STREBEL** [Engl]
Dumbarton Central Area hs, 1965–70

* **GASSON, Barry, with J MEUNIER and
B ANDRESON** [Engl]
Burrell Collection, G, p1971, f1983

GAULDIE, William (1876–1945) [of D]
*Practice established 1898; by 1950, known as Gauldie,
Hardie, Wright & Needham. Later: Gauldie, Wright
& Partners.*
Potter's shop, Murraygate, D, 1911; Fife County
Buildings, Cupar, 1950s; Royal Exchange Assurance
office, D, 1955–8; Belmont university hall of
residence, D, 1963–5; Regional police headquarters,
D, 1966–8

GEDDES, Patrick (1854–1932) [of E]
See also F Mears.
Scottish National Zoological Pk, E, p1913 (with
F Mears; compl by Mears, 1927)

* **GENERAL ELECTRIC CO. LTD and
SIMON-CARVES LTD** [Engl] (e)
Hunterston 'A' Nuclear Power Sta, 1957–64

* **GIBB, Alexander & PARTNERS** [Engl] (e)
Tongue Br and causeways, 1971; (second) Drygrange
Br, 1971–3

GIBBS, James (1682–1754) [of London]
Scottish works: Balvenie Ho, 1724; St Nicholas West
Ch, A, p1741, b1752–5. Principal English works: St
Mary-le-Strand Ch, London, 1714–17; Sudbrook Ho
a/a, 1715–19; St Martin's-in-the-Fields Ch, London,
p1720, b1722–6; Ditchley Ho, 1720–42; Cambridge
Senate Ho, 1722–30; King's Coll New Building,
Cambridge, 1724–49; Radcliffe Library, Oxford,
1737–48

* **GIBSON, John** (1817–92) [Engl]
National Bank, Queen St, G, 1847 (relocated 1902–3
as Langside Halls)

GIBSON, Miles S (1848–1906) [of G]
Barrowfield weaving factory, G, 1889–99

GIBSON, Richard G [of Lerwick]
*Prior to 1972, was Depute County Architect, Zetland
County Council.*
Hamnavoe Sch, Shetland, f1980; Hill La hs, Lerwick,
Shetland, f1982; Hanseatic Booth restr, Symbister,
Shetland, f1984; Hamnavoe sheltered hs, f1984; Pony
Pund restr, Noss, Shetland, f1985; North End hs,
Lerwick, f1985 and 1990; Gibblestone Ho hs,
Scalloway, Shetland, f1990; The Crafty hs, Kirkwall,
Orkney, f1991; Art Centre, Weisdale, Shetland, f1993;
Symbister Sch, f1993; Commercial Rd hs, Lerwick,
f1996; Knab Rd hs, Lerwick, f1996

GIBSON, T Bowhill (c.1895–1949) [of E]
Dominion Cinema, E, 1937–8; County Cinema,
Portobello, E, 1939

* **GIBSON, Thomas** [Engl]
Marchmont Ho, 1750–3 (with 3rd Earl of
Marchmont).

GIBSON, Thomas (d.1896) [of E]
Warrender Pk Rd hs (part), E, 1878

GILLESPIE, KIDD & COIA [of G]
Successor firm to Salmon & Son & Gillespie.
St Anne's RC Ch, Dennistoun, G, 1931–3; St Patrick's
RC Ch, Greenock, 1934–5; St Columbkille's RC Ch,
Rutherglen, 1934–40; St Columba's RC Ch, Maryhill,
1937; St Peter in Chains RC Ch, Ardrossan, 1938 (by
Warnett Kennedy); †RC Pavilion of 1938 Glasgow
Empire Exhibition (by Warnett Kennedy); †Palace of
Industries North, Empire Exhibition (by Coia, with T
S Tait); St Lawrence's RC Ch, Greenock, 1951–4; St

Michael's RC Ch, Dumbarton, 1952; Freeland La hs, Murray 1st development, East Kilbride, f1953; St Paul's RC Ch, Glenrothes, 1956–7; Simshill Sch, G, 1956–63; Kildrum 1 hs, Cumbernauld, s1957; Our Lady and St Francis RC Sch, G, 1958–64; St Charles's RC Ch, G, 1959–60; St Martin's RC Ch, Castlemilk, G, 1959–61; Bellshill Maternity Hosp, 1959–62; St Peter's Seminary, Cardross, 1959–66; Kildrum Primary Sch, Cumbernauld, 1960–2; Howford Sch, G, 1961–3; St Benedict's RC Ch, Easterhouse, G, 1962–5; Our Lady's RC High Sch, Cumbernauld, 1963–4; St Bride's RC Ch, East Kilbride, 1963–4; Halls of Residence, University of Hull (Engl), 1963–7; St Patrick's RC Ch, Kilsyth, 1964; Sacred Heart RC Ch, Cumbernauld, 1964; Round Riding Rd hs, Dumbarton, s1964; Our Lady of Good Counsel RC Ch, G, 1965; †St Benedict's RC Ch, G, 1965–7; Notre Dame Coll, Bearsden, 1969; BOAC Building, G, 1970; Wadham Coll, Oxford (Engl), a/a, 1971–7; St Margaret's RC Ch, Clydebank, f1972; Cumbernauld Technical Coll, 1972–5; Robinson Coll, Cambridge (Engl), p1974, b1977–80; Bonar Hall, D, 1975; Glasgow Sch of Art refectory, 1981

GILLESPIE, James (1854–1914) **& SCOTT, James** (1861–1944) [of St Andrews]
St Andrews Post Office, 1891–2; Kirkcaldy Sheriff Court, 1893–4 (by Gillespie); University Hall, St Andrews, 1895–6; St Andrew's Rectory, St Andrews, 1896; Monimail Free Ch, 1897–8; Markinch Municipal Buildings, 1897–9; Bute Medical Sch, St Andrews, 1897–9; Queen Victoria Memorial Hall, Coaltown of Balgonie, 1905–6; Hepburn Gardens, St Andrews (part), 1906–10; The Ridge, St Andrews, 1913; UF Ch, St Andrews, 1926–8; St Leonards Sch Music Wing, St Andrews, 1930; New Picture Ho, St Andrews, 1930; 166 South St, St Andrews restr, 1955–7

GLASGOW TOWN COUNCIL/ CORPORATION/DISTRICT COUNCIL: WORKS BY CITY ARCHITECT AND EQUIVALENT POSTS
Postholders: John Carrick (1819–90), Superintendent of Works/CA 1844–90; A B MacDonald (1847–1915), City Engineer 1890–1914; Thomas Nisbet, Master of Works and CE 1914–24; Thomas Somers, MOW & CE 1925–41; Robert Bruce, MOW and CE 1941–8; James Riddet, MOW and CE from 1950; Archibald Jury, CA and Planning Officer/Dir. of Planning 1951–6, CA 1967–71; James Kernohan, CA/Director of Architecture 1972–7; William Worden, DoA 1977–85; Christopher Purslow, DoA from 1985. For Carrick's own pre-1844 work, see separate entry.
†Bell St Police Office, 1850; City Halls and Markets, 1852–3 (and a/a 1882–6); Western Police Office,

Cranston St, 1859; †Abercromby Lodging Ho, G, 1860; Queen's Pk plan (with J Paxton) and Queen's Drive feuing plan, 1860; Cattle Market, 1866; Glasgow City Improvement Act scheme, s1866; Tobago St Police Building, 1868–9; †Drygate Lodging Ho, 1869; Belvidere Hosp, 1874–7 and 1887; Meat Market, *c*.1875; †Yate St Police Office, 1878; †Clyde St Lodging Ho, 1878; High St hs, 1878; 109–29 Saltmarket CIT hs, p1880, f1887; †Gorbals Public Baths, 1884–5; City Hall, Candleriggs front, 1885; †Northern Police Office, Maitland St, *c*.1890; High St City Improvement hs, 1891–3; Trongate blocks, 1891–1900; People's Palace, 1893–8; Botanic Gardens lodges, 1894; Bell St City Improvement hs, 1895–6; Sanitary Chambers, G, 1895–7; Ruchill Hosp, 1895–1900; Southern Police Building, G, 1896–7; Whitevale St Baths, 1899–1903; Partick Pumping Sta, 1904; Kingston Halls, 1904–5 (by R W Horn); Mearnskirk Hosp, 1921–30 (by J A T Houston); Shettleston Hall, 1922–5; Cathcart Library, 1923–4 (by J A T Houston); King George V Bridge, 1924–8; Kelvin Hall, 1926–7; Crookston Cottage Homes, 1936–8 (by W Barrie); Cowglen Hosp, s1937; Gartloch Hosp Nurses' Home, 1937–9; Calfhill Court hs, Pollok, 1950–3; Moss Heights hs, 1950–3; cottage hs, Cranhill, s1951; Hutchesontown/Gorbals Area A hs, 1956; Smithycroft Secondary Sch, 1964–6; Springburn CDA Area B hs, p1964; Darnley hs, s1970; St Stephen's Primary Sch, Sighthill, 1971–2; Doncaster St hs, 1980–2; Queens Cross East and West hs, G, 1985–9; Oran St hs, f1986; Tormusk Community Renewal, Castlemilk, 1987–91

GLASGOW TOWN COUNCIL/ CORPORATION: WORKS BY DIRECTOR OF HOUSING
Postholders: Peter Fyfe, 1919–23; John Bryce, 1923–8; Robert W Horn, 1928–31; William McNab, 1932–41; Ronald Bradbury, 1943–8; Archibald Jury, 1948–51.
Kennyhill and Riddrie hs, 1919–27 (by R W Horn); Mosspark hs, p1920; Knightswood, s1921; Hamiltonhill rehousing scheme, s1923; Blackhill rehousing scheme, 1935–6; Pollok Section A hs, s1937; Great Western Rd hs, 1937–42; Penilee hs (by J H Ferrie, Chief Housing Architect), 1939–47; Sannox Gardens hs, 1946–51; Pollok Section C Area X hs, type T/1/3 blocks (first Glasgow post-war flats), f1948; Queen's Pk Drive old people's cottage hs, 1949–50; Fyvie Av hs, Eastwood, 1949–51; Crathie Drive hs, 1949–52

GLEAVE, Joseph L (1907–64) [of G]
1958–64, J L Gleave & Partners; from 1964 to 1987, Dorward Matheson Gleave & Partners; from 1987, Matheson Gleave Partnership. For work between 1949

and 1958, see Keppie & Henderson.
Columbus Memorial Lighthouse (Dominican Repub), p1931, b1939–92; Inverness County Buildings, 1961–3; Blackfriars and St Francis Primary Schools, G, 1961–4; Queen Mother's Hosp, G, 1961–4; Prestwick International Airport, 1964; Fort William hosp, 1965; Pollokshaws CDA Unit 1 hs, G, s1966; Mathematics Building, University of Glasgow, 1969; Boyd Orr Building, University of Glasgow, f1972; Geology Building, University of Glasgow, 1980; Central (Raigmore) Hosp, Inverness, f1983

GLENROTHES NEW TOWN DEVELOPMENT CORPORATION
Chief Architects: Peter Tinto, 1950–64; Merlyn C Williams, 1965–72; John Coghill, 1972–7; Jack Baird, 1977–80; Sandy Bannerman, 1980–92.
Initial town plan, 1951; Woodside shopping precinct and hs, 1951–2 (by H A Wheeler); Auchmuty Precinct 2nd development hs, s1953; The Beeches hs, f1954; Auchmuty High Sch, 1954–7; Town Centre first shopping block, s1955

GLOVER, John Hardie (d.1994)
See B U Spence.

* GOLDIE, George (1828–87) [Engl]
St Mary's RC Ch, Lanark, 1856–9 (with M Hadfield); Our Lady's Ch, Fetternear, 1859; St Mary's Ch, Greenock, 1862

GORDON, A Esme (1910–93) & DEY, William G [of E]
†Transport and Travel Pavilion, 1938 Glasgow Exhibition; Methil Ch, 1939; Scottish Life Assurance Company offices, E, 1960; St David's Ch, Broomhouse, E, 1960; George St electricity office, E, 1960–4; Moray Ho Coll of Education extensions, E, 1960–80 (including gymnasium, 1968–70)

GORDON, John (1835–1912) [of G]
Latterly in partnership with D Bennett Dobson.
5 Cleveden Gardens, G, *c*.1877; Grovepark Mills a/a, G, 1878–1900; Calton Public Sch, G, 1890; Subway Power Sta, G, 1895–6; Miller & Lang Art Publishers, G, 1901–3 (by Dobson); Dungoyne St, Barra St, and Crosbie St hs, G, 1901–3; Scotland St bonded warehouse, G, 1903; 53 Pentland Terr, E, 1904

GOWANS, James (1821–90) [of E]
Gowanbank, 1842–62; Rosebank Cottages, E, 1854 (with Alexander MacGregor); †Rockville, E, 1858; Grange Cemetery tomb, E, 1858; 23–5 Blacket Pl, E, 1859–60; Lammerburn, E, 1860; Creetown Sta, *c*.1860; Castle Terr hs, E, 1866; Edinburgh Winter Garden, 1875 (with F T Pilkington); Waverley, Colinton Rd, E, 1884; 1–4 Lockharton Gardens, E,

1884; demonstration dwellings and Melville Drive masons' pillars, Edinburgh Exhibition, 1886; 64–78 and 157–9 Colinton Rd, E, 1886–7

GRAHAM, James Gillespie (1766–1855) [of E]
Snizort Parish Ch, 1800–1; Achnacarry Cas, s1802 (compl 1837 by Peter Manual); Howard Pl layout, E, 1807; Culdees Cas, 1809; Erskine lands feuing plan, E, 1809 (b1830s); County Buildings, Cupar, 1810; Drumtochty Cas, *c*.1810–12; Ross Priory, 1810–16; Collace Ch, 1813 (attr); St Mary's RC Ch, E, 1813–14; St Andrew's RC Chapel, G, 1814–17; Liberton Parish Ch, E, 1815; Clackmannan Parish Ch, 1815; Gray's Hosp, Elgin, 1815–19; †Armadale Cas, *c*.1815–20; †Duns Market Ho, 1816; Old Parish Ch, Dunoon, s1816; Cambusnethan Priory, 1816–19; Inveraray Courthouse, 1816–20 (with R Reid); Alloa Parish Ch, 1817; †West George St Independent Ch, G, 1818; Duns Cas a/a, 1818; Logie Easter Old Parish Ch, 1818–19; Dunbar Parish Ch, 1818–21; The Lee, 1820; Nicolson St Ch, E, 1820; plan for area south of St Vincent St, G, 1820s; Moray estate feuing plan and elevations, E (including Moray Pl, Randolph Cres, Ainslie Pl, Great Stuart St), 1822–36; Dunninald Ho, 1823–4; Blacket Pl, E, layout s1825; Hamilton Sq, Birkenhead (Engl), s1825; Walker lands feuing plan, E, 1826 (mostly built s1862); Dunino Ch, 1826–7; Muthill Parish Ch, 1826–8; Greenside Ch, E, 1830–9; †Murthly Ho, s1831 (with Sir James Drummond Stewart); Errol Parish Ch, 1831–3; Montrose Old Ch steeple, 1832–4 (with A W N Pugin); Taymouth Cas a/a, 1834–8; St Margaret's Convent, E, 1835; Tolbooth St John Ch, E, 1839–44 (with A W N Pugin); Brodick Cas a/a, 1844–6; St Anthony the Eremite Chapel, Murthly, a/a, 1846–8; Ayton Ho, 1846–51. For full list of works, see Colvin, *Dictionary*, 1995 edn, pp. 420–5

GRAINGER, Thomas (1795–1852) [of E]
Entry includes work by/with John Miller, 1805–83.
Haymarket Sta, E, 1840 (by Miller); North Leith Sta, E, 1846; Burntisland Sta, 1847 (with Miller); Cupar Sta, 1847; Ladybank Sta, 1847–8 (with Miller); Melrose Sta, 1847–9 (by Miller).

GRANT, Sir Archibald
Monymusk Village, p1716

GRANT, John A W (1885–1959) [of E]
Westerton Garden Suburb, 1912–15 (with R Unwin); Westquarter Model Village, 1936–8; Fountainbridge Library, E, 1938; Ae village hs, p1947; Moredun hs, E, s1947; Salvesen Gardens hs, E, 1948; Clermiston hs, E, 1952–61; Muirhouse hs scheme first development, E, s1953

GRATTON & McLEAN [of G]
Castlemilk West Ch, G, 1957–9

GRAY, Charles W [of E]
Ch of the Holy Name, Oakley, 1958

GROVES-RAINES, Nicholas [of E]
Moncrieff Terr, E, 1979; Balfour Ho, Cameron Cres, E, 1982–3; 16–18 Blackfriars St, G, 1984–5; Spiers Wharf, G, p1984, s1988 (with J Cunning Young); †Historic Gardens Pavilion, Glasgow Garden Festival, 1988; Saltmarket hs, G, 1993

* HABERSHON, W (1818–92) **& PITE, A R** [Engl]
All Saints Epis Ch, Challoch, 1871–2

HALLEY, Charles J and NEIL, Hamilton
[of Clydebank]
Argyll Motor Works, Alexandria, 1905–6; Free High Ch, Dumbarton, 1907–8

HAMILTON, David (1768–1843) [of G]
In partnership latterly with his son James (1818–61).
Ardenconnel Ho, *c.*1790 (attr); Union St viaduct approaches, A, s1800 (with Charles Abercrombie); Hutcheson's Hosp, G, 1802–5; Nelson Monument, G, 1806; Aikenhead Ho, 1806 (attr; with later a/a); Kenmure Ho, *c.*1806; †Gorbals Parish Ch, G, 1806–10; Ayr New Ch, 1807–12; Crawford Priory, p1809 (compl J Gillespie Graham); Camphill Ho, *c.*1810; Kincaid Ho, 1812; †Glasgow Tolbooth a/a, 1813; Old Erskine Ch, 1813–14; Falkirk Town Steeple, 1813–14; Kilmardinny Ho, *c.*1815; Port Glasgow Town Buildings, 1815–16; Hafton Ho, 1816; Larbert Ch, 1817; †St John's Ch, G, 1817–19; Castle Toward, 1820–1; Castle Ho, Dunoon, 1822; †Hamilton Palace a/a, 1822–6 (with Francesco Saponieri); Bothwell Ch, 1825–33; †St Enoch's Ch, G, 1827; High Ch of Campsie, 1827–8; Royal Exchange, G, 1827–9; Priory Lodge, Largs, 1829–30; Warriston and Northfield (attr), Largs, *c.*1830; Royal Exchange Sq facades, G, 1830–9 (with James Smith); Dunlop Ho, 1831–4; Ballimore Ho, *c.*1832; Glasgow Necropolis gateway and bridge, 1833; 151–7 Queen St, G, *c.*1834; Dunoon High Kirk a/a, 1834; Cleland Testimonial Building, G, 1834–6; †St Paul's Ch, G, 1835; Free Normal Seminary, G, 1836–7; Lennox Cas, 1837–41; Hamilton Riding Sch, 1838 (attr); Mosesfield, Springburn, G, 1838; Glasgow Necropolis lodge, 1839–40; †Western Bank, G, 1840; Bank of Scotland, Cadzow St, Hamilton, *c.*1840; Brooksby, Largs (attr), *c.*1840; †British Linen Bank, G, 1840–1; Western Club Ho, G, 1840–1; Union Bank (Lanarkshire Ho) Ingram St, G, 1841; †Glasgow & Ship Bank, G, 1842; St Fillan's Villa, Largs, 1843; †Muirshiel Ho, *c.*1843–5

HAMILTON, John (1851–1935) [of G]
Sir John Maxwell Sch, G, fl907

HAMILTON, Thomas (1784–1858) [of E]
Burns Monument, Alloway, 1818–23; Kinghorn Town Ho, 1822; John Knox Memorial, G, 1825; Royal High Sch, E, 1825–9; †Hopetoun Rooms, E, 1827; Salisbury Cottage (Arthur Lodge), E, *c.*1827–30 (attr); Cumstoun Ho, 1828–9; Ayr Municipal Buildings and Steeple, 1828–32; Kinghorn Sch, 1829; 45 George St, E, 1829; King's Br and George IV Br, E, s1829 (compl George Smith); 45 George St, E, 1829; Burns Monument, E, 1830; Ayrshire Bank, Ayr, *c.*1830; Wallace Tower, Ayr, 1830–3; 93 George St, E, 1833; Dean Orphanage, E, 1833–6; Alyth Ch, 1837–9; Egyptian Vaults, Glasgow Necropolis, *c.*1840; Royal Coll of Physicians, E, 1844–6; Free St John's Ch, E, 1845; New North Free Ch, E, 1846–8; South Leith Parish Ch a/a, 1847–8

HAMILTON-PATERSON, Robert (b.1843)
& DUNCAN RHIND, Sir T (1871–1927) [of E]
83 George St, E, 1901; 9 Randolph Pl, E, a/a, 1901–2; Charlotte Ho, E, 1903 (by Rhind)

* HANE, Joachim [Ger] (e)
†Inverness Citadel, s1652

* HANSOM, Joseph (1803–82) [Engl]
St David's RC Ch, Dalkeith, 1853; St Mary's RC Ch, Lochee, D, 1865

* HARRISON, J Stockdale (d. *c.*1952) [Engl]
Usher Hall, E, 1911–14

* HARRISON, Thomas (1744–1829) [Engl]
†Kennet Ho, 1795–9; Broomhall, 1796–9 (compl 1865–74 by Thomson & Wilson)

HARVEY & SCOTT [of G]
Rothesay Academy, 1956–9; Gallowgate area A hs, G, 1963–9

HASTIE, William (1755–1832) [of St Petersburg]
Kolpino ordnance works (Rus), 1801–8; Tsarskoe Selo new town (Rus), p1809; from 1812, numerous town plans across Russian Empire; Contract Ho, Kiev (Ukr), 1815–17

HASWELL, George (d.1784) [of Inveraray]
Castlehill Ch, Campbeltown, 1778–80

HAY, Charles
St Joseph's Coll, Dumfries, 1907

HAY, John (d.1861), **James Murdoch** (*c.*1823–1915) **and William Hardie** (*c.*1813–1900) [of Liverpool]
St John's Epis Ch, Perth, 1851; South Free Ch, Stirling, 1851–5; Well Park Free Ch, Greenock, 1853; Chalmers Ch, Stirling, 1853; Bridge of Allan Free Ch, 1853–4; Old High Ch, Stirling, 1854–6; East Free Ch, Brechin, 1856; Buccleuch and Greyfriars Free Ch, E,

1856–7; St John's Free Ch, Gourock, 1857; Tarfside Free Ch, 1859; St Kentigern's Ch, Lanark, 1883

HAY, William (1818–88) [of E, Toronto, and again E]
From 1878: in partnership with George Henderson (1846–1905)
St John's Epis Ch, Longside, 1854; †General Hosp and †Gould St UP Ch, Toronto (Can), 1855; St Michael's Coll, Toronto, 1856; St George's Anglican Ch, Newcastle, Ontario (Can), 1857; †Yorkville Town Hall (Can), 1859–60; Kingsknowes, Galashiels, 1868–9; St Giles Cath, E, restr, 1871–84; Old Parish Ch, Galashiels, 1878–81 (by Henderson); Old St Paul's Epis Ch, E, 1881–1906; Government Ho, Hamilton (Bermuda), 1883; Holy Trinity Cath, Hamilton (Bermuda), 1885–1905; Craiglockhart Parish Ch, E, 1889–99

* **HAYWARD, John** (1808–91) [Engl]
St John's Chapel, Jedburgh, 1843–4

HEITON, Andrew (1823–94) [of Perth]
Includes earlier work of A Heiton & Son.
Dunalastair, 1852; Dunkeld and Birnam Sta, 1856; Union Bank, George St, Perth, 1857–8; †Springburn railway village, G, 1863; †Castleroy, D, 1867; Orchill Ho, 1868; Kinfauns Parish Ch, 1868–9; St Mary's Monastery, Perth, 1868–70; Giffen Ho, 1869; †Ravenscraig, West Ferry, 1874; Vogrie Ho, 1875; Atholl Hydropathic, Pitlochry, 1875–8; Kinnoul Primary Sch, Perth, c.1876; Keillour Cas, c.1877; Perth Municipal Buildings, 1877–9; Bonskeid, 1881; Druidsmere Ho, Blairgowrie, 1885; Station Hotel, Perth, 1888

HEITON, Andrew Grainger [of Perth]
Trinity Coll, Glenalmond, a/a, 1889 and 1904–6; Perth Guildhall, 1907–8

HENDERSON, A G (c.1882–1963)
See Keppie & Henderson.

HENDERSON, David (d. c.1787) [of E]
Inverleith Ho, E, 1774; Auldgirth Old Br, 1781–2

HENDERSON, George (1846–1905)
See W Hay.

HENDERSON, John (d.1786) [of E]
Assembly Rooms, E, s1787

HENDERSON, John (1804–62) [of E]
See also W Hay.
Samuel Douglas's Free Sch, Newton Stewart, 1834; Newhaven Parish Ch, 1836; Montrose Natural History Museum, 1837; Holy Trinity Ch, E, 1837–8; St Mary's Ch, Dumfries, 1837–9; Brechin Mechanics' Institute, 1838; Panmure Testimonial, Camustane Hill, 1839; North Ch, Stirling, 1841; Trinity Coll, Glenalmond

(initial works), 1843–51; St Mary's Epis Ch, Dunblane, 1844; St Mary's Epis Ch, Hamilton, 1846–7; St Columba's by the Castle Ch, E, 1846–7; St Mary's Epis Ch, Arbroath, 1847; Christ Ch (Epis), Lochgilphead, 1852; St Peter's Epis Ch, Galashiels, 1853; St Mary's Epis Ch, Port Glasgow, 1856; St Baldred's Epis Ch, North Berwick, 1861–2

HENDERSON, Peter Lyle (1848–1912) [of E]
12–17 Earlston Pl, E, 1882; 41 Marchmont Cres, E, 1883; †St Leonard's Brewery, E, 1889–90; Deacon Brodie's Tavern, E, 1894; †North British Brewery, E, 1897; Central Bar, Leith, E, 1899; †Aitken's Brewery, Falkirk, 1900; †Masonic Temple, E, 1900; The Abbotsford public house, E, 1902

HENRY, David (1835–1914) [of St Andrews]
Successor practice: Walker & Pride.
Gibson Hosp, St Andrews, 1880–2; Anstruther Town Hall, 1883; †Chalmers Memorial Ch, Anstruther, 1890

HENRY, J Macintyre (d.1929) [of E]
†Palace Hotel, E, 1888; Café Royal interior, E, 1900–1; Midlothian County Buildings, E, 1904; Blair Atholl Village Hall, 1907

* **HILL, Oliver** (1887–1968) [Engl]
Cour House, Saddell, 1928

HISLOP, Alexander David (1876–1966) [of G]
Later, Hislop Welsh & Humphreys.
See also J A Campbell.
Phoenix Assurance office, G, 1912–13; Carrongrove hs, Denny, 1919–25

HISTORIC SCOTLAND [of E]
Formed 1991. Successor to Scottish Development Department Ancient Monuments Division (1978–84) and Historic Buildings and Monuments Directorate (1984–91). For pre–1969 state conservation organisations, see Public Works (Office of Works); and R Reid.
Stirling Cas Great Hall restr, s1964, ongoing 1996; Jedburgh Abbey visitor centre, 1983–7; St Andrews Cas visitor centre, 1991–2 (by C McGregor); Stirling Cas restaurant, 1992–4 (by J Rahil and I Malcolm).

HOLMES, Jack [of G]
1951–5, sole partner; 1955–85, Jack Holmes & Partners; from 1985, Holmes Partnership.
Deil's Craig Dam, Blanefield, 1956–7; Lyford, Strathblane, 1957–8; St Gregory's and Wyndford Primary Schs, G, 1963–7; Milngavie development plan, 1964; Anderston Industrial Zone, G, 1965–9; Carbrain Primary Sch, Cumbernauld, 1966; Anniesland Cross hs, G, 1966–7; Woodlands Estate hs, Milngavie, 1971–4; Milngavie Central Redevelopment Scheme, 1973

(with W Gillespie, landscape architect); 100 Bothwell St, G, s1987 (with Newman Levinson & Partners)

HONEYMAN, Dr John (1831–1914) [of G]
Solo practice, 1854–89; from 1889, Honeyman & Keppie (see separate entry).
†St Mark's Ch, Greenock, 1861; †Charlotte St Ch, G, 1862; Park Ch, Helensburgh, 1862; Lansdowne UP Ch, G, 1862–3; Dumbarton Free Ch, 1863–4; Trinity Cong Ch, G, 1863–4; St Silas's Epis Ch, G, 1863–4; 24–30 Jamaica St, G, 1864; Barony Free Ch, G, 1866; Helenslee, Dumbarton, a/a, 1866–7; Sir Peter Coats Library and Museum, Paisley, 1866 and 1881; Knockderry Cas, Cove, a/a, 1869; Belmont Cres, G, 1869–70; Admiral St Wesleyan Ch, G, 1870; St Matthew's Ch, Perth, 1871; Ca d'Oro, G, 1872; Craigie Hall, G, 1872; †Stoneleigh, Greenock, 1872; †Riccartsbar Asylum, Paisley, 1872; Fairfield and †Henderson St Schs, G, 1874; Skelmorlie Manse, 1874; Moreland, Skelmorlie, a/a, 1874 and 1893; Rockvilla Sch, G, 1874–7; Candlish-Polmadie Ch, G, 1874–7; Tureen St Sch, G, 1875–6; Free (St Philip's) Ch, Portobello, E, 1875–7; Port of Menteith Parish Ch, 1876; Buchanan Memorial Ch, G, 1877–8; St Anthony's RC Ch, Govan, G, 1877–9; Helensburgh Municipal Buildings, 1878 (extended 1906 by A N Paterson); Cathedral Sq UP Ch, G, 1878–80; Clyde Ho, Greenock, 1880; Westbourne Free Ch, G, 1880–1; †Skipness Ho, 1881; St Michael's Ch, Slateford, E, 1881–3; Coats Observatory, Paisley, 1883; †Achamore Ho, Gigha, 1884; Castle Knock (Roundelwood), Crieff, 1885

HONEYMAN, James M, JACK, William A P & ROBERTSON, George [of G]
See also J B Wilson.
St Matthew's Ch, Knightswood, 1950–2; Broom Parish Ch, Newton Mearns, 1958–9; Ladywell housing, G, 1961–4; Victoria Drive Secondary Sch a/a, G, 1962–8; Anderston Kelvingrove Ch, G, 1970–2

HONEYMAN & KEPPIE, John (1863–1945) [of G]
In partnership 1889–1901 and 1914–17. Between 1901 and 1913, known as Honeyman, Keppie & Mackintosh; for work designed wholly by C R Mackintosh, see separate entry. Post–1917: see Keppie & Henderson.
Fairfield Shipbuilding offices, Govan, G, 1889–91 (by Keppie); James Sellars monument, Lambhill Cemetery, G, 1890 (by Keppie); Greendyke St Auction Mart, G, 1890; Craigie Hall interiors, s1892 (by Keppie & Mackintosh); Glasgow Arts Club a/a, 1892–3; Glasgow Herald Building, 1893–4 (partly by Mackintosh); Conservative Association, Helensburgh, 1894 (partly by Mackintosh; attr); Martyrs' Sch, G, 1895 (partly by Mackintosh); Skelmorlie Parish Ch, f1895 (by Honeyman); Queen Margaret Coll Medical

Building, G, 1895 (partly by Mackintosh); Saracen Tool Works, G, 1896; Beauly, Bridge of Weir, 1898–9; Brechin Cath restr, 1899–1902 (by Honeyman); The Mary Acre, Brechin, 1901–2; Easterhill, Bridge of Weir, 1902–3; 518 Sauchiehall St, G, 1903–4; 137–43 Sauchiehall St, G, c.1903–6 (by Keppie); Barony Parish Ch, Auchterarder, 1904; McConnel's Building, G, 1905–6 (by Keppie); 307–33 Hope St, G, 1906–7 (by Keppie); Glasgow Savings Bank, Parkhead Cross, G, 1908 (by Keppie); gallery, Broughton Place, Kirkcudbright, 1909–10 (by Keppie); Pinehurst, Bearsden, c.1912; Jordanhill College Sch, G, p1913, b1920

HOPE, John C [of E]
Edinburgh Old Town Renewal Trust offices, Advocates Close, E, 1984–6; Sealoft, Kinghorn, a/a, 1992–3 and 1996; Canongate masterplan, E, s1993; 3–5 Northumberland Pl, E, s1993

HOUSTON, James (1893–1966) [of Kilbirnie]
The Moorings, Largs, 1936; Radio Cinema, Kilbirnie, 1937; Viking Cinema, Largs, 1939

HOUSTON, John Alfred Taylor (1878–1927)
See Glasgow Corporation.

HUGHES, Edith M Burnet (1888–1971) [of G]
Coatbridge War Memorial, 1926; Glasgow Mercat Cross, 1930; St Mary's Epis Cath, Song Sch, Choir Sch, E, furniture and restr, 1956–65

HUGHES, T Harold (1887–1947) [of G]
Garscadden Sports Pavilion, G, 1936; St Matthew's Epis Ch, G, 1936; Glasgow University Chemistry Building, 1936–9 and 1950–4 (with D S R Waugh); Glasgow University Library Reading Room, 1938–40 (with D S R Waugh)

HUNTER, James Kennedy (1863–1929) [of Ayr]
Later in partnership with J A Morris.
Black Clauchrie, 1898; Templetonburn, 1901/1908; Dunskey Ho, 1901–4; Portpatrick Hotel, 1905; Carnegie Library, Maybole, 1906; High Greenan, 1910; Ayr Pavilion, 1910–11; Hotel de Croft, Dalry, 1912; Treesbank, 1926

HUNTER, Rob [of E]
Buchanan Ct, E, 1991–2

HURD, Robert (1905–63) [of E, Leven, Burntisland]
Partnership details: for several years from 1933, in partnership with Norman A G Neil; later, Robert Hurd & Partners. From 1963 to 1965, sole partner: Ian Begg. From 1965, merged with L A Rolland & Partners, retaining separate practice names, but under joint senior partnership of Ian Begg and Laurence Rolland. From 1988, formally merged as Hurd Rolland Partnership. This entry includes post–1965 works of both Robert Hurd

& *Partners* (H) *and L A Rolland & Partners* (R).
See also Ian Begg.
Ravelston Garden, E, 1935–7; Acheson Ho restr, E, 1936–7; Tolbooth Area Redevelopment, E, 1953–8; Morocco Land Redevelopment, E, 1956–7; Aigas and Kilmorack hydro power stations, 1958–63; Chessel's Court Redevelopment, E, 1958–66; Kyle of Lochalsh Primary Sch, 1959–60 and 1978; The Plock hs, Kyle of Lochalsh, 1966–9 (H); Auchtermuchty redevelopment, 1967–9 (R); Marygate hs, Pittenweem, 1968–70 (R); St Katharine's Court hs, Newburgh, 1968–70 (R); 23–4 Fettes Row restr, E f1973 (H); Duncansland restr, E, 1973–4 (H); Rapid Housing Programme, West Highlands (Kyle, Erbusaig, Rattagan), p1974 (H); Provost's Land, Leslie, 1975 (R); Rossend Cas restr, s1975 (H); Madras Rd hs, Auchtermuchty, 1975–7 (R); Skye and Lochalsh hs schemes (Dornie, Balmacara, Plockton, Uig, Dunvegan, Kyleakin), 1975–80 (H); Malta Green hs, E, 1981–3 (H); Towerwell hs, Newburgh, 1981–3 (R); Aboyne Cas restr, 1982 (H); Golf Museum, St Andrews, 1990; General Accident Life headquarters, York (Engl), 1990–2; Carndubh hs, Dornie, 1991–2; Balmacara Sq hs, 1991–3; Duff Ho restr, 1992–4.

HUTCHEON, John [of Montrose]
Montrose Town Ho, 1763 (a/a 1818 by William Smith)

HUTCHISON, Robert (*c.*1769–1845) [of Coaltown of Balgonie]
Town Hall and St Catherine St, Cupar, 1815–17; Markinch Free Ch, 1843–4

* HUTCHISON, David, LOCKE, Graham & MONK, Anthony [Engl]
Paisley Civic Centre, p1964, b1966–71

* IMPERIAL TOBACCO COMPANY, ENGINEERS' OFFICE [Engl]
W.D. & W.O. Wills factory, G, 1946–53

INGLIS, William Beresford
See Weddell & Inglis.

INGRAM, James [of Kilmarnock]
Later, J & R S Ingram; see also R S Ingram.
Irvine Town Hall, 1859; Palace Theatre, Kilmarnock, 1862–3; Kilmarnock Opera Ho, 1874; Hurlford Parish Ch, 1875

INGRAM, Robert S [of Kilmarnock]
Later: Ingram & Brown.
Burns Monument, Kilmarnock, 1879; Maybole Town Hall, 1887; Darvel Central Ch, 1888; Dick Institute, Kilmarnock, 1897–1901; Dean Cas restr, s1905 (compl J S Richardson).

IRVINE NEW TOWN DEVELOPMENT CORPORATION
Chief Architects: David Gosling, 1968–72; John K Billingham, 1973–9; Ian C Downs, 1979–96; George Wren, 1996. This entry lists project architects, where known.
Nethermains Advance Factories, 1969 (by A Dickson); Dreghorn hs Phase 1, 1969–71 (by G Hesketh); Bourtreehill hs, 1973–80 (by G Simister and others); Town Centre first phase, f1976; Magnum Centre, 1976; Braehead hs, 1977–9 (by R Rutherford); Beach Pk maintenance depot, 1981 (by G Malvenan); Towerlands Centre, 1982 (by D McDonald, A Kerr); Glasgow Vennel, 1983 (by D Hutchison, R Punton); Main St, Kilwinning restr, 1984 (by A McLean, R Rutherford); Montgomerie St hs, 1984; Caley Ho, Kilwinning, 1984 (by R Rutherford); Heathfield sheltered hs, 1985–6 (by R Rutherford); Hawthorn Pl sheltered hs, 1988 (by R Rutherford); Littlestane sheltered hs, 1990–1 (by R Rutherford); Lawthorn hs, 1990–1 (by R Rutherford); Red Cross Ho, 1991–2 (by R Rutherford, A Stewart); 68–106 Harbour St, 1992–4 (by R Rutherford)

JACKSON, Nicholas (m)
Ladykirk Ch, *c.*1500

JAFFRAY, Alexander (b.1677)
Monymusk Ho a/a, 1719–20; St Paul's Epis Chapel, A, 1721

JAFFRAY, George [of A]
Old Aberdeen Town Ho, 1788; Powis Ho, Old Aberdeen, 1802–4 (attr)

JAMIESON, Ernest Arthur Oliphant Auldjo (*c.*1880–1937) **& ARNOTT, James Alexander** (1871–1950) [of E]
See also Arnott & Morrison.
Astley Ainslie Hosp, E, 1925–39; Louise Carnegie Memorial Gates, Dunfermline, 1928

JENKINS, George Gordon (1848–1923) **& MARR, George** [of A]
Partnership commenced 1878; chief partner from 1915 to World War II was Harbourne Maclennan (1871–1951).
Mannofield Ch, A, 1882; Royal Br, Ballater, 1885; Ashley Rd Sch, A, 1887; Aberdeen Masonic Temple, 1909–10; 100 Queens Rd, A, 1927; Commercial Bank, Union St, A, 1936; St Katherine's Centre, A, 1937; Wick redevelopment areas, 1960–7; Total Oil offices, A, 1978; Chevron offices, A, 1980; Bon–Accord Centre, A, 1987–9

JERDAN, James (1839–1913) [of E]
From 1904, Jerdan & Son, with John Jerdan (1875–1947).

James Court restr, E, 1891; Gogarburn Ho, 1893; Balnowlart, 1905; tower and hall, Candlish UF Ch, E, 1913; The White Ho, Gullane, 1933; Napier Ho, E, 1934

JOASS, John James (1868–1952) [of G, London]
Dingwall War Memorial, 1922
Selected English works (in partnership from 1898 with J Belcher): Mappin & Webb building, London, 1906–8; Royal Insurance building, London, 1907–9.

JOASS, William Cumming (d.1919) [of Dingwall]
Ross Memorial Hospital, Dingwall, f1873; Strathpeffer Spa Pavilion and (attr) Ben Wyvis Hotel, 1879; Strathpeffer Free Ch, 1886; Fodderty Parish Ch, 1888–90

JOHNSON-MARSHALL, Percy & ASSOCIATES [of E]
Development Plan, Edinburgh University, p1962 (with RMJM)

JOHNSTON, J M (1871–1934) [of E]
Later: J & F Johnston, with Frank Johnston (d.1994)
Wardie Sch, E, 1931–2; Ainslie Pk Sch, E, 1938; †Goldberg store, E, 1960; Coll of Commerce and Stevenson Coll, E, 1965–70; Leith Nautical Coll, E,1975–7

JOHNSTON, Ninian (1912–90)
See G Boswell.

JOHNSTON, Alexander (1839–1922) **& BAXTER, David, senior** (1870–1957) [of D]
Practice formed 1867. Partner from 1928: David Baxter junior (b.1907). Successor practice: Baxter, Clark & Paul, q.v.
Errol Pk Ho, 1875–7; Murraygate/Commercial St block, D, 1877; Robertson's Bond, D, 1897; Loyal Order of Ancient Shepherds, D, 1907; Watson's Bond, D, 1907; Vernonholme, D, 1910; Alexandra St hs, Alyth, f1938

JOHNSTON, Edwin (d.1994) **& GROVES-RAINES, N** [of E]
See also N Groves-Raines.
Landmark Visitor Centre, Stirling, 1971

JUSTICE, John and JUSTICE, John (junior) [of D] (e)
Glen Isla Sch Br, 1824; Haughs of Drimmie Br, *c*.1830; Crathie Br, 1834

* **KAHN, Albert** (1867–1942) [Amer]
Administrative building, G & J Weir Holm Foundry, 1912; Gates factory, Heathhall, Dumfries, 1913; 44 Kilbirnie St, G, 1913–14 (with Richard Henderson)

KAY, Robert (1740–1818) [of E]
South Br and Hunter Sq, E, 1786–8 (with R Adam)

KAYE, Stewart (*c*.1891–1952) [of E]
Gogarburn Hosp, E, s1929; Lothian Ho, E, 1935–6; Learmonth Court, E, 1937; Comely Bank hs, E, 1938/46

KEIR, Mr [of Whithaugh]
Newcastleton village layout, 1793

KELLY, Dr William (1861–1944) [of A]
In partnership with W Smith, then with J B Nicol (q.v.); Aberdeen Corporation Director of Housing, 1918–23.
Cornhill Lunatic Asylum, 1893; 60–4 Rubislaw Den North, A, 1896; Aberdeen Savings Bank head office, 1896; St Mary's Chapel, St Nicholas Ch, A, restr, 1898; St Ninian's Ch, A, 1898; Joint Infectious Diseases Hosp, Portsoy, 1903–4; Aberdeen Savings Bank George St branch, 1908; Tudor Lodge, Stonehaven, 1909; Harlaw Memorial, Inverurie, 1913–14; Torry hs, A,1920–6; Royal Aberdeen Hosp for Sick Children, A, 1926–8

KEMP, George Meikle (1795–1844) [of E]
West Parish Ch, Maybole, 1836–40; Millburn Ch, Renton, 1840–5 (attr); Scott Monument, E, 1840–6

KENNEDY, Warnett
See Gillespie, Kidd & Coia.

KENNEDY, George R M & PARTNERS [of A, G]
Latterly: Kennedy Partnership.
Haugh hs, Elgin, 1974–6; Coppice Ct hs, Grantown–on–Spey, 1975–7; Granary St hs, Huntly, 1977; Wilsness Terminal, Sumburgh Airport, 1978–9; Hanover Ct hs, Stonehaven, 1978–80; Corpach hs, 1980–2; Hanover Ct hs, Tarves and Buckie, 1981–3; The Glebe hs, Kingussie, 1982–3; The Closes area restr, Elgin, 1982–4; Lord Todd public ho and Strathclyde University residences, G, 1982–92; Airlie Gardens hs, Banff, 1985; Doune Ct hs, Macduff, 1985; National Hyperbaric Centre, A, 1985–6; Scottish Life Assurance office, E, 1991–2

KEPPIE & HENDERSON [of G]
Partnership from 1917 to 1949. Subsequent partnerships: Keppie Henderson & J L Gleave, 1949–58; Keppie Henderson & Partners/Architects, 1958–89; SBT Keppie, 1989–95; Keppie Design, from 1995. See also Honeyman & Keppie; J L Gleave.
Glasgow Cross scheme, p1914, b1922–32 (including Mercat Building, 1925–8); David Elder Infirmary, G, 1925–8; Bank of Scotland, Sauchiehall St, G, 1929–31; Cloberhill Elementary Sch, G, 1929–32; Vale of Leven General Hosp, 1952–5 (by Gleave); Fleurs Av Sch, G, s1956; Burroughs Adding Machines Ltd Factory, Cumbernauld, 1956–8; Littlewoods store, Argyle St, G, 1956–60; James Watt Engineering Building, University of Glasgow, 1957–8; Glasgow Sch of Art extension (Foulis Building), f1963; Biochemistry

Buildings, University of Glasgow, 1963–4; Falkirk Royal Hosp, experimental ward, 1963–6; Hydrodynamics Laboratory and Astronomy Building, University of Glasgow, 1964–7; Maternity Unit, Southern General Hosp, G, 1964–7; Western Infirmary Redevelopment Phase I, G, 1965–74; †Cranhill Secondary Sch, G, 1966; Glasgow University Engineering block, 1966–8; Henry Wood Building, Jordanhill Coll, G, 1967–8; Gartnavel General Hosp, 1968–73; Glasgow Sch of Art extension (Newbery Tower), 1970; Glasgow Coll of Food Technology, G, 1970–8; Airdrie District (Monklands) General Hosp, 1977; Beaumont Hosp (Irl), 1977, s1978; Sheriff Court of Glasgow, 1980–6; The Forge Centre, G, 1986–8; Loreburne Centre, Dumfries, 1988–91; Ayr Hosp, f1992; Eagle Building redevelopment, Bothwell St, G, f1992

KERR, Andrew (d.1887) [of E]
Rosslyn Chapel a/a and restr, 1880; Doune Cas restr, 1883

KERR, David (m)
Steeple Building, Kilbarchan, 1755, a/a 1782

KERR, Henry Francis (1854–1946) [of E]
St Mark's Ch, E, 1899–1900; St Peter's Epis Ch, Inverkeithing, 1903; Dalziel North UF Ch, Motherwell, 1915; Greyfriars Ch, E, restr, f1938

KERR, William (1866–1940) [of Alloa]
Kilncraigs Mills offices, Alloa, 1904, and extension, 1936; Sauchie Public Hall, 1911, and extension, 1925; Lethangie Ho a/a, 1911/1923/1935; The Gean Ho, Alloa, 1912–13; Townhead Institute, Alloa, 1914; Cochrane Hotel, Alva, 1929; Town Council Gas Undertaking offices, Alloa, 1934–8

KIDNER, William (1841–1900)
Lesmurdie, 1881–5; The Haugh, Elgin, 1882

KING, J Thomson (d. *c*.1900), **MAIN, Thomas B** (d. *c*.1992) **& ELLISON, Eric D** (d.1995) [of G]
Fitzpatrick Ho, G, 1965–8; Scottish Amicable office, G, 1973–6; Corunna Ho, G, 1982–8

KINGHORNE, Patrick Lyon, 3rd Earl of (1642–95)
Glamis Cas a/a, 1670–9

KININMONTH, Sir William H (1904–88)
See Anderson (Rowand) Paul & Partners; Anderson (Rowand) Kininmonth & Paul

* KINIPPLE, Walter R [Engl] (e)
James Watt Dock, Greenock, 1878–86

KINROSS, John M (1855–1931) [of E]
1 Cluny Gardens, E, 1886; Falkland Palace restr, 1887;

Manderston a/a, s1891; St Peter's Epis Ch, Fraserburgh, 1891–2; Our Lady of Perpetual Succour RC Ch, Braes of Glenlivet, 1897; St Peter's Epis Ch, Torry, A, 1897–8 (by H O Tarbolton); Carlekemp, North Berwick, 1898; Mortonhall Rd/Oswald Rd hs, E, 1898; Fairfield, Arboretum Rd, E, 1901; Peel Ho, 1904–9; Ardtornish a/a, 1908

KIRKCALDY BURGH COUNCIL
Valley Gardens and Esplanade multi–storey hs, s1954 (by Burgh Engineer Robert Meldrum, with Wimpey)

KIRKLAND, Alexander (*c*.1824–92) [of G, Chicago]
Stobcross feuing layout, G, s1849; 4–26 Bothwell St, G, 1849–52 (with John Bryce); St Vincent Cres, G, 1850–5; South Portland Street Suspension Br pylons, G, 1851–3; Minerva St, G, 1853–8; †37–51 Miller St, G, 1854; †Eagle Buildings, Bothwell St, G, 1854; †County Building, Chicago, Ill. (Amer), f1882 (with J J Egan)

KYLE, Rt Revd James Francis (1788–1868) [of A]
(RC) Bishop, Vicar Apostolic, Northern District.
St Margaret's RC Ch, Huntly, 1834; St Peter's RC Ch, Buckie, 1850–7 (with A & W Reid)

LAING, Alexander (d.1823) [of E]
Archer's Hall, E, 1776; Edinburgh High Sch, 1777; Inverness Tolbooth and Town Steeple, 1789; Darnaway Cas, s1802; Dysart Ch, 1802–3; Peterhead Old Ch, 1804–6; Huntly Ch, 1805

* LAING, John [Engl]
St John Epis Ch, Eastriggs, 1916

LAIRD, Michael D & PARTNERS [of E]
Later: Michael Laird Partnership.
Music Sch, George Watson's Sch, E, 1964–7; Standard Life Assurance Extension Phase 1, E, 1964 (with R H Matthew); Standard Life Phase 2, 1968 (with R H Matthew); Ethicon Factory, Sighthill, E, 1968; Argyle Ho, E, 1969; Central Facilities Complex (including boiler ho), Kings Buildings, University of Edinburgh, 1970–5; India Pl redevelopment, E, 1972–6; Creative Arts Centre, Merchiston Cas Sch, E, f1975; Royal Bank Data Centre, E, 1978; Cameron Toll Centre, E, 1982–4; Goretex Factory, Livingston, f1984; Tanfield offices, E, 1988–91; Drummond Ho, South Gyle, E, 1990; Standard Life offices, Lothian Rd, E, 1995–6

* LAMB, Edward B (1806–69) [Engl]
Carnsalloch Chapel, 1847; St Ninian's Epis Ch, Castle Douglas, 1856–61

LAMB, James [of Paisley]
Renfrew Town Hall, 1871–3

LAMOND, William Gillespie (1854–1912) [of
Arbroath, D]
Entry includes his work for Charles Ower 1896–8,
T M Cappon 1898–1904, and J H Langlands (Architect
of Dundee Sch Board) 1904–12. See also T M Cappon.
Keptie Hill Water Tower, Arbroath, 1885; Pearl
Insurance office, D, c.1897; Whitehills Hosp, Forfar,
1899; Airlie Memorial Tower, Tulloch Hill, 1901; RC
Ch, Broughty Ferry, D, 1904; Ancrum Rd Sch, D,
1905; St Joseph's Sch, D, 1905–6; Stobswell Sch, D,
1906; Technical Institute (Coll of Technology), D,
1907; Dens Rd Sch, D, 1907; Glebelands Sch, D,
c.1908; Eastern Sch, Broughty Ferry, 1911

LANARK COUNTY COUNCIL [of Hamilton]
Lanark County Buildings, Hamilton, 1959–64 (D G
Bannerman, County Architect); Cardinal Newman RC
High Sch, Bellshill, 1972

LANE, BREMNER & GARNETT [of G]
Dunbarton County Council headquarters, Dumbarton,
p1960, s1965; Gartocharn Primary Sch, 1967; Kirkhill
Primary School, Broxburn, 1968–9 (with Scottish
Education Department architects); John Neilson
Institute, Paisley, a/a, 1991–2

LAW, William [of A]
Marischal St viaduct and bridge, A, 1766–7

**LAW, Graham C & DUNBAR-NASMITH,
Sir James D** [of E]
Practice formed 1958.
Leuchie, 1960; Cramond Brig Cottages, E, 1963–4;
Glen Tanar, 1970; Milnwood hs, Bellshill, Phase I,
1970–2; Eden Ct Theatre, Inverness, 1973–6; Festival
Theatre, Pitlochry, f1980; Fort George restr, 1983–5;
Maltings Arts Theatre, Berwick upon Tweed, 1986–90;
Balmoral visitor centre, hs, 1986–91; Cromarty Arts
Centre, 1988–90; Sunninghill Pk (Engl), 1989–91;
Scottish Mining Museum, Newtongrange, s1991;
Gilcomston South Ch steeple restr, A, 1992–3; Loch
Loyal boathouse, 1992–4; Edinburgh Festival Theatre,
1992–4; Mundipharma GmbH, Limburg (Ger),
1992–4; Culloden Visitor Centre, 1993–4; Hotel
Unter den Linden a/a, Berlin (Ger) 1995–7

LEADBETTER, Thomas G (d.1931) **& FAIRLEY,
James McLellan** [of E]
Also as Greenshields, Leadbetter & Fairley.
8 Castle St, E, 1889; Grandtully Cas a/a, 1892; Blair
Ho, Ayrshire, a/a, 1893; St Paul's Ch, Milngavie,
1898 (by Fairley); Stobieside Ho, 1907 (by Fairley);
Drumclog Ch, 1912 (by Fairley); Bedrule Ch, 1914;
The Holmes, St Boswells, a/a, c.1914

LEIPER, William (1839–1916) [of G]
See also W H McNab.
Partick Burgh Halls, p1865, b1872; Dowanhill UP Ch,
G, 1865–6; Dumbarton Burgh Academy (Burgh Halls),
1865–6 (by Melvin & Leiper); The Elms, Arbroath,
1869; Coll–Earn, Auchterarder, 1869–70; Cairndhu,
Helensburgh, 1871; Cornhill Ho a/a, 1871; Terpersie,
Helensburgh, 1871; Bonnyton, Helensburgh, c.1872;
Dalmore, Helensburgh, 1873; The Lodge, Loch Goil,
c.1874; Cairns Ch, Lanark, 1875; Camphill UP Ch,
1875–8; Livadia (Russian imperial yacht) interiors,
p1880; Castlepark, Lanark, 1880; Wheatpark, Lanark,
a/a, 1882; Ruthven Tower, Auchterarder, 1882;
Kinlochmoidart Ho, 1883; Hyndland Parish Ch, G,
1885–7; Templeton Carpet Factory, G, 1889; Sun Life
Assurance office, G, 1889–94; Clarendon,
Helensburgh, 1891; Victoria Infirmary, Helensburgh,
1894–5; Brantwoode, Helensburgh, 1895; Knockderry
Cas, Cove, a/a, c.1897; Red Tower, Helensburgh, 1898;
Auchenbothie, 1898; Piersland Lodge, Troon, 1898–9;
Ballimore Ho a/a, 1900; Endrick Lodge, Stirling,
1900; †Glendaruel Ho, 1901; St James's (St
Columba's) Ch, Kilmacolm, 1901–3; Morar Lodge,
Helensburgh, 1902; Drumadoon, Helensburgh, 1903;
Uplands, Bridge of Allan, 1907

LEITCH, Archibald (1866–1939) [of G, London]
Hampden Pk stadium, G, 1903 (with James Miller);
Sentinel Works (including reinforced-concrete pattern
shop), G, 1903–5; Stamford Br stadium, London,
1905; White Hart La stadium, London, s1905; Ibrox
Pk stadium, G, 1927–9; Parkhead stadium, G, 1929;
White Hart La stadium east stand, London, 1936–7

LENNOX, Gavin & McMATH, Daniel W [of G]
Renfrew Masonic Temple, 1931; New Bedford Picture
Ho, G, 1932

LESLIE, Alexander (1754–1835) [of Largo]
Carnbee Parish Ch a/a, 1793; Ceres Ch, 1806;
Kilrenny Ch, 1807; Newburn Ch, 1813–15; Largo Ch
a/a, 1816–17; Wester Durie steading, n.d.

LESLIE, James (1801–89) [of D, E]
†Wood's Hosp, Largo, 1830; Customs Ho, D:
see J Taylor

LESLIE, William (1802–79) [of A]
Dunrobin Cas a/a, s1845 (with Sir C Barry and the
2nd Duke of Sutherland); Congregational Ch, A, 1865
(with James Souttar)

LESSELS, John (1808–83) [of E]
Later in partnership with his son James and, in turn, with
Harry Ramsay Taylor (c.1864–1922). Entry includes
post–1883 work of Taylor.
Salisbury Green Ho, E, 1860–7; Chester St, E,
1862–70; Coates Pl, E, 1864; Manor Pl (west side), E,
1864–92; St Leonard's, E, 1869–70; 108–10 Princes St,

E, 1869; 3–21 Palmerston Pl, E, 1870–6 (attr); Smith Gallery, Stirling, 1872; Drumsheugh Gardens, E (part), 1874–82; Tweedsmuir Parish Ch, 1875; Royal Cres, E, 1881–8 (compl J Lessels); 39 Jeffrey St, E, 1886; Stockbridge Library, E, 1898–1900; St Andrew Hotel, E, 1900 (by Taylor); Nelson Hall and library, E, 1902; Stirling Public Library, 1904 (by Taylor); Edinburgh Geographical Institute, 1909

* LETHABY, William R (1857–1931) [Engl]
Melsetter Ho and Chapel, Hoy, Orkney, 1898–1900

* LIMBRICK GRAYSHON ASSOCIATES [Engl]
Monklands Time Capsule, Coatbridge, 1991

LINDSAY, Ian Gordon (1906–66) [of E]
Latterly, with John H Reid; pre-1945 work, see Orphoot, Whiting & Bryce.
Iona Abbey conventual buildings restr, 1939–56; Livingston Station Ch, 1949; St John's Epis Ch, Moffat, 1951–3; Colinton Mains Parish Ch, E, 1954; The Cross, Cathedral St, Dunkeld, restr, s1955; Druminnor restr, 1958; Inveraray town restr, 1958–63; Cramond Village restr, 1959–61; Newhaven CDA, E, 1960; New Lanark restr, *c*.1964–8; Mylne's Ct, E, restr, 1966–70; Isaac S Mackie hs, Elie, 1976–8

LINDSAY, Joseph [of D] (e)
Engineer to Gilroy Bros.
Tay Works New Mill, D, 1863–5.

LIVINGSTON NEW TOWN DEVELOPMENT CORPORATION
Chief Architect and Planning Officer: Peter Daniel, 1962–5; W Newman Brown, 1965–82; Gordon Davies, from 1982.
Craigshill South hs (with Laing/12M Jespersen), s1965; Integrated Power factory, 1985

LOCHHEAD, Alfred G (*c*.1888–1972) [of E]
Cleghorn block, E, 1924–5

LOGAN, David [of Montrose]
Montrose Old Ch, 1791; Arbroath Town Ho, 1803; Montrose Academy, 1815; Forfar Academy, 1815

LORIMER, Sir Robert Stodart (1864–1929) [of E]
Entry includes pre-1929 work of Lorimer & Matthew.
Earlshall restr, 1890–4; Colinton Cottage, 23 Pentland Av, E, 1893; The Grange, North Berwick, 1893 and 1904; Stronachullin Lodge, 1894; Pentland Cott and Roxobel, E, 1895; †Clousta Hotel, Shetland, 1895; Good Shepherd Ch, Murrayfield, E, 1897; Acharra, Spylaw Av, E, 1897; Briglands Ho, 1898; Hermitage, Spylaw Av, E, 1898; Ch of the Good Shepherd, E, 1899; Hartfell and Huntly, Spylaw Av, E, 1899; 1–7 Rustic Cottages, E, 1900–2; Brackenburgh (Engl), 1901; Rowans and Westfield, Spylaw Av, E, 1901; 8 Great

Western Terr, G, a/a, 1901; Wayside, St Andrews, 1901–4; Rowallan, 1902; Pitkerro a/a, 1902; Craigmyle Ho, 1902–4; 54 Melville St, E, a/a, 1903; Lundie Cottage, Arncroach, 1903; Hyndford, North Berwick, 1903; Dunderach, E, 1903–4; Bunkershill, North Berwick, 1904; Whiteholm, Gullane, 1904; Wemyss Hall a/a, s1905; Ardkinglas, 1905–7; Shieldaig, E, 1905–7; Glenlyon, E, 1906; St Peter's RC Ch, Edinburgh, 1906; New Library, St Andrews University, 1907–8; Kirklands, Ancrum, 1907–8; 47–53 Woodhall Rd, E, 1907–10; Lympne Cas a/a (Engl), 1907–12; Galloway Ho a/a, 1909; Thistle Chapel, St Giles's Cath, Edinburgh, 1909–11; Rhu–na–Haven, Aboyne, 1911–12; Dunderave restr, 1911–21; Lennoxlove restr, 1912–14; Formakin, 1912–14; Laverockdale Ho, E, 1912–14; Midfield Ho a/a, s1914; Marchmont Ho a/a, 1914; Dunnottar, Pentland Av, E, 1914–15; Dunrobin Cas a/a, 1915–21; Balmanno restr, 1916–21; Imperial War Graves cemeteries at various locations, 1918–28, including 8 in Egypt, 5 in Germany, 8 in Greece, 4 in Italy; Thessaloniki War Memorial (Gre), 1920–4; Naval War Memorials at Chatham, Plymouth and Portsmouth (Engl), 1920–4; Paisley War Memorial, 1922; Queenstown War Memorial (S Afr), 1922; Paisley Abbey restr, 1923–8; Galashiels Municipal Buildings Extension, 1924; Scottish National War Memorial, Edinburgh Castle, 1924–7; St John's Kirk, Perth, restr, 1926; University of Edinburgh (West Mains site) Departments of Zoology, Geology, Agriculture, Animal Genetics, Animal Breeding, 1927–30 (by J F Matthew); Kinfauns Home Farm Dairy, 1928.

LORIMER & MATTHEW [of E]
Post–1929 work. Partners: John F Matthew (1875–1955); Stuart R Matthew (1912–96), sole partner from 1955. See also Carr & Matthew.
Warriston Crematorium, E, 1928–9 (and a/a 1946 and 1956); St Margaret's Ch, Knightswood, G, 1929–32; Walpole Hall, E, 1931–3; Loretto Sch Memorial Hall, 1933–5; Wheatsheaf Inn, E, 1933–4; Granton Parish Ch, E, 1934 (by J F Matthew); 8 Picardy Pl, E, a/a, 1934–5 (by R H Matthew); Kemp Smith Ho, Kilgraston Rd, E (by R H Matthew), 1937; Thistle Foundation, E, 1947–8 (main group by S R Matthew; Robin Chapel, 1950–3, by J F Matthew); Linburn Estate, for Scottish War Blinded, 1947–9; Cornton and Borestone hs schemes, Stirling, 1950–3

LOTHIAN REGIONAL COUNCIL ARCHITECTURAL SERVICES [of E]
Balerno High Sch, E, 1983; Tollcross Fire Sta, E, 1986; Bathgate Fire Sta, 1991; Leith Academy, E, f1991

LOUDON, John Claudius (1783–1843) [of London, Great Tew]

†Barnbarroch Ho a/a, 1806; †Garth, Welshpool (Wal), 1809–10

* LUGAR, Robert (*c*.1773–1855) [Engl]
Tullichewan Cas, 1808; Balloch Cas a/a, 1809; Hensol, 1822–4

* LUTYENS, Sir Edwin (1869–1944) [Engl]
Ferry Inn, Rosneath, 1896; Greywalls, Gullane, 1901

* LYNN, William Henry (1829–1915) [Irl]
George A Clark Town Hall, Paisley, 1879–92

McANALLY, Alexander & PARTNERS [of G]
St Pius Ch, G, 1954–7; St Teresa of Lisieux RC Ch, G, 1956–60 (presbytery 1934–5); St Mark's Ch, Rutherglen, 1957–61; St James's RC Ch, Crookston, G, 1965–8

McARTHY, Charles & WATSON, John [of E]
Bo'ness Public Library, 1901; Roseburn Cliff, E, 1911

McCAIG, John Stuart [of Oban]
McCaig Monument, Oban, s1897

McCANDLISH, William (*c*.1779–1855) [of New Galloway]
Kells Parish Ch, 1822; Dalry Parish Ch, 1830–2; Glencairn Parish Ch, 1836–7; Corsock Free Ch, 1851–2

McCARRON, Richard J [of E]
Our Lady of Sorrows RC Ch, Garrynamonie, South Uist, 1964–5

McCLYMONT, Brian
House, Lamington, Easter Ross, 1993

McDONALD, J R H [of G] (builder)
Carseview Drive hs, Bearsden, 1933–6

MacDONALD, F A & PARTNERS [of G] (e)
Glen Br, Dunfermline, 1930–2; Guardbridge Br, 1935–8; Queens Br, Perth, 1960

MacDONALD, Sinclair & SON [of Thurso]
Thurso Post Office, 1916; Lybster Sch, 1934–7; Orkney rural hs (Evie, etc.), s1937; Manse Park hs, Kirkwall, s1949; Castletown Rd/Queens Terrace hs, Thurso, 1950s; Buttquoy hs, Kirkwall, 1951; Dounreay power station workers' hs, Thurso, s1954; Palace Rd hs/restr, Kirkwall, p1966; Thurso Swimming Pool, 1967; Central development, Thurso, 1969–75; Papdale hs, Kirkwall, s1973; Spence's Sq restr, Kirkwall, 1976–8

MacDOUGALL, Leslie Grahame
See L G Thomson.

McDOWELL, William (d.1579) (R)MOW
Alternative spellings: McDowall, McDougall.
Edinburgh Cas palace block a/a, *c*.1566; Mar's Wark, Stirling (attr), 1570–2; Edinburgh Cas Regent Morton Gateway and Half–Moon Battery, after 1573; new gallery, Holyrood Palace, E, 1576–7

McGIBBON, William Forsyth (1856–1923) [of G]
Blacklock & McArthur warehouses, G, 1888–1900; †Corn Exchange, G, 1895; St Cuthbert's Ch, G, 1898; Scotstoun Flour Mills a/a, G, 1898; Shettleston Old Parish Ch, G, 1898–1903

MacGIBBON, David (1831–1902) **& ROSS, Thomas** (1839–1930) [of E]
MacGibbon's practice established 1856; Ross a partner from 1872. Pre–1872 designs all by MacGibbon.
Biggar Corn Exchange, 1860; †Cormiston Towers, Biggar, 1860; National Bank of Scotland branches at †Alloa, Falkirk, Forfar, Girvan, Montrose, 1861–3; Merchant Company estate plans, E, s1862; Grindlay St/Lothian Rd, E, 1864–5; †Theatre Royal, E, 1865; George Watson's Colinton and Merchiston estate plans, E, s1867; Drumdryan estate plans, E, 1867–70 (Glengyle Terr, Leven Terr, etc.); Merchiston Terr, E, 1868; 12 Morningside Rd, E, 1868; Bruntsfield Cres, E, 1869–3; Gillespie Cres, E, 1870; Royal Maternity and Simpson Memorial Hosp, E, 1871; †Osborne Hotel, Princes St, E, 1873; Kilravock Lodge, E, *c*.1874; 92 George St, E, 1879; Edinburgh Parish Council Chambers, E, 1887

McGILL, Alexander (d.1734)
Edinburgh Town's Architect, 1720–5; for joint works with James Smith, see Smith entry.
House of Gray, 1714–16 (attr); Blairdrummond, 1715–17; †Duke of Montrose's townhouse, G, a/a, 1718–19; †Mount Stuart, 1718–22; Greyfriars West Ch, E, 1719–22; †Donibristle Ho, 1719–23; †Montrose Epis Chapel, f1724; Donibristle Chapel, 1729–31; †Picardy weaving village, E, 1730–1; Mount Stuart Chapel, early 18th century (attr)

McGURN, LOGAN, DUNCAN & OPFER [of G]
Stratford St hs, Maryhill, G, 1984–8 (with Ken MacRae); Pelican Blonde café, 523 Sauchiehall St, G, 1985; Glassford Ct, G, 1985; Virginia Ct, G, 1988; Gillieston Farm a/a, 1990; Ledlewan barn a/a, 1992; Caledonian University refectory, G, 1994; Bellgrove St West hs, G, 1996; National Piping Centre and Museum, G, 1996

McKAY, John Ross (1884–1962)
See Peddie (Dick) & Walker Todd.

McKELLAR, John Campbell (1859–*c*.1938) [of G]
Falkland St, Lauderdale Gardens, Polwarth St, Airlie

St hs, Hyndland, G, *c*.1890–1914; 23–53 Camphill Av hs, G, 1903; 28–40 Cleveden Drive hs, G, 1904–5

MACKENZIE, Alexander G R (1879–1963) [of A] Post–1933 works: All Saints Epis Ch, Hilton, A, 1936; Jackson's Garage, Bon–Accord St, A, 1937; Northern Hotel, A, 1937–8; St Mary's Ch, King St, A, 1937–9; University Sports Pavilion, A, 1939–41; Candacraig a/a, 1952; Provost Ross's Ho restr, A, 1954

MACKENZIE, Alexander Marshall (1847–1933) [of A, London] *In partnership with James Matthews 1877–93 (as Matthews & Mackenzie); A Marshall Mackenzie & Son (with A G R Mackenzie) from 1904; see also A G R Mackenzie.* Church of Scotland Training Coll, A, 1874; Terracing, etc., Union Terr Gardens, A, 1877–8; St Machar's Epis Ch, Bucksburn, 1878–80; 23 Queens Rd, A, 1879; St Margaret's Epis Ch, Leven, 1879–80; Craigiebuckler Ch, 1882–3; Aberdeen Harbour Offices, 1883–5; Northern Insurance, A, 1883–5; 74 Riverside Dr, A, 1885; Aberdeen Art Gallery and Museum, 1885; †Elgin Town Hall, 1885; Trinity Free Ch, A, 1891; Aberdeen South UF Ch, 1892; Crathie Parish Ch, 1893–5; Marischal Coll Extension, A, 1893–1906 (with Greyfriars Ch, 1903); 33–51 Queens Rd, A, 1895; Mar Lodge, 1895; Aberdeen Sch Board offices, 1896; 53–63 Queens Rd, A, 1896–9; Aberdeen Parish Council offices, 1897; 31 Forest Rd, A, 1899; Scott's Hosp, Huntly, 1901; Kingseat Asylum, 1901–4; 17 Rubislaw Den North, A, 1905; Waldorf Hotel, London, 1906–7; St Kentigern's Epis Ch, Ballater, 1907; King's Coll a/a, A, 1912; Ladyhill, A, 1912 (for himself); Lowson Memorial Ch, Forfar, 1912; Lecht Lodge, 1913; Connet Hill, Elgin, 1913; Australia Ho, London, 1913–18; Cults West Ch, A, 1914–16; Victory Hall, Aboyne, 1920; War Memorial and Cowdray Hall, A, 1923–5; Elphinstone Hall, King's Coll, A, s1928; Capitol Cinema a/a, A, 1932–4

MACKENZIE, J Russell (d.1889) [of A] Inverurie Town Hall, 1862; 1 Queen's Cross, A, 1865; St Paul's Epis Ch, A, 1867; Thorngrove, A, 1867; First Free Ch, Thurso, 1868–71; Torphins North Ch, 1874–5; Rubislaw Parish Ch, A, 1874–81; Queen's Gardens, A, *c*.1880; Norwood, A, 1881

MACKENZIE, Thomas (1815–54) [of Elgin and A] *Partner of Mackenzie & Matthews; see also J Matthews.* Elgin Museum, 1842; Drummuir Cas, 1846–50; Caledonian Bank, Inverness, 1847; Ballindalloch Cas a/a, 1849–51; Christ's Coll, A, 1850; St John's Epis Ch, A, 1849–51; St Drostan's Epis Ch, Old Deer, 1851; †Dess Ho, 1851; Rubislaw Terr, A, 1852; Banff Town Hall, 1852–3; Fraserburgh Town Ho, 1853; Milne's Sch, Fochabers, 1854; Cawdor Cas a/a, 1854–5

MACKENZIE, William Macdonald (1797–1856) [of Perth] Perth Exchange Coffee Rooms, 1836; City and County Infirmary, Perth, 1836–8; †City Hall, Perth, 1845

MacKIE, RAMSAY & TAYLOR [of A] Zoology Department, Aberdeen University, 1969; Medical Sciences Institute, Dundee University, 1970

MACKINTOSH, Charles Rennie (1868–1928) [of G] *This list includes works designed by Mackintosh under aegis of Honeyman & Keppie/Honeyman, Keppie & Mackintosh; for works designed jointly with J Keppie, see Honeyman & Keppie. Most interior schemes listed here were jointly designed with M Macdonald.* 140–2 Balgrayhill Rd, G, 1890; Glasgow Sch of Art, first stage, 1896–9; interiors, Miss Cranston's Tearooms, Buchanan St, G, 1896; interiors, Miss Cranston's Tearooms, Argyle St, G, 1897; Queen's Cross Ch, G, 1897; Dunglass Cas a/a, 1899; 120 Mains St, G, a/a, 1899; Ruchill Ch Hall, G, 1899; Windyhill, Kilmacolm, 1899–1900; Daily Record printing works, G, 1900; Miss Cranston's Tearooms, Ingram St, G, 1901; *Haus eines Kunstfreundes* design, 1901 (built from 1988 as 'Art Lover's Ho', Bellahouston Pk, G, by Andrew MacMillan); Hill Ho, Helensburgh, 1902–4; Scotland St Sch, G, 1902–6; Willow Tearooms, G (a/a: converted warehouse), 1903–4; Glasgow Sch of Art west wing, 1905–9; Mosside, Kilmacolm, 1906; Auchenibert, 1906; 5 Blythswood Sq a/a, G, 1908; Ingram St Tearooms a/a, G, 1910–11; 78 Derngate, Northampton (Engl), 1916

MacKINTOSH, David [of Oban] Oban Sheriff Courthouse, 1889

MACKISON, William (1833–1906) [of D] *Dundee Burgh Engineer; see Dundee Town Council.*

McKISSACK, John (*c*.1844–1915) **& ROWAN, William G** (*c*.1846–1924) [of G] *Partnership dissolved c.1890; afterwards, John McKissack & Son (with James McKissack, 1875–1940). Most pre–1890 church designs were by Rowan.* Pollokshields West (Free) Ch, G, 1875–7; Livingstone Memorial UP Ch, Blantyre, 1880–2; Grangemouth Zetland Free Ch, 1882–4; †St John's Methodist Ch, G, 1883; Craigmailen Free Ch, Bo'ness, 1883; Scone New Ch Hall, New Scone, 1885; Tarbert Parish Ch, 1885–6; Queen's Park Baptist Ch, G, 1886; Strathbungo Parish Ch, G, 1886–7; McKechnie Institute, Girvan (by McKissack), 1887–8; †(St Ninian's) Wynd Ch and Dr Still Medical Mission, G, 1888; Trinity UP Ch, Pollokshields, G, 1890–1; King St warehouses, G, 1893–1902; Eastbank Academy, G, 1894; Caer–Edin, Bo'ness, 1899 (attr, by Rowan); St

Margaret's Ch, Tollcross, G, 1900–2; Eastbank Parish Ch, G, 1901–4; Strathclyde Sch, 1903; Barnbeth Ho, Bridge of Weir, 1913–14; Kingsway Cinema, Cathcart, G, 1929; Vogue Cinema, Rutherglen, 1935–6; Cosmo Cinema, G, 1938–9 (with W J Anderson)

McLACHLAN, Ewen and Fiona [of E]
91 Marchmont Rd, E (tenement flat), a/a, 1988–91; Matthew Gallery, 20 Chambers St, E, 1992; Mid Gogarloch Syke hs, E, 1995–6

McLACHLAN, John (d.1893) [of E]
Royal Bank, 179 High St, E, 1892–3

MacLAREN, James (1829–93) [of D]
Established practice 1850. 1873–7, with G S Aitken (q.v.); later, as James MacLaren & Sons; MacLaren Sons & Soutar; MacLaren Soutar & Salmond (q.v.). See also G S Aitken.
†Beechwood, D, 1850s; Clement Pk, D, s1854; Savings Bank, D, 1867; Balthayock Ho, 1870

MACLAREN, James M (1853–90) [of G, London]
Avon Hall and Avondhu Ho, Grangemouth, 1877–8; The Park, Ledbury (Engl), 1886; Stirling High School, 1887–8; 22 Avonmore Rd, London, 1888; Aberfeldy Town Hall, 1889–90; 10–12 Palace Court, London, 1889–90; Santa Catalina Hotel, Las Palmas (Canary Islands), 1889–90; Glenlyon farm buildings, 1889–91; Heatherwood, Sussex (Engl), 1890–1

MacLAREN, John Turnbull (1864–1948), **SOUTAR, Charles G** (d.1952) **& SALMOND, William** (d. *c.*1955) [of D]
Also with Andrew Patrick.
Medical Schools, University Coll, D, 1902; Craigiebarns, West Ferry, 1911; Bellfield St Sch, D, 1915; Longcroft, D, 1922; Logie Sch, D, 1927; Farington, 1929

MACLENNAN, Thomas Forbes (1874–1957) [of E]
Scottish Veterans' hs, Longniddry, *c.*1920 (with J Macintyre Henry); Hanover Buildings, E, 1929

McLENNAN, William David (1872–1940) [of Paisley]
Bull Inn, Paisley, 1900; St George's UF Ch, Paisley, 1905; †Crosslee Mill, Houston, 1916–17

MacLEOD, John (d.1888) [of G, Dumbarton]
Christian Institute, G, 1878; Garnethill Synagogue, G, 1878–9; Bridgend U P Ch, Dumbarton, 1887–8

MacLERAN, James (d. *c.*1795) [of E]
Ochtertyre Ho, 1784–90; Dunrobin Cas a/a, 1785; Tarbat Ho, 1787; Over Rankeillor Ho, Cupar, 1792

MacMILLAN, Andrew
See Gillespie, Kidd & Coia; and C R Mackintosh.

MacMILLAN, Duncan (1840–1928) [of A]
Ferryhill Free Ch, A, 1872; 8–12 Queens Rd, A, 1876; North Parish Ch, Buckie, 1880

McNAB, William Hunter (d.1937) [of G]
Also in partnership with W Leiper.
Argyll Mansions, Oban, 1906; Beneffrey, Springkell Av, G, 1910

McNAIR, Charles J (b.1881) **& ELDER** [of G]
State Cinema, Shettleston, G, 1937; State Cinema, Kings Park, G, 1937; Lyceum Cinema, Govan, G, 1937–8; Ascot Cinema, Anniesland, G, 1938–9

MACNAUGHTAN, Alexander W (d. *c.*1911) [of E]
Bruntsfield Place hs (part), E, 1889; 109–19 High St, E, 1902

McNAUGHTAN, Duncan (1845–1940) [of G]
Latterly with Alan G McNaughtan.
Maryhill Burgh Hall, G, 1876–8; Burnbank UP (Gilmour Memorial) Ch, G, 1882–4; Baltic Chambers, G, 1899–1900; St Rollox Public Sch, G, 1906

McNEISH DESIGN PARTNERSHIP
[of Motherwell]
RNIB Coll, Loughborough (Engl), 1990; Challenge Ho, G, f1993; Bothwell Evangelical Ch a/a, f1993; Castleglen hs, East Kilbride, 1994–5; Principal's Residence, University of Strathclyde, Jordanhill Campus, G, 1996

MACPHERSON, Archibald (1851–1927) [of E]
St Aloysius' Coll, G, 1883; St Joseph's Convent, D, 1892; St Nathalan's RC Ch, Ballater, 1905; St Matthew's Ch, Rosewell, f1926; Our Lady's Ch, Bannockburn, 1927

MacRAE, Ebenezer J (1881–1951)
Edinburgh City Architect; see Edinburgh Corporation.

McWHANNELL, Ninian (*c.*1860–1939) **& ROGERSON, John** (*c.*1862–1930) [of G]
Royal Samaritan Hosp, G, 1896–1907; Renfrew Combination Poorhouse, G, 1902; Barrhead Police Buildings, 1902–4

MAITLAND, Andrew (1802–94) **& SONS** [of Tain]
Tain Parish Ch, 1891–2

MAITLAND, James Steel (1887–1982)
[of Montréal, Paisley]
From c.1923, partner of T G Abercrombie (q.v.).
Bleury and Herald Buildings, Montréal (Can/Qué), *c.*1910 (with Brown & Vallance); Russell Institute, Paisley, 1926–7; Cochrane's, Paisley, 1927; Fulbar La hs, Renfrew, 1932; Porterfield Rd Schemes 1–8 hs, Renfrew, 1935–9; West Sch, Paisley, 1936; Woodside Crematorium, Paisley, 1937; Cocklesloan hs, Renfrew, 1940s; Kirklandneuk hs, Renfrew, 1951

MAR, John Erskine, 11th Earl of (1675–1732)
House of Alva, after 1700 (attr); Alloa estate,
landscaping and industrial works, s1701; Craigiehall
ancillary work, after 1701; Alloa Tower a/a, *c*.1706
(with A Edward); Craigiehall gateway, 1708 (with A
McGill); House of Dun, s1730 (with W Adam);
Tullibody Ho and Tillicoultry Ho, d/u (attr)

* **MARTIN, Sir Leslie** [Engl]
Royal Scottish Academy of Music and Drama, G,
1982–7 (with W Nimmo); Royal Concert Hall, G,
1987–90 (with RMJM)

* **MARTIN, Mogin** (d.1538) [Fr] (m)
Dunbar Cas, d/u; Falkland Palace a/a, after 1637
(with N Roy, J Scrymgeour)

MARTIN (HUGH) & PARTNERS [of D, E]
Eastgate Centre, Inverness, 1981–3; Britoil Building,
G, 1982–6; Princes Sq development, G, 1985–7

MARWICK, Thomas Purves (1854–1927) **& SON**
(Thomas Craigie Marwick) [of E]
*Practice carried on by T C's son, Thomas Waller
Marwick (1901–71).*
Warrender Pk Terr hs (part), E, 1880; Warrender Pk
Rd hs (part), E, 1881–2; Bruntsfield Pl hs (part), E,
1885/1890; National Bank, Trongate, G, 1902–3;
Gresham Ho, George St, E, 1908; St Cuthbert's
Association Slaughterhouses and Edinburgh City
Markets, E, 1909; Bread St Co–operative office, E,
1914; National Bank of Scotland, George St, E, 1936;
Bread St Co–operative store, E, 1937; †Atlantic
Restaurant, Garden Club and Physical Fitness
Pavilion, 1938 Glasgow Empire Exhibition (by T W
Marwick); Jay's store, E, 1938–9; Sun Alliance office,
E, 1954–5

* **MATCHAM, Frank** (1854–1920) [Engl]
†Empire Theatre, G, 1895–7; King's Theatre, G,
1901–4; His Majesty's Theatre, A, 1904–8

MATHESON, Donald A (1860–1935) [of G] (e)
Chief engineer of Caledonian Railway.
Central Sta, G, a/a, 1899–1906

MATHESON, Robert (1808–77)
*Principal architect to Office of Works: see Public Works:
Office of Works.*

MATTHEW, John F (1875–1955) **and Stuart R**
See Lorimer & Matthew.

MATTHEW, Sir Robert Hogg (1906–75) [of E,
London, and again E]
*See also Lorimer & Matthew; and Department of
Health for Scotland.*
Principal Scottish works prior to formation of Robert
Matthew Johnson-Marshall (RMJM) practice in 1956:

Town–planning exhibition at Royal Scottish Academy,
1937; Turnhouse Airport Terminal, E, p1952, b1954–6;
Swinton Sch (Engl), s1953; Ruddington Sch (Engl),
1955–6; Burtons Shop, High St, Hawick, 1955–6;
Crombie Hall, University of Aberdeen, 1955–60.
Principal works as Architect to London County
Council (1946–53): Royal Festival Hall (with L
Martin, P Moro, E Williams), 1948–51; Lansbury
neighbourhood, 1948–51; County of London develop-
ment plan, 1951; Roehampton hs scheme (with O J
Cox, C Lucas, H J Whitfield Lewis and others), s1951

**MATTHEW (ROBERT), JOHNSON-
MARSHALL (Stirrat) & PARTNERS** [of E]
*Later: RMJM Scotland; see also R H Matthew. Entry
does not include work of London branch, headed by
Stirrat Johnson-Marshall. Principal design work to
c.1960 by Matthew and Tom Spaven; thereafter only
selected projects personally designed by Matthew.*
Kincardine Power Sta, p1954, b1958–60; New Zealand
Ho, London, p1955–6, b1959–63 (with Maurice Lee
of London office); Royal Infirmary redevelopment, E,
p1955, b1975–81 (Phase I only); Firrhill High Sch, E,
s1957; Lochay hydro power sta, 1957–9; Cashlie hydro
power sta, 1957–60; Barshare hs and comprehensive
town plan, Cumnock, 1957–61; Queen's Coll Dundee
tower, 1958 61; Hutchesontown/Gorbals Area B hs, G,
1958–64; University of Edinburgh, George Square
redevelopment, Arts Tower, 1960–3; Belfast Regional
Plan (Irl), 1961–4; Ninewells Hosp, p1961, f1974;
Loretto Sch Chapel a/a, 1962–5; Cockenzie Power Sta,
1962–8; Coll of Nautical Studies, G, 1962–70;
Administrative sector plan, Islamabad (Pak), p1964
(with Percy Johnson-Marshall); Central Area
Redevelopment hs, Jarrow (Engl), 1964–6; Ferguson
Pk hs, Blairgowrie, 1964–6; George Sq Theatre and
Faculty Buildings, University of Edinburgh, 1964–7;
Adelphi St Coll of Nautical Studies, G, s1965; Central
(Royal Commonwealth) Pool, E, p1965–7, b1967–70;
Longannet Power Sta, 1965–6; British Home Stores, E,
1966–8; Stirling University, 1966–73; Midlothian
County Buildings Extension, E, s1967; Hunterston B
Power Sta, 1967–76; Scotstoun Pk hs, South
Queensferry, 1968–70; New University of Ulster,
Coleraine (Irl), 1968–77 (by Matthew); Inverkip Power
Sta, 1970–9; British Home Stores and Market, A,
1971–4; IBP hs project, Tripoli (Libya), s1972;
Edinburgh Airport, 1975–7; Linkburn hs, East Craigs,
E, 1977–9; Aberdeen Airport, 1978; United Distillers
headquarters, E, 1981–4; Scottish Gallery of Modern
Art, E, 1982–4; Peterhead Power Sta, 1985; Falkirk
Sheriff Court, 1990; Motorola works, Bathgate, phase
I, f1991; museum and Mills Mount restaurant,
Edinburgh Cas, 1992–6; Victoria Quay Scottish Office
headquarters, E, 1993–5

MATTHEWS, James (1820–98) [of A, Inverness]
*Also partner of Thomas Mackenzie (1844 to 54), and
A M Mackenzie (1872 to 1893). See also A M Mac-
kenzie (post–1877) and T Mackenzie (pre–1854 work).*
Rubislaw Terr, A, 1852; Kincardine O'Neil Parish Ch,
1860–2; Aberdeen Grammar Sch, 1861; Inverness
District Asylum, 1861–4; 60–2 Union St, A, 1862–3; St
Machar's Cath, A, a/a, 1867; Advocates Hall, A, 1869;
West Ch of St Andrew, A, 1869; St Andrew's Epis Ch,
Alford, 1869; St Margaret Epis Ch, A, 1870; 11 Queens
Rd, A, 1875; Inverness Town Ho, 1876–82 (with
William Lawrie); Ardo, 1877; Aigas, 1877 (with
Lawrie); St Brycedale (Free) Ch, Kirkcaldy, 1877–81;
Stonehaven Town Hall, 1879 (with Lawrie)

MEARS, Sir Frank (1880–1953) [of E]
*1928–34, with Charles D Carus-Wilson; from 1953, with
H A Rendel Govan and Robert James Naismith (as Sir
Frank Mears & Partners).*
Scottish National Zoological Pk, E, p1913, f1927 (with
P Geddes); Hebrew University, Jerusalem, 1919–29
(with P Geddes; only Einstein Institute and Wolfson
Library were built to their designs); David
Livingstone Memorial Buildings restr, Blantyre, 1927;
Huntly Ho restr, E, 1927–32; Lucy Sanderson Homes,
Galashiels, f1934 (with Carus-Wilson); Gladstone's
Land restr, E, 1934–6; Broad St area improvement,
Stirling, s1936 (compl by Rendel Govan and
Naismith); New Br of Awe, 1938–9; King George VI
Br, A, 1939; Royal Scots Memorial, E, 1950–2; Second
Ch of Christ Scientist, E, 1952; White Horse Close
restr, E, 1961–4; Dalkeith central redevelopment,
s1962–4 (by R J Naismith); Dalnottar Crematorium,
Clydebank, 1964–7; Selkirk central redevelopment,
p1965; master plan for Wester Hailes, E, s1967;
Mitchell Library extension and St Andrew's Halls
restr, G, 1972–80; Ore terminal, Hunterston, f1979

* MEASURES, Harry B (1862–1940) [Engl]
See also Public Works (London).
Pinkston Power Sta, G, 1900–1

* MEIER, Richard [Amer]
Edinburgh Pk masterplan (with Campbell & Arnott), p1993

MELVILLE, William (e, 1850–1920) [of G]
St Enoch Sta extension, G, 1898–1902

MENART, Charles J [of G, Perth]
108–12 High St, Perth, 1904 (by Menart & Jarvie);
St Leonard's Manse, Perth, 1905; St Aloysius's Ch, G,
1908–10; Blairs Coll New Chapel interiors, 1910–11;
Sacred Heart RC Ch, Torry, A, 1911; Sacred Heart RC
Ch, G, 1912; St Joseph's Coll Chapel, Dumfries, 1923

MENELAWS, Adam (c.1750–1831)
[of St Petersburg]

Gorenki estate, near Moscow (Rus), c.1800; Yahotyn
estate, near Kiev (Ukr), 1806; works at Tsarskoye Selo
(Rus) from 1818, including Arsenal, 1819–34, and
Chapel, 1825–38 (with I Ivanov); Alexandria palace
and park, Peterhof (Rus), including Cottage Palace,
1826–9

MERLZIOUN, Walter (m)
Stirling Cas, King's Ho (with John Merlzioun), f1496;
Holyrood Palace gatehouse, E, 1502

MERRYLEES, Andrew [of E]
Formerly of Spence, Glover & Ferguson.
National Library of Scotland, Causewayside Building,
E,1985–7 (phase 1), and 1993–4 (phase 2); Heriot–Watt
University, James Watt Centre, E,1990 (and other
linked buildings, 1987–9)

* MERZ & McLELLAN [Engl] (e)
Chapelcross Power Sta, 1955–60 (with UKAEA)

METZSTEIN, Isi
See Gillespie, Kidd & Coia.

MILLAR, George
South Africa pavilion, 1938 Glasgow Empire
Exhibition (later moved to Ardeer)

MILLAR, T Andrew (c.1880–1922) [of G]
Boghall, Bardowie, 1907; Deasholm, 1912

MILLER, James (1860–1947) [of G]
Later James Miller & Son.
Bridge St Sta, G, 1889–90; West Highland line sta-
tions, 1889–94; Aberfoyle Epis Ch, 1893; Botanic
Gardens entrance pavilions and †sta, 1894; Caledonian
Mansions, G, 1895–7; St Enoch's Underground Sta, G,
1896; 2 Lancaster Cres, G, 1898; Govan Linthouse UF
Ch, 1899–1900; 8 and 10 Lowther Terr, G, 1900;
Lintwhite Sch, Bridge of Weir, 1900; Clydebank
Municipal Buildings, 1900–2; Central Hotel a/a, G,
1900–8; †Glasgow International Exhibition main
buildings, 1901; Sunlight Cottages, Kelvingrove Pk, G,
1901; Caledonian Chambers, G, 1901–3 (with D
Matheson); Glasgow Royal Infirmary redevelopment,
p1901, b1907–14; 136–48 Queen St, G, 1902;
Noddsdale, Largs, 1902 (a/a 1911); Hampden Pk
Stadium, G, 1903 (with Archibald Leitch); St
Andrew's East Ch, G, 1903–4; Wemyss Bay Sta,
1903–4; Jordanhill Ch, 1904; Turnberry Hotel,
1904–5; Peebles Hydropathic, 1904–5; Dalmuir
Garden City, 1905–6; Anchor Line Building, G,
1905–7; 'Lusitania' liner interiors, 1906–7 (by
Alexander McInnes Gardner); Prince of Wales
Museum of Indian Art, Bombay (India), initial design
1908; North British Locomotive Co. offices, G, 1909;
Monktonhead, Monkton, 1910; Institute of Civil
Engineers, London, 1910–12; Perth Royal Infirmary,

1911–14; Gleneagles Hotel, p1913; Stirling Sta, 1913–15; Blanefield, 1913–15; Cranston's Picture Ho, G, 1914–16; Kildonan Ho, Barrhill, 1915–23; Union Bank headquarters, G, 1924–7; Forteviot Village, 1926; Stirling Royal Infirmary, 1926–8; Wryggeston Sch, Leicester (Engl), p1927; 28–36 Renfield St, G, 1929; Synagogue, Salisbury Rd, E, 1929–32; Royal Bank, 92–8 West George St, G, s1930; Troon Town Hall, 1932; Commercial Bank, Bothwell St, G, 1934; Canniesburn Auxiliary Hosp and Convalescent Home, 1935–8; BBC Broadcasting Ho, G, 1936–8; Leyland Motor depot, Salkeld St, G (attr), c.1937; Holy Rude Ch, Stirling, restr, 1937–9; Nairn headquarters, Kirkcaldy, 1938

MILLER, John (1805–83)
See T Grainger.

MILLER PARTNERSHIP [of G]
Murrayfield Stadium redevelopment, E, 1992–4

MILLS, John Donald (1872–1958) **& SHEPHERD, Godfrey D B** (1874–1937) [of D]
92 Hepburn Gardens, St Andrews, 1904; Ardvreck, D, 1905–7; 102 Hepburn Gardens, St Andrews, 1906; University Hall a/a, St Andrews, 1910–11; The Swilken, St Andrews, 1914; Fingask Cas restr, 1925; St Salvator's Hall, St Andrews, 1927–30 and 1937–40

MILNE, James [of E]
Ann St, E, s1814 (attr); Lynedoch Pl, E, 1820–3; Saxe–Coburg Pl, E, 1821–3; St Bernard's Parish Ch, E, 1823; St Bernard's Cres, Carlton St, Danube St, Deanhaugh St, Dean Terr, E, p1824

MILNE, John [of St Andrews]
Royal Arch, Fettercairn, 1864–5; Public Hall, Fettercairn, 1890–1

* **MILNE, Oswald** (1881–1968) [Engl]
Tirinie Ho, 1934

* **MINERS' WELFARE COMMISSION** [Engl]
Architect: F Frizzel.
†Arniston baths, 1933; †Polkemmet baths, 1934

MINISTRY OF WORKS/PUBLIC BUILDING AND WORKS
See: Public Works.

MITCHELL, Arthur George Sydney (1856–1930) [of E]
From 1887, with George Wilson (1845–1912).
3 Rothesay Terr, E, 1883; Well Court, E, 1883; Edinburgh Mercat Cross restr, 1885; Leithen Lodge, 1885–7; †'Old Edinburgh' exhibit at Edinburgh Exhibition, 1886; Warrender Pk Rd hs, 1886 (part; by Wilson); Commercial Bank, Gordon St, G, extension, 1886–8; Scone Free Ch, 1887; †Wood Memorial Ch,

Elie, 1897; Edinburgh University Students' Union, 1887–8; Dean Free Ch, E, 1888; New Craig Ho, E, 1889; †Duntreath a/a, 1889; †Sauchieburn, 1889–90; Parson's Green Free Ch, E, 1890; Crichton Memorial Ch, Dumfries, 1890–7; 2 South Lauder Rd, E, 1892; Greenfield Ho, Alloa, 1892–4; Ramsay Garden, E, (part), 1893–4; Roxburgh District Asylum, s1895; Westfield, Pentland Av, Colinton, E, 1897; 18 Corrennie Gardens, E, 1897; Crichton Royal Hosp Extension buildings, 1897–1914; Royal Bank, North Br, E, 1898; Shiel Bridge Cas, 1898; St John's FC, Port Ellen, 1898; Craigmillar Pk Free Ch, E, 1898; Candlish UF Ch, E, 1898–1900 (tower by Jerdan & Son, 1913); Glenborrodale, 1898–1902; Ophthalmological Pavilion, Edinburgh Royal Infirmary, 1899; Alastrean (Ho of Cromar), Tarland, 1899–1905; Glenkindie Ho a/a, 1900; Caledonian United Services Club, E, 1900; Elder Memorial UF Ch, Leith, E, 1901; Scottish Life Building, A, 1902; The Pleasance, Gullane, 1902; 16 Hermitage Drive, E, 1902; Royal Victoria Hosp a/a, E, 1903–6; Chalmers Memorial UF Ch, Cockenzie, 1904; 9 Lowther Terr, G, 1904–6; Chirnside Ch a/a, 1906; Arngask Parish Ch, 1906–7; St Cuthbert's Parish Ch, Colinton, E, a/a, 1907–8; Gullane UF Ch, 1908; United Free Church headquarters offices, E, 1911 (with E A O Auldjo Jamieson)

MITCHELL, Joseph [of Inverness] (e)
Nairn (railway) Viaduct, 1856–7; Alness Viaduct, 1861–3; Conon Br Viaduct, 1862; Dalguise Viaduct, 1862–3 (with W Fairbairn); Killiecrankie Viaduct, 1863; Tilt Viaduct, 1863; Castle Grant Br, 1863–4; Shin Viaduct, 1867 (with M Paterson)

MITCHELL, Robert [of London]
Preston Hall, 1791; Silwood Pk (Engl), 1796; Nelson Column, Montréal (Can/Qué), 1808–9

MOIRA, Richard (d.1988) **and Betty Lydia C** (d.1989) [of E]
Heddell's Pk and Annsbrae hs, Lerwick, 1956–9; Leog hs, Lerwick, 1958–60; Fraserburgh General & Maternity Hosp, 1961–8; Wishart Av hs, North Berwick, f1962; Greenfield hs, Lerwick, s1963; Kveldsro hs, Lerwick, 1965; Ptarmigan restaurant, Cairngorm, s1966; Sound hs, Lerwick, s1969; Strontian village development, 1969–74; Ben Lawers Interpretation Centre, s1970; Hanover Sq hs, Stranraer, s1971; St Mary's St development, E, s1971; Glencoe Visitor Centre, 1973; Torridon Youth Hostel, 1975; Loch Morlich Water Sports Centre, 1979

MONROE, John (m)
Inverkeithing Town Ho Steeple (attr), 1754–5

MONTGOMERY, John, of Old Rayne
Aberdeen Mercat Cross, 1686

MORHAM, Robert (1839–1912)
See Edinburgh Town Council.

MORISON, David [of Perth]
Perth Art Gallery and Museum, 1824

MORRIS, James A (d.1942) [of Ayr]
See also J K Hunter.
South Ch, Prestwick, 1882–4; Savoy Croft, Ayr, 1894; Savoy Pk, Ayr, s1896; Ayr lodging ho, 1899; drill hall, Burns Statue Sq, Ayr, 1901; Art sch, Ayr Academy, 1907; Conheath Ho a/a, 1909; Conheath Chapel, 1909 (compl by R S Lorimer 1928); St Ninian's Epis Ch, Troon, 1913

MORRIS, Roger (*c.*1716–92) [Engl]
Inveraray Cas, p1744, s1746; Garron Br, Inveraray, 1747

MORRIS, James, & STEEDMAN, Robert [of E]
Tomlinson Ho, E ('Avisfield'), 1956–7 (a/a 1964); Wilson Ho, 16 Kevock Rd, Lasswade, 1958–9; Sillitto Ho, 32 Charterhall Rd, E, 1960; Royal Victoria Hosp, E, a/a, s1960; Cheyne Ho, North Berwick, 1961; Berry Ho, 10 St Thomas's Rd, E, 1961; Princess Margaret Rose Hosp Clinical Unit, E, 1960–5; Holden Ho, East Kilbride, 1962; 65–7 Ravelston Dykes Rd, E, 1963; †Carron Ho, George St, E, 1963; The Quarry, Gullane, 1964; Snodgrass Ho, Silverburn, 1964; Students' Amenity Centre, Edinburgh University, 1966–73; Principal's Ho, Stirling University, 1967; Christian Salvesen offices, E, 1969–70; Wolfson Centre, Strathclyde University, G, 1970–1; Almondell Footbridge, 1971; Countryside Commission centre, Battleby, 1971–3; Barend Ho, s1972; Shell office building, Mossmorran, 1976–7; Morris Ho, Fala, f1977; Peebles Swimming Pool, 1982–3; Music Sch, St Leonards Sch, St Andrews, 1983–4; Kinnaird Head Lighthouse Museum, 1993–5; House of Formartine, 1994–5

MORTON, John Gibb [of G]
Howard St warehouse, G, 1903

* MOTT, HAY & ANDERSON [Engl] (e)
Forth Road Br (with Sir Giles G Scott), 1958–64

MOTTRAM, Arthur Hugh (1886–1953) [of E]
Later: Mottram, Patrick & Dalgleish.
Rosyth garden city hs, s1914; Rosyth Parish Ch, 1929–31; Bonnington Av hs, E, 1936; Craigroyston High Sch, E, 1960 and 1972; Life Association of Scotland, George St, E, 1966

* MOUCHEL, Louis Gustav & PARTNERS [Engl] (e)
Tower Br, Cockburnspath, 1929 (with T A Gourlay); Dalreoch Br (Perthshire), 1931–2

MURPHY, Richard [of E]
29 Inverleith Gardens, E, a/a, 1991; Fruitmarket Gallery, E, a/a, 1992–3; 49 Gilmour Rd, E, a/a, 1994; 17 Royal Terr Mews, E, a/a, 1995

MURRAY, Sir James (d.1634) (R)MOW
†Berwick Ho (Engl), after 1607; Edinburgh Cas palace block a/a, 1615–17; Linlithgow Palace north quarter, s1618 (with W Wallace); Winton, 1620–7 (attr, with W Wallace); Kilbaberton, E,1623; Pitreavie, 1630 (attr); Parliament Ho, E, 1632–9; Holyrood Palace a/a, E, s1633 (with Sir Anthony Alexander MOW)

MURRAY, J L [of Biggar]
District Asylum for Lanark, Hartwood, s1890

MURRAY, John G T & MINTY, J Andrew (b.1857) [of London]
Wallace Memorial, Elderslie, 1912

MYLNE, John (1611–67) (m)
Tron Kirk, E, 1636–47; Cowane's Hosp, Stirling, 1639 (attr); †Leith fortifications, 1649–50 (attr); Methven Cas a/a, 1663–4 (attr); Fort Charlotte, Lerwick, 1665–6; Panmure Ho, s1666; Leslie Ho a/a, 1667–72 (compl R Mylne and W Bruce)

MYLNE, Robert (1633–1710) (m)
John Mylne Monument, Greyfriars Churchyard, E, 1674; South Leith Parish Ch steeple a/a, E,1674; Mylne's Land, Leith, E,1678; Mylne Sq, E, 1684–8; Mylne's Court, E, s1690

MYLNE, Robert (1733–1811) [of London]
Blackfriars Br, London, 1760–9; St Cecilia's Hall, E, 1761–3 (with George Paterson); Cally Ho, 1763–5 (with a/a by Thomas Boyd, 1795); New (Jamaica) Br, G, 1768–72 (with William Mylne); Whitefoord Ho, Canongate, E, 1769; Inveraray new town tenement hs, 1774–6; Inveraray estate works, 1774–84; Aray Br, 1775; Inveraray Cas interiors, 1782–9; Pitlour Ho, 1783–4; Dubh Loch Br, 1785; Maam Steading, 1787–90; Glenaray and Inveraray Parish Ch, *c.*1800–5

MYLNE, William (1734–90) [of E]
North Br, E, s1763

NASMYTH, Alexander (1758–1840) [of E]
St Bernard's Well, E, s1788; Rosneath Home Farm, 1803; Tongland Br, 1804–8 (with T Telford); Almondell Br, *c.*1810; †Elleray (Engl), *c.*1820;

NATIONAL COAL BOARD, SCOTLAND [of E]
Egon Riss, Chief Production Architect during 1950s/early 1960s.
Bilston Glen Colliery, f1952; †Killoch Colliery, f1953; †Rothes Colliery, f1957 (with Fife Coal Company); Seafield Colliery, f1965; Monktonhall Colliery, f1965

NEAVE, David (1773–1841) [of D]
Dundee Town's Architect from 1813 to 1833.
Monikie Ch, 1811–12; Logie Ho, *c.*1813; 5–19 King St, D, 1815–19 (attr); 1–27 South Tay St, D, 1818–20; Forfar Sheriff Courthouse, 1824; Union, Dock, Exchange Streets, D, layout, p1828

NEWALL, Walter (1780–1863) [of Dumfries]
Hannayfield, Dumfries, 1812; Borgue Ch, s1814; Buittle Parish Ch, 1817–19; Douglas Mausoleum, Kelton, *c.*1820 (attr); Kirkmahoe Ch, 1822–3; St Mary's RC Ch, New Abbey, *c.*1824; Anwoth Parish Ch, 1826–7; Cardoness Ho, 1828; Sidmount Cottage, Moffat, 1832; Parton Parish Ch, 1832–4; Blacket Ho, *c.*1835; Dumfries Observatory, 1835–6; British Linen Bank, Dumfries, 1839; Kirkpatrick Durham Ch, 1849–50

NICHOLSON, Peter (1765–1844) [of G, London]
Carlton Pl, G, 1802–4 and 1813–18; †timber bridges over Clyde, G, 1803 and *c.*1805; †Yorkhill Ho, Partick, 1806; Ardrossan town plan, 1806; †Hamilton Building, Old Coll, University of Glasgow, 1811–13 (executed by J Brash)

NICOL, J B [of A]
Partner of W Kelly (q.v.).
Aberdeen Royal Infirmary and Maternity Hospital, Foresterhill, A, 1928–37

NICOLL RUSSELL STUDIOS [of D]
Bayne & Duckett shop, West Ferry, D, 1977; The Mary Acre a/a, Brechin, 1979; Dundee Repertory Theatre, 1979–82; Lazarin, West Ferry, D, 1982; Arbroath Market Pl environmental improvements, 1985–6; 'Grianan' Building, Dundee Technology Park, 1986–7; Trustee Savings Bank, St Andrews branch, 1988; Scrymgeour's Corner, Crieff, 1990–2; White Top Centre, D, 1992–4

NISBET, James (d.1781) [of Kelso]
Paxton Ho, 1757–63 (builder, and possibly designer); Ednam Ho, Kelso, 1761; Ford Cas (Engl) a/a, 1771; Kelso Parish Ch, 1771–3; †Twizell Cas (Engl), s1771, compl *c.*1830

NISBET, John [of G]
Hyndland hs (part), G, *c.*1890–1914; Kelmscott, Springkell Av, G, *c.*1903; Springhill Gardens and Camphill Gate hs, Shawlands, G, 1904–6

NISBET, Robert (d.1831) [of Musselburgh]
Inveresk Ch, 1803–10

NIVEN, Douglas and CONNOLLY, Gerard [of G]
St John Ogilvy Ch, Irvine, 1982

NIVEN, David Barclay (1864–1942) &
WIGGLESWORTH, Herbert (1866–1949)
[of London]
Kincardine Ho, 1894–1906; Courier Building, D, 1902

NOAD, R Mervyn (b.1906) [of G]
Some works with Alastair Wallace.
Broadmeadows, Symington (Hansel Village), 1931–4; †Renfrew Aerodrome and Club Ho, 1934; †Model Flats, Oil Pavilion, Interior of Scottish Pavilion North, and Epis Ch Pavilion, 1938 Glasgow Empire Exhibition; Good Shepherd Ch, Hillington, 1939–40; St Aidan's Epis Ch, Clarkston, 1951

NOBBS, Percy Erskine (1875–1964) [of E, Montréal]
Principal works in Québec: Centre social des étudiants de l'université McGill, Montréal, 1904–6; †Maison C W Colby, Montréal, 1905–6; Maison P E Nobbs (with G T Hyde), Westmount, Qué, 1913–15

NORTH-EASTERN REGIONAL HOSPITAL BOARD [of A]
Regional Architect, 1960s: C C Wright.
Aberdeen Royal Infirmary new buildings, Foresterhill, 1963–6 (Phase I), 1971–84 (Phase II).

NORTHERN LIGHTHOUSE BOARD [of E]
Engineers to Board, up to 1938: Thomas Smith, 1786–99; Robert Stevenson (RS), 1799–1843; Alan Stevenson (AS), 1843–53; David Stevenson (DS), 1853–5; David and Thomas Stevenson (TS), 1855–78; Thomas Stevenson, 1878–85; Thomas and David Alan Stevenson (DAS), 1885–7; David Alan Stevenson, 1887–1938.
Lighthouses by RS: Bell Rock, 1807–11; Corsewall, 1815; Mull of Kintyre, 1815; Rinns of Islay, 1825; Mull of Galloway, 1828–30; Tarbat Ness, 1830; Girdleness, 1833. By AS: Hynish Harbour and Lighthouse Establishment, 1837–40; Skerryvore, 1838–44; Cromarty and Fortrose, 1846; Covesea Skerries, 1846; Ardnamurchan, 1848; Noss Head, 1849. By DS and TS: North Unst, 1852; Butt of Lewis, 1863; Dubh Artach, 1867–72. By DAS: Killantringan, 1900; Barns Ness, 1901

OCHTERLONY, Sir Matthew M (1880–1946)
[of E]
For later work, see also H O Tarbolton.
Balmadies, 65 Spylaw Bank Rd, E, 1915

OFFICE OF WORKS
See Public Works: Office of Works.

OLDRIEVE, William Thomas (1853–1922)
Principal architect, Office of Works; see Public Works: Office of Works. For post–retiral works, see Oldrieve, Bell & Paterson.

OLDRIEVE, William T, BELL & PATERSON,
William [of E]
26 Kinnear Rd, E, 1932; Bristo Baptist Ch, E, 1933–5;
Edinburgh Savings Bank, Hanover St, E, 1939

ORPHOOT, WHITING & BRYCE [of E]
Later Orphoot, Whiting & Lindsay.
Haystoun Ho, Peebles, a/a, 1924–5; Eventyr,
Longniddry, 1936 (by Lindsay); Arisaig Ho a/a,
1936–7; St Finnan's RC Ch, Invergarry, 1938 (by
Lindsay)

OWER, Charles, senior (1813–76) [of D]
Dundee & Arbroath Railway, 1850–7; Dundee
Harbour, 1850–68; Montrose Lunatic Asylum, 1855

OWER, Charles, junior (*c.*1849–1921) **and Leslie**
(*c.*1852–1916) [of D]
See also W G Lamond.
Seymour Lodge, D, 1880; Trinity UF Ch,
Newport–on–Tay, 1881; Pitlochry West Ch, 1884;
Duncraig, D, 1890; Inglis Memorial Hall, Edzell,
1897–8

PAGE & PARK [of G]
Glasgow Cath precinct masterplan, 1984–91;
Sinderins hs, D, 1986–9; Italian Centre, G, p1988,
f1992 (with extension, 1993–4); Brodick Cas Visitor
Centre, 1989–90; John Knox St hs, G, 1990;
Kilmarnock town centre improvements, 1991–5;
Edinburgh Royal Mile improvements, 1992–6; Gorbals
East masterplan, G, 1994; Port Glasgow Town
Buildings a/a, 1994–5; Newall Ho, Rhu, 1994–6

PAISLEY CORPORATION
George St and Canal St redevelopment hs, Paisley,
s1955 (by J A McGregor, Burgh Engineer)

* PALEY, E G (1823–95) **& AUSTIN, H J**
(1841–1915) [Engl]
St John Epis Ch, Greenock, 1878

PARR James, & PARTNERS [of D]
Latterly: The Parr Partnership.
95 Dundee Rd, West Ferry, D, 1964; Derby St
multi–storey hs, D, 1964–5; Balgay Rd hs, D, f1972;
Agnes Sq hs, Broughty Ferry, D, 1972–4; Bellrock Sq
hs, West Ferry, D, 1973; Wellgate CDA centre and civic
library, D, 1974–7; Commercial St hs, Perth, 1974–8;
Tayside Ho, D, 1976–7; Scottish Exhibition Centre, G,
1984–5; General Accident World Headquarters,
Pitheavlis, Perth, 1986–9; Digital micro–electronics
plant, South Queensferry, 1986–9; King St hs,
Broughty Ferry, D, 1988; Supreme Courts Extension,
E, 1988–90; Britannic Ho, Greenock, 1990–1; Glasgow
Airport a/a, 1992–4

PATERSON, Alexander Nisbet (1862–1947) [of G]
*In partnership with Campbell Douglas 1903–7, and
Donald McKay Stoddart (c.1876–1930) 1918–30.
Entry includes works designed during these partnerships.*
Arngask Library, 1893; Bank St UF Ch, Clydebank,
1901; The Longcroft, Helensburgh, 1901; Golfhill Sch,
G, 1902–3; Barr & Stroud works, G, 1903–6; Clyde St
Sch, Helensburgh, 1905; National Bank, St Enoch Sq,
G, 1906–8; Liberal Club, G, 1907–9; Colquhoun Arms
Hotel, Arrochar, 1908; Drum-Millig, Helensburgh,
1910; Renfrew Police Sta, 1910; Scalescleugh (Engl),
1912; Albion motor works, G, 1912; 23 Kempock Pl
and 2–8 Bath St hs, Gourock, 1915; Camis Eskan,
Helensburgh, 1915; Gateway and Aquarium, Zoological
Pk, E, 1923–7; Muirend Savings Bank, 1925

PATERSON, David [of Airlie]
Cortachy Ch, 1828–9

PATERSON, George (d.1789) [of E]
Marlefield Ho a/a, s1754; Bothwell Cas a/a, 1759–60

PATERSON, John (d.1832) [of E]
†Dundee Infirmary, 1794–8; Monzie, *c.*1795–8;
Eglinton Cas, 1796–1803; †Coilsfield (Montgomerie)
Ho, 1798; St Paul's Ch, Perth, a/a, *c.*1800–7; Leith
Bank, Leith, 1804–6 (attr); Fetteresso Cas a/a, 1808;
Fasque, *c.*1809 (attr); Fetteresso Parish Ch, 1810–12;
Brancepeth Cas (Engl) a/a, 1818–19; Lennel Ho,
*c.*1820 (attr)

PATERSON, John Lamb (1931–89) [of E]
†Le Corbusier exhibition, 1966, and †New Town
bicentenary exhibition, E, 1967; Visitor Centre,
Carrbridge, 1969–70

PATERSON, Murdoch (d.1892) [of Inverness] (e)
Chief Engineer of Highland Railway.
Thurso and Wick (railway) stations, 1873–4; Nairn Sta,
1885; Strathpeffer Sta, 1885; Dingwall Sta, 1886; Clava
Viaduct, 1893–8 (with J Fowler); Findhorn, Slochd and
Tomatin Viaducts, 1897; Culloden Viaduct, 1898

PATERSON, Robert (1825–1889) [of E]
Café Royal, E, 1861; †North Morningside Ch, E, 1862;
Portobello Police Sta, 1877; Windsor Hotel, Princes
St, E, 1879; Warrender Baths, E, 1886–7 (by R
Paterson & Son)

PATON, David (1801–82) [of E, New York City]
York Place block, E, 1824; †Summerfield Ho, E,
*c.*1824–5; Senate Capitol, Raleigh, North Carolina
(Amer), 1833–4

PAUL, Arthur F Balfour (1875–1938) [of E]
*See also Anderson (Rowand) & Balfour Paul/Paul
& Partners.*
Sir William Fraser Homes, E, 1898–9

PAULL, William and HUNTER, Andrew
St Andrew's by the Green Ch, G, 1750–2

PEACE, T S (1844–1934) [of Kirkwall]
Kirkwall Municipal Buildings, Orkney, 1884

PEARCE BROTHERS [of D] (e)
Baltic Works, D, 1864–72; Wallace Craigie Works a/a,
D, s1865; Taybank Works a/a, D, 1873–4; Titaghur
Mill (India), s1884

* PEARSON, John L (1817–97) [Engl]
Holy Trinity Epis Ch, Ayr, s1898

PEDDIE, John Dick (1824–91) **& KINNEAR,
Charles George Hood** (1830–94) [of E]
*Partnership founded 1848. From 1878, Kinnear &
Peddie. Later, with J M Dick Peddie. Entry includes
work of partnership/partners before 1896; post–1896,
see Peddie & Washington Browne.*
National Bank, Hawick, 1852; Pollok St Ch, G, 1856,
Cockburn St, E, p1856; b1859–64; Sydney Pl UP Ch,
G, 1857; Telling Hall, Royal Bank (former Dundas
Mansion), St Andrew Sq, E, 1857; 114–16 Trinity Rd,
E, 1858 (Kinnear's own house); Ebenezer Erskine
Monument, Stirling, 1859; Glen Gorm Cas, Mull,
1860; Leith Corn Exchange, 1860–3; Fife & Kinross
District Asylum, Springfield, 1861–6; Chalmers Hosp,
E, 1861–4; Pilrig (New) Free Ch, E, 1861–4; National
Bank, Stirling, 1863; Crawfordton Ho, 1863–6;
Kinnettles Ho, 1864; †Lathallan a/a, 1864; Hope Pk
Ch, St Andrews, 1864; Greenock Sheriff
Courthouse/County Buildings, 1864–7; Moat Park
Ch, Biggar, 1865; Morgan Hosp, D, 1866 (by
Kinnear); University Club, E, 1866; Aberdeen County
and Municipal Buildings (Town House, county and
municipal offices and courthouses), 1866–74; Crown
Insurance office, 67 George St, E, 1867; St Cuthbert's
Poorhouse, E, f1868; Melrose District Asylum, s1869;
Glenmayne, 1869; Cargen Ho, c.1870; Royal Bank,
Leith, 1871–2; Threave Ho, 1871–3 (by Kinnear);
Rothesay Pl and 1–2 Rothesay Terr, E, s1872;
†Auchmore, Killin, a/a 1872; †City of Glasgow
Assurance, 28a Renfield St, G, 1872; Threave Ho,
1872; 20–40 Gordon St, G, 1873; Palmerston Pl Ch, E,
1873–5; Grahamston Ch, Falkirk, 1874–5;
Drumsheugh Gardens, E (part), 1874–8; Leckie
Memorial Ch, Peebles, 1875–6; Dunblane
Hydropathic, 1875–7; 91–115 Hope St, G, 1876–7 (and
a/a 1890); Craiglockhart Hydropathic Institution, E,
1877–80; Kirkcudbright Town Hall, 1878; Royal Bank
buildings, Falkirk, 1879; Bank of Scotland, George St,
E, 1883–5; McMillan Hall, Newton Stewart, 1884;
Airds Ho, 1884; Pitreavie Ho a/a, 1885; Glasclune,
North Berwick, 1889; Keith Marischal a/a, 1889;
National Bank, Buchanan St, G, 1890; Cardoness Ho,

1889; Southwick Parish Ch, 1889–91; Dalton Parish
Ch, 1895 (by J M Dick Peddie); †Philpingstone Terr,
Bo'ness, 1895–6 (by J M Dick Peddie)

PEDDIE (DICK) & WALKER TODD (from
1921)**/TODD & JAMIESON** (from 1936)**/McKAY**
(from 1942; with John Ross McKay, 1884–1962) [of E]
Hopetoun Terr hs, Gullane, 1920; Aberlady hs, 1920;
St Catherine's Epis Ch, Bo'ness, 1921; Bank of
Scotland, South Bridge, E, 1923; Macmerry hs, 1925;
St Peter's Epis Ch, Linlithgow, 1928; Binns store, E,
1935 (by J R McKay), 1935; Linlithgow County
Buildings and Police Sta, s1936; St Aidan's Epis Ch, E,
1936; Royal Bank, Kilmarnock, 1937; Royal Bank,
Galashiels, 1940–6 (by McKay); Royal Insurance
building, George St, E, 1969

PEDDIE (DICK), John More, (1853–1921) **&
WASHINGTON BROWNE** [of E]
*In partnership from 1896 to 1908; this entry includes
Peddie's own 1896–1908 work, Browne's pre-partnership
works (from the start of his own practice in 1885) and
post-partnership works, and Peddie's 1908–21 work.
For Browne, see also R R Anderson.*
Pre–1896 work by Browne: Cossar Ewart Ho,
Penicuik, 1885–9; Braid (UP) Ch, E, 1886; Edinburgh
Public Library, 1887; Bruntsfield Pl hs (part), E, 1887;
†Redferns, E, 1891; Drumsheugh Toll, E, 1891;
Langlees, 1891; Maisondieu Ch, Brechin, 1891; Royal
Hosp for Sick Children, E, 1892–5
    Work by Peddie and Browne, 1896–1908: Miss
Cranston's Tearooms, Buchanan St, G, 1896 (by
Browne); British Linen Bank, Melrose, 1897 (by
Browne); Standard Life Assurance office, E,
1897–1901; Carnegie Library, Jedburgh, 1898 (by
Browne); National Bank Chambers, St Vincent St, G,
1898–1906 (by Peddie); Caledonian Hotel, E,
1898–1902; Scottish Equitable Building, St Andrew
Sq, E, 1899; Cargilfield Sch, 1899; British Linen Bank,
Renfrew, 1899; Royal Bank, D, 1899; Johnsburn,
Balerno, c.1900 (by Browne); British Linen Bank,
Crieff, 1900 (by Browne); Bank of Scotland, Ayr, 1901;
Bo'ness Town Hall and Carnegie Library, 1901–4 (by
Browne); British Linen Bank, George St, E, 1902–5
(by Browne); Scottish Provident Institution, G,
1904–8 (by Peddie); †North British & Mercantile
Assurance Building, E, 1905; British Linen Bank,
Alloa, 1906 (by Browne); Liberton Hosp, E, f1906;
Edinburgh Coll of Art, 1906 (by Peddie); Coldstream
Parish Ch a/a, 1906 (by Peddie); 72–4 Main St, Largs,
1907 (by Browne)
    Post–1908 work by Browne: 72–4 Main St, Largs,
1907; Daniel Stewart's Coll Library, E, 1908; YMCA,
St Andrew St, E, 1914–15; Scottish National
Monument to King Edward, Holyrood, E, 1920–2

Post–1908 work by Peddie: Edinburgh Life Assurance Co. office, E, 1908–9; Davidson's Mains Epis Ch, E, 1908–14; Westerdunes, North Berwick, 1909; Blervie Ho, 1909–10; St Cuthbert's Ch, Melrose, 1911; Coldstones, Gullane, 1912; County Buildings, Dumfries, 1912–14

PETRIE, Alexander (d.1905) [of G]
Gordon Pk hs, G, s1885 (compl by George Anderson, 1888–95); Niddrie Sq and Balvicar St hs, G, 1895; St Enoch Sq offices, G, 1895; Glencairn Drive and Gardens hs, Terregles Av hs, G, 1897; Willowbank Sch, G, 1899–1901

PILKINGTON, Frederick T (1823–98)
[of E, London]
In partnership with J Murray Bell between 1839 and 1877.
Broomhill, Burntisland, 1858; Inchglas, Crieff, 1859; Bridge St hs, Penicuik, 1860; Barclay Free Ch, E, p1861; Trinity Free Ch, Irvine, 1861–3; Penicuik Free Ch, 1862; †Woodslee Ho, Penicuik, 1862; †Glassingal, 1864; Fountainbridge and Grove St hs, E, 1864–5; St John's Free Ch, Kelso, 1864–6; Innerleithen Parish Ch, 1865–7; Scottish National Institution for the Training of Imbecile Children, Larbert, 1865–9; 38 Dick Pl, E, 1865–70; Craigend Pk, E, 1867–9; †Dundee Eastern Club, 1867–70; Stoneyhill, 1868; St Mark's Ch, D, 1868–9; 1–7 Coltbridge Terr, E, 1869; Free Ch, Gilmore Pk, E, 1871; Clock Tower, Gatehouse of Fleet, 1871; McCheyne Memorial Ch, D, 1872; Dean Pk Ho, E, 1872; Moffat Hydropathic, 1875–7; †Windsor Hotel, Victoria St, London, 1881–3

PIRIE, John B (1852–90) **&CLYNE, Arthur** (1852–1923) [of A]
After 1890, Clyne practised on his own.
South Ch, Fraserburgh, 1878–80 (by Pirie); 24 Rubislaw Den South, 1879 (by Clyne); Hamilton Pl hs, A, 1880s; Argyll Pl and Cres hs, A, 1880–5; Queen's Cross Free Ch, A, f1881; Millbrex Ch, 1881–2; Anderson Library, Woodside, A, 1883 (by Clyne); Macduff Town Hall, 1884; St Palladius's Epis Ch, Drumtochty, 1885; 46–8, 52–4 Queens Rd, A, 1885; 50 Queens Rd, A, 1886; 2 Rubislaw Den South, A, 1899; 56 Rubislaw Den South, A, 1900; St Devenick's Epis Ch, A, 1902–3; 24 Forest Av, A, 1902–3

PLAYFAIR, James (1755–94) [of London]
Raith Ho a/a, 1785; Kinnaird Cas a/a, 1785–93; Langholm Lodge, 1786–7; Forfar Town and County Hall, 1785–8; Kirriemuir Parish Ch, 1786–90; Melville Cas, 1786–91; †Bothwell Cas a/a, 1787–8; Farnell Ch, c.1789; Kinnaird Temple c.1790 (attr); St Peter's Epis Chapel, E, 1790–1; Cairness Ho, s1791; Lynedoch Mausoleum, Methven Ch, 1793

PLAYFAIR, William Henry (1790–1857) [of E]
University Coll (Old Coll), E, compl, p1815, b1819–27; City Observatory, E, s1818; Dollar Academy, 1818–20; extension plan north of Calton Hill, E (including Royal Terr, Hillside Cres, Brunswick St, Blenheim Pl), p1819, s1821; Signet/Advocates' Library, staircase hall, E, a/a, 1819–20; Royal Circus, E, p1819–20, b1821–3; Royal Institution, E, 1822–6, a/a 1832–5; 8 Inverleith Row, 1824–5; Playfair Monument, E, 1826; National Monument, E, 1826–9 (with C Cockerell); Minto Manse, 1827; St Stephen's Ch, E, 1827–8; St Ronan's Well, Innerleithen, c.1828; Belmont, E, 1828–30; George Heriot's Hosp a/a, 1828–30; Dunphail, 1828–33; †Drumbanagher (Irl), p1829; Surgeons Hall, E, 1829–32; †Grange Ho a/a, 1830; Prestongrange Ho a/a, 1830; †Relugas Ho a/a, 1830; Dugald Stewart Monument, E, 1831; Dalcrue Ho and Br, 1832; Brownlow (Irl), 1833–5; Craigcrook Cas a/a, 1835; Bonaly Tower, 1836–8; Barmore (Stonefield), 1836–40; Floors Cas a/a, 1837–45; Islay Ho, a/a and lodge, 1841–5; Donaldson's Hosp, E, 1841–51; Mound Railway Tunnel, E, 1844–6; Free Church Coll, E, 1846–50; National Gallery and Royal Academy, E, 1850–8

* POULSON, John G L [Engl]
Aviemore, Four Seasons Hotel and complex, 1965–6

PRENTICE, Andrew Noble (1866–1941)
[of London]
15 Cleveden Cres, G, 1902–6; Symington Ho, c.1915

PUBLIC WORKS: MINISTRY OF WORKS (to 1963)/**MINISTRY OF PUBLIC BUILDING AND WORKS, SCOTLAND** (1963/4–1970)/**PSA SCOTLAND** (from 1970) [of E]
Works by Stewart Sim, Senior Architect: Fountainbridge Telephone Exchange, E, 1948–50; Montrose Ho, G, 1951–3; Greyfriars Ho, A, 1953; St Rollox Post Office, G, 1954–5; Carstairs State Institution, 1956–8; Tulliallan Police Coll a/a, f1960. Works by others: Kirkwall Post Office, 1960; Royal Botanic Gardens offices, herbarium and library, E, 1960–4; †Centre 1, East Kilbride, p1964, f1968 (by R Stevenson); Plant Exhibition Houses, Royal Botanic Garden, E, 1965–7 (team leader, George A H Pearce); Courthouse extension, Cowgate, E, 1992; Dreghorn Barracks, E, 1992

PUBLIC WORKS: OFFICE OF WORKS
For state–sponsored restoration works, see R Reid (earlier); see Historic Scotland (later).
New works by Robert Matheson, principal architect 1851–77 (and succeeded by W W Robertson 1877–1904): Palm Ho, Botanic Gardens, E, 1855; New Register Ho, E, 1856–62; Head Post Office, E, 1861–6; Wester Coates feuing plan, E (including Grosvenor St

and Lansdowne Cres), 1865; Aberdeen Old Post Office, 1875; General Post Office, G, 1875–6. Restoration work by W M Nixon and Robert Matheson: Dunfermline Abbey restr, 1845–8. Work by Royal Engineers Office, E: Cameron Barracks, Inverness, 1880–6. Works by William T Oldrieve, principal architect 1904–14: Waterloo St Post Office, G, 1906; Aberdeen Post Office, 1907; Eskdalemuir Observatory, 1908; Oban Post Office, 1909; Lerwick Post Office, 1910. By E M Carmichael, engineer: Earlston Power Sta, 1936. New works by J Wilson Paterson: Scottish United Services Museum, Edinburgh Cas, 1928–30; Sheriff Courthouse, E, 1934–7 (with A J Pitcher). Principal restoration works (of state 'guardianship monuments') by J Wilson Paterson: Jedburgh Abbey restr, 1923; Blackness Cas restr, 1926–35; Inchcolm Abbey restr, 1927/31

* PUBLIC WORKS (LONDON): OFFICE OF WORKS/MINISTRY OF PUBLIC BUILDING AND WORKS/DIRECTORATE OF WORKS/PSA [Engl]
Principal Scottish projects designed in London; see also F Fowke.
Infantry and Cavalry Barracks, Redford, E, 1909–15 (by Harry B Measures, Director of Barrack Construction); Clyde Submarine Base, Faslane, 1963–70; Coulport armaments depot, 1964–70; Rosyth, HMS Caledonia and Cochrane, 1965–70; RAF Lossiemouth a/a, 1974–6 (and ASM project, 1983–9); RAF Leuchars a/a, 1984–9; RAF Kinloss a/a, 1985–8; Loch Long RNAD Trident Site, 1985–94 (including Shiplift by Babtie, Shaw & Morton, f1994)

* PUGIN, Edward Welby (1834–75) [Engl]
Glenfinnan RC Ch, 1873

* PUGIN & PUGIN (Cuthbert Welby Pugin, 1840–1928; Peter Paul Pugin, 1951–1904; Sebastian Pugin Powell, b.1866) [Engl]
Entry includes some works by P P Pugin alone.
St Francis RC Ch, Friary and Sch, G, 1878–95; St Patrick's RC Ch, Coatbridge, 1896; St Patrick's RC Ch, North St, G, 1898; St Mary's RC Ch, Stirling, 1902; St Peter's RC Ch, Partick, G, 1903; St Alphonsus RC Ch, G, 1905; Holy Cross RC Ch, Govanhill, G, 1909–11

RAE, George (1811–69) [of St Andrews]
Playfair Terr, St Andrews, 1846–52; Edgecliffe, St Andrews, 1864–6

RAILTON, William [of Kilmarnock]
Cunninghame Combination Poorhouse, *c.*1847; Kilmarnock Sheriff Courthouse, 1852; Kilmarnock Infirmary, 1867

RAMAGE, William (1820–66) [of A]
St Ternan Epis Ch, Banchory, 1851; St Margaret Epis Ch, Forgue, 1856; St Congan's Epis Ch, Turriff, 1862

RAMSAY, James [of E]
Cathkin Ho, 1799

RAMSAY, Walter N W [of G]
Edinburgh University Medical Sch, p1951; Glasgow University Arts Building, p1953; Queen Margaret Hall, G, s1964

RANKEINE, Theophilius
Ayr Old Parish Ch, 1652–4

RANKINE, W J McQuorn
†St Rollox Stalk, G, p1839

* REES, W Beddoes [Wal]
Arthur Memorial Ch, New Cumnock, 1912

REIACH, Alan (1910–92) [of E]
In partnership with George McNab and Stuart Renton from 1959. From 1965, with Eric Hall, as Alan Reiach, Eric Hall & Partners (later: Reiach & Hall).
Whitemoss, East Kilbride, shops and hs, s1949 (with T R Spaven); Edinburgh and East of Scotland Agricultural Coll, p1949–50, b1954–60 (with Ralph Cowan); Easthouses Ch, 1951; Coillesdene Av hs, E, 1955; St John's Parish Ch, Oxgangs, E, 1956; Veterinary Field Sta, Roslin, 1962; Haddington Central Area improvement, f1962 (by Eric Hall, prior to partnership); Kildrum Parish Ch, Cumbernauld, f1962; Golspie High Sch, 1962–3; 1 and 3 Winton Loan, E, 1962–4; First Year Science Building (Appleton Tower), University of Edinburgh, 1963–6; Silverknowes Golf Club, E, 1964; St Mungo's Ch, Cumbernauld, 1964–6; Royal Victoria Hospital redevelopment, E, 1966; New Club redevelopment, E, 1966–9; Denny Civic Theatre, 1967–70; Heriot–Watt University, Riccarton Campus, s1968; Art Block, St George's Sch, E, 1983–4; Borders General Hosp, 1985–7; St Enoch Centre, G, 1985–9 (with GMW Partnership); Yeaman Pl hs, E, 1988; Midlothian District headquarters, Dalkeith, 1988–91; Life Association of Scotland offices, E, 1990; Oxgangs Library, E, 1991; Sainsbury store, E, 1992–3; 10 George St, E, 1993; Oban Hosp, 1993–4

REID, Robert (1774–1856) [of E]
Architect and Surveyor to the King in Scotland, 1808–40; head of Scottish Office of Works, 1827–40.
Marshall Pl, Perth, s1801; New Town northern extension, E, layout p1801–4 (with William Sibbald); Bank of Scotland headquarters, E, 1802–6 (with R Crichton); Heriot Row, E, p1802, f1808; Parliament Sq and Law Courts a/a, s1803; Perth Academy, 1803–7; Great King St, E, p1804, s1812; Drummond Pl, E,

p1804 (revised by T Bonnar 1817–18); Rose Terr, Perth, 1805; Abercromby Pl, E, p1805, b1807–19; London St, E, p1806, s1807; Leith Customs Ho, E, 1810–12; Perth Prison, 1810–12; St George's Ch, E, 1811–14; United Coll, St Andrews, east range, 1829–31 (with a/a by William Nixon, 1845–9); Arbroath Abbey and Elgin Cath restr, p1834 (by Office of Works); Glasgow Cath restr, p1836 (by Office of Works)

REID, G & FORBES, J Smith [of E]
See also R Fairlie.
Leith Academy, E, 1929; Royal High Primary Sch, E, 1931; Inverness High Sch, 1934; Craigmillar Intermediate Sch, E, 1936; Kelso High Sch, 1936; Chirnside Sch, 1937; Wilkie's store, Shandwick Pl, E, 1937

RENNIE, John (1761–1821) [of London] (e)
Kelso Br, 1800–3; †Waterloo Br, London, 1811–17; Cree Br, 1812–13; Ken Br, 1821–2; †London Br, 1824–31 (built by son, Sir J Rennie; later moved to Arizona, USA)

RENTON, James Stuart [of E]
See also A Reiach.
Clapperfield, Liberton, E, 1971

RHIND, David (1808–83) [of E]
Scott Monument, G, 1837; Haggs Ch, 1840; Maxwellton Sch, East Kilbride, *c.*1840; Commercial Bank Head Office, E, s1843; Central Bank Buildings, Perth, 1846; Daniel Stewart's Hospital, E, 1848–53; Christie Miller Mausoleum, E, 1848–56; West Pollokshields feuing plan, G, 1849; Dr Guthrie's Ragged Sch, E, 1850; Carlowrie Cas, 1851–5; Commercial Bank, Hawick, 1852; Outlook Tower a/a, E, 1853; Commercial Bank, Gordon St, G, 1853–7; †Life Association of Scotland, E, 1855–8; Oban Sheriff Courthouse, 1856; Commercial Bank, Linlithgow, 1859; Wick Sheriff Courthouse, 1862–8; Commercial Bank, Ayr, 1863; Commercial Bank, Kirkwall, *c.*1863; Dumfries Sheriff Courthouse, 1863–6; Kirkcudbright Sheriff Courthouse, 1866–8; Commercial Bank, Jedburgh, 1868; Selkirk Sheriff Courthouse, 1868–70; Belhaven and Stenton Mausoleum, Cambusnethan, 1869 (attr); Watt Institution, E, 1872–4

RHIND, James R [of Inverness]
Woodside and Maryhill Libraries, G, 1902–5; Govanhill Library, G, 1902–6; Dennistoun Library, G, 1903–5; Bridgeton Library, G, 1903–6; Parkhead and Hutchesontown Libraries, G, 1904–6

RHIND, John (*c.*1836–89) [of Inverness]
Dingwall Free Ch, 1867–70; Macdonald Monument, Cille Choruill, Roy Bridge, 1873; Ardverikie, 1873–9

RHIND, Sir T Duncan (1871–1927)
See Hamilton-Paterson & Duncan Rhind.

RICHARDS, John and Margaret
See R H Matthew; Matthew (Robert), Johnson-Marshall & Partners.

RICHARDSON, James S (1883–1970) [of E]
Inspector of Ancient Monuments for Scotland.
Teampull Mholuidh, Eoropaidh (Lewis), restr 1912; Caley Cinema, E, 1922–3 (with J R McKay); Dean Cas gatehouse, Kilmarnock, 1936–7

* RICKMAN, Thomas (1776–1841) [Engl]
St David's (Ramshorn) Ch, G, 1824–6 (with J Cleland); Terraughtie Ho, 1825; The Grove, 1825

RISS, E (d.1964)
See National Coal Board, Scotland.

ROBBIE, H Pearce & WELLWOOD, Martin M [of D]
Later: Wellwood & Leslie. See also J M Robertson; J Findlay.
Dundee Dental Hosp, 1962–8; Deanhead hs, Eyemouth, 1969–76; Spittal hs, Berwick (Engl), 1972; Alloway Terr hs, D, 1979–80; Finlarig Terr hs, D, 1980–1

ROBERT MATTHEW, JOHNSON-MARSHALL (RMJM)
See Matthew (Robert), Johnson-Marshall & Partners.

ROBERTSON, David [of E]
North Morningside Ch, E, 1879–81

ROBERTSON, James [of E]
Redhall Ho, 1758

ROBERTSON, John [of Inverness]
St Anne's Epis Ch, Strathpeffer, 1890–9; Assynt Parish Ch, Inchnadamph, 1901–3; Old Town Hall, Stornoway, Lewis, 1903–5; St Laurence Ch, Forres, 1904; Invergowrie Parish Ch, 1909

ROBERTSON, John Murray (1844–1901) [of D]
Succeeded by James Findlay (q.v., for post-1901 works).
India Buildings, D, 1874; Beachtower, West Ferry, D, 1875; The Cottage, Lochee, D, 1880; The Bughties, Broughty Ferry, D, 1882; Caledonian Insurance Building, D, 1886; Glamis Ho, D, 1891; Lochee Library and Baths, D, 1894–6; Royal Victoria Hosp, D, 1899

ROBERTSON, Thomas Saunders (1835–1923) [of D]
Partner of C Edward (q.v.).
Carbet Cas, D, a/a, after 1861; Catholic Apostolic Ch, D, 1867; †St Enoch's Ch, D, 1874; St Stephen's Ch, Broughty Ferry, D, 1875; Westgreen Asylum, Liff, D,

1877–82; Rossie Ch a/a, 1880; Gowrie Ho, West Green, D, 1901

ROBERTSON, William (1786–1841) [of Elgin]
Successor practices: A & W Reid; J & W Wittet.
Temple of Pomona, Cullen Ho, 1822; Cullen Town Hall, 1822; Anderson's Institution, Forres, 1823; Holy Trinity Epis Ch, Elgin, 1825; Dufftown RC Chapel, 1825; Boharm Ch, 1828; South Villa, Elgin, 1830; St Thomas's RC Ch, Keith, 1831–32 (with Father Walter Lovi); Collie Lodge, Banff, 1836 (attr); National Bank, Dingwall, 1836; St Mary's RC Chapel, Inverness, 1836–7; Wilson's Academy (Old Academy), Banff, 1837; Elgin Courthouse, 1837–8; Aberlour Ho, 1838; Forres Tolbooth, 1838–9; Stornoway Gaol, Lewis, *c.*1839; Dochfour Ho a/a, 1839–40; Dr Bell's Academy, Inverness, 1839–41

ROBERTSON & ORCHAR [of D] (e)
Bowbridge Works, D, s1857; Seafield Works, D, s1857; Den Burn Works, Brechin, s1864; Victoria Rd Calender, D, 1874–5

ROBSON, Neil [of G] (e)
Pollokshaws and Barrhead viaducts, 1847; St Andrew's Suspension Br, G, 1853–5

ROCHE, John (m)
St Columba's Ch, Burntisland, 1589–96 (attr)

ROCHEAD, John T (1814–78) [of G]
†St John's Free Ch, G, 1845; Minard Cas, Loch Fyne, 1848; Kew Terr, G, 1849 (with James Brown); †Victoria Royal Arch, D, 1849–50; Blairvadach, Shandon, *c.*1850; Davidson Memorial, Glasgow Necropolis, 1851; Knock Cas, 1851–2; West Shandon Ho, 1852; Buckingham Terr, G, 1852–8; Levenford Ho, Dumbarton, 1853; Grosvenor Terr, G, 1855; City of Glasgow Bank, Trongate, G, 1855; Park Ch, G, 1856–7; Duncan Ban McIntyre Monument, Beacon Hill, 1859; †St Mary's Free Ch, E, 1859–60; John St UP Ch, G, 1859–60, National Wallace Monument, Stirling, 1859–69; Renfrew Old Parish Ch, 1861–2; Hawick Corn Exchange, 1865; Bank of Scotland, St Vincent Pl, G, 1867–70; North Park Ho, G, 1869; St Andrew's Free Ch, Hawick, 1871

ROGERSON, Robert, & SPENCE, Philip [of G]
Ruchazie Ch, G, f1955; SOGAT House, G, 1961–5; St Mary Tron Parish Ch, G, 1964–6; †Victoria Park Parish Ch, G, 1968–70; Hillhead Public Library, 1972; Shieldhall Sewage Works, G, *c.*1980–2

ROLLAND, L A & PARTNERS [of Leven]
Previously A & A C Dewar; from 1932, L A Rolland & Partners. From 1965, see R Hurd.

ROSS, Alexander (1834–1925) [of Inverness]

Entry also includes Ross & Macbeth, Alexander Ross & Son.
St Andrew's Epis Cath, Inverness, 1866–9; St Paul's Epis Ch, Croachy, 1867–9; Inverness Market and arcade, s1870; Avoch Parish Ch, 1870–2; St Saviour's Epis Ch, Bridge of Allan, 1871–2; Ardross Terr and St, Inverness, 1873–88; All Saints Epis Ch, Buckie, 1875; St Olaf Epis Ch, Kirkwall, 1875–6; St Margaret's Epis Ch, Aberlour, 1875–9; Largs Epis Ch, 1876; St Andrew's Epis Ch, Fort William, 1879–84; Epis Sch, Fort William, 1880; Ardross Cas, 1880–1; Lerwick Town Hall, 1881–3; St Peter's Epis Ch, Thurso, 1883–4; Cawdor Cas a/a, 1884; St Columba's Ch, Portree, 1884; Free Ch, Halkirk, 1884–6; Loch Torridon Hotel, 1884–7; Ardtornish Ho, 1885–9; Palace Hotel, Inverness, 1890; Free North Ch, Inverness, 1890; St John the Evangelist Epis Ch, Inverness, 1890–1; Skibo Cas a/a, 1900; Seaforth Sanatorium, Maryburgh, f1908; St Finnbarr's Epis Ch, Dornoch, 1912

ROSS, Launcelot Hugh (1885–1956) [of G]
Later: Ross & Lindsay. See also T S Tait.
North of Scotland Bank, St Vincent St, G, 1926–8; Drumchapel Old Ch, 1936–9; †Tower of Empire (with T S Tait), †Palace of Engineering and Palace of Art at 1938 Glasgow Empire Exhibition; Stewarts & Lloyds offices, Bellshill, 1958–9

ROSS, William (m)
Lovat Mausoleum, Kirkhill, 1633–4

ROSS-SMITH, Stanley & JAMIESON, R J C [of E]
Carnegie Ct, Pleasance, E, 1966

ROWAN, W G (1845–1924)
See McKissack & Rowan.

**ROWAND ANDERSON & BALFOUR PAUL/&
PARTNERS/KININMONTH & PAUL**
See Anderson (Rowand).

* **ROY, Nicholas** [Fr] (m)
Falkland Palace a/a, after 1537 (with M Martin and J Scrymgeour)

RUSSELL, Clement (MOW), **COCHRANE,
Patrick, and others**
Greyfriars Ch, E, s1602

RUSSELL & SPENCE (e)
Blackford Brewery Maltings, *c.*1887; †Great Canal Maltings, G, 1888

RUST, John (1853–1919) [of A]
Aberdeen City Architect from 1892.
City Hosp, A, a/a, 1892–5 (for Town Council); 60–2 Queens Rd, A, 1901

RUTHERFORD, Roan
See Irvine New Town Development Corporation.

SALMON, James, senior (1805–88) [of G]
Partnerships: 1843–c.1854, with Robert Black (1800–69); from the mid–1860s, as James Salmon & Son, with W Forrest Salmon; between c.1870 and 1872, with James Ritchie. Work with Black: see Black & Salmon.
†Catholic Apostolic Ch, G, s1852 (with A W N Pugin); Dennistoun feuing layout, G, 1856; Auchingramont Ch, Hamilton, 1860; Mechanics' Institute, Bath St, G, 1861; †Anderston Parish Ch, G, 1864–5; Langside Coll, G, 1870; †Gallowhill Ho, Paisley, 1867; Free (St George's North) Ch, Greenock, 1870–1; Barony Parochial Asylum, Woodilee, Lenzie, 1871–5 (extended W F Salmon, 1890–4); Dennistoun Sch, G, 1883

SALMON & SON & GILLESPIE [of G]
Partners: W Forrest Salmon (1843–1911); ceased designing c.1892. From the late 1890s to 1913: James Salmon junior (1873–1924) and John Gaff Gillespie (1870–1926). Successor firm: Gillespie, Kidd & Coia.
Scottish Temperance League, 106–8 Hope St, G, 1894; Mercantile Chambers, G, 1897; 22 Park Circus, G, a/a, 1897–9; British Linen Bank, Govan, G, 1897–1900; Marine Hotel, Troon, 1897–1901; Rowantreehill, Kilmacolm, 1899 (for W F Salmon by J Salmon jun); St Vincent Chambers, 142a–44 St Vincent St, G, 1899; St Andrew's East Ch Hall, G, 1899; Glasgow Savings Bank, Anderston, G, 1899–1900; 162–70 Gorbals St, G, 1899–1900; 12 University Gardens, G, 1900; †Lloyd Morris Memorial Ch, G, 1902; British Linen Bank heightening, Queen St, G, 1902–5; Miyanoshita, Kilmacolm, 1904; Lion Chambers, G, 1904–7; Den o'Gryffe, Kilmacolm, s1905; Edzell North Lodge, 1906; †Cartsburn Sch, Greenock, 1906–8; The Pantiles, Kilmacolm, 1907; Stirling Municipal Buildings, p1907; Pollok Golf Clubhouse, G, 1911; Steel Co. of Scotland offices, Blochairn, G, 1913; Cong Ch Hall, Dalmarnock, G, 1914

SCHAW, William (d.1602) (R)MOW
†Seton Palace north–east quarter, after 1585; Dunfermline Palace a/a, 1590s; Stirling Cas Chapel Royal, 1594 (attr); Fyvie Cas a/a, s1596 (attr; with Alexander Seton)

* SCHILDT, Alfred [Ger]
Evangelische Kirche deutscher Sprache, Chalmers Crescent, E, 1967

SCHULTZ, Robert Weir (1861–1951) [of London]
After 1914, changed name to Robert Schultz Weir.
Falkland Ho a/a, 1890–1900; Wester Kames Tower, Bute, restr, 1897–1902; Scoulag Lodge, Bute, 1898;

Woolmer Green Ch (Engl), 1899–1900; Old Place of Mochrum a/a, 1903–8; Edinburgh RC Archepiscopal Chapel, 1904–7; All Saints' Cath, Khartoum (Sudan), 1909; St Andrew's Chapel, Westminster Cath, London, *c.*1912

* SCOTT, Sir George Gilbert (1811–78) [Engl]
St Paul's Epis Ch (Cath), D, 1852–65; St Cuthbert's Epis Ch, Hawick, 1858; Trinity Coll Glenalmond, hall, 1861–3; St James's Epis Ch, Leith, E, 1862–5 (with R R Anderson); Glasgow University, p1863, b1864–70 (executed with J O Scott; spire by J O Scott, 1887); Albert Institute, D, 1864–7; St Mary's Epis Cath, G, s1871 (spire by J O Scott, 1893); St Mary's Epis Cath, E, p1872, b1874–1917 (Song Sch by J O Scott)

* SCOTT, Sir Giles (1888–1960) [Engl]
St Ninian's RC Ch, E, 1929; No. 6 telephone kiosk, standard design, p1935 (various locations); St Columba's RC Cath, Oban, 1935–52

SCOTT, John (d.1666) (wright)
Great Hall roof, Parliament Ho, E, 1634–9

SCOTT, John Oldrid (1844–1913)
See G G Scott.

* SCOTT, Mackay Hugh Baillie [Engl]
The White Ho, Helensburgh, 1899–1900; Sandford Ho, Wormit, a/a 1913

SCOTT, W M
303–25 High St, Linlithgow, 1937

SCOTT, Walter Schomberg [of E]
Partnerships: first, with I G Lindsay; on his own, c.1960; latterly, with A C S Dixon.
Northfield Ho restr, s1954; Monteviot a/a, 1957–63; Falkland Palace restr works, 1960s; Poolewe Visitor Centre, 1963; Membland, 1966; Pan Ha restr, Dysart, 1968–9; Dupplin, *c.*1970; Gannochy Lodge, 1973; 7 Charlotte Sq, E, restr, f1975

SCOTT, John Nichol (b.1863) **and CAMPBELL, Alexander Lorne** (*c.*1871–1944) [of E]
The Grange, Linlithgow, 1904–9; St Andrew's UF Ch, Bo'ness, 1905; 65 George St, E, 1907–8

SCOTT FRASER & BROWNING [of G]
East Kilbride Civic Centre, 1966–8

SCOTT, John Nichol & WILLIAMSON, J Anderson [of E]
See also Scott & Campbell; and J A Williamson.
North Bridge plan, E, p1896

SCOTT WILSON & KIRKPATRICK (SCOTLAND) [of G] (e)
Glasgow Inner Ring Rd, North Flank, s1965 (with W Holford, consultant architect)

SCOTTISH CO-OPERATIVE WHOLESALE SOCIETY [of G]
Morrison St warehouse, G, 1919–33 (by James Ferrigan); SCWS Warehouse, 138–40 Seagate, D, 1934 (by W Cornelius Armour); Luma factory, G, 1936–8 (by W Cornelius Armour); Taybank Works extension, D, 1949; Centenary Ho, G, 1962–9 (by Kenneth F Masson, chief architect)

SCOTTISH DEVELOPMENT DEPARTMENT/SSHA JOINT HOUSING DEVELOPMENT UNIT
See Scottish Special Housing Association.

SCOTTISH EDUCATION DEPARTMENT [of E]
CLASP Hostel programme, Highlands and Islands (prototypes, Oban and Dunoon), s1967 (with National Building Agency)

SCOTTISH SPECIAL HOUSING ASSOCIATION [of E]
Architectural design overseen by Chief Technical Officers: Walter Fairbairn, 1937–9; J Austen Bent, 1945–59; Harold Buteux, 1959–78; J H Fullarton, from 1978. From 1990, merged with Housing Corporation, to form Scottish Homes.
Toryglen tower blocks, G, s1955 (with Dr Ludwig Kresse, Stuttgart); Central CDA (Radnor Park), Clydebank, s1960 (with Sir Frank Mears & Partners); Wyndford, G, 1961–9; Hutchesontown/Gorbals Area D, G, 1961–8; Fortrose St, G, 1962–4 (Joint Housing Development Unit, with SDD); Broomhill, G, 1963–9; Anderston Cross CDA, G, s1965 (Joint Housing Development Unit); Meikle Arden Site, Cove, 1966–8; Kinneil Pk, Bo'ness, f1970; Tweedbank Phase 1, Galashiels, 1972–6; Park Mains, Erskine, 1977–9; Lamer St, Dunbar, 1981–3; Kirkland St, G, 1983–5; Bowling Green St, E, 1983–5; Firrhill Drive, E, 1985–7; Ralston Rd, Campbeltown, 1989

SCRYMGEOUR, John, of Myres (R)MOW
New tower, Holyrood Palace, E, 1529–32; new forework and chapel, Holyrood, E, 1535–6; Falkland Palace a/a, after 1537 (with N Roy, M Martin); Midcalder Ch *c.*1540 (attr)

SHAIRP, Alexander [of Oban]
Eader Glinn, Oban, 1892; Oban Old Parish Ch, 1893; Oban Municipal Buildings, 1897

SHAW, Richard Norman (1831–1912) [of London]
Key English works: Leyswood, 1868–9; Cragside, 1870–85; Lowther Lodge, London, 1873–5; Adcote, 1876–81; 170 Queens Gate, London, 1887–8; New Scotland Yard, London, 1887–90; Chesters, 1889–91; Bryanston, 1889–93; Piccadilly Hotel, London, 1905–8

SHAW-STEWART, BAIKIE & PERRY [of E]
Leith Fort hs, E, p1957, b1960–6; house at Newlands, 1960–1 (by Perry)

SHEARER, James Grant (1881–1962) [of Dunfermline]
From 1950 to 1962, in partnership with George Annand.
Carnegie Birthplace Memorial, Dunfermline, 1925–49; Elgin Hostel, Portree, Skye, 1931–3; Dunfermline Fire Sta, 1934; boys' school hostel, Lerwick, 1939; Lochalsh hydro power sta, 1948; Conon Valley hydro power scheme, 1951–6 (including Achanalt sta, 1951–5); Fasnakyle hydro power sta, 1946–52; Cannich model village, *c.*1952; War memorial and Abbey war memorial chapel, Dunfermline, 1953; David Marshall Lodge, Aberfoyle, 1958; Fisher's Close, E, restr, f1964; Kinross central redevelopment, 1970–3

* SHEKHTEL, Fedor [Rus]
†'Russian Village', 1901 Glasgow Exhibition

SHEWAN, Michael [of A]
Gray's Sch of Art, A, 1964–8; Holburn Bar, A, 1965

SHIELLS, R Thornton & THOMSON, James M [of E]
St Peter's Epis Ch, Musselburgh, 1865 (by Paterson & Shiells); 9–16 George IV Bridge, E, 1868 (by Shiells); 7–25 Forrest Rd, E, 1870; King's Pk UP Ch, Dalkeith, 1871 (by Shiells); Buccleuch St Ch, Dalkeith, 1879 (by Shiells); Bo'ness Old Kirk, 1885; Dumbarton Cottage Hosp, 1898

SIBBALD, William (d.1809) [of E]
Edinburgh City Superintendent of Works, 1790–1809
Beechwood, E, a/a, *c.*1799; Dublin St, E, p1799, s1801; New Town extension plan, E, 1801–4 (with R Reid); Lady Yester's Ch, E, 1803; Portobello Baths, E, 1805–6; Portobello Old Parish Ch, E, 1808–10

* SIEFERT, Richard [Engl]
Anderston Commercial Centre, G, 1967–73; Charing Cross redevelopment phase 1, G, 1971–5

SIM, Stewart (1898–1988)
See Public Works: Ministry of Works

SIMISTER MONAGHAN [of G]
85–93 Govanhill St hs, G, 1980–83; Elderpark hs, G, 1984–6; Edzell St hs, G, 1985–8; Methil St hs, G, 1989–91; Sandy Rd hs, G, 1989–91; Buttery and Weaver Buildings hs, Argyle St, G, 1989–91; Duddingston Manor hs, E, 1989–91; Byres Road and University Av hs, G, 1991–4; Drumchapel and Castlemilk hs rehab projects, G, 1991–6; Lynedoch St hs, Greenock, 1992–4; Brechin St hs, G, 1993–5

SIMPSON, Archibald (1790–1847) [of A]
40–4 Union St, A, 1811; Castle Forbes, 1814–15; St
Andrew's Epis Ch, A, 1816–17; Medico–Chirurgical
Society's Hall, A, 1818–20; †Aberdeen Asylum,
1819–22; Assembly Rooms (Music Hall), A, 1820–2;
Park Ho, Drumoak, 1822; Union Buildings
(Athenaeum), A, 1822–3; Bon–Accord Sq/Cres, A,
1823; Murtle Ho, 1823; Crimonmogate, c.1825;
Stracathro Ho, 1827; St Giles's Ch, Elgin, 1827–8;
Letham Grange Ho, 1828; Boath Ho, c.1830;
Anderson's Institution, Elgin, 1830–3; Royal
Infirmary, A, 1832–40; St Andrew's Epis Ch, Banff,
1833; St Nicholas East Ch, A, a/a, 1833–5; Gordon
Epis Chapel, Fochabers, 1834–5; Linton Ho, 1835;
Elgin Pauper Lunatic Asylum, c.1835; Drumoak
Parish Ch, 1835–6; †Carnousie New Ho, c.1835–40;
Woodside North Ch, 1836; Westburn Ho, 1836–7;
Marine Terr (part), A, s1837; Marischal Coll, A,
1837–42; Conservative Club, A, 1838; Gordon Schs,
Huntly, 1839; Northern Insurance office, A, 1839–40;
North of Scotland Bank, A, 1839–42; Thainstone,
1840; Market St and †New Market, A, 1840–2; North
of Scotland Bank, Huntly, 1842; St Machar's Parish
Ch, Aboyne, 1842; East, West and South Free
Churches, A ('Triple Kirks'), 1843–4; Trinity (Free)
Ch, Rothesay, 1843–5; Glenferness, 1844–5;
†Mechanics' Institute, A, 1845; St Mary's Free Ch, A,
1845–6; Woodside New (South) Ch, A, 1846–9; Union
Bank, Lerwick, 1846

SIMPSON, James (1831–1934) [of E]
Leith Burgh Architect.
Links Pl Sch, Leith, E, 1875; Fort Primary Sch, Leith,
E, 1875; Gladstone Pl, Leith, E, 1880; Leith
Improvement Scheme hs (Henderson St, etc.), E, s1885;
25 Learmonth Terr, E, 1891–3 (interiors by W Scott
Morton); Leith Infectious Diseases Hosp, E, s1894

* SIMPSON, Sir John W (1858–1933) **and ALLEN,
Edmund John Milner** (1859–1912) [Engl]
Glasgow Art Gallery and Museum, 1897–1901

**SIMPSON, James Walter Thorburn & BROWN,
Andrew Stewart** [of E]
St Giles Cath restr, E, 1977–80; Conservative Club
redevelopment, E, 1978–82; Rosslyn Cas restr,
s1984–8; Trotters shop, George St, E, 1985; 8 Queen
St restr, E, 1988; Tyninghame a/a, 1989–93; Royal
Lyceum Theatre a/a, E, 1990–2

SIMPSON & WILSON [of G] (e)
Spean Bridge-Mallaig railway viaducts, 1897–1901

SINCLAIR, Colin (1878–1957) [of G]
Successor practice to H & D Barclay (q.v.).
† 'Clachan' pavilions at 1911 and 1938 Glasgow
exhibitions; Stag Hotel, Lochgilphead, 1937

* SKINNER, Colonel William (1700–1780) [Engl]
Fort George, 1748–69

SKIRVING, Alexander (d.1919) [of G]
6–12 Broomielaw, G, 1883; Battle Monument,
Langside, G, 1887–8; 76–84 Wilson St, G, 1889; 5
Kensington Rd, G, 1893; Langside Hill Free Ch, G,
1894–6

* SLATER, William (1819–72) **& CARPENTER**
[Engl]
St Peter's Epis Ch, E, 1857–65; St John's Epis Ch,
Dumfries, 1868

* SLOAN & BALDERSTON [Amer]
UP Ch, Dalmeny St, E, 1882 (with Archibald
Thomson)

SMART, David (1824–1914) [of Perth]
Sharp's Institution, Perth, 1860; Battleby, 1861–3;
Good Templar Hall, Perth, 1894–5; Royal Bank
Buildings, Perth, 1899; Arngask Hotel, 1899–1900

SMART, STEWART & MITCHELL [of Perth]
Perth Art Gallery & Museum a/a, 1929–35

* SMEATON, John [Engl] (e)
Coldstream Br, 1763–6; Perth Br, 1766–72; Br of
Banff, 1779

SMELLIE, Thomas (1860–1938) [of Kilmarnock]
Henderson Ch, Kilmarnock, 1905

* SMIRKE, Sir Robert (1780–1867) [Engl]
Kinmount Ho, 1812; Newton Don, 1815–18;
Strathallan Cas, 1817; Whittingehame, 1817–18;
Cultoquhey, c.1819; Perth Sheriff Court, 1819;
Kinfauns Cas, 1820–2; Erskine, 1828

SMITH, George (1793–1877) [of E]
Blythswood Sq, G, 1823–9 (attr; with J Brash/W
Burn); Exchange Coffee Ho, D, 1828; Woodside Cres,
Terr and Pl, G, 1831–42; Newton Pl, G, 1837;
†Melbourne Pl, E, 1840–1; Victoria St, E, 1840–6;
Lynedoch Cres and St, G, 1845

SMITH, James (c.1645–1731) (R)MOW
Kinneil Ho a/a, fl677 (attr); Drumlanrig Cas a/a,
1679–90; †Hamilton Palace a/a, 1684–c.1700; †con-
version of Holyrood Abbey, E, for Order of Thistle,
1686–8; Whitehill Ho (later Newhailes), after 1686;
Canongate Parish Ch, 1688; Mackenzie of Rosehaugh
Mausoleum, Greyfriars Churchyard, E, 1691; Raith
Ho, 1693–6; Queensberry Aisle, Durisdeer Ch, 1695;
Surgeons Hall, E, 1696–7; Keith Hall a/a, 1697–9
(attr; or by Alexander Jaffray); Melville Ho, 1697–1702
(with W Bruce); Yester Ho, c.1699–1715 (with A
McGill); Dalkeith Palace a/a, 1702–5; Strathleven Ho
c.1708 (attr); †Dryden Ho, before 1715 (attr);

Durisdeer Ch a/a, 1716–20 (attr; possibly with A McGill); barracks at Inversnaid, Cille Chuimin, Ruthven, and Glenelg, 1718–1723; †New Ch, Dumfries, 1724–7 (with A McGill); Newbattle Parish Ch, 1727–9 (with A McGill); †Smith's Land, E, d/u.

SMITH, James (1779–1862) [of E]
Rosskeen Ch, 1828–32; Torrisdale Cas offices, 1841–5

SMITH, James (1808–63) [of G]
Victoria Baths, West Nile St, G, 1837; McLellan Galleries, G, 1855–6; Overtoun Ho, Dumbarton, 1860–3; Stirling's Library, Miller St, G, 1863–5; Bellahouston Ch, G, fl863

SMITH, John (m)
Linlithgow Tolbooth, 1668–70; Linlithgow Grammar Sch, 1670

SMITH, John (1781–1852) [of A]
Aberdeen Trustees' Assistant/Town's Architect and Superintendent of Public Works from 1807.
Phesdo Ho, 1814–15; Raemoir Ho, 1817 and 1844; †Aberdeen Courthouse, 1818–20; †Strichen Ho, 1818–21; Aberdeen Mercat Cross restoration, 1820; Tillydrone Ho, A, 1820; Dunecht Ho, 1820; Udny Ch, 1821; Mercat Cross restr, A, 1821–2 (relocated 1841–2); King St facades, A, 1825–30; King's Coll, A, a/a, 1825–32; Fordoun Parish Ch, 1827–9; Br of Don (with T Telford and J Gibb), 1827–30; St Clement's (East) Ch, A, 1828; Nigg Ch, 1828–9; St Nicholas Churchyard Screen ('Facade'), A, 1829; †Fintray, 1829; Newhills Ch, 1829; Wellington Suspension Br pylons, 1829–31; Aberdeen North Ch, 1830; Aberdeen South Ch, 1830–1; St Nicholas Ch gates and lodges, A, 1830–1; Robert Gordon's Hosp a/a, A, 1830–3; Castle Fraser a/a, c.1830–8; Easter Skene, 1832; St Machar's Cath gatehouses, A, 1832; Old Catholic Sch, A, 1833 (attr); †Balmoral, 1834–9; Cluny Cas, 1836; Manse of Drumoak, 1836; Advocates' Hall, A, 1836; Menie Ho, 1836; St Devenick Suspension Br, 1836–7; Learney Ho a/a, 1838; Banchory Ho, 1839; Town's Schools, A, 1840; Craigellie Ho, 1840–1; Br of Dee widening, 1840–1; Forglen Ho, 1840–5; Blind Asylum, A, 1841; Inverurie Ch, 1841–2; Trinity Hall, A, 1845–6 (with W Smith)

SMITH, William (1817–91) [of A]
Worked with John Smith II. Aberdeen Town's Architect.
Trinity Hall, A, 1845–6 (with J Smith); Balmoral, new house, 1853–5 (with Prince Albert); Aberdeen Town & County Bank, Evan St, Stonehaven, 1854; Dunecht Ho a/a, 1855–9; Gilcomston Free Ch, A, 1868; Tarland Parish Ch, 1869–70; Boys and Girls' Hosp, A, 1869–71; City Hosp, A, s1874; Rosemount Ch, A, 1875–7; 39–45 Union St, A, 1877; Auchterless Ch, 1877–9 (by W & J Smith); St Nicholas Steeple, A, 1878–80.

SMITH, John (1782–1864) **& Thomas** (1785–1857) [of Darnick]
Melrose Ch, 1809–10; Dryburgh Chain Br, 1817; Chiefswood, 1820–1; Holylee, 1825–7; Yarrow Br, 1833; Westruther Ch, 1839–40

SOUTAR & PATRICK
See MacLaren, Soutar & Salmond.

SOUTH–EASTERN REGIONAL HOSPITAL BOARD [of E]
Regional Architect, 1940s–60s, John Holt.
Radiotherapeutic Institute, Western General Hosp, E, 1952–4; Neurosurgical Department, Western General Hosp, E, s1954; Royal Victoria Hosp a/a, Kirkcaldy, 1955–67

SOUTTAR, James (d.1922) **and James Augustus** [of A, London]
Cong Ch, A (with W Leslie), 1865; Imperial Hotel, A, 1869; Baptist Ch, Crown Terr, A, 1870; Aberdeen Town and County Bank, Montrose, c.1870; Wellfield Cemetery lodge and gates, A, 1882; 96–120 Rosemount Viaduct, A, 1887; Salvation Army Citadel, A, 1893–6; Heugh Hotel, Stonehaven, 1898; Torr Hall, 1903–5

SPEED, John [of Newburgh] (m)
Newburgh Town Ho, 1808

SPENCE, Sir Basil U (1907–76) [of E, London]
Pre-war work: see Anderson (Rowand) & Balfour Paul/Paul & Partners. This entry is concerned with Spence's post-1946 works, including Basil Spence, Glover & Ferguson (office in E) and Basil Spence & Partners (office in E, then London).
Bannerfield hs, Selkirk, 1946–8; † 'Britain Can Make It' exhibition, London, 1947; Natural Philosophy Department, University of Glasgow, 1947–51; Lamer St hs, Dunbar, 1949–52; Sunbury-on-Thames hs (Engl), f1950–1; †Exhibition of Industrial Power, Kelvin Hall, G (with J A Coia), and †Sea and Ships/Heavy Industries pavilions, South Bank, London (both Festival of Britain), 1951; Anglican Cath, Coventry (Engl), p1951, b1954–62; 'The Cottage', Longniddry, 1952–5; Duncanrig Sch, East Kilbride, 1953; Sydenham comprehensive sch, London, f1954; Durham University Physics Building, f1956; Thurso High Sch, 1956–8; Annfield hs, Newhaven, E, 1957; University of Edinburgh Staff Club, 1957–8; St Andrew's Parish Ch, Clermiston, E, 1957–9; Rossie Priory a/a, c.1958; Basildon New Town (Engl) planning, s1958; University of Sussex (Engl), s1960; †Hutchesontown-Gorbals Area C hs, G, 1960–6; Department of Genetics, University of Glasgow, 1961–2; Institute of Virology, University of Glasgow, 1961–4; Scottish Widows Building, St Andrew Square, E,1962; Abbotsinch Airport Terminal

Building, 1963–6; Crookfur Homes, Newton Mearns, 1964–7; Mortonhall Crematorium, E, 1964–7; Edinburgh University Library, 1965–7; Newcastle Central Library (Engl), 1966–9; 79–121 Canongate hs, E, 1966–8; Stirling University, 1966–73; †British Pavilion, Expo 67, Montréal (Can/Qué), 1967; Knightsbridge Household Cavalry Barracks, London, fl970; Chancellery of British Embassy, Rome, fl971; Glasgow Royal Infirmary, 1971–82; Scottish Widows Fund, E, 1972–6; Parliamentary Building Extension, Wellington (N. Zeal), fl974; Queen Anne's Mansions offices, London, fl976;   Royal Bank West End Branch, E, 1976; Manse Court, East Calder, 1982–4

SPENCE, William (1806–83) [of G]
Coulter Mains, 1838; †Dalmarnock Gas Works, G,1843 (and later extensions); Rhu Parish Ch, 1851; †Paisley's Building, G, 1855–6; †Randolph, Elder & Co engine works, G, 1858; UP Ch, Helensburgh, 1865; Cameron Ho a/a, 1865; 250 Wallace St warehouse, G, 1871–2; Dunlossit Ho a/a, fl874; Clydesdale Bank, High St, D, 1876; Stewart & Macdonald warehouse, Buchanan St, G, 1879

STARFORTH, John (1823–98) [of E]
University Ho, St Andrews, 1864–6; Greyfriars Ch, Dumfries, 1865–8; Dumfries Royal Infirmary, Dumfries, 1869–73; Trinity Ch, Greenock, 1871; British Linen Bank, Dumfries, a/a, 1872; Free Ch, Galashiels, 1875; Greenock Poorhouse, 1876–9; †Peebles Hydropathic, 1878–81; UP Ch, Kelso, 1885–6; St Andrew's Parish Ch, Moffat, 1884–7; Nairn Old Parish Ch, 1893–7

STARK, Malcolm [of G]
Gilfillan Memorial Ch, D, 1887–8; Govan District Asylum, Hawkhead, G, 1893–5

STARK, William (1770–1813) [of G, E]
†Hunterian Museum, G, 1804–5; †Glasgow Asylum, Bell's Park, G, p1804–6, b1807–20; Dunfermline Abbey, a/a, 1807; St George's Tron Ch, G, 1807–8; Saline Ch, 1809–10; Glasgow Courthouse, 1809–14; Advocates' and Signet Libraries, E, s1812; †Dundee Royal Asylum, 1812–20; Gloucester Asylum (Engl), 1813–23 (executed by J Collingwood)

STEEDMAN, Robert
See Morris & Steedman.

STEELE, Matthew [of Bo'ness]
Bo'ness Masonic Hall, 1909; 131–5 Stewart Av, Bo'ness, 1909; Hippodrome Cinema, Bo'ness, fl912

STEPHEN, James P [of Glamis]
Architect Studio, Glamis, 1982–4; Servite Ho, D, 1985–7; St Anthony's RC Ch, Kirriemuir, 1986–7; Northwood Ct, Broughty Ferry, D, 1989; St Peter & St

Paul's RC Ch, Rosyth, 1989–91; West Pk estate, D, 1990–2; Camperdown Works High Mill a/a (as hs), D, 1992–5

STEPHEN, John (*c*.1807–50) [of G]
Partner of Scott, Stephen & Gale.
Sighthill Cemetery gates and chapel, G, 1839–40; St Jude's Ch, G, 1840; Blythswood Testimonial Sch, Renfrew, 1840; Queen's Tea Store, York St, G, 1843; Muter Monument, Glasgow Necropolis, 1844; Gartsherrie Academy, Coatbridge, 1845; 65–7 (attr) and 68–72 James Watt St, G, *c*.1848

* STEPHENSON, Derek & PARTNERS [Engl]
Heron Ho, G, 1967–71; Bank of Scotland building, Lynedoch Pl, G, 1968; Pegasus Ho, G, *c*.1970; Langside Av hs, G, fl976

STEVENS, Alexander, the elder (*c*.1730–96) [of Prestonhall]
Drygrange Br, 1779–80; Br of Dun, 1785–7; Hyndford Br, 1785–7; Ayr Br, 1786–9; 1–3 New Bridge St, Ayr, 1787

STEVENS, Alexander, the younger [of E]
Raehills Ho, 1782 (a/a by W Burn, 1830–4); St Cuthbert's Ch Steeple, E, 1789–90; Monreith Ho, 1790–4; Moffat Ch a/a, 1795

STEVENSON, Alan (1807–65) (e)
See Northern Lighthouse Board.

STEVENSON, David (1815–66) **and Thomas** (1818–87) (e)
See Northern Lighthouse Board.

STEVENSON, David Alan (1854–1938) (e)
See Northern Lighthouse Board.

STEVENSON, John J (1831–1908) [of G, later London]
See also Douglas (Campbell) & Stevenson.
Kelvinside Parish Ch, G, 1862; The Red Ho, London, 1872; 67–79 St Vincent St, G, *c*.1875–8; Ken Hill (Engl), 1879–80; Crieff Free Ch, 1880–2; Fairlie Parish Ch, 1883; St Leonard's Ch, Perth, 1885; Fairlie Sch, 1887; Fairlie Village Hall, 1892; Nathaniel Stevenson Memorial Free Ch, G, 1898–1902; Peter Memorial Ch, Stirling, 1901

STEVENSON, Robert (1772–1850) (e)
See Northern Lighthouse Board.

STEWART, John (1869–1954) **& PATERSON, George Andrew** (1876–1934) [of G]
Broomhill UF Ch, G, 1902–5; Anderston Library, G, 1904–6; MacLaren High Sch, Callander, 1907 (and a/a 1924); Anniesland Cross hs, G, 1908–10; Ardchullary Mhor,

1910; Ho of Elrig, 1912–14; Scottish Veterans' Garden Settlement, Callander, 1919–20; Netherlee Ch, 1933–9; East King St hs, Helensburgh, 1936 (and other schemes)

STEWART, TOUGH & ALEXANDER [of Greenock]
Municipal Buildings and Police Sta, Gourock, 1923

* STIRLING, James (1926–92) [Engl]
St Andrews University residences, 1964–7

STIRLING, William (1772–1838) [of Dunblane]
Logie Ch, 1805; Airth North Ch, 1818–20; Kippen Ch, 1823–7; Garden Ho, 1824; Lecropt Ch, 1824–6 (with David Hamilton); Dron Parish Ch, c.1825; Holmehill Ho, Dunblane, 1826; Creich Parish Ch, 1829–32; Monzie Parish Ch, 1830–1

STIRRAT, Frank [of G]
Dixon Halls, G, 1878–9

* STOKES, Leonard Aloysius (1858–1925) [Engl]
Rose St telephone exchange, E, 1901–3; Western telephone exchange, G, 1907 (with C Menzies); Aberdeen telephone exchange, 1908–9

STRANG, Alexander (1916–84) **& PARTNERS** [of Stirling]
Chief Housing Architect to Stirling County Council, 1946–57.
Silverburn, Dunblane, 1967; Kildean Cattle Market, 1967

* STRATTON DAVIS, David & YATES [Engl]
The Inch hs, E, 1946–9

* STREET, George Edmund (1824–81) [Engl]
Dunecht Ho a/a, 1870s; St Mary's Epis Ch, Ellon, 1871; St John's Epis Ch, New Pitsligo, 1871; Haddo Ho chapel, 1876–81

STRONACH, Alexander (m)
Portmahomack store houses, 1699 (extended 1779); Tain Tolbooth, 1706–8

* STROZZI, Peter [Ital] (e)
†Leith fortifications, 1548

SUTHERLAND, Eric A (1870–1940) [of G]
Govan Savings Bank, G, p1904; British Ropes Office, Rutherglen, 1912; Hillhead Savings Bank, G, p1939

SUTHERLAND, George [of A]
Victoria Sch of Science and Art, Elgin, 1890

SUTHERLAND, T Scott (1899–1963) [of A]
Odeon Cinema, A, 1927; Regent Cinema, A, 1932; Anderson Drive speculative hs, A, c.1932 (and elsewhere, e.g. Broomhill); 250–2 Union St, A, c.1933; Architecture School conversion, Garthdee, f1956

SUTHERLAND, James & WALKER [of E]
Hope Park Cong Ch, E, 1875–6; Rosehall UP Ch, E, 1877

SWAN, T Aikman (d.1945) [of E]
Stenhouse Saughton Ch, E, 1935; High St hs, Dalkeith, 1935; 2–8 Lothian Rd, Dalkeith, 1938

SWANSTON, J D (1869–1956) **and DAVIDSON, James** [of Kirkcaldy]
King's Theatre, E, 1905–6

* SWIFT, Arthur & PARTNERS [Engl]
St Andrew's Ho, G, 1961–4

TAIT, John (1787–1856) [of E]
Clarendon Cres, E, 1850–3; Eton Terr, E, 1855; Oxford Terr, E, 1858–9

TAIT, Thomas S (1882–1954) [of London]
See also Sir J J Burnet.
Overall plan/co-ordination of 1938 Glasgow Empire Exhibition, and design of †Tower of Empire/Treetop Restaurant (with Launcelot Ross), and Palace of Industries (with J A Coia; re-erected at Prestwick Airport 1941)

TARBOLTON, Harold Ogle (1869–1947) **& OCHTERLONY, Sir Matthew M** (1880–1946) [of E]
See also G Bodley; J M Kinross; M Ochterlony.
Bangour Village Ch, 1924–30; Elsie Inglis Memorial Hosp, E, f1925; Ch of Ascension (Epis), G, 1925; Harmony, Longniddry, 1933; Bank of Scotland, Dumfries, c.1933; Inverewe Ho, 1937; St Salvador's Epis Ch, E, 1939–42; St Fillan's Epis Ch, E, 1940; St David's Epis Ch, E, 1941; Sloy hydro scheme, 1946–50 (including Sloy Power Sta); Tummel-Garry hydro scheme, 1947–53 (including Pitlochry Power Sta); Mount Royal Hotel, E, 1955 (by later partners)

TAYLOR, Alexander [of E, G]
Layout of Hyndland, G, 1830s/40s (attr); †Baingle Brae, Tullibody, 1834; Royal Terr, G, 1839–49; Clarendon Pl, G, 1839–41

* TAYLOR, John (d. c.1841) [Irl]
Dundee Customs Ho, 1839–40 (with James Leslie); Glasgow Customs Ho, 1840

TELFORD, Thomas (1757–1834) [of London]
Westerhall Ho, a/a 1783 (his first major work); Tongland Br, 1804–8 (with Alexander Nasmyth); Caledonian Canal, 1804–22; Pulteneytown layout plan, Wick, 1808; Craigellachie Br, 1814–15; programme of 32 Highland churches and manses, 1825–34 (with J Smith and W Thomson); Dean Br, E, 1831–2; Jamaica Br, G, 1833. For complete list of Telford

works, including the numerous parliamentary roads and bridges constructed in the Highlands under his direction from 1804, see Sir A Gibb, *The Story of Telford*, 1935

* TESSIN, Hans Ewald [Ger] (e)
Ayr Citadel, s1652

THOMAS, William R [of Burntisland]
Easterheughs, 1946–55 (with W Williamson)

THOMS, Patrick (1873–1946) **& WILKIE, William Fleming** (1876–1961) [of D]
Edzell Free Ch, 1900; The Boreen, D, 1901; Morar, D, 1905; Nyoora, D, 1905; Grayburn Ho, Benvie, 1905–7; Kinpurnie Cas, 1908–11; Ferncroft, D, 1912; Hill Rise, D, 1913–14; Farington Hall, 1914; The Priory, Crail, 1915; Harris Academy, D, 1926–8; Greywalls, D, 1929; Draffen & Jarvie, D, 1935; Northern Coll, D, 1974

THOMSON, Alexander (1817–75) [of G]
Partnerships: 1849–56, with John Baird II (1816–93); 1856–71, with George Thomson (q.v.); 1873–5, with Robert Turnbull (c.1839–1905). After 1877: Turnbull in partnership with David Thomson; R Turnbull & Son from 1883/4.
Seymour Lodge, Cove, 1850; Craig Ailey, Cove, 1850; The Knowe, Albert Dr, G, s1852; Langside feuing lay-out, G, 1853; Rockland, Helensburgh, 1854; Craigrownie Cas, Cove, 1854; Tor Ho, Rothesay, 1855; Caledonia Rd UP Ch, G, 1856–7; Maria Villa ('Double Villa'), Mansionhouse Rd, G, 1856–7; Holmwood, Cathcart, 1857–8; St Vincent St UP Ch, G, 1857–9; †Queen's Park Terr, Eglinton St, G, 1857–60; Walmer Cres, G, 1857–62; Beattie Monument, Glasgow Necropolis, 1858; 1–10 Moray Pl, G, s1859; †Chalmers Free Ch, G, 1859; Strathbungo feuing layout, G, 1859; Grosvenor Building, G, 1859–61; †Cairney Building, Bath St, G, 1860; Buck's Head Building, G, 1862–3; †Dunlop St warehouse, 1864; Eton Terr, 41–53 Oakfield Av, G, 1865; Grecian Buildings, G, 1865; Northpark Terr, Hamilton Dr, G, 1866; Arran View, Airdrie, 1867; Queen's Park UP Ch, G, 1867–9; Great Western Terr, G, s1869; Castlehill, 202 Nithsdale Rd, G, 1870; Kelvinside Terr steps, G, 1870s (attr); Westbourne Terr, G, 1871; Ellisland, 200 Nithsdale Rd, G, 1871; Egyptian Halls, G, 1871–3; †122 Wellington St, G, a/a, 1872; †Cowcaddens Cross Building, G, 1872; 84–112 Nithsdale Rd, G, 1873–8 (attr); 94–106 Otago St, G, 1874; †Gorbals St and Norfolk St hs, G, 1874; 99–107 West Nile St, G, 1874; †87–97 Bath St, G, 1874–6; †Maryhill Rd and Garscube Rd hs, G, 1875; Millbrae Cres, G, 1875 (attr; by Turnbull); Dunluce and Woodend, Dullatur Village, 1875–6 (attr; by Turnbull); Winton Ho, c.1889 (by Turnbull)

THOMSON, Alexander George [of G]
Penkill Cas a/a, s1857; St John's Epis Ch, Girvan, 1859; Pearce Lodge, G, 1885–8

THOMSON, David [of G]
Partnerships: from late 1850s to 1862, with C Wilson; 1877–84, with Robert Turnbull. From 1948, practice merged with Weddell Inglis.
Knockdow Ho, 1867; St Margaret's Ch, Dalry, 1871–3; St Ninian's Epis Ch, G, 1872–7; St Andrew's Epis Ch, Ardrossan, 1873–5; Gourlay St Sch, G, 1873–5; Kinning Pk Sch, G, 1886.

THOMSON, Frank (1882–1961) [of D]
Partner of H & F Thomson; son of James Thomson. For libraries: see Dundee Town Council.
St John's Cross Ch, D, 1911; Stewarts' Offices, Castle St, D, 1921.

THOMSON, George (d.1878) [of G, Cameroon]
See also Alexander Thomson.
Missionary Hosp, Victoria (Cameroon), c.1874

THOMSON, James (c.1784–1832) [of Dumfries]
Sanquhar Parish Ch, 1822–4; Dunscore Ch, 1823–4

THOMSON, James (1835–1905)
See Baird & Thomson.

THOMSON, James (d.1927)
Dundee City Architect and Engineer; see Dundee Corporation.

THOMSON, James Taylor (c.1888–1953) [of G]
Metro–Vick Ho, G, 1925–7; St John's Renfield Ch, G, 1927–31; Possil Sch, G, 1930–4; Links Ho, Wilson St, G, 1931; †Church of Scotland Pavilion, Palace of Industries West, and Concert Hall, 1938 Empire Exhibition

THOMSON, Leslie Grahame (1896–1974) [of E, Oban]
Adopted name MacDougall from 1953.
Reid Memorial Ch, E, 1929–33; 6 Easter Belmont Rd, E, 1932; Srongarbh, West Linton, 1935 (for himself); Isobel Fraser Home, Inverness, 1936; National Bank of Scotland head office, E, 1936–42 (with Arthur Davis); Fairmilehead Ch, E, 1937; The Pantiles Hotel, West Linton, 1937–9; Caledonian Insurance office, E, 1938–40 (with F J Connell); Canonmills Clock, E, 1947; Queensferry Rd multi–storey hs (Maidencraig Court), E, 1953–5; Longstone Ch, E, 1954; Christ Church Dunollie, Oban, 1954–7

THOMSON, John (1859–1933) **& SANDILANDS, Robert D** (d.1913) [of G]
Later Thomson, Sandilands & McLeod.
UP Ch, Whithorn, 1884–92; City of Glasgow District Asylum, Gartloch, G, 1890–7; Sherbrooke Cas Hotel, G, 1896; Royal Insurance Building, Buchanan St, G,

1897–8; Govan Municipal Buildings, G, 1897–1901; Parish Council Chambers, G, 1900–2; Stobhill Hosp, 1901–4; Hutcheson's Girls Grammar Sch, G, 1910–12; New Bridgegate UF Ch, G, 1923

THOMSON, Robert (d. *c*.1924) **& WILSON, Andrew** [of G]
Daily Record Office, G, 1899–1900

THORNLEY, Michael and Sue [of G]
31–45 Peel St, G, 1991–3

TINDALL, Benjamin [of E]
Hermits and Termits restr, E, 1980–2 (for himself); The Vaults, Leith, E, restr, 1982–5; Fringe Office, High St, E, 1986–90; Royal Coll of Physicians restr, E, 1993–4; Botanics Shop, E, 1994

TINDALL, Mary C [of Haddington, Pathhead]
1 Nungate, Haddington, restr, 1953; Ford Ho restr, 1961; Harbour warehouses conversion, North Berwick, 1970

* TITE, Sir William (1798–1873) [Engl]
Perth Sta, 1848

TODD, W J Walker [of E]
See also Peddie & Walker Todd.
St Columba's Epis Ch, Bathgate, 1916

TRAQUAIR, Ramsay (*c*.1874–1952) [of E, Montréal]
Mackenzie Ho, Kinnear Rd, E, 1910; Ch of Christ Scientist, E, 1911; Skirling Ho, 1912

TROUP, F W (1859–1941) [of London]
Blucairn, Lossiemouth, 1906; Blackfriars Ho, London, 1913; Art Workers Guild Hall, London, 1913

TURNBULL, Robert (*c*.1839–1905)
See A Thomson; D Thomson.

TURNBULL, Thomas W [of E]
Architect to Edinburgh Royal Infirmary.
Nurses' home and maternity hosp, Royal Infirmary, E, 1935–9 (with J Miller)

* UBALDINI, Migiorino [Ital] (e)
†Edinburgh fortifications, 1547–8

* UK ATOMIC ENERGY AUTHORITY [Engl]
Dounreay Experimental Research Establishment, s1955 (by R S Brocklesby, Chief Architect, Engineering Group)

UNDERWOOD, Walter & PARTNERS [of G]
Fulton Building, University of Dundee, 1962–3; Queen Margaret Union, University of Glasgow, 1968; Cowcaddens CDA hs, G, s1968; Dale Ho, West George St, G, 1981; Fountain Ho, G, 1981

* UNWIN, Sir Raymond (1863–1940) [Engl]
See also C M Crickmer.
Gretna Village, 1916–17 (with C M Crickmer, T G Lucas, C E Simmons and others); Eastriggs Village, 1916–18; All Saints Epis Ch, Gretna, 1917

WALFORD, J T [of London, E]
St John the Evangelist RC Ch, Portobello, 1903–6

WALKER, James Campbell (*c*.1822–88) [of E]
Galashiels Poorhouse, 1859; Upper Strathearn Poorhouse, Auchterarder, 1862–3; County Buildings, Stonehaven, 1863–5; Blair Drummond, 1868–72; Waverley Cas Hotel, Melrose, 1869–71; Dunfermline Municipal Buildings, 1875; Dunfermline Central Library, 1881–3; Hawick Town Hall, 1883

WALKER, R J
†Scottish Exhibition of National History, Art and Industry, G, 1911

WALKER, Robert [of G]
Monument to American Soldiers, Mull of Oa, Islay, 1918

WALLACE, Robert (*c*.1790–1874) [of London]
County Buildings, Ayr, 1818–22; Derby Athenaeum, Royal Hotel, post office and bank (Engl), 1837–9

WALLACE, William (d.1631) (m)
George Heriot's Hosp, E, from *c*.1628 (attr; possibly with J Murray; compl W Aytoun); Byres of Coates Monument, Greyfriars Churchyard, E, *c*.1629

* WALLIS, GILBERT & PARTNERS (Amer)
India Tyre Factory, Inchinnan, 1929–30

WALTON, George (1868–1933) [of G, London]
Interiors of houses at †Ledcameroch and at York (Engl), 1897–8; Kodak shop interiors in Glasgow, London, overseas, 1899; The Leys, Elstree (Engl), 1901; Wern Fawr (Wal), 1907–10.

WARDROP, Hew Montgomery (1856–87) [of E]
See also R R Anderson.
Tilliefour a/a, 1885–6; All Saints Epis Ch, Inveraray, 1886; Ballochmyle Ho a/a, 1886–8; St Anne's Epis Ch, Dunbar, 1889–90 (executed by Anderson)

WARDROP, James Maitland (1824–82) [of E]
In partnership with Thomas Brown from 1849, Charles Reid from 1873.
County Buildings and Town Hall, Wigtown, 1862–3; Linlithgow Courthouse, 1863; County and Police Buildings, Alloa, 1863; Lochinch Cas, 1864; Forbes Rd, E, *c*.1865; Methlick Parish Ch, 1865–7; Falkirk Sheriff Courthouse, 1866; †Stichill Ho, 1866; Cumnock Old Ch, 1867; St Leonard's Hall,

St Andrews, 1867–8; Nunraw, 1868; Reid Hall, Forfar, 1869; Forfar Sheriff Courthouse, 1869–71; Callendar Pk a/a, 1869–77; St Mary of Wedale Parish Ch, Stow, 1873–6; Stirling Sheriff Courthouse, 1874–6; Fairburn Ho, 1874–8; Kinnordy, 1879; Cambo, 1879–81; Beaufort Cas, 1880; Dalquharran Cas a/a, 1880; Barskimming, 1883

WARDROP & REID
See J M Wardrop.

* WARE, Isaac (1704–66) [Engl]
Carnsalloch Ho, 1754–9 (attr); †Amisfield Ho, East Lothian, 1756–9

* WATERHOUSE, Alfred (1830–1905) **& SON**
(Paul Waterhouse, 1861–1924) [Engl]
Entry also includes later works by Paul Waterhouse.
Prudential Building, D, 1875; Arnsbrae Ho, Alloa, 1885; Alloa Town Hall, 1888; Prudential Building, G, 1888–90; Prudential Building, E, 1892–5; Mount Melville, 1902; Prudential Building, A, 1910; Prudential Building, Dunfermline, 1914–16; All Saints Epis Ch, St Andrews, 1923; Younger Graduation Hall, St Andrews, 1923–9; St Gregory's Ch, St Andrews, 1925

WATSON, George Mackie (1859–1948) [of E]
Bardrochat Ho, 1893; Eilean Donan Cas, restr, 1913–32

WATSON, Thomas, of Old Rayne
Aberdeen Tolbooth, 1615

WATSON, Thomas Lennox (*c.*1850–1920) [of G]
Adelaide Pl Baptist Ch, G, 1875–7; †Kilmacolm Hydropathic, 1879–80; North Ch, Perth, 1880; Wellington UP Ch, G, 1882–4; Hillhead Baptist Ch, 1883; St Andrew's Ch, Crieff, 1883; †Red Hall, 1014 Great Western Rd, G, 1885; Clyde Yacht Club (Royal Marine Hotel), Hunter's Quay, 1888; Woodcroft, Larbert, 1888; Citizen Building, 24 St Vincent Pl, G, 1889; Adelphi Terrace Sch, G, 1894; 396–450 Sauchiehall St, G, 1900–8 (with Henry Mitchell)

WATSON, John (1873–1936), **SALMOND, David** (1876–1938) **& GRAY, James H** (1885–1938) [of G]
Glasgow City Chambers extension, 1913–23; Davidson Hosp, Girvan, 1921; Philipshill Hosp, 1929–31

* WEBB, Philip (1831–1915) [Engl]
Arisaig Ho and steading, 1863–4

WEDDELL, James W (b.1879) **& INGLIS, William Beresford** [of G]
Partnership from 1932. From 1948, became Weddell & Thomson.

Toledo Cinema, Muirend, G, 1933; Rogano's Oyster Bar, G, 1935–6; Beresford Hotel, G, 1937–8

WEDGWOOD, Roland, ASSOCIATES [of E]
Ravelston Ho Rd hs, E, 1966–8; Craigmount Av North hs, E, 1968; 69–85 Ravelston Dykes Rd, E, 1969; Scottish Agricultural Industries headquarters, E, f1971; 61 St Alban's Rd, E, 1975; Lynedoch Ho, E, 1977–9

* WEEDON, Harry [Engl]
†BMC Factory, Bathgate, s1960

WEEKES, Joseph (d.1949)
See Dunbarton County Council.

WEIR, James [of E]
†St Cuthbert's Ch, E, 1773–5

WEIR, Robert Schultz (1861–1951)
See R W Schultz.

WHEELER, Sir H Anthony, & SPROSON, Frank [of Kirkcaldy, E]
See also Glenrothes New Town Development Corporation.
Bowery hs, Leslie, 1953–6; Burntisland redevelopment, 1955–62; Priory Acres, St Andrews, 1957; Lochgelly Central Area Redevelopment, 1957–64; Dysart redevelopment, 1958–71; St Columba's Ch, Glenrothes, 1960–1; The Gyles hs, Pittenweem, 1962; Kinghorn redevelopment, 1962–6; Broad St hs, Cowdenbeath, f1963; School Pl hs, Uphall, f1963; Oxgangs Av hs, E, 1964; Torbain Parish Ch, Kirkcaldy, 1964–8; Old Buckhaven hs, 1964–73; Boghall Ch, Bathgate, 1965; Stirling Rd hs, Milnathort, f1967; Grangemouth Central Area development, 1967–8; Blackburn Town Centre, 1968; Broxburn Old Town Redevelopment, 1968–70; Backcauseway hs, Culross, 1968–70; Abronhill 4 hs, Cumbernauld, 1968–70; St John's Ch, Galashiels, 1972; Edinburgh Coll of Art, Hunter Building, 1972–6; Hawthornbank Ho, E, 1974; Royal Bank, Dunfermline, 1983–5; Bedford Court, Alloa, 1983–5; Edinburgh High St Phase 3, 1983–6; Low Port Centre, Linlithgow, 1985–7; Heriot Watt University Union, E, 1989–91; St Andrews University Residences, 1992–3

WHISTON, Peter [of E]
St Margaret's RC Ch, Davidson's Mains, E, 1950; Sancta Maria Abbey, Nunraw, s1951; St Mark's Ch, Fairmilehead, E, 1956; St Mark's RC Ch, Oxgangs, E, 1959; St Columba's RC Ch, Cupar, 1964

* WHITFIELD, Sir William [Engl]
Glasgow University Library, 1965–81

WHITIE, William B (d.1946) [of G]
Springburn Public Halls, G, 1899–1902; Springburn Library, G, 1902–6; Mitchell Library, G, 1906–11; †Metropole Theatre, G, 1910

WHYTE, David A (d.1830) [of Newtyle]
Keithick Ho, 1818–23; Glenisla Ch, 1821

WHYTE, W M [of G]
Balmoral Cres, G, 1884–6

WILKIE, Thomas (m)
Gallery Ho, s1677

* WILKINS, William (1751–1815) [Engl]
Dalmeny Ho, 1814–17; Dunmore Pk, 1820

* WILLIAMS, Sir E Owen (1890–1969) [Engl]
Strathy Br, 1920–30; Findhorn Br, 1925–6 (with
Maxwell Ayrton); Duntocher Burn Br, 1925–7;
(second) Montrose Br, 1928–31; Daily Express
Building, G, 1936

WILLIAMSON, James Anderson (1860–1935)
See Edinburgh Corporation; and Scott & Williamson.

WILLIAMSON, William (1871–1952)
[of Kirkcaldy]
See also Williamson & Hubbard.
Inniscarra, D, 1905; Burntisland Public Library, 1906;
Mission Institute, Kirkcaldy, 1909–10; Tayside
Institute, Newburgh, 1923

WILLIAMSON, William & HUBBARD, Henry
(1888–1959) [of Kirkcaldy]
St Mungo's Ch, Alloa, 1936; Kirkcaldy Ice Rink, 1937;
North East Fife County Infectious Diseases Hosp,
Windygates, 1938; Westfield Court, E, p1938,
b1949–51; Wellbraehead hs, Forfar, 1967–9

WILLIAMSON, James & PARTNERS [of G] (e)
Awe Hydro-Electric Project, Cruachan, 1962–5

* WILLSON, Thomas [Engl]
†St Enoch Hotel, G, 1879 (with M S Gibson)

WILSON, Alexander [of St Petersburg]
Alexandrovsk Works Flax Mill, St Petersburg (Rus),
1812

WILSON, Charles (1810–63) [of G]
†Hutchesontown Ch, G, 1837; Strathbungo Ch, 1839
(parts later incorporated into McKissack & Rowan
church); Glasgow Botanic Gardens, layout and
Curator's House, 1840; Gryffe, Bridge of Weir, 1841;
City Lunatic Asylum, Gartnavel, G, 1841–3; McBride
Free Ch, Rothesay, 1845; †247 St Vincent St, G, 1845;
Windsor (Kirklee) Terr, G, 1845–64; Breadalbane Terr,
G, 1845–6 and 1855–6; Glasgow Academy, 1846;
Argyle Free Ch, G, 1846; Greenhead Ho, G, 1846;
Helensburgh Old Parish Ch, 1846; Lews Cas,
Stornoway, 1848; Raasay Ho, 1848; Rutherglen West
(Free) Ch, 1848–50; Alexander's Mill, Duke St, G
(later Great Eastern Hotel), 1849; Southern
Necropolis Gateway, G, 1849; Shandon Ho, 1849; John

Neilson Institution, Paisley, 1849–52; St Helen's, D,
1850; Dudhope Ho, D, a/a, 1850; Meadowside St
Paul's Ch, D, 1850; †Woodside Ho, Paisley, 1850–1;
Royal Bank, Buchanan St, G, 1850–1; Kelvingrove Pk
and Woodlands Hill layout plan, G, p1851–4 (with
Thomas Kyle; J Paxton consultant); †Lochton, 1852;
North St tenement, G, 1853; 901–3 Sauchiehall St, G,
1853; Royal Faculty of Procurators Hall, G, 1854; Park
Gardens, Quadrant, Terr, Circus, Woodlands Terr, and
monumental stairway, G, s1855; Park Circus Pl, G,
p1855–6, b1872–3; Free Church Coll, G, 1856–61; 2–5
La Belle Pl, G, 1857; Queen's Rooms, G, 1857–8; Park
Gate, G, 1857–9; Duncarse, D, 1858; Wester Moffat
Ho, 1859–62; Rutherglen Town Hall, 1861–2;
Benmore Ho, 1862 (and a/a 1874 by David Thomson);
Eastwood Parish Ch, 1862–3; Great Western Hotel
and Terr, Oban, 1862–3; St John's Epis Ch, Oban,
1863

WILSON, John Bennie (*c*.1848–1923) [of G]
*Partnership details: from 1879 to 1929: J B Wilson/
J B Wilson & Son. Later: Honeyman, John B Wilson
& Son; Wilson, Honeyman & Jack; Honeyman, Jack
& Robertson (q.v.).*
Stockwell Free Ch, Pollokshields, G, *c*.1886; Albert Rd
UP Ch, G, 1886–7; New Jerusalem Ch, Queens Dr, G,
1895 7; Ivy Pl UP Ch, Stranraer, 1896–8; UP ch, Ayr,
1898–1902; Cathcart Free Ch, G, 1898–1908;
Dunnikier Free Ch, Kirkcaldy, 1899; Grange UP Ch,
Grangemouth, 1900–3; Erskine UF Ch, Burntisland,
1900–3; Scotstoun UF Ch, G, 1902; Cairns UF Ch,
Milngavie, 1903; Institute of Engineers, G, 1906–8

WILSON, Robert (d.1901)
See Edinburgh School Board.

WILSON, Robert G (1844–1931)
See Ellis & Wilson.

WIMPEY LTD, SCOTTISH DIVISION [of E]
Divisional Architect, 1950s/60s: Tom Smyth.
Royston Area A hs, G, 1960; Lincoln Av and Scotstoun
Ho hs, G, 1962–3

WINTER, James
Blair Cas a/a, 1747–58

WOMERSLEY, Peter (1923–93) [of Melrose]
Farnley Hey (Engl), 1952–4; The Rig, Gattonside,
1956 (for himself); High Sunderland, 1956–7; Port
Murray, Maidens, 1960–3; Central Area
Redevelopment, Galashiels, 1961–5; Fairydean
Stadium, Galashiels, 1963–5; Psychiatric admission
unit, Haddington, 1963–5; Nuffield Transplantation
Surgery Unit, Western General Hosp, p1963,
b1965–8; Hull University Sports Centre (Engl),
1964–7; Roxburgh County Buildings Phase I, 1966–8;

Edenside Group Practice Surgery, Kelso, 1967; Bernat Klein Studio, High Sunderland, 1969–72; Monklands Leisure Centre, Coatbridge, 1977; Dingleton Hosp Boiler Ho, 1977

* WOODHOUSE & MORLEY [Engl]
Finishing Mill, Anchor Mills, Paisley, 1886; Half Time Sch and †No. 1 Spinning Mill, Ferguslie Mills, Paisley, 1887; Mile End Mill, Anchor Mills, Paisley, 1899–1900

WRIGHT, John P M
1–55 Harrison Terr, Elgin, 1947–9

WRIGHT, Robert [of E]
39–43 Castle St, E, 1793 (with James McKain)

WYLIE, Edward Grigg (*c*.1885–1954) [of G]
From 1937, consultant architect to Scottish Industrial Estates/SDA. Entry also includes work of Wright & Wylie (1914–28), Wylie Wright & Wylie (1928–36), Wylie Shanks & Wylie (1936–57), Wylie Shanks & Underwood (1957–60), Wylie Shanks & Partners (1960–85). See also Walter Underwood & Partners.
55 Mitre Rd, G, 1924; Glasgow Dental Hosp, 1926–31; Scottish Legal Life Assurance Society headquarters, G, 1927–31; Hillhead High Sch, G, 1928–31; Lennox Cas Mental Defectives' Institution, 1931–6; Hillington Industrial Estate, s1937; Weir amenity block, G, 1937; Carfin and Larkhall Industrial Estates, s1938; NCR Factory extension, D, 1949; Rolls Royce Factory, East Kilbride, 1951–3; Newhouse Industrial Estate buildings, 1952; James Weir Building, Strathclyde University, G, 1957–8 and 1963–4; Stow Coll of Building and Printing, G, 1960–4; Stow Coll of Distributive Trades, G, 1960–4; Motherwell Civic Centre, b1965–70; Clydesdale Bank interior, Buchanan St, G, 1968–71; Fortronic factory, Donibristle, 1983–4

YEOMAN McALLISTER [of E]
High Green, Dean Village, E, 1990–1; Kingscrest, Colinton Rd, E, 1991–2; Gayfield Sq hs, E, 1992–4

* YORKE, ROSENBERG & MARDALL [Engl]
1 Castle St, E, 1993–5

YORKSTOUN, J and LOCKHART, J (m)
Forework, Stirling Cas, *c*.1500–10

YOUNG, George P K (1858–1933) [of Perth]
St Stephen's Ch, Perth, 1895; General Accident Assurance Building, High St, Perth, 1899–1901; Perth Fever Hosp, 1904–6; 1–7 York Pl, Perth, 1907; Northern District Sch, Perth, 1908–10

YOUNG, John (d.1801) [of E]
79–89 Hanover St, E, 1787

YOUNG, William (1843–1900) [of London]
Glasgow Municipal Buildings, 1883–8; Peebles Parish Ch, 1885–7; Sefton Lodge, Newmarket (Engl), *c*.1890; Chevening Pk interiors (Engl), *c*.1890; Gosford Ho a/a, 1891; Duncombe Pk a/a (Engl), 1895–8; War Office, London, 1898–1906; Elveden Hall a/a (Engl), 1899–1903

L.2 *The public architect*: senior staff of Glasgow Corporation Housing Department, 1948. At front centre, the Director, Dr. Ronald Bradbury, flanked by T. Robb, Assistant Director (on left), and F. C. Scott, Chief Architect (on right; later Chief Architect to East Kilbride Development Corporation). Both Bradbury and his successor, Archibald Jury, were architects; Jury was subsequently re-designated City Architect and Planning Officer.

Subject Index

Name Index

Name Index